Accounting
Desk Book
Ninth Edition

The Accountant's Everyday
Instant Answer Book

Tom M. Plank, MBA
Douglas L. Blensly, CPA, CMA

PRENTICE HALL
Englewood Cliffs, New Jersey 07632

Prentice-Hall International (UK) Limited, *London*
Prentice-Hall of Australia Pty. Limited, *Sydney*
Prentice-Hall Canada, Inc., *Toronto*
Prentice-Hall Hispanoamericana, S.A., *Mexico*
Prentice-Hall of India Private Limited, *New Delhi*
Prentice-Hall of Japan, Inc., *Tokyo*
Simon & Schuster Asia Pte. Ltd., *Singapore*
Editora Prentice-Hall do Brasil, Ltda., *Rio de Janeiro*

Ninth Edition

© 1989 *by*

PRENTICE-HALL, Inc.

Englewood Cliffs, NJ

10   9   8   7   6   5

Special thanks to KMG Main Hurdman for their technical assistance
with the applications of the Tax Reform Act of 1986.

Library of Congress Cataloging-in-Publication Data

Plank, Tom M.
  Accounting desk book: the accountant's everyday instant answer
book / Tom M. Plank and Douglas L. Blensly. — 9th ed.
    p. cm.
  Includes index.
  ISBN 0-13-003559-9
  1. Accounting.   I. Blensly, Douglas L.   II. Title.
HF5635.B668   1989
657′.02′02—dc19   88-39352
                                                              CIP

ISBN 0-13-003559-9

9 780130 035592

PRENTICE HALL
BUSINESS & PROFESSIONAL DIVISION
A division of Simon & Schuster
Englewood Cliffs, New Jersey 07632

Printed in the United States of America

About the Authors

Tom M. Plank is President of Pasadena Business Institute, Inc., a consulting firm. He holds his degrees from the Graduate School of Management, University of California (Los Angeles).

Mr. Plank is a specialist in SEC Accounting Rules and Regulations, new security issues registrations, and annual report filings with the SEC. He gives in-house seminars on accounting rules and SEC disclosure requirements to the accounting personnel of companies in commerce and industry and in public accounting firms.

Mr. Plank has served on the accounting and finance faculties of various major universities in Chicago and Los Angeles. His business experience includes that of an officer for a large commercial bank, a securities analyst for an investment banking firm, and a consultant for various corporations.

Mr. Plank has published over 25 articles in various journals, and is the author of seven business books: *SEC Accounting Rules and Regulations, The Age of Automation, The Science of Leadership*, and four accounting books. He is an accounting editor for a major publishing house.

Douglas L. Blensly is a Certified Public Accountant and a Certified Management Accountant. He graduated "cum laude" from California State University, Los Angeles, and currently is the accounting and auditing partner for the public accounting firm of Martin, Werbelow and Co., Pasadena, California.

Mr. Blensly is on the Accounting Principles and Auditing Standards committee of the California Society of CPAs and is a member of the Auditing Section of the American Accounting Association.

Mr. Blensly is the author of *The New Look in Financial Statements*, monographs on various accounting and business topics, and the author of four accounting books. He speaks regularly on accounting and auditing matters before various professional groups in California. He is a member of the accounting faculty, California State Polytechnic University (Pomona), and formerly was on the accounting faculty of Pasadena City College.

Mr. Blensly is an editorial advisor for the *Journal of Accountancy*.

Introduction

This ninth edition of the *Accounting Desk Book* has its origins in two sources. First, the passage of time has required the updating and substantive revision of the material from prior editions. We have merely to cite the continuing inundation of the accounting profession with new rules (Generally Accepted Accounting Principles— "GAAP"). New practices introduced in the rules that were never before required and their interpretation and application must be understood in order to ensure compliance.

Second, the inclusion of new topics in this edition is necessary because accounting and associated disciplines, e.g., finance, management, taxes, etc., are dynamic areas of business administration with a continuing number of new practices, standards, rules, regulations, technical terminology, and an ever-expanding body of technical knowledge. Accordingly, nine new Sections have been added to the three Sections in prior editions, as well as substantial revision and updating of the material in those three Sections.

Objectives. The original objective of the *Desk Book* continues to be to provide a reference manual *useful* to meet the specific and varied needs of accountants, attorneys, controllers, financial officers, bankers, credit analysts, securities analysts, government administrators, business managers generally, and others who require accuracy and clarity, and equally important, who want—and need instantly while working at their desks—a *succinct* clarification of significant areas of their responsibilities that requires a minimum of time for the information they are seeking.

Structure of the book. To further the objective and to contribute to the quality, application, and usefulness of accounting and financial principles, the book's coverage is broad in scope, and is organized for quick and convenient access by the user.

The Section titles are suggestive of the substance of the book: 1) Accounting Principles and Practices; 2) Cost Accounting; 3) Governmental (Fund) Accounting; 4) Internal Controls; 5) Business Combinations; 6) Management Principles; 7) Budgeting for Profiles; 8) Financial Statement Analysis and Interpretation; 9) Securities and Exchange Commission Organization and Filing Requirements; 10) Materiality and Financial Statement Disclosure; 11) Taxes-The Tax Reform Act of 1986; 12) Tax Accounting

There are seven Appendixes:

A. Index for Journal Entries Examples
B. Concise Guide to the Tax Reform Act of 1986
C. Accounting Methods—Advantages and Disadvantages
D. Table of Contents—The Current Text (Accounting and Industry Standards)
E. Monetary and Nonmonetary Items
F. Guide to Income Tax Records Retention Requirements
G. Financial Planning Tables

Each of the twelve Sections is formatted in a topical arrangement. There are 143 topics and sub-topics discussed in the twelve Sections. Each topic is titled; many are further subdivided into sub-topics which also are titled.

The discussions of the material have been developed from a *user* approach. They are concise in substance and applicable to all types of business enterprises, both manufacturing and service industries.

Timeliness.   The authors recognize the importance of current information to keep pace with the fast moving state-of-the-arts. The coverage of the topics, application, illustrations, examples, and definitions of terms (where necessary because of the unique vernacular in many of the specialized topics) are consistent with the contemporary literature in accounting and finance. Care has been taken to avoid abstract theory, technical jargon, complex "legaleze," or textbook type of dissertations which create more confusion than simplication of, in some instances, complex rules and procedures. All topics have been covered in as straightforward a presentation as possible.

However, it should be emphasized that the *Desk Book* is not a textbook; rather, it is essentially a reference manual to help the user to have at arm's length (between two covers) immediate answers to a large number of practical accounting, finance, tax, and other management questions. The discussions for the most part are self-contained, e.g., an explanation of a topic does not require any reference nor is linked to a preceding topic in another location in the book.

Contents

What Accounting Is All About • Accounting Principles • Seven-Step Cycle • The Accountant • Who Determines the Standards • Generally Accepted Accounting Principles (GAAP) • GAAP Outline • Measurement Principles • Employee Benefits • Pension Fund Accounting • FASB STATEMENT NO. 87, *Employers' Accounting for Pension Plans* • FASB STATEMENT NO. 88, *Employers' Accounting for Settlements and Curtailments of Defined Benefit Pension Plans and for Termination Benefits* • Deferred Compensation Plans • Information Systems • Accounting Information System Outline • Payrolls • Long-Term Construction Contracts • Completed Contract Method • Current Assets • Cash • Inventory • LIFO Terminology • FIFO • Retail Method • Lower of Cost or Market • LIFO Conformity Rule • Marketable Securities • Non-Current Assets • Equipment and Plant • Depreciation Methods • Intangible Assets • Research and Development Costs • Goodwill • Organization Expenses • Current Liabilities • Long-Term Debt • Bond Premiums and Discounts • Early Extinguishment of Debt • Troubled Debt Restructurings • Stockholders' Equity • Prior Period Adjustments • Contingency Reserves • Recapitalizations • Quasi-Reorganizations • Treasury Stock • Going Concern Concept • Revenue • Expenses • Extraordinary Items • Imputed Interest • Present Value Computation and Application

Objectives of a Cost System • Developing a System • Foundation of a Cost Accounting System • A Model • Cost Accounting Terminology • Standard Cost System • Job Order Cost System • Process Cost System • How to Use Standard Costs • Direct Costing • Break-Even Point Analysis • Summary

Government vs. Commercial Accounting • Terminology • Eight Types of Funds • Accounting Procedures for the Eight Funds • Journal Entries Illustrations

Section 4—Internal Controls

Definitions • Foreign Corrupt Practices Act of 1977 • Accountant's Responsibility • Compliance Problems • Accounting vs. Administrative Controls • Inventory Controls • Expense Controls • Cash Controls • Accounts Receivable Controls • Notes Receivable Controls • Bank Reconciliations • File Maintenance • Computer Files • Internal Controls for a Small Business Enterprise • Controls Checklist for Small Business • Embezzlement • Prevention Procedures • Check-Kiting • Payroll Frauds • Clues for Dishonest Practices

Section 5—Business Combinations

Cost Method • Equity Method • Consolidation Method • Combined Statements • Exceptions • Purchase Method • Pooling-of-Interest Method • Foreign Subsidiaries • Discs • Intercompany Transactions • Indefinite Reversal Criteria • Undistributed Earnings of Subsidiaries • Goodwill in Business Combinations • Negative Goodwill • Summary

Section 6—Management Principles

Capital Structure • Business Structure Considerations • Leases and Leasebacks • Lease Accounting Terminology • Lease or Buy • Plant Leasebacks • Acquisition Decisions • Buy-Sell Agreement for a Business Acquisition • Credit Lines • Commercial Finance Companies • Factor Financing • Inventory Loans • Long-Term Bonds • Bank Term Loans • Working Capital Management • Financially Troubled Businesses • Bankruptcy Procedures • Corporate Reorganization

Section 7—Budgeting for Profits

Budgetary Controls • Types of Budgets • Sales Budget • Forecasting Sales • Production Budget • Materials Budget • Labor Budget • Captial Expenditures Budget • Cash Budget • Manufacturing Expense Budget • Illustration

Section 8—Financial Statement Analysis
and Interpretation

Purpose of Statement Analysis • Four Groups of Ratios • Analysis Techniques • Balance Sheet Analysis • Income Statement Analysis • Evaluation of Financial Ratios • Cash Flow Analysis

Section 9—Securities and Exchange Commission
Organization and Filing Requirements

Organization Chart • SEC Accounting Definitions • 1933 Act (Synopsis) • 1934 Act (Synopsis) • Truth in Securities Laws • Integrated Disclosure System •

Independent Auditors • Aging • Basic Information Package • Projections and Forward-Looking Information • Safe Harbor Rule • SEC Forms • Going Public • Preparation and Filing of a Registration Statement • Regulation D—Small Business Can Now Go Public • SEC Definition of a Small Business • Small Business Registration Form S-18 • Accountants Form S-18 Responsibilities • Shelf Registration • Purpose • Updating • Going Private • Accountant's Participation in Going Private Transaction • Income Statement Requirements • Balance Sheet Requirements • Per Share Disclosure Requirements • Information Required of the Issuer

Materiality—An Elusive Concept • What's Material? • 17 Financial Statement Disclosure Requirements—a Listing • Financial Accounting Standard Board Conceptual Framework—Disclosure Guidelines • Full Disclosure Principle • Disclosure Requirements Detailed • Restatements • Income Tax Disclosure • Permanent Differences • Timing Differences • Auditing Standards • Reporting Earnings Per Share—Computation Illustration • Segment Reporting • Statement of Cash Flows • Foreign Currency Translations • Interim Statements—Guidelines for Interim Reporting • Price-Level Financial Reporting • Accounting Changes • 86 Accounting and Financial Statement Disclosure Deficiencies

The New Law—Significant Provisions Listed • Accumulated Earnings Tax • Uniform Capitalization Rule • The Simplified Method (Illustrated) • Inventories • Change in Inventory Method • LIFO • Securities and Other Intangibles • Accelerated Cost Recovery System • Property Classifications • Investment Tax Credit Repealed • At-Risk Rule • Safe Harbor • Tax Guidelines in Capitalization • "1244" Stock • S Corporations • Sub S 1982 Tax Revisions • S Corporations 1986 Code Changes • Passive Investment Income • Safe Harbor Rule • Professional Corporations • Tax-Free Recapitalizations • Bad Debt Method—New Law Change • Employee Benefits • Deferred Compensation Arrangements • ERISA • Research and Development Code Changes • Alternative Minimum Tax • Business Acquisitions—Sales and Purchases • Acquiring Companies with Tax Losses • Consolidated Tax Returns • Golden Parachute Contracts—Code Changes • State Taxes

The Accountant's Problem • Accountants' Responsibility • Tax Return Preparation • Choosing a Taxable Year—Code Changes • Change of Accounting Method • Income Recognition • Premature Accruals—Code changes • Timing Income and Expenses • Installment Sales—Code Requirements • Proportionate

Disallowance Rule—New Requirements • Consignment Sales • Imputed Interest •
Accounting for Income Taxes

Appendixes **567**

1

The Accountant and Accounting

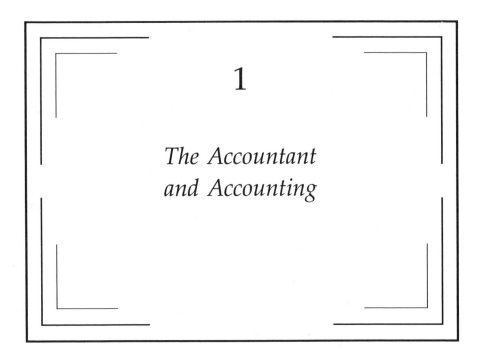

1

The Accountant
and Accounting

WHAT ACCOUNTING IS ALL ABOUT

In the AICPA Professional Standards for Accounting ("The Environment of Financial Accounting") that definition was superseded as follows (October 1970):

> Accounting is a service activity. Its function is to provide quantitative information, primarily financial in nature, about economic entities that is intended to be useful in making economic decisions, in making reasoned choices among alternative courses of action. Accounting includes several branches, for example,
>
>
>
> Financial Accounting
> Managerial Accounting
> Governmental Accounting
>
>

Accounting Information

Accounting information can be classified into two categories—financial accounting and managerial accounting. Financial accounting is information for the users of financial statements, i.e., creditors, stockholders, financial analysts, governmental regulatory agencies, trade associations, customers. (This is not to say, however, that the same information is not of interest to management.) Financial

3

accounting, then, concerns the financial position, earnings, liquidity, and operating performance generally of the enterprise.

Managerial accounting is primarily for internal control purposes: cost-volume-profit analysis, efficiency, productivity, planning and control, pricing decisions, operating and capital budgets, and a variety of specialized reports which management needs for the decision-making process.

Accounting Principles

Accounting can be thought of as a system—a system of assumptions, doctrines, tenets, and conventions, all included in the concept "Generally Accepted Accounting Principles" commonly referenced by the acronym GAAP. These principles developed by a process of evolution over a long period of years much in the same way that the common law developed, by way of an analogy. Very few accounting rules are embodied in statutory law, as government has for the most part deferred the promulgation of accounting standards to the private sector of the economy. Let's examine a few of the fundamental notions (concepts) that underlie accounting principles and practices as they exist today.

For the financial accounting standards required for external reporting, GAAP encompasses the conventions, rules, and procedures necessary to define accepted accounting practices at a particular time, and includes not only broad guidelines of general application, but also detailed practices and procedures. The conventions, rules, and procedures provide a standard by which to measure financial presentations.

The significant principles are that accounting information be relevant, reliable, comparable, and consistent. Relevant information helps users to predict events, or to confirm or correct prior expectations. Reliable information can be verified, is accurate and objective. Comparable information is measured and reported in a similar manner for different enterprises, particularly in the same industry. Consistent information is reported in the same manner from period-to-period, i.e., the same accounting methods are consistently applied.

Accounting Concepts

The *matching principle* requires that the revenues of the accounting period be precisely matched with the expenses of that same period that were incurred to generate the revenues.

The *accrual principle* considers revenues and expenses to be an inflow and outflow of *all* assets, not just the flow of cash in and out of the enterprise.

The *historical cost principle* requires that economic resources be entered into the system at cost, when the transaction occurs. The price paid is, on the face of it, considered to be the value of the asset.

The *realization* notion means economic events are accounted for only when the enterprise has been a party to one side of a *bona fide* transaction. For example, if a parcel of land has appreciated in value, the gain cannot be recognized until the land has been sold.

Associated with the realization concept is the idea of *substance-over-form* standard. All transactions must have "economic substance" as opposed to "sham" transactions entered into for some "creative accounting" purpose.

The *entity* concept concerns any person or group of persons having a name, common purpose, and *transactions with outsiders*. A relationship between the entity and external parties must be clearly established. The form of organization of the enterprise is not relevant with respect to the entity being an *accounting unit*.

The *going-concern* assumption considers the entity as one that will operate indefinitely.

The *consistency* standard requires the accounting procedures applied during a given accounting period be the same procedures that were applied in previous periods. The purpose of the consistency principle is to ensure that the statements of the enterprise for the current and prior periods are comparable.

The *conservative doctrine* directs that when the enterprise is exposed to uncertainty and risk that are material, accounting measurement and disclosure should be approached with a high degree of caution and in a prudent manner, until evidence develops that there is a significant reduction or elimination of the uncertainty.

Finally, is the all-important *disclosure* principle. The financial statements must present for the users all the relevant information that is necessary in order *not* to be misleading. This includes not only errors of commission, but also errors of omission of material information.

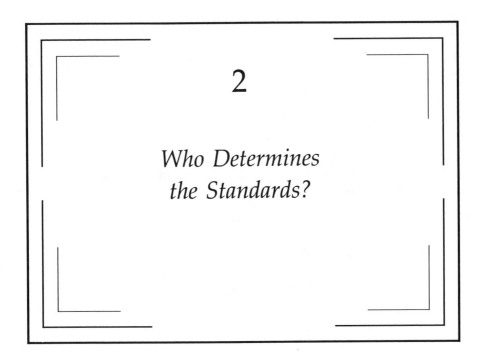

2

*Who Determines
the Standards?*

AMERICAN INSTITUTE OF CERTIFIED PUBLIC ACCOUNTANTS

In society at large, citizens are not praised for *upholding* laws; they are condemned or punished for *breaking* laws or *failure* to conform to the laws. On a smaller scale, the professional accountant is not applauded for adhering to standards; he is, or may be, criticized, reprimanded, ostracized or faced with monetary or criminal penalties for noncompliance with the standards or for *failure* to conform with accounting standards.

Most professional accountants will agree that, despite criticism for certain actions or nonactions, the AICPA is the one dominant organization of accountants. The Institute speaks with recognized authority for the *entire* profession of accounting (for members and nonmembers alike). When the AICPA speaks "officially," on-the-record, adherence is compulsory for members. When the AICPA speaks "unofficially," off-the-record, adherence is *not* compulsory. BUT—(and to emphasize it)—*but*—a member who violates an *unofficial* pronouncement had best have a good defense for his alternate position if it conflicts even with this *unofficial* AICPA position.

The AICPA is the national organization of certified public accountants in the United States. Its membership is made up of thousands of certified public accountants engaged in one or more of every conceivable phase of the accountant's function in society.

There are two requirements for membership:

1. Possession of a valid certified public accountant certificate issued by a state, territory or territorial possession of the United States or the District of Columbia, and
2. Passing an examination in accounting and other related subjects, satisfactory to the Board of Directors of the AICPA.

Members are governed by *four* sets of standards:

1. The Bylaws of the AICPA; (not discussed)
2. The Code of Professional Ethics; (discussed briefly)
3. Auditing Standards; (discussed briefly)
4. Financial Accounting Standards (discussed and enlarged in this entire section of the book).

FINANCIAL ACCOUNTING STANDARDS

Financial accounting standards, since May 7, 1973, have been determined by the Financial Accounting Standards Board (the FASB), which, by action of the Council of the AICPA, was designed to replace the old Accounting Principles Board (the APB).

> *Status of FASB interpretations.* Council is authorized under Rule 203 to designate a body to establish accounting principles and has designated the Financial Accounting Standards Board as such body. Council also has resolved that FASB Statements of Financial Accounting Standards, together with those Accounting Research Bulletins and APB Opinions which are not superseded by actions of the FASB constitute accounting principles as contemplated in Rule 203.
>
> In determining the existence of a departure from an accounting principle established by a Statement of Financial Accounting Standards, Accounting Research Bulletin or APB Opinion encompassed by Rule 203, the division of professional ethics will construe such Statement, Bulletin or Opinion in the light of any interpretations thereof issued by the FASB.

The FASB is *not* a division of the AICPA or a committee thereof. It is an autonomous organization in which the AICPA has representation. It is one of a three-part rule-making process, with each part performing important and distinct functions in the process of setting accounting standards:

The Financial Accounting Foundation is governed by a nine-member board of trustees comprised of five CPAs, two financial executives, one financial analyst, and one accounting educator. The president of the AICPA is a trustee. The trustee's primary duties are to appoint members of the Standards Board and the Advisory Council, to arrange financing, to approve budgets and periodically to review the structure of the organization.

The Financial Accounting Standards Board (FASB) is an independent body with seven full-time, salaried members, at least four of whom are CPAs drawn from public practice; the other members are persons well versed in financial reporting. The FASB's primary duty is to issue statements on financial accounting standards, including interpretations of those standards.

The Financial Accounting Standards Advisory Council comprises not less than 20 members who are experts in the field. The Council works closely with the FASB in an advisory capacity, consulting with the Board to identify problems, set agenda priorities, establish task forces, and react to proposed financial accounting standards.

The net result of the recognition of the new FASB was to make the following designated pronouncements the *official*, binding standards to be observed:

Those *prior* pronouncements of the *old* Accounting Principles Board (the APB) which were *not* changed by the new FASB:

1. APB Opinions
2. APB Statements
3. Accounting Research Bulletins:
   Plus the new pronouncements (rules) of the FASB:
4. FASB Statements
5. FASB Interpretations

An Important Distinction

The (old) "Accounting Interpretations" (that is the terminology used) were prepared by the AICPA staff and were *not*, when issued, considered to be official. They were answers to practitioners' questions. These "Accounting Interpretations" are *still* in effect, still unofficial, but recommended for use, with the burden of departures on the individual accountant. There will no longer be any new "Accounting Interpretations,"—at least not under that title.

The new terminology for these unofficial answers to practitioners' questions (since June 1973) is *"Technical Practice Aids."* These have been added to the body of *unofficial* interpretations of standards.

Note that the "interpretations" issued by the FASB, however, carry the title, "FASB Interpretations" and, under Rule 203 cited previously, *are official* pronouncements.

Unofficial Pronouncements

The following are the unofficial pronouncements issued by the AICPA as guidance for members (who might have to explain departures therefrom):

The Accounting Interpretations (up to June 1973)

The Technical Practice Aids (from June 1973 on)

Terminology Bulletins

Guides on Management Advisory Services

Statements on Responsibility in Tax Practice

Statements of Position of the Accounting Standards Division

Accounting Research Studies (these are different from "Accounting Research Bulletins" which *are* official)

Industry Audit Guides

Most other publications of the AICPA, unless clearly specifying their official nature. (Reference here is to *accounting* publications.)

Reiterating the concept of the first paragraph of this chapter, the responsibility to know the standards and to follow them rests with the individual accountant.

The whole body of compulsory rules and interpretations (though some are unofficial) is surprisingly small in terms of printed material.

GENERALLY ACCEPTED ACCOUNTING PRINCIPLES (GAAP)

GAAP represents the accounting profession's efforts to establish a body of theory and practice that provides a guide in the form of a common set of standards and procedures. The term *generally accepted* has two meanings: 1) an accounting rule-making authority has developed a principle of financial reporting for specific areas and 2) an accounting practice has been accepted as appropriate for a given procedure or standard because of its widespread application over a long period of time. In both cases the established principles are said to have "substantial authoritative support."

The primary sources of authoritative pronouncements are the Financial Accounting Standards Board *Statements* and *Interpretations*, the Accounting Principles Board, Committee on Accounting Procedures, and Accounting Research Bulletins, (for rules that have not been superseded by FASB Statements), AICPA Statements of Position, AICPA Industry Accounting and Auditing Guides, and FASB Technical Bulletins.

The importance of the accountant complying with GAAP is set forth in Rule 203 of the Code of Professional Ethics, which prohibits an accountant from stating in an opinion that financial statements conform with GAAP if the statements in fact contain a significant departure from a principle.

The substance of GAAP concerns two areas of accounting; i.e., measurement and disclosure principles. Conservatism, verifiability, and objectivity are the primary attributes of the rules that govern the preparation and disclosure of financial statements.

There are other areas of accounting specialization, such as: income taxes, cost accounting, SEC filings, statistical sampling, computers, mathematical "decision-making," etc., which require unique education and research. Though peripheral and adjunct, they are guided by the main body of standards, but not explicitly spelled out by them.

The FASB is developing a series of Statements of Financial Accounting Concepts. Four statements have been issued through December 1981:

1. Objectives of Financial Reporting by Business Enterprises
2. Qualitative Characteristics of Accounting Information
3. Elements of Financial Statements of Business Enterprises
4. Objectives of Financial Reporting by Nonbusiness Organizations

PRELUDE TO GAAP OUTLINE

Standards and Regulations

Until 1973, accounting principles had been established by the American Institute of Certified Public Accountants. In 1973, the Financial Accounting Standards Board was organized as an independent standard-setting body, with the AICPA continuing to set the standards for auditors. Corporations whose securities are publicly held must conform to rules set by the Securities and Exchange Commission, a federal government agency. The Internal Revenue Service administers the tax statutes and regulations at the federal level. There is no standard setting authority for managerial accounting, but there is a program available for accountants to qualify for a certificate in management accounting (CMA). The Institute of Internal Auditors administers an examination for an accountant to be designated a certified internal auditor (CIA).

A well-defined body of knowledge and precise, for the most part, methodology has been developed for accounting procedures over a long period of time. Existing techniques and new approaches continue to be studied by the authorities in an effort to keep accounting standards consistent with changes and innovations in business practices, legislative changes, and socioeconomic changes in our society.

The following is an outline of Generally Acceptable Accounting Principles (GAAP):

I. OBJECTIVES OF FINANCIAL ACCOUNTING

II. BASIC FEATURES AND BASIC ELEMENTS OF FINANCIAL AC-
COUNTING

   A. Basic Features—The Environment

   B. Basic Elements—The Individual Company

      1. Economic resources, obligations and residual interests

      2. Changes in those resources—events that cause them to increase or
decrease

    *3. GAAP—for recording and reporting them:

      *A) The Pervasive Principles

      *B) The Broad Operating Principles

        *1) Selection and measurement

        *2) Financial statement presentation

      C) Detailed Operating Principles

*3(A) and 3(B)(1) & (2) are covered in the outline below. They pertain to the practi-
cal application of the principles, which are described in more theoretical and
historical-development terms in the prior sections of the outline.

GAAP

(Generally Accepted Accounting Principles).

THE PERVASIVE MEASUREMENT PRINCIPLES

Six principles establish the basis for implementing *accrual* accounting:

   1. *Initial Recording*: of assets and liabilities, income determination, revenue and
realization.

   2. *Realization*:

     Revenue —when earning process is complete.

           —when an exchange has taken place.

     Expenses —gross decreases in assets.

           —gross increases in liabilities.

     Classes of expenses:

     Costs of assets used to produce revenue—cost of goods sold, selling—
administrative expense, interest expense.

     Expenses from non-reciprocal transfers—taxes, thefts, floods.

     Costs of assets other than product disposed of—plant, equipment.

     Costs of unsuccessful efforts.

Declines in market prices of inventories.

Does *not* include repayments of borrowings, expenditures to acquire assets, distributions to owners (including treasury stock) or adjusting prior period expenses.

3. *Associating Cause and Effect.*
4. *Systematic and Rational Allocation.*
5. *Immediate Recognition:*
   Costs of the current period which provide no future benefits (those which have been incurred *now* or *prior*) or when allocating serves no useful purpose.

   Measurement is based on its own exchanges: contracts not recorded until *one* party fulfills commitment; not all changes are recorded, not internal increases and not price changes in productive resources.

   Assets usually are recorded at cost, or unexpired portion of it. When sold, difference increases the firm's net assets. The cost principle: use acquisition price (historical cost). Cost also refers to how asset was originally recorded, regardless of how determined.
6. *The Unit of Measure*—U.S. Dollar—no change is recognized for change in general purchasing power of the dollar.

The Pervasive Principles—Modifying Conventions

Modifying conventions are applied because too rigid adherence to the measurement principles might produce undesirable results, exclude other important events, or even at times be impractical.

The modifying conventions are:

1. *Conservatism*
2. *Emphasis on the importance of income* (LIFO is an example)
3. *Judgment of the accounting profession as a whole* with regard to:
   The usual revenue recognition rule—recognition of contracts in progress.
   Segregation of extraordinary items.
   Avoiding undue effect on net income in one single period (installment sales).

BROAD OPERATING PRINCIPLES

Two broad principles are:

1. The Principles of Selection and Measurement.
2. The Principles of Financial Statement Presentation.

THE PRINCIPLES OF SELECTION AND MEASUREMENT

These principles guide the selection of the *events* to be accounted for; they determine *how* the selected *events* affect items; and they guide the *assignment of dollars* to the effects of the *events*.

The types of *events*, classified, are:

1. External Events
   A. *Transfers* to or from *other* entities
      (1) Exchanges (reciprocal transfers)
      (2) Non-reciprocal transfers
         (A) With owners
         (B) With outsiders
   B. *Other-than-transfers*
2. Internal Events
   A. Production of goods or services
   B. Casualties

The outline presented next breaks down each of the types of events above and briefly highlights, where appropriate:

When to record the transaction

How it is *measured*—what value to use

Some *discussion* and/or *examples*

In that order: when to record, how to value, discussion, examples. In addition to the events themselves (above), there are:

3. *Additional* principles which relate to the *changes* in events, which determine their effects.
4. Principles governing assets and liabilities that are not resources or obligations (such as deferred taxes).

1A External Events—Transfers To or From Other Entities

(1) Exchanges (reciprocal transfers)
   Assets—Acquisitions: Record as acquired (some not carried forward are expenses); cost, face amount, sometimes discounted value; sometimes fair value in non-cash exchanges (allocate fair values for individual assets in group)—excess in goodwill. Cash, accounts receivable, short-term receivables at discounted amount when no or low interest stated.

Assets—Dispositions: When disposed of, at cost adjusted for amortization and other changes; in partial dispositions value is based on detailed principles (FIFO, LIFO, average).

Liabilities—Increases: When obligation to transfer assets or provide services is incurred in exchanges; value is established in the exchange, sometimes discounted (long-term)—pension obligations, loans under capitalized long-term leases, bonds, notes bearing little or no interest (the difference is amortized over period to maturity).

Liabilities—Decreases: When discharged through payments or otherwise; use recorded amounts. If partial, may have to apportion to recorded amount.

Commitments—Not recorded when unfulfilled on both sides, unless: one party fulfills its part: some leases are recorded: *losses* on firm commitments are recorded. Long-term leases are recorded as assets by the lessee, with the corresponding liability.

Revenue from Exchanges—When product is sold, service performed, resource used by others, and when asset is sold producing gain (or loss); recorded at price in the exchange, sometimes reduced for discounts or allowances. Exceptions: long-term construction contracts, revenue not recognized on purchases, certain products with an *assured* selling price—sometimes recorded over long periods without reasonable assurance of collection (installment method; cost recovery method). (Under the installment method, proceeds collected measure the revenue, but expense is measured by multiplying cost by ratio of collection to sales price. In cost recovery method, use all proceeds collected until all costs are recovered.)

Expenses—Directly associated with revenue from exchanges—use costs of assets sold or services provided, recorded when related revenue is recognized. If other than a product, the remaining *undepreciated* cost is subtracted from the revenue obtained.

(2) Non-reciprocal transfers:

(A) *With owners*: Investments and withdrawals recorded as they occur:

Increases—by amount of cash received; the discounted value of money claims received or liabilities canceled; fair value of non-cash assets received (often, the fair value of *stock issued*).

Decreases—cash paid; recorded amount of non-cash assets transferred; discounted present value of liabilities incurred.

In "pooling," assets and liabilities are combined as on books (no change); "purchase" method entails use of fair value.

Investments of non-cash assets recorded when made; sometimes measured at cost to founder (rather than fair value).

(B) *With outsiders*: assets, when acquired, when disposed of, when discovered; for non-cash assets given, usually use fair value; liabilities, at face value, sometimes discounted.

1B External Events—Other Than Transfers

Examples are: Changes in prices of assets, changes in interest rates, technological changes, damage caused by outside influences.

Favorable events—Generally not recorded, except at time of later exchange. Retained on books at recorded amounts until exchanged (assets) or until satisfied (liabilities). Exceptions are: When using the equity method; foreign currency translations; marketable securities under new rules, written down to market, up to cost, as fluctuates; obligations under warranties.

Unfavorable events—Decreasing market price or utility of asset, adjusted to lower market price or recoverable cost, usually governed by specific rules such as cost or market for inventories. A loss is recognized when utility is no longer as great as its cost, obsolescence; adjust write-offs or write-off entirely currently if it is completely worthless, or down to recoverable cost. Damage caused by others, record when occurs or discovered—to recoverable cost. Increases in amounts currently payable because of higher interest rates only generally not recorded until liquidated. Increases in non-U.S. Dollar liabilities are recorded in terms of U.S. Dollar because of currency translation.

2A Internal Events—Production of Goods or Services

Production is the input of goods and services combined to produce an output of product which may be goods or services. It includes: manufacturing, merchandising, transporting and holding goods.

Recorded at historical or acquisition costs (previously recorded) as used in the production process during the period; deducted from revenue to which related in the period sold. Costs are usually shifted or allocated from initially recorded asset accounts to other accounts in a *systematic* and *rational* manner.

Costs of manufacturing or providing services—Costs of assets completely used plus allocated portions of assets partially used; allocations are assumed, based on relationship between assets and activities; note that "costs" refers to amounts charged initially to assets—they become "expenses" when allocated to expense as follows:

If benefit only one period—expense then.

If benefit several periods—expense over periods involved (depreciation, depletion, amortization).

Expenses—Some items are recognized as expenses immediately and charged directly thereto. Enterprises never "acquire" expenses, as they acquire assets. Costs may be charged as expenses immediately under the principle of immediate recognition when they pertain to the period involved and cannot be associated with any other period, such as officer salaries and advertising.

Revenue—Under certain conditions and special standards, revenue may be recognized at completion of production or as production progresses (precious metals industry; long-term construction contracts). Ratio of performance to date must be capable of being reasonably estimated and collection *reasonably* assured. Take losses *immediately*. Revenue is measured by an allocated portion of a predetermined selling price, less product or service costs as they progress.

2B Internal Events—Casualties

Sudden, substantial, unanticipated reductions in assets *not* caused by other entities, such as:

Fires, floods, abnormal spoilage.

Recorded when they occur or when they are discovered.
Measured by writing them down to recoverable costs and a *loss* is recorded.

3 Additional Principles Which Related to the Changes in Events, Determine Their Effects

Dual effect—Every recorded event affects at least *two* items in the records. *The double-entry system is based on this principle.*

INCREASES IN ASSETS ARISE FROM:

A. Exchanges in which assets are acquired
B. Investments of assets by owners
C. Non-reciprocal transfers of assets by outsiders
D. Shifts of costs during production
E. External events (equity method)
F. Increases ascribed to produced assets
with *opposite effect* of:
1. Decrease in other assets
2. Increase in liability
3. Revenue recognition
4. Sometimes, neutral effect—production costs shifted.

DECREASES IN ASSETS ARISE FROM:

A. Exchanges in which assets are disposed of
B. Withdrawals of assets by owners
C. Non-reciprocal transfers to outsiders
D. External events which reduce market price

E. Shifts and allocations
F. Casualties
with *opposite effect* of:
1. Increase in other assets
2. Decrease in liabilities
3. Increases in expenses:
Immediately, if used up:
Or if future benefit cannot be determined.

INCREASES IN LIABILITIES ARISE FROM:

A. Exchanges in which liabilities are incurred
B. Transfers with owner (dividend declaration)
C. Non-reciprocal transfers with outsiders
with *opposite effect* of:
1. Decrease in other liabilities
2. Increase in assets
3. An expense.

DECREASES IN LIABILITIES ARISE FROM:

A. Exchanges in which liabilities are reduced
B. Transfers with owners
C. Non-reciprocal transfers with outsiders (forgiveness of indebtedness)
with *opposite effect* of:
1. Increases in other liabilities
2. Decreases in assets
3. Revenue

INCREASES IN OWNERS' EQUITY ARISE FROM:

A. Investments in enterprise
B. *Net* result of all revenue and expenses in a period
C. Non-reciprocal transfers with outsiders (gifts)
D. Prior period adjustments.

DECREASES IN OWNERS' EQUITY ARISE FROM:

A. Transfers to owners (dividends)
B. Net losses for a period
C. Prior period adjustments.

REVENUE ARISES:

A. Primarily from exchanges

B. Occasionally from production

C. Rarely from transfers or external events with *opposite effect* of:

1. Usually an asset increase

2. Decrease in liability (called "unearned revenue").

EXPENSES ARISE FROM:

A. Exchanges—costs directly associated with revenue are recognized when assets are sold or services provided

B. Non-reciprocal transfers with outsiders

C. External events other than transfers

D. Production:

1) Costs of manufacturing products and providing services *not* included in product costs (example—overhead)

2) Expenses from systematic and rational allocation, excluding those assigned to product costs of manufacturing

3) Expenses recognized immediately on the acquisition of goods or services

4) Costs of products for which revenue is recognized at *completion* of production or as *production* progresses (precious metals, percent-of-completion contracts).

4 Principles Governing Assets and Liabilities That Are Not Resources or Obligations

Certain items are shown as assets that are not in reality resources, such as deferred charges for income taxes; and certain items are shown as liabilities that are not in reality liabilities, such as deferred credits for income taxes.

Accounting for them is governed by detailed principles, such as accounting for deferred federal income taxes.

The effect of recording these items is an increase or a decrease in assets or liabilities, with a corresponding decrease or increase in expenses on the income statement.

3

Employee Benefits

INTRODUCTION

After over 12 years of studying the issue, the Financial Accounting Standards Board in December, 1985, issued FASB Statement No. 87 *"Employers' Accounting for Pension Plans,"* and Statement No. 88 *"Employers' Accounting for Settlements and Curtailments of Defined Benefit Pension Plans and for Termination benefits."*

These two Statements are the applicable GAAP for pension fund accounting and disclosure for fiscal years beginning after December 15, 1986.

PENSION FUND ACCOUNTING TERMS

The Statements have their own, unique vernacular. The terminology used in the new rules should be reviewed as many familiar words and terms have shades of meaning in the pension fund accounting rules somewhat different from common, everyday usage, as well as the technical meaning of terms in a completely new vocabulary.

Definitions

ACCUMULATED BENEFIT OBLIGATION: The actuarial present value of benefits (whether vested or nonvested) attributed by the pension benefit formula to employee service rendered before a specified date and based on employee service and compensation (if applicable) prior to that date. The accumulated benefit obligation differs from the projected benefit obligation in that it includes no assumption about future compensation levels. For plans with flat-benefit or non-pay-related pension benefit formulas, the accumulated benefit obligation and the projected benefit obligation are the same.

ACTUAL RETURN ON PLAN ASSETS COMPONENT OF NET PERIODIC PENSION COST: The difference between the fair value of plan assets at the end of the period and the fair value at the beginning of the period, adjusted for contributions and benefits during the period.

ACTUARIAL FUNDING METHOD: Any of several techniques that actuaries use in determining the amounts and incidence of employer contributions to provide for pension benefits.

ACTUARIAL GAIN OR LOSS: (See *GAIN OR LOSS*)

ACTUARIAL PRESENT VALUE: The value, as of a specified date, of an amount or series of amounts payable or receivable in the future with each amount adjusted to reflect (1) the time value of money (through discounts for interest) and (2) the probability of payment by means of decrements for events such as death, disability, withdrawal, or retirement between the specified date and the expected date of payment.

ALLOCATED CONTRACT: A contract with an insurance company under which payments to the insurance company are currently used to purchase immediate or deferred annuities for individual participants. (See *ANNUITY CONTRACT*)

AMORTIZATION: In pension accounting, amortization is used to refer to the systematic recognition in net pension cost over several periods of previously unrecognized amounts, including unrecognized prior service cost and unrecognized net gain or loss.

ANNUITY CONTRACT: A contract in which an insurance company unconditionally undertakes a legal obligation to provide specified pension benefits to specific individuals in return for a fixed consideration or premium. An annuity contract is irrevocable and involves the transfer of significant risk from the employer to the insurance company. Annuity contracts are also called *allocated* contracts.

ASSUMPTIONS: Estimates of the occurrence of future events affecting pension costs, such as mortality, withdrawal, disablement and retirement, changes in compensation and national pension benefits, and discount rates to reflect the time value of money.

ATTRIBUTION: The process of assigning pension benefits or cost to periods of employee service.

BENEFIT APPROACH: One of two groups of basic approaches to attributing pension benefits or costs to periods of employee service. Approaches in this group assign a distinct unit of benefit to each year of credit service. The actuarial present value of that unit of benefit is computed separately and determines the cost assigned to that year. The accumulated benefits approach, benefit/compensation approach, and benefit/years-of-service approach are benefit approaches.

BENEFIT FORMULA: (See *PENSION BENEFIT FORMULA*)

BENEFITS: Payments to which participants may be entitled under a pension plan, including pension benefits, death benefits, and benefits due on termination of employment.

BENEFIT-YEARS-OF-SERVICE APPROACH: One of three benefit approaches. An equal portion of total estimated benefit is attributed to each year of service. The actuarial present value of the benefits is derived after the benefits are attributed to the periods.

CAPTIVE INSURANCE SUBSIDIARY: An insurance company that does business primarily with related entities.

CAREER AVERAGE PAY FORMULA (CAREER AVERAGE PAY PLAN): A benefit formula that bases benefits on the employee's compensation over the entire period of service with the employer. A career average pay plan is a plan with such a formula.

CONTRIBUTORY PLAN: A pension plan under which employees contribute part of the cost. In some contributory plans, employees wishing to be covered must contribute; in other contributory plans, employee contributions result in increased benefits.

COST APPROACH: One of the two groups of basic approaches to attributing pension benefits or costs to periods of service. Approaches in this group assign net pension costs to periods as level amounts or constant percentages of compensation.

COST COMPENSATION APPROACH: One of two cost approaches. Net pension costs under this approach are attributed to periods so that they are a constant percentage of compensation for each period.

CURTAILMENT: (See *PLAN CURTAILMENT*)

DEFINED BENEFIT PENSION PLAN: A pension plan that defines an amount of pension benefit to be provided, usually as a function of one or more factors such as age, years of service, or compensation. Any pension plan that is not a defined contribution pension plan is, for purposes of Statement No. 87, a defined benefit pension plan.

DEFINED CONTRIBUTION PENSION PLAN: A plan that provides pension benefits in return for services rendered, provides an individual account for each participant, and specifies how contributions to the individual's account are to be determined instead of specifying the amount of benefits the individual is to receive. Under a defined contribution pension plan, the benefits a participant will receive depend solely on the amount contributed to the participant's account, the returns earned on investments of those contributions, and forfeitures of other participants' benefits that may be allocated to such participant's account.

ERISA: The Employee Retirement Income Security Act of 1974.

EXPECTED LONG-TERM RATE OF RETURN ON PLAN ASSETS: An assumption as to the rate of return on plan assets reflecting the average rate of earnings expected on the funds invested or to be invested to provide for the benefits included in the projected benefit obligation.

EXPECTED RETURN ON PLAN ASSETS: An amount calculated as a basis for determining the extent of delayed recognition of the effects of *changes* in the fair value of assets. The expected return on plan assets is determined based on the expected long-term rate of return on plan assets and the market-related value of plan assets.

EXPLICIT APPROACH TO ASSUMPTIONS: An approach under which each significant assumption used reflects the best estimate of the plan's future experience solely with respect to that assumption. (See also *IMPLICIT APPROACH TO ASSUMPTIONS*)

FAIR VALUE: The amount that a pension plan could reasonably expect to receive for an investment in a current sale between a willing buyer and a willing seller; that is, other than in a forced or liquidation sale.

FINAL-PAY FORMULA (FINAL-PAY PLAN):   A benefit formula that bases benefits on the employee's compensation over a specified number of years near the end of the employee's service period or on the employee's highest compensation periods. For example, a plan might provide annual pension benefits equal to 1 percent of the employee's average salary for the last five years (or the highest consecutive five years) for each year of service. A final-pay plan is a plan with such a formula.

FLAT-BENEFIT FORMULA (FLAT-BENEFIT PLAN): A benefit formula that bases benefits on a fixed amount per each year of service. A final-pay plan is a plan with such a formula.

FUND: Used as a *verb*, to pay over to a funding agency in order to fund future pension benefits or to fund pension cost. Used as a *noun*, fund means assets accumulated in the hands of a funding agency for the purpose of meeting pension benefits when they become due.

FUNDING METHOD: (See *ACTUARIAL FUNDING METHOD*)

FUNDING POLICY: The program regarding the amounts and timing of contributions by the employer(s), participants, and any other sources, e.g.; state subsidies or federal grants, which will provide the benefits a pension plan specifies.

GAIN OR LOSS: A change in the value of either the projected benefit obligation or the plan assets resulting from experience different from that assumed or from a change in an actuarial assumption. (See also *UNRECOGNIZED NET GAIN OR LOSS*)

GAIN OR LOSS COMPONENT OF NET PERIODIC PENSION COST: The sum of (1) the difference between the actual return on plan assets and the expected return on the assets; (2) the amortization of the unrecognized net gain or loss from previous periods. The gain or loss component is the net effect of delayed recognition of gains and losses (the net change in the unrecognized net gain or loss) except that it does not include changes in the projected benefit obligation occurring during the period and deferred for later recognition.

IMPLICIT APPROACH TO ASSUMPTIONS: An approach under which two or more assumptions do not individually represent the best estimate of the plan's future experience with respect to those assumptions. Instead, the aggregate effect of their combined use is presumed to be approximately the same as that produced by an explicit approach.

INTEREST COST COMPONENT OF NET PERIODIC PENSION COST: The increase in the projected benefit obligation due to passage of time.

INTEREST RATE: (See *DISCOUNT RATE*)

LOSS: (See *GAIN OR LOSS*)

MARKET-RELATED VALUE OF PLAN ASSETS: A balance used to calculate the expected return on plan assets. Market-related value can be either fair market value or a calculated value that recognizes changes in fair value in a systematic and rational manner over not more than five years. Different ways of calculating market-related value may be used for different classes of assets, but the manner of determining market-related value shall be applied consistently from year to year for each asset class.

MEASUREMENT DATE: The date as of which plan assets and obligations are measured.

MORTALITY RATE: The proportion of the number of deaths in a specified group to the number living at the beginning of the period in which the deaths occur. In estimating the amount of pension benefits that will become payable, actuaries use mortality tables, which show the death rates for each age.

MULTI-EMPLOYER PLAN: A pension plan to which two or more unrelated employers contribute, usually in compliance with one or more collective bargaining agreements. A characteristic of multi-employer plans is that assets contributed by one participating employer may be used to provide benefits to employees of other participating employers since assets contributed by each employer are not segregated in a separate account or restricted to provide benefits only to employees of that employer. A multi-employer plan is usually administered by a board of trustees composed of management and labor representatives and are referred to as a ''joint trust'' or ''union'' plan. Generally, many employers participate in a multi-employer plan, and an employer may participate in more than one plan. The employers participating in multi-employer plans usually have a common industry bond, but for some plans the employers are in different industries and the labor union may be their only common bond.

MULTIPLE-EMPLOYER PLAN: A pension plan maintained by more than one employer but not treated as a multi-employer plan. Multiple-employer plans are not as prevalent as single-employer and multi-employer plans, but some of the ones that do exist are large and involve many employers. Multiple-employer plans are generally not collectively bargained and are intended to allow participating employers, usually in the same industry, to pool their assets for investment purposes and reduce the costs of plan administration. A multiple-employer plan maintains separate accounts for each employer so that contributions provide benefits only for employees of the contributing employer. Some multiple-employee plans have features that allow participating employers to have different benefit formulas, with the employer's contributions to the plan based on the benefit formula selected by the employer.

NET PERIODIC PENSION COST: The amount recognized in an employer's financial statements as the cost of a pension plan for a period. Components of net periodic pension cost are service cost, interest cost, actual return on plan assets, gain or loss, amortization of unrecognized prior service cost, and amortization of the unrecognized net obligation or asset existing at the date of initial application of Statement No. 88. The Statement uses the term *net periodic pension cost* instead of *net pension expense* because part of the cost recognized in a period may be capitalized along with other costs as part of an asset, such as part of the cost of inventory.

NONPARTICIPATING ANNUITY CONTRACT: An annuity contract that does not provide for the purchaser to participate in the investment performance or in other experience of the insurance company. (See also *ANNUITY CONTRACT*)

NONPUBLIC ENTERPRISE: An enterprise other than one (1) whose debt or equity securities are traded in a public market, i.e., either on a stock exchange or in the over-the-counter market, or (2) whose financial statements are filed with a regulatory agency (federal or state) in preparation for the sale of any class of securities.

PARTICIPANT: Any employee or former employee, or any member or former member of a trade or other employee association, or the beneficiaries of those individuals, for whom there are pension plan benefits.

PARTICIPATING ANNUITY CONTRACT: An annuity contract that provides for the purchaser to participate in the investment performance and possibly other experience (the mortality rate, for example) of the insurance company.

PARTICIPATION RIGHT: A purchaser's right under a participating contract to receive future dividends or retroactive rate credits from the insurance company.

PBGC: The Pension Benefit Guaranty Corporation.

PENSION BENEFIT FORMULA (PLAN'S BENEFIT FORMULA OR BENEFIT FORMULA): The basis for determining payments to which participants may be entitled under a pension plan. Pension formulas usually refer to the employee's service or compensation, or both.

PENSION BENEFITS: Periodic, usually monthly, payments made pursuant to the terms of the pension plan to a person who has retired from employment or to that person's beneficiary.

PLAN AMENDMENT: A change in the terms of an existing plan or the initiation of a new plan. A plan amendment may increase benefits, including those attributed to years of service already rendered. (See also *RETROACTIVE BENEFITS*)

PLAN ASSETS: Assets—usually stocks, bonds, and other investments—that have been segregated and restricted, usually in a trust, to provide benefits. Plan assets include amounts contributed by the employer (and by employees for a contributory plan) and amounts earned from investing the contributions, less benefits paid. Plan assets cannot ordinarily be withdrawn by the employer except in certain circumstances when a plan has assets in excess of obligations and the employer has taken certain steps to satisfy existing obligations. Assets not segregated in a trust, or otherwise effectively restricted so that they cannot be used by the employer for other purposes, are not plan assets even though it may be intended that such assets be used to provide pensions. Amounts accrued by the employer as net periodic pension cost, but not yet paid to the plan, are not plan assets. Securities of the employer held by the plan are includable in plan assets provided they are transferable. If a plan has liabilities other than for benefits, the nonbenefit obligations are considered as reductions of plan assets.

PLAN ASSETS AVAILABLE FOR BENEFITS: (See *PLAN ASSETS*)

PLAN CURTAILMENT: An event that significantly reduces the expected years of future service of present employees or eliminates for a significant number of employees the accrual of defined benefits for some or all of their future services.

PLAN'S BENEFIT FORMULA: (See *PENSION BENEFIT FORMULA*)

PLAN SUSPENSION: An event in which the pension plan is frozen and no further benefits accrue. Future service may continue to be the basis for vesting of nonvested benefits existing at the date of suspension. The plan may still hold assets, pay benefits already accrued, and receive additional employer contributions for any unfunded benefits. Employees may or may not continue working for the employer.

PLAN TERMINATION: An event in which the pension plan ceases to exist and all benefits are settled by purchase of annuities or by other means. The plan may or may not be replaced by another plan. A plan termination with a replacement plan may or may not be in substance a plan termination for accounting purposes of accrued net pension cost.

PREPAID PENSION COST: Cumulative employer contribution in excess of accrued net pension cost.

PRIOR SERVICE COST: The cost of retroactive benefits granted in a plan amendment. (See also *UNRECOGNIZED PRIOR SERVICE COST*)

PROJECTED BENEFIT OBLIGATION: The actuarial present value as of a date of all benefits attributed by the pension benefit formula to employee service rendered prior to that date. The projected benefit obligation is measured using assumptions as to future compensation levels if the pension benefit formula is based on those future compensation levels, e.g., pay-related, final pay, final average pay, career average pay plans.

RETROACTIVE BENEFITS: Benefits granted in a plan amendment that are attributed by the pension benefit formula to employee services rendered in periods prior to the amendment. The cost of the retroactive benefits is referred to as *prior service cost.*

RETURN ON PLAN ASSETS: (See *ACTUAL RETURN ON PLAN ASSETS COMPONENT; EXPECTED RETURN ON PLAN ASSETS*)

SERVICE: Employment taken into consideration under a pension plan. Years of employment before the inception of a plan constitute an employee's past service; years thereafter are classified in relation to the particular actuarial valuation being made or discussed. Years of employment, including past service, prior to the date of a particular valuation constitute prior service; years of employment following the date of the valuation constitute future service; a year of employment on the date of valuation, or in which such date falls, constitutes current service.

SERVICE COST COMPONENT OF NET PERIODIC PENSION COST: The actuarial present value of benefits attributed by the pension benefit formula to services rendered by employees during that period. The service cost component is a portion of the projected benefit obligation and is unaffected by the funded status of the plan.

SETTLEMENT: An irrevocable action that relieves the employer (or the plan) of primary responsibility for a pension benefit obligation and eliminates significant risks related to the obligation and the assets used to effect the settlement. Examples of transactions that constitute a settlement include (1) making lump-sum cash payments to plan participants in exchange for their rights to receive specified pension benefits; (2) purchasing nonparticipating annuity contracts to cover vested benefits.

SINGLE-EMPLOYER PLAN: A pension plan that is maintained by one employer. The term also may be used to describe a plan that is maintained by related parties such as a parent and its subsidiaries.

SPONSOR: A pension plan established or maintained by a single employer, *the employer*; a plan established or maintained by an employee organization, *the employee organization*; a plan established or maintained jointly by two or more employers or by one or more employers and one or more employee organizations, *the association, committee, joint board of trustees, or other group of representatives* of the parties who have established or who maintain the pension plan.

TURNOVER: Termination of employment for a reason other than death or retirement.

UNALLOCATED CONTRACT: A contract with an insurance company under which payments to the insurance company are accumulated in an unallocated fund which is a fund not allocated to specific plan participants. An unallocated fund is to be used either directly or through the purchase of annuities to meet benefit payments when employees retire. Funds held by the insurance company under an unallocated contract may be withdrawn and otherwise invested.

UNFUNDED ACCRUED PENSION COST: Cumulative net pension cost accrued in excess of the employer's contributions.

UNFUNDED ACCUMULATED BENEFIT OBLIGATION: The excess of the projected benefit obligation over plan assets.

UNRECOGNIZED NET GAIN OR LOSS: The cumulative net gain or loss that has not been recognized as a part of net periodic pension cost. (See *GAIN OR LOSS*)

UNRECOGNIZED PRIOR SERVICE COST: That portion of prior service cost that has not been recognized as a part of net periodic pension cost.

VESTED BENEFIT OBLIGATION: The actuarial present value of vested benefits.

VESTED BENEFITS: Benefits for which the employee's right to receive a present or future pension benefit is no longer contingent on remaining in the service of the employer. Other conditions, such as inadequacy of the pension fund, may prevent the employee from receiving the vested benefit. Under graded vesting, the initial vested right may be to receive in the future a stated percentage of a pension based on the number of years of accumulated credited service; thereafter, the percentage may increase with the number of years of service or of age until the right to receive the entire benefit has vested.

FASB STATEMENT NO. 87

Employers' Accounting for Pension Plans

1. Companies presently using other than the prescribed plan-based benefit approach to attributing pension costs to periods will be faced with a method change with potential significant effect on amounts recognized in the income statement.
2. Each significant assumption affecting the pension computation is required to be the best estimate of that factor alone. Under this explicit approach, the use of assumptions known to be inaccurate but with offsetting effect is unacceptable. Major assumptions that must be developed and continuously updated for significant changes include the discount rate (the current rate at which benefits could be effectively settled) used to measure pension obligations and portions of periodic pension cost; the expected long-term rate of return on plan assets necessary for the gain or loss calculation; and where determined by the plan's benefit formula, assumed future compensation levels.
3. Provided the accounting policy adopted is followed consistently, No. 87 allows a number of choices. The market-related value of plan assets, a factor in the gain or loss computation, may be either fair market value or a calculated value that recognizes changes in fair value of plan assets over not more than five years; different methods of calculating market-related value can be used for different classes of plan assets. Prior service costs may be amortized by

the declining method prescribed for general use or by an alternative that reduces the unrecognized balance more rapidly. Subject to specified conditions, unrecognized net gains or losses may be amortized by any systematic method. The measurement date for requirements can be the date of the financial statements, or a date not more than three months earlier.

4. Beginning in 1989, calendar-year companies will be required to report any minimum unfunded pension liabilities, offset by intangible assets and/or reductions in shareholders' equity in their balance sheets. The potential effect of these changes on existing or proposed loan and other financing agreements should be evaluated and, where indicated, arrangements to avoid noncompliance should be initiated.

5. The income statement effects of adopting No. 87, which may include recording pension income instead of pension costs, may have unanticipated effects on bonus, profit-sharing, incentive, and similar plans. These effects should be estimated promptly and decisions made on whether the plans should be amended.

6. The new rules for foreign plans become effective in 1989. They are the same as the rules for domestic plans. Because a substantial effort may be necessary to develop the information for foreign plans, planning for conversion to the new rules should begin now.

7. Compliance with rules for determining the tax deductibility of pension costs might require data for IRS different from that needed for reporting under No. 87. Supplemental actuarial valuations may be needed for tax purposes.

Of the several types of pension plans covered by the new rules, the most significant impact of the new Standard will be on single-employer defined benefit plans.

A single-employer plan is maintained by one employer. The term is also used to describe a plan that is maintained by related parties such as a parent and its subsidiaries.

The main requirements of single-employer plans follow:

1. Effective in 1989 for calendar-year companies, balance sheet recognition of a minimum pension liability must be recognized. The "unfunded accumulated benefit obligation" equals the excess of the present value of benefits earned to date, calculated without reference to future compensation levels over the fair value of plan assets. Recording the minimum liability generates an intangible asset to the extent of unrecognized prior service cost; any excess is recorded as a reduction of equity.

2. Development of a standardized method for attributing pension cost to service periods. In requiring that the attribution method be based on the plan's benefit formula, the use of a "benefit" instead of a "cost" approach to determining periodic cost must be applied.

3. Recognition of future compensation levels in calculating the unrecognized net asset or obligation at the transition date, in determining net period cost and in disclosing the "projected benefit obligation" but not in calculating a minimum liability displayed in the balance sheet.

4. Linkage of current and delayed cost recognition to employee service periods. A liability must be recognized if net pension cost *exceeds* employer contribution. An additional minimum liability is recognized as an intangible asset. In limited circumstances, cost allocation is determined instead by the remaining life expectancy of inactive plan participants.

5. Prospective recognition of prior service cost and of the unrecognized net obligation or net asset determined at the transition date.

6. Delayed recognition of gains and losses. Those from all sources are aggregated and amortized by any systematic method consistently applied, subject to a floor set by the Standard's "corridor" approach. In an attempt to reduce volatility, the Board compounded the Standard's complexity by basing the gain or loss computation on the expected return on plan assets. That factor is determined by applying the expected long-term rate of return on plan assets to the market-related value of plan assets, which are defined as either fair value or a calculated value that spreads changes in fair value over not more than five years.

7. Separate calculation of numerous components of net periodic pension cost and separate disclosure of four items: service cost, interest cost, actual return on plan assets, and the net total of all other components.

8. Disclosure requirements are significantly expanded from present practice.
   - There should be a brief description of the plan and the type of benefit formula applied.
   - Financial statements should disclose the nature and effects of significant changes in the factors affecting the computation of the net pension liability (or asset) and net periodic pension cost recognized in the financial statements.
   - The funding policy should be disclosed. (APB Opinion No. 8 and FASB Statement No. 36 can be helpful in understanding differences between *funding* pension plans and *accounting* for plans.)
   - Net periodic pension costs and their components should be disclosed.
   - The actual return on plan assets should be shown.
   - Disclosure of the components of the pension benefit obligation is required.
   - The plan assets should be described.
   - A reconciliation of the amounts included in the funded status of the plan's projected benefit obligation is essential to understanding the relationship between the accounting and the funded status of the plan.
   - An assumed weighted-average discount rate and rate of compensation increase should be disclosed.
   - The following disclosures are *suggested* by the Rule:

    a. The ratio of net periodic pension cost to covered payroll.

    b. The separate amounts of amortization of unrecognized prior service and amortization of unrecognized net gain or loss.

    c. Information about cash flows of the plan separately showing employer contributions, other contributions, and benefits paid during the period.

    d. The amounts of plan assets classified by major asset category.

    e. The amounts of the vested benefit obligation owed to retirees and to others.

    f. The change in the projected benefit obligation that would result from a one-percentage-point change in (1) the assumed discount rate and (2) the assumed rate of compensation increase.

    g. The change in the service cost and interest cost components of net periodic pension cost that would result from a one-percentage-point change in (1) the assumed discount rate and (2) the assumed rate of compensation increase.

  9. Pension expense is reflected on the accrual basis.

  10. Actuarial gains and losses applicable to a single event not related to the pension plan and not in the ordinary course of business are recognized immediately in earnings. (Examples are plant closing; segment disposal).

FASB STATEMENT NO. 88

Employer's Accounting for Settlements and Curtailments of Defined Benefit Pension Plans and for Termination Benefits

The reason for this separate Statement to be applied simultaneously with Statement 87 is the FASB's decision that a separate Statement on employer's accounting for a settlement of a pension obligation, or a curtailment of a defined benefit pension plan, or a termination of benefits would provide a better understanding of the accounting procedures than to include them in the scope of Statement 87.

This Statement applies to an employer that sponsors a defined benefit pension plan accounted for under the provisions of Statement 87 if all or part of the plan's pension benefit obligation is settled or the plan is curtailed. It also applies to an employer that offers benefits to employees in connection with their termination of employment.

(Note: While Statements 87 and 88 include some of the rules in Statement 74, the new Statements supersede that rule.)

The significant requirements of this Statement follow:

• Statement 88 requires that unrecognized balances of prior service costs and net gains and losses computed under No. 87's delayed recognition model be considered to the extent specified in determining the effect on the income statement of a settlement or curtailment meeting the Standard's criteria.

- Restatement of previously issued financial statements is prohibited, except for one provision that has a retroactive effect; e.g., at the time of transition to No. 87 companies having deferred gains resulting from previous asset reversions are required, subject to limitations, to recognize them as income.
- A settlement and/or a curtailment may occur separately or together.
- The maximum gain or loss subject to recognition in earnings when a pension obligation is settled is the unrecognized net gain or loss plus any remaining unrecognized net asset existing at the date of initial application of Statement 87.
- The projected benefit obligation may be decreased (a gain) or increased (a loss) by a curtailment (see definition of *CURTAILMENT*). To the extent that a gain exceeds any unrecognized net loss, it is a curtailment gain. To the extent that a loss exceeds any unrecognized net gain, it is a curtailment loss.
- An employer can provide benefits to employees in connection with their termination of employment. The benefits can be either *special termination benefits* offered only for a short period of time, or *contractual termination benefits* required by the terms of a plan only if a specified event (a plant closing, for example) occurs. The employer that gives special termination benefits must recognize a liability and a loss when the employees accept the plan and the amount can be reasonably estimated. Termination benefits can take various forms including lump-sum payments, periodic future payments, a combination of both, paid directly from the employer's assets, from an existing pension plan, or from a new employee benefit plan.
- The Statement sets forth the events that require previously unrecognized amounts to be recognized in earnings and as adjustments to assets and liabilities. The previously unrecognized net gain or net loss and the previously unrecognized prior service cost should be recognized in the period when *all* of the following conditions are met:
  (1) All pension obligations are settled.
  (2) Defined benefits are no longer accrued under the plan.
  (3) The plan is not replaced by another defined benefit plan.
  (4) No plan assets remain.
  (5) The employees are terminated.
  (6) The plan ceases to exist as an entity.

Disclosure Requirements

An employer recognizing a gain or loss must make the following disclosures:

(1) A description of the nature of the event(s) associated with the gain or loss.
(2) The amount of the gain or loss that is recognized.

Effective Dates

Both Statements are effective for fiscal years beginning after December 15, 1986. Both Statements must be implemented simultaneously. Except for the delay permitted in reporting a minimum unfunded liability in the balance sheet, the new rules cannot be phased in through partial adoption. APB Opinion 8 is to be followed until the new rules are applied.

DEFERRED COMPENSATION PLANS

Non-Compensatory Plans

A plan is considered to be non-compensatory when it possesses all four of the following characteristics:

1. Almost all full-time employees may participate;
2. Stock is offered to employees equally based on a uniform percent of wages;
3. The time for exercise is limited to a reasonable period;
4. The discount from the market price of the stock is not greater than would be reasonable in an offer to stockholders or others.

Compensatory Plans

Stock issued to an employee under any plan *except* a non-compensatory plan (above) is considered to be a compensatory plan and calls for the recognition of *compensation expense* by the employer.

The time of earliest measurement (issuance, date of grant) is the determining factor as to when to record the compensation. The fact that the employee may not be able to receive or sell the stock for some years does *not* affect the compensation.

At the time of issuance (the date of the agreement), if the facts of the option price and a market price are known, the difference between a *higher* market price and the option price (the price at which the employee may buy the stock from the company) is considered to be compensation—at that time, not later. However, if the granting of the options is predicated upon the rendering of *future services*, the compensation calculated may be deferred to the period of future benefit (to be derived from those services). The excess (or bargain) is the theoretical benefit availed to the employee for his services, past, present or future.

For example, assume the employee's services would extend over two years (current and next year), the entry would be:

Current Year		
Employees Compensation (current expense)	50.	
Unearned Compensation (holdover)	50.	
Paid-In Capital		100.
Market Price at issuance	$ 10.	
Option price	9.	
Excess per share	$ 1.	
100 shares @ $1.	$100.	

Next Year		
Employees Compensation (expense)	50.	
Unearned Compensation		50.

Any "unearned compensation" should be shown as a separate reduction of stock options under the stockholders' equity.

No compensation is recognized if the option price equals or exceeds the market price at option issuance date.

Note again that the *exercise* date is not pertinent—yet.

For *tax* purposes, the amount deductible by the corporation is not applicable or determinable until the time the employee must pick up ordinary income, a factor which varies according to the plan as specified under IRS regulations. Thus, both the period and amount of expensing will probably differ for tax purposes, thus creating timing differences. Also, the difference between the compensation originally recorded and the tax-deductible amount goes to Capital Surplus.

The accounting for stock options follows:

Assume a stock option plan for an officer of the corporation which is for 1000 shares of $25 par value common stock. The stock can be purchased for $20 a share after 5 years. The market price on January 1, 1988, is $37.50 per share. January 1, 1988, is the measurement date, because the option price of $20 and the number of shares that can be acquired (1000) are both known. The compensation per share to be recognized is the difference between the market price $37.50 and the option price ($20), as the officer is employed over the five-year period.

Entry at the end of Year 1:			
Dec. 31, 1988	Salary Expense	3,500	
	Stock Options		
	Exercisable		3,500

To record portion of compensatory stock option plan earned as of 12/31/88. (1000 × $17.50 = $17,500 × 1/5 = $3,500)

(This entry is repeated each year until the options are exercised.)

The options are exercised on December 31, 1992, and the officer remits the $20 per share option price.

Dec. 31, 1992	Cash	20,000	
	Stock Options		
	Exercisable	17,500	
	Common Stock ($25 Par)		25,000
	Paid-in Capital in		
	Excess of Par Value		12,500

Earnings Per Share

All shares which could be issued under the arrangement are considered "as if" issued, and considered to be common stock equivalents and outstanding for earnings per share computations. If applicable, the treasury stock method is used to determine the incremental shares.

Compensatory stock options may thus affect *both* factors in the EPS formula: The numerator, for the compensation expense; and the denominator, by the addition of the equivalent shares.

Both primary and fully diluted computations are affected, if 3% or more.

PROFIT SHARING PLANS

Contributions are based upon independent action taken by the corporate Board of Directors, tied to the profit of the year, under a profit sharing agreement approved by both management and employees. The authority for the contribution is reflected in the minutes of the corporation. The IRS also approves the plan.

The IRS imposes a combined maximum tax-deductible limit for companies having *both* plans.

ACTUARIAL GAINS AND LOSSES

Reported gains or losses within the plans should be considered, generally on the average method, and only to the extent that they might necessitate a change in the contribution requirement. These gains or losses are usually reflected in the computations made by the fund administrator in the determination of the amount needed to be contributed by the corporation to keep the plan properly funded, subject to the minimum and maximum considerations.

DEFINED CONTRIBUTION PLANS

These plans specify either:

1. Benefits will be based on defined *contributions*, or
2. Contributions will result in defined *benefits*.

In circumstance (1), the contribution is the pension cost for the year. Circumstance (2) requires the determination of pension cost in the same detailed manner just described.

INSURED PLANS

Usually the amount of net premium payment determined by the insurance company is the proper pension cost for the employer, provided dividends, termination costs and other factors are handled properly by the insurance company.

COMPANIES WITH MORE THAN ONE PLAN

Actuarial methods may differ, but accounting for each plan should follow the stated standards.

SOCIAL SECURITY BENEFITS AND PENSION PLANS

Some pension plans provide for reduced benefits to the extent of Social Security benefits. In estimating future benefits for present value purposes under the plan, estimate must also be made for the Social Security benefits applicable.

ERISA REQUIREMENTS

No change in accounting standards is necessitated by the new participation, vesting or funding requirements of the 1974 Act because the determination of proper cost still falls under the minimum-maximum rules. However, significant increases in the dollar amount of the pension cost contribution caused by the requirements should be disclosed when the plan first becomes subject to the Act.

OTHER DEFERRED COMPENSATION CONTRACTS

Other contracts should be accounted for individually on an accrual basis, with the estimated amounts to be ultimately paid systematically, and rationally allocated over the period of active employment from the time the contract is effective until services are expected to end or the contract expires. However, deferring expenses is permissible to match future services.

For annuity or lump-sum type settlements in these plans, the annual accrual should still be accrued over the time of active employment. Thus, the total expenses booked to the end of employment should equal the estimated present value of the money to be paid to the employee (or beneficiaries).

When payments extend beyond the period of active employment (such as annuity payments to a beneficiary), the present value of all said payments should be accrued and expensed.

KEY-PERSON LIFE INSURANCE

The acceptable method of accounting for premium costs incurred in buying key-person (non-term) life insurance is to first charge an asset account for the period's increase in the cash surrender value of the policy, and then expense the difference between that increase and the premium paid. The ratable charge method is not acceptable. This procedure applies only to those policies under which the corporation is the ultimate beneficiary. But the procedure also applies to those policies which may be taken on ''debtor-corporation'' officers.

A loan on a life insurance policy of an officer can be shown in either of two ways:

1. As a current liability if the company intends to repay it within the current year; or
2. As a deduction from the amount shown as cash surrender value if the company does *not* intend to repay it within a year. If it runs to the death of the insured, it is deducted from the proceeds, if the corporation transmits them to the survivors.

Although the corporation is the beneficiary of these funds on a pay-out of the policy, the proceeds are usually used to pay benefits to the employee's family, to redeem stock, or for some other purpose beneficial to the employee.

MISCELLANEOUS CONSIDERATIONS

In a business combination, the rule for assigning an amount for the assumption of pension cost accruals should be the greater of:

1. The accrued pension cost computed in conformity with the accounting policies of the acquiring company, or
2. The excess, if any, of the actuarially computed value of the vested benefits over the amount of the fund.

In the disposal of a business segment, costs and expenses directly associated with the decision to dispose should include such items as:

1. Severance pay;
2. Additional pension costs;
3. Employee relocation expenses.

In pooling of interest, employee compensation and stock option plans, if reasonable, may carry over to the acquiring company without violating the precepts of pooling.

401(k) PLANS

Definition: Section 401(k) of the Internal Revenue Code authorizes an employee benefit plan, under which an employee can elect to defer current taxes on the portion of his taxable income contributed on his behalf by his employer.

The main features of 401(k) plans follow:

- Current tax savings for employers and employees.
- Employees can accumulate a substantial retirement fund by putting a portion of their income into a tax-deductible plan.
- Suitable for companies with a high percentage of employees who are willing to save a portion of their pay. 70 percent of all employees, or 80 percent of eligible employees, must choose to participate in the plan.
- Companies contributing to a profit-sharing plan can also contribute to a 401(k) plan, as the plan can be combined with an existing pension or profit-sharing plan.
- Employee's contribution can be a portion of pay, or in lieu of a pay increase.
- All funds placed in the plan are deductible by the employer. And the employee's contribution and subsequent earnings on the plan's investments are tax free to the employee until withdrawal.
- Lump-sum withdrawals qualify for 10-year averaging.
- Employer and employee's contributions can be as much as 15 percent of the employee's pay, up to an annual dollar limit on profit-sharing plans.
- Employer's costs associated with establishing and administering the plan are deductible as ordinary business expenses.
- 401(k) plans must be part of a qualified profit-sharing or stock bonus plans. A qualified plan must meet the following requirements:
    1. The plan must permit the employee to elect to have the employer's contribution made to an employee trust.
    2. The plan must prohibit a distribution of trust benefits attributable to employer contributions made merely because of the completion of a stated period of participation, or the lapse of a fixed number of years.

3. The employee's right to the accrued benefit derived from employer contributions must be nonforfeitable.
4. The plan must meet nondiscrimination rules pertaining to employee coverage.

A plan meets the nondiscrimination rule if:

1. The plan prohibits contributions and benefits from discriminating in favor of employees who are officers, shareholders, or highly compensated employees.
2. The plan either covers a certain minimum percentage of employees, or does not discriminate in its coverage.
3. The plan must cover a certain minimum percentage of eligible employees.
4. The contributions made to the plan must satisfy one of two *actual deferral percentage* tests: 1) The test for eligible highly compensated employees must not be more than the deferral percentage of all other eligible employees multiplied by 1.5; or 2) The excess of the actual deferral percentage for the highly compensated employees must not be more than the actual deferral percentage of all other eligible employees multiplied by 2.5.

Definitions

HIGHLY COMPENSATED EMPLOYEE: An eligible employee who receives more compensation than two-thirds of all other eligible employees.

ELIGIBLE EMPLOYEE: An employee who in any year is eligible for employer contributions under the plan for that year.

ACTUAL DEFERRAL PERCENTAGE: For the eligible highly compensated employee (top ⅓) and all other eligible employees (lower ⅔) for a plan year: the average of the ratio, calculated separately for each employee in such group, of the amount of employer contributions paid under the plan on behalf of each employee for such year to the employee's compensation for the same year.

EMPLOYEE COMPENSATION: An employee's compensation is the amount taken into account under the plan prior to calculating the contribution made on behalf of the employee under the deferral election.

COVERED EMPLOYEES: Those employees in any year whose accounts are credited with a contribution under the plan for that year.

- Employees *may* borrow from the plan, but under strict guidelines set forth in the Code and in IRS regulations.
- 401(k) plan may impact other qualified plans. If an employee is a participant

in a 401(k) plan and elects to defer a portion of his pay into the plan, the reduction in his compensation for federal income tax purposes may affect his potential benefits under other plans in which he is a participant. For example, if the employee is in a profit-sharing plan under which employer contributions are geared to pay, a reduction in pay due to a 401(k) contribution may reduce the employer's contribution to the profit-sharing plan. The same is true with defined benefit pension plans in which potential benefits are based upon current compensation, and which could be affected by deferrals into a 401(k) plan.

- Participation in a 401(k) plan does not affect an employee's right to set up an IRA.

- The plan cannot discriminate in favor of "key" or highest paid officers, executives, the "highly compensated," or shareholders.

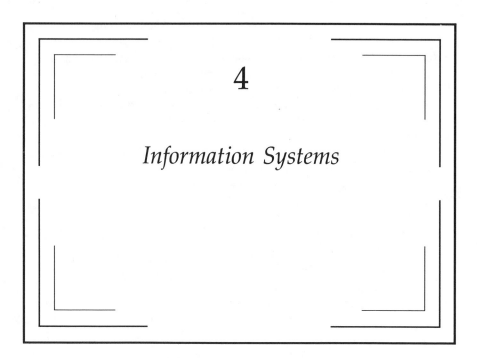

4

Information Systems

THE FLOW OF DOCUMENTS

Paper. The forest primeval—milled and pressed to industrial use.

Contracts, certificates, invoices, correspondence, memos, rules, ledgers, machine-tapes, flow charts, advertising catalogs, computer runs, time-cards, checks, statements, tags, cards, sheets, rolls—scratch paper—envelopes, boxes, cartons. Unused paper supplies; paper-in-process; paper filed. Microfilm. Tax returns. Tape and red tape.

An avalanche, if uncontrolled.

Logic, purpose and usefulness, when held in check. A systematized schematic designed to control the economic current which generates the power of the business entity. Periodically to be monitored and tested for resistance, weakness, stability and storage capacity.

The aim—the goal—is to focus all paper into a group picture—one still-life, the photo at a given moment in time—the year-end for the financial statements, as posed by the figures in the general ledger, adjusted and dressed for that split-second closing moment. The numerical characters in a tableau, arranged and described in narration in conformity with professional standards.

Throughout the year, the numerical characters which will ultimately be stilled for one moment—to be counted and accounted for—to be placed in proper perspective for that financial statement group photograph—these characters keep moving, refusing to stand still, adding, accumulating, building, sometimes detracting and withdrawing—darting in and out of the books of account.

A firm hand is needed to guide these figures, to direct their movements, to prevent the inanimate from taking on life of its own, stop the machine before it becomes the master.

The chart of the anatomical business blood-line, in terms of recorded circulation, must be clearly directed, delineated and controlled:

The veins: through which information flows to the heart—
The books of original entry:

1. General Journal
2. Cash Receipts Book
3. Cash Disbursements Book
4. Sales Book with its corollary Accounts Receivable sub-ledger
5. Purchases Book with its corollary Accounts Payable sub-ledger
6. Payroll Register and Summaries

The heart: which stores and pumps out the information—
The general ledger (with its associated valves):

7. General Ledger and Subsidiaries:

    Inventory Control
    Fixed Assets Ledger
    Cost Sub-Ledger Control
    Schedules to supplement

The arteries: which take that flow for digestion to the body and members of the community—owners, bankers, creditors, government, the general public—
The financial statements:

8. Balance Sheet
9. Income Statement
10. Statement of Changes in Financial Position
11. Statement of Changes in Retained Earnings (or Capital interests)
12. Financial notes

The following pages outline an approach to the development of an information system, which is sufficiently broad in its components, so that the accountant can apply it as a starting point for a study. Following this general outline are the components of an accounting information system in detail.

AN ACCOUNTING INFORMATION SYSTEM OUTLINE

What is an Information System?

I. A network of *procedures* for processing raw data in such a way as to generate the information required for management use.

    (A) Procedures—the logical steps for accomplishing a job.

    (B) System—a network of related procedures, the sum of which result in the accomplishment of the objective.

Objective of an Information System

I. To reduce the range of uncertainty in the decision-making process.

The Nature of Information

I. Understanding the nature of information.

    (A) What is information?

        1. Information includes *all* the data and intelligence—financial and nonfinancial—that management needs to plan, operate and control a particular enterprise.

        2. Information is not just the accounting system and the forms and reports it produces. An efficient information system must move beyond the limits of classical accounting reports, and conceive of information as it relates to two vital elements of the management process—planning and control.

            (a) Information about the future.

            (b) Data expressed in nonfinancial terms, e.g., share of market, performance of personnel, adequacy of customer service.

            (c) Information dealing with external conditions as they might bear on a particular company's operations.

    (B) Data is not information. Information *is* data presented in a useful form.

        1. A report is a device which communicates information, not data.

II. Information is quantitative (statistical) or qualitative (nonstatistical).

    (A) Quantitative information—concerns selected data; data selected with respect to the problem, the user, time, place and function.

    (B) Qualitative—concerns information that can be expressed in nonstatistical terms; i.e., adequacy of customer service, environmental conditions.

The Economics of Information

I. Think of information as a *resource* used in a way that improves the organization's other resources—its personnel and physical facilities. Proper information can help to achieve the goals of the organization in the most efficient manner.

II. Like any other resource, information is not a free commodity. Accordingly, the same criteria should be applied to the development of an information system as to the development of any other resource.

(A) Will the additional benefits expected from an information system justify the additional costs of developing and implementing the system (marginal cost vs. marginal utility)?

III. In regard to paragraph II, information is available to the organization at some cost. Generally, the initial information is of great value. However, as more and more information is "bought," it becomes increasingly difficult to make use of these incremental units. Therefore, the utility of additional information decreases as more and more information becomes available.

IV. As more information is searched for, the cost of each *additional* unit of information tends to increase.

V. *The Problem*: Determining the amount of information you need from an information system becomes a balancing act. The maximum amount of information that the system can provide isn't necessarily the best. The additional costs of *one* more unit of information should be *exactly* equal to the assigned monetary value of the last unit of information provided.

Impact of the Information System on Organizational Structure

I. The system must tie together information requirements of the organizational structure.

II. The information system will produce changes in personnel working environment.

III. Usually, there is a gap created by a changing organization structure and a static information system.

Three Elements of an Information System

I. Syntheses of three subsystems of an information system.
(A) The computer
(B) Data processing
(C) The language

Approach

I. Cornerstone for developing a management information system is the determination of the organization's information needs.
(A) Requires a clear understanding of each decision-maker's role in the organization. This includes responsibilities, authority, and relationships with other executives.

      1. This cannot be accomplished by the open approach of simply asking an executive what information he requires.

      2. Information systems analyst must help management determine its information needs.

      3. Must be related to the manager's planning and control functions.

II. Analyze and evaluate the system *currently* in use.

    (A) Procedures

    (B) Forms used

    (C) Costs

Planning Information

I. Planning means setting objectives, formulating strategies, and deciding among alternative courses of action.

    (A) The information required to do planning is of three basic types.

      1. *Environmental Information.* Describes the social, political, and economic aspects of the climate in which a business operates, or may operate in the future.

      2. *Competitive Information.* Explains the past performance, programs, and plans of competing companies.

      3. *Internal Information.* Indicates a company's own strengths and weaknesses.

II. Planning information.

    (A) The strategic (as opposed to operating) information about critical business problems.

    (B) Flows to the top executive level.

    (C) The information required for executive-level decisions, e.g., policies.

    (D) Policy maker will be faced with less uncertainty, in the sense that he is better informed about what is going on.

    (E) Organization discipline is tightened as operating methods and results come under instantaneous observation of top management.

III. Determine the decision-making levels in the organization. How many "tiers" are to be included in the information system?

IV. Is the current system adequate?

    (A) Twenty tests to determine if the current system is adequate.

      1. Does the current system produce useful reports, or just listings of numbers?

      2. Do all individuals, or stations, who receive reports use them for decision-making purposes, or do they receive them because they are interesting, or because it is ego-filling to be on the distribution list?

      3. Does the same report go to different levels of decision makers? Does the information system take into account the different needs for information at the different organizational levels?

4. If an organization has automated, is the data processing subsystem simply a bookkeeping tool of the conventional accounting system? Is the automatic data processing system being used for information purposes, or merely as computing hardware?

5. Are the managing officers completely familiar with the current system? Are they devoting personal interest and talent to this area?

6. Is the system viewed as a decision-making resource, or narrowly as only a means to reduce accounting costs?

7. Is the fact realized that conventional accounting systems fail to provide *all* the information necessary for the decision-making process?

8. When was the system last analyzed?

9. Is the information system centralized or decentralized? If the latter, is there a duplication of information processing?

10. Can stored information be retrieved efficiently by users?

11. How good are the internal data for planning purposes?

12. How do costs behave in response to volume changes?

13. Are the factors that condition success in the organization explicitly stated and widely communicated among the management group?

14. Has the organization's structure remained *unchanged* during the past 15 years?

15. Does the organization regularly collect and analyze information about population, price level, labor, and other important trends affecting the general profitability of the organization?

16. What analyses are currently reported to operating management? Are they reported in a manner that permits their utilization in the planning process?

17. Is significant information about competitors regularly collected and analyzed?

18. How is current information "factored into" the planning process?

19. To what extent are decisions based upon fact vs. belief and opinion?

20. How is current information communicated? In a formal or informal manner?

V. Analyze the current system to discover weaknesses.

(A) Analyze the flow of information through the system.

(B) Analyze the operations (termed "events") performed by individuals (or stations) in the system.

(C) Combine (A) and (B) by locating the *origin* of documents, measuring the effort needed to produce them, data needed for correct preparation, number of individuals, or stations, in the system that need copies, and the events that cause documents to be prepared.

1. Compare the output that results with the output desired.

2. Consider modifications that can reduce input, or will result in more desirable output, or both.

(**D**) Study all the operations of the business in order to understand clearly the *processes* within the company.

Use of Linear Programming

I. Linear programming can be used to maximize resource allocation.
  (**A**) Linear programming is a systematic way of finding the best course of action when many variables and many conditions must be taken into consideration.
  (**B**) An approach to maximizing an objective (profits) which is subject to many restrictions—legal, safety, service, and policy.
  (**C**) Four advantages of using linear programming:
    1. Construction of the model will give management additional insight into its everyday operations.
    2. The model gives management a way of testing and quantifying the effects of policy decisions.
    3. Linear programming stimulates the setting of goals and criteria for evaluating performance.
    4. Linear programming is an effective technique for long-range planning in the face of uncertainty.

Feedback Control

I. Controls involve *techniques* such as financial controls, costs, and other types of controls.
II. Based on pertinent and timely information.
III. Information for Feedback Control. Three basic flows of information needed.
  (**A**) Provides a constant check on day-to-day results to be compared with expected or forecasted standards.
  (**B**) Fulfills most of the decision-making information for middle and lower echelons of operating personnel.
  (**C**) The information provided is usually historical in nature—deals with money, materials, people, performance.
  (**D**) Introduces management by exception techniques.*
    1. Establishes criteria, standards, forecasted or expected performance.
    2. Directs management attention *only* to off-target performance. Keeps useless information from the top. Only relevant facts, as they arise, will reach management, enabling control of circumstances as they are developing.

*Incidentally, this technique is hardly new in concept. See Exodus XVIII, Jethro to Moses, ". . . every great matter they shall bring to you, but any small matter they shall decide themselves."

3. Reduces volume of information needed, because on-target performance can proceed without further action.

(a) Relieved of unnecessary data-gathering and other unproductive routines, so manager is freed for other work—particularly where his human abilities are needed, such as working with and helping employees under him.

SUB-LEDGERS AND SCHEDULES

Some accounts in the general ledger are, by their very nature *summaries* of important supplemental data which, because of bulk alone, would, if not entered in summary form, make the physical ledger too huge to handle. Items such as individual accounts receivable and payable, inventory units, machinery and equipment—though each represents an individual asset or liability—are best displayed in one or more summary accounts, with full details being maintained in a separate book or ledger, individually tended, the total of which ties to the control account.

Some, like accounts receivable and accounts payable, are automatic products of the internal system. (The computer updates the accounts receivable file with sales and with payments received, with the monthly summaries of changes going to the general ledger control account.) Sometimes, a one-write system updates subsidiaries simultaneously. Others must be maintained manually, like the fixed asset ledger or the manual inventory control card-system. Others may be generated by outside sources, like payroll records and summaries. Others are as basic as a petty cash summary.

SYSTEMS—MANUAL, MECHANIZED OR COMPUTERIZED

The number of different methods used for keeping records is almost as varied as the personalities of the people designing, operating and maintaining the system. With the exception of those larger entities where work is so divided that each employee performs only one small function in a huge system overviewed by few, except top management and outside auditors—few businesses use a standard text-book approach.

Most private systems are the result of accumulations of changing bit-by-bit adaptions to the needs and demands of the business itself and outside influences (taxes, AICPA and SEC guides and requirements, state and federal laws, competitive practices, advanced technology, market conditions, good-bad sales/profit results, etc.). Except where the availability of funds and skills is unlimited (practically nowhere), most systems in use today are evolvements and combinations of good old basic hand-written techniques, now partitioned into piecemeal refinements, combining mechanical, electronic and manual skills.

Complete automation of the *entire* accounting process is a rarity.

Ultimately, the nature of the system used depends upon one or more of these factors:

Time and expediency

Skill required

Cost

Facilities and space available

The degree of in-depth coverage *wanted* by owners/management.

Note the emphasis on the word "wanted." Many weaknesses need correction for better tax-review backup or for more efficient reporting, but management, in weighing the costs involved, wisely chooses not to refine. For example, if the *cost* of instituting a highly complex standard costing system outweighs the advantages to be gained from it, management may choose to retain its current, less complex, less specific costing system, which has understandable, but controllable tolerances of error.

The Evolutionary Process of the Machine

The evolutionary process of systematized accounting record maintenance might use the following piecemeal add-on progression:

All Manual System

1. The *"shoebox" system.* The owner transacts all business in cash—buying, selling, paying expenses—and tosses invoices, documents, and receipts into a box.
2. The *checkbook.* The owner stops paying bills with cash, now pays by check. Still uses shoebox for receipts for sales. Notes deposits in checkbook.
3. *Cash disbursements book.* Has now hired someone to do his payroll tax reporting. Lists each check in a book, from which he can obtain a columnar breakout distribution of each type of expense.
4. *Payroll register.* Supplements the above by transferring the weekly payroll items to separate sheets for each employee where total earnings and deductions are accumulated as required for payroll tax reports.
5. *Cash receipts book.* Owner now lists each day's receipts separately and distributes to columns by type of sale or income.
6. *General ledger.* Owner sets up a ledger sheet for each column category in his disbursements and receipts book. "Posts" summary totals periodically.
7. *General ledger expanded.* The owner goes back to the old shoebox and digs out the cost information needed to set up the value of permanent items bought then (assets: equipment, fixtures, etc.) Sets up asset accounts, long-term liabilities and a balancing net worth account.

8. *Sales book/accounts receivable ledger.* To get more sales, owner finds he must start giving credit. He uses sequentially numbered invoices, lists charge sales daily in numerical order in Sales Book. Makes a separate page for each customer in an accounts receivable subsidiary ledger. For this, he uses a carbonized two-part preprinted statement, which he updates manually every day or so.

In the Cash Receipts Book, he adds a column for "received on account" from customers. Line-by-line, these credits are posted to the above subsidiary ledger-statement. Also, he includes a column for cash discounts and allowances taken by customers. At month-end, he mails original to customer and keeps the copy of the statement as his ledger sheet and starts a new sheet for the new month with the balance from the old sheet.

9. *Periodic financial statements.* Owner now wishes to see how he progresses. Finds he needs further information for an accurate statement. He must, in a side computation, compute or estimate:
Any unpaid bill to creditors
Inventory on hand
Taxes due to date on payrolls, etc.
Possible bad debts among his stated receivables
Depreciate his equipment

At this point, he probably seeks outside assistance.

10. *Purchase book/accounts payable ledger.* As business expands, his debts accumulate, and he wants to know the exact status of when and to whom payments are due. He adds these books to the system. In the Cash Disbursements Book, he puts a column for payment on account to accounts payable and another for cash discounts taken.

11. *Perpetual inventory cards.* His on-hand stock of unsold items grows daily, and he can no longer trust his memory to recall the exact cost of items in stock, nor the quantities on hand. He sets up one card for each type of merchandise on hand, goes to the storage area, counts and lists everything, checks his purchase invoices and assigns a cost to each item. On the card, he provides all the details pertaining to that item, so that he knows what's on hand and what cost it represents. Periodically, he takes a physical count to verify the perpetual cards.

12. *General journal.* He rounds off the system by putting in here any entry which does not appropriately go in the other books of original entry. He posts from here and the other books directly to the General Ledger.

13. *Worksheet entries and worksheet trial balance.* As an adjunct to the preparation of the now monthly financial statements, accruals, recurrent adjustments and accrual reversals (when necessary) are made to the balances taken from the ledger—all on workpapers—to determine monthly position and progress.

14. *Imprest petty cash system.* Adds this to tighten up on loose expenditures.

15. *Fixed asset subsidiary ledger.* To better detail them for depreciation investment tax credit, gains or losses on dispositions, and basis on trade-ins.

Mechanizing

16. *A one-write system for check disbursements.* Here, he combines the old check book and his Cash Disbursements Book into one writing process, instead of two. He also opens a separate bank account for the payroll and uses a one-write system for it also. At month-end, he summary posts to the General Ledger.

17. *A billing machine.* Rented or bought. Mechanizes his invoices, customer statements, sales book and subsidiary receivable ledger.

18. *Service bureau.* He assigns numbers to his general ledger accounts in an ascending series covering assets, liabilities, equity, income, costs and expenses in that order. He is assisted in setting up framework numbers for captioning and totaling functions so the computer-produced financial statement conforms with the special format he wants. Monthly, he sends to the service bureau:
A copy of his one-write check listing, with account numbers assigned for the debiting (in lieu of the columnar distribution spread);
Manual summary entries for each other book of original entry;
Manual entries for accruals, adjustments, recurrent monthly entries, reversals of accruals.

All this is submitted in simple debit/credit style with account numbers indicated. He adds each page, gets totals for debits, credits and *account numbers*, and gets an overall batch control total for each. The Service Bureau cross-checks the inputting to the batch totals, and posting to wrong accounts is virtually eliminated.

He receives from the Service Bureau a printed Cash Disbursements listing, a General Ledger with alpha description (brief, as inputted), and financial statements with detailed supporting schedules.

19. *Computer terminal.* A typewriter-like console, which is hooked via telephone lines into an outside-owned computer. He may put his sales and receivables on it, his check-processing and disbursements run, his purchase-vendor invoices and purchase book, his inventory, the payroll, or general ledger—practically anything desired, depending upon the programming availability and the costs. The techniques used are compatible with those learned in the use of the service bureau, with the addition of a few typewriter-input techniques.

20. *Video scope*. May supplement the computer terminal, so he can call for almost instantaneous display of that off-premises storage in the central processor's electronic file. He may request a printout for later delivery.

21. *The in-house computer*. The final decision is made. He rents or buys a computer for total in-house use. The extent of options available is vast. Basically, the type of in-house computer obtained should depend upon the more important of the following features:

The output wanted.

The capacity of the central processing unit for permanent program storage.

The additional adjunct program storage possibilities.

The type of storage—cassette, disc, tape and on down to magnetic cards or punched-paper tape, with each having advantages in terms of cost or access.

The type of input—punched cards, direct input from console, intermediate from console-to-tape-to-computer, etc.

The extent of printout capabilities and demands (speed, size of paper, etc.).

The adaptation of video screens at the console or remote locations—branches, warehouse.

The cost factor—initial investment, machine and programs, maintenance, personnel needed, space necessitated.

The extent of skill needed.

The imagination of the owner or management—willingness to learn, try, develop new methods, new talents.

PAYROLLS AND PAYROLL TAXES

Legal requirements have made the maintenance of accurate earnings records a mandatory function of any financial accounting system. The preparation of payrolls is now, in many companies, a segregated division of duty. Regular periodic summary information from detailed payroll records is needed for entry into the general ledger.

Details of each payroll are usually summarized monthly in a general journal entry and posted to the general ledger with distribution of the debits going to various salary-expense areas (for the gross salary) and the credits going to various withholding accounts (sometimes netted against corresponding employer-expense accounts, such as unemployment insurance) and the cash account upon which the net payroll checks are drawn.

The employer later pays the amounts withheld (hopefully as due) to the various taxing or other authorities, including his employer's added share (expense) as determined in the preparation of the required form for filing.

To support the filings, each payroll item must be isolated and collated for *each* individual employee to accumulate that individual's record of earnings as required for these quarterly, semi-annual and annual reports to federal, state and city taxing arms. The Fair Labor Standards Act and state laws also set standards of minimum pay for work hours and overtime for some or all employees.

Many payrolls are now prepared by outside processors, such as banks and service bureaus. Controls should be as strong as possible to assure accurate, protected input and output. All voided checks, for example, should be surrendered to the employer and accounted for in bank reconciliations.

Individual personnel permanent files should be maintained and would probably include:

Name and address, Social Security number, date of birth, date hired, occupation, work week, regular and overtime rates, basis of pay (day, week, month), authorized increases, vacation time, bonuses, injuries and compensation claims and settlements, pension and profit-sharing information (deductions, rights, and vested interests), W-4 and other withholding authorizations, references and correspondence, educational transcripts, unemployment claims and reports, medical records, health claims, expense-account authorizations, separation information (date, circumstances, etc.) and other information.

Time cards are usually filed separately and tied to specific payrolls by reference identification.

Payroll tax reports usually required are:

Federal:

Card-form 501 for payroll tax deposits with local bank

Quarterly 941 for withholding and FICA

W-2's

W-3

Annual 940 (Federal Unemployment)

1099—information returns with summary 1096

State:

Withholding tax—interim and annual

Unemployment insurance—usually quarterly

Disability insurance—usually quarterly, sometimes combined with unemployment report

Annual reports covering individual earnings; possibly annual information returns also.

The entire process of payroll preparation is an area which is conducive to effective statistical sampling techniques. Management (as well as outside auditors) should periodically sample all phases of the payroll routine, from initial authorizations through to the canceled-check returns. The discovery of one flaw might prove significant.

THE GENERAL LEDGER, CHART OF ACCOUNTS AND TRIAL BALANCE

In the world of mechanical figures, uniformity offers many advantages, especially the one of eliminating hard-knock costly errors experienced by forerunners in the field of experimentation. One such area of "uniformity" in standard usage, which is most beneficial, is the conventional layout of the general ledger.

As shown below, accounts in the general ledger are most useful if arranged and numbered in the order sequence indicated. Any firm which has gone to an outside computer service or installed its own in-house computer for the generation of machined financial statements will attest to the necessity for this format. The machines, unthinking as they are, can easily be programmed to add, subtract, combine, sub-total, balance, and print these accounts according to numerically sequential instructions each step of the way down the line-by-line financial balance sheet and income statement. (Moreover, sub-ledgers can be added as needed.)

> Assets:
>   Current
>   Non-current
>   Other
> Liabilities:
>   Current
>   Long-term
> Equity:
>   Capital stock
>   Retained earnings
> Income—revenue from operations
> Cost of sales items
> Expenses:
>   Selling
>   Administrative
> Non-operating income and expense
> Federal income tax
> Extraordinary items:
>   Less applicable income tax
>   Net income

Limitations and definitions of the entries into each account should be spelled out for anyone with responsibility for booking entries into the general ledger. Most large firms have drawn up internal "charts of accounts" which pinpoint exactly which accounts should be debited or credited and the sources from which the entry might come. At the least, someone should be charged with the responsibility of making the decision, and written authorizations (sometimes, voucher-type general journal entries) should be prepared and signed by that authority.

Many modern systems call for the manual booking of summaries of all the books of original entry, recurrent monthly journal entries, adjustments, accruals and reversals onto loose-leaf-type numbered journal sheets, batch-totaled, with a copy going to the computer department for processing to monthly hard-copy ledger cards. Sometimes, a yearly re-run is made showing all the action in each account for the entire year. A trial balance is usually a by-product of the computer-run general ledger.

Summary entries may be by-passed for cash disbursements, sales or purchases, if the input of this material is programmed for direct summation of monthly activity, being stored and posted to the general ledger when run with the other input from the summary general journal sheets.

Some systems in use today even by-pass the use of a general ledger, producing all the same pertinent information and references in comprehensive, detailed financial statements. Controls here should assure proper input, output and traceable audit trails.

LONG-TERM CONSTRUCTION CONTRACTS

Revenue is usually recognized at the time of exchanges in which cash is received or new claims arise against other entities. However, exceptions are made, for example . . . for long-term construction-type contracts.

There are two methods available to commercial organizations engaged wholly or partly in the contracting business for handling long-term construction contracts:

1. The completed-contract method; and
2. The percentage-of-completion method.

These contracts generally entail the construction of a specific project.

THE COMPLETED-CONTRACT METHOD

The completed-contract method recognizes income only when the contract is completed or substantially completed. Costs of contracts in process and current billings are accumulated, but there are no charges or credits to income except for provisions for losses. If remaining costs are not significant in amount, a contract may be regarded as substantially completed.

General and administrative expenses are not charged off to periodic income but are allocated to the contract. This is especially important when no contracts are completed in a year in which there are general and administrative expenses. It is not as important when there are numerous contracts. However, there should be no excessive deferring of overhead costs which might occur if total overhead was assigned to few or small contracts in process.

Even though the completed-contract method does not permit recording any income before completion, provision should be made for expected losses. Any excess of accumulated costs over related billings should be shown in the balance sheet as a current asset. Excess of accumulated billings over related costs should be shown in most cases as a current liability. Where there are many contracts, and costs exceed billing on some and billings exceed costs on others, the contracts should be segregated so that the figures on the asset side include only those contracts in which costs exceed billings and on the liability side, only those in which billings exceed costs. The assets should be described as ''costs of uncompleted contracts in excess of related billings'' rather than as inventory or work in process. On the liability side, the item should be described as ''billings and uncompleted contracts in excess of related costs.'' The standards state that the excess accumulated billings over related costs should be shown as a current liability *in most cases*. Noncurrent classification is discouraged, but would nevertheless be within GAAP.

The advantage of the completed-contract method is that since it is based on results as finally determined, it is generally more accurate than if it were based on estimates for unperformed work which could involve unforeseen costs or other possible losses. It is generally used for contracts lasting less than one year. But where accurate estimates of completion costs aren't available, it may be used for longer term contracts. The disadvantage of the completed-contract method is that in a period where no contract has been completed, current performance is not reflected. This results in showing high profits one year and little or no profits in other years.

Percentage-of-Completion Method

The percentage-of-completion method recognizes income as work on a contract goes along. Recognized income should be *that percentage of estimated total income* that either (a) incurred costs to date *bear to total costs* after giving effect to estimates of costs to complete based upon most recent information or (b) which may be indicated by such other measures of progress to completion as may be appropriate (see illustration). Under the percentage-of-completion method current assets may include costs and recognized income not yet billed for certain contracts, and liabilities (usually current liabilities) may include billings in excess of costs and recognized income with regard to other contracts.

The principal advantages of the percentage-of-completion method are (1) periodic recognition of income instead of the irregular recognition of income on completed contracts, and (2) the reflection of the status of the uncompleted contracts through the current estimates of costs to complete or of progress toward completion. In the *completed-contract method* there is no reflection of status of uncompleted contracts.

ILLUSTRATION
Income reflected under percent-of-completion method:

	Accumulated Percent Completed (1)	Expenses allocable to contract (2)	Year's assigned portion of contract (1)	Net income to report
Year 1	30%	$ 305,000	$ 300,000	$ (5,000)
Year 2	75%	385,000	450,000	65,000
Year 3	100%	210,000	250,000	40,000
Totals		$ 900,000	$ 1,000,000	$ 100,000

Total contract price is $1,000,000.

(1) A Percentage of completion is a certified percentage furnished by the architect. The percent increases each year until 100% is completed. The difference between one year and the next is that year's completed portion.

(2) Includes supplies used during year, with consideration given to opening and closing inventories. Expenses are those ascertainable as incurred to bring the contract to the stage of completion.

The chief disadvantage of the percentage-of-completion method is that it depends upon estimates of ultimate costs and, consequently, of currently accruing income which is subject to uncertainties inherent in long-term contracts.

Note that *billings* are not shown because reportable income is *not* predicated on them, though in some cases billings may coincide with the percentage completed.

Income under the "Completed Contract" Method

Using the same example above, the net income of $100,000 would be reported only in the final year (Year 3), together with details. No reflection of partial completion is shown on the income statement for the first and second years.

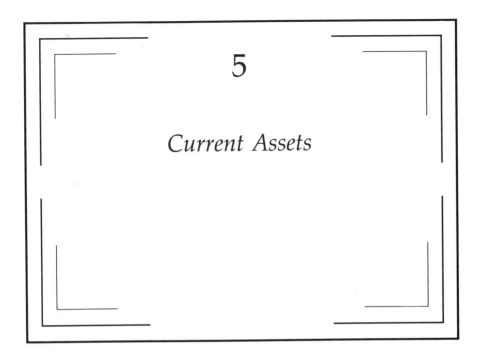

5

Current Assets

CLASSIFICATION OF CURRENT ASSETS

Classification of current assets is important since the more the current assets exceed the current liabilities, the higher becomes the working capital. There is considerable variation and inconsistency among companies in the way assets are classified in financial statements.

For accounting purposes, the term "current assets" is used to designate cash and other assets or resources which are reasonably expected to be realized in cash, sold or consumed during the normal operating cycle of the business.

Here are some examples:

(1) Cash available for current operations and items which are the equivalent of cash; (2) inventories of merchandise, raw materials, goods in process, finished goods, operating supplies, and ordinary maintenance materials and parts; (3) trade accounts, notes and acceptances receivable; (4) receivables from officers, employees, affiliates and others if they are collectible in the ordinary course of the business within one year; (5) installment or deferred accounts and notes receivable if they conform generally to normal trade practices and business terms; (6) marketable securities representing the investment of cash available for current operation; and (7) prepaid expenses, such as insurance, rent, taxes, unused royalties, current paid advertising services not yet received, and operating supplies.

Prepaid expenses are not current assets in that they will be converted into cash, but in the sense that, if not paid in advance, they would require the use of current assets otherwise available during the operating cycle.

The operating cycle is defined as the average time between the acquisition of materials or services until the time that cash is finally realized on sale of the materials or services. Where there are several operating cycles occurring within a year, a one-year time period is used as the criterion for a current asset. Where the operating cycle is more than 12 months (i.e., in the tobacco, distillery, and lumber businesses), a longer period is used. Where a business has no clearly defined operating cycle, a one-year period is used.

Assets Excluded from "Current Assets"

The following types of items are to be excluded from the current asset classification:

(1) Cash and claims for cash which are (a) restricted as to withdrawal or use for other than current operations, (b) earmarked for expenditure in the acquisition or construction of noncurrent assets, or (c) segregated for the liquidation of long-term debts. Even though funds may not actually be set aside in separate accounts, funds that are clearly to be used in the near future for the liquidation of long-term debt, sinking fund payments, or other similar purposes should be excluded from current assets, unless the maturing portion of debt is being shown as a current liability.

(2) Investments in securities (marketable or not), or advances which have been made for the purposes of control, affiliation, or other continuing business advantage.

(3) Receivables arising from unusual transactions (e.g., sale of capital assets, loans or advances to affiliate companies, officers or employees) not expected to be collected within a one-year period.

(4) Cash surrender value of life insurance policies.

(5) Land and other natural resources.

(6) Depreciable assets.

(7) Long-term prepayments which are chargeable to the operations of several years or deferred charges, such as bonus payments under a long-term lease and costs of rearranging a factory or removal to a new location.

Accounts and notes receivable due from officers, employees or affiliated companies should not be included under the general heading "Accounts Receivable." They should be shown separately. The basic reasoning behind this is that accounts receivable are classified as a current asset presuming they will be converted into cash within one year. Except in the case where goods have actually been sold to them on account, for collection according to the regular credit terms, amounts due from officers, directors and stockholders are not likely to be collected within one year. Therefore, they should be shown under a noncurrent caption.

The same is true of accounts receivable from affiliated companies. These amounts are not likely to be paid off currently and are usually of a more permanent nature. Showing them as current assets is misleading. Also, there is an overstatement of current assets and consequently of working capital.

Sometimes current assets are carried at values which do not represent realizable values. For example, accounts receivable should be net of allowances for uncollectible accounts or net of earned discounts when discounts are expected to give an *estimated* receivable value.

Also, some current assets should now reflect *unrealized* gains or losses. (See both Marketable Securities and Foreign Currency Translations in this Accounting Section.)

Assets and liabilities in the balance sheet should not be offset unless a legal right of setoff exists.

Inventory is valued at cost unless its utility value has diminished to a lower market replacement cost. Standard costing is acceptable, if it reasonably approximates actual cost. The flow of inventory costs may be predicated upon FIFO, LIFO, or average assumptions.

CASH

GAAP requires accounting for cash to include money that is represented by actual coins and currency on hand or demand deposits available without restriction. It must be management's intention that the cash be available for current purposes. Cash in a demand deposit account that is being held for retirement of long-term debts not currently maturing should be excluded from current assets and shown as a noncurrent investment.

Another common restriction on a company's cash balance is in borrowing arrangements with banks. A business entity will be required to maintain a minimum amount of cash on deposit, usually an agreed upon percentage of the cash balance. This requirement is termed a *compensating balance*. The compensating balance is not available to the company for unrestricted use as it would be a violation of the loan contract with the lender. The compensating balance must be disclosed as a noncurrent asset, if the related borrowing is a noncurrent liability. If the borrowing is a current liability, it is permissible to show the compensating balance as a separately captioned current asset to enable other creditors, suppliers for instance, to see that a portion of the cash balances of their customer is unavailable.

Cash in a savings account subject to statutory notification before withdrawal and cash in certificates of deposits maturing during the current operating cycle or within one year can be included as current assets, but should be separately captioned in the balance sheet to avoid the misleading disclosure that the funds are available immediately upon demand. Such items usually are disclosed in the *short-term in-*

vestments caption, but they can also be labeled *Time Deposits* or *Restricted Cash Deposits*.

INVENTORY

The term "inventory" is used to designate tangible personal property which is: (1) held for sale in the ordinary course of business, (2) in the process of being produced for later sale, or (3) currently consumed directly or indirectly in the production of goods or services to be available for sale.

Manufacturing firms have many types of inventory; for example, finished goods, work in process, raw materials and manufacturing supplies. Finished goods of a manufacturing company are comparable to the merchandise of a non-manufacturing company. Excluded from inventory are long-term assets subject to depreciation and depreciable fixed assets retired from regular use and held for sale. Raw materials which become part of a finished product become part of that inventory cost. Trade practices and materiality are usually the determining factors in either inventorying production supplies on hand or expensing them as part of product costs.

In accounting for inventories we try to match appropriate costs against revenues. This gives a proper determination of realized income. Another way of putting it is to say that by applying the best method of costing inventory, we are measuring out "cost of goods sold," by associating cause and effect.

Inclusion of Goods in Inventory Should Follow the Legal Rule of Title

Whatever the location of goods, if title is legally held by the company, the goods should be included in inventory. If title to the goods has passed to a customer, the goods should not be included in inventory.

Cost of Inventory

The primary basis of accounting for inventories is cost. This means the sum of the expenditures and charges, directly or indirectly, incurred in bringing the inventory to its existing condition and location.

As applied to inventories, cost means acquisition and production costs. However, there are many items which, although related to inventory, are not included in the cost of the inventory; for example, idle facility expense, excessive spoilage, double freight, rehandling costs. If these costs are abnormal, they should be treated as expenses of the current period rather than carried forward as part of the inventory cost. General and administrative expenses should be treated as expenses of the period. Likewise, selling expenses should not be included in inventory. The cost of inventory, however, should include an applicable portion of manufacturing overhead. The exclusion of *all* overhead from inventory cost is not an acceptable accounting procedure.

Cost, however, *must not* be used when the market value of inventory items is lower than the cost.

Flow of Cost Assumptions

Costs for inventory may be determined under any one of several assumptions as to the flow of costs; for example, FIFO, average, and LIFO. The method selected should be the one which most clearly reflects periodic income.

The "flow of costs" and "flow of goods" are usually not the same. But we use a "flow of cost"—such as FIFO, average, or LIFO—because to identify the cost of a specific item sold is often impossible, impractical, or even misleading. Where similar goods are purchased at different prices at different times, it would be difficult to identify specific goods sold except in a case of valuable jewelry, automobiles, pianos or other large items. Even perpetual inventory records would not make identification possible. Therefore, an assumption is made with respect to the flow of costs in order to provide a practical basis for measuring period income.

LIFO is considered an appropriate method for pricing inventory during extended inflationary periods, when costs continue accelerating. When the economy is deflationary or relatively stable, the FIFO or average methods are usually preferred by management. Practices of the other companies in the same industry should also be considered. Financial statements would be more useful if all companies within a given industry used uniform methods of inventory pricing.

The method used must be consistently applied and disclosed in financial statements. (See Disclosures and Restatements in this text.)

LIFO TERMINOLOGY

The accounting terminology for LIFO inventory accounting is unique to the topic. The appropriate definitions of terms follow.

BASE YEAR: The year in which LIFO was adopted for a particular item or pool of items.

BASE-YEAR COST OF AN ITEM: The average cost of the item at the beginning of the base year.

BASE-YEAR COST OF A POOL: The current year quantity of all items in a pool, priced at base-year cost.

CURRENT COST: The cost basis of items may be determined by reference to actual cost of goods purchased or produced:
* Most recently in the year.
* Earliest in the year.

- Throughout the year.
- Any method which in the Commissioner's opinion that clearly reflects income.

DECREMENT: A decrease in an inventory pool at base-year prices.

DOLLAR-VALUE METHOD: A method for pricing inventory that uses comparison of total dollars in inventory adjusted for price level changes, rather than a comparison of specific items. This method applies the double-extension technique, the link-change technique, and the LIFO retail method (these methods defined below).

DOUBLE-EXTENSION TECHNIQUE: The approach by which an index is developed by double pricing the ending inventory at base-year cost and at current-year cost.

DOUBLE-EXTENSION INDEX: When applied to a pool, as used in the dollar-value method, is a measure of the change in the value of the ending inventory between the base year and the current year. The index is obtained by dividing the current year by the base year.

DOUBLE PRICING: The procedure of costing items in the ending inventory pool of a given year at both current-year cost and the cost of a prior year, either the base year or immediately prior year.

INCREMENT: An increase in a pool at base-year prices.

INDEX-METHOD: The use of a LIFO index by reference to outside sources or by double pricing a statistical or judgmental sample.

ITEM: A classification of either an inventoriable product or the raw material cost component of the LIFO inventory.

LIFO COST LAYER: An increase in the LIFO value of a pool in a given year resulting from an increase in total base-year cost multiplied by the current-year LIFO index.

LIFO RESERVE: The difference between the FIFO cost and LIFO cost of an item or pool.

LIFO RETAIL METHOD: This method combines the LIFO dollar-value method with the retail inventory method resulting in the determination of LIFO inventory increments or decrements in terms of base-year retail value rather than base-year cost.

LINK-CHAIN TECHNIQUE: The technique of developing a cumulative index by double pricing the ending inventory at current-year costs and beginning-of-year costs instead of base year costs as for the double-extension techniques.

NATURAL BUSINESS UNIT: A manufacturer or processor ordinarily engaged in the entire production of one product line, or two or more related product lines.

POOL: A group of similar items of inventory accounted for as a unit under the dollar-value method.

RAW MATERIALS CONTENT POOL: A pool of raw materials, including raw materials in work-in-process and finished goods.

SPECIFIC IDENTIFICATION METHOD: A comparison of the quantity of a specific item in the ending inventory with the quantity of the same item in the beginning inventory. This is also called the *Unit Method.*

First-In, First-Out (FIFO)

This is probably the most common method of valuing inventories. The latest costs are assigned to the goods on hand; thus, the earliest costs become the costs of the goods sold. The theory here is that goods are disposed of in the same order as acquired.

Here is a simple illustration of FIFO. Opening inventory and purchases during the year were as follows:

Opening inventory	1,000 units at $10, or	$10,000
First purchase	800 units at $11, or	8,800
Second purchase	500 units at $14, or	7,000
Third purchase	400 units at $12, or	4,800
Fourth purchase	300 units at $13, or	3,900
Totals	3,000	$34,500

The closing inventory consists of 1,100 units. Under the FIFO method of costing, the closing inventory is considered to be made up of:

300 units of the fourth purchase (at $13)	$3,900
400 units of the third purchase (at $12).......................	4,800
400 units of the second purchase (at $14).....................	5,600
Cost of 1,100 units in closing inventory..................	$14,300

Last-In, First-Out (LIFO)

In recent years, LIFO has become a very popular method. In years of rising prices and high taxes, the LIFO method keeps profits (and taxes) down. It has the virtue of applying the current price structure to the cost of goods sold, thus matching the high price structure of the sales with the high price structure of costs.

The basic approach to LIFO costing is to assign the *earliest* costs to the *closing* inventory, as if the latest-acquired items were the first sold. For example, if we use the figures set forth above in the FIFO illustration, the costs of our closing inventory of 1,100 units under the LIFO costing approach would be:

1,000 units of the opening inventory (at $10).....................	$10,000
100 units of the first purchase (at $11)	1,100
Cost of 1,100 units in closing inventory....................	$11,100

Note that the 100-unit incremental increase over the inventory might, in the LIFO method, have been valued under *any* one of the following four options:

1. In the order of acquisition (as illustrated)
2. At the most recent purchase cost
3. At an average cost for the year
4. At the "dollar-value" method which converts the incremental increase by means of an index based on the LIFO base year prices.

Average Costs

A weighted average is sometimes used to determine the cost of the closing inventory. This method is generally not approved for tax purposes. Under the weighted average method, you determine an average unit cost and then multiply that average unit cost by the number of units in the closing inventory. To get the weighted average, the number of units in each purchase is multiplied by the unit price for that purchase. And the total units purchased and the total of all purchase costs are added to the units and costs in the opening inventory. Then the total of all the costs is divided by the total of all the units. The resulting figure is the average cost per unit.

For example, in the FIFO illustration above, the total number of units involved in the opening inventory plus the four purchases was 3,000. The total cost of the 3,000 units was $34,500. Dividing $34,500 by 3,000, we come up with an average cost per unit of $11.50. Since our closing inventory consisted of 1,100 units, if we priced it at average cost (1,100 × $11.50), the cost of our closing inventory would be $12,650.

Thus, depending on the method of cost used, our closing inventory could have been $11,100, $12,650, or $14,300.

The Retail Inventory Method

This method of inventory pricing is sometimes most practical and appropriate. It is used principally by retail establishments. This inventory valuation has as its initial starting point the retail or selling price of the merchandise rather than the cost. It arrives finally at the cost valuation entirely on the basis of average relationships of retail and cost figures over the period involved.

When merchandise is purchased, the retail selling price is placed on the price tag attached. At inventory time, the inventory is taken at the selling price. The cost is then arrived at by multiplying the inventory by the cost complement percentage, which is the difference between the mark-up % and 100%. It is arrived at as follows:

	Cost	Retail	Mark-up	Mark-up %	Cost Complement %
Beginning inventory	$ 50,000	$ 75,000	$ 25,000	33⅓%	66⅔%
Purchases	72,000	120,000	48,000	40 %	60 %
Total to Date	122,000	195,000	73,000	37.4%	62.6%
Markdowns		3,000	3,000		
Total to Date	$122,000	$192,000	$ 70,000	36.5%	63.5%
Sale for period		95,000			
Ending inventory		$ 97,000			

At the end of the period, the retail inventory of $97,000 will be reduced to cost by applying the cost complement percent of 63.5. Thus, the inventory figure at cost is $61,595.

The gross margin tabulation follows:

Sales		$ 95,000
Opening inventory	$ 50,000	
Purchases	72,000	
	122,000	
Closing inventory	61,595	
Cost of sales		60,405
Gross margin		$ 34,595

Lower of Cost or Market

A departure from cost basis of pricing inventory is *required* when the disposal of the goods in the ordinary course of business will be at less than cost. This calls for valuing the inventory at the lower cost or market.

As used in the phrase, "lower of cost or market," market means current replacement cost (by purchase or reproduction) with the exception that: (1) market is not to exceed the net realizable value which is the estimated selling price in the ordinary course of business less reasonably predictable costs of completion and disposal, and (2) market should not be less than net realizable value reduced by an allowance for a normal profit margin. Here, for example, are the prices to be used in carrying out the lower of cost or market concept (the price to be used in each case is the one in boldface):

	1	2	3	4	5
(a) Cost	**.82**	.95	.95	**.78**	.94
(b) Market—cost to replace at inventory date	.86	**.90**	.80	.75	.94
(c) Selling price less estimated cost to complete and sell	.92	.92	.92	.92	**.92**
(d) Selling price less estimated cost to complete and sell and normal profit margin	.83	.83	.83	.83	.83

In applying the cost or market rule, no loss should be recognized unless the evidence indicates clearly that a loss has been sustained. Where evidence indicates that cost will be recovered with a normal profit margin upon the sale of merchandise, no loss should be recognized even though replacement cost is lower. It should also be remembered that pricing goods at the lower of cost or market is not to be followed literally in all cases. Rather, it is to be applied realistically with regard to the form, content, and composition of the inventory.

There are three ways of applying the lower-of-cost-or-market rule: The rule may be applied on (1) each item in the inventory, (2) the total cost of the major categories in the inventory, or (3) the cost of entire inventory.

Each of these methods would produce different results, and all of them are considered acceptable for financial statement purposes. The method used should be the one which most clearly reflects periodic income. For example, if there is only one product, rule (3) would seem to have the greatest significance. Where there is more than one major product, rule (2) would seem to be the most useful. Rule (1), application of the lower of cost or market to each item of inventory, is the most common in practice.

When substantial and unusual losses result under the cost or market rule, it is desirable to disclose them separately from normal cost of goods sold.

Any procedure adopted for the treatment of inventory items should be applied consistently and disclosed in the financial statement. Without such consistency there is no basis with which to compare the results of one year with another. Any change in the basis of stating inventories will probably have an important effect on the statements, and full disclosure of such a change should be made.

There are some instances when inventories are properly stated above cost. Exceptions are made in the case of precious metals (e.g., gold and silver), agricultural or mineral products or the packing industry.

Where a company has firm purchase commitments for goods in inventory, losses which are expected to arise from such uncancellable and unhedged commitments for future purchase of inventory should be reflected in the current period in the same way as losses on inventory.

LIFO CONFORMITY RULE
(IRS TITLE: "REPORT RULE")

If a company adopts LIFO for tax purposes, then LIFO *must* be applied for determining income, profit (or loss) for financial reporting purposes. IRS regulations does permit a few exceptions to the conformity rule:

1. The use of an inventory method other than LIFO when the taxpayer is presenting information as a supplement, or an explanation of the taxpayer's primary presentation of income in financial reports to outside parties. The supplemental information must be in notes to the financial statements, not in the body of the income statement.
2. An inventory method other than LIFO can be used to determine the value of the taxpayer's inventory for reporting the value of the inventory as an asset on the balance sheet.
3. An inventory method other than LIFO can be used for information reported in internal management reports.
4. The application of an inventory method other than LIFO for financial reports for a period of less than one year.
5. The use of LIFO lower of cost or market valuation of inventories when applying LIFO for tax purposes.

The Code also includes a rule covering related corporations. All members of the same group of *financially* related corporations shall be treated as a single taxpayer when applying the conformity rule. Formerly, the rule enabled taxpayers to circumvent the conformity rule by having a subsidiary on LIFO, while the non-LIFO parent presented combined non-LIFO financial statements. The Code considers this treatment a violation of the conformity requirement. One exception resulting from a Tax Court case is allowable for tax and reporting purposes. Parent corporations can convert their inventories to the *moving-average method* in the consolidated annual report to shareholders. The Court ruled that the conformity rule is satisfied because the financial report is *not* attributable to the subsidiaries, so the right of the subsidiaries to use the LIFO method in a consolidated tax return is allowable.

The IRS permits companies on LIFO to explain the inventory amount on the balance sheet and the primary presentation of income by disclosing what income would have been had another inventory method been used.

Example:	Inventory on FIFO method	$1,000
	Less adjustment to LIFO method	500
		$ 500

When a company discloses what its income would have been under an alternative inventory valuation method, the company should state the reasons for the disclosure. One reason, for example, might be to enable users of the financial statements to compare the company's reported income with that of other companies in the industry.

During the period of double-digit inflation there was widespread adoption of the LIFO inventory method, changing from FIFO and other methods. The objective is to charge the most current inventory costs against sales revenues, or closer compliance with the matching principle. The Code provides taxpayers with an election to account for inventories under the LIFO method, the essence of which is the requirement that companies electing LIFO for tax purposes cannot use another method of inventory valuation for purposes of reporting income, profit or loss in credit statements, financial reports to shareholders, partners, or other proprietors or beneficiaries. This is the essential requirement of the conformity rule.

There are a number of exceptions permitted by the Code where another method of inventory valuation can be used without violating compliance with the conformity rule.

1. As a supplement to or explanation of the primary presentation in statements of income for a taxable year, *but not on the face of the income statement.*

2. To ascertain the value of inventory of specified goods on hand for purposes of reporting such value on the balance sheet.

3. For purposes of information reported in internal management reports.

4. Market value may be used each year in lieu of the LIFO cost assigned to inventory items for federal income tax reporting when the market value is *less than* the LIFO cost.

In defining what will be considered supplemental or explanatory information, and therefore allowed to be shown, the regulations provide that information reported on the face of the income statement cannot be included in order to eliminate all parenthetical information being considered supplemental by the user of the statements. Hence, the regulation explicitly spells out that the footnotes to the statement are not a part of the face of the statement. This allows another method of inventory valuation to be used and disclosed in a footnote, but cost of goods sold using the FIFO method cannot be disclosed parenthetically. The footnote disclosures should be issued with the income statement as part of a single report.

A company that changes to LIFO is required to explain the change and its effect on earnings. The following is a sample of a footnote:

> "In order not to overstate profits as a result of inflation during the year, the company changed its method of accounting for inventory from First-in, First-out to Last-in, First-out. This was necessary because of the rapid increase in prices in recent years which caused inventories sold to be replaced at substantially higher prices. The effect

of the change was to decrease reported earnings by $XXX,XXX, or $X.XX per share.''

Another example:

"The company has changed its method of accounting for inventories to Last-in, First-Out (LIFO) method. This was done because the rapid increase in prices during the year would result in an overstatement of profits if use of the First-in, First-out (FIFO) method were continued since inventories sold were replaced at substantially higher prices. The effect on reported earnings of the change for the year was a decrease of $XXX,XXX, or $X.XX per share.''

It is worth repeating that any supplementary information on the face of the income statement *other than footnotes* is a violation of the conformity rule. For column format, for example, one for LIFO earnings and the other for FIFO earnings for comparative purposes would be a violation.

Earnings information on a FIFO basis is more representative of actual performance than LIFO-based information. This is of special concern when a company has recently changed to LIFO under the presumption that LIFO is the preferable method for this particular situation. An addition to the above footnote could read

"Many of the company's competitors use the FIFO method of inventory valuation. Had the company reported its LIFO inventories under the FIFO method, and had a 44 percent tax rate been applied to changes in income, **and had no other assumptions been made as to changes in income** (emphasis added), net income for 19XX would have been $XXX,XXX ($X.XX per share) and for 19XX $XXX,XXX ($X.XX per share).''

This addition to the footnote disclosure is informative because items in the financial statements other than just income tax expense could change as a result of the difference in earnings using FIFO rather than LIFO. Accordingly, the point specified in the phrase "and had no other assumptions been made as to changes in income" is a significant qualification.

Under the current rule, companies are encouraged, but are not required, by the conformity rule to disclose on a pro forma basis the effect on earnings that LIFO would have had if applied in the year prior to the actual change to LIFO. The reason is there was no conformity problem since LIFO was not used for tax purposes in the year preceding its adoption.

MARKETABLE SECURITIES

The traditional precept of stating assets at historical costs has, in the area of marketable equity securities, been changed by the AICPA. Effective for statements ending on or after December 31, 1975, marketable securities are to be shown at the *lower* of historical cost or current market value (statement date), through the use of offsetting valuation allowance accounts (separated as to current and noncurrent).

There are several ramifications to be considered in accomplishing this periodic write-down (or possible write-up) to historical costs:

1. Management decides whether to classify securities as current or noncurrent assets, *generally* basing the classification upon its intent or non-intent of one-year disposition.

2. All current equity securities held are considered to be a single portfolio. All noncurrent equity securities are considered to be another single portfolio.

3. In unclassified balance sheets, securities are considered to be noncurrent.

4. Entire portfolios are considered to be *one unit* for the purpose of determining the overall lump-sum value to be shown. This entails an *item-by-item comparison* between *cost* and *market price* for each holding. When an *entire* portfolio's market value sinks *below* its cost (some holdings may be *over* cost), a valuation allowance account is *credited* for the difference (and serves as an offsetting asset account for net balance sheet display purposes)—with the *debit* for the unrealized loss going to:

    A. An *income* statement unrealized loss account for those securities in the *current* portfolio;

    B. An *equity section* unrealized loss account for those securities in the *noncurrent* portfolio. This account is a separate (debit) component of retained earnings and is shown in the Statement of Retained Earnings, or in the more expansive Statement of Stockholders' Equity.

5. At each subsequent year end, the new market values are compared again with cost, and the valuation allowance accounts for the entire portfolios are adjusted for:

    A. Further declines, or

    B. Increases up to, but not exceeding, cost.

6. When securities are sold, the difference between *cost* and *selling price* becomes an income statement *realized* gain or loss, the asset cost being deleted from the portfolio and the valuation allowance account at year end being subsequently adjusted to reflect the temporary decline in the market value of the remaining securities held.

7. Permanent declines should be reflected immediately upon discovery as an income statement realized loss and a reduction of the asset cost account. The newly reflected written-down cost-basis becomes the portfolio value, and it should not be changed for later recoveries in market value.

8. When reclassifying portfolios from one category to another (current to noncurrent or vice-versa), permanent entries should be made to reflect the change as of the date of reclassification.

9. Timing differences should be recognized unless there is reasonable doubt that unrealized losses will be offset by subsequent capital gains.

10. Disclosure is required.
11. *No* restatement of prior year is necessary.
12. *Not* mandatory for not-for-profit organizations, except investor-owned hospitals.
13. *Not* applicable to immaterial items.
14. Equity securities do not include bonds, treasury stock, or redeemable preferred stock.
15. Does *not* pertain to those holdings treated under the equity method.
16. See illustrative journal entries in Appendix A.

Marketable securities are securities that can be sold readily because of an established market, i.e., securities listed on a national securities exchange or traded regularly in the over-the-counter market. The Marketable Securities classification (a current asset) in a statement of financial condition includes U.S. government securities and corporate stocks and bonds. The accounting entries when an investment is made are:

Marketable Securities	XXX	
Cash		XXX
If the securities are sold at a gain:		
Cash	XXX	
Marketable Securities		XXX
Gain on Sale of		
Marketable Securities		XXX
If the securities are sold at a loss:		
Cash	XXX	
Loss on Sale of Marketable		
Securities	XXX	
Marketable Securities		XXX

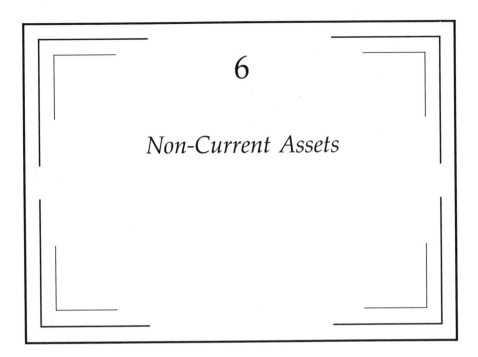

6

Non-Current Assets

CLASSIFICATION OF NON-CURRENT ASSETS

Noncurrent assets are assets which have a useful life of more than one accounting period. Equipment, land and buildings are examples of this category.

EQUIPMENT AND PLANT—ACQUISITIONS AND DISPOSITIONS

Acquisitions

Assets acquired in exchanges are measured at the exchange price, that is, acquisition cost. Money and money claims are measured at their face amount or sometimes at their discount amount.

In exchanges in which neither money nor promises to pay money are exchanged, the assets acquired are generally measured at the fair value of the assets given up. However, if the fair value of the assets received is more clearly evident, the assets acquired are measured at that amount.

Under the above standards, equipment and plant are therefore valued:

1. At cost, if purchased for cash or its equivalent, or
2. If an exchange of non-cash property is involved (wholly or partially), preferably at the fair value of the asset acquired, or, if that is not clearly evident, of the asset surrendered (an example of the latter would be the use of the market price of the company's own stock given in exchange for an asset whose fair value cannot reasonably be determined), or
3. If a group of assets is acquired in one exchange, the total price is allocated to the individual assets based on their relative fair values. Excess paid over fair value is treated as goodwill. In the opposite case, any excess of fair value of the assets acquired over the exchange price is used to reduce the value of the non-current assets (except investment securities) proportionately.

Dispositions

Decreases in assets are recorded when assets are disposed of in exchanges.

Decreases in assets are measured by the recorded amounts that relate to the assets. The amounts are usually the historical or acquisition costs of the assets (as adjusted for amortization and other charges).

The disposing of equipment and plant assets usually results in a gain or loss and is reported as such on the financial statements. In an exchange, for financial purposes, losses should be recognized, but gains should be used to adjust the basis of the new acquisition.

On straight dispositions, depreciation is usually calculated to the date of disposal (approximately) and both the accumulated depreciation and the asset account are then netted to the amount recovered to arrive at the gain or loss, which, for tax purposes may require special consideration, such as recapture of depreciation and investment tax credits.

Other Considerations

Self-constructed assets should not be depreciated while under construction. The cost basis should be determined not only by the material and labor expended, but also by apportionment of overhead items, such as depreciation on any fixed assets used in that construction process (which application in turn reduced the depreciation expense for that particular fixed asset).

Detailed sub-ledgers or worksheets should be maintained for all fixed assets, showing date acquired, cost or basis, investment tax credit, estimated life, salvage value (if any), depreciation taken by year, accumulated depreciation and gains or losses on dispositions or trade-in information.

Appraisal write-ups are contrary to generally accepted accounting principles, but when circumstances necessitate write-ups, the offset goes to "appraisal surplus" and becomes part of the equity capital. Depreciation then must be based on the higher, appraisal values.

DEPRECIATION

If an asset provides benefit for several periods, its cost is allocated to the periods in a systematic and rational manner in the absence of a more direct basis for associating cause and effect. . . . This form of expense recognition always involves assumptions about the pattern of 'matching costs to benefits' because neither can be conclusively demonstrated.

Depreciation is the term applied to the allocation of a fixed asset's cost over its beneficial useful life. It is a method of accounting which aims to distribute the cost or other value of tangible or capital assets, less salvage (if any), over the estimated useful life of the asset (which may be a single asset or a group of assets in a single account) in a systematic and rational manner. It is a process of allocation, not of valuation, applied on a consistent basis.

Rather than increasing expenses immediately, depreciation might also *increase* other asset values temporarily, such as in the application of overhead depreciation to inventory or to self-constructed assets.

From a tax viewpoint, the deduction for depreciation (which requires no annual cash outlay) reduces the amount of tax we have to pay. This has the effect of increasing the accumulation of cash at our disposal—i.e., the "cash flow."

Before we can determine the amount of our depreciation deductions, we have to know the following three elements: (1) the method of depreciation that we will use, (2) the amount we can recover (depreciable basis), and (3) the period over which we can take deductions (useful life).

The depreciation is usually applicable only to property which approaches, by wear and tear, business ineffectiveness. "Depreciation" and "repairs and maintenance" are not the same. It is necessary to distinguish between repairs and maintenance costs to keep the asset in operation and repairs which are capital expenditures and increase the life of the asset. The former are expense deductions in the year incurred; the latter must be amortized over the life of the asset. What repairs increase the life of the asset and what repairs are necessary for its operation is often a matter of judgment. Examples of repairs which are classified as capital expenditures are the costs of remodeling or reconditioning a building.

The determination, or estimation of useful life, may be based on: (1) IRS guidelines, such as in Bulletin F or ADR rules, basically determined by estimated physical durability, longevity or unit-productive capability; (2) statutory law, as in the case of a patent; (3) contract, as in the case of some leases; (4) utility, as in the case of an airport built for military training during war.

Although write-up of fixed assets to reflect appraisal, market or current values is not in accordance with GAAP, where such appreciation has been recorded, depreciation should be based on the written up amounts for financial statement purposes.

Methods of Depreciation

Following the passage of the Internal Revenue Act of 1954, which permitted the use of the declining-balance and similar accelerated methods of depreciation, the AICPA stated such methods met the requirement of being systematic and rational and could be used for general accounting purposes, with appropriate disclosure to be made of any change in method when depreciation is a significant factor in determining net income.

The declining-balance and the sum-of-the-year-digits methods of depreciation are appropriate and most used in those cases where the expected productivity or revenue-earning power of an asset is greater during earlier years of life or when maintenance charges tend to increase during later years.

Accounting methods of depreciating assets may differ from tax methods used. It is the practice of many firms to use straight-line depreciation for accounting purposes and an accelerated one for tax purposes. When this happens, disclosure should be made of the timing differences.

Straight-line method. The depreciation expense is the same from period to period. The formula followed for this method is:

$$\text{Depreciation expense} \quad = \quad \frac{(\text{Cost - Salvage Value})}{\text{Estimated Life}}$$

For example, if the asset costs $10,000, has a salvage value of $100, and an estimated life of ten years, the depreciation expense for the year would be computed as follows:

$$\frac{(\$10,000 - \$100)}{10} \quad = \quad \$990$$

The straight-line method depends upon the hypothesis that depreciation will be at a constant rate throughout the estimated life.

200%-Declining-balance method. Under this method (also called the double-declining-balance method), the amount of depreciation expense decreases from period to period. The largest depreciation deduction is taken in the first year. The amount then declines steeply over succeeding years until the final years of estimated useful life when the depreciation charge becomes relatively small. Code § 167 restricts the taxpayer to a rate not in excess of twice the straight-line rate if the straight-line method had been employed.

While true declining-balance method requires the application of a complex formula, if you are going to use the maximum declining-balance depreciation—i.e., the 200% method—you need not go through these mathematical computations. Just do this: (1) determine the straight-line percentage rate; (2) double it; (3) apply it against your full basis (undiminished by salvage value) to get your first year's deduction. In the second year, (1) reduce your basis by the previous year's depreciation deduction; (2) apply the same percentage rate to the new basis you arrived at in step (1). In the third year and later years, repeat the same process.

Example: You buy a truck for the business. It costs $5,500 and has a five-year useful life. We'll assume you bought it January 1, 1979. Since it has a five-year life, the percentage of depreciation by the straight-line method is 20%. Using 200%-declining-balance, you'll use a 40% rate. So, for 1979, you'd deduct $2,200 (40% of $5,500). For 1980, you reduced your $5,500 basis (original cost) by the $2,200 1979 depreciation deduction. That gives you a basis for 1980 of $3,300. For 1980, your depreciation deduction would be 40% of that $3,300, or $1,320. That cuts your basis for 1981 to $1,980 and your depreciation deduction for that year becomes $792 (40% of $1,980). This process continues on for the future years you continue to hold this truck.

Sum-of-years-digits method. Here, diminishing rates, expressed fractionally, are applied to the total depreciable value (cost—salvage).

Under sum-of-the-digits, the annual depreciation charge decreases rapidly; since maintenance charges, on the other hand, increase rapidly, the effect is to level off the annual costs of depreciation and maintenance.

To use sum-of-the-digits, you proceed as follows. Using, for purposes of illustration, a depreciation account of $5,500 with a 10-year life and ignoring salvage, add the numbers of the years: $10 + 9 + 8 + 7 + 6 + 5 + 4 + 3 + 2 + 1 = 55$. Depreciation the first year will be 10/55 of $5,500, or $1,000. For the remaining years, you can follow one of two practices. Either you continue to base depreciation on original cost, using 55 as the denominator of your fraction and the number of the year as the numerator—9/55 of $5,500, 8/55 of $5,500, and so on, or you apply a fraction with a diminishing denominator to unrecovered cost —9/45 of $4,500, 8/36 of $3,600, and so on.

Note that in the second method, the amount by which the denominator for a given year diminishes is always the amount of the numerator for the preceding year. Denominator 45 in the second year is denominator 55 for the first year, less numerator 10 for the first year; denominator 36 for year 3 is denominator 45 for year 2, less numerator 9 for year 2.

Regardless of which method is used, annual depreciation will be the same: 9/55 of $5,500 and 9/45 of $4,500 both give $900 of depreciation; 8/55 of $5,500 and 8/36 of $3,600 both give depreciation of $800.

Sinking-fund method. The sinking-fund method of computing depreciation has been generally preferred by independent businessmen. An imaginary sinking fund is established by a uniform end-of-year annual deposit throughout the useful life of the asset. The assets are assumed to draw interest at some stated rate, e.g., 6%, sufficient to balance the fund with the cost of the asset minus estimated salvage value. The amount charged to depreciation expense in any year consists of sinking fund plus the interest on the imaginary accumulated fund. The book value of the asset at any time is the initial cost of the asset minus the amount accumulated in the imaginary fund.

Assume that an asset costs $1,000 and has no salvage value but has an estimated life of 25 years. The interest rate is assumed to be 6%. By using conversion tables, the sinking fund deposit is $1,000 × .01823 or $18.23. In the second year, the depreciation charge will be $18.23 + ($18.23 × .06) = $19.32; in the third year, it will be $18.23 + ($18.23 + $19.32) × .06 = $20.48, and so forth. The $18.23 represents the sinking fund deposit and remains the same for the period of depreciation. In other words, under this method the businessman anticipates earnings and profits on his capital investment and thus increases his capital.

This method is permissible for Federal income tax purposes provided it does not exceed the rate as computed under the declining-balance method, during the first two-thirds of the asset life.

Units-of-production method. This method is used for the depreciation of assets used in production. Under this method, an estimate is made of the total number of units the machine may be expected to produce during its life. Cost less salvage value, if any, is then divided by the estimated total production to determine a depreciation charge for each unit of production. The depreciation for each year is obtained by multiplying the depreciation charge per unit by the number of units produced. Here's how it works on a $10,600 machine good for 300,000 units of output:

$$R = \frac{\text{Cost - Salvage Value}}{\text{Estimated Units}}$$

$$R = \frac{\$10{,}600 - \$600}{300{,}000}$$

$$R = \$.03\tfrac{1}{3}$$

Units produced for 1 year = 24,000
Depreciation = 24,000 × $.03⅓ = $800

A severe obstacle to the use of this method is the difficulty of ascertaining the total number of units which the asset will produce. The production method is most applicable to fixed assets like airplane engines, automobiles, and machinery where wear is such an important factor. It is useful for fixed assets that are likely to be exhausted prematurely by accelerated or abnormal use.

BASIS

Normally, the basis for depreciation (i.e., the capital amount on which you figure your depreciation deductions) is what you paid for property. To the cost of the property itself is added the cost of transporting the property to your premises, the cost of installation, and acquisition related costs.

For tax purposes, the basis for depreciation can be different from the basis used for financial reporting purposes. This difference often arises when there are trade-ins involved. According to GAAP, the entity paying any monetary consideration on a trade-in should recognize losses immediately, but, for gains, should adjust the basis of the acquisition to the extent of the gain. For tax purposes, neither gain nor loss is usually recognized, with neither serving to adjust the basis of the new acquisition. Hence, there may be a timing difference with respect to the different bases used for depreciation.

Allocation of Basis

When property is acquired, it is often necessary to allocate basis. Here are the instances when allocation is necessary:

(1) When improved real estate is purchased, there must be an allocation made as to land (nondepreciable, because land doesn't wear out) and buildings;

(2) When more than one asset is purchased for a lump sum;

(3) When a group of assets (or possibly a business) is purchased for a single sum involving depreciable and nondepreciable assets.

Improved real estate. Whenever you acquire a piece of improved real property, you have an immediate need for an allocation. Land is not depreciable; and in order to determine your basis for depreciating the building, you have to reduce your overall basis by an amount which represents a reasonable basis for the land. The usual method of making the allocation is in proportion to the respective fair market values.

If you have in fact paid proportionately more for the building for some special reason and can establish the fact, you can use the higher amount as your depreciation basis. The best way to secure such an advantage, however, is by specific allocation in the contract which spells it out in detail.

If any of the contents of the building are included in the purchase transaction, you need a further allocation between the structure and the contents. Then the amount allocated to the contents must be further broken down among the various items which are included in the sale.

This latter allocation may require all parties to consider the investment credit and depreciation recapture provisions of the tax law.

Acquisition of more than one asset. In the purchase of more than one asset (mixed assets) the same rules which have been discussed above apply. The cost of a group of assets which is stated as a single sum must be broken down and allocated among the separate items or groups. This permits the proper allocation of useful lives to different assets or groups, and separates depreciable from nondepreciable assets. Again, the possible effects of the investment credit and depreciation recapture provisions must be watched.

Appraisal

Accounting for an appraisal write-up
  Building 350,000
    Appraisal Capital 350,000
    (Equity Section. Raises building from
    cost of 400,000 to appraised value of 750,000)

Year 2
Depreciation Building $21,667
    Accumulated Depreciation-Building $21,667
Depreciation based on *appraised value:* $400,000 for
40 years; $350,000 for 30 years. Building 10 years old
at time of appraisal.

INTANGIBLE ASSETS

Intangible assets are a group of long-term assets that do not have physical existence or tangible form, but are considered to have value to the entity. Examples are patents, copyrights, trademarks, and goodwill.

Intangible assets are categorized into two classes:

1. Indentifiable intangible assets—those having specific identity and usually a known limited life. The limitation may be a legal regulation, a contractual agreement or the nature of the intangible itself, for example, a patent, copyright, franchise, trademark and the like.
2. Unidentifiable intangible assets—those having no specific identity and an unknown life. Goodwill is the most notable example.

Identifiable intangible assets should be recorded at their cost. If the asset is acquired in a transaction other than a purchase for cash, it is to be valued at its fair value or the fair value of the consideration given, whichever is more definitely determinable. If several identifiable intangible assets are acquired as a group, a separate cost should be established for each intangible asset. The cost or assigned basis should be amortized by systematic charges to income over the expected period of economic benefit usually set by law or by contract. If it becomes apparent that the period of economic benefit will be shorter or longer than that originally used, there should be an appropriate decrease or increase in annual amortization charges.

The costs of *unidentifiable* intangible assets (such as goodwill) are normally amortized on a straight-line basis over a period not exceeding forty years. Arbitrary shorter periods are not to be used unless specific factors pinpoint a shorter life.

Unidentifiable intangible assets are usually measured as the excess paid over the identifiable assets.

The cost of an intangible asset, including goodwill acquired in a business combination, should not be written off to income in the period of acquisition nor charged as a lump sum to capital surplus or to retained earnings, nor be reduced to a nominal amount at or immediately after acquisition.

The question of whether other costs of internally developed identifiable intangible assets are to be capitalized or expensed is not delineated by the Standards Board. Questions have arisen regarding the capitalization of the cost of a large initial advertising campaign for a new product or capitalizing the cost of training new employees. The interpretation is that there is no encouragement to capitalize these costs under existing standards.

Expected Period of Benefit. Some intangibles have the length of their beneficial lives set by law, or contract. Patents have a beneficial life of 17 years. Copyrights are granted for the life of the creator plus 50 years. Trademarks have a legal life of 20 years, but can be renewed an indefinite number of times. A franchise can be for a definite period of time specified in a contract, as is a lease.

Separability from the Enterprise. Patents, copyrights, licenses, franchises, etc., are salable and therefore are separable from the business entity. Goodwill is a part of the enterprise and therefore is not separable.

RESEARCH AND DEVELOPMENT COSTS (AND PATENTS)

Under the latest standards of financial accounting and reporting for research and development costs adopted in October, 1974, and the subsequent extensions of that section to cover applicability to business combinations accounted for by the "purchase" method, and applicability to computer software, research and development costs are to be *charged as expenses when incurred*. (Note that this is diametrically opposed to the old system of deferral and amortization.) (Note also that in changing to the direct expense method, previously amortized "R & D" costs should be treated as prior period adjustments.)

Research is planned search or critical investigation aimed at discovery of new knowledge with the hope that such knowledge will be useful in developing a new product or service or a new process or technique or in bringing about a significant improvement to an existing product or process.

Development is the translation of research findings or other knowledge into a plan or design for a new product or process or for a significant improvement to an existing product or process whether intended for sale or use. It includes the conceptual formulation, design and testing of product alternatives, construction of prototypes, and operation of pilot plants. It does not include routine or periodic alterations to existing products, production lines, manufacturing processes, and other on-going operations even though those alterations may represent improvements; and it does not include market research or market testing activities.

Typical activities which would be included in research and development costs (excluding those done for others under contract) are:

Laboratory research aimed at finding new knowledge

Searching for applications of findings

Concepts-forming and design of new product or processes

Testing of above

Modifications of above

Design, construction and testing of prototypes

Design of new tools, dies, etc, for new technology

Pilot plant posts not useful for commercial production

Engineering activity to the point of manufacture

Certain activities, however, are *excluded* from the definition of research and development and are either expensed or amortized depending upon the apparent periods benefited:

1. Engineering costs during early commercial production.
2. Quality costs during commercial production.
3. Break-down trouble-shooting costs during production.
4. Routine efforts to improve the product.
5. Adapting to a customer's requirement, if ordinary.
6. Existing product change-costs for seasonal reasons.
7. Routine designing of tools and dies, etc.
8. Costs of start-up facilities other than pilot plant or those specifically designed only for research and development work.
9. Legal work involved in patent applications or litigation, and the sale or licensing of patents.

In the following list, the *italicized* portions represent those elements of research and development costs and expenditures which should be *capitalized* and not expensed immediately. The non-italicized items are those which should be expensed immediately:

1. MATERIALS, EQUIPMENT AND FACILITIES: *The costs of materials (whether from the enterprise's normal inventory or acquired specially for research and development activities) and equipment or facilities that are acquired or constructed for research and development activities and that have alternative future uses (in research and development projects or otherwise) shall be capitalized as tangible assets when acquired or constructed.* The cost of such materials consumed in research and development activities and the depreciation of such equipment or facilities used in those activities are research and development costs. However, the costs of materials, equipment, or facilities that are acquired or constructed for a particular research and development project and that have no alternative future uses (in other research and development projects or otherwise) and therefore no separate economic values are research and development costs at the time the costs are incurred.

2. FASB No. 86, *Accounting for the Costs of Computer Software to be Sold, Leased, or Otherwise Marketed*, requires all costs associated with the development of a computer software product to be sold, leased, or otherwise marketed to be charged to expense as required by FASB No. 2, *Accounting for Research and Development*. The costs of maintenance and customer service is charged to expense when the related revenue is recognized, or when these costs are incurred, whichever occurs first.

3. PERSONNEL: Salaries and wages and other related costs of personnel engaged in research and development activities shall be included in research and development costs.

4. TANGIBLES PURCHASED FROM OTHERS: *The costs of intangibles that are purchased from others for use in research and development activities and*

that have alternative future uses (in research and development projects or otherwise) shall be capitalized and amortized as intangible assets in accordance with Section 5141. The amortization of those intangible assets used in research and development activities is a research and development cost. However, the costs of intangibles that are purchased from others for a particular research and development project and that have no alternative future uses (in other research and development projects or otherwise) and therefore no separate economic values are research and development costs at the time the costs are incurred.

5. CONTRACT SERVICES: The costs of services performed by others in connection with the research and development activities of an enterprise, including research and development conducted by others in behalf of the enterprise, shall be included in research and development costs.

6. INDIRECT COSTS: Research and development costs shall include a reasonable allocation of indirect costs. However, general and administrative costs that are not clearly related to research and development activities shall not be included as research and development costs.

Research and development costs should *not* be charged as part of factory overhead because this handling would result in partial deferral to closing inventory. The standard requires expensing as incurred.

Writing Off a Patent

A patent has a legal life of 17 years. However, most companies write off patents in much shorter periods since their useful lives are generally shorter than 17 years. Reasons for writing off patents in less than 17 years are as follows:

(1) The patent could have been purchased many years after issuance.

(2) The patent is for a current-fad-type item and sales can be expected to last for only a year or two.

(3) A newer patented item appears on the market which puts an end to the economic usefulness of the patent.

(4) The legal costs to defend a patent must be capitalized.

Some companies buy a patent just to protect an older patent they have from becoming outmoded. The cost of the new patent purchase should be written off over the remaining life of the old patent.

Copyrights

A copyright has a legal life of 50 years after author's death, with those prior to December 31, 1977, renewable for 47 years. However, here, as in the case of patents, copyright costs are usually written off in a much shorter period since the economic usefulness of a copyright usually is only a few years. Since the cost of obtaining a copyright usually is nominal (unlike a patent), the amount is usually not amortized but is written off immediately to income. Publisher-held copyrights last 75 years, unless reassigned to the author.

Franchises

Franchises are identifiable intangibles and, by contract, have a certain number of years to run. They should be written off over that contractual period. Sometimes, a franchise can be terminated by the will of the licensor. In such case, an immediate write-off may be justified.

Trademarks

A trademark is an identifiable intangible, usually with an indeterminable life and should, therefore, be written off over forty years unless a shorter life can be determined with reasonable certainty.

In the same category are trade names, brand names, secret formulae and processes, designs, and the right to use certain labels.

GOODWILL

In acquiring a business in an exchange or combination, each individual asset is measured at its fair value. The excess exchange price over those values assigned to individual assets is termed and recorded as 'goodwill.'

Goodwill is an unidentifiable intangible asset. It has no permanent existence (such as land). It has no definite, measurable life. It has neither limited nor unlimited usefulness. Thus, delaying write-off until a loss is certain may cause a dilemma, as would an early write-off. Therefore, the AICPA, in recognition of this problem, has, for conformity, suggested the arbitrary period of write-off at forty years, or less. In addition, the straight-line method of amortization should be used in expensing goodwill.

The amortization of goodwill is not deductible for tax purposes. Since the expensing of goodwill creates a lower net income for financial statement purposes than the taxable income for tax purposes, there arises a *permanent* difference as opposed to a timing difference.

The value of a company is derived from the ability of the business to earn more than an assumed normal rate of return. Goodwill is recognized in the accounts *only* when acquired through specific purchase and payment. It cannot be generated internally and capitalized in the accounts because reassuring the variables that contribute to goodwill and associating costs and future benefits to those variables is considered to be too high a degree of guesswork and estimation. The usual calculation to value goodwill when an acquisition by the purchase method is being negotiated is to determine the *acquired* company's earning power and a "normal" rate of return on the fair market value of the company's assets. Assume the five-year average earnings to be $100,000 per year and 10 percent is agreed upon as a normal rate of return. Capitalizing the earnings (100,000/.10) gives a value of $10,000,000 for the acquired company. Assume the *acquiring* company pays $12,000,000 for the company. Goodwill under the purchase method may then be taken onto the books at a value of $2,000,000.

Establishing the Goodwill Factor

Goodwill is generally based upon the assumption that earnings will continue, but not forever. The good name and reputation of the sellers will continue to influence the business for a while in the hands of the new owners. It is this lingering influence which is the nature of goodwill. It may be the result of any of, or a combination of, the following:

1. A prized location;
2. Exceptional operating efficiency;
3. Unusually satisfactory relations with customers or personnel;
4. Special expertise in business techniques;
5. An unusual product with customer acceptance.

In negotiation to buy or sell a business, one of the problems is always the setting of a mutually satisfactory price on the value of goodwill—over and above the net fair value of the identifiable assets (minus liabilities).

Here are six varied methods of computing goodwill:

Assumed facts for computing the goodwill value; net assets, $1,000,000; profits of last 5 years: $190,000, $195,000, $190,000, $215,000, $210,000; total $1,000,000; average, $200,000

(1) *Years' purchase of past annual profits*	
Profits of second preceding year	$ 215,000
Profits of first preceding year	210,000
Total and price to be paid for goodwill	$ 425,000
(2) *Years' purchase of average past profits*	
Average profits of last 5 years (as stated above)	$ 200,000
Multiply by number of years of purchase	2
Goodwill	$ 400,000

(3) *Years' purchase of excess profits*

	Profits	12½% of Net Assets	Excess
Year Preceding Sale	*Profits*	*Net Assets*	*Excess*
Third	$190,000	$125,000	$ 65,000
Second	215,000	125,000	90,000
First	210,000	125,000	85,000
Total Payment for Goodwill			$ 240,000

(4) *Years' purchase of average excess profits*

Average profits of past 5 years	$ 200,000
Deduct 12½% of $1,000,000	125,000
Excess	75,000
Multiply by number of years of purchase	3
Goodwill	$ 225,000

(5) *Capitalized profits, minus net assets*

Capitalized value of average net profits, or total value of business:

$200,000 ÷ 12½%	$1,600,000
Deduct agreed value of net assets other than goodwill	1,000,000
Goodwill	$ 600,000

(6) *Excess profits capitalized*

Average profits of past 5 years	$ 200,000
Deduct profits regarded as applicable to net assets acquired—12½% of $1,000,000	125,000
Remaining profits, regarded as indicative of goodwill	$ 75,000
Goodwill = $75,000 ÷ 25%	$ 300,000

ORGANIZATION EXPENSES

When a corporation is created, there are numerous expenses involved in its creation. Among these are legal fees, stock certificate costs, underwriters' fees, corporation fees, commissions, promotion expenses, etc.

Under Section 248 of the tax law, organization expenses are to be written off over a minimum five-year period. This is the factor which causes many corporations to write organization costs off over that period, though the standards permit immediate write-off.

SECRET FORMULAS AND PROCESSES

A formula or process known only to a specific producer may be a valuable asset even though there is no patent involved. Such property usually has economic benefit which continues indefinitely instead of a limited period.

In those instances in which the life is indeterminate, the forty-year period should be used, amortizing on a straight-line basis, as long as benefit continues and cannot be reasonably pinpointed or rejected.

RETAIL LAND SALES

For periods ending on and after December 31, 1972, new requirements for financial reporting of retail land sales were promulgated by the Committee on Land Development Companies of the AICPA. Under the guides (which apply to retail lot sales on a volume basis with down payments smaller than those involved in casual sales), payments made on such sales are treated as deposits and not recognized as sales under either the accrual method or the installment method until they equal at least 10% of the contract price, the cancellation period has expired, and promised performance becomes predictable.

Accrual Method

The accrual method is required on a project-by-project basis if *all* the following conditions are met:

1. The properties clearly will be useful for residential or recreational purposes without legal restriction when the payment period is completed, and
2. The project's planned improvements must have progress beyond preliminary stages and there is evidence that the work will be completed according to plan, and
3. The receivable cannot be subordinated to new loans on the property, except for construction purposes and collection experience on such contracts is the same as on those not subordinated, and
4. Collection experience of the project indicates that collectibility of receivable balances is reasonably predictable and that 90% of the contracts in force six months after sales are recorded will be collected in full.

All other contracts must be accounted for by the installment method under which revenue is recognized as payments are received, and related selling costs may be deferred.

There are three principal aspects with respect to reporting land sales. They are: (1) timing of revenue, (2) deferral of revenue for future performance obligations, and (3) measurement of revenue. The earlier practice was to count as income the full contract price at the time the contract was executed, even though a buyer made only a small down payment and the completion of the contract was uncertain.

For example, a buyer entered a contract with a land development company for the purchase of a $20,000 homesite. He made a $500 down payment and promised to pay the balance before completion. Under prior rules, the land development company would have counted the entire $20,000 as income, even though a large percentage of such contracts might never have reached completion.

Timing of Revenue

Under the present rules, the development company doesn't count the $20,000 as income unless there is a reasonable probability of completion and it collects a down payment of at least 10%.

Each company looks to its own experience to provide a reasonable prediction of the percentage of all the contracts that will be completed. The past sales experience will indicate how much should be deducted from the overall gross sales figure and provided for in an allowance for contract cancellations. When a contract is canceled, the receivable from the contract is charged to the allowance account.

The rules also include a criteria for determining when a contract cancellation has occurred. According to the guidelines, a contract is considered canceled if less than 25% of the contract price has been paid and the buyer is in default for 90 days or more. If more than 25% but less than 50% of the contract price has been paid, the default period is 120 days; more than 50%, the default period is 150 days.

Where a company's collection experience cannot provide a reasonable prediction of completions, the installment method must be used, not the accrual method. Where refund period policies exist, no portion of the deposit receipts should be reported until the refund period has passed.

Deferral of Revenue for Future Performance Obligations

Where there are significant future-performance requirements, the earning process is incomplete. Therefore, the portion of the income representing reasonable compensation for the improvement effort and risk must be deferred until the work is performed. The amount deferred is in the ratio of revenue that the unexpected costs bear to the total costs expected to be incurred.

Measurement of Revenue

Here, we deal with the specific value that should be ascribed to long-term receivables where the interest rate is less than the prevailing rate for an obligation with similar terms, security, and risk.

The credit ratings of retail land purchasers generally approximate those of users of retail consumer installment credit provided by commercial banks and established retail organizations. Accordingly, the effective annual yield on the net investment in land contract receivables should not be less than the minimum annual rate charged to installment borrowers by commercial banks and established retail organizations.

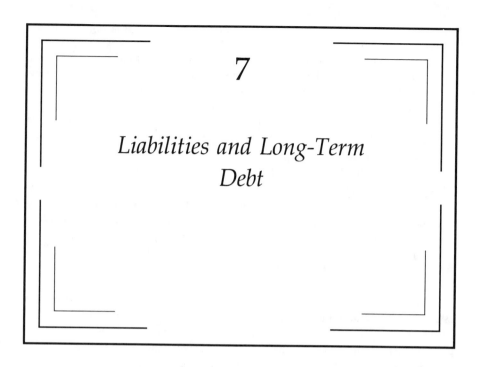

7

Liabilities and Long-Term Debt

IDENTIFICATION OF CURRENT LIABILITIES

The category of current liabilities normally consists of obligations which must be paid within one year. Some other current liabilities are as follows:

(1) Obligations whose liquidation is reasonably expected to require the use of existing current assets or the creation of other current liabilities.

(2) Obligations for items such as payables incurred in the acquisition of material and supplies which are to be used in the production of goods, or in providing services which are offered for sale.

(3) Collections received in advance pertaining to the delivery of goods or the performance of services which will be liquidated in the ordinary course of business by delivery of such goods or services. But note that advances received which represent long-term deferments are not to be shown as current liabilities. An example of this would be a long-term warranty or the advance receipt by a lessor of rentals for the final period of a ten-year lease as a condition to the execution of the lease.

(4) Debts which arise from operations directly relating to the operating cycle. Examples are accruals for wages, salaries, commissions, rentals, royalties, and income and other taxes; short-term debts which are expected to be liquidated within a relatively short period of time, usually one year; short-term debts arising from acquisition of capital assets; the current portion of a serial note; amounts required to be expended within one year under a sinking fund; loans accompanied by a pledge of a life insurance policy which by its terms is to be repaid within one year. When the intent is to repay a loan on life insurance from the proceeds of the policy received upon maturity or cancellation, the obligation should not be included as a current liability.

(5) Amounts which are expected to be required to cover expenditures within the year for known obligations, the amount of which can only approximately be determined. An example is a provision for accruing bonus payments. When an amount is expected to be required to be paid to persons unknown (for example, in connection with a guarantee of products sold), a reasonable amount should be included as a current liability.

It does not include debts to be liquidated by funds accumulated in noncurrent assets, or long-term obligations incurred to provide working capital for long periods. A contractual obligation falling due within a one-year period which is expected to be refinanced on a long-term basis should also be excluded from current liabilities. Bonds maturing within a one-year period which are to be refinanced by the issuance of new bonds should not therefore be included as current liabilities. Doing so would give a wrong impression of the company's working capital. The bonds should remain among long-term liabilities, with a footnote indicating the maturity date and the contemplated refinancing.

(6) Accounts payable for goods purchased before the end of the accounting period and for which title has passed but which have not been received.

(7) Liabilities for services rendered to your company before the end of the period but not yet billed.

(8) Dividends which have been declared but have not yet been paid.

(9) Liabilities to be liquidated in merchandise arising from the issuance of due bills, merchandise coupon books, and gift certificates.

(10) A liability must be accrued for employees' rights to receive compensation for future absences under certain conditions:

a. If the employees' right to compensation for future absences is related to services already rendered to the company.

b. The obligation relates to accumulated or vested rights.

c. Payment of the compensation is probable.

d. The amount of the compensation can be reasonably estimated.

Vacations, illness, and holidays are examples of liabilities to be accrued, if compensation is expected to be paid.

This rule does not apply to such items as termination pay, deferred compensation, stock (or stock options) issued to employees, nor to such fringe benefits as group insurance or long-term disability pay.

LONG-TERM DEBT

Bond Premium or Discount

Liabilities are measured at amounts established in exchanges, usually the amounts to be paid, sometimes discounted. Conceptually, a liability is measured at the amount of cash to be paid discounted to the time the liability is incurred . . . Bonds and other long-term liabilities are in effect measured at the discounted amount of the future cash payments for interest and principal.

The difference between the face amount of the liability to be paid in the future and the actual net proceeds received in the present for incurring of this debt is amortized over the period to the maturity due-date. When this amount of periodic calculated interest is combined with the nominal face-amount of interest actually paid to debt-holders, the difference is amortized, giving a level, "effective" rate, and is called the "interest" method of amortization and is an acceptable method to be used.

Statement presentation. Unamortized discount or premium or debentures or other long-term debt should be shown on the balance sheet as a direct deduction or addition to the face value. It should *not* be shown as a deferred item. The amortized portion of either premium or discount should be shown as an interest item on the income statement. Issue costs should be treated as deferred charges.

The accounting method for bonds issued at a premium follows.

Year 1		
Cash	2,025,000	
Unamortized Bond Issue Costs	15,000	
Bonds Payable (8%, 10 years)		2,000,000
Unamortized Premium on Bonds		40,000
(Entries for the face value of the bonds,		
issue costs, and net cash proceeds received)		

Year 2		
Unamortized Premium on Bonds	4,000	
Unamortized Bond Issue Cost		1,500
Interest Expense (difference)		2,500
Interest Expense	160,000	
Cash		160,000

EARLY EXTINGUISHMENT OF DEBT

Bonds and other long-term obligations often contain provisions giving the bond issuer an option to retire the bonds before their maturity date. This option is often exercised in connection with the issuance of new bonds at favorable rates (a refunding).

Usually, the amount paid for early extinguishment will be different from the face amount due and also different from the "net carrying value" of the debt. The "net carrying value" is the sum due at maturity plus or minus the remaining unamortized premium or discount (and cost of issuance).

On January 1, 1973, standards were adopted for the treatment of this early extinguishment of debt:

1. The difference between the reacquisition price and the *net carrying amount* of the debt (face value plus/minus unamortized items) should be recognized currently *in income* as gain or loss and shown as a separate item, and, if material, shown as an *extraordinary item*, net of related income tax effect.

2. Disclosure of pertinent details should be made.

3. Gains or losses should not be amortized to future periods. A gain or loss from the early extinguishment of debt made to satisfy sinking fund requirements that must be met within one year of the date of extinguishment is an ordinary item.

4. The extinguishment of *convertible* debt before maturity should be handled in the same manner.

5. The criteria of "unusual nature" and "infrequency of occurrence" do *not* apply here for the classification of the early extinguishment of debt as extraordinary. The determining factor for classification is *"materiality."*

These existing standards, in effect, prohibit the old practice of applying gains or losses on debt refunded to any new issues of similar obligations.

TROUBLED DEBT RESTRUCTURINGS

A restructuring of debt constitutes a troubled debt restructuring if the creditor, for economic or legal reasons related to the debtor's financial difficulties, grants a concession to the debtor that it would not otherwise consider. That concession stems either from an agreement between the creditor and debtor, or is imposed by law or a court.

Debtors.   A debtor that transfers its receivables from third parties, real estate, or other assets to a creditor to settle fully a payable, shall recognize a gain on restructuring of payables. The gain shall be measured by the excess of (1) carrying amount of payable settled (the face amount increased or decreased by the applicable accrued interest and applicable unamortized premium, discount finance charges or issue costs), over (2) the face value of the assets transferred to the creditor. This difference is a gain or loss on the transfer of assets. The debtor shall include that gain or loss in measuring net income for the period of transfer, reported as provided in APB #30 (section 2012) "Reporting Results of Operations."

A debtor that grants an equity interest to a creditor to settle fully a payable shall account for the equity interest at its fair value. The difference between fair value of the interest granted and the carrying amount of the payable is recognized as a gain on restructuring of payables. Gains on restructuring of payables shall be aggregated and, if material, shall be classified as an extraordinary item, net of related income tax effect.

Creditors.   When a creditor receives from a debtor in full satisfaction of a receivable, either (1) receivables from third parties, real estate, or other assets, or (2) shares of stock, the creditor shall account for those assets at their fair value at the time of restructuring. The excess of the recorded investment in receivables satisfied, over the fair value of assets received, is a loss to be recognized and included in net income for the period of restructuring and reported according to APB #30 (section 2012).

A creditor shall disclose the following information pertaining to troubled debt restructurings:

1. For outstanding receivables whose terms have been modified, by major category:
   (a) the aggregate recorded investment,
   (b) the gross income that would have been recorded in the period then ended, if those receivables had been current in accordance with their original terms and had been outstanding throughout the period, or since origination, if held for part of the period, and
   (c) the amount of interest income on those receivables that was included in net income for the period.
2. The amount of commitments to lend additional funds to debtors using receivables whose terms have been modified in troubled debt restructurings.

Commitments that are associated with a supplier's financing arrangements which involve an unconditional purchase obligation must be disclosed. These obligations are terms "take-or-pay" contracts.

The following must be disclosed:

1. The nature of the obligation.
2. The amount of the fixed and determinable obligation in the aggregate and for each of the next five years.

3. A description of the obligation that is variable, and the purchases in each year for which an income statement is presented.

Disclosure of future payments on long-term borrowings and redeemable stock must also be disclosed. The maturities, sinking fund requirements (if any), and redemption requirements for each of the next five years must be shown.

For additional situations and more detailed information, see FASB Statement No. 15, *Accounting by Debtors and Creditors for Troubled Debt Restructuring*, June, 1977.

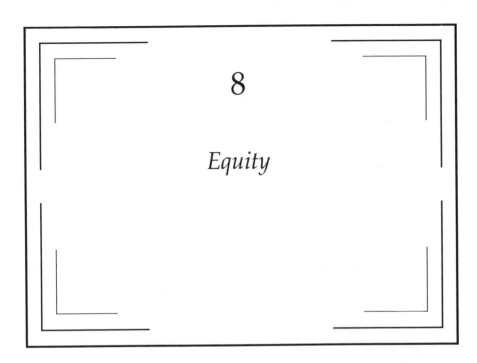

8

Equity

STOCKHOLDERS' EQUITY

"Stockholders' equity" is the most commonly used term to describe the section of the balance sheet encompassing the corporation's capital and retained earnings. Other terms used are "net worth" or "capital and surplus."

Stockholders' equity consists of three broad source classifications:

1. Investments made by owners:

   Capital Stock (Common and/or Preferred)—at par value (legal value) or stated amount

   Additional Paid-In Capital—"In Excess of Par," "Capital Surplus," etc.
2. Income (loss) generated by operations:

   Retained Earnings—the accumulated undistributed annual profits (losses), after taxes and dividends
3. Appraisal Capital—resulting from the revaluation of assets over historical cost (*not* in conformity with GAAP)

   Changes in shareholders' equity, primarily in retained earnings, are caused by:

1. Periodic net income (loss) after taxes
2. Dividends declared
3. Prior period adjustments of retained earnings
4. Contingency reserves (appropriations of retained earnings)
5. Recapitalizations:
   A. Stock dividends and split-ups
   B. Changing par or stated value
   C. Reducing capital
   D. Quasi-reorganizations
   E. Stock reclassifications
   F. Substituting debt for stock
6. Treasury stock dealings
7. Business combinations
8. Certain unrealized gains and losses
9. Donations

CAPITAL STOCK

Capital stock is the capital contributed by the stockholders to the corporation.

Common Stock

The common stockholders are the residual owners of the corporation; that is, they own whatever is left after all preceding claims are paid off. By definition, common stock is "a stock which is subordinate to all other stocks of the issuer."

When a corporation has a single class of stock, it is often called "capital stock" instead of "common stock." The three aspects of stock ownership are (1) dividends, (2) claims against assets on liquidation, and (3) shares in management. As to these aspects of ownership, common stockholders have the following rights: to dividends, common stockholders have no fixed rights but, on the other hand, are limited to no maximum payment; their claim against the assets of the corporation on liquidation is last in the order of priority, following all creditors and all other equity interests. The common stockholders, by statute, must have a voice in management. Their voice is often to the exclusion of all other equity interests, but they may also share their management rights with other classes of stock.

Common stock may be classified:

(1) Par and no-par stock. Par stock is stock with a stated, legal dollar value, whereas no-par stock lacks such a given value. The distinction today is largely an academic one. However, state laws regarding stock dividends and split-ups and the adjustments of par value may affect the accounting treatment of such dividends.

(2) Classes of common stock.   Common stock may be divided into separate classes—e.g., class A, class B, etc. Usually, the class distinction deals with the right to vote for separate directors, or one class may have the right to vote and one class may not. Class stock is a typical technique used where a minority group wishes to maintain control.

Preferred Stock

The second major type of capital stock is preferred stock, stock which has some preference with regard to dividend payments or distribution of assets on liquidation. In the usual situation, preferred stock will have a preference on liquidation, to the extent of the par value of the stock. In addition, its right to dividends depends on the following classification:

(1) Participating and nonparticipating right.   If the preferred has a right to a fixed dividend each year but has not the right to share in any additional dividends over and above the stated amount, it is nonparticipating preferred. If it is entitled to a share of any dividends over and above those to which it has priority, it is called participating. For example, a preferred may have the right to a 5% annual dividend and then share equally with the common stock in dividends after a dividend (equal to the preferred per-share dividend) has been paid to the common stockholders.

(2) Convertible preferred stock.   Convertible preferred is stock which may, at the holder's option, be exchanged for common. The terms of the exchange and the conversion period are set forth on the preferred certificate. Thus one share of $100 par preferred may be convertible beginning one year after issue into two shares of common. If the preferred stockholder converts, he will own two shares of common at a cost to him of $50 per share (this assumes he purchased the preferred at par). A company will issue a convertible security at a time when it needs funds but for one reason or another cannot or does not wish to issue common stock. For example, in a weak stock market, common may be poorly received while a convertible preferred can be privately placed with a large institutional investor. The conversion privilege, from the point of view of the purchaser, is a ''sweetener'' since it affords the opportunity to take a full equity position in the future if the company prospers. The issuer may be quite satisfied to give the conversion privilege because it means that (assuming earnings rise) the preferred stock, with a prior and fixed dividend claim, will gradually be eliminated in exchange for common shares.

Accounting for a convertible preferred issue follows the usual rules. That is, when the preferred is first issued, a separate capital account will be set up, to which will be credited the par value of the outstanding stock. When conversion takes place, an amount equal to the par of the converted stock is debited to the preferred account. The common stock account will be credited with an amount equal to the par or stated value of the shares issued in exchange for the preferred. Any excess will go to capital surplus.

Both participating (1) and convertible (2) preferred stocks above must be considered in the computation of earnings per share.

(3) Cumulative and noncumulative.

A corporation which lacks earnings or surplus cannot pay dividends on its preferred stock. In that case, the question arises whether the passed dividend must be paid in future years. If past dividends do accumulate and must be paid off, the stock is cumulative; otherwise, noncumulative.

The preferred may share voting rights equally with the common stock, it may lack voting rights under any circumstances, or it may have the right to vote only if one or more dividends are passed. In the latter case, the preferred may have the exclusive right to vote for a certain number of directors to be sure that its interests as a class are protected.

For cumulative stock, the dividends must be accrued each year (even if unpaid), unless issued with an "only as earned" provision. The effect on earnings per share is the extent of the reduction of net income for this accrual.

Par Value, Stated Capital, and Capital Stock Accounts

The money a corporation receives for its stock is in a unique category. It is variously referred to as "a cushion for creditors," "a trust fund," and similar expressions. The point is that in a corporation which gives its stockholders limited liability, the only funds to which the creditors of the corporation can look for repayment of their debts in the event the corporation suffers losses is the money received for stock, which constitutes the stated capital account. Consequently, most state corporation statutes require a number of steps to be taken before a corporation can reduce its stated capital. These steps include approval by the stockholders and the filing of a certificate with the proper state officer, so that creditors may be put on notice of the reduction in capital.

Stated capital is actually divided into separate accounts, each account for a particular class of stock. Thus, a corporation may have outstanding a class A common, a class B common, a first preferred, a second preferred, etc. Each class would have its own account, which would show the number of shares of the class authorized by the certificate of incorporation, the number actually issued and the consideration received by the corporation.

It is at this point that the distinction between par and no-par stock becomes important. Par stock is rarely sold for less than its par value, although it may be sold for more. In many states, it is illegal to sell stock at a discount from par, and even when not illegal, there may be a residual stockholder liability for that original discount to the creditors. In any case, an amount equal to the par value of the stock must be credited to its capital account, with any excess going into a surplus account.

In the case of no-par stock, the corporation, either through its board of directors or at a stockholders' meeting, assigns part of the consideration received as stated capital for the stock and treats the rest as a credit to a capital surplus account. Treating part of the consideration received as stated capital is the equivalent of giving the stock a par value.

Capital Stock Issued for Property

Where capital stock is issued for the acquisition of property in a non-cash transfer, measurement of owners' investment is usually determined by using the fair market value of the assets (and/or the discounted present value of any liabilities transferred).

When the fair value of the assets transferred cannot be measured, the market value of the stock issued may be used instead for establishing the value of the property received.

When the acquisition is an entire business, the principle of "fair value" is extended to cover each and every asset acquired (other than goodwill). If the fair value of the *whole* business is considered to be *more* than the individual values, that excess is considered to be goodwill.

The difference between fair value put on the assets received and the *par value* (stated) of the stock issued goes to the Capital-in-Excess of Par Value account (or Additional Paid-in Capital, etc.) as either a positive or negative (discount) amount. Note that this does *not* pertain to any "negative" goodwill which might have been created; said negative goodwill, if any, should be used to reduce, immediately, the non-current assets (except investment securities), proportionately to zero, if necessary, with any remaining excess to be deferred and amortized as favorable goodwill is amortized.

Capital in Excess of Par or Stated Value
(Capital Surplus)

The term "capital surplus" is still widely used, although the preferred terminology is "capital in excess of par" or "additional paid-in capital."

The capital in excess of par account is credited with capital received by the corporation which is not part of par value or stated capital. It is primarily the excess of consideration received over par value or the amount of consideration received for no-par stock which is not assigned as stated capital.

In addition, donations of capital to the corporation are credited to this account. If stated capital is ever reduced as permitted by law, the transfer is from the capital stock account to this capital surplus account.

This account is also credited for the excess of market value *over* par value for stock dividends (which are not split-ups) and for the granting of certain stock options and rights.

RETAINED EARNINGS

Accounting Terminology Bulletin No. 1 (August, 1953) recommended the following (terminology bulletins do not have authoritative status, but are issued as useful guides):

1. The abandonment of the term "surplus";
2. The term "earned surplus" be replaced with such terms that indicate the source such as:
   Retained Earnings
   Retained Income
   Accumulated Earnings
   Earnings Retained for Use in the Business

Retained earnings are the accumulated undistributed past and current year's earnings, net of taxes and dividends paid and declared.

Portions of retained earnings may be set aside for certain contingencies, appropriated for such purposes as possible future inventory losses, sinking funds, etc.

A Statement of Changes in Retained Earnings is one of the basic financial statements *required* for fair presentation of results of operation and financial condition to conform with GAAP. It shows net income, dividends, prior period adjustments. A Statement of Other Changes in Owners' Equity shows additional investments by owners, retirements of owners' interests and similar events (if these are few and simple, they are put in the notes).

Regardless of how a company displays its undistributed earnings, or the disclosures thereof, for tax purposes, the actual earnings and profits which could have been or are still subject to distribution as "dividends" *under IRS regulations* may, under some circumstances, retain that characteristic for the purpose of ordinary income taxation to the ultimate recipient. (See Tax Section of this book.) The AICPA has no requirement for this disclosure other than normal requirement for the "periods presented," which would usually show the activity in retained earnings for only two years and not prior.

PRIOR PERIOD ADJUSTMENTS

Under FASB Statement #16 *Prior Period Adjustments*, issued June 1977, only the following rare types of items should be treated as prior period adjustments and *not* be included in the determination of current period net income:

1. Correction of an error (material) in prior financial statements; and
2. Realization of income tax pre-acquisition operating loss benefits of *purchased subsidiaries*.

Corrections of errors are *not* changes in accounting *estimates*. Error corrections are those resulting from:

1. Mathematical errors;
2. Erroneous application of accounting principles;
3. Misuse of, or oversight of, facts existing at a prior statement period.

(Changes in accounting *estimates* result from *new* information or developments, which sharpen and improve judgment.)

Litigation settlements and income tax adjustments *no longer* meet the definition of prior period adjustments. However, for *interim periods only* (of the current fiscal year), material items of this nature should be treated as prior interim adjustments to the identifiable period of related business activity.

Goodwill may not be written off as a prior period adjustment.

Retroactive adjustment should be made of all comparative periods presented, reflecting changes to particular items, net income and retained earnings balances. The tax effects should also be reflected and shown. Disclosure of the effects of the restatement should be made.

Prior period adjustments must be charged or credited to the opening balance of retained earnings. They cannot be included in the determination of net income for the current period. (APB Opinion 9. FASB Statement 16)

Beginning Retained Earnings		$1,000
Correction Depreciation Error		
$300 x .50 (net of tax)		150
Adjustment Beginning Retained Earnings		1,150
Net Income		400
Ending—Retained Earnings		$1,550
Accumulated Depreciation	$300	
Taxes Payable		150
Retained Earnings		150

CONTINGENCY RESERVES

A "contingency" is defined as "an existing condition, situation, or set of circumstances involving uncertainty as to possible gain or loss to an enterprise that will ultimately be resolved when one or more events occur or fail to occur."

Loss contingencies fall in three categories:

1. Probable
2. Reasonably possible
3. Remote.

In deciding whether to accrue the estimated loss by charging income or setting aside an appropriation of retained earnings, or merely to make a disclosure of the contingency in the notes to the financial statement, the following standards have been set:

Accrue a charge to income if *both* of the following conditions are met at the date of the financial statements:

1. Information available *before* the issuance of the financial statements indicates that probably the asset will be impaired or a liability incurred; and
2. A *reasonable* estimate of the loss *can* be made.

(When a contingent loss is probable but the reasonable estimate of the loss can only be made in terms of a range, the amount shall be accrued for the loss. When some amount within the range appears at the time to be a better estimate than any other amount within the range, that amount shall be accrued. When no amount within the range is a better estimate than any other amount, the minimum amount in the range shall be accrued.)

If discovery of the above impairment occurs *after* the date of the statements, disclosure should be made and pro-forma supplementary financial data presented giving effect to the occurrence as of the balance sheet date.

When a contingent loss is only *reasonably possible* or the probable loss cannot be estimated, an estimate of the *range* of loss should be made or a narrative description given to indicate that *no* estimate was possible. Disclosure should be made; but no accrual.

When the contingency is *remote*, disclosure should be made when it is in the nature of a guarantee. Other remote contingencies are not required to be disclosed, but they may be, if desired, for more significant reporting.

General reserves for unspecified business risks are not to be accrued and no disclosure is required.

Appropriations for loss contingencies from retained earnings must be shown, with the stockholders' Equity section of the balance sheet and clearly identified as such.

Examples of loss contingencies are:

1. Collectibility of receivables.
2. Obligations related to product warranties and product defects.
3. Risk of loss or damage of enterprise property by fire, explosion, or other hazards.
4. Threat of expropriation of assets.
5. Pending or threatened litigation.
6. Actual or possible claims and assessments.
7. Risk of loss from catastrophes assumed by property and casualty insurance companies including reinsurance companies.

8. Guarantees of indebtedness of others.

9. Obligations of commercial banks under "standby letters of credit."

10. Agreements to repurchase receivables (or to repurchase the related property) that have been sold.

Handling of these loss contingencies depends upon the nature of the loss probability and the reasonableness of estimating the loss. (Gain contingencies are not booked, only footnoted.)

RECAPITALIZATIONS

Essentially, a recapitalization means changing the structure of the capital accounts. It can also mean a reshuffling between equity and debt. A recapitalization may be done voluntarily by the corporation; or it may be part of a reorganization proceeding in a court, pursuant to a bankruptcy or a reorganization petition filed by the corporation or its creditors.

In almost all cases of recapitalizations, stockholder approval is required at some point during the process. This is because a recapitalization may affect the amount of stated capital of the corporation or change the relationships between the stockholders and the corporation or between classes of stockholders. The different categories of recapitalizations are discussed in the following paragraphs.

Stock Split-Ups

A split-up involves dividing the outstanding shares into a larger number; for example, two for one. In a two-for-one split, each stockholder receives a certificate for additional shares equal to the amount of shares he is presently holding. The split-up is reflected in the corporate books by reducing the par value or the stated value of the outstanding shares. Thus if shares with a par value of $10 are split two for one, the new par becomes $5. No entry is necessary, other than a memo entry. The stockholder adjusts his basis for the unit number of shares.

Reverse split. The opposite of a split-up is a reverse split, which results in a lesser number of outstanding shares. Stockholders turn in their old certificates and receive a new certificate for one-half former holdings. The par value or stated value is adjusted to show the higher price per share. A reverse split is sometimes used in order to increase the price of the stock immediately on the open market.

Stock Dividends

As far as the stockholder is concerned, a stock dividend is the same as the stock split; he receives additional shares, merely changing his unit-basis of holding.

But the effect is quite different from the point of view of the corporation. A stock dividend requires a transfer from retained earnings of the *market value* of the shares. Capital stock is credited for the par value and capital in excess of par value is credited for the excess of market price over par. (When the shareholder has the option of receiving cash, he must report the dividend as ordinary income.)

Dividends are presumed to be distributions which do not affect the market price because they are *less* than 20% to 25% of the number of previously outstanding shares.

Stock Split-up Effected in the Form of a Dividend

Usually, a stock distribution is either a dividend or a split-up. However, there is another type of distribution, which, because of certain state legal requirements pertaining to the minimum requirements for or the changing of par value, necessitates a different nomenclature.

In those instances where the stock dividend is so great as to materially reduce the market value, it is by nature and AICPA definition a "split-up." However, because certain states require that retained earnings must be capitalized in order to maintain par value, the AICPA standards recommend that those types of transactions be described by the corporation as a "split-up effected in the form of a dividend." The entry would then be a reduction of retained earnings and an increase in capital stock for the *par value* of the distribution. For income tax purposes, the corporation may be required to show this reduction of retained earnings as a Schedule M adjustment and may technically still have to consider it as available for ordinary-rate ultimate distribution.

CHANGING PAR OR STATED VALUE OF STOCK

This type of recapitalization involves changing from par to no par or vice versa. This is usually done in conjunction with a reduction of stated capital. A corporation, for example, may decide to change its stock from par stock to no-par stock in order to take advantage of lower franchise fees and transfer taxes. Or no-par shares may be changed to shares having par value to solve legal problems existing under particular state statutes. A par value stock which is selling in the market at a price lower than its par must be changed if the corporation intends to issue new stock, because of some state laws which prohibit a corporation from selling its par value stock for less than par value. In such case, the corporation may reduce par value or may change the par to no par, thereby, the new stock can be given a stated value equivalent to the price it can bring in the open market.

QUASI-REORGANIZATIONS

Current or future years' charges should not be made against capital surplus (as distinguished from "retained earnings") however created, instead of the income accounts.

An exception to this rule (called "readjustment") occurs when "a corporation elects to restate its assets, capital stock and retained earnings and thus avail itself of permission to relieve its future income account or retained earnings account of charges which would otherwise be made there against." In which event, the corporation "should make a clear report to its shareholders of the restatements proposed to be made; and obtain their formal consent. It should present a fair balance sheet as at the date of the readjustment, in which the readjustments of the carrying amounts are reasonably complete, in order that there may be no continuation of the circumstances which justify charges to capital surplus."

As an example of how this readjustment might occur, suppose that a company has a deficit in its retained earnings (earned surplus) of $100,000. By revaluing its assets upward, it is possible for this company to create a capital surplus account for the write-up to fair value, then write-off the deficit in retained earnings to that account. From then on, a new retained earnings account should be established and the fact be disclosed for ten years.

STOCK RECLASSIFICATIONS

Another category of stock recapitalization involves reclassifying the existing stock. This means that outstanding stock of a particular class is exchanged for stock of another class. For example, several outstanding issues of preferred stock may be consolidated into a single issue. Or, common stock may be exchanged for preferred stock, or vice versa. The object in this type of reclassification is to simplify the capital structure, which in many cases is necessary in order to make a public offering or sometimes to eliminate dividend arrearages on preferred stock by offering a new issue of stock in exchange for canceling such arrearages.

SUBSTITUTING DEBT FOR STOCK

One form of recapitalization that has become popular in some areas involves substituting bonds for stock.

The advantage to the corporation is the substitution of tax-deductible interest on bonds for nondeductible dividends on preferred stock. Of course, where we are dealing with a closely-held corporation, substituting debt for stock in a manner to give the common stockholders a pro rata portion of the debt may be interpreted for tax purposes as "thin" capitalization, and the bonds may be treated as stock anyhow.

Also, to attract new money into the corporation, it is advantageous to consider the issuance of convertible debt securities—bonds to which are attached the rights (warrants) to buy common stock of the company at a specified price. The advantages of this type of security are:

1. An interest rate which is lower than the issuer could establish for nonconvertible debt;
2. An initial conversion price greater than the market value of the common stock;
3. The conversion price which does not decrease.

The portion of proceeds from these securities which can be applied to the warrants should be credited to paid-in capital (based on fair value of both securities) and discounts or premiums should be treated as they would be under conventional bond issuance.

TREASURY STOCK

Treasury stock is stock which has previously been issued by a corporation but is no longer outstanding. It has been reacquired by the corporation and, as its name implies, held in its treasury. Treasury stock is not canceled because cancellation reduces the authorized issue of corporation stock.

In some circumstances, it is permissible to show treasury stock as an asset if adequately disclosed. However, dividends on treasury stock should not be treated as income.

Treasury Stock Shown at Cost

When a corporation acquires its own stock to be held for future sale or possible use in connection with stock options, or with no plans or uncertainty as to future retirement of that stock, the cost of the acquired stock may be shown separately as a deduction from the total of capital stock, capital surplus and retained earnings. Gains on subsequent sales (over the acquired-cost price) should be credited to capital surplus and losses (to the extent of prior gains) should be charged to that same account, with excess losses going to retained earnings. State law should be followed if in contravention.

Treasury Stock Shown at Par of Stated Value

When treasury stock is acquired for the purpose of *retirement* (or constructive retirement), the stock should be shown at par value or stated value as a reduction in the equity section and the excess of purchase cost over par (stated) value should be charged to capital surplus to the extent of prior gains booked for the same issue, together with pro-rata portions applicable to that stock arising from prior stock dividends, splits, etc. Any remaining excess may be either applied pro-rata to common stock or to retained earnings.

Treasury Stock as an Asset

If adequately disclosed, it is permissible in some circumstances to show stock of a corporation held in its own treasury as an asset. (This rule was adopted in 1934 upon recommendation of the New York Stock Exchange.)

For example, pursuant to a corporation's bonus arrangement with certain employees, treasury stock may be used to pay the bonus, and, in accordance with the concept of a current asset satisfying a current liability, that applicable treasury stock might be shown as current asset. However, dividends on such stock should not be treated as income while the corporation holds the stock.

Treasury stock has no voting rights nor the right to receive dividends. (Note: Treasury stock remains *issued* stock, but not *outstanding* stock). Treasury stock can either be retired or resold. Treasury stock is an owners' equity account and is deducted from the stockholders' equity on the balance sheet.

When a company buys its own stock:		
Treasury Stock	XXX	
Cash		XXX
If the stock is resold:		
Cash	XXX	
Treasury Stock		XXX
(The credit is the amount paid for the stock when purchased by the corporation		

If there is a difference between the corporation's acquisition of the stock and the resale price, the difference is debited or credited to an account Paid-In Capital from Treasury Stock Transactions for the amount of the difference between the proceeds of the resale and the amount paid by the corporation.

Under the cost method, treasury stock is shown as the last item before arriving at Stockholders' Equity, while under the par value method treasury stock reduces the common stock account directly under the capital stock section of Stockholders' Equity.

THE GOING CONCERN CONCEPT

There is an underlying presumption in the standards set for financial accounting that a business, once started, will continue functioning and operating as a going concern. For example, the use of historical costs for building and property, which are currently more valuable, presupposes that the *use* of that property will generate more advantages than would present disposition. Deferrals to future periods through systematic allocations also indicate a presumption of longevity.

This presumption of continuance as a going concern is never stated by the independent auditor—never worded in his own opinion. On the *contrary*, it is when there appears to be danger of the firm's *not* being able to continue as a going concern that the auditor makes the assertion that "the statements have been prepared on the basis of a going concern," and that he is *unable* to express an opinion because of major uncertainties, which he describes. Therefore, the actual use of the terminology, "going concern," in the auditor's opinion indicates trouble.

Some factors which may be indicative of *possible* failure to continue as a going concern are:

Inability to satisfy obligations on due dates.

Inability to perform contractual obligations.

Inability to meet substantial loan covenants.

A substantial deficit.

A series of continued losses.

The presence of major contingencies which could lead to heavy losses.

Catastrophes which have rendered the business inoperable.

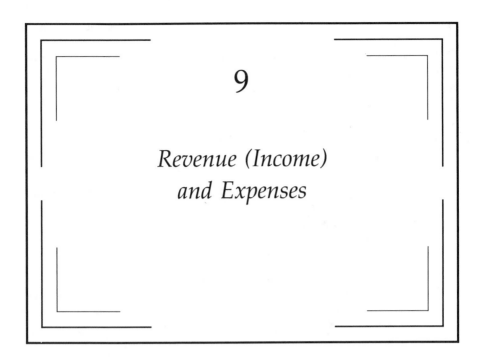

9

Revenue (Income) and Expenses

REVENUE (INCOME)

The principles upon which net income is determined derive from the pervasive measurement principles, such as realization, and the modifying conventions, such as conservatism.

The entire process of income determination (''matching'') consists of identifying, measuring and relating revenue and expenses for an accounting period. Revenue is usually determined by applying the realization principle, with the changes in net asset value interrelated with the recognition of revenue.

Revenue arises from three general activities:

1. Selling products;
2. Rendering services or letting others use owned resources, resulting in interest, rent, etc;
3. Disposing of other resources (not products), such as equipment or investments.

Revenue does not include proceeds from stockholders, lenders, asset purchases or prior period adjustments.

Revenue, in the balance sheet sense, is a gross increase in assets or a gross decrease in liabilities recognized and measured in conformity with GAAP, which results from those profit-directed activities that can change owners' equity.

Revenue is considered *realized* when:

1. The earning process is complete or virtually complete, and
2. An exchange has taken place.

The objectives of accounting determination of income are not always the same as the objectives used for tax purposes.

There are various acceptable ways of determining income, all of which are discussed in other parts of this book:

Revenue (see three general activities above):

1. Accrual method—this is financial accounting and GAAP.
2. Cash method—this is *not* considered financial accounting, and not GAAP, since one of the characteristics of GAAP is the *accrual* of appropriate items.
3. Installment sale method—generally for retail stores.
4. Completion of production method—used for precious metals.
5. For long-term construction contracts:
    A. Completed contract method.
    B. Percentage-of-completion method.
6. For leasing activities:
    A. The direct financing method.
    B. The operating method.
    C. The sales method.
7. The cost recovery method (used for installment sales).
8. Consolidation method—for majority-owned subsidiaries (over 50%).
9. Equity method—for non-consolidated subsidiaries and for controlled non-subsidiaries.

Other types of income requiring special determination:

1. Extraordinary items of income.
2. Unrealized income arising from:
    A. Foreign currency holdings or transactions.
    B. Ownership of marketable securities shown as current assets.

A *shareholder* in a corporation does *not* have income when that corporation earns income (except for a Sub-S corporation). The shareholder has, and reports for tax purposes, income only upon *distribution* of that income in the form of dividends. Generally, distributions of stock—stock dividends and stock splits—are *not* income to the shareholder, but merely an adjustment of the number of shares he holds (for the same original cost plus token costs, if any). However, there are some situations which call for the stockholder to report stock dividends as income. (See Tax Section.)

If a buyer has a right of return to the seller, revenue is recognized if *all* of the following criteria are met:

1. Buyer is obligated to pay (and not contingent upon resale of the product) or has paid the seller.
2. Buyer's obligation would not be changed by theft, damage, or destruction of the product.
3. Seller does not have any significant obligation to buyer related to resale of the product by the buyer.

4. Buyer's business must have economic substance separate from the seller's business.

If these criteria are met, sales revenue and cost of sales reported in the income statement are reduced to reflect estimated returns; expected losses are accrued.

EXPENSES

Expenses are one of the six basic elements of financial accounting, along with assets, liabilities, owners' equity, revenue and net income.

> Expenses are determined by applying the expense recognition principles on the basis of relationships, between acquisition costs [the term "cost" is commonly used to refer to the amount at which assets are initially recorded, regardless of how determined], and either the independently determined revenue or accounting periods. Since the point in time at which revenue and expenses are recognized is also the time at which changes in amounts of net assets are recorded, income determination is interrelated with asset valuation.

All costs are not expenses. Some costs are related to later periods, will provide benefits for later periods, and are carried forward as assets on the balance sheet. Other costs are incurred and provide no future benefit, having expired in terms of usefulness or applicability—these expired costs are called "expenses." All expenses, therefore, are part of the broader term "cost." These expired costs are not assets and are shown as deductions from revenue to determine net income.

> Expenses are gross decreases in assets or gross increases in liabilities recognized and measured in conformity with GAAP that result from those types of profit-directed activities that can change an owner's equity.

Recognizing Expenses

Three pervasive principles form the basis for recognizing expenses to be deducted from revenue to arrive at net income or loss:

1. Associating cause and effect ("matching"):

For example, manufacturing cost of goods sold is measured and matched to the *sale* of the product. Assumptions must be made as to how these costs attach to the product—whether on machine hours, space used, labor expended, etc. Assumptions must also be made as to how the costs flow out (LIFO, FIFO, average costs).

2. Systematic and rational allocation:

When there is no direct way to associate cause and effect and certain costs are known (or presumed) to have provided benefits during the accounting period, these costs are allocated to that period in a systematic and rational manner and to appear so to an unbiased observer. The methods of allocation should be consistent and systematic, though methods may vary for different types of costs. Examples are: Depreciation of fixed assets, amortization of intangibles, interperiod allocation of rent or interest. The allocation referred to here is not the allocation of expired manufacturing costs with the "cost" area to determine unit or job costs; it is rather the broader area of allocation to the manufacturing area from the unexpired asset account: Depreciation on factory building, rather than overhead-depreciation on Product A, B, or C.

3. Immediate recognition (period expenses):

Those costs which are expensed during an accounting period because:

A. They cannot be associated on a cause-and-effect basis with revenue, yet no useful purpose would be achieved by delaying recognition to a future period, or
B. They provide no discernible future benefits, or
C. They were recorded as assets in a prior period and now no longer provide discernible future benefits.

Examples are: Officer salaries, most selling expenses, legal fees, most general and administrative expenses.

OTHER EXPENSES (AND REVENUE)

Gains and losses.   Expenses and revenue from *other* than sales of products, merchandise or services may be separated from (operating) revenue and disclosed net separately.

Unusual items.   Unusual items of expense or income not meeting the criteria of "extraordinary" should be shown as a separate component of income from continuing operations.

Extraordinary items. Extraordinary items are discussed elsewhere in this book. They should be shown separately—net of applicable taxes—*after* net income from continuing operations. If there are any disposals of business segments, they should be shown immediately prior to extraordinary items—also with tax effect.

IMPUTED INTEREST ON NOTES RECEIVABLE OR PAYABLE

Accounting Considerations

The AICPA sets forth the appropriate accounting when the face amount of certain receivables or payables ("notes") does not reasonably represent the present value of the consideration given or received in certain exchanges. The objective of these rules is to prevent the form of the transaction from prevailing over its economic substance.

(*Present value* is the sum of future payments, discounted to the present date at an appropriate rate of interest.)

APB Opinion No. 21 states that:

(1) When a note is received or issued solely for cash, the note is presumed to have a present value equal to the cash received. If it is issued for cash equal to its face amount, it is presumed to earn the stated rate of interest.

(2) When a note is received for cash and some other rights or privileges, the value of the rights or privileges should be given accounting recognition by establishing a note discount or premium account, with the offsetting amount treated as appropriate. An example is a five-year noninterest-bearing loan made to a supplier in partial consideration for a purchase of products at lower than prevailing market prices. Under such circumstances, the difference between the present value of the receivable and the cash lent to the supplier is regarded as (a) an additional cost of the purchased goods, and (b) interest income, amortized over the life of the note.

(3) When a note is exchanged for property, goods, or services and (a) interest is not stated, or (b) it is stated but is unreasonable, or (c) the stated face amount of the note is materially different from the current cash sale price of goods (or services), the note, the sales price, and the cost of the property (goods or services) should be recorded at their fair value, or at an amount that reasonably approximates the market value of the note, whichever is more clearly determinable.

Any resulting discount or premium should be regarded as interest expense or income and be amortized over the life of the note, in such a way as to result in a constant effective rate of interest when applied to the amount outstanding at the beginning of any given period.

Opinion No. 21 also provides some general guides for determining an "appropriate" interest rate and the manner of amortization for financial reporting purposes.

IMPUTED INTEREST: When a sale is made for an amount that is collectible at a future time giving rise to an account receivable, the amount is regarded as consisting of a sales price *and* a charge for interest for the period of the payment deferral. APB Opinion No. 21 requires that in the absence of a stated rate of interest, the present value of the receivable should be determined by reducing the face amount of the receivable by an interest rate that is approximated under the circumstances for the period that payment is deferred.

This rate is the *imputed rate.* It is determined by approximating the rate the supplier pays for financing receivables, or by determining the buyer's credit standing and applying the rate the borrower would have to pay if borrowing the sum from, say, a bank.

The process of arriving at the present value of the receivable is referred to as *discounting* the sum. If the total present value of the receivable (face amount plus the imputed interest) is less than the face amount, the difference between the face value of the receivable and its present value is recognized as a discount. If the present value exceeds the face amount of the receivable, the difference is recognized as a premium.

The sale is recorded as a debit to a receivable account, a credit to a discount on the receivable, and a credit to sales at the present value as reported for the receivable. The discount is amortized as a credit to interest income over the life of the receivable. On the balance sheet any unamortized discount at the end of the accounting period is reported as a direct subtraction from the *face amount* of the receivable.

Example: Seller ships merchandise totaling $10,000 to a customer with payment deferred for five years. Seller and customer agree to impute an interest charge of 10 percent for the $10,000. The journal entries follow.

Accounts Receivable	10,000	
Sales (Present value at 10%)		6,209
Unamortized Discount		3,791
(To record the sale of merchandise		
at the present value of the receivable)		

The *interest method* is applied to amortize the discount.

End of Year 1		
Unamortized Discount	620.90	
Interest Income		620.90
(10% of $6,209.00)		
End of Year 2		
Unamortized Discount	682.99	
Interest Income		682.99
(10% of $6,829.90)		
End of Year 3		
Unamortized Discount	751.29	
Interest Income		751.29
(10% of $7,512.89)		

End of Year 4		
Unamortized Discount	826.42	
Interest Income		826.42
(10% of $8,264.18)		
Unamortized Discount	909.06	
End of Year 5		
Unamortized Discount	909.06	
Interest Income		909.06
(10% of $9,090.60)		

At the end of five years full amortization of the discount has been recorded and the face amount of the receivable results. (*Note*: Opinion No. 21 does not require the imputed interest method when ". . . receivables and payables arising from transactions with customers or suppliers in the normal course of business which are due in customary trade terms not exceeding approximately one year.")

CLASSIFYING AND REPORTING EXTRAORDINARY ITEMS

Income statement presentation requires that the results of *ordinary operations* be reported first, and applicable provision for income taxes provided for.

In order, the following should then be shown:

1. Results of discontinued operations:
   A. Income or loss from the operations discontinued for the portion of the period until discontinuance—shown net of tax, with the tax shown parenthetically;
   B. Loss (or gain) on disposal of the business segments, including provision for phase-out operating losses—also shown net of tax parenthetically.
2. Extraordinary items.
   Should be segregated and shown as the last factor used in arriving at net income for the period. Here, the caption is shown net of applicable income taxes, which are shown parenthetically.
   Note that extraordinary items do *not* include disposal of business segments as such, because they are segregated and shown separately prior thereto (as above).

An example of the reporting of the above:

	1987		1986
Income from continuing operations before income taxes	$ xxx		$ xxx
Provision for income taxes	xx		xx
Income from continuing operations		$ xxx	xxx

	1987	1986
Discontinued operations (Note):		
Income from operations of discontinued		
Division B (less applicable taxes of $xx)	$ xx	
Loss on disposal of Division B, including provision		
for phase-out operating losses of $xx (less		
applicable income taxes of $xx)	xx	xx
Income before extraordinary items		xxx
Extraordinary items (less applicable income taxes		
of $xx)		
(Note)		xx
Net Income		$ xxx $ xxx
Earnings per share:		
Income from continuing operations	$ x.00	$ x.00
Discontinued operations	x.00	x.00
Extraordinary items	x.00	x.00
Net Income	$ x.00	$ x.00

Note that earnings per share should be broken out separately for the factors of discontinued operations and extraordinary items, as well as for income from (continuing) operations.

The criteria for classifying a transaction or event as an "extraordinary item" are as follows:

Extraordinary items are events and transactions that are distinguished by their unusual nature *and* by the infrequency of their occurrence. Thus, *both* of the following criteria should be met to classify an event or transaction as an extraordinary item:

1. *Unusual nature*—the underlying event or transaction should possess a high degree of abnormality and be of a type clearly unrelated to, or only incidentally related to, the ordinary and typical activities of the entity, taking into account the environment in which the entity operates.

2. *Infrequency of occurrence*—the underlying event or transaction should be of a type that would not reasonably be expected to recur in the foreseeable future, taking into account the environment in which the entity operates.

Items which are *not* to be reported as extraordinary, because they may recur or are not unusual, are:

1. Write-downs of receivables, inventories, intangibles, or leased equipment.
2. Effects of strikes.
3. Gains or losses on foreign currency translations.
4. Adjustment of accruals on long-term contracts.
5. Gains or losses on disposal of business segments.

6. Gains or losses from abandonment or sale of property, plant or equipment used in the business.

Note that some highly unusual occurrence might cause one of the above types of gains or losses and should be considered extraordinary, such as those resulting from: major casualties (earthquake), expropriations, and legal restrictions. Disposals of business segments, though not extraordinary in classification, should be shown separately on the income statement, just prior to extraordinary items, but after operations from continuing business.

Miscellaneous data pertaining to extraordinary items:

Bargain sales of stock to stockholders are *not* extraordinary items, but they should be shown separately.

A gain or a loss on sale of coin collections by a bank is *not* an extraordinary item.

PRESENT VALUE COMPUTATION AND APPLICATION

The procedure of computing interest on principal *and interest on interest* underlies the concept of *compounding*. There are a number of accounting procedures (accounting for bonds, accounts receivable, accounts payable, and leases, for example) to which the compound interest formula (and variations) can be applied.

1. The *future value* of a sum of money. If $1,000 (the principal P) is deposited in a bank today, what will be the balance (S) in the account in *n years* (or *periods*) if the bank accumulates interest at the rate of i percent per year?

2. The *present value* of a sum of money due at the end of a period of time. What is the value *today* of the amount owed if $1,000 has to be paid, say to a creditor, n years from today?

3. The *future value of an annuity* which is a series of *equal* payments made at *equal* intervals. If $1,000 a year is deposited for n years, how much will have accumulated at the end of the n-years period if the deposits earn interest at the rate of i percent per year?

4. The *present value of an annuity* which is a series of *equal* payments made at *equal* intervals. If we are to be paid $1,000 a year for n years, how much is this annuity worth today, given i percent rate of interest?

The formula for the future value of a sum of money is the familiar compound interest formula. In the four examples to follow let:

S = The future worth of a sum of money invested today.
P = Principal, or the sum of money that will accumulate to S amount of money.

i = The rate of interest (r may be substituted).

n = Number of periods of time.

It is important to understand that a "period of time" is not necessarily one year, even though rates of interest in the United States are always understood to mean the rate for a period of one year. A period can be any length of time—i.e., day, week, month, year, second, minute, hour. Time is a *continuous*, not a *discrete* function.

With compound interest the total amount accumulated (S in the formula) at the end of one period earns interest during the subsequent period, or "interest on interest." The formula is:

$$S = P(1 + i)^n$$

At this point it should be emphasized that the user no longer must do the arithmetic. Not only can the problem types be solved by the use of tables, but now inexpensive hand calculators will perform the computations and give the answers. The user has simply only to enter the numbers that represent the letters in the formula. Users with computers can, of course, program the formulas for permanent storage and simply "call out" whichever formula applies to the problem at hand. With respect to the arithmetic, however, three of the variables in the equation are always known quantities; therefore, finding the value of the fourth and *un*known variable follows.

A word of caution. Computational errors caused by entering the wrong value for n are not uncommon. If i = 12% and the compounding period is every six months, n in the formula is 6. If the compounding period is quarterly n is 3. If the compounding period is daily (as is the case in many financial institutions savings policies) n becomes i/360—360 days in the year are applied in this country for interest calculations instead of 365. This is because the *smaller* the denominator, the bit more interest the *lender* collects. However, if the formula applies to a problem involving U.S. Government bonds, a 365-day year must be assumed because it enables the government to borrow a bit cheaper, relatively.

Annuities

The previous discussion considers the accumulation of interest on a *single* payment, however the single payment may be invested. *Annuities* apply to problems that involve a series of *equal payments* (or investments, savings, etc.,) made at *equal intervals* of time. The period of time between payments is called the *payment period*. The period of time between computation of the interest accumulation is called the *interest-conversion period*. When the payment period exactly equals the interest-conversion period, the annuity is an *ordinary annuity*. The equal payments are termed *rents*, which are spread over equal periods of time, the first rent payment made at the *start* of the annuity, and the last payment made at the *end* of the annuity.

The *future worth* of the annuity is the sum of the future worths of each of the separate rents. Assuming $100 invested we have $100 at time 1. At time 2 we have the $100 invested that day, plus the $100 invested at time 1, plus the interest earned during the period between time 1 and time 2. At time 3 another $100 is deposited; we now have the $100 deposited that day, the $100 deposited at time 2 plus the interest earned for one period, and the $100 deposited at time 1 plus the interest earned during the period between time 1 and time 2.

The formula for the future worth of an annuity of $1 is:

$$S = \frac{(1 + i)^n - 1}{i}$$

Note that the formula for the accumulation of interest on an ordinary annuity has the same variables as the compounding formula for a single payment.

To obtain S for any amount more than $1, multiply both sides of the equation by the amount invested, by P. In this case multiply both sides of the equation by 100. As above the amount for $1 can be found in tables (or by the use of a hand calculator).

The *present worth* of an annuity concerns the same question as the present worth of a single payment for *n years at i rate of interest*. How much would we pay today for an annuity in order to receive a given number of equal payments at equal intervals for a given number of periods in the future?

The formula for $1 is:

$$S = \frac{1 - (1 + i)^{-n}}{i}$$

The method for accounting for the premium or discount on bonds payable are compound interest procedures. The resultant interest charges are the product of the net balance of bonds payable and the effective interest rate at the time the bonds were issued. For bonds issued at a premium, the computed interest charges will *decrease* each year as the bonds approach maturity because the net balance of the liability decreases each year due to the amortization of the premium. Conversely, for bonds issued at a discount, the computed interest charges will *increase* each year as the bonds approach maturity because of the accumulation of the discount.

A straight-line method is used for the amortization of premiums or accumulation of discounts which involves simply dividing the original premium or discount by the number of years until maturity to determine the constant annual amount of amortization or accumulation.

The most frequent application of the above formula for accounting procedures is the present value formula. For example, when a company issues bonds, cash is debited for the proceeds of the bond issue and a liability account is credited for the amount. The entries will be the present value of the bonds. Assume a bond issue sold at a premium, or for more than the typical $1,000 par value, the present value of which we assume to be $1,200. The entries at the time of the sale of the bonds are:

Cash	$1,200	
Bonds Payable		$1,200

An alternative treatment is permissible by rule:

Cash	$1,200	
Bonds Payable		$1,000 (par)
Premium on Bonds		200

The Premium Account is an adjunct account (an addition) to Bonds Payable. The interest charge each year is computed by multiplying the bond liability *at the end of each year* by the effective rate of interest (see the definition). The adjunct account at the end of each period is debited for the amount of interest which reduces the liability each period. *The interest charge calculation is computed on the reduced amount of the liability that occurs each year as the adjunct account is debited.* At maturity the Premium Account has a zero balance and the liability will be reduced to the maturity, or face amount (the par value of $1,000) of the bond.

Assume the bond is sold at a $200 *discount*, i.e., $200 less than the $1,000 par value. The journal entry is:

Cash	$800	
Bond Discount	200	
Bonds Payable		$1,000

The Bond Discount account is a *contra* account to bonds payable with the liability at time of issue $800.00. Again, for an amount deposited for the annuity of more than $1 multiply both sides of the equation by that amount. Also, again note the same variables as in the compound interest formula.

2

Cost Accounting
Systems

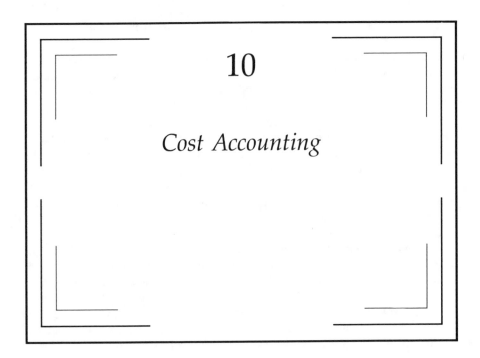

10

Cost Accounting

IF YOU DON'T KNOW YOUR COSTS . . .
YOU'LL NEVER SEE YOUR PROFITS

What is cost accounting? The cost accounting function in an organization is a system broadly defined in terms of procedures—i.e., the gathering, sorting, classifying, processing (computations), summarizing, reporting, and filing of information relevant to a company's costs, mostly in the form of data (numbers).

What is the function of a cost accounting system? Primarily, the system accepts disorganized, meaningless raw data (input) from the environment and processes (transforms) the data into understandable form. The information then leaves the system (output) in an organized form of reports required by management.

Specifically, cost accounting explicitly sets forth data which relate to the *costs* associated with the business. This includes the assignment of costs to a particular product, to a particular process, to a particular operation, or to a particular service, in the case of a service business.

The objective of a cost accounting system. The primary objective of cost accounting is to provide information useful to management for the decisions necessary for the successful operation of the business. The system should be designed to achieve this objective by providing management with information concerning the efficiency and effectiveness of production and service processes in order that cost reduction and increased profits can be attained. An analysis of accurate cost data is the essence of profit planning—*what* to produce, what *price* to charge, whether to *continue* producing a certain product.

Management should expect cost reports to show the results of past operations in terms of costs per unit of product, costs per unit of production in each operating department, or costs per unit of service in the case of a service organization. The system should provide immediate feedback information on changes in costs from accounting period to accounting period, and comparisons of costs with *predetermined estimates or norms*. With the proper cost information management can adjust operations quickly to changing economic and competitive conditions.

Developing a cost accounting system.   The task of developing a cost accounting system is to determine the specific needs of management, and the extent to which it is economically feasible to add detailed procedures to a basic system.

The system must be easily understood by all individuals in the organization who are involved in the use of control procedures, and flexible in its application. First, the system should be simple—i.e., must not include procedures that accumulate information that might be interesting, but *not particularly useful.* (A common pitfall is a cost system which, itself, is more expensive than the costs to be saved.) Second, the cost system must provide useful information in the most efficient manner. *Accurate* accounting records are particularly significant. Third, the cost accounting system must be flexible. Businesspeople often are required to adjust and adapt their operations to meet changing needs of customers, changes in production methods due to improved technology, changes in the economic and social environment in which the business operates, and changes in governmental regulations. Likewise, all businesses hope to grow and become larger. New cost accounting control requirements will appear by the nature of the growth process. Any system should be planned to meet changing needs with the least possible alteration of the present system.

There are fundamental cost control methods that apply to any business and include principles applicable to an individual business. The type of production, the number of products manufactured, the size of the business, the types of costs associated with the business, and the desires, capabilities, and attitudes of the individuals involved in the business will all have a part in determining the structure of the cost control system. Personnel responsible for the procedures within the business for the accounting and control techniques must be constantly aware of the unique characteristics of the particular business.

No right answer.   It is a rare instance that there is just one obviously right answer to any business problem. Certainly alternative choices for the allocation of an enterprise's limited resources confront the business manager every day. Information for selecting the "right" choice is provided by a cost accounting system. Is the product profitable? Is the product priced to yield a predetermined profit margin? What are the per unit costs of the product? Could it profitably be sold at a lower, more competitive price? Should production be expanded, reduced, discontinued? Are costs out of line? What are the controllable costs? Uncontrollable costs? These are only a few items of significant information that are furnished by a well-developed cost accounting system.

FOUNDATION OF A COST ACCOUNTING SYSTEM

What input does a cost accounting system accept?

There is an infinite amount of data within the business environment that can be entered into the system. It should be emphasized that the choice of data to be entered is not random; that is, chance or guesswork is not the determinant of the selection of data input. Rather, the selection of data is done within a carefully designed framework of the information needed to provide the required output (reports), with the framework continually subject to modification by a *feedback* system. The framework is governed by a set of *controls* to ensure compliance with the procedures, policies, and objectives which the system has been designed to carry out.

The elements of the framework of a set of books to track costs are briefly described as follows:

- The system is for a specific organization and accepts data relating only to that organization.
- Precautions should be taken against superfluous (and expensive) input.
- The system accepts information about transactions generated by events which have actually occurred, a purchase, for example.
- The system accepts information which has numbers assigned to it, with dollars and cents the most common measurement.
- The system accepts only information that has been predetermined to meet the needs of the users of the information.
- Information entered into the system should be completely free of bias; only absolutely objective information is acceptable.
- Information must be *verifiable*. Verifiability means transactions that are recorded in the same way by two or more qualified personnel acting independent of each other.
- Information entered into the system must be *consistent*. Consistency prevents manipulation of data in the accounts, as well as makes the financial information comparable from one period of time to another.

Four group classifications. Most businesses of any size can be classified as to production activities into one of the following four groups:

1. *Jobbing Plants*. Jobbing plants specialize in products that are made to order, i.e., not conducive to a repetitive operation. Some examples are machine shops, printers, repair shops of all kinds, and custom made products of any kind, generally.

2. *Continuous Processing Plants*. Continuous processing is concentrated upon products that are produced for inventory and sold at a later date, instead of ordered in advance. The significant aspect of continuous processing is that the production of the product is adaptable to a *repetitive* operation which is sequential in steps in the conversion of raw materials into finished products, all the units of which are the same; mass production techniques apply. Examples are shoe manufacturers, food processors, glass, soap, paper, textiles, and automobiles.

3. *Assembly Plants*. Products are made up of many component parts, either manufactured by the assembler or purchased from other manufacturers. Aircraft manufacturers are one of the best examples, as they subcontract various parts of the aircraft to literally hundreds of subcontractors. Automobile production is an example of both continuous processing and assembling, as many parts for automobiles are purchased from other manufacturing suppliers.

4. *Service Establishments*. Service establishments include businesses that provide various services to the public, rather than manufactured products. Medical, legal, accounting, architectural, transportation, food, and recreational services are examples of service businesses.

The cost control problems of each of these groups are different. Control and cost procedures for each must be designed, as well as for individual businesses within a group.

Cost Accounting System—A Model
(An Outline)

Job Order Costs
   Need for a job order cost system.
   Use of journals and ledgers.
   Cost control reports.
   Recording job costs.

Process Costs
   Need for a process cost system.
   Advantages of a process cost system.
   Accuracy of data provided by the system.
   Characteristics of a process cost system.
   Production controls.
   Flow assumptions (FIFO or alternatives).
   Conversion cost components.
   Per unit cost information.
   Spoilage problems, shrinkage, breakage, theft, defective units, etc.
   Units of production.

Cost Accounting System—A Model
(An Outline) (cont.)

Accounting for Raw Materials
Determining raw materials requirements.
Purchasing.
Recording materials' costs.
Counting and pricing materials.
Accounting for materials used.
Materials contol procedures—storing, issuing, etc.

Accounting for Labor Costs
Labor and payroll records.
Purpose for accounting for labor costs.
Timekeeping.
Allocating labor costs.
By-products.
Joint products.
Distribution costs.
Transfer pricing.
Payroll preparation.
Recording payrolls.
Paying the payroll.
Individual employee earnings' record.
Salaried employees payroll records.
Fringe benefits.

Responsibility Accounting
Cost centers.
Profit centers.

Accounting for Overhead Costs
What is overhead? Manufacturing overhead?
    Administrative overhead?
Overhead costs and tight control systems important.
Allocating overhead costs.
Overhead budgets (determining overhead rates).
Administrative (nonmanufacturing) overhead, e.g., accounting and other support functions.

Cost Targets
Predetermined costs.
Determining cost estimates (the cost standards).
Use of the standards in ledger accounts.
Analyzing cost deviations from the standards.
Standard costs for a job system.
Standard costs for a process system.

Break-Even Analysis
Cost-price-volume relationships.
Fixed costs.
Variable costs.
Production capacity levels.
Effects of changes in product price.
Effects of changes in product costs.
Unit costs.
Total costs.

Cost Accounting System—A Model
(An Outline) (cont.)

Graphic method.
Incremental costs.
Single or multi-product firms.

Budgeting and Profit Planning
Various types of budgets, i.e., operating and capital budgets.
Cash flow planning.
Cash budget.

Cost Allocation Techniques
Direct costing and contribution approach.
Absorption costing.
Contribution approach.

Ratio Analysis for Control
The most commonly applied ratios, with the emphasis on the ratios for the expense elements of
the income statement.
How to interpret and apply the ratios to business decisions.
Ratios as warning signals (red flags).

Summary of Operations
Promptness.
Accuracy.
Comparative reports, i.e., current vs. past trends highlighted.
Cost trends highlighted and explained.
Cost reports for areas of specific responsibility.
    Report contents:
        Direct labor hours and costs.
        Indirect labor hours and costs.
        Direct materials used.
        Production overhead applied.
        Actual overhead expense.
        Variances.
        Idle time costs, if any.
        Overtime costs.
        Spoilage costs.
        Maintenance hours and costs.
        Scrap costs.
        Inventory status report.
        New order book.
    Orders shipped during the period.
    New order bookings.
    Interim expense and income statements. (For predetermined periods of time—week, month.
        Actual versus budgeted costs for the period. Comparisons with prior determined periods of
        time. Year-to-date totals and comparisons with prior years).

The topics listed below are the essential elements of a cost accounting system;
they are reviewed in the discussion that follows.

• Cost Accounting Terminology.
• Integrating a Cost System.

- Historical and Standard Cost Systems.
- Job and Process Cost Systems.
- Standard Costs—Illustration.
- Direct Costing.
- Effects of Costing on Financial Statements.
- Break-Even Point Analysis.
- Summary.

Cost Terminology (for quick reference)

Here are some brief definitions of various types of costs:

(1) *Historical*—measured by actual cash payments or their equivalent at the time of outlay.

(2) *Future*—expected to be incurred at a later date.

(3) *Standard*—scientifically predetermined.

(4) *Estimated*—predetermined.

(5) *Product*—associated with units of output.

(6) *Period*—associated with the income of a time period.

(7) *Direct*—obviously tradeable to a unit of output or a segment of business operations.

(8) *Prime*—labor and material directly traceable to a unit of output.

(9) *Indirect*—not obviously traceable to a unit of output or to a segment of business operations.

(10) *Fixed*—do not change in the total as the rate of output varies.

(11) *Variable*—do change with changes in rate of output.

(12) *Opportunity*—measurable advantage foregone as a result of the rejection of alternative uses of resources whether of materials, labor, or facilities.

(13) *Imputed*—never involve cash outlays nor appear in financial records. Involve a foregoing on the part of the person whose costs are being calculated.

(14) *Controllable*—subject to direct control at some level of supervision.

(15) *Noncontrollable*—not subject to control at some level of supervision.

(16) *Joint*—exists when from any one unit source, material, or process come products which have different unit values.

(17) *Sunk*—historical and not recoverable in a given situation.

(18) *Discretionary*—avoidable and unessential to an objective.

(19) *Postponable*—may be shifted to future period without affecting efficiency.

(20) *Out of pocket*—necessitate cash expenditure.

(21) *Differential*—changes in cost that result from variation in operations.

(22) *Incremental*—those added or eliminated if segments were expanded or discontinued.

(23) *Alternative*—estimated for decision areas.

(24) *Replacement*—considered for depreciation significance.

(25) *Departmental*—production and service, for cost distributions.

HISTORICAL AND STANDARD COST SYSTEMS

Cost accounting systems vary with the type of cost (present or future) used. When present costs are used, the cost system is called an *historical* or *actual cost* system. When future costs are used, the cost system is called a *standard cost* system. In practice, combinations of these costs are used even in actual or standard systems. Where there is an intentional use of both types of costs, we sometimes refer to the system as a *hybrid cost* system.

Actual cost system.   Since an actual cost system uses only those costs which have already been incurred, the system determines costs only after manufacturing operations have been performed. Under this system the product is charged with the actual cost of materials, the actual cost of labor, and an *estimated* portion of overhead (overhead costs represent the future cost element in an actual cost system).

Standard cost system.   A standard system is based upon estimated or predetermined costs. There is a distinction between estimated and standard costs, however. Both are "predetermined" costs, but estimated costs are based upon average past experience, and standard costs are based upon scientific facts that consider past experience and controlled experiments. Arriving at standard costs involves careful selection of material, an engineering study of equipment and manufacturing facilities, and time and motion studies.

In either system, adjustment must be made at the financial statement date to the *closing inventory* so that it is shown at actual cost or reasonably approximate actual cost, or at market if lower. Also, the inventory must bear its share of the burden of overhead. "The exclusion of all overheads from inventory costs does not constitute an accepted accounting procedure."

For interim statements, estimated gross profit rates may be used to determine cost of goods sold during the interim, but this fact must be disclosed.

It must be emphasized that whatever cost accounting method is chosen by a company, its purpose is primarily an internal management tool directed at controlling costs, setting production goals, measuring efficiencies and variances, providing incentives and establishing realistic relationships between unit costs, selling prices and gross margins. Regardless of costing methods used, generally accepted accounting standards must be followed for the preparation of the financial statements, wherein the valuation must be cost or market, whichever is lower.

Also, either the FIFO or LIFO methods (or the average method) may be used under any cost system. These methods pertain to the assumption of the *flow* of costs, not to the actual costs themselves. Note that *both* methods may be used within one inventory, as long as the method is applied to that portion of the inventory consistently from period to period. Disclosures should be made of any change in method.

Integrating A Cost System

It is not essential to integrate a cost system with the rest of the accounting system, but it is highly desirable. A cost system is really an extension of the regular system. With an integrated system, entries in the inventory account in the general ledger should represent the sums of figures taken from the cost accounting data. The general ledger inventory accounts (e.g., finished goods, work in process, and raw materials) are the control accounts and they should tie in with the amounts of physical inventories actually on hand. Discrepancies may result from errors, spoilage, or thievery.

Elements of cost.   Production costs consist of three elements: direct materials, direct labor, and manufacturing (overhead) expenses:

Direct Materials: Those materials which can be identified with specific units of the product.

Direct Labor: That labor which can be identified with specific units of the product.

Manufacturing Expenses (Overhead): Those costs (including indirect material or labor) which can not be identified with specific units of the product. These costs represent expenses for the factory and other facilities which permit the labor to be applied to the materials to manufacture a product.

Sometimes, overhead is further subdivided into:

Direct overhead—Those manufacturing costs other than material and direct labor which specifically apply to production and require no allocation from other expense areas;

Indirect overhead—Those expenses which have been allocated into the manufacturing expense area from other more general areas.

For financial statement purposes, overhead should not include selling expenses or general or administrative expenses.

JOB ORDER OR PROCESS COST SYSTEMS

There are distinctions between cost systems other than the use of present or future costs.

A *job order system* compiles costs for a specific quantity of a product as it moves through the production process. This means that material, labor, and overhead costs of a specific number or lot of the product (usually identifiable with a customer's order or a specific quantity being produced for stock) are recorded as the lot moves through the production cycle.

A *process system* compiles costs as they relate to specific processes or operations for a period of time. To find the unit cost, these figures are averaged for a specified period and spread over the number of units that go through each process. Process costing is used when large numbers of identical products are manufactured, usually in assembly-line fashion.

Keep in mind that actual or estimated costs can be used with either a job order or process cost system.

Benefits and Drawbacks

Whether the job order or process system is used depends on the type of operation. The job order system is rarely used in mass production industries. It is invariably used when products are custom made. Process costing is used where production is in a continuous state of operation as for: Paper, baking, steel making, glass, rubber, sugar, chemicals, etc. Here are some of the relative merits and shortcomings of each method:

Advantages	
Job Order	*Process*
(1) Appropriate for custom-made goods	(1) It is usually only necessary to calculate costs each month
(2) Appropriate for increasing finished goods inventory in desired quantities	(2) Minimum of clerical work required
(3) Adequate for inventory pricing	(3) If there is only one type of product cost computation is relatively simple
(4) Permits estimation of future costs	
(5) Satisfies "cost-plus" contract requisites	

Disadvantages	
Job Order	*Process*
(1) Expensive to use—a good deal of clerical work required	(1) Use of average costs ignores any variance in product cost
(2) Difficult to make sure that all materials and labor are accurately charged to each specific job	(2) Involves calculation of stage of completion of goods in process and the use of equivalent units
(3) Difficult to determine cost of goods sold when partial shipments are made before completion	

HOW TO USE STANDARD COSTS

Smith Company manufactures only one product, glubs—a household article made out of a certain type of plastic. Glubs are made from D raw material which goes through a single process. Glubs are turned out from D material in a fraction of a day. Smith Company has a process-type cost setup integrated with its other financial records. D material is charged to work in process through requisitions based upon actual cost. Direct labor is charged to work in process based upon payroll. Manufacturing expense is charged to work in process based upon the number of payroll hours. Each day a record of the number of glubs manufactured is kept. This is the responsibility of the production department.

Here's the way the Smith Company process cost system operates: Every month, total figures are worked up for raw material, payroll, factory expenses. Each of these figures is then divided by the total number of glubs produced for that month to arrive at a unit cost per glub. Here is what the unit cost accumulation for the four months shows (this example assumes no work-in-process inventory and no equivalent units):

Unit Cost per Glub Manufactured

	First Month	Second Month	Third Month	Fourth Month	Weighted Average
Material D	$ .94	$ .91	$ .97	$1.10	$ .95
Direct Labor	1.18	1.22	2.00	.70	1.29
Manufacturing Expenses	1.22	1.47	2.11	.82	1.42
	$3.34	$3.60	$5.08	$2.62	$3.66

Right now, glubs are being sold at $4.30, and the present profit appears sufficient. T.O. Smith, the president and major stockholder of the corporation, feels that if glubs were sold at $3.30 each, four times as many could be sold. He also reports that he has learned that Glubco, Inc., Smith's competitor, is going to market glubs for $3.60. Smith thinks that $3.30 is a good sales price since the cost records indicate that glubs were manufactured for as low as $2.62 in the fourth month. Smith Company's accountant says the president is incorrect. He points out that the average cost is somewhere in the area of $3.55 to $3.80 based upon the cost records for six months. Selling glubs for $3.30 would create losses. The factory foreman says that during the third and fourth months there was an error in calculating the number of glubs put into finished goods inventory. From the figures for the fourth month, it appears that the foreman is correct. The unit cost per glub is unusually low. Mr. Smith wants to know the lowest at which he can sell glubs and still make a reasonable profit. The accountant suggests setting up a cost system based upon standard costs. He outlines the following steps:

(1) Purchasing department records indicate that material D should cost no more than 15¢ per pound. (According to the chief engineer, it takes approximately two pounds of D to produce one glub.) The 15¢ figure takes future market conditions into account.

(2) A time study of half a dozen workers who produce glubs is made. The average time it takes each of these six men to produce one glub is one-third of an hour. The average hourly wage of these men is $3.00.

(3) Based upon reasonable level of production for the following year, a departmental manufacturing expense or overhead is estimated to be 100% of direct labor.

Based upon the above determinations, the standard cost per glub is $2.30. It is calculated as follows:

Raw Material D: two pounds at 15¢ per pound	$ .30
Direct Labor: ⅓ hour at $3.00 per hour	1.00
Manufacturing Expense: 100% of direct labor	1.00
Total	$2.30

In order to produce glubs at this cost, the following points are agreed upon:

(1) When more than 15¢ a pound is paid for raw material D, the excess is to be charged to a special variance account instead of the raw material account. These excesses are to be explained periodically by the purchasing department.

(2) Requisitions for raw material D are to be limited to two pounds of D for each glub to be manufactured. If more than two pounds per glub is issued to meet scheduled production, the excess over two pounds is to be charged to a separate variance account. The reason for any excess will also have to be explained.

(3) The daily number of direct labor hours spent making glubs is to be multiplied by three. This should equal the number of glubs produced that day. Any discrepancy here is probably due to inefficiency. The number of inefficient hours at the standard $3 rate times the 100% manufacturing expense rate is to be charged to a special variance account.

(4) Payroll over $3 an hour is to be charged to a variance account. Only $3 an hour is to be charged to the work-in-progress account. The factory foreman will have to explain hourly labor figures over $3 periodically.

(5) Departmental variations in the 100% of direct labor manufacturing expense burden are to be charged or credited to separate variance accounts. This is to be done each month.

Here's what happened each month after this system was instituted:

Variance Accounts	Fifth Month	Sixth Month	Seventh Month	Eighth Month	Ninth Month
(1) Material D Price	$ 2,100	$ 300	$ 750	$ 0	$ 0
(2) Material usage	19,500	13,000	5,000	500	400
(3) Labor efficiency	8,000	5,050	800	700	300
(4) Labor rate	400	150	(50)	400	100
(5) Mfg. Expense	0	5,000	1,000	300	(100)
	$ 30,000	$ 23,500	$ 7,500	$ 1,900	$ 700
Unit Manufactured	48,000	48,000	48,000	48,000	48,000
Variance per Unit	.63	.49	.16	.04	.01
Standard Unit Cost	2.30	2.30	2.30	2.30	2.30
Actual Cost	$ 2.93	$ 2.79	$ 2.46	$ 2.34	$ 2.31

Here is what was elicited from discussion with the persons responsible for the different variance accounts:

(1) The purchase price for raw material D exceeded 15¢ per pound mainly because of the distance of Smith Company from where D is obtained in the south. The head of purchasing feels that D could be purchased for no more than 15¢ if he could have a small office in the south with one assistant who would remain there. It was decided to go ahead and give him the office and the additional employee.

(2) The factory foreman, together with the chief engineer, has been going over the requisitions of raw material D. More D was needed because some of the glubs had air holes in them and weren't usable. It seems that the pressure used to extrude them wasn't sufficient. The chief engineer says that he can replace the present air die channels with larger ones so that these defects do not recur. The foreman knew that some glubs were scrapped in the past, but it wasn't until this switch to standard costs that he knew how much waste there really was.

(3) The foreman and the industrial engineer who performed the time and motion study discussed the labor efficiency loss. It was their opinion that there were more factory employees than needed to carry out various operations to convert D into finished glubs. It was also learned that some employees could use more training, while others were overskilled for their particular functions. Still others were not producing enough for some reason or other. Both men felt that a training program instructing employees in the efficient use of available tools would increase efficiency. Further time and motion studies on every phase of the production process were initiated.

(4) There was not much variance in labor rate, but it was hoped that the training program would release more technically skilled and higher paid employees for use in the more complicated production steps.

At the end of the seventh month, it was obvious that the steps taken were beginning to pay off. The additional costs incurred in carrying out these steps (for example, the additional employee in purchasing and the southern office) created a manufacturing overhead variance where none had existed before; but the success in other areas outweighed this.

At the end of the ninth month, everyone agreed that the switch to standard costs had exceeded expectations. The new lower production cost would help expand the market for glubs. Smith Company was also in a good competitive position compared with Blubco since it probably could now undersell it.

This illustration shows the advantages of standard costs:

(1) Control and reduction of costs;

(2) Promotion and measurement of efficiencies;

(3) Calculation and setting of selling prices;

(4) Evaluation of inventories;

(5) Simplification of cost procedures.

DIRECT COSTING

Another type of cost accounting which is used for internal purposes but not for financial or tax reporting purposes is "direct costing." This is a method in which only those costs which are a consequence of production of the product are assigned to the product—direct material cost, direct labor cost, and only variable manufacturing overhead. All fixed manufacturing costs are treated as expenses of the period.

The methods of recording costs for direct material and direct labor are similar under direct costing and conventional costing. It is in the method of reflecting manufacturing overhead that the systems differ. In a direct costing system, overhead costs are classified as fixed or variable. In conventional costing, only one overhead control account is used. In direct costing, two control accounts are used—a direct overhead account and an indirect overhead account. The direct overhead account is for variable expenses—those that vary with the volume of production. The indirect overhead account is for fixed expenses—those that do not vary with production. These are charged as expenses of the period rather than as costs of the finished product. Research costs, some advertising costs, and costs incurred to keep manufacturing and nonmanufacturing facilities ready for use are considered expenses of the period. Under direct costing, direct labor, direct material, and overhead costs that vary with production find their way into the inventory. The other manufacturing overhead expenses are charged off currently against income. The important reason behind direct costing is not to value inventories, but to segregate expenses.

Effect of Direct Costing on Financial Statements

Direct costing, if used on the financial statements (for internal use), would produce the following results:

(1) Where the inventory of manufactured goods does not fluctuate from one accounting period to the next, there should be no difference between net income using direct costing or net income using conventional costing.

(2) Where the inventory does fluctuate and is increased, net income under direct costing will be lower. *Reason*: Fixed overhead costs under direct costing will have been charged to the current period instead of deferred by increasing the value of inventory. Under conventional costing, the value of the ending inventory will have been increased by these fixed overhead costs.

(3) Where inventory decreases, net income under direct costing will be higher than conventional costing. *Reason*: Fixed overhead costs included in the value of the inventory under conventional costing will now increase the cost of goods sold, thereby reducing income.

BREAK-EVEN POINT ANALYSIS

One type of budget which provides useful supplementary statistics is the break-even analysis. Although a complete and adequate budget may be developed without using a break-even analysis, its use adds to the understanding of estimates.

The break-even point is that amount of sales necessary to yield neither income nor loss. If sales should be less than indicated by the break-even point, a loss would result.

Where the total cost of goods sold and other expenses is less than sales and if this total varied in direct proportion to sales, operations would always result in net income. For example, in a company in which the cost of goods sold and expenses amounts to $1.80 per unit sold and the sale price is $2, on the first unit there would be net income of 20¢. On a million items, the net income would amount to $200,000.

As a practical matter, the simple example cited above is not realistic. The reason is that although some expenses may vary with volume of sales (e.g., salesmen's commissions, traveling expenses, advertising, telephone, delivery costs, postage, supplies, etc.), there are many other types of expenses which are not affected by the variations in sales. These expenses are called "fixed" expenses. Examples are depreciation, rent, insurance, heat, etc.

If, going back to the above illustration, we assume that fixed costs and expenses amount to $40,000, we have at least $40,000 of costs and expenses before even one unit is sold. If we sell a million units, however, we have an income before deducting fixed expenses of $200,000. After fixed expenses, our net income is

$160,000. So, our income picture goes from a loss of $40,000 (where no units are produced) to a profit of $160,000 (where one million units are produced). Somewhere between these, however, is a point represented by a certain number of units at which we will have neither income nor loss—the break-even point.

How to Compute the Break-Even Point

Here is how we determine the break-even point. Let S equal the sales at the break-even point. Since sales at this point are equal to the total fixed costs and expenses ($40,000) plus variable costs and expenses ($1.80 per unit or 90% of sales).

$$S = \$ 40,000 + .9S$$
$$S - .9S = \$ 40,000$$
$$.1S = \$ 40,000$$
$$S = \$400,000$$

Even the above illustration oversimplifies the problem. It makes the assumption that all costs and expenses can be classified as either *fixed* or *variable*. However, in actual operations, expenses classified as fixed expenses may become variable where sales increase beyond a certain point, and some variable expenses may not vary in direct proportion to the sales.

Rent expense, for example, may not always be a fixed expense. A substantial increase in sales may create a need for additional showroom or salesroom space or, perhaps, salesmen's offices, or salesmen's commissions may rise unexpectedly when they have gone above a certain quota.

Then, there are types of hybrid expenses which may be classified as *semifixed*. For example, executives' salaries, association dues, subscriptions to periodicals and many other expenses are not in proportion to sales. Another unreality in the above problem is that as sales increase, there is a likelihood that sale prices will decrease because of larger orders. Now let's take a look at another situation:

Net sales		$2,500,000
Costs and expenses:		
Fixed	$ 250,000	
Variable	1,500,000	1,750,000
Net income		$ 750,000

This company currently has under consideration an investment in a new plant which will cause an increase in its fixed expenses of $200,000.

The present break-even point is as follows:

$$S = \$250,000 + .6S$$
$$S - .6S = \$250,000$$
$$.4S = \$250,000$$
$$S = \$625,000$$

If the company builds the plant, the break-even calculation will be:

$$
\begin{aligned}
S &= \$450,000 + .6S \\
S - .6S &= \$450,000 \\
.4S &= \$450,000 \\
S &= \$1,125,000
\end{aligned}
$$

If the plant expansion is undertaken, then the sales must be increased by $500,000 for the company to maintain its net income of $750,000, as follows:

$$
\begin{aligned}
S &= \$450,000 + .6S + \$750,000 \\
S - .6S &= \$1,200,000 \\
.4S &= \$1,200,000 \\
S &= \$3,000,000 \\
\text{Increase} &= \$500,000 \ (\$3,000,000 \text{ less } \$2,500,000)
\end{aligned}
$$

Now let's analyze the situation under two alternatives. The maximum production with the present plant is 1,500,000 units. At an average sale price of $2 per unit, sales would be $3,000,000. With the new plant, sales are estimated to hit $5,000,000 (2,500,000 units @ $2 per unit).

	Without New Plant	With New Plant
Net sales	$3,000,000	$5,000,000
Less: Fixed costs and expenses	250,000	450,000
	2,750,000	4,550,000
Less: Variable costs and expenses (60% of sales)	1,800,000	3,000,000
Net income	$ 950,000	$1,550,000

If sales do not increase, the increase in fixed costs and expenses of $200,000 would cut the net income to $550,000. The break-even point will have been boosted $500,000, and the sales will have to be increased by this amount to produce the current $750,000 of income. Alternatively, the net income can be increased by $600,000 if the sales figure is increased by $2,000,000. Although these figures are based on an assumption that all costs and expenses are fixed or variable, the break-even analysis focuses attention on the factors involved in costs and income and provides a basis for consideration of various problems.

SUMMARY

When a business enterprise becomes as operationally and financially complex as even most small and medium-sized companies are today, fairly sophisticated control and evaluation techniques must be developed to ensure an adequate level of operational efficiency and financial stability.

The historical essence of cost accounting systems has been upon the *flow* of financial resources *into, through,* and *out* of the business. It cannot be over-emphasized that the ultimate objective of cost accounting is to provide relevant, valid, and timely information of the cost of manufactured products, or to the cost of services provided by service organizations.

3

Governmental (Fund) Accounting

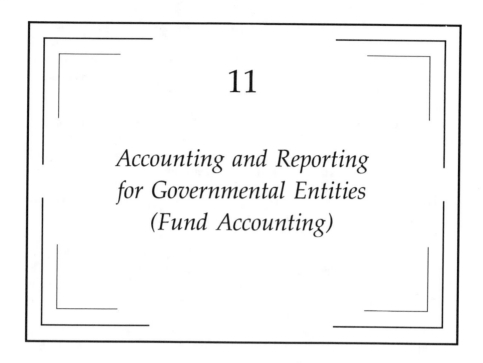

11

Accounting and Reporting for Governmental Entities (Fund Accounting)

DIFFERENCES BETWEEN GOVERNMENTAL AND COMMERCIAL ACCOUNTING

While both types of entities use double-entry bookkeeping procedures and either cash or accrual methods, and both prepare balance sheets and operating statements, there are many differences between commercial and governmental systems.

Governmental accounting is associated with: 1) an absence of a profit; 2) compliance with statutory and/or legal requirements; 3) a fundamental difference in the treatment of net worth. Commercial accounting provides accounting for preferred and common stock and retained earnings, with a paid-in capital account where appropriate. Governmental accounting treats "net worth" under account classifications *Reserve for Encumbrances or Unappropriated Surplus*; 4) characteristically, government accounts will include a *Reserve for Contingencies* account since the projected (budgeted) reserve may not materialize as the accounting year progresses.

LEGAL PROVISIONS

In governmental accounting, legal provisions relate to budgeting and to the disposition of assets. The preparation and implementation of the projected budget and related accounting procedures are governed by certain legal provisions expressed specifically in legislation (statutory) or restrictions imposed by a nonlegislative (regulatory) authority. The accounting system must have built-in safeguards that expenditures will comply with both types of restrictions. Governmental accounting must also include revenue and expense data which facilitates the preparation of budgets for the future.

As will be seen certain *funds* are considered less flexible in their accounting treatment. The least flexible type is the one created by a state constitution or by legislation, because the accountant must keep the books as determined by law. The most flexible is the type established by executive authority, since such authority can make changes in a fund without prior legislative approval.

In fund accounting *estimated and actual revenues* and *expenditures* are compared on an ongoing basis, e.g., reviewed by the governing bodies approving the initial budget and the appropriation for the fund. Comparisons reveal the extent to which the "actuals" are in line with the estimates (the budget) and will show significant deviations, if any, during the fiscal year of actual revenues and expenditures from the budgeted amounts.

Assets and liabilities incurred by a fund are similar to those in a commercial enterprise. Asset accounts, for example, will include cash, accounts receivable, etc., while liabilities will show accounts or vouchers payable, notes payable, bonds payable, etc.

A separate *general ledger* must be maintained for each fund related to the governmental entity's budget. Each general ledger has a self-balancing account that brings the revenue and appropriation accounts into balance at the end of the fiscal year.

As a general rule independent auditors will insist on the entity using an *accrual* system, unless the financial authorities for that specific fund can demonstrate that the financial reports would not *materially* differ if a cash accounting system is used.

IS GOVERNMENTAL ACCOUNTING COMPLEX? NO!

Rather, fund accounting is perceived to be complicated. It is not in the least any more difficult than commercial accounting. In fact, fund accounting is easier to understand if thought is given to the basic concept that underlies governmental accounting:

> Governmental accounting simply involves *two* sets of books instead of one set. There is a set of books for the projected budget for the upcoming fiscal year and a separate set of books for recording *actual* revenues and expenditures as the fiscal year progresses. The two sets of books are synchronized, so that as the actuals materialize and are recorded in the actual set, the complementary account in the budgeted set is appropriately debited or credited.

That's all there is to governmental accounting. Why then is it thought to be complicated? The answer is for the same reason that we initially think any totally new and unfamiliar discipline appears difficult—the *terminology* is the culprit. It is well-settled that learning the terminology of a new discipline is 50 percent or more of the learning battle of anything new that one endeavors to learn. Governmental accounting terminology is indeed entirely different from commercial accounting terminology; it has a vocabulary that is totally unique to governmental accounting; no governmental accounting term can be found in any other system of accounting, whether commercial, industrial, or otherwise.

The first step, then, to acquire an understanding of fund accounting procedures is to review and become familiar with the terms. The following list of definitions will enable the user to easily apply the accounting methods for the various types of funds which are covered in the material following the definitions.

TERMINOLOGY

Here is a listing of definitions applicable only to fund accounting:

ABATEMENT.   Cancellation of amounts levied or of charges made for services.

ACCRUED ASSETS.   Assets arising from revenues earned but not yet due.

ACCRUED EXPENSES.   Expenses resulting in liabilities which are either due or are not payable until some future time.

ACCRUED REVENUES.   Levies made or other revenue earned and not collected.

ALLOTMENT LEDGER.   A subsidiary ledger which contains an account for each allotment showing the amount allotted, expenditures, encumbrances, the net balance, and other related information.

APPROPRIATION.   An authorization granted by the legislative body to make expenditures and to incur obligations for specific purposes.

APPROPRIATION EXPENDITURE.   An expenditure chargeable to an appropriation.

APPROPRIATION LEDGER.   A subsidiary ledger containing an account with each appropriation.

ASSESSMENT.   The process of making an official valuation of property for the purpose of taxation.

AUTHORITY BONDS.   Bonds payable from the revenues of a specific public authority.

BETTERMENT.   An addition or change made in a fixed asset which prolongs its life or increases its efficiency.

BUDGET. A plan of financial operation embodying an estimate of proposed expenditures for a given period or purpose, and the proposed means of financing them.

BUDGETARY ACCOUNTS. The accounts necessary to reflect budget operations and condition, such as estimated revenues, appropriations, and encumbrances.

CAPITAL BUDGET. An improvement program and the methods for the financing.

CLEARING ACCOUNT. An improvement program and the methods for the financing.

CLEARING ACCOUNT. An account used to accumulate total charges or credits for the purpose of distributing them among the accounts to which they are allocable, or for the purpose of transferring the net difference to the proper account.

CURRENT SPECIAL ASSESSMENT. Assessments levied and due during the current fiscal period.

CURRENT TAXES. Taxes levied and becoming due during the current fiscal period—from the time the amount of the tax levy is first established, to the date on which a penalty for nonpayment is attached.

DEBT LIMIT. The maximum amount of gross or net debt legally permitted.

DEBT SERVICE REQUIREMENT. The amount of money necessary periodically to pay the interest on the outstanding debt and the principal of maturing bonded debt not payable from a sinking fund.

DEFICIT. The excess of the liabilities of a fund over its assets.

DELINQUENT TAXES. Taxes remaining unpaid on and after the date on which a penalty for nonpayment is attached.

DIRECT DEBT. The debt which a governmental unit has incurred in its own name, or assumed through the annexation of territory.

ENCUMBRANCES. Obligations in the form of purchase orders, contracts, or salary commitments which are chargeable to an appropriation, and for which a part of the appropriation is reserved.

ENDOWMENT FUND. A fund whose principal must be maintained inviolate, but whose income may be expended.

EXPENDABLE FUND. A fund whose resources, including both principal and earnings, may be expended.

EXPENDITURES. If the fund accounts are kept on the accrual basis, expenditures are the total charges incurred, whether paid or unpaid, including expenses, provision for retirement of debt not reported as a liability of the fund from which retired, and capital outlays.

FRANCHISE. A special privilege granted by a government permitting the continuing use of public property.

FULL FAITH AND CREDIT. A pledge of the general taxing body for the payment of obligations.

FUND ACCOUNTS. All accounts necessary to set forth the financial operations and financial condition of a fund.

FUND GROUP. A group of related funds.

GOVERNMENTAL ACCOUNTING. The preparation, reporting, and interpretation of accounts for governmental bodies.

GRANT. A contribution by one governmental unit to another unit.

GROSS BONDED DEBT. The total amount of direct debt of a governmental unit, represented by outstanding bonds before deduction of sinking fund assets.

INDETERMINATE APPROPRIATION. An appropriation which is not limited either to any definite period of time, or to any definite amount, or to both time and amount.

INTER-FUND ACCOUNTS. Accounts in which transactions between funds are reflected.

INTER-FUND LOANS. Loans made by one fund to another fund.

INTER-FUND TRANSFERS. Amounts transferred from one fund to another.

JUDGMENT. An amount to be paid or collected by a governmental unit as the result of a court decision, including a condemnation award in payment for private property taken for public use.

LAPSE. As applied to appropriations, this term denotes the automatic termination of an appropriation.

LEVY. To impose taxes or special assessments.

LUMP-SUM APPROPRIATION. An appropriation made for a stated purpose, or for a named department, without specifying further the amounts that can be spent for specific activities or for particular expenditures.

MUNICIPAL. An adjective applying to any governmental unit below or subordinate to the state.

MUNICIPAL CORPORATION. A body or corporate politic established pursuant to state authorization, as evidenced by a charter.

NET BONDED DEBT.   Gross bonded debt less applicable cash or other assets.

NON-EXPENDABLE FUND.   A fund the principal, and sometimes the earnings, of which may not be expended.

NON-OPERATING INCOME.   Income of municipal utilities and other governmental enterprises of a business character, which is not derived from the operation of such enterprise.

OPERATING EXPENSES.   As used in the accounts of municipal utilities and other governmental enterprises of a business character, the term means the costs necessary to the maintenance of the enterprise, or the rendering of services for which the enterprise is operated.

OPERATING REVENUES.   Revenues derived from the operation of municipal utilities or other governmental enterprises of a business character.

OPERATING STATEMENT.   A statement summarizing the financial operations of a municipality.

ORDINANCE.   A bylaw of a municipality enacted by the governing body of the governmental entity.

OVERLAPPING DEBT.   The proportionate share of the debts of local governmental units, located wholly or in part within the limits of the reporting government, which must be borne by property within such government.

PREPAID TAXES.   The deposit of money with a governmental unit on condition that the amount deposited is to be applied against the tax liability of the taxpayer.

PROPRIETARY ACCOUNTS.   Accounts which show actual financial condition and operations such as actual assets, liabilities, reserves, surplus, revenues, and expenditures as distinguished from budgetary accounts.

PUBLIC AUTHORITY.   A public agency created to perform a single function, which is financed from tolls or fees charged those using the facilities operated by the agency.

PUBLIC TRUST FUND.   A trust fund whose principal, earnings, or both, must be used for a public purpose.

QUASI-MUNICIPAL CORPORATION.   An agency established by the state primarily for the purpose of helping the state to carry out its functions.

REFUNDING BONDS.   Bonds issued to retire bonds already outstanding. The refunding bonds may be sold for cash and outstanding bonds redeemed in cash, or the refunding bonds may be exchanged with holders of outstanding bonds.

RELATED FUNDS. Funds of a similar character which are brought together for administrative and reporting purposes.

RESERVE FOR ENCUMBRANCES. A reserve representing the segregation of surplus to provide for unliquidated encumbrances.

REVENUE BONDS. Bonds the principal and interest on which are to be paid solely from earnings, usually the earnings of a municipally owned utility or other public service enterprise.

REVOLVING FUND. A fund provided to carry out a cycle of operations.

SPECIAL ASSESSMENT. A compulsory levy made by a local government against certain properties, to defray part or all of the cost of a specific improvement or service, which is presumed to be of general benefit to the public and of special benefit to the owners of such properties.

SPECIAL DISTRICT BONDS. Bonds of a local taxing district, which has been organized for a special purpose—such as road, sewer, and other special districts—to render unique services to the public.

SUSPENSE ACCOUNT. An account which carries charges or credits temporarily pending the determination of the proper account or accounts to which they are to be posted.

TAX ANTICIPATION NOTES. Notes issued in anticipation of collection of taxes, usually retired only from tax collections as they come due.

TAX LEVY. An ordinance or resolution by means of which taxes are levied.

TAX LIENS. Claims which governmental units have upon properties until taxes levied against them have been paid.

TAX RATE. The amount of tax stated in terms of a unit of the tax base.

TRUST FUND. A fund consisting of resources received and held by the governmental unit as trustee, to be expended or invested in accordance with the conditions of the trust.

UNENCUMBERED APPROPRIATION. An appropriation or allotment, or a part thereof, not yet expended or encumbered.

UTILITY FUND. A fund established to finance the construction, operation, and maintenance of municipally owned utilities.

WARRANT. An order drawn by a legislative body, or an officer of a governmental unit, upon its treasurer, directing the treasurer to pay a specified amount to the person named, or to the bearer.

GOVERNMENTAL ACCOUNTING SYSTEMS

Governmental Accounting Standards Board (GASB)

The GASB was established in 1984, under the oversight of the Financial Accounting Foundation which, in turn, oversees the Financial Accounting Standards Board (FASB). Before the establishment of the GASB, the reports of governmental entities were criticized by the accounting community because they could not be interpreted in a manner consistent with the financial reports of private business organizations. The primary purpose of the GASB is to develop standards of reporting for state and local government entities; its organizational and operational structure is similar to that of the FASB, and its objective is to make the combined general purpose financial reports of governmental entities as comparable as possible to those of private business.

As a general rule the GASB will promulgate standards that parallel GAAP. However, there are instances that require a governmental entity to comply with a state law or regulatory accounting requirement that is in noncompliance with GAAP. Such reports are classified as *Special Reports or Supplemental Schedules*, which are not a part of the general purpose statements. In these cases governmental units can publish two sets of statements, one in compliance with legal requirements and one in compliance with GAAP. (An example of this problem is that it is not uncommon for some governmental entities to be required by law to apply the cash basis of accounting.)

Governmental accounting systems are developed on a *fund basis*. A fund is defined as an independent fiscal and accounting entity with a self-balancing set of accounts recording cash and other resources together with all related liabilities, obligations, reserves, and equities that are segregated for the purpose of carrying on specific activities or attaining specified objectives in accordance with applicable regulations, restrictions, and other statutory and regulatory limitations.

In addition to each fund's transactions within the fund itself, each fund in a governmental unit can have financial transactions with other funds in the same entity. The financial statements must reflect interfund transactions which result from services rendered by one fund to another.

The accrual basis of accounting is recommended for matching revenues and expenditures during a designated period of time which refers specifically to the time when revenues and expenditures are recorded as such in the accounting records.

Governmental revenues should be classified by fund and source. Expenditures should be classified by fund, function, organization unit, activity, character, and principal classes of objectives in accordance with standard recognized classifications. Common terminology and classifications should be used consistently throughout (1) the budget; (2) the accounts; and (3) the financial reports. These three elements of governmental financial administration are inseparable and can be thought of as the "cycle" of governmental financial transactions and final product of the accounting system.

Eight Types of Funds

1. The *General Fund* which accounts for all transactions not accounted for in any other fund.
2. *Special Revenue Fund* which accounts for revenues from specific sources or to finance specific projects.
3. *Debt Service Fund* which accounts for the payment of interest and principal on long-term debt.
4. *Capital Project Fund* which accounts for the receipt and disbursement of funds used for the acquisition of capital facilities.
5. *Enterprise Funds* which account for the financing of services to the public paid for by the users of the services.
6. *Fiduciary Funds: Trust and Agency Funds* which account for assets held by a governmental unit as trustee or agent for individuals, private organizations, or other governmental units.
7. *Internal Service Funds* which account for the financing of special projects and services performed by one governmental entity for an organization unit within the same governmental entity.

The accountant should:

- Maintain complete and adequate files for the initial documentation which established or restricted the fund, together with any special reporting requirements demanded.
- Keep separate detailed books of entry for each fund, separate bank account for that fund, separate identification of all property and securities.
- Under *no* circumstances should assets of separate funds be commingled. Transfers between funds should not be permitted without documentary authorization, and inter-fund receivables and payables should, in contra-effect, be equal and clearly identified, always maintaining the original integrity of each fund.
- Interest accruals, cooperative-share funding (example: government 80%—college 20% in Work Study Program), expense allowances or allocations—all should be made timely.
- Federal, state and local reporting requirements should be studied, met and reported as due to avoid stringent penalties, interest and possible loss of tax-exempt status. Options may exist regarding the handling of payroll and unemployment taxes; they should be studied and explored for money-saving possibilities.
- Independently audited annual financial statements by fund are usually required both by organizational charter and governmental departments (espe-

cially where grant-participation is involved). Publication of the availability of these statements is sometimes mandatory (foundations).

- One area of discussion and dispute is the "compliance" feature of audits involving certain governmental agency grants. Here, the independent auditor is called upon to measure the agency's compliance with certain non-accounting rules, such as eligibility of money-recipients, internal controls and other matters not ordinarily associated with a financial audit. The integrity of the auditor's financial opinion should never be compromised by peripheral compliance requirements. In most cases, he should qualify his opinion indicating the results and *extent of tests* made for compliance. The AICPA, to some extent, has spelled out guidelines for "compliance" opinions in Section 9641 of its "Statements on Auditing Standards."

- Municipal accounting techniques, procedures, format and demands are not discussed here. Their overall application involves the use of fund accounting. The main distinction is the entering of the budget—the anticipated revenues and the appropriations thereof—directly on and as part of the books of account. Progress reports then show how actual compares with anticipated. The estimates are then zeroed out at year-end. The meaning and use of "encumbrances" should also be understood. Reports for some local subdivisions, such as school-boards, usually involve a strict accounting of each receipt and disbursement, including the detailing of outstanding checks.

Accounting for the general fund (GF).   The General Fund is the type most frequently used as it accounts for revenues not allocated to specified activities by law or by contract. Every governmental entity *must* have a General Fund; none of the other types of funds are required, but are established as needed.

Entries in the GF system originally are made to Estimated Revenues and Appropriations and simultaneously a debit or credit, whichever is the case, is recorded in the Fund Balance account. For proper controls the encumbrance system is used with entries recorded when commitments are made or orders placed. This procedure has the effect of setting aside the money for the payment of future purchase orders and payment vouchers. When a purchase is actually made, the entries to an Encumbrances and Reserve for Encumbrances are reversed and those accounts cleared. (The later expenditure is not always the same as the encumbrance). Simultaneously, the actual expenditure is recorded by a Debit to an Expenditures account and a credit to Vouchers Payable.

Taxes and service charges are budgeted in a Taxes-Receivable—Current Account. The estimated amounts should be recorded after the estimate and posting of uncollectibles, so the entries are a credit to Revenues and a credit to Estimated Uncollectible Taxes. When collections are actually received during the fiscal year, they are recorded with a debit to cash and a credit to Taxes Receivable—Current. Subsequently, it is determined that a certain amount of taxes will become delinquent as the year progresses. These amounts are recorded in a Taxes Receivable—Delinquent account (debit) and a credit to Taxes Receivable-Current. At this point an Interest and Penalties account should be opened for fees, penalties and other charges associated with the collection of delinquent taxes.

Taxes Receivable—Delinquent	xxx	
Estimated Uncollectible Current Taxes	xxx	
Taxes Receivable—Current		xxx
Estimated Uncollectible Delinquent Taxes		xxx
Interest and Penalties	xxx	
Estimated Uncollectible Interest and Penalties		xxx

At the end of the fiscal year, the accounts of the General Fund are closed out. Any differences are recorded for or against the Fund Balance.

Accounting for Special Revenue Funds (SRF).   Special Revenue Funds account for revenues obtained via specific taxes or other designated revenue sources. They are usually mandated by statute, charter, or local ordinance to fund specific functions or activities. Examples are parks, museums, highway construction, street maintenance, business licensing.

Revenue Funds resources cannot be used for any purpose other than the purpose for which the bonds were sold.

Journal entries:		
Encumbrances	xxx	
Reserve for Encumbrances		xxx
Reserve for Encumbrances	xxx	
Encumbrances		xxx
Expenditures	xxx	
Vouchers Payable		xxx
Vouchers Payable	xxx	
Cash		xxx

Taxes and service charges are budgeted in a Taxes-Receivable—Current account. The estimated amounts should be recorded after the estimate and posting of uncollectibles, so the entries are a credit to Revenues and a credit to Estimated Uncollectible Taxes; e.g.,

Taxes Receivable—Current	xxx	
Estimated Uncollectible Current Taxes		xxx
Revenues		xxx

When collections are actually received during the fiscal year they are recorded with a debit to Cash and a credit to Taxes Receivable—Current.

Accounting for Debt Service Funds (DSF).   Debt Service Fund accounts for the payment of interest and principal on long-term debt resulting from the sale of general obligation bonds. This fund does not include the accounting for special assessments and service debts of governmental enterprises.

There are three types of long-term debt:

- Term or sinking fund bonds.
- Serial bonds.
- Notes and time warrants having a maturity of *more than one year* after issuance.

The first entry in the accounting cycle for a bond fund is to record the bond authorization:

Bonds Authorized—unissued	xxx	
Appropriations		xxx
The bonds are sold:		
Cash	xxx	
Bonds Authorized—unissued		xxx

If the bonds are sold at a premium, a Premium on Bonds account is credited. If sold at a discount, a Discount on Bonds account is debited.

Accounting for the Capital Projects Fund (CPF).   Capital Projects Funds are a set of accounts for all resources used to acquire *capital* facilities (except funds financed by special assessment and enterprise funds). There must be Capital Project Funds for each authorized project to ensure that the proceeds of a bond issue, for example, are expended only as authorized. There is also a separate budget for the CPF, usually labeled the Capital Budget.

The accounting process begins with project authorization which is in memorandum form, no entry is necessary. Assuming the project is financed by the proceeds of a bond issue (as most of them are), the proceeds of the borrowing is an entry to the Cash account and a credit to Revenues for the *par value* of the bonds. If the bonds were sold at a premium, there is a credit to a Premium on Bonds account for the amount of the premium. Since GAAP requires bond premiums to be treated as an adjustment to the interest costs, the premiums are transferred *to* the Debt Service Fund established to service the debt. The entry to record the transfer is:

Premium on Bonds	xxx	
Cash		xxx

If the bonds are sold at a discount, the discount is eliminated by a transfer of the amount of the discount *from* the Debt Service Fund *to* the Capital Projects Fund.

Accounting for Enterprise Funds (EF). Enterprise Funds finance self-supporting (not taxpayers) activities of governmental units that render services on a user charge basis to the general public. Common enterprises are water companies, electricity, natural gas, airports, transportation systems, hospitals, port authority, and a variety of recreational facilities.

In most jurisdictions, utilities and other enterprises are required to adopt and operate under budgets in the same manner as non-enterprise operations of governmental units. A budget is essential for control of each enterprise's operating results and to ensure that the resources of one enterprise are not illegally or improperly utilized by another.

The accrual basis of accounting is the required method for Enterprise Funds. As customers are billed Accounts Receivable accounts are debited and revenue accounts *by sources* are credited.

Four financial statements are required to disclose fully the financial position and results of operations of an Enterprise Fund:

- Balance Sheet
- Revenue and Expenses
- Changes in Financial Position
- Analysis of Changes in Retained Earnings

Accounting for Trust and Agency Funds (TAF). Trust and Agency Funds are similar; the primary difference is that a Trust Fund is usually in existence for a long period of time, even permanently. Both have fiduciary responsibilities for funds and assets that are not owned outright by the funds.

There are two types of Trust Funds, i.e., expendable and nonexpendable funds. The former allows the principal and income to be spent on designated operations, while nonexpendable funds must be preserved intact. Pension and various retirement funds are examples of expendable funds; a loan fund from which loans are made for specific purposes and must be paid back, which requires maintaining the *original amount* of the fund is a nonexpendable fund.

Trust Funds are operated as required by statutes and governmental regulations established for their existence. Accounting for Trust Funds consists primarily of the proper recording of receipts and disbursements. Additions are credited directly to the Fund Balance account and expenditures charged directly against the Fund Balance.

An Agency Fund can be thought of as sort of a clearinghouse fund established to account for assets received for and paid to others; the main asset is cash which is held only for a brief period of time, so is seldom invested because cash is usually paid out shortly after receipt.

An Agency Fund simplifies the complexities that can result from the use of numerous fund accounting entities; e.g., instances in which a single transaction affects several different funds. All Agency Fund assets are owed to another fund, a person, or an organization. The entries for receipts and disbursements in Agency Funds are easy:

Upon receipt:		
Cash	xxx	
Fund Balance		xxx
Upon disbursement:		
Fund Balance	xxx	
Cash	xxx	

Accounting for Intergovernmental Service Funds (ISF).

ISF, also referenced as Working Capital Funds and Internal Service Funds, finances and provides accountability for services and commodities provided by a designated agency of a governmental unit to other departments, agencies, etc., of the same governmental entity. Examples are motor pools, centralized garages, central purchasing, storage, facilities, and central printing services.

Funds for the establishment of ISF usually originate from three sources:

- Contributions from another operating fund—e.g., the General Fund or an Enterprise Fund.
- The sale of general obligation bonds.
- Long-term advances from other funds, which are to be repaid over a specific period of time from the earnings of a revolving fund.

As cash is expended for the benefit of other fund-users, the users are charged with the cost of the materials or services furnished by the ISF and the ISF is then reimbursed by interdepartmental cash transfers from the departments of other funds to which materials or services have been furnished.

The accounting for ISF should include all accounts necessary to compile an accurate statement of the outcome of its financial operations, and of its financial position at any given time. These accounts will usually include the fixed assets owned by the fund, accounts for buildings financed from capital Project Funds, depreciation recorded on fixed assets to obtain an accurate computation of costs and to preclude depletion of the fund's capital. The accrual basis must be used for all ISF accounting, with all charges to departments of various funds billed at the time materials or services are rendered and expenditures are recorded when incurred. Encumbrances may or may not be formally recorded in the books of account; if they are the entries would be:

Encumbrances	xxx	
Reserve for Encumbrances		xxx

If encumbrances are not recorded in the accounts, memorandum records of orders and commitments should be maintained to preclude over-obligation of cash and other fund resources.

When an ISF is established, the entry to be made will depend upon the service the fund is to provide. If the fund's capital is obtained from the General Fund, the entry would be:

Cash	xxx	
Contribution from General Fund		xxx

If a general obligation bond issue is a source of the fund's capital:

Cash	xxx	
Contribution from		
General Obligation Bonds		xxx

If fund capital is obtained from another fund of the same governmental unit the entry is:

Cash	xxx	
Advance from (name of fund)		xxx

Accounting for the General Fixed Assets Account Group (GFA).

The fixed asset accounts are maintained on the basis of original cost, or the estimated cost if the original cost is not available, as in the case of gifts. The appraised value at the time of receipt of the asset is an acceptable valuation. Otherwise, initial costs of fixed assets are obtainable from contracts, purchase vouchers, and other transaction documents generated at the time of acquisition or construction.

Depreciation on fixed assets should not be recorded in the general accounting records. Depreciation charges are computed for unit cost purposes, provided such charges are recorded in memorandum form and do not appear in the fund accounts.

Different from depreciation accounting for commercial enterprises, the depreciation of fixed assets is not recorded as an expense because there is no purpose in doing so. Property records should be kept, however, for each piece of property and equipment owned by the fund. The sum of the cost value of the properties—buildings, improvements, machinery, and equipment—should equal the corresponding balances of those accounts carried in the general ledger.

Accounting for the Long-Term Debt Group (LTD).

General Obligation Bonds and other types of long-term debt supported by general revenues are obligations of the governmental unit as a whole, not of any of the entity's constituent funds individually. Additionally, the monies from such debt can be expended on facilities that are used in the operation of several funds. Accordingly, the total of long-term indebtedness backed by the "full faith and credit" of the government should be recorded and accounted for in a separate self-balancing group of accounts titled General Long-Term Debt Group of Accounts. Included in this debt group are general obligation bonds, time warrants, and notes that have a maturity date of *more than one year* from the date of issuance.

Long-term debt is recorded in the self-balancing accounts, so do not affect the liabilities of any other fund. The reason for these accounts is to record a governmental unit's long-term debt at any point in time from the date the debt is incurred until it is finally paid. Under GAAP the proper valuation for the long-term debt liability is the sum of 1) the present discounted value of the principal payable at the stipulated maturity date in the future and 2) the present discounted value of the periodic interest payments to the maturity date.

The entries to be made at the time the bonds are sold are:

Amounts to be Provided for		
the Payment of Term Bonds	xxx	
Term Bonds Payable		xxx

The proceeds of the bond issue are entered in a Capital Projects Fund account to be expended as authorized in the Authorized Capital Outlay account.

(Note: Not-for-profit accounting for other than governmental entities use the accrual basis of accounting—e.g., colleges and universities, voluntary hospitals, health and welfare organizations, etc.)

4

Internal Controls

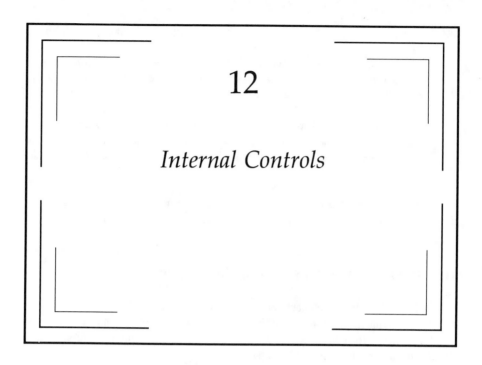

12

Internal Controls

When considering a topic of the magnitude of importance and complexity of internal control systems (ICS), it can be helpful at the outset first to understand what we are dealing with before getting into the technical aspects of the discussion. In the case of ICS it can be thought of as a "way of thinking." That is to say ICS involves the *evaluation* of both the methods and the application of those methods to an entity's controls system. Evaluation techniques require thoughtful consideration, rigorous study and research, and objective analysis. These three attributes are "ways of thinking," which in turn provide us with the guidance and direction of an orderly approach to a review of the techniques and procedures for the *judgmental* appraisal of the "adequacy" of an organizations's ICS.

The development of an internal accounting control system should be made in relation to the *objectives* of accounting controls. The objectives are set forth in the Statements on Auditing Standards No. 1, Section 320.28:

> *Accounting control* comprises the plan of organization and the procedures and records that are concerned with the safeguarding of assets and the reliability of financial records and consequently are designed to provide reasonable assurance that:
>
> **a.** Transactions are executed in accordance with management's general or specific authorization.

    b. Transactions are recorded as necessary (1) to permit preparation of financial statements in conformity with generally accepted accounting principles or any other criteria applicable to such statements and (2) to maintain accountability for assets.

    c. Access to assets is permitted only in accordance management's authorization.

    d. The recorded accountability for assets is compared with the existing assets at reasonable intervals and appropriate action is taken with respect to any differences.

Two levels of objectives are implicit in the Statement. The primary objectives are the *safeguarding* of assets and the *reliability* of financial records.

THE FOREIGN CORRUPT PRACTICES ACT OF 1977

Primarily as a result of the enactment of the Foreign Corrupt Practices Act of 1977 (FCPA), internal accounting controls have in recent years become a significant point of concern for corporate management, the public accounting profession, and the Securities and Exchange Commission.

Section 102 of the FCPA titled *Accounting Standards* specifies that all corporations required to file with the SEC must:

> Make and keep books, records, and accounts, which, in reasonable detail, accurately and fairly reflect the transactions and dispositions of the assets of the issuer.

The significance of this statutory requirement is that it represents the first time, historically, that the U.S. Congress has legislated an accounting Rule. The promulgation of accounting principles and practices (GAAP) have always been developed by "private sector" authorities, i.e., the AICPA, the FASB, the AAA (American Accounting Association), and "other authoritative sources." Other authoritative sources are, essentially, highly specialized industries to which the general principles (GAAP) cannot be fully applied as it would be impractical to incorporate procedures unique to just one industry into GAAP. Banking, insurance, and financial institutional accounting is an example; railroad accounting is another as is the motion picture industry.

Accountant's Responsibility

Again, the significance of the Act is the explicit statutory recognition by the Federal Government given to accounting controls and control systems. The accountant's responsibility is to plan a system which constantly monitors for errors, irregularities, malfeasance, embezzlement, and fraudulent manipulation of the accounts. The accountant is in fact the "monitor." He must continually evaluate the effectiveness of the system and monitor compliance with the requirements of the statute, which of course also includes compliance with GAAP since the statute explicitly includes GAAP in the Act.

The fact that the statutory requirement applies to publicly-held corporations has led, initially, to the misunderstanding that it is of no concern to public accountants who are not involved in auditing public corporations. But auditors must be mindful of the *Statement on Auditing Procedure No. 1*, which applies to the scope of the examination of *all* companies, whether public or private corporations, partnerships, or other forms of business organizations. This Statement specifically references creditors, for example, who are a primary user of financial statements and to whom an auditor has a potential liability for materially misleading financial statements accompanying applications for credit to financial institutions, regardless of honest error or fraudulent intent.

Compliance Problems

What can an accountant do to ascertain compliance with the 1977 Act? Compliance can be demonstrated by an *intent* to comply, since neither the Act nor the professional literature specify criteria for evaluating a system's adequacy or materiality levels. This makes it difficult for management, directors, independent auditors, and legal counsel to be sure of compliance with the Act.

The following suggestions may be helpful both to the accountant and to management for establishing intent to comply.

There should be:

1. Records of memos and minutes of meetings held by management, the board of directors, and the audit committee (if any) concerning internal accounting control concepts. The discussions should include legal counsel, internal auditors, and independent auditors.

2. Statements for the record of intention to comply.

3. A record of all meetings within the company of the accounting personnel and internal audit staff to ensure that they understand the importance of compliance and are able to monitor compliance.

4. A written program for continuing review and evaluation of the accounting controls system.

5. Letters from the independent auditors stating that no material weaknesses in internal accounting controls were discovered during the audit, or that suggested needed improvements have in fact been made. If necessary, the independent auditors' comments should include other deficiencies, and management's written plans to correct them should be included.

6. A record of periodic review and approval of the evaluation of the system by senior management, the audit committee, and the board of directors.

7. Instructional manuals for the development of methods and techniques for describing, testing, and evaluating internal controls.

8. Training programs conducted for internal auditors and other company personnel responsible for internal controls.

9. Changes in internal controls to overcome identified deficiencies that are initiated and documented.

10. A formal written code of conduct appropriately communicated and monitored. (Note: the SEC regards a corporate written code of conduct as imperative.)

11. Documentation that compliance testing was done by direct *visual* observations during the period being audited.

INTERNAL ACCOUNTING AND ADMINISTRATIVE CONTROL

Internal control, according to the Professional Auditing Standards, is subdivided as follows:

(a) Accounting control, which comprises the plan of organization and all methods and procedures that are concerned mainly with, and relate directly to, safeguarding assets and the reliability of the financial records.

(b) Administrative control, which comprises the plan of organization and all methods and procedures that are concerned mainly with operational efficiency and adherence to managerial policies, such as sales policies, employee training and production quality control. This is usually only indirectly related to the financial records.

Administrative control includes, but is not limited to, the plan of organization and the procedures and records that are concerned with the decision processes leading to management's authorization of transactions. Such authorization is a management function directly associated with the responsibility for achieving the objectives of the organization, and is the starting point for establishing account control of transactions.

Accounting control comprises the plan of organization and procedures and records that are concerned with safeguarding assets and the reliability of financial records, and consequently are designed to provide reasonable assurance that:

(a) Transactions are executed in accordance with management's general or specific authorization.

(b) Transactions are recorded as necessary (1) to permit preparation of financial statements in conformity with generally accepted accounting principles or any other criteria applicable to such statements, and (2) to maintain accountability for assets.

(c) Access to assets is permitted only in accordance with management's authorization.

(d) The recorded accountability for assets is compared with the existing assets at reasonable intervals and appropriate action taken with respect to any differences.

Fundamentals of a System of Internal Accounting Control

(1) Responsibility: There should be a plan or an organizational chart which places the responsibility for specified functions on specific individuals in the organization.

The responsibility for establishing and maintaining a system of internal accounting control rests with management. The system should be continuously supervised, tested and modified as necessary to provide reasonable (but not absolute) assurance that objectives are being accomplished, all at costs not exceeding benefits.

(2) Division of duties: The idea here is to remove the handling and recording of any one transaction from beginning to end from the control of any one employee. Further, making different employees responsible for different functions of a transaction actually serves as a cross-check which facilitates the detection of errors, accidental or deliberate.

(3) Use of appropriate forms and documents: Efficient design of forms and documents aids in the administration of the internal control system. Mechanical or electronic equipment can also be used to expedite the process of checking. Both of these methods provide control over accounting data.

(4) Internal auditors: Periodic review of all the above elements of the internal control system should be carried out by an internal audit staff. The function of this staff would be to periodically check the effectiveness of above items (1), (2), and (3).

There is a relationship between the size of an organization and the degree of development of its system of internal control. Complete separation of functions and internal auditing department may not exist in smaller companies. The objective in these smaller companies is to divide the duties in the way that creates the greatest amount of internal check.

Elements of a Satisfactory System of Internal Accounting Control

The elements of a satisfactory system of internal control include:

(1) A plan of organization which provides appropriate segregation of functional responsibilities.

(2) A system of authorization and record procedures adequate to provide reasonable accounting control of assets, liabilities, revenues and expenses.

(3) Sound practices to follow in the performance of duties and functions of each of the organizational departments.

(4) Personnel of a quality commensurate with responsibilities.

One important element in the system of internal control is the independence of the operating, custodial, accounting and internal auditing functions. There should be a separation of duties in such a way that records exist outside each department to serve as controls over the activities within that department. Responsibilities for various functions and delegation of authority should be clearly defined and spelled out in organizational charts and manuals. Conflicting and dual responsibility is to be avoided. The function of initiation and authorization of an activity should be separate from the accounting for it. Custody of assets should be separated from the accounting for them.

Relationship of Your Internal Control System to Your Outside Accountants

The efficiency of your internal control system becomes important to your outside, independent auditors. Before determining how much of an audit they should make, they must review the internal control system. An efficient system may do away with certain audit procedures which might otherwise be necessary. A poor internal control system may necessitate greater checking on the part of the auditor with a consequent additional cost for the audit.

INTERNAL CONTROL FOR INVENTORIES

Some internal control procedures that can be used in conjunction with different types of inventories—finished goods, work in process, materials, goods for resale—are detailed in the paragraphs that follow.

Inventories of Merchandise Purchased for Resale and Supplies

(1) The purchasing department approves the purchase orders for merchandise to be bought. In a small company, the owner or manager may be the one to approve these purchase orders. Purchase orders should be sequentially numbered and traced to final disposition.

(2) After okays from purchasing manager have been received, requests for price quotations are usually sent out. These requests should go to various companies, and the company quoting the lowest price will be the one from which the purchases are made, unless there are other overriding considerations.

(3) In the selling department, an updated individual quantity record for each type of unit is kept on perpetual inventory stock cards. It is usually the responsibility of inventory clerks to keep these cards up to date. These stock cards indicate the need for reorders and they should be checked against purchase requisition by the manager of the selling department or other person in control of the merchandise stock. In a business too small to have a separate selling department, the owner or manager is the one to perform these functions. The number of units of merchandise ordered is then entered on the inventory stock cards by one clerk. The number actually received is entered from the receiving list by another clerk. The number sold or used is entered on the stock cards by still another clerk from sales lists or salesmen's orders. After giving effect to the number ordered, received and issued on the inventory stock records the balance represents the number of units actually on hand. A well-rounded perpetual card system usually includes detailed unit costs for ready computation under either LIFE, FIFO, or average methods.

(4) In the receiving department, the receiving clerk should not be allowed to see purchase order records or purchase requisitions. Receiving reports are checked against the perpetual inventory stock records and a notation is made on these stock record cards indicating the date, order number and quantity received. Even where a business is too small to have a perpetual inventory, a receiving report should be made, which should then be checked against the purchase orders and a notation as to the day and quantity received made on those purchase orders.

(5) In the accounts payable department, the receiving report is checked against the merchandise stock record, then sent to the accounts payable department where it is verified against the seller's invoice. The purchasing agent should have approved the price on the seller's invoice before that invoice was sent to the accounts payable department. A clerk in the accounts payable department should verify all extension totals on the invoice. If the vendor's invoice and receiving report are in agreement the invoice is then entered into a purchase journal or voucher register for future payment. Any discrepancy between quantity received and quantity on the seller's invoice will hold up payment until an adjustment is made by the seller.

The departments involved in internal control in merchandise and supplies inventories are purchasing, sales, receiving, accounts receivable and accounts payable.

Finished Goods Inventories

(1) Ascertain the quantity of units which have been completed from the production record and transferred to the shipping department or warehouse. The daily report of finished goods units transferred to the warehouse or shipping department indicates the number of finished units available to the sales department.

(2) Compute the unit cost of finished goods delivered to the sales department. This information is obtained from the unit cost sheet (for a process cost accounting system) or from the job-order cost card (in a job order cost accounting system).

(3) Set up finished goods inventory cards and for each item record the quantity

received at the warehouse, the quantity shipped on orders and the balance remaining at specified unit costs. The number of finished goods units in the warehouse or stockroom should tie in with this finished goods inventory file.

(4) Periodically, physically count the finished goods inventory and see that it ties in with the finished goods inventory file.

The departments involved in internal control of finished goods inventories are manufacturing, cost accounting, accounts receivable and sales.

Raw Materials and Supplies Inventories

(1) In the stores department, the storekeeper must safeguard the raw materials and supplies inventories—both physically and by accounting control. No raw materials or supplies can leave without a stores requisition. Quantity control at minimum levels is also the responsibility of the storekeeper.

The storekeeper should keep a stores record for each item, listing the maximum and minimum quantities, quantity ordered and number, quantity received, quantity issued, and balance on hand. When stores cards show minimum quantities, a stores ledger clerk pulls those cards from the file to make sure that materials or supplies are ordered to cover the minimum needs. Quantities shown on the stores record should be verified by making an actual count of the stores items which are to be ordered; than a purchase requisition is filled out from the stores records. The quantity of each item ordered is approved by the storekeeper. He knows the average monthly consumption of each item. The ordering of special equipment by department heads also goes through the storeroom after having the necessary executive approval. The purchase requisition is then sent to the purchasing agent.

In the stores department, a receiving report is prepared in triplicate by the receiving clerk. One copy goes to the stores ledger clerk, another to the accounts payable department; the third is kept by the receiving clerk. The receiving clerk puts the stores items in proper places within the storeroom after preparing his receiving report. Sometimes, location numbers are used to facilitate ready accessing.

The stores ledger clerk gets a copy of the receiving report and makes a record of the quantity and the order number on the stores ledger card affected by the items received.

(2) In the purchasing department, the purchase agent places the order for the quantity needed on the quantity requisition. If he feels the quantity ordered is excessive, he may look into the storekeeper's purchase requisition. He then requests price quotations from various supply companies, placing his order with the lowest bidder. The purchase agent also verifies the prices on the seller's invoices by comparing them with the price quotations.

(3) In the accounts payable department, no bill should be approved for payment until materials ordered have actually been received, are in good condition, and the prices of the seller's invoice match his quotations.

(4) In the manufacturing department, different individuals have authority to sign stores requisitions to withdraw materials from the storeroom. Usually, a fore-

man prepares a stores requisition where raw materials or supplies are needed in any of the manufacturing departments. This requisition contains the account name and number, department name and number, job order number, quantity of material issued, the stores item name and classification symbol, the name of the person to withdraw materials from the storeroom, the unit price of the item and the total cost of items withdrawn from the storeroom.

The departments involved in internal control for raw materials and supplies inventory are stores, purchasing, accounts payable and manufacturing.

Work-in-Process Inventory

(1) In the manufacturing department, stores requisitions are prepared by shop foremen for materials which are to be charged to the work-in-process inventory account. Quantities of materials are obtained from engineering or administrative departments. Specifications for raw materials are usually shown on a bill of materials (a list of different items required to complete an order). The stores requisition will specify the quantity, price, cost of each item of raw material requisitioned and the job order number.

Time tickets are prepared by the workmen and approved by a foreman in the department in which work is performed before it is charged to the work-in-process inventory account. Each labor operation may have a standard time to perform a certain operation which has been predetermined by the engineering department. There also may be a predetermined standard wage rate, determined by the head of the manufacturing department and known by the payroll department. The cost accounting department is responsible for the amount of manufacturing expense charged to the work-in-process inventory account.

(2) In the cost department, raw material cost is computed from sales requisitions, direct labor costs from time tickets, and manufacturing expense is estimated from prevailing overhead rates.

Internal control methods for the work-in-process inventory account depend on whether the firm has a process cost accounting or job-order cost accounting system.

The chief point of internal control for work-in-process inventories is computing costs. Product costs are analyzed by operations, departments and cost elements. This permits measurement of the cost of products at different stages of completion. The number of partly finished units when multiplied by a cost at a particular stage should come close to the value in the work-in-process inventory account.

The departments involved in internal control of work-in-process inventories are manufacturing and cost accounting.

Taking Count—The Physical Inventory

The two most significant factors of inventory control are:

1. Knowing what *should* be on hand, based on paper controls; and
2. Verifying *what actually is on hand*; by a physical count.

The Perpetual System—Knowing What Should Be on Hand

In many firms, not enough effort and emphasis are put into the timely keeping of detailed perpetual inventory stock records, thus ignoring the most basic control available.

The nature and extent of the records to maintain vary from company to company. At the least, there should be a constant updated record of the *units* handled—a card or a loose-leaf sheet to which are posted the "ins" and "outs" always showing the new morning's balance on hand—or rather, the balance which *should* be on hand. If expanded to the fullest, the system would also include unit-costs of acquisitions (or, in manufacturing, detailed material, labor and overhead costs assigned), unit-sales deleted at cost (based on the company's "flow-of-cost" assumption of LIFO, FIFO or average costs) and balance on hand extended at cost. Also, the individual record would show back-order positions, write-downs, destructions, and, most importantly, locations in the storage area (by location number or description). It may show the total sales income for that particular unit, displaying unit gross profits. Retail stores using the gross profit method of valuing inventories usually maintain controls over entire departments, or sections of departments, rather than by individual units, and extended values are at retail, showing markups and markdowns, as well as bulk cost figures.

The general ledger summary inventory asset account should (where the system provides cost-flowing movement) always tie to the total of the subsidiary perpetual system (at least monthly). They should be matched as often as possible and all differences traced to eliminate any weaknesses in the system.

The point is—know what *should be on hand!*

The Physical Count—Verifying What is Actually on Hand

At least once a year, a physical count of the entire inventory should be taken, usually as of the balance sheet date. Management, not the auditor, is responsible for taking this physical inventory. The auditor is an *observer* of methods, count and valuation, but he may help establish the system of counting, the tags to use, the methods of assuring a full count, the cutoff procedures, the pricing, etc., so as to satisfy himself of the reasonableness of the total value he can accept for his attestation.

The method of tagging, counting, weighing or measuring, locating, recounting—the assignment of personnel—all the procedures should be set in advance and followed (unless properly authorized changes develop).

The auditor should familiarize himself with the nature of the products handled, the terminology, the packaging, the principles of measurement. His "education'' in the client's processes should not be obtained at the sacrifice of counting-time.

The auditor is concerned with the final evaluation of that *physical* inventory. The perpetual records, as such, and errors therein are not a necessary part of the audit process, though weaknesses should be commented upon in the management letter.

However, a history of *accurate* internal paper control of inventory can substantially reduce the extent of testing by the auditor. When it can be expected that variations from perpetual inventories will be small and within tolerable limits, the auditor may choose to use statistical random sampling in testing either an immediately prior physical count or in counting only those items *drawn by the auditor* (without advance notice) for random selection. If the sample then indicates a rate of error unacceptable to the auditor, he may request another (or full) physical count, or he may, with management's consent, adjust the overall value of the inventory to an amount indicated by the sample (see Journal Entries in Appendix A), with management promising to investigate the error in the ensuing fiscal year.

When an effective perpetual inventory control is in use, management usually "cycle" counts the inventory once, or several times over, during the year, testing bits and pieces throughout the year, covering it entirely at least once.

There are often *portions* of an inventory which may require more time and effort to physically count than the relative merit of those portions warrants. Such items may be *reasonably* estimated (with joint approval of management and auditor), based on such elements as: last year's value, movement during the year, space occupied, weight, or, considering sales and purchases, using an estimated gross profit method.

Summary Thoughts

The accuracy of a physical inventory even with the most sophisticated computerized system, may always be in doubt if there is *no* perpetual record for comparison. A perpetual inventory is meaningless unless tested periodically to a physical count. A history of accurate perpetual records can be justification for an auditor's using statistical sampling for year-end evaluation. Moreover, management itself can use statistical sampling techniques for cycle counting. Tie-in to the general ledger asset account should be made regularly by management. The financial statement value of the inventory must be at cost or market, whichever is lower. Standards are *not* acceptable, unless approximating cost.

INTERNAL CONTROL FOR EXPENSES

Each of the various types of expenses requires special internal control procedures. These procedures are covered in the following paragraphs.

Manufacturing Expenses

(1) In the manufacturing service and producing department, small tools which are not constantly being used should be kept in the toolroom. Each workman requiring such tools is given metal checks, each stamped with his number. The toolroom attendant will release a tool to a workman in exchange for a metal check bearing the workman's number. The check is kept in the toolroom until the tool is returned, at which time the check is returned to the workman.

The department foreman has the responsibility for approving a requisition for a new tool when one wears out.

(2) Charges for freight and shipping on incoming supplies should be charged to the account to which the supplies are charged. Copies of the freight or shipping bills should be attached to supply invoices. Supplies inventory is, therefore, charged for these freight and shipping charges instead of an expense account.

(3) Numerous types of shop supplies, such as brooms, oil, waste, solder, wire, are part of the raw materials and supplies inventory. They should be kept in the storeroom and issued only by a stores requisition, signed by an authorized individual. The individual who indicates the need for such supplies (usually a foreman) should indicate the job order number or departmental expense account number to which the material is to be charged on the stores requisition.

(4) Workmen categorized as indirect laborers should have an identification number when they work in a specific department. A time clock card should be kept and verified by a foreman or timekeeper.

The departments involved in internal control of manufacturing expenses are factory production, factory service and accounts payable.

Selling Expenses

(1) Salesmen's salaries should be okayed by the sales department manager before a summary is sent to the payroll department. The basis for the summary is the salesmen's daily report. Commissions earned by salesmen are verified from duplicate sales invoices mailed to the customer. These are computed in the sales department and approved by the sales department manager.

(2) To prevent padding of travel expenses, many companies allow flat rates or maximum amounts for each day of the week. Unusual amounts should require an explanation from the salesman.

(3) The office manager retains control over outgoing mail and postage. A mail clerk usually affixes the postage. A point to keep in mind as a control of postage expenses is not to permit every office worker access to stamps or a postage meter.

(4) Telephone expenses can be controlled by having the switchboard operator record all outgoing calls by departments on a call report sheet. Long distance calls should be reported on a special form indicating the party making the call and where the call is going to. From the long distance call record, telephone expenses are distributed by departments.

(5) Subscriptions to publications and dues of various organizations and professional societies should be approved by the sales manager before a voucher is prepared for them.

(6) All bills approved by the sales manager are sent to the accounting department for payment.

The departments involved for internal control of selling expenses are sales and accounts payable.

Administrative Expenses

Internal control for administrative expenses is very similar to the material for the sales department. Bills for administrative expense items should be approved by an administrative department executive before they are sent to the accounts payable department for payment.

The departments involved in internal control of administrative expenses are administrative and accounts payable.

Financial and Other Expenses

In corporations which have special departments to control financial problems in the company, a treasury department or similar department will handle expenses in the nature of interest, discount and dividends and may even supervise handling of cash. The financial department may also have the responsibility for authorizing credit extended to customers.

(1) A credit manager in the financial department should have the responsibility for approving sales orders above a specific amount. The manager should be in constant touch with the accounts receivable department to determine whether or not a customer has been regular in his payments. The treasurer has the responsibility for authorizing bad debt writeoffs. The writeoff itself should be made by someone in the accounts receivable department on the authority of the financial department executive—not the sales manager.

(2) The financial department executive or office manager approves expenditures such as interest and bank discounts, office expenses and supplies. After approval of these items, invoices are sent to the accounts payable department.

The departments involved in internal control for factory payrolls are timekeeping, payroll, accounts payable and the particular manufacturing division.

Salaries and Wages

(1) In the timekeeping department each workman is given an identifying number which will serve to identify the department within which he works. A badge with this number identifies him when his presence within the factory is checked each day.

(2) It is the duty of a time clerk to check the presence of each workman once

or twice a day, every day. This is to eliminate the possibility of one man punching the time clock for another workman who is absent. Absences are noted in a time book. These are then checked against the employee's time ticket, time clock card or payroll sheet at the end of each specific pay period.

(3) Care should be taken to prevent one worker punching another worker's time clock card. The time clock card indicates the number of hours the workman is present each day in the plant. The time clock card can be used to verify the hours shown on daily time tickets. This may be done daily or weekly.

(4) In the manufacturing department, a time ticket which lists the workman's name, number of hours worked on different jobs and labor operations and total hours worked is prepared. It must be approved by the foreman of the department in which work is performed.

(5) In the payroll department, time tickets are verified against the time clock cards and the time keeper's time clock book. The time ticket is then given to a clerk who inserts the hourly or piece-work rate of each workman. Another clerk computes the earnings. The time tickets are then used for working up the payroll sheet. Then, the time tickets are sent to the cost accounting department to prepare a payroll distribution sheet. The payroll sheet becomes the record by which the workman is paid. After the payroll sheet has been completely okayed, it is sent to the accounts payable department for payment. Payment to each worker, either by check or cash, should be receipted.

In the accounts payable department the payroll sheet serves as the basis for payment.

The departments involved in internal control for factory payrolls are timekeeping, payroll, accounts payable and the particular manufacturing division.

Office Payroll

(1) In the sales department, the sales manager approves the daily sales reports. From these reports, a record of the salesperson's days is prepared. The record is sent to the payroll department after approval by the sales manager. The manager in the sales department also approves the records of work performed by the sales office force before sending it to the payroll department.

(2) In the administrative department, the office manager approves time worked by the office force and then sends it to the payroll department. Salaries of top executives are often placed on a special payroll. Their salaries are usually known by the paymaster who prepares their checks and sends them directly to the executives' offices.

(3) The treasurer or financial department office manager similarly approves the work performed by the clerical personnel in his department.

(4) Upon receiving these authorized reports from the various departments, the paymaster sets them up on a payroll sheet and after computing the applicable salary

for each office worker, takes all applicable deductions and indicates a net salary for each employee.

(5) In the accounts payable department, payment for these office workers' salaries is prepared from the payroll sheets.

INTERNAL CONTROL FOR CASH

Where currency is available, internal control is needed the most. Incoming checks may be used in manipulating accounts receivable and must be controlled. Accounts receivable control becomes part of cash control, and vice versa. Cash disbursements and petty cash also need special internal controls. The details on internal control for these cash or cash-connected items follow.

Cash Receipts

(1) In the selling department, cash sales should be recorded in a register. A numbered sales slip should be made up for each sale. These slips should be used in numerical order.

(2) In the cashier's department, an employee should count the cash in each register at the end of the day. Except for a small amount left to make change, all cash should be removed. The total daily cash receipts should be recorded on slips and placed in the same pouch as the cash itself. The pouch should then be turned over to a clerk (a different employee from the one who counted the cash in the register) who will make out a bank deposit slip. Still another clerk in the cashier's department should read the cash register totals of the day or remove the cash sales slips. The cash removed from the register must agree with the tape and the total of cash slips which are numbered sequentially (all numbers must have been accounted for). The sales readings are then compared with the amount of cash removed from the registers by the cashier. Small discrepancies are charged to a cash, short or over account. Larger discrepancies call for an explanation.

(3) In the accounts receivable department, incoming mail should be opened by a bonded clerk. All checks, currency, money orders are listed by this clerk on a cash-received record. The cash-received record lists date of receipt, name of sender and amount. The record and totals are then sent to the accounts receivable department to be properly applied to the customers' accounts. The cash is sent to the cashier's office and subsequently given to the deposit clerk.

(4) In the accounts receivable department, the record of cash received is used to credit against customers' accounts. This record then goes to the general accounting department where it is compared with daily deposit slips of cash received from customers before it is entered on the books.

The departments involved in internal control of cash receipts are selling, treasury or cashier's and accounts receivable.

Cash Disbursements

In the accounts payable department, purchase of any item must have prior approval from the authorized person in charge of the department in which the expenditure originates before it comes to the accounts payable department. Where a voucher system is in operation, vouchers are prepared for each expenditure. Information on the voucher matches that shown on the seller's invoice. Vouchers are entered in the voucher register after having been approved by the head of the voucher department and then placed in a pending file for future payments.

The departments involved in the internal control of cash disbursements are accounts payable and voucher.

Petty Cash

In any department where it is necessary to have a petty cash fund, at least two individuals should have the responsibility for handling petty cash. One individual inspects and approves the item for payment. The other has charge of the petty cash fund and pays the vouchers as they are presented. Each petty cash voucher should list the date, amount paid and name of the account to be charged. A bill or other receipt, if there is one, should be attached to the voucher. The employee who controls the petty cash fund should compare the receipts attached to the petty cash vouchers with the vouchers.

When the petty cash fund needs reimbursement, the person who controls the fund totals those petty cash vouchers which have been paid out and presents them to the accounts payable department, which then arranges for the necessary reimbursement.

The departments involved in the internal control of petty cash are selling, administrative, or others in which there is a need for such petty cash funds, and accounts payable.

Accounts Receivable

Copies of sales slips from the sales department are used to charge customers' accounts. Copies of any credits due customers come from the sales department. These records are sent to the accounts receivable department, where, if possible, one clerk should have the responsibility for entering only debits to customers' accounts and another for posting credits for returned merchandise, receipt of a note, etc. Still a third employee should enter the credit in the customer's account for cash received.

Sending statements at the end of each month is a good way to check the accuracy of the customer's accounts.

The departments responsible for internal control of accounts receivable are the accounts receivable and sales.

Notes Receivable

In the treasury department, a record of notes held from customers is made. A record is then sent to the accounts receivable division where a clerk makes the proper credits. A copy is sent to the general accounting department to reflect the charge to the control account—notes receivable. The treasurer keeps the notes until maturity date or until discounted with the bank. A subsidiary note register should be kept if the company receives a large number of such notes.

The departments responsible for internal control of notes receivable are treasury and accounts receivable.

Cash and Bank Reconciliations

Cash is the lifeblood of the company. It is the center upon which the whole circle of business activity is pivoted. Here is the reservoir into which all flows—in and out.

It is surprising to find that tests of cash receipts and cash disbursements are usually limited by management (through intermediaries) to monthly bank reconciliations.

Nothing is more effective than unannounced, non-routine, spot-tests of the cash-handling procedures (for that matter, *any* business procedure) by the highest working or non-working authority within the company. Think of the impact made on an employee when he *knows* he may be facing an impromptu test of his work by the president of the company—at any time! Called in, for example, to explain the purpose of a canceled check he now holds; imagine the psychological impact if this is done periodically, but irregularly? A test of application of payments on account—receivables and payables—almost any awareness of constant high-level review has an alerting effect. Peak, honest, performance is encouraged.

Bank reconciliations by and of themselves can not stand alone as proof of cash authenticity. They prove only the activity *within* that one period and serve to lend to prior reconciliations substantiation of then-listed outstanding checks. The current reconciliation is technically unproved until the outstanding checks and uncredited deposits in transit appear.

Reconciliations should be tested by someone other than the original preparer.

Block-proofs of cash should also be used occasionally to test an entire year's transactions. Here, all deposits are matched to all receipts recorded (in total); and all recorded disbursements are matched to total bank charges for cleared checks and minor items, with consideration, of course, given to opening and closing transit items.

The theory behind the mechanics of the bank reconciliation is to *update* the *bank* figures (on a worksheet) to reflect all transit items which have not yet cleared the bank, as follows:

Bank shows a balance of	$ 10,500
Add deposits in transit	2,000
	12,500
Less checks outstanding (itemized)	600
Adjusted bank balance	$ 11,900
Balance per books shows	$ 11,909
Difference	$ 9 (more on books)

Having taken the preliminary steps of determining the deposits in transit (by checking the bank credits against recorded receipts) and the outstanding checks (by checking off all returned canceled checks against the listing of those issued or carried over), we note a remaining difference of $9.

In *order*, the following are the *most expedient* ways of finding this difference:

1. Look at the bank statement for any bank charge (D/M's or combination)—not yet recorded in the general ledger;
2. Look at the books for any $9 debit (or combination) on the books and not on the statement;
3. $9 may be indicative of a transposition. Match the bank's opening pickup balance to the closing one on the last statement:
   Match deposits to receipts recorded;
   Check general ledger footings and subtraction;
   Check summary postings into the general ledger from the original source;
   Check footings in the books of original entry (Receipts, Disbursements, General Journal);
4. Having exhausted the above possibilities and still not having found the difference, check the face amount of each check to the amount charged by the bank (each check is canceled with a clearance date).
5. Now match your own listing of the check to the actual check. (Steps 4 and 5 are interchangeable).
6. Not yet? Prove the bank's additions.
7. If still elusive, you've probably missed it above or made a transposition error in listing transit checks or deposits; or, it may be an error made last month which was missed.

FILE MAINTENANCE

One of the most important, yet least emphasized, facets of the business enterprise is the establishment and proper maintenance of an effective, accurate filing system. How costly is the time wasted in frustrating searches for misfiled data, when initial precautions and firm rules might have assured quick access to and retrieval of needed documents by competent, authorized personnel!

Suggestions

Establish firm rules for filing.

Provide adequate accessible filing space for current files.

Pinpoint responsibilities for filing and accessing files.

Follow legal requirements for record retention. Establish an annual policy of removing out-dated files.

Utilize flow charts when appropriate.

Have sufficient copies of documents such as purchase orders, sales shipping papers, and all papers ultimately tied to a sales or vendor's invoice, to allow for a complete numerical file of each document.

A List of File Categories

Sales invoices to customers—both alphabetic and numeric files;

Vendor invoices—alphabetic, sometimes with copy of paid voucher check or numbered voucher. Some firms keep invoices segregated in an "unpaid" file until paid;

Canceled checks—keep by month in reconciled batches. Do not intermingle different batches;

Correspondence files—for customers, vendors, others;

Permanent files—organizational information, legal documents, leases, minutes, deeds, etc. Usually in fireproof areas, accessibility limited.

Other:

Tax files

Payroll and personnel files

Backup for journal entries

Investment files—security transactions

Petty cash voucher files

Purchasing department files—supplies, bids, etc. (costs)

Credit department files

Prior years' books of entry

Data from subsidiary companies owned

Advertising programs, literature, etc.

Computer Files—Considerations

1. Security protection—access, codes, permanent tapes/ discs of programs, updated balance files for accounts receivables, payables, general ledger,

payrolls. Keep enough of these changing files for re-runs or accumulation runs, as needed for emergencies.

2. Keep hard copy until sure replacement hard copy is accurate, or as necessary for continuous file.
3. Be prepared for manual emergency work, if computer goes down suddenly.
4. Pinpoint responsibility for keeping logs, storage, etc.

One of the most significant developments in public accounting in recent years is the provision in the Foreign Corrupt Practices Act of 1977 (FCPA) requiring publicly-held companies to develop and maintain a system of internal accounting controls sufficient to provide:

1. That transactions are executed in accordance with management's general or specific authorization.
2. That transactions are recorded as necessary to permit preparation of financial statements in conformity with generally accepted accounting principles, or any other criteria applicable to such statements.
3. That the system maintains accountability for assets.
4. That access to assets is permitted only in accordance with management's general or specific authorization.
5. That the recorded accountability for assets is compared with existing assets at reasonable intervals, with appropriate action taken with respect to any difference.

Auditor's Objective: The significance of the Act, insofar as auditors are concerned, is the explicit statutory recognition given to accounting controls. The auditor's objective is to plan the examination to search for errors or irregularities that would have a material effect on the financial statements, and to use skill and care in the examination of the client's internal control system. While the independent auditor is not part of a company's internal accounting control system, the auditor must evaluate the effectiveness and monitor compliance of internal accounting control systems.

INTERNAL CONTROLS FOR A SMALL BUSINESS ENTERPRISE

There are many definitions of a "small business." The most commonly accepted one is the U.S. Department of Commerce classification of an enterprise of less than 500 employees as a small business concern. Using this definition there is something over 5 million nonagricultural small business establishments in the United States.

In a small business organization of only a few people, little reliance can be placed on internal controls involving a segregation of duties such as among several persons in a large organization. However, that is no excuse to ignore the importance of some degree of internal controls; rather, limited personnel with a few wearing more than one hat and associated with the handling of a company's money can be the reason for a review of the need and the establishment of the control function.

A plan of organization which provides at least a limited segregation of functional responsibilities within the constraint of limited staff should be developed. In a small business the segregation is not so much between employees as between the owner and employees. An alert and able owner can provide about as much control as the segregation of duties does in a large organization.

The owner of a small business usually is the key person in its management. Different from a large organization, the small business person represents one of the effective components of a control system, e.g., that of *personal observation*. Principally, the owner can personally focus attention upon selective areas of the business. One example would be reconciling the bank statement—one of the prime areas of control for a manager with limited time.

The selection of a few areas for control is an important step. A tendency to over-control must be avoided in order to avoid a negative cost-benefit allocation of time and expense. There is no need to control pencils and paper clips; the effort should be directed toward areas where the risk of error and material loss are greatest. Careful evaluation can uncover areas over which no control is exercised, but which are significant enough to establish procedures for their control.

The checklist which follows has been developed by the authors as an economic and simplified guide for the responsible person in a small business to conduct periodic internal audits for the implementation and continuous review of the activities in the various areas of the business. From this checklist, which includes the significant areas of any business, can be selected those areas most important to the individual user. While a small business does not need accounting controls as sophisticated and expensive as those of a large company, neither can a small business be lax and informal with respect to procedures that can prevent possible mismanagement of assets or even embezzlement or fraud. The checklist, itself, is a set of procedures that can be a suitable system.

AN INTERNAL CONTROLS CHECKLIST
FOR SMALL BUSINESS

(After selecting the areas that are considered to be necessary for some degree of control, the user can refer a few pages back for additional detail for each item selected).

Question	Remarks	N/A	Yes	No
GENERAL				
1. Are accounting records kept up-to-date and balanced monthly?		——	——	——
2. Is a standard chart of accounts with descriptive titles in use?		——	——	——
3. Are adequate and timely reports prepared to insure control of operations:				
a. Daily reports		——	——	——
b. Monthly financial statements		——	——	——
c. Ratio analysis such as C/S or gross profit?		——	——	——
d. Comparison of actual results with budget		——	——	——
e. Cash and other projections		——	——	——
4. Does the owner/Board take an active interest in the financial affairs and reports available?		——	——	——
5. Are personal expenses kept separate from business expenses?		——	——	——
6. Are employees who are in a position of trust bonded?		——	——	——
7. Are director/employees required to take annual vacations and are their duties covered by another?		——	——	——
8. Are monthly bank reconciliations reviewed by owner/director?		——	——	——
9. Do employees appear to be technically competent?		——	——	——
10. Are job descriptions prepared?		——	——	——
11. Are volunteers properly trained and supervised?		——	——	——
12. Is there any separation of duties?		——	——	——
13. Is there utilization of machine accounting and/or EDP in the preparation of financial reports accounts receivable, etc.?		——	——	——
14. Are Minutes up to date and complete?		——	——	——
15. Are transactions with stockholders at arms' length?		——	——	——
16. Are governmental reporting requirements being complied with in a timely manner?		——	——	——
17. Is insurance maintained in all major cases and is this coverage reviewed periodically by a qualified individual?		——	——	——

Question	Remarks	N/A	Yes	No

Conclusions:

CASH RECEIPTS

1. Is mail opened by director/owner or someone other than the bookkeeper?

2. Are receipts taped or listed prior to turning them over to the bookkeeper, and are they subsequently traced to the cash receipts journal?

3. Does the client have adequate documentation of cash receipts?

4. Are checks immediately endorsed for deposit only, deposited promptly and intact?

5. Are over the counter receipts controlled by cash register, prenumbered receipts etc., and are these reviewed by owner/ director?

6. Are checks returned by the bank followed up for subsequent disposition?

Conclusions:

INVENTORIES

1. Are perpetual inventories maintained?

2. Are they verified periodically by someone not normally in charge of inventories?

3. Where perpetual records are not in use:

   a. Are periodic physical counts taken by responsible employees?

   b. Is owner exercising control by review of gross profit margins?

Question	Remarks	N/A	Yes	No
4. Are physical facilities such as to discourage pilferage by employees and others?		——	——	——
5. Are off-premises inventories controlled?		——	——	——
6. Is customers' merchandise on the premises physically segregated and under accounting control?		——	——	——
7. Are inventories reviewed periodically for old, obsolete, or excessive items?		——	——	——

ACCOUNTS RECEIVABLE & SALES

Question	Remarks	N/A	Yes	No
1. Are work orders, sales orders, shipping documents and invoices prenumbered and controlled?		——	——	——
2. Would the existing system disclose shipments being made without recording a sale? (Sales on consignment, samples, etc.)		——	——	——
3. Is a credit check approved by owner?		——	——	——
4. Are sales invoices reviewed for price, terms, extensions and footings?		——	——	——
5. Is an aged trial balance prepared monthly, reconciled to the general ledger, and reviewed by the owner?		——	——	——
6. Are monthly statements:				
a. Reviewed by owner?		——	——	——
b. Mailed to all accounts?		——	——	——
c. Are zero and credit balance statements mailed?		——	——	——
7. Are write-offs, credit memos and special terms approved by the owner/director?		——	——	——
8. Is there sufficient separation of the receipts function and the application of payments to the accounts receivable?		——	——	——
9. Are notes and other receivables under separate control?		——	——	——
10. If there are any pledges receivable:				
a. Are they properly recorded?		——	——	——
b. Is there collection follow-up?		——	——	——

Question	Remarks	N/A	Yes	No
c. Are write-offs properly approved?		___	___	___
11. Is pricing of sales invoices from standard price lists?		___	___	___
12. Are variations from standard prices approved by owner/director?		___	___	___
13. Do adequate controls exist to assure receipts from miscellaneous sales (scrap, fixed assets, rents, vending machines, etc.)?		___	___	___

Conclusions:

_____

_____

	Remarks	N/A	Yes	No
ACCOUNTS PAYABLE, PURCHASES, DISBURSEMENTS				
1. Are prenumbered purchase orders used and are these approved by owner/director?		___	___	___
2. Are competitive bids required above prescribed limits?		___	___	___
3. Are payments made from original invoices?		___	___	___
4. Are supplier statements compared with recorded liabilities?		___	___	___
5. Are all disbursements made by prenumbered checks?		___	___	___
6. Is the owner/director's signature required on all checks?				
a. Does he sign checks only when they are accompanied by original supporting documentation?		___	___	___
b. Is the documentation adequately cancelled to prevent reuse?		___	___	___
7. Is there evidence that the following items have been checked before invoices are paid?				
a. Prices, discounts, sales tax		___	___	___
b. Extensions and footings		___	___	___
c. Receipt of goods or services		___	___	___
d. Account distribution		___	___	___

Question	Remarks	N/A	Yes	No
8. Are voided checks retained and accounted for?		——	——	——
9. Is there an imprest petty cash fund?		——	——	——
a. If so, is there a responsible employee designated as a custodian of the fund?		——	——	——

Conclusions:

_____

_____

INVESTMENTS				
1. Does owner have sole access to certificates, notes, etc.?		——	——	——
2. In case of non-profit organizations:				
a. Is dual control exercised over certificates?		——	——	——
b. Is there a written investment policy?		——	——	——
c. Does the board approve sales and purchases?		——	——	——
d. Is the return on investment checked periodically by the board?		——	——	——
3. Is there effective utilization of temporary excess funds?		——	——	——
4. Is income from investments accounted for periodically?		——	——	——

Conclusions:

_____

_____

PROPERTY, PLANT & EQUIPMENT				
1. Are there detailed, and updated records to support general ledger totals for assets and accumulated depreciation?		——	——	——
2. Is the owner/Board acquainted with assets owned, and is approval required for sale or acquisition?		——	——	——
3. Are there physical safeguards against theft or loss of small tools and other highly portable equipment?		——	——	——

Question	Remarks	N/A	Yes	No
4. Is there a policy distinguishing capital and expense items?		——	——	——

Conclusions:

_____

_____

PAYROLL				
1. Is owner/director acquainted with all employees and does he approve all new hires and changes of pay rates?		——	——	——
2. Is there a folder for each employee that contains an employment application, W-4, authorizations for deductions, etc.?		——	——	——
3. Are there controls to prevent the payroll from being inflated without the knowledge of owner/ director either by fictitious employees or padded hours?		——	——	——
4. Does the owner/director sign all payroll checks?		——	——	——
5. If payroll is prepared by a bank or service bureau, does the owner/director periodically review each check and related journals prior to distribution to employees?		——	——	——
a. Are unusable checks properly voided or redeposited?		——	——	——
6. Is the payroll bank reconciliation prepared by someone other than the bookkeeper?		——	——	——
7. Is the payroll paid from a separate imprest bank account?		——	——	——

Conclusions:

_____

_____

_____

REVIEW OF THE CHECKLIST

Review the checklist and record below the items and comments that appear to need attention both with respect to increased control and improved efficiency.

1. _____

_____

_____

Question	Remarks	N/A	Yes	No
2. _____				
3. _____				
4. _____				
5. _____				

EMBEZZLEMENT—ITS PREVENTION

Definition: Embezzlement is the fraudulent appropriation of property by a person whom management has *trusted*. ''Trusted'' is the key word.

A company can be losing money before suspecting that an embezzlement might be taking place, because this crime is usually committed by someone in a position of trust. Losses can be a small amount taken from a cash register, or a large sum of money stolen through manipulating the books. A set of simple controls built into the accounting system can prevent an embezzling operation. At the least proper controls can document incriminating evidence, in the absence of which it would be difficult to estimate a loss for insurance purposes, or to prove in the courts that the losses resulted from a crime.

This discussion reviews procedures for the detection and prevention of dishonest practices. It can be helpful first to understand a few of the usual methods that embezzlers commonly use to divert company funds to their own pockets. Such an understanding can be a framework for developing the record-keeping and control procedures to safeguard the company's money and other property vulnerable to misappropriation by an employee. (In general, however, an embezzler's methods are limited only by his creativity.)

1. By definition an embezzler is usually a trusted employee enjoying the complete confidence of his employer. Usually, the embezzler has authority in such important areas as managing the checkbook. The easiest opportunity is sales for cash with no recording of the transaction in the books and no relevant paperwork. Prenumbered invoices or simply cash register receipts can be used for all sales with appropriate monitoring procedures to assure that cash sales are being recorded. Also, when employees know written records are maintained, the temptation to embezzle is lessened.

2. A complicated method of embezzlement is termed *lapping*. Lapping involves temporarily withholding receipts, such as payments by a customer on ac-

counts receivable, and is a continuing process that usually starts with a small amount and runs into thousands of dollars before it is detected.

Example: An employee opens mail or receives cash and checks as payment on open accounts. The employee pockets a $100 cash payment by a customer named Paul. To avoid Paul complaining at a later time about failure for his account to be credited, $100 is next taken from a *$200* subsequent payment by a customer named Peter and credited to Paul's account and the embezzler pockets the $100 difference. (Note that the amount pyramids; it has to in order for the embezzler to continue to profit.) The lapping procedure continues with the employee absconding with increasingly larger amounts of money involving a steadily increasing number of customer accounts.

Prevention requires detailed recordkeeping procedures of invoices and other supporting working papers and periodic unscheduled audits of the accounts, along with confirmation of accounts receivables. Without adequate procedures, detection of lapping is difficult and can continue for years. One red flag, however, is the discovery that an employee is keeping personal records of transactions outside of the established accounting system. Another indication that is a common practice is for an embezzler to decline vacations, and even leave the premises for lunch. Many companies require employees responsible for funds management to take regular vacations with the substitute employee discovering irregularities.

3. *Check-kiting* is one of the most popular operations in small and large companies alike. For a successful check-kiting operation, the employee must be in the position both to write checks and to make deposits in two or more bank accounts. One account is the embezzler's personal account and the other is the business checking account.

The check-kiter plays the *float*: e.g., the number of days between the deposit of a check and collection of funds. There may be several days between the date when a check drawn on Bank A is deposited in Bank B and the date the check clears Bank A for payment. A simple kite is accomplished simply by cashing a check at Bank B and covering the morning of the day the check is expected to reach Bank A. As the process is repeated the kited checks become increasingly large, more cash is withdrawn from Bank B and the kiting continues as long as the shortage is covered on time in Bank A. Finally, the kite "breaks"; this is when Bank A refuses to honor a check because the funds on deposit are insufficient to cover the kited check, or because the check reached Bank A a day earlier than usual.

A temporary kite can be used by a dishonest employee who has stolen cash in a separate operation. The cash shortage can be concealed at the end of an accounting period by depositing a kited check into the company account. This deposit brings the bank balance into reconciliation with the book balance on the statement date.

The best preventive measure against kiting (or to detect suspected kiting) is for the owner of the business to request "cut-off" statements from the bank at periodic intervals which, in turn, should be irregular intervals.

4. Payroll frauds are a frequent source of loss. The usual practice is to add the names of relatives or fictitious individuals to the company payroll, enabling the em-

bezzler to draw several weekly paychecks instead of one. The best preventive measure is a policy that no person is added to the payroll without the personal authorization of the owner, or a responsible personnel manager in the organization. Also, frequent and regular payroll audits can reveal more pay checks being drawn than the company has employees.

5. A typical embezzling procedure is for the dishonest employee to open an account on the books for a dummy supplier and issue checks to the nonexistent supplier for fictitious purchases. Established purchase procedures and an inventory controls system can discourage an employee from using false vouchers to process purchases of nonexistent merchandise.

There are a number of clues that can alert the owner or manager of a business to suspect dishonest practices.

- An unusual increase in sales returns can conceal accounts receivable payments.
- Unusual bad-debt write-offs can cover a fraudulent practice.
- A decline in credit sales that is unusual can indicate possible unrecorded sales.
- Unexpected large drop in profits or increase in expenses can be a red flag.
- An increasing rate of slow collections of receivables can conceal an embezzlement.

In addition to an accounting system that incorporates a system of internal controls, there are a number of precautions an owner can take to reduce the possibility of fraudulent losses.

- Careful checks of prospective employees' background.
- Know the employees' personal lifestyles, insofar as possible.
- Have company mail addressed to a post office box, and only the owner has access to the box.
- Have only the owner or a key person collect and open company mail.
- The owner can be the only person to manage the funds, write checks, and make deposits.
- Examine periodically all cancelled checks, especially the endorsements on them.
- Unusual discounts and bad-debt write-offs should be approved by the owner, or manager.
- All employees responsible for company funds should be bonded.
- If possible, the preparation of the payroll and payment of employees should be done by different persons, especially if cash is disbursed on payday.
- Avoid the *cardinal* sin—*Never sign blank checks!* Not even to your *Mother*.

5

Business Combinations

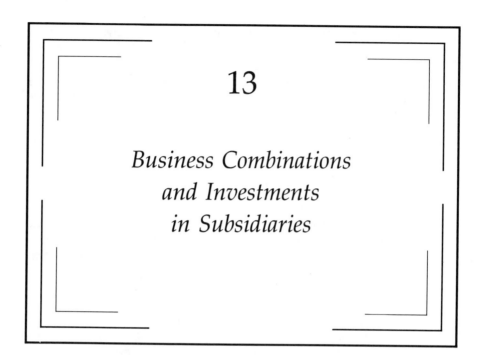

13

Business Combinations and Investments in Subsidiaries

BUSINESS COMBINATIONS AND ACQUISITIONS

This section deals with the *accounting* treatment of dealings involved with the following types of business combinations and acquisitions:

1. Those *combinations* occurring when a corporation and one or more *incorporated* or *unincorporated* businesses *are united into one* accounting entity, with that single entity then carrying on the activities of the prior separate entities. Two methods of accounting are applicable here:
   A. The Purchase Method, or
   B. The Pooling of Interests Method.
2. Those *stock acquisitions* (or stock investments) wherein one corporation *buys the voting common stock* of another corporation—sometimes acquiring voting control, sometimes not—with both entities continuing as separate, individual, distinct operating corporations. Three methods of accounting are applicable here:
   A. The Consolidation Method (or the alternate Combining Method),
   B. The Equity Method, or
   C. The Cost Method.

In each of these methods, the investment in the subsidiary's stock appears on the books of the owning company as an investment asset.

In order to clarify the distinctions involved—as a quick reference—these major points should be considered:

1. Consolidation, the Equity Method and the Cost Method all pertain to the acquisition of *voting stock* by the buying company.

   Pooling and Purchase pertain to the acquisition of *assets* and usually liabilities (inventory, plant, equipment, etc.).

2. How to distinguish between pooling and purchase:

   A. With *pooling*, the *acquiring* company uses its *own capital stock* to exchange for the capital stock of the acquired company. For example, a stockholder of Company B (the *acquired* company) will, after pooling, hold stock in Company A, the acquiring company. Company B's stock will have been cancelled. Or, a third Company C might be formed with both A & B companies folding into Company C. Pooling is usually a tax-free combination, provided all requirements are met.

   B. With *purchase*, the acquiring company buys the assets (usually net of liabilities), and the acquired company (the one selling the assets) must usually account for gain or loss on the sale of the individual assets, involving the recapture provisions of the tax law.

   C. Pooling involves the exchange of stock. Purchase can involve either stock, cash or property.

   D. In *purchase*, the assets are valued at *fair value*, usually creating goodwill. In *pooling*, there is no change in asset value, since they are picked up at net *book* value.

   E. Under both pooling and purchase, the acquired company is subsequently liquidated.

   F. A combination of *both* methods is unacceptable.

3. With *stock acquisitions*, all companies continue separate operations even though under new ownership or managerial control. Accounting records are maintained for each distinct company, and each company prepares financial statements independent of the other company. However, public release of those statements is guided by the rules of consolidation or the equity method.

4. With stock acquisitions:

   A. Use the *cost method* when owning less than 20% of the stock *and* exercising *no* effective managerial control.

   B. Use the *equity method* when owning 20% or more (influence is presumed)—or when owning less than 20% *but with substantial managerial* influence. Also, use the equity method when owning *over 50%* and *not using the consolidation method*.

   C. Use the *consolidation method* when ownership is *over 50%* (majority interest), *unless* conditions exist (described later) which constitute exception to the rules of consolidation and permit the use of the equity method.

D. An acquiring enterprise should account for contingencies that can be reasonably estimated and considered probable as an allocation to the purchase price of the acquired company.

Note that financial accounting (and the SEC) require consolidation for over 50% holdings, with exceptions noted, but the IRS requires a minimum 80% voting control for consolidated tax returns.

Consolidation must also be used for subsidiaries whose principal activity is leasing property or facilities to the parent or other affiliates.

FASB Statement No. 94, *Consolidation of All Majority-Owned Subsidiaries*, eliminates most of the exceptions from consolidation formerly permitted by Accounting Research Bulletin No. 51, *Consolidated Financial Statements*. The most significant exception that has been eliminated is the ''nonhomogeneity exception,'' i.e., excluding majority-owned subsidiaries whose business is unrelated to either the business of the parent or of other members of the consolidated group. Essentially, Statement No. 94 permits only two exceptions: 1) subsidiaries under *temporary* control, and 2) subsidiaries *not* controlled by the majority owner.

When *not* using consolidation, and the holdings are over 50%, the equity method must be used for all unconsolidated subsidiaries (foreign as well as domestic).

When holdings are 50% or under, down to 20%, you must use the equity method, since significant managerial voice is presumed (unless you prove the contrary).

Further details of each of these methods are now presented.

THE COST METHOD—STOCK ACQUISITIONS

The cost method: An investor records an investment in the stock of an investee at cost, and recognizes as income dividends received that are distributed from net accumulated earnings of the investee, since the date of acquisition by the investor.

Dividends from the investee's earnings are entered as income;

Dividends in *excess* of investee's earnings after date of investment reduce the cost of the investment;

Losses of the investee (after acquisition) should be recognized under the ''marketable security'' standards.

For the investor, under the *cost method*, dividends only are to be picked up as income (with cash being debited).

THE EQUITY METHOD—STOCK ACQUISITIONS

The equity method: An investor initially records an investment in the stock of an investee at cost and adjusts the carrying amount of the investment to recognize the investor's share of the earnings or losses of the investee after the date of the acquisition. The amount of the adjustment is included in the determination of net income by the investor, and such amount reflects adjustments similar to those made in preparing consolidated statements including adjustments to eliminate intercompany gains and losses, and to amortize, if appropriate, any difference between investor cost and underlying equity in net assets of the investee at the date of the investment.

Proportionate share of earnings, whether distributed or not, increases the carrying amount of the investment and is recorded as income;

Dividends reduce the carrying amount of the investment and are *not* recorded as income;

After investment, a series of losses by the investee may necessitate additional reduction in the carrying amount.

Under the equity method, the proportionate share of earnings (losses) of the investee (subsidiary) is picked up as income (loss), with the investment asset account being debited (or credited for a loss). Dividends, when received, are thus merely a conversion of part of that increased investment value to cash.

Both the investment and the share of earnings are recorded as single amounts. Market devaluation is *not* applicable.

The Equity Method Should Be Used (For Foreign or Domestic Subsidiaries):

1. When owning *20% or more* of the voting stock of the investee (significant control is presumed); or
2. When owning *less than 20%* and the investor can demonstrate the exercise of significant control; or
3. When not consolidating those investees in which more than 50% is owned; but the equity method should not be used if consolidation is justified; or
4. For participant's share of joint ventures.

The equity method *should not* be used:

1. When consolidation is proper for over 50% control; or
2. When ownership is below 20% and there is *no* demonstrable control (use the cost method); or
3. When the principal business activity of the subsidiary is leasing property or facilities to the parent or other affiliates (consolidate instead).

"Voting stock interest" is based on the *outstanding* shares without recognition of common stock equivalents.

Applying the Equity Method

1. Follow the rules of intercompany profit and loss eliminations as for consolidations;

2. At purchase of stock, adjust investment to reflect underlying equity and amortize goodwill, if any;

3. Show investment as a single amount, and show income as a single amount, except for (4) below;

4. Show share of extraordinary items separately, net of tax;

5. Any capital structure change of the investee should be accounted for as in consolidations;

6. When stock is sold, account for gain or loss based on the carrying amount then in the investment account;

7. Use the investee's latest financial statement;

8. Recognize non-temporary declines in the value of the investee's stock by adjusting the investment account;

9. Do not write investment account below zero; hold over any losses until future gains offset them;

10. Before picking up share of investee's income, deduct any cumulative preferred dividends (paid or unpaid) not already deducted by the investee;

11. If the level of ownership falls to the point which ordinarily calls for the cost method, stop accruing earnings undistributed, but apply dividends received to the investment account;

12. If changing from the cost method to the equity method for any one investment (because of change in ownership), make the necessary retroactive adjustments;

13. If goodwill is created in (12) above, it should be amortized.

Equity Method: A method of accounting by a parent company for investments in subsidiaries in which the parent's share of subsidiary income (or loss) is recorded in the parent company's accounts.

The accounting procedures for the equity method follow:

Investment—X Co.	275,000	
Cash		275,000
(To record the purchase of 25% of X Co. stock at cost; 25,000 shares @ $11.00)		
Investment—X Co.	40,000	
Goodwill		40,000
(Additional equity in X Co. at date of acquisition)		
Cash	5,000	
Investment—X Co.		5,000
(To record receipt of 20. per share cash dividend from X Co.).		
Investment—X Co.	27,500	
Investment from Parent share of X Co. undistributed earnings.		25,000

Income from Parent share of X Co.		
undistributed extraordinary item.		2,500
(To record 25% of X Co. net income of		
$100,000 from continuing operations and		
$10,000 extraordinary income; total income		
$110,000.)		
Income Tax Expense (on operation)	12,500	
Income Tax Expense (Extra. item)	1,250	
Deferred Taxes		13,750
(To record 50% of reported income as accrued		
taxes.)		

The following entry is made for the depreciation of the excess of fair value of assets less book value of the acquired assets:

Equity of Earnings of Investee	xxxx	
Investment in Investee		xxxx

Income Taxes

1. Set up a deferred tax based on the investor's proportion of the subsidiary's net income (after tax), based on the investor's rate of tax, *unless*: If it appears that the *undistributed earnings* of the investee meet the *indefinite reversal criteria* (see elsewhere in this text), do *not* accrue taxes, but make disclosure.
2. For dividends received, pull applicable tax out of deferred taxes and put in tax payable account;
3. Disclose applicable timing differences.

(See also Journal Entries in Appendix A, Timing Differences and Disclosures in this text.)

THE CONSOLIDATION METHOD—STOCK ACQUISITIONS

There is a presumption that consolidated statements are more meaningful than separate statements and that they are usually necessary for a fair presentation when one of the companies in the group directly or indirectly has a controlling financial interest in the other companies.

Assets, liabilities, revenues and expenses of the subsidiaries are combined with those of the parent company. Intercompany items are eliminated.

Earned surplus of a subsidiary company from *prior* to acquisition does *not* form part of the parent's consolidated earned surplus, and dividends therefrom do not constitute income.

The purpose of consolidated statements is to present the financial data as if it were one single unit.

Rule for Consolidation

The usual condition for a controlling financial interest is ownership of a majority voting interest and, therefore, as a general rule ownership by one company, directly or indirectly, of over 50% of the outstanding voting shares of another company is a condition pointing toward consolidation.

Do *not* consolidate:

1. When control is likely to be temporary; or
2. Where control does *not* rest with the *majority* holder (example: subsidiary is in reorganization or bankruptcy); or
3. Usually, for foreign subsidiaries (See later in this chapter); or
4. Where subsidiary is in a dissimilar business (manufacturer vs. financing); or
5. When the equity method or the cost method is more appropriate for the four conditions named above.

Note that the equity method should *usually* be used for all majority-held subsidiaries which are not consolidated, unless the cost method is necessitated by lack of influential control.

Foreign subsidiaries come under special standards and cost (with proper disclosure) may sometimes be used. (See later in this chapter.)

Other Considerations

A difference in fiscal period is no excuse for *not* consolidating. When the difference is no more than 3 months, use the subsidiary's fiscal-period report. Where greater than 3 months, corresponding period statements should be prepared for the subsidiary.

Intercompany items should be eliminated. (See later in this chapter.)

For partial years:

1. The year of acquisition: Consolidate for the year and, on income statement, deduct pre-acquisition earnings not applicable to the parent.
2. The year of disposition: do not consolidate income; show only equity of parent in the subsidiary's earnings prior to disposal as a separate line item.

Shares held by the parent should *not* be treated as outstanding stock in the consolidation.

When a subsidiary capitalizes retained earnings for stock dividends or split-ups effected as dividends, such transfer is not required for the consolidated balance sheet which reflects the accumulated earnings and capitalization of the group (not the subsidiary).

Combined Statements

This is the showing of the individual company statements *plus* the combined consolidation, which combination reflects all intercompany eliminations.

Examples of when to use combined statements:

1. Where one individual owns controlling interest in several related corporations; or
2. Where several companies are under common management; or
3. To present the information of a group of unconsolidated subsidiaries; or
4. When it is necessary to show the individual operations of parent as well as subsidiaries, as well as the consolidated results—for creditors usually. This type is also called a "Parent-Company" statement.
5. A subsidiary whose primary business is leasing to a parent should always be consolidated.

Limitations of Consolidated Statements

Along with their advantages, consolidated statements have certain limitations:

1. The separate financial position of each company is not disclosed.
2. The dividend policy of each company cannot be ascertained.
3. Any financial ratios derived from the consolidated statements are only averages and do not represent any particular company.
4. A consolidated income statement does not show which companies have been operating at a profit and which have been losing money.
5. Creditors who are concerned with the financial resources of individual companies would not get the information they desire.
6. Disclosing liens or other particulars of individual companies may require extensive footnotes.

(See Journal Entries, Appendix A, for example of Consolidating Entries.)

THE PURCHASE METHOD—BUSINESS COMBINATIONS

The Purchase Method accounts for a business combination as the acquisition of one company by another. The acquiring company records at its cost the acquired assets less liabilities assumed. A difference between the cost of an acquired company and the sum of the fair values of tangible and intangible assets less liabilities is recorded as goodwill. The reported income of an acquiring corporation includes the operations of the acquired company after acquisition, based on the cost to the acquiring corporation.

The financial statements should be supplemented after purchase with pro forma statements showing:

1. Results of operations for the current period as if the combination had occurred at the beginning of the period; and
2. Results for the immediately preceding period, presented as if they had combined.

The AICPA has listed some general guides for the assigning of values to certain individual items, as follows:

Receivables at present values of amounts to be received, less allowances for uncollectibles.

Marketable securities at net realizable values.

Inventories:

Finished goods at selling prices, less disposal costs and reasonable profit to the acquirer;

Work in process at selling price, less cost to complete, disposal cost and reasonable profit;

Raw materials at current replacement prices.

Plant and equipment at current replacement cost if to be used or, if to be disposed of, at net realizable value.

Intangibles (identifiable, excluding goodwill) at appraised values.

All other assets at appraised values (including land).

Accounts and notes payable, long-term debt and other claims payable at *present values*, using current rates.

Accruals at present values.

Other liabilities and commitments, at present values, determined by using appropriate current interest rates.

Goodwill should be amortized on a straight-line basis over a period not to exceed 40 years, and only to a shorter period if benefit can be pinpointed. Goodwill of the *acquired* company is not brought forward.

THE POOLING-OF-INTERESTS METHOD—BUSINESS COMBINATIONS

The pooling-of-interests method accounts for a business combination as the uniting of ownership interests of two or more companies by exchange of equity securities. No acquisition is recognized because the combination is accomplished without disbursing resources of the constituents. Ownership interests continue and the former bases of accounting are retained. The recorded assets and liabilities of the constituents are carried forward to the combined corporation at their recorded amounts. Income of the combined corporation includes income of the constituents for the entire fiscal period for which the combination occurs. The reported income of the constituents for prior periods is combined and restated as income of the combined corporations.

A pooling involves the combination of two or more stockholder interests which were previously *independent* of each other.

The AICPA has said that a business combination which meets *all* of the following 12 conditions should be accounted for as a pooling:

1. Attributes of the combining companies:
   A. Each is autonomous and not a subsidiary or division of any other company for the prior two years; and
   B. Each is independent (10 percent) of the other combining companies.
2. Manner of combining interests:
   A. Effected within one year in a single transaction per a specified plan; and
   B. The corporation issues only common stock identical with its majority outstanding voting stock in exchange for substantially all (90% or more) of the voting common stock of the acquired company at the date of consummation; and
   C. None of the combining companies changes the equity interest of the voting common stock in contemplation of the combination within two years *before* the plan or between the dates the combination is initiated and it is consummated; and
   D. No company re-acquires more than a normal number of shares and only for purposes other than for business combinations between the dates of initiation and consummation; and
   E. Legal costs of pooling are expensed; and
   F. The ratio of interest remains the same for each common stockholder, with nothing denied or surrendered, with respect to his proportion before the combination; and
   G. Stockholder voting rights are not restricted nor deprived of by the resulting combination; and
   H. The plan is resolved at the planned date and no provisions remain pending or carried over after the combination.
3. There is the absence of the following planned transactions:
   A. The combined corporation does not intend to retire or re-acquire any of the common stock issued to effect the combination; and
   B. The combination does not enter any financial arrangements to benefit former stockholders (such as a guaranty of loans secured by stock issued in the combination); and

C. There is no intent or plan to dispose of any of the assets of the combination within two years after the combination other than those in the ordinary course of business or to eliminate duplicate facilities of excess capacity.

Financial statements of the current period, and of any prior period, should be presented as though the companies had been combined at the earliest dates presented and for the periods presented.

Disclosure should cover all the relevant details.

Purchase Method

Accounts Receivable	50,000	
Inventory	40,000	
Building	110,000	
Equipment	30,000	
Investments	5,000	
Goodwill	16,200	
Accounts Payable		25,000
Long-Term Debt		30,000
Unamortized discount on long-term debt		(3,800)
Common Stock (Par $10; 10,000 Shares)		100,000
Additional Paid-In Capital		100,000

Entry to apply the purchase method to account for the purchase of XYZ Co. assets and liabilities for 10,000 shares of common stock. Total purchase price $200,000 based on market price of the stock at date of consummation of $20 per share.

Amortization of Goodwill (1/40)	405	
Goodwill		405
Unamortized discount on long-term debt	760	
Discount Income		760
(Goodwill amortized on straight-line basis.)		

Pooling Method

It must be recognized that the two methods are not alternatives and it should not be inferred that there is a choice of one or the other method. Rather, the pooling of interests method can be applied only when 12 restrictive criteria as set forth in APB Opinion No. 16 "Accounting for Business Combinations" are met. GAAP requires *compliance* with *all* 12 of the conditions. If one or more of the criteria is not met, the purchase method of accounting for the combination *must* be applied.

Inventory	43,000	
Cash	5,000	
Accounts Receivable	60,000	
Allowance for Doubtful Accounts		7,000
Building	75,000	
Accu. Depreciation		15,000
Equipment	100,000	
Accu. Depreciation		60,000
Investments	4,000	
Accounts Payable		25,500
Long-Term Debt		30,000
Common Stock (Par, $10; 10,000 shares)		100,000
Additional Paid-In Capital		49,500

(Entries to reflect the pooling of XYZ Co. per the *book* value of the *items* on the date of *consummation*.) Note: *Goodwill cannot* be acquired by the *pooling method*.

The principal difference between the different methods of business combinations is the resulting corporate entity. In an *acquisition* both the acquired and acquiring companies remain as separate legal entities after the combination, with the acquiring company being the *parent* and the acquired company the *subsidiary*. In a *merger* two or more companies combine and one legal entity results, which can be any one of the combining companies. In a *consolidation*, the combining companies form a new legal entity.

APB Opinion No. 16 prohibits the use of treasury stock transactions for a business combination when a pooling of interest method is used. Treasury stock purchases are restricted to be used for purposes other than for business combinations for a period of two years before and during the period of the combination plan. Treasury shares acquired during this period are "tainted" and only a very small number of treasury shares can be used in a pooling. The restrictions on treasury stock purchased after the start of a plan are to prevent backdoor agreements to buy out certain stockholders.

FOREIGN SUBSIDIARIES

The following are the possible methods of providing information about foreign subsidiaries:

1. Exclude foreign subsidiaries from consolidation. Include a summary of their assets, liabilities, income and losses for the year and the parent's equity in such foreign subsidiary. The amount of investment in the foreign subsidiary and the basis by which it was arrived should be shown. If the foreign subsidi-

ary is excluded from consolidation, it is not proper to include intercompany profits (losses) which would have been eliminated by consolidating.
2. Consolidate domestic and foreign subsidiaries furnishing information of the foreign subsidiaries' assets, liabilities, income and losses, as stated above.
3. Furnish complete consolidated statements:
A. Including only domestic companies, *and*
B. Including the foreign subsidiaries.
4. Consolidate domestic and foreign subsidiaries and furnish, in addition, parent company statements showing the investment in and income from foreign subsidiaries separately from those of domestic subsidiaries.

DISCS

A Domestic International Sales Corporation (DISC) is typically a 100%-owned domestic subsidiary corporation of a parent manufacturing or sales company, created especially for the purpose of benefiting from special tax provisions under IRS Code Section 991–997, and electing to be taxed thereunder.

The DISC income is derived predominantly (95% by tax law) from export sales and rentals. The primary accounting aspects are:

1) A DISC is a wholly owned *domestic* subsidiary and should be consolidated with the parent's financial statement (the IRS prohibits it for tax purposes).
2) Portions of the DISC's earnings are considered to be distributed by the IRS and taxable to the parent. Therefore, for accounting purposes, clear distinction should be made on the DISC's books setting up a "previously taxed dividend payable." The parent should set up a contra "previously taxed dividends receivable" until such time as the cash transfer is made.
3) For the remaining portion of the DISC's earnings, which are not deemed distributed but which will be picked up as part of the consolidated income, *no entry* should be made for the deferral of applicable income taxes, *unless* there is indication of impending distribution of those earnings. Since the main purpose of the DISC option is to *defer* taxability of those undistributed earnings, the presumption of non-distribution prevails, and the indefinite reversal criteria apply.

Changes in the Tax Law have replaced the DISC system with the Foreign Sales Corporation system (FSC) starting in 1985 (see Internal Revenue Code sections 921–927).

INTERCOMPANY TRANSACTIONS

In Consolidations:

Since consolidated statements reflect the position and results of operations of what is considered a single economic entity, all intercompany balances and transactions must be eliminated. Some of these are obvious. Others are not.

Here are some of the items to be eliminated (done on worksheets which combine the company and its subsidiary figures):

1. The investment account in the subsidiary and its corresponding equity offset (capital stock and applicable retained earnings).
2. Intercompany open account balances, such as loans, receivables, payables arising from intercompany sales and purchases.
3. Intercompany security holdings, such as bonds, including related bond discount or premiums.
4. Intercompany profits where goods or services are exchanged for over cost, such as profits on transfers of inventory or fixed assets. Intercompany profits on fixed asset transfers might also involve adjustments to the accumulated depreciation account. Intercompany profits on inventory may affect both opening and closing inventories of raw materials, work in process and finished goods, as well as cost of sales.
5. Intercompany dividends.
6. Intercompany interest, rents, and fees.
7. Intercompany bad debts.

The amount of intercompany profit or loss eliminated is not to be affected by the existence of minority interests. Such items must be eliminated. However, in eliminating them, they may be allocated proportionately between the majority and minority interests.

If "bottom-line" accumulated losses occur to the extent of wiping out the minority interest, any excess losses should then be reflected against the *majority* interest, rather than showing a negative minority interest. However, future earnings should then first be applied to that excessive loss and the positive remaining earnings apportioned between the majority and minority interests.

In the Equity Method

Intercompany gains and losses should be eliminated in the same manner as if the subsidiary were consolidated. It is not necessary to eliminate intercompany gain on sales to such subsidiaries if the gain on the sales does *not* exceed the *unrecorded* equity in the *undistributed* earnings of the unconsolidated subsidiary. However, do *not* eliminate intercompany holdings or debt.

In Combined Statements

Intercompany transactions and intercompany profits and losses should be eliminated following the same manner as for consolidated statements.

GOODWILL IN BUSINESS COMBINATIONS

Goodwill arises only from the purchase method; no goodwill is created in the "pooling-of-interests" method of combining businesses, since assets and liabilities are carried forward to the combined corporation at their recorded amounts.

With respect to the purchase method and stock acquisitions treated under either the consolidation method or the equity method, accounting for goodwill requires its amortization over a period not in excess of forty years.

Goodwill is the amount assigned to the excess paid over the fair value of the identifiable net assets acquired.

NEGATIVE GOODWILL

Negative Goodwill: When one company purchases another, negative goodwill arises where there is an excess of the assigned value of identifiable assets over the cost of an acquired company. The goodwill account has a credit balance. When the purchase price is less than the sum of the fair market value of the net assets acquired, the valuation of the noncurrent assets, except investments in Marketable Securities, must be reduced on a proportionate basis until the purchase price for the acquisition equals the adjusted valuation of the fair market value of the net assets acquired. If after the adjusted valuation of noncurrent assets is reduced to zero and the purchase price is still less than the net assets acquired, the difference is disclosed in the balance sheet as negative goodwill (a credit balance) and is amortized to income over a period not to exceed 40 years. (APB Opinion 16)

SUMMARY

Consolidated Financial Statements: The combination of the financial positions and earnings reports of the parent company with those of various subsidiaries into an overall statement as if they were a single entity, i.e., the financial statements should reflect a group of affiliated companies as a single business enterprise—a single economic entity. The consolidated statements are in substance summations of the assets, liabilities, revenues, and expenses of the individual affiliates calculated on the basis of transactions with nonaffiliates. Intercompany transactions (transactions among the affiliates), intercompany investments, and account balances must be eliminated to avoid double-counting of resources, account balances, and operating results.

6

Management
Principles

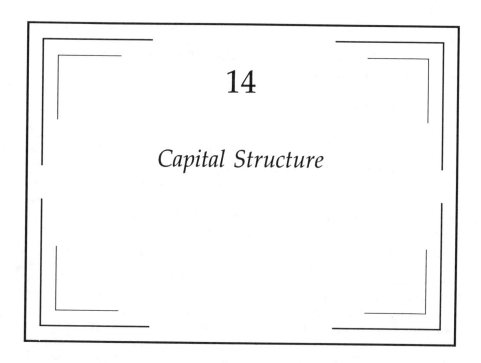

14

Capital Structure

MANAGEMENT'S RESPONSIBILITY

By capital structure, we mean the division of the corporation's capital between debt and equity and the various classes within those categories.

Essentially, the capital structure is a means of allocating risk of loss, participation in profits and financial control by management. The final decision on the capital structure is usually governed by the kind of money available (debt or equity money) and the terms on which it can be obtained. Nevertheless, in organizing a new corporation, or in raising additional financing for an existing company, management should make an effort to formulate the financial structure which will be most desirable for the business in the long run.

Basic Principles to Follow

It is easier to obtain money from both equity and debt sources if the financial plan reflects basic economic principles. Generally, bonds are issued when future earnings of a corporation promise to be large and reasonably certain; preferred stock is issued when earnings are irregular but show promise of exceeding preferred stock dividend requirements; common stock is issued when earnings are uncertain and unpredictable. These principles are not automatic. Tax considerations may alter them. Debt financing has tax advantages.

Highest Return on Capital

The highest potential return on equity capital investment and the largest potential for capital appreciation are produced by the combination of the smallest possible proportion of equity investment—common stock—and the highest proportion of fixed amount debt. This is called trading on the equity, also commonly termed "leverage." A business borrows money in the hope that the borrowed funds will produce more earnings than the interest rate paid for the money. The danger is that failure to earn a rate of return higher than the interest cost of the borrowed money will consume basic capital and possibly result in creditors taking the business assets.

As an illustration, a business with $100,000 in capital stock can make 10% on capital. If it borrows another $100,000 and keeps its 10% earnings rate on the capital it uses, common stockholders will get a 14% return after paying 6% on the borrowed money. If the earnings rate can be increased to 15%, common stockholders will get a 24% return. But if the earnings rate on the capital employed declines to 5%, common stockholders will receive only 4%. If the corporation earns only 2% on its $200,000, 6% will still be payable on the $100,000 of borrowed money and the common stockholders' capital will be dissipated by 2% a year.

Increased earning power, inflation, or any other factor which operates to increase the dollar value of assets benefits common stockholders exclusively—not the holders of fixed-value notes or bonds, or of preferred stock. So the owners of the business will profit to a greater degree from appreciation in value and sustain any loss at a faster rate when there is a low proportion of common stock and a high proportion of fixed value obligations.

Taking Minimum Risks

Maximum safety calls for all common stock and no fixed obligations to pay interest and redeem loans. But debt may be advantageous to raise capital and to maximize income and capital gain possibilities. So a business may have to make a judgment on how far it can go into debt. Caution and prudence of lenders may, to a considerable extent, determine this factor. In general, a lender will want the borrower to have as much money at risk as the lender has; so this may restrict borrowing to no more than equal to the amount of invested capital. Often the owners will want to advance money to their business on a temporary basis, and this could increase the proportion of debt to equity.

Wise limits on the proportion of capital to debt vary in each situation, depending on the earnings prospects, stability of the business, and the financial position and skill of its management. The presence of one or more of the following factors, where a loan is required, would suggest caution before lending funds:

(1) Instability of prices and volume.

(2) Abnormally high percentage of fixed cost.

(3) High rate of turnover.

(4) Low ratio of profits to sales.

For example, a retail store should borrow proportionately less than an apartment house venture or a printing plant with a large fixed investment in heavy machines.

When expansion seems necessary or advantageous, good financing requires a high ratio of stocks to debt to provide borrowing power for future needs. However, if the owners are sure of their future earnings prospects and earning power and feel that a relatively short operating period will prove their judgment, they may borrow as much capital as they need—or can get—and hold off issuing stock until they can get a higher price for it. Because the capital requirements of a successful business can be expected to increase sharply, it may be wise to hold back enough stock for future expansion needs without heavy dilution of the owner's interest and control.

Maintaining Control of a Company

A financing plan that will bring in enough outside funds and also maximize control is often accomplished by giving sole voting power to a small common stock issue. The danger always exists that the owners' control will be lost and their interest diluted if they do not foresee and prepare for the rising financial requirements that successful operation brings. When further capital is needed, the owners may have to release too large a portion of their stock holdings to keep full control.

A preferred stock issue is usually used to secure the investor's money when some of the investing group contribute intangibles such as services, special skills, patent rights, etc., and so are entitled to a share of the profits over and above the normal return for cash investment. Again the owner of the underlying equity must anticipate and make sure that the financial requirements of a successful business can be obtained without loss of his control and dilution of his interest. The use of preferred stock allows the owner to retain a larger proportion of the common. As the business grows, issuance of additional voting stock may reinforce the owner's control by making it more difficult for another to purchase a controlling stock interest.

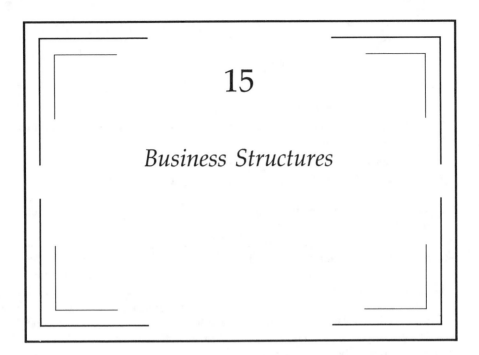

15

Business Structures

BUSINESS STRUCTURE CONSIDERATIONS

Any business enterprise is internally composed of two distinct human elements:

Employers—the owners of the business;
Employees—those employed by the owner.

(Sometimes, an owner is an employee of his own firm, but his classification as an owner is unaffected.)

The owner (employer) of a business may be the founder—the one who initially organized and funded the operation—or a successor to that original founder. The founder, in starting the business, has several, but limited, options as to the *type* of legal business-structure format to be used for the operation. (Also, the founder or his successor may choose to change the structure from one type to another at a subsequent date.)

The primary considerations are:

1. The extent of personal liability should the business fail;
2. The comparative tax advantages offered by different methods of organization.

And the available options are:

1. Sole proprietorship
2. Partnership—in combination with one or more other owners
3. Corporation—in combination with others for legal formation, but he might in fact be subsequently the sole owner
4. Sub-chapter S Corporation—with others, or alone
5. Professional Corporation or Association—with others, or alone.

(A Joint Venture is merely a stop-gap entity from which profits flow to one of the above types of entity.)

If the owner places a priority on *tax-savings*, any format would be chosen in preference to the corporation format, which historically has been taxed on both the *earnings* and the *distribution (dividends)* of those same earnings. The Sub-S corporation and the Professional corporation (if electing the Sub-S option) do eliminate the double-taxation feature (and also offer the advantage of full corporate deductions for executive salaries, if paid timely), but they also involve personal taxation on all the undistributed earnings, which pass through to the individuals (with certain exceptions) effectively as in a partnership.

If the owner places priority on the *limitation* of personal liability, he will choose the corporate form (possibly with the Sub-S option). But he cannot choose the Professional corporation to limit liability, since most states prohibit this limitation by law (as for doctors, accountants, etc.).

Once the legal format is set, the method of financial accounting and reporting for that particular type of business is applied.

Most accounting textbooks and the guidelines seem to be directed toward the corporate method of accounting. The standards of maintaining records for most assets, liabilities and items of income and expense are generally applicable to any type of business structure. Whatever guidelines apply to the corporation also apply to most of the other forms of business entity, *except* in these areas:

1. The Capital or Equity section:
   A. Initial investment
   B. The sharing of profits/losses
2. Salaries/Drawings of owners
3. Income tax on the entity's profit
4. How to account for investments in subsidiaries or controlled nonsubsidiaries
5. Dissolution of the entity.

Here, in brief, are the major differences to recall or research for the various structures:

Clearly distinguish between *personal* expenditures and business expenditures.

In proprietorships and partnerships, personal items are to be treated as drawings or withdrawals or as loans. In a corporation, treat as a loan or dividend.

In partnerships, the *partnership agreement* takes precedence and establishes all the rules, especially of distribution. The agreement should spell out: Capital contributions requirements and basis of assets or liabilities assumed, duties of the partners, time to be spent in the business, limitations on drawings, the ratio of sharing profits and losses, death provisions, insurance protection, loans and interest on loans. Salaries might, for example, be allotted to each working partner before the ratio-splitting of profits, but the salary plus the split-share of the remaining profit effectually go into that partner's capital account and are reduced by *actual drawings* (salary plus profit-withdrawal).

In *disslolution* of partnerships, liabilities to/from partners are paid before distribution, and *no* distribution is made in excess of each partner's just share needed for liquidation of liabilities.

Death usually dissolves a *partnership*, unless the agreement makes specific contingent provisions.

Financial statements for either a proprietorship or partnership should provide a "Statement of Capital Changes" (similar to a corporation's "Changes in Retained Earnings").

The valuation of assets (and/or liabilities) at original cost should be stated at fair value, in any structure. Goodwill is set up, if pertinent, and the Capital or Capital Stock section credited for the agreed ownership portion. (Law requires corporations sometimes to distinguish between "par value" and "excess of par.") "Negative goodwill should be used to write down non-current (fixed) assets in an immediate proportion. Goodwill, if any, should be amortized for financial purposes over 40 years unless there is proof of a shorter benefit period. Goodwill is not deductible for tax purposes.

The *trade name*, if any, should be used on proprietorship or partnership statements, with disclosure of the type of business structure.

The "cash basis" of accounting is *not* a generally accepted accounting principle, and proper financial statements, when carrying an independent auditor's opinion, are either qualified ("subject to") or with a disclaimer, depending on the materiality of the difference had the accrual method been used.

Financial accounting for sole proprietorships and partnerships *should not* record accruals or deductions for the income tax which that owner or co-owner must pay on his respective share of the earnings. However, financial footnotes should make such a disclosure if the funds for such payment may deplete those belonging to the entity (as future "withdrawals").

The *equity method* of accounting for investments in subsidiaries or controlled non-subsidiaries is *not* permitted for sole proprietors, trusts or estates. Proprietors should carry investments *at cost*. Partnerships and joint-ventures should use cost adjusted for accumulated undistributed earnings.

Deferred taxes on undistributed earnings of subsidiaries or non-subsidiaries should *not* be set up for partnerships, because of the factor of "personal taxing" mentioned above.

Financial statements for sole proprietorships may show a "reasonable" salary allowance for the owner to arrive at a financial operating income. But the salary is still a withdrawal.

Consolidations are permitted a proprietorship (over 50% ownership):

1. If owning 100%, the investment is eliminated against equity;
2. If less than 100%, the minority interest is shown on the income statement before extraordinary items, and on the balance sheet between liabilities and net worth.

Other eliminations should be as in consolidations.

Joint ventures are usually not majority-controlled by any of the participants. Hence, consolidation is not in order. The equity method is used by partnerships or corporations that participate in a joint venture. Proprietors should use the cost method of investment. Sometimes, however, upon proper disclosure, "proportionate" consolidation is used. Here, a pro-rata share of assets, liabilities and income is consolidated.

LEASES AND LEASEBACKS

Leases today loom large in financing the acquisition of plant and equipment. The lease may be part of a sale-leaseback package or it may be the alternative to an outright purchase. A lease is preferred by some lessees because it does not usually require a large outlay of cash.

There are a number of terms in lease contracts that must be understood when considering a lease arrangement. These unique terms are defined below.

BARGAIN PURCHASE OPTION. A provision allowing the lessee, at his option, to purchase the leased property for a price that is sufficiently lower than the expected fair value of the property at the date the option becomes exercisable, provided that exercise of the option appears, at the *inception of the lease*, to be reasonably assured.

BARGAIN RENEWAL OPTION. A provision allowing the lessee, at his option, to renew the lease for a rental sufficiently lower than the fair rental value of the property at the date the option becomes exercisable. The exercise of the option must appear, at the inception of the lease, to be reasonably assured. ("Fair rental" means the expected rental for equivalent property under similar terms and conditions.)

CONTINGENT RENTALS. The increases or decreases in lease payments that result from changes occurring subsequent to the inception of the lease in the factors affecting the lease, other than the passage of time. Any factors that occur subsequent to the inception of the lease that materially affect the original minimum lease payments in the contract become contingent rentals, and must be considered in their entirety separately from the minimum lease payments.

ESTIMATED ECONOMIC LIFE OF LEASE PROPERTY. The estimated remaining period during which the property is expected to be economically usable by one or more users, with normal repairs and maintenance, for the purpose for which it was intended at the inception of the lease without limitation by the lease term.

ESTIMATED RESIDUAL VALUE OF LEASED PROPERTY. The estimated fair value of the leased property at the end of the lease term.

EXECUTORY COSTS. Costs such as insurance, maintenance, taxes, and other costs associated with the lease property, whether paid by the lessor or lessee.

FAIR VALUE OF LEASED PROPERTY. The price for which the property could be sold in an *arm's-length transaction* between *unrelated* parties. Usually, the value is determined by the market price of similar property under market conditions prevailing at the time the lease is negotiated.

INCEPTION OF THE LEASE. The date of the lease agreement, or commitment, if earlier. A commitment must be in writing, signed by the parties to the transaction, and specifically set forth the principal provisions of the transactions. No principal provision still to be negotiated qualifies for purposes of this definition.

INCREMENTAL BORROWING RATE. The rate of interest at the inception of the lease that the lessee would have had to pay to borrow the funds over a time period similar to the life of the lease for the funds necessary to have purchased the lease asset.

INITIAL DIRECT COSTS. Costs incurred by the lessor that are directly associated with negotiating and consummating the completed transaction.

INTEREST RATE IMPLICIT IN THE LEASE. The discount rate applied to (1) the minimum lease payments, excluding that portion of the payments representing executory costs of the lessor, together with any profits thereon, and (2) the unguaranteed residual value accruing to the benefit of the lessor, causing the aggregate *present value* at the beginning of the lease term to be equal to the fair value of the leased property to the lessor at the inception of the lease, minus any investment tax credit retained by the lessor and expected to be realized by him.

LEASE TERM.   The fixed noncancelable term of the lease, plus all periods, if any, covered by bargain renewal options.

MINIMUM LEASE PAYMENTS.   The payments that the *lessee* is obligated to make for the leased property over the lease term. Also, any payments that the lessee must or can be required to make upon failure to renew or extend the lease at the expiration of the lease term, whether or not the payment would constitute a purchase of the leased property.

RELATED PARTIES.   A parent company and its subsidiaries, an owner company, and joint ventures (corporate or otherwise), and partnerships, and an investor and its investees, provided that the parent company, owner company, or investor has the ability to exercise significant influence over operating and financial policies of the related party.

RENEWAL OR EXTENSION OF A LEASE.   The continuation of the original lease agreement beyond the original lease term, including a new lease under which the lessee continues to use the same property.

UNGUARANTEED RESIDUAL VALUE.   The estimated residual value of the leased property exclusive of any portion guaranteed by the lessee or by any party related to the lessee or by a third party unrelated to the lessor.

UNRELATED PARTIES.   All parties that are not *related parties* as defined.

LEASE OR BUY?

This is a decision that many taxpayers are often faced with. And it cannot necessarily be made on the basis of lowest net-after-tax cost alone—although, of course, the net-after-tax cost is a big consideration. Often the scales may be tipped in favor of rental, because (1) the burden of maintenance is usually on the lessor, and (2) it's easier to switch to a new machine. The latter option may be of great importance where the possibility of a newer machine may make the previous one obsolete.

But the cost is undoubtedly a big factor. And in arriving at the net-after-tax cost, we have to take into account the impact of the various tax factors on each type of acquisition.

Before making the comparison, however, let's get straight just what we are comparing. On the one hand, we have a rental of a machine we do not own. On the other hand, we acquire ownership. What's more, we can acquire ownership by financing our purchase—a very large initial cash outlay of company funds may not be necessary. Most acquisitions today are made via the financing route. So, in a sense, in comparing rentals with purchases, we are comparing two different costs of money—the interest factor that's built into the rental structure and the interest that is paid for the equipment loan. And the tax factors have a considerable effect on determining the net cost.

Making the comparison.   Insofar as the rent paid is concerned that's generally fully deductible for tax purposes. In addition, the lessor can pass through to the lessee the investment tax credit. Thus, the net cost is the gross rent less the tax benefit derived from both the deduction for rent and the investment credit.

On the purchase side, the buyer is paying both purchase price and interest. The interest is tax deductible. In addition, he gets an investment credit and depreciation deductions. Thus, his net cost is the total of purchase price and interest, reduced by the tax benefits derived from the investment credit, the interest deductions and the depreciation deductions.

How to Set Up the Figures to Make the Comparison

There are a variety of rental arrangements available, and there are numerous financing arrangements available, as well. Rather than attempt to deal with a specific illustration that may or may not apply to the type of equipment you are

---

Worksheet for Determining First-Year, After-Tax Cost of Renting

1. Gross rent	$ _____
2. Applicable tax rate	_____
3. Tax saved via rent deduction (Line 1 × Line 2)	$ _____
4. Net after-tax cost for first year (Line 1 minus Line 3)	$ _____

Worksheet for Determining First-Year, After-Tax Cost of Buying

1. Total cost of acquired assets[1]	$ _____
2. Cash down payment in first year	$ _____
3. Other first-year installments paid	$ _____
4. Interest paid on unpaid balance	$ _____
5. Total cash outlay in first year (total of Lines 2, 3, and 4)	$ _____
6. Regular depreciation	$ _____
7. Interest paid (same as Line 4)	$ _____
8. Total deductible items (total of Lines 6 and 7)	$ _____
9. Total tax saved by deductions (Line 8 × tax rate)	$ _____
10. Investment tax credit	$ _____
11. Net after-tax, first-year cost (Line 5 minus Lines 9 and 10)	$ _____

---

[1]Normally the total cost will be the contract price for the acquired assets. But if there is a trade-in, use adjusted basis—i.e., basis of the assets traded in plus balance paid or payable. If a trade-in is involved, substitute for the amount on Line 1 (for the purposes of this computation) the amount paid or payable for the equipment over and above the amount allowed by the seller for the trade-in.

likely to rent or buy, we have set forth two worksheets. One is for determining the first-year, after-tax cash cost of renting and the other for determining the first-year, after-tax cash cost of buying. Thus, you can insert your own figures on the worksheets and come up with a comparison that has meaning for you.

PLANT FINANCING VIA LEASEBACKS

Here is a hypothetical example of a typical sale-leaseback deal. By working through it, we can see how the figures affect both buyer and seller.

A corporation uses a plant in its business which it has owned for 15 years. Original cost was $1,000,000, of which $700,000 was allocated to the building and $300,000 to the land. It has taken $440,000 of depreciation, so its basis for the whole property is now $560,000. In January 1984, it decides to sell the property to an investor corporation if it can get a 15-year leaseback. The sale price is $760,000, with a net rental under the lease equivalent to a 15-year amortization of the $760,000 at a 9% return—or a rental of $77,225. Assume that the investor corporation can allocate $500,000 of its purchase price to the building for depreciation purposes.

The seller.   The seller corporation has a $200,000 gain on the sale and pays a capital gains tax of $60,000. If it has borrowed $700,000 (the new amount it gets after the capital gains tax) at 9% interest payable over 15 years, on a constant payment basis, the yearly payment would have been $67,450. Over the 15-year period, the seller would have paid a total of some $1,012,000 instead of $1,158,000 (15 times $77,225) which it pays on the sale-leaseback. But in the case of the mortgage, the seller only gets a tax deduction for the $312,000 interest that it pays. This, together with the $260,000 depreciation that the seller had left on the property would have meant a total tax deduction of $527,000 or, at least 46% corporate rates, a saving of $263,000. The mortgage would have cost the seller $749,000 ($1,012,000 minus the tax saving). But, under the leaseback, the seller gets a tax deduction for the entire rental paid, so it gets a saving of $533,000 (46% of the entire 15-year rental), which would mean a cost to the seller of the leaseback of $625,000 ($1,158,000 minus $533,000). The result is that the sale-leaseback costs the seller $124,000 less than what the mortgage would have cost.

The buyer.   The buyer, under the sale-leaseback, gets a deduction over the 15-year period of the lease of $500,000, the amount that it allocated to the building. This means that $500,000 of the rent income is protected from tax. The tax on the remainder is $302,000, so the net to the buyer on the sale-leaseback over the 15-year period is $856,000. If the buyer had taken a mortgage position in this particular property for $760,000 at 9% interest, it would have received $1,084,000 with $334,000 interest taxable to it (the remainder would have been mortgage amortization). This would have meant a total tax of $153,600 or a net after taxes to the buyer of $930,400. This is almost $74,400 more than the buyer's net in the case of the leaseback.

What the figures mean to both parties: Figures don't always tell the whole story. Here are some additional factors that can mean a great deal to one, or both, parties.

To the seller.   The seller pays $124,000 less (net after tax deduction) than it would in the case of a mortgage. But to get this, the seller has given up its owner-ship of the property at the end of the lease. At present, the land is valued at $260,000. So, it appears, the seller actually loses $136,000. But this is deceptive. The seller's building wears out at the end of the lease and, because of the favorable aspects of the deal to the buyer, the buyer would be able, at the time of the sale-leaseback, to give the seller an option to renew for, say, another 10 or 15 years at a very low rental. Any improvements constructed by the seller during the renewal term would be depreciated by the seller. Also, the sale-leaseback provides the seller with the maximum amount of financing, since with the property worth $760,000, it would be hard (due to legal limitations on the amount of the mortgage in relation to market value and to the desire by the mortgagees for protection), in most states, to get a mortgage for the full market value.

To the buyer.   In effect, the buyer has $74,400 of his investment left in the property at the end of the original lease term. The buyer has gotten out his 9% yield, plus the rest of his "principal" and will own the property worth at least $260,000, if land values don't change. The buyer can afford to give the seller a renewal lease at a rental of only $7,000 a year, and still get a 9% before-tax return on his $74,000. By this method, during the renewal lease term, the seller will have the land on a tax-deductible basis. And if the renewal lease is set up properly, any improvements will not be income to the buyer. At the end of the renewal term, or the original lease if the seller does not renew, the buyer still owns the land.

Special Forms of Sale-Leasebacks

Besides the conventional sale-leaseback between two unrelated parties, there are some specialized forms of setting up this type of transaction.

New construction.   Here a builder may arrange the financing for a new plant he is constructing for a business corporation by getting that corporation to agree to lease the property, and by interesting an investor in the purchase of the property upon completion. In the meantime, the builder will obtain construction financing unless the investor is an insurance company or pension trust which can handle the financing from commencement of construction.

Exempt organizations.   Educational and charitable organizations and other tax exempts have been heavy buyers in these deals They enjoy a favorable tax status and so can afford to offer the seller a good deal—the seller deducts the rent, but the charity is not ordinarily taxed on it as income unless it is unrelated to its exempt functions. Consequently, the charity will be able to charge less rent than an ordinary investor. Also a charity or educational institution is exempt from local realty taxes, usually.

When you sell to a tax-exempt organization, it will pay you to hold on to the furniture and equipment and any other depreciable property which the buyer doesn't want. The buyer gets no benefit from the depreciable deduction since he pays no tax. You might as well keep these deductions for yourself.

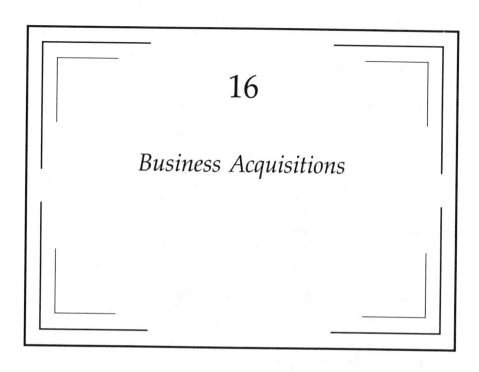

16

Business Acquisitions

The accounting and financial officers of the company will be involved in any arrangements to buy a business or sell the existing business. Questions of value, technique (purchase or sale of assets or stock), accounting treatment (will the acquisition qualify as a "pooling of interest"?), tax consequences, desirability of the acquisition or sale all may be within the province of the chief financial officer and his staff.

FORCES BEHIND BUSINESS SALES AND ACQUISITIONS

Many businesses diversify and build up sales volume by acquiring other businesses. Capital values can be built by acquiring additional product lines, moving into new territory, etc. Financial statements may be improved. Taxes may be saved by acquiring companies with operating loss carry-forwards. This is done through tax-free exchanges.

We see an increasing use of a combination of methods that include leases, mortgage financing, and percentage and deferred purchase arrangements. They give a maximum retention of capital for regular business operations.

Benefits of Merging

Here's a list which will orient your own thinking and help you in any trade or negotiations with other firms:

(1) *Many young companies just don't have the cash* to realize their potential. This is particularly true in areas which require nationwide merchandising, heavy development work, and expensive productive equipment.

. (2) *Diversification* is a major reason for acquisitions. The reasons for seeking diversification are numerous. For example, a company may be seeking to get into the so-called areas of today: e.g., electronics, chemicals, atomic energy. By picking up a company already in one of these fields, it may get into the desired area much more economically than otherwise. Diversification may also be sought where a company needs funds to expand into a new field. By first diversifying, it hopes to broaden its profit base and increase its growth, with the new funds generated by growth used to get into the areas the company originally sought to enter. Diversification may also be sought by companies in cyclical business by acquiring companies not subject to severe ups and downs. In this way, the acquiring company hopes to make its financial problems less burdensome in the periods when it needs substantial financing and to overcome periods of low revenue when business is contracted.

(3) *Some firms merge with others to get into a new line because investors do not value the industry or its earnings very highly.* Unless such companies can substantially convert into another industry, they cannot realize a large mark-up in capital values.

(4) *Many companies realize that they must have more volume to carry the research and overhead staff necessary to stay competitive today.* The volume required to carry necessary research will vary industry by industry. For example, one company doing about $12 million a year acquired enough additional lines of business to bring its volume up to $20 million. Anything less would have made the firm hard-pressed to carry on the research and staff services needed to compete with others in its industry.

(5) *Plants become idle* as a result of a company's product lines becoming obsolete, or volume drops off for some other reason. The company finds itself with excess plant capacity. Where this plant capacity—e.g., machinery, equipment, etc.—is in good shape, and is not itself obsolete, acquiring a new business may be the best way of making use of this excess plant capacity. This may be a far better solution than a gradual shutdown and a contraction of the existing business.

(6) *Companies are sometimes acquired to get their special attributes.* For example, it may be desirable to get the key personnel of a particular company, and the only way is to get the company as well. In other cases, an acquired company may have special machinery already available which might cost a considerable amount in dollars and time to reproduce. Sometimes the acquired company may have a sales

organization which would be just what the acquiring company needs. It may be more economical to acquire the company than to try to build up a similar sales organization.

(7) *Some new, successful companies are taxed so high that there's very little left for investors and expansion.* These make ideal buys for other firms with loss carryovers, which might be used to protect subsequent profits earned by the combined operation.

(8) *Some companies have found that it doesn't pay to continue a product line which doesn't yield a specified volume.* One company decided to dispose of all subsidiaries and divisions which did less than $10 million a year. Many companies are trying to earn the premium which investors pay for stability of earnings. They seek diversification which will allow one line to hold up and balance off other lines which run through recessions.

(9) *Many companies go on the block because their owners are faced by a personal estate tax squeeze* and aren't able to get money out of a profitable business to make their personal portfolio liquid. The only solution is to sell part or all the business at capital gains rates or merge with a publicly traded company.

(10) *Many businesses don't want to distribute dividends* but would prefer to use accumulated earnings to acquire other products and expand into new territory or product lines.

(11) *Closely-held companies, or companies with cash and mortgagable assets locked up in the corporation, offer a good buying opportunity*—(a) to companies with fairly marketable stock, which can acquire the locked-up assets by an exchange of stock, or (b) to companies with a cash surplus which permits them to buy stock or assets at a discount (likely because the original owner has to pay a heavy tax rate if he taps the assets by taking a dividend distribution).

(12) *Some companies with strong earnings position can reap big advantages by picking up a smaller company.* Suppose the market values a firm 15 times earnings. If the firm can then pick up a smaller company for 5 or 6 times earnings (frequently possible), it will realize an automatic profit for its stockholders and still be able to plow some earnings into building up the new acquisition.

(13) *When two companies in the same business merge, they can often bring about a number of operating economies.* Bulk purchasing for both companies may cut the unit cost of purchases. In some cases, duplicating facilities may be eliminated—e.g., one warehouse may serve the purposes of both businesses and one warehouse may therefore be eliminated.

BUY-SELL AGREEMENT FOR A BUSINESS ACQUISITION

When you sign on the dotted line. . . .
You are inflexibly obligated. . . .

What This Discussion Is About

This discussion concerns the negotiations and completed agreement for the sale-purchase of a business enterprise. Before an agreement of any kind is signed, the respective parties have freedom of choice and action. After a contract is signed, the principals are committed to perform precisely according to the terms of the agreement—options are no longer available.

What Is A Contract?

Before discussing the specifics of a business acquisition, it might be helpful to remind ourselves of the salient aspects of a contract generally, as a buy-sell agreement for a business is a contract.

A contract is simply a set of legal rules, the rules of a business transaction which two, or more, parties agree to live by. Buyers and sellers are adversaries, albeit, friendly in most instances. Each one wants the best deal he can get. That is why each side must be careful, because each side will strive for terms favorable to his own interests and objectives.

Two Common Pitfalls. Broadly, there are two common pitfalls that should be avoided:

- A contract may obligate you in ways you did not expect, or intend when you signed.
- A contract may *not* obligate the other party in ways you expected him to be obligated.

Obligating yourself in unexpected ways can be avoided by careful scrutiny of the document before signing. (Details to watch out for will be covered in the next few pages.)

Failure to obligate the other party in proper ways is a more elusive pitfall. You tend to know more precisely what you are obligating yourself to do than what you think the other party should do. The inherent danger of this pitfall is that the failure to obligate the other party as you intended is not discovered until it is too late. Be mindful! You have no chance to make changes in a contract after you have signed on the dotted line. (Details concerning how to protect yourself against this pitfall will also be discussed in subsequent pages.)

Essential Ingredients of a Contract. Let's briefly examine the essential elements of any type of contract.

- A contract offers flexibility. That is to say, the law does not specify the exact wording of contracts. The parties concerned structure and furnish the wording for the agreed upon terms of a transaction.
- Contracts can be bilateral (two opposite parties), or multilateral (more than two parties involved).

- A contract starts from different positions of the parties; the signed contract brings the parties together because it represents agreement to the same set of *promises.*

- Note, again, the word "promises" above. A contract must contain promises of the parties concerned to do something: "I promise to do this if you promise to do that."

- A contract must be supported by *consideration.* Consideration is something of value received (or given) at the request of the promisor in reliance upon and in return for his promise.

- Most formal contracts have a uniform format consisting at least of:
  A heading such as, *Sale of Business Assets.*
  Date and geographic location of the agreement.
  The names of the parties involved.
  Recitals of facts.
  The promise clause(s).
  The body of the contract.
  Signatures of the contracting parties.
  Signatures of witnesses, with the calendar day and year.

- The law does not guarantee that every promise in a contract is enforceable. A contract to commit a crime, for example, is unforceable because the commitment is an illegal act in the first place.

It should be noted that the general pattern of contracts developed more as a matter of practice than of any legal requirements for a set format. A contract can be valid and binding without any formal design. For example, an exchange of letters containing the agreed upon terms can be a valid and binding contract.

Negotiation

A contract is preceded by negotiations between the parties. What is negotiation? Negotiation can be thought of as the bargaining prelude to the final agreement, during which "opposite" parties become "alike." The negotiation process clarifies alternatives, resolves issues, establishes promises, determines future courses of conduct, and results in legally-enforceable obligations explicitly written into the document. Negotiation ends when the contract is signed.

In the course of negotiating the sale, the seller usually makes statements of fact to the buyer regarding the business and its assets. The buyer should verify the facts regarding such items as:

- The dollar amount of sales.
- Title to property being sold.
- Number and specific facts about the seller's customers.
- Manner of operation of the business.

- Validity of patents or other intangible rights.
- All contracts to which the seller is a party.
- Other material information.

Where such facts are important to the buyer, he should consult with his accountant for the financial aspects and with his attorney for the legal ramifications in order to incorporate the appropriate details into the contract.

Be Mindful. Protections that *might* have been included, possibilities that *might* have been considered, choices that *once* were available, all are foreclosed when you sign the contract at the completion of negotiations. Experience has demonstrated that most disputes relating to buy-sell agreements arise because significant details of the agreement were not precisely defined, or omitted entirely by oversight.

BUY-SELL AGREEMENT FOR A BUSINESS ACQUISITION

A Complex Transaction

The purchase and sale of an ongoing business is a complex transaction. It can involve the transfer from the seller to the buyer of many different kinds of items, commonly among which are:

- Inventory.
- Accounts receivable.
- Contracts of various sorts.
- Plant, machinery, equipment.
- Goodwill.
- Leaseholds.
- Patents and copyrights.
- Payables.
- Long-term liabilities.
- Equities.

Time-Lag Problem. The transaction usually involves a time-lag. There is a period of time between the date of agreement of the parties and the actual transfer of the business. It is not uncommon, for example, for payment to be not always entirely in cash. The manner of paying the deferred balance is a significant item in the negotiations, with final transfer to the buyer delayed until payment is completed. The basic problem is: Who runs the business until then?

Two Methods. When a going business is a corporation, two methods of sale and purchase exist. The corporation can sell the assets or the shareholders can sell their shares of stock. Under either method, the buyer gets a going business, but there are significant differences in results and tax consequences in these methods for both the buyer and seller.

The Buyer's Position. Ordinarily, the buyer prefers to purchase the assets of a going business, *net* of liabilities. The buyer then acquires only assets and none (or as few as possible) of the existing debt of the seller's company. If the purchaser buys all outstanding shares of stock, he acquires a corporation with all its known and unknown (beware!) liabilities.

The tax situation is different between the two methods. The cost of shares of stock is a capital expenditure, no part of which is depreciable. But when the net assets are purchased, the tax treatment of the cost of business assets depends upon the kinds of assets purchased. Capital items, like machinery, are depreciable. Inventory is part of the cost of goods sold. Generally, the tax statutes and regulations tend to favor purchase of business assets rather than shares of stock.

On the other hand, an important advantage in the purchase of corporate shares is the simplicity of the transaction. Only one item—the stock—is involved, which can be transferred with the stroke of a pen. When the assets are purchased, negotiations involve the complication of determining price, which in turn involves evaluation techniques of the business assets and liabilities. The latter tends to be the number one cause of breakdowns in the negotiations and withdrawal of the parties from the proposed acquisition, because of the extended negotiations and agreement on the value of such items as inventory, capital assets, real estate, goodwill, and other assets, tangible and intangible. In addition, there must be agreement regarding the valuation of liabilities, especially contingent liabilities, such as the outcome of ongoing litigation against (or for) the company, warranties outstanding, and the like.

The Seller's Position. The seller of a business usually wants to sell the corporation's stock when disposing of the business, primarily because of the simplicity, as noted, of a stock transaction compared to the complication of assets and liabilities valuation problems. The sale of assets leaves the owner-stockholder with a corporate entity, commonly termed a *corporate shell*. If the shell is the sole asset of the corporation, there is no reason for the corporation's continued existence after the assets are sold. But three problems still can remain for the seller:

- To convert any unsold assets, if any, to cash. Some assets might not have been sold—accounts receivable, for example.
- To dissolve the corporation and distribute remaining assets to the shareholders.
- Enter income taxes. The sale of corporate shares involves only one taxable event. The sale of assets is one taxable event, the disposition of remaining assets, if any, is another taxable event, and corporate dissolution is still another taxable event.

Mechanics. The parties must reach agreement, not only upon the substance of the sale and purchase, but also upon the terms by which the deal will be consummated. It is possible that the consent of other persons may be required, for example, when the seller is a lessee and is assigning a leasehold interest. Documents in proper form must be prepared, signed, and ready for delivery by one party to the other.

There is frequently a lapse between the time the parties agree and the completion of the transaction. The time lapse is more critical in the sale of a going business than in most other routine sale-purchase transactions, simply because of the nature of the commodity being sold; i.e., an ongoing business. Does the seller continue the operation until the sale is final? Does the buyer want to take over promptly because he does not want others to operate the business that he will ultimately own?

Both parties usually want the business to continue during the transition period as it has been operated to date. The negotiations and final contractual agreement regarding the operation of the business during the transition period can be fully as complex as the negotiations for the sale price.

Professional Assistance

The seller and buyer of a business will become associated (presumably) with at least two odd species of advisors throughout the process of negotiating and closing a business acquisition. Who? An accountant and a lawyer! Who else?*

In a more serious context, both can perform services valuable to the principals. In fact, it would be foolhardy for a businessperson to attempt to sell (or buy) a business without accounting and legal services.

The Accountant—How to Use Him. The traditional habitat of an accountant has been that of a backroom office, with the accountant leaning over a long-legged desk with a green visor, thick-rimmed glasses, and pouring over an endless stack of accounting worksheets. Today their responsibilities and services to clients have considerably broadened to include tax preparation and advisory and consultative services on financial matters.

Specifically, the accountant can:

- Determine the integrity of the financial statements. Even a simplified (but audited) balance sheet can be very informative. The explanatory footnotes to the financial statements can particularly be a gold mine of information. It is only half in jest to say that if business managers took the time to read the footnotes, they could avoid the distasteful task of analyzing and interpreting the inundation of numbers in the financial statements.
- Audited statements oftentimes represent long (and not always amicable) discussions between the company's independent auditor and executive management agreeing upon whether or not certain "material" matters, particularly negative financial information, should be disclosed in financial reports.

---

*The authors once heard the following definitions of lawyers and accountants. "A lawyer is one who uses incomprehensible language." "An accountant is one who uses incomprehensible figures."

- Assist in the analysis of the financial data and other financial information furnished by the other side.
- Prepare *pro forma* financial information; i.e., financial statements based upon the assumption that the acquisition had already taken place.
- Assist in asset and liability valuations.
- Assist in income tax considerations, along with the attorney.
- A fundamental technical determination concerns the acquisition method—"pooling-of-interest" or "purchase" methods. (The technical considerations and consequences of the two methods are book-length in their aspects, far beyond the scope of this paper. The accountant is familiar with the rules that must be applied to these choices.)
- Impartially apply "Generally Acceptable Accounting Principles" (acronym: GAAP). However, the accountant has broad leeway in the principles to be applied. Therefore, the accountant can advise entirely legitimate accounting methods which can, in fact, cause differences in results; i.e., differences in income, tax liabilities, capital (equity) changes, for example.

The Lawyer—How To Use Him. Lawyers, too, have had their traditional habitat—the courtroom. But over the years legal services have expanded; in fact, many attorneys never see a courtroom, rather they specialize in different aspects of the law. As related to the substance of this paper, sellers and buyers of a business well could engage the services of a lawyer who specializes in the law of contracts; a lawyer who actually makes a career solely of helping clients to negotiate and develop the terms of a buy-sell agreement for a business acquisition.

Specifically, the lawyer can:

- Draft a letter of intent, if utilized.
- Raise questions to be answered by the parties to the transaction (as well as questions for other professional advisors being retained).
- Suggest techniques for structuring the transaction.
- Develop the basic terms of the agreement as negotiations proceed.
- Advise on the form of the acquisition from the standpoint of legal considerations.
- Handle the preparation and closing of the acquisition documents (the final contract for signatures).

Two Common Errors. There are two common errors associated with the employment of accountants and lawyers in an acquisition.

- The first is to fail to use their services at all. Or, to give them a minor technical role, i.e., asking the accountant to check only if the financial statements make sense or asking the attorney only if the written agreement is legally binding as written.

- The second is a more common error—too much reliance on professional advisors. The business aspects of an acquisition are primary areas of responsibility for the managing officers of the seller's and buyer's respective companies. The parties concerned are in charge throughout the acquisition process, and should be totally independent of their professional advisors when making decisions along the way.

SUMMARY OF POINTS TO REMEMBER

- The sale of a business is a complicated transaction. Any number of items of material amounts of money are included in the sale of a business.
- Seller and buyer should agree at least on the items being sold and purchased, price, payment method, date and place of transfer of possession to the buyer, and the mechanics of continued operation of the business between the date of agreement and date when the sale is completed.
- Seller will usually prefer to sell his shares of stock, rather than have the corporation sell its assets.
- Not all of the business assets will necessarily be sold.
- Both parties should understand clearly their obligation as set forth in the agreement. *Minds cannot be changed after the contract has been signed.*
- Seller should be secured with respect to deferred payment of any balance of the purchase price.
- Buyer should make certain that he purchases the assets necessary to conduct the business.
- Buyer should be aware of all the obligations that he may be assuming.
- Buyer should have explicit covenants (items) in the contract regarding future competition from the seller. A covenant for the seller not to compete, usually for some specified period of time or within the confines of a specified geographic area, is not uncommon in a sale-purchase contract of a business.
- Negotiate all the provisions you want before signing.
- Be certain the appropriate promises and consideration are in the terms of the contract.
- Both parties should recite all facts; all of the facts should be verified.
- Each party to the agreement should be clearly identified—no "hidden" principals.
- Take care to ascertain if possibly a trustee, incompetent, receiver, executor, or other parties might be involved.
- All signatures should be clearly legible and readable.

- Preserve the completed and fully-signed contract, with all accompanying documents.
- There is no legal difference with respect to the format and design of a contract. A contract can be typed, printed, handwritten, or an exchange of letters.

Broadly. Both the seller and buyer of a business should:

- Ask the lawyer: "What is the worst that can happen?"
- Ask the accountant: "What financial information do I need?"

CONCLUSION

An agreement for the sale-purchase of a business should at least tell the seller of a business what he should do, when he should do it, and what will happen if he doesn't do it.

The acquisition contract should at least tell the buyer what he should do, when he should do it, and what will happen if he doesn't do it.

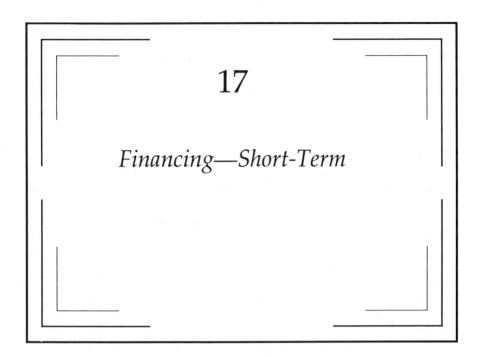

17

Financing—Short-Term

SOURCES OF SHORT-TERM FUNDS

Banks, finance companies and factors are the usual sources of short-term funds, although some finance company loans and bank term loans may run for a fairly long term or provide for a continuing line of credit.

Short-term credit may be available on the strength of the overall financial soundness of the borrower or for specific collateral—often, accounts receivable.

ARRANGING FOR CREDIT LINES WITH BANKS

The most readily available and frequently used source of money for a business is a bank loan. For most businesses, banks are only a source of temporary short-term money. To qualify for an unsecured bank loan, a company has to be substantially established and adequately supplied with equity money. The exceptions are cases in which the bank is lending on the strength of the personal credit of the proprietor, or principal stockholder, or somebody else who underwrites the loan for the borrowing business.

In dealing with banks, it is important to understand the nature of a commercial banking operation. The money it lends is that placed with it by depositors plus its own capital. A portion of the deposited money is set aside in reserves, another portion is held to meet the depositors' regular demands for cash, and the remainder is available for loans. Neither banking laws nor banking practice permit investment in a business or making capital loans in lieu of equity capital.

Selecting a Bank

The choice of a bank is important in the development of proper credit facilities, and a good banking connection once made is a valuable asset. As a general rule, it is not necessary to shop around for a banking connection—a local bank can usually meet the company's banking needs in a satisfactory manner. Some companies deliberately patronize more than one bank with the idea that if one bank turns down a request for a loan, the other will grant the loan. But this may backfire. One bank may want quick repayment for fear that the other will get repayment first. Where the local bank has restrictions which make it unable to meet the company's requirements, it is wise to go to another bank. But ordinarily it pays to give one bank all your business, in the expectation that the bank will take care of a good customer in time of financial stress. Banks prefer the exclusive arrangement. In times of financial need the bank whose officials have a good working knowledge of a company's operations and financial background can take care of its credit needs more quickly and effectively.

How the Banker Judges a Borrower

The banker will study the financial statements of the borrower, using many of the ratios described in this book.

In addition, he will want further information which he will get partially from discussion with the prospective borrower, partially from checking his credit files, and partially from checking with other creditors. The customer's or prospect's credit file, which contains the accumulated information about a particular business and its owner, is of tremendous importance in every loan decision. It is a marked trail which leads the experienced lending officer back through the history of the organization and its officers and enables him to uncover and evaluate information that might not otherwise be made available to him.

The banker will want to know these things about the prospective borrower:

(1) Its character, ability, and capacity.

(2) What kind of capital resources does it have?

(3) What kind of business organization is it? How good are its executives? What has been its sales trend?

(4) Will the loan be a sound one? Are any of the following conditions present to an extent which would throw doubt on the financial soundness of the business:

    (a) Heavy inventories in relation to sales.

    (b) Excessive dividends and salary withdrawals.

(c) Heavy loans to officers of subsidiary organizations.
(d) Large past-due receivables.
(e) Top-heavy debt.
(f) Too much invested in fixed assets.
(g) An overextended position—i.e., scrambling to apply income and funds to pay the most insistent creditors.

Types of Bank Accommodations

A company should familiarize itself with the various kinds of loan accommodations a bank is willing to extend, the interest rates, terms, and security requirements of each.

A line of credit.   A line of credit is merely a declaration by a bank that, until further notice, it is prepared to lend up to a stated maximum amount on certain terms and conditions to the prospective borrower. Since the line of credit is only a declaration of intent, it can be canceled at any time. The availability of a line of credit is very valuable because, instead of fixed credits which call for continuing interest, only amounts of money actually used, plus a small commitment fee on any portion of the original commitment not actually borrowed, are charged, which add up to inexpensive financing.

The application for a line of credit is not an application for a loan but simply an arrangement under which the bank agrees to make loans if funds are needed. But even so, a bank conducts an intensive investigation before granting the line of credit.

Term loans.   A business loan which runs for a term of more than one year with provisions for amortization or retirement over the life of the loan is a term loan. Such a loan, even if secured, will depend upon the bank's appraisal of the long-range prospects of the company, its earning power and the quality of its management. The term is usually a maximum of ten years.

Short-term loans.   Short-term bank loans are obtained either by individual borrowing or by obtaining a *line of credit* against which advances may be obtained. Short-term borrowing is available to companies that have sufficient credit to minimize the bank's risk. The loan is granted on the basis of a study and analysis of the financial position of the company. The security for these loans is a series of promissory notes which evidence the cash advance. These notes have maturity dates calling for repayment within one year, at which time they are reviewed, repaid, reduced or extended. Short-term loans are particularly effective for seasonal financing and the financing of inventories, or to keep things running smoothly during spurts of seasonal activity. Before granting a short-term loan, the bank may require that between 10% and 20% of the loan actually made be kept on deposit (called a compensating balance), or that the loan be cleaned up at least once a year to prevent the use of bank credit as permanent funds.

Character loans. These are short-term, unsecured loans, generally restricted to companies or individuals with excellent credit reputations.

Installment loans. Large banks generally grant this type of loan. Installment loans are made for almost any productive purpose and may be granted for any period that the bank allows. Payments are usually made on a monthly basis; as the obligation is reduced, it often may be refinanced at more advantageous rates. The installment loan can be tailored to the seasonal requirements of the company.

Equipment loans. An increasingly popular method of raising funds is to borrow money against machinery and equipment. There are two main ways of handling equipment loans. The first is to pledge equipment to which the company has an unencumbered title as security for the loan. The second method is via an installment financing plan.

Time purchase loans. Many special types of time purchase loans are available to finance both retailer and consumer purchase of automobiles, household equipment, boats, mobile homes, industrial and farm equipment, etc., and are made for varying periods of time, depending on the product. This category also includes accounts receivable financing, indirect collections and factoring.

Inventory loans. These loans are available if the merchandise or inventory can qualify as collateral. The requirements are stiff and the loans are limited to certain classes of inventory.

Accounts receivable loans. Small banks are not usually equipped to offer this type of loan, and the majority of their business customers are too small to take advantage of it. Under this loan, the bank takes over the company's accounts and notes receivable as collateral for the loan.

Warehouse receipt loans. Under this plan, goods are stored in warehouses and the warehouse receipts are used as security for a loan to pay off the supplier. As fast as the company is able to sell the merchandise, it pays off the bank loan. This loan permits the company to get along without a large amount of working capital.

Collateral loans. A company may be able to obtain bank loans on the basis of such collateral as chattel mortgages, stock and bonds, real estate mortgages, and life insurance (up to the cash surrender value of the policy). Even with collateral, the bank will still give great weight to the company's ability to repay. The bank may turn down the application for a loan, no matter how good the collateral, if there is not a clear showing of ability to repay.

SHORT-TERM BORROWING FROM COMMERCIAL FINANCE COMPANIES

A commercial finance company will frequently step in where a commercial bank will not. Commercial finance companies charge a higher rate and will sometimes take more risk and almost always take on more clerical work to protect their money. Because many companies in the commercial finance field are also engaged in factoring, there is a tendency to confuse the two. Factoring is the service rendered through the assumption of the credit risk on sales purchased from the factored company and the acceptance of the bookkeeping and collection responsibilities for the resulting receivables. In contrast to factoring, the commercial finance company does not guarantee against credit losses on sales to customers.

Finance companies do not "lend" money—they provide revolving working capital. Perhaps this is a subtle distinction, but if a company requires borrowed money it should, if qualified, resort to the many commercial banks throughout the country to satisfy that need. Banks and commercial finance companies are not in competition with one another. Finance companies are among the largest borrowers of money from commercial banks, and commercial banks very frequently refer their customers to finance companies when the capital position of the prospective borrower is insufficient for the bank to grant the credit lines needed.

Funds advanced by commercial finance companies are secured by collateral—mainly accounts receivable—and the finance company has recourse to the borrowing firm. The decision to advance the necessary funds is based, among other things, upon the character and ability of the company's management, its diversification and performance, the quality of the assets pledged, and the ability of the company to operate at a profit if the funds are made available to it.

Commercial financing of accounts receivable and other collateral provides a flexible borrowing arrangement whereby a borrower will receive the funds needed, in the amounts needed, and at the time needed. The accounts receivable outstanding are self-liquidating through their collection. To keep interest charges at a minimum, the financed company may borrow only the funds it needs as and when needed. This method can be contrasted with the fixed-dollar loan, which carries a constant interest cost that must be met.

Accounts Receivable Financing

Accounts receivable are accepted by some banks and most commercial credit companies as collateral for a line of credit. Individual banking practices vary, however, and the borrower should become familiar with local banking requirements. The financing of accounts receivable involves the assignment by the borrower to the lender of the borrower's accounts receivable. These accounts receivable are security for advances which the lender makes to the borrower simultaneously with each assignment. As the proceeds of the assigned accounts are collected, they are turned over to the lender and applied to reduction of the indebtedness, the excess being returned by the lender to the borrower. The borrower remains responsible for the payment of the debt, even though the primary source of payment are the proceeds of the assigned accounts receivable. If the proceeds of the assigned accounts receivable are insufficient to repay the amount advanced, the borrower is liable for the deficiency. This is one important difference between accounts receivable financing and factoring. The factor purchases the accounts receivable from the borrower and assumes the risk of loss from any bad accounts.

Accounts receivable may be financed on a notification or a non-notification basis. Under a notification plan, the receivables are pledged and payment is made directly to the lender, but the borrower remains responsible for the payment. The lender notifies the borrower's customers that their accounts have been assigned and directs them to make payments directly to him. Under the more satisfactory and more commonly used non-notification plan, the borrower collects as agent for the lender. This method is preferable because the relationship between the borrower and his customers is not disturbed and the financing arrangement remains confidential.

Functions of Accounts Receivable Financing

The primary function of accounts receivable financing is to release funds tied up in these accounts, thereby giving a company working capital. Financing of receivables may put a borrowing company in a stronger position for sales expansion and may improve its credit standing by providing funds to discount its own payables.

Accounts receivable financing should be employed in conjunction with a cash forecast and financial plan. The financing will be used according to the plan's estimate of how much cash will be required before the expended cash comes back from customers. Whenever there is a shortage of working capital but available accounts receivable that are not yet due, the borrower is in a position to raise cash to meet his current needs. Of course, this financing aid is not the final answer to the problem of inadequate working capital; but it is a means of temporary relief, especially in seasonal industries where receivables are concentrated in a short period of the year and unacceptable collateral for long-term financing.

Mechanics of Accounts Receivable Financing

Before accepting accounts receivable as collateral, the lending agency will evaluate the risks and investigate the facts involved. Through analysis and investigation of the borrower's financial history and related factors, the lending agency can decide if it wants to assume the risk and how the risk can be minimized. At the outset it should be emphasized that certain types of businesses do not lend themselves to receivable financing. Most service enterprises fall into this category. This is because a serviceman may damage the customers' goods and offset any receivable that may be due. The same risk appears in businesses that furnish special orders. And generally factors do not look with favor on unstable industries.

Other considerations involve the accounts themselves. The lender will look to see if the accounts are acceptable for financing. Usually any account that represents a bona fide obligation owed to the borrower from a creditworthy customer, without the probability of setoff or the like, is available for financing. Under certain conditions, partial billings against unfinished contracts may be financed. The lender will have to be assured that these invoices are payable on regular terms and won't be unduly delayed. Under most circumstances, long-term dating will not disqualify the receivables unless there is undue hazard in their collection.

After the lender has satisfactorily completed his investigation, a basic contract between the lender and the borrower will be executed defining the rights and obligations of the parties. The contract is generally needed because accounts receivable financing contemplates a series of transactions rather than a single isolated loan. Many lenders require yearly contracts. While the agreements vary with the situations, a typical agreement might provide that the borrower assign all accounts receivable, or a selected group of them, to the lender as security. In return the lender agrees to advance funds up to 80% of the face value of the accounts receivable pledged, usually specifying a dollar maximum which can be borrowed. Periodically, schedules of customers' invoices are submitted to the lender to replenish borrowing power. Under this type of arrangement, the borrower, when cash is needed, simply lists the invoices which he wants to finance on the lender's standardized form and the lender advances the cash upon presentation of the form. The borrower should avoid arrangements where it is necessary to get clearance on each individual invoice. Blanket deals are much easier to administer, since invoice schedules are simply submitted periodically on accounts that have blanket approval and the lender worries about individual account limits.

Equity Adjustments

Upon the collection of the accounts, the financing company generally receives a larger amount than the percentage advanced. The excess, known as "equity," is credited to the client's accounts. (However, the full difference between the gross amount of the invoice and the percentage advanced is seldom realized upon payment because of returns, allowances and discounts.)

Cost of Accounts Receivable Financing

There are various methods of computing charges on open accounts receivable. The most common are:

(1) Straight interest on the amount of funds advanced expressed either as a rate per annum, per month or per diem. The rate of interest is applied to the average daily balances;

(2) A commission on the accounts assigned plus, in some cases, interest on the funds advanced. The logic behind the commission is that regardless of the amount of funds advanced against the assigned accounts, a major expense is incurred in handling the bookkeeping involved. The commission more accurately reflects the cost of maintaining the account;

(3) Charges may be expressed as a percentage of the average balance of the collateral assigned;

(4) A minimum charge may be required as assurance that the financing company will meet its expense in initiating and servicing the account;

(5) Gradually decreasing rates may be applied in any of the above methods, reflecting the decreasing operating costs per dollar advanced as the account grows larger.

Rates on the accounts receivable loan vary widely. Commercial bank rates may range from prime to 2% over prime or higher per annum on the balance in the loan account. Some banks add a small service charge to cover the sizable amount of clerical work involved, such as one-half on one percent based on total receivables pledged or a flat amount for originally setting up the loan. As pointed out, banks do not often go into accounts receivable financing, so that the borrower will probably have to turn to a commercial finance company for the loan. The cost of financing accounts receivable through a finance company is high. This may cost the borrower 2% to 4% over prime on a loan where the advance is 75% of the face value of the receivables. The rates may range from 4% to 8% over prime, or higher, depending on the overall interest cost of money.

Split Loans

There may occasionally be a situation where a company's credit standing may no longer entitle it to unsecured borrowing, but its financial position may still be far better than that of the usual finance company client, and therefore the company may not be willing to pay the high finance company charge. In this case the finance company may be able to work a *split loan* with a bank at a reduced rate for the borrower. The finance company will approach the bank and do all the preliminary work of setting up the loan. The split loan is a three-way arrangement among the borrower, the finance company and the bank. Under this arrangement, the finance company advances half the needed funds and takes full charge of administering the accounts receivable, which are the security for the entire arrangement. The bank does no work except to lend the other half of the needed funds without guarantee by the finance company. The bank relies on the judgment of the finance company and is able to employ its funds at a good rate with no more expense than any unsecured loan would entail and with greater safety because both lenders are protected by the lien on the accounts receivable. The benefit to the borrower can be seen from the following figures:

Assume the finance company rate is 20%, the prime bank interest rate is 16% and the rate for a split loan is 18%. If the borrower had used the finance company exclusively, he would have paid 20%. Here, he pays 20% on half the loan and 16% on the other half, or a net rate of 18%.

FINANCING THROUGH A FACTOR

Factoring is primarily a credit business in which the factor checks credits and makes collections for his client. He also purchases his client's accounts receivable without recourse, thereby guaranteeing the client against credit losses. This is the basic service of a factor for which the factor receives a fee. Normally the account debtor is notified that the account was purchased by the factor and that payment thereon is to be made directly to the factor.

In this operation the factor checks the credits, makes the collections and assumes the loss in the event the accounts are not paid. Up to this point, however, the factor has passed no funds to his client. He has purchased the accounts and has agreed to pay for them on their net due dates.

Under the standard factoring contract, the factor buys the client's receivables outright, without recourse, as soon as the client creates them by shipping merchandise to customers whose credit the factor has investigated and approved. Cash is made available to the client immediately on shipment; thus, in effect, he sells for cash and can turn his receivables into cash as far as he creates them. The arrangement is flexible, however, to the extent that the client may withdraw the full proceeds of the sale or leave the proceeds with the factor until their due date. He is charged interest only for money withdrawn prior to the due date. Thus he has a 100% demand privilege on the funds available to him but pays interest only on funds actually used.

However, the factor will make cash advances to the client on the receivables prior to their maturity. For example, suppose that the factor purchases accounts receivable amounting to $40,000 from his client, without recourse, due in 60 days. In this case, the factor owes the client $40,000 which must be paid in 60 days. The factor, however, will advance, say, $35,000 to the client immediately, to make operating cash available. The other $5,000 will be paid when due. The factor will charge interest on the funds advanced to the client, and at current rates. If these advances are not enough to meet the needs of the client—and this occurs frequently in seasonal business—the factor will also make short-term, supplementary loans secured by inventory, fixed assets or other acceptable collateral.

Non-Notification Factoring

Non-notification factoring is now available to clients in many fields who sell directly to customers in the retail trade. In this type of factoring, the factor purchases the receivables outright without recourse but does not assume the collection function without specific request. The client makes collections himself, and the customer is not notified of the factoring arrangements. The fee for non-notification factoring may be less than that charged for notification factoring.

Bank and Factor in Combination

Frequently, a commercial bank cannot provide all the loan funds a growing company needs. Its balance sheet is not liquid enough or it can't clear off the bank debt every six or twelve months. A factor can provide funds to clear off bank loans periodically or make additional bank credit possible by guaranteeing accounts or replacing accounts receivable with cash.

When Should You Factor?

First, can you factor? Yes if:

(1) You sell on normal credit terms;
(2) 80 to 90% of your customers are rated;
(3) Your annual volume is sufficiently large for profitable factoring.

What will factoring do for you? It converts your sales into cash sales. It can give you additional working funds to expand, modernize or whatever will improve your business.

Now, what will it cost you? You pay a service charge and interest. Interest will be 22% or 24% or more per annum on money actually used on a daily basis. The service charge, depending on the risk in your accounts and the amount of handling required, will be from three-quarters of one percent to one and one-half percent of the receivables purchased. But against this, you can credit savings:

(1) On the salaries of credit and collection people;
(2) On the elimination of bad debt writeoff;
(3) On the interest on money borrowed to carry sales and accounts receivable.

What the Factor Wants to Know

The first points a factor considers are the type of sales and the selling terms of the borrower. The sales should be on open account, so as to create accounts receivable that can be sold. The terms of the sale determine the value of the account to the factor. The shorter the terms of payment, the faster the factor can expect to turn over his investment and the lower his rates. If payment terms are extended, the factor will have a long wait to realize his investment and will charge a higher rate, one that might be prohibitive.

Credit information on the accounts should be available. The credit rating determines the risk assumed by the factor when he purchases the accounts without recourse. The factor will expect some credit losses and will include a loss reserve in his charges. A factor will not enter into a factoring agreement unless almost all of the borrower's regular customers seem to be good credit risks.

The arrangement should continue over an extended period of time—something more than a few months. Factors do not like to get involved in short-term deals.

The volume of accounts is important. Just as in any business the larger the earnings propsect, the more attractive the deal is. It does not pay a factor to handle a small volume. The size of the individual accounts controls the factor's costs. The greater the balance of the accounts, the smaller the percentage of fixed cost in its collection.

The factor will examine the records to determine if there is an abnormal percentage of returns and complaints. If the percentage of returns as compared with sales is too high, the factor may take this as a warning signal and back out of the transaction.

Provisions of Factoring Contract

The business of the present-day factor is to purchase accounts receivable upon much the same basis that tangible assets are bought and sold. The typical contract first provides that the client agrees to sell to the factor as absolute owner, and the factor agrees to purchase from the client without recourse to the client (with certain exceptions), all accounts receivables created by the client in the ordinary course of his business. The factor usually has recourse to the borrower for returns or allowance for bad debts or errors in pricing.

INVENTORY LOANS

Inventories are not as liquid as accounts receivable, and a bank or finance company will generally want to secure its advances by accounts receivable and go to inventories only after the business has exhausted its ability to borrow on receivables. Receivables convert into cash automatically, they present fewer legal problems, and they don't go out of style or become technologically obsolete or suffer drastic price declines. But inventory financing is important, particularly to businesses that must build up a stock to meet a seasonal demand.

Inventory is acceptable as collateral usually if the following conditions are met:

   (1) The inventory is readily salable—that is, no great sales effort would be required to turn it into cash to satisfy the loan if that should become necessary;
   (2) The inventory consists of basic commodities that will not deteriorate or become obsolete within the period of the loan;

(3) The necessary legal technicalities to protect the lender's position in the event of bankruptcy are available.

You will be able to borrow, if at all, only on your stock of raw materials or finished merchandise. Work in process has little value for borrowing purposes. No lender wants the responsibility for finishing up and selling work in process.

Here's what a lender will want to know about your inventory before he decides whether and how much he can lend on it:

(1) Is the price fairly stable or does it fluctuate sharply?

(2) How broad a market is there for the commodity?

(3) Are there any governmental restrictions on its sale?

(4) Under what conditions may the commodity be stored and for how long?

(5) Is the item closely graded by the trade?

(6) How does the condition of the commodity affect its value?

(7) Is the commodity usually sold in certain standard sizes, and does the commodity under consideration comply with those standards?

(8) Is there any danger of obsolescence in the near future due to technological changes?

(9) What should the costs of liquidation be, such as sales commissions, parking and transportation charges?

(10) Can the commodity be hedged by the purchase of futures?

The Problem of Protecting the Lender

The Uniform Commercial Code, already adopted in most jurisdictions and all the leading commercial and industrial states, has eliminated a lot of legal problems that formerly existed in connection with inventory financing.

The Code rules relating to after-acquired property, future advances, dominion and control of the collateral by the debtor, commingling of goods, and transferring the lien on the collateral to the proceeds make possible so-called "floating liens." The concept of a floating lien is that of a lien on a shifting stock of goods or inventory; that is, a lien on collateral in more or less constant flux and undergoing quantitative and qualitative changes. It is a concept that responds to a long-felt need of businessmen for an effective device giving a lender a security interest on goods and materials which the debtor is permitted to retain, process, manufacture or otherwise change and sell, and also covering the proceeds of the sale and the new goods and materials bought by the debtor with the proceeds in a continuing cycle of business activity. The chattel mortgage has been unable to satisfy this need because of problems in connection with description of the property covered, after-acquired property, and the power of the debtor to sell the collateral and to use the proceeds.

The fact that the Code makes legally possible a floating lien does not mean that the secured creditor's interest in collateral covered by the lien will necessarily be entitled to priority over all liens subsequently attaching or perfected in the same collateral. It may be subordinate to subsequent purchase money interests, and there will be problems of priority as against federal tax liens.

Also, a purchaser from the debtor in the ordinary course of business will get good title. However, the lender's lien may attach to the proceeds of the sale or the resulting account receivable.

In jurisdictions that have not adopted the Code, the lender will be looking to protect his lien under a Factors' Lien Act or the Uniform Trust Receipt Act or by taking actual or constructive possession of the inventory. The lender's actual possession of the goods is rarely feasible, and it will not be often that he can be given constructive possession by having the goods placed in a regular public warehouse and having him hold warehouse receipts. This can be cumbersome and expensive because it necessitates transferring the goods to and from the borrower's premises, plus storage charges. Field warehousing may be a more feasible alternative. Both these continue to be used in Code jurisdictions, although the underlying legal requirements may vary somewhat from pre-Code law.

Field Warehouse Financing

At field warehouse is created by a warehouse company leasing, at a nominal rent, a portion of the buyer's premises where the pledged inventory is to be stored. This space is segregated from the rest of the buyer's premises by a partition, wire fence or other appropriate means. Separate locks are installed to prevent any person from entering the storage space without the consent of the warehouse company. Signs can be posted all about the leased premises indicating that the space is under the control of the warehouse company and not the borrower. The purpose of this is to assure that the borrower's creditors will not be misled into thinking that they can lay claim to this inventory, or that they are secured by the fact that this inventory is on the borrower's premises.

The warehouse company hires a custodian, usually putting on its payroll a stockman who has been looking after the inventory for the borrower. Warehouse receipts are issued to the lender.

Commercial finance companies have developed a method of handling the whole chain of transactions from the acquisition of raw material to finished inventory for accounts receivable. Withdrawals from the warehouse are replaced by a steady stream of new raw materials and finished goods going into the warehouse. The sales invoice goes into the hands of the commercial finance company to replace finished goods shipped out of the warehouse. The net effect is to add a substantial increment of working funds to the business. As the finance company furnishes funds to buy raw materials, it is repaid out of advances on the finished product and then gets repaid for these advances out of cash paid upon the collection of the accounts receivable created when the finished product is sold.

The Factor's Lien

The use of a field or other warehouse is usually not practical where the borrower must retain possession of the inventory for further processing. Field warehousing is unnecessary in states where there are factor's lien laws, because the procedure where a factor's lien is available can be much less cumbersome and less expensive than field warehousing.

The lien agreement between the borrower and the lender must be placed on public record and usually provides that the borrower will report to the lender at frequent intervals the nature and value of the inventory in the hands of the borrower at that time. The borrower agrees that it will, upon a reduction in its inventory, make payments to the lender on its loans equal to or greater than the amount of the inventory reduction. The law usually requires that a notice, in a specified form, of the existence of the factor's lien be posted in a conspicuous place at the principal entrance to the place of business of the borrower. For obvious reasons, the lending agency usually requires a liberal margin of inventory values against its advances, inspects the inventories at frequent intervals and follows loans of this kind with exceptional care.

This procedure gives the lender in good lien on practically every piece of inventory located on the premises. A factor's lien is not operative against bona fide purchasers for value of the merchandise, who purchase it from the borrower in the ordinary course of business without actual notice of the lien. These purchasers get good title to the merchandise free and clear of the lien, but the lien of the lender attaches to the account receivable created by the sale. It is very important that the lender adhere strictly to the notice, posting, and filing requirements of the statute which makes the factor's lien available.

The usual transaction involving the financing of inventory on a factor's lien contemplates a combined inventory and accounts receivable financing operation. The lender expects the inventory advances to be repaid out of the proceeds of the accounts receivable created by the sale of the inventory after it has been processed. The borrower expects to finance part of his cost of production by receiving additional advances on accounts receivable as they are created and assigned to the lender.

Trust Receipts

A trust receipt is a financing instrument in the form of an agreement between a bank (the lender), called the entruster, and a person, firm, or corporation (the borrower), called the trustee. It shows that certain goods or property, or evidence of title to these goods or property, having been acquired for financing purposes by the lender are released by it under specified conditions to the borrower.

While the goods are in the borrower's possession, the lender retains ownership until the goods or property, or the evidence of title to goods or property, are properly accounted for by the trustee to the entruster. This accounting is through payment or otherwise, as set out in the instrument.

The trust receipt is used for interim financing of staple commodities when it is necessary to release pledged goods from a warehouse in order to sell or process them. Another use is in financing, under a "floor-planning" arrangement.

Floor planning.   This term refers to the use of the trust receipt to finance the purchase by dealers or distributors of motor vehicles, household appliances and other products that may be readily identifiable as to specific units and that have other than a nominal unit value.

Under such a financing arrangement, the products are actually paid for by a bank or other lending agency, which obtains title through the payment of a draft with bill of lading attached, for the purchase price, or through a bill of sale or otherwise. In effect, the products are released by the lender to the borrower for inventory and sales purposes against the borrower's note and trust receipt. The trust receipt provides, in effect, that the borrower will hold the products in trust for the lender for the purpose of sale at not less than a specified minimum sale price per unit and will, pending sale, return the products to the lender upon demand. Or, upon sale, the borrower will keep the proceeds of sale segregated and deliver such proceeds to the lender immediately.

Floor plan terms.   Frequently, the lender will advance for the original purchase no more than 90% or less of the invoice cost of the products to be financed. It will usually require the monthly curtailment of any advances outstanding at the end of three months, with complete liquidation required within six months after the date of purchase. Interest on daily loans outstanding is usually billed to the borrower at regular monthly intervals.

Floor plan procedures.   During the period of outstanding advances, the lender will have a valid security interest (except against an innocent purchaser for value) in the products held by the borrower under trust receipt, provided they are clearly identifiable and the lender has observed all requirements of law surrounding trust receipt financing. These requirements may vary to some extent with the laws of each state but usually they include the necessity of placing on public record a "Statement of Trust Receipt Financing" which, in effect, is merely a notice that the borrower is engaged in trust receipt financing with a specified lender. At frequent but irregular intervals, the lender will make a detailed physical check of the products held by the borrower under trust receipt to establish their continued availability and to inspect their condition.

Observing floor plan terms and procedures.   The business using this method of inventory financing must take exceptional care to see that, when floor-planned products are sold, the proceeds of sale are delivered promptly to the lender to apply on outstanding advances. As the name implies, a trust receipt arrangement requires the trust of the lender in the integrity of the borrower. The latter must avoid any appearance of irregularities that might lead to the destruction of the confidence.

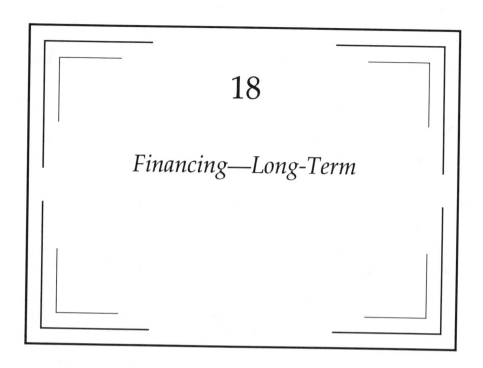

18

Financing—Long-Term

DIFFERENCES BETWEEN LONG-TERM AND SHORT-TERM DEBT

The basic distinction within a corporation's capital structure is that between equity (common and preferred stocks) and long-term debt. Short-term debt, even though it is anticipated that it will be renewed, is normally considered a current liability.

Long-term debt is generally shown as a separate category of liabilities and is distinguished from a stock issue in the following ways: (1) the corporation makes an absolute promise to pay the full amount of maturity; (2) the corporation promises to pay a fixed interest at periodic intervals; (3) the debt is frequently, but not necessarily, secured by specific assets of the corporation or by its assets generally; (4) the debt is frequently, but not necessarily, issued under an indenture under which a trustee is appointed to act as the creditors' representative in dealing with the corporation. Long-term debt is ordinarily in the form of bonds, although there is today a greater use of notes.

LONG-TERM BONDS

Long-term bonds are normally issued either in registered or coupon form. A coupon bond contains a coupon for each interest payable date during the life of the bond.

When the interest date is reached, the bondholder clips the coupon and sends it to the corporation and subsequently receives his interest payment. Coupon bonds are transferable merely by delivery (like cash) and, hence, create a problem of safe-keeping for the bondholder. A registered bond is registered with the corporation, and interest payments will be made directly to the registered owner until such time as the corporation is notified of a transfer. Registered bonds can only be transferred by negotiation (i.e., endorsement by the present owner) and are therefore less risky to hold.

Principal, Interest, and Maturity of Long-Term Bonds

A bond issue will normally be made up of a large number of bonds identical in all respects (except sometimes as to maturity). The usual denomination (par value) for a bond is $1,000, although in some cases "baby bonds" of $100 denominations have been issued to appeal to the smaller investor. The bond's stated, or "nominal" interest rate is selected on the basis of two considerations: (1) the current scale of money rates; (2) the quality of the company issuing the bonds. If the interest rate is set too low, the bond issue will be salable only at a substantial discount from par or may not be salable at all. If the interest rate is too high, the corporation will be paying more than necessary for money it obtains. Once the bonds have been issued, their price will fluctuate depending on changes in money rates and in the financial and operating condition of the company. It is unusual for a publicly traded bond to have the same market rate as the nominal rate—that is, it is unusual for the bond to be traded at exactly par value.

The current range of money rates plays a role in determining whether a long-term bond issue should be considered at all. Current interest rates are plotted on a graph according to the maturity of the various issues. This is called a "yield curve." An upsweeping yield curve means that the longer maturities yield the highest interest rates (the "normal" situation, since there must be some inducement for lenders to tie up their money for the longer periods). However, there are occasions when the yield curve will be downsweeping; i.e., interest rates for the shorter maturities will be higher than for the longer maturities. Obviously, the best time from the borrower's viewpoint for a long-term bond issue is when the yield curve is downsweeping, since long-term money is then cheaper than short-term money. On the other hand, if the yield curve is sharply upwards, short-term money may be so much cheaper that it would be wise to arrange the necessary financing through short-term loans (assuming they are available) with the intention of refinancing with long-term debt at some later date when the yield curve is more favorable.

The maturity of long-term debt may range anywhere from five years to 100 years. A bond issue may have a single maturity date for all the bonds or may be a serial issue, with a certain proportion of the bonds maturing at different dates. With a single maturity, the company must be prepared to pay off the entire issue at one time or refinance, called *refunding*. A serial issue spreads the corporation's obligation over a period of years and can be thought of as somewhat similar to a sinking fund.

Secured Bonds

For blue-chip corporations of the very highest quality, specific security for a bond issue is usually of little importance to the market because of the high credit standing of the company. But for other companies, the security underlying a bond may be an important factor in determining its marketability. Secured bonds can be divided into four classes:

(1) Real property mortgage bonds. These are bonds secured by real estate owned by the corporation. The face amount of the bonds will normally not exceed two-thirds of the appraised value of the real estate in the case of first mortgage bonds. In addition, second or third mortgage bonds can be issued.

(2) Equipment obligation bonds. These are bonds secured by chattel mortgages on personal property owned by the corporation. A special form of such bond is the equipment-trust certificate under which title to the property remains with the lender who leases it to the corporation until such time as the debt is paid. Equipment-trust certificates are most often used in the railroad industry.

(3) Collateral trust bonds. These are bonds secured by investment securities in companies other than the borrower. The borrower is entitled to the interest or dividends from the securities, but they may be sold by the lender in case of the borrower's default.

(4) General or blanket mortgage bonds. These are bonds secured by all of the corporation's assets. These bonds normally preclude any further issues of secured debt by the corporation unless they specifically provide that they may be subordinated to future bond issues secured by specified assets.

One major problem that frequently occurs in secured bonds is the inclusion of an after-acquired property clause. This clause provides that the mortgage securing the bond issue will automatically be expanded to include all property or specified property subsequently acquired by the corporation. Sometimes this is limited to new property which is acquired to replace property originally included under the mortgage, but on other occasions the clause covers all new property acquired by the corporation and thus increases the security of the bondholders. If a corporation has such a bond indenture in existence and wishes to avoid subjecting new property to the outstanding mortgage, it may be able to proceed in one of the following ways:

(1) Acquire the new property subject to a purchase money mortgage, which ordinarily has priority over the after-acquired property clause;

(2) Organize a subsidiary company to hold the new property;

(3) Lease instead of buy the new property;

(4) Acquire the new property in connection with a merger or consolidation, which frequently renders the after-acquired clause inoperative;

(5) As a last alternative, the outstanding bonds can be redeemed.

Guaranteed Bonds

The guarantee is a less common form of creating security for a bond issue. A guarantee differs from a mortgage in that the creditor is entitled to look to another person rather than to specified property as additional protection for his loan. The three most common types of guarantee bonds are:

(1) Individual guarantees.   These are most often used in closed corporations where all or some of the stockholders may sign the bonds or notes individually. They assume personal liability in addition to the corporate liability.

(2) Guarantees by corporate parents.   A corporation may decide to carry out some of its operations via subsidiary corporations. In that case, if the subsidiary sells a bond issue, the parent corporation by guaranteeing the bonds can sometimes make the bonds salable at a lower interest rate. Although corporations cannot, as a general rule, guarantee the obligations of others, most states make an exception for subsidiary corporations or for guarantees made within the scope of the corporation's business operations.

(3) Joint guarantees.   These are most common in the railroad industry where two or more railroad corporations may guarantee the bonds of a facility which is jointly used by them, such as a terminal building.

Debenture Bonds

These are unsecured bonds backed only by the general credit of the corporation. In the case of small and many medium-sized companies, debenture bonds are considerably riskier than either secured or guaranteed bonds. There are two primary categories of debentures:

(1) Nonsubordinated debentures.   These, on their face, make no provision for subordination to any future bond issues. However, if the bond indenture says nothing further, these bonds will automatically be junior in lien to any future bond issues which are secured by specific corporate assets. To prevent this from happening, the lender may insist that the indenture contains a provision limiting the total amount of future debt which the corporation may issue or a provision that the debenture bonds will have an equal status with the claim of any future mortgage bonds or secured bonds issued by the corporation.

(2) Subordinated debentures.   Of all the types of debt, these most resemble a stock issue. The subordination clause places the lender last among all the creditors of the company, past or future. The advantage to the corporation is that it preserves its future borrowing power, while at the same time creating deductible interest rather than nondeductible dividends. This type of bond issue will appeal to persons who are prepared to assume greater risk than the usual bondholder, but who also want a priority position as against the common stockholders. Debenture bonds are very similar, therefore, to preferred stock. In fact, the debentures will frequently carry a conversion privilege as a "sweetener," thus giving the bondholder the option to change his interest to stock in the event the company is successful.

Discount Bonds

Sometimes bonds may be issued at a discount instead of calling for interest. For example, a bond with a face of $1,000 may be issued at $750. At maturity, the bond will be redeemed for $1,000.

This type of bond is not usually used except by closely-held companies. But tax problems may be created by a discount bond.

For bonds issued on or before July 18, 1984, to the extent there is an "original issue discount" and the bondholders realize this discount, either on redemption or through sale to other holders, the gain realized is treated as ordinary income. Gain not attributable to the original issue discount—i.e., gain that might arise from purchasing a bond as between bondholders, at a further discount—is treated as capital gain. Note: There's a major new law change for bonds issued after July 18, 1984 and purchased on resale at a discount. The gain is ordinary income to the extent of the accrued market discount.

From the corporation's point of view, discount should be amortized over the life of the bond, thereby increasing proportionately each year's interest expense. Where a premium is received, it too is amortized over the life of the bonds, thereby decreasing each year's interest expense.

Special Features of Bond Issues

Any or all of the following special types of provision may be found in a bond issue:

(1) Sinking funds.   A sinking fund requires the corporation to set aside a certain amount of cash each year so that, at the maturity of the bond issue, there will be sufficient funds to pay off the bondholders. The annual contribution may be set up in one of several different ways. For example, an increasing amount may be required each year on the theory that the underlying asset becomes more productive. Or, higher amounts may be required in the earlier years because increasing maintenance charges are anticipated as the asset grows older. If the sinking fund reserve is retained by the corporation until the maturity of the bond issue, the corporation may invest the funds in some form of investment which is both safe and liquid, such as Treasury obligations. On the other hand, the indenture may provide that the sinking fund cash is to be used to purchase bonds on the open market or from individual bondholders drawn by lot. Whatever the specific use of the sinking fund, it acts to increase the security of the remaining bondholders.

(2) Restrictions on cash payments.   A bond indenture frequently prohibits the corporation from paying out cash dividends or using cash to reduce working capital unless a minimum amount of surplus is retained. Stock dividends, however, are normally not prohibited since they do not involve the overflow of cash.

(3) Convertibility to stock.   This has already been mentioned in connection with debentures. In setting conversion terms (the price of conversion), the corporation determines whether or not it wishes to force conversion. If it is issuing the bonds only as a temporary measure, it will give relatively easy conversion terms so that the bondholders are encouraged to take stock as soon as possible. On the other hand, if the corporation prefers the bonds (for example, because the interest is deductible), it may set the conversion terms to be attractive only after a period of years.

(4) Call feature.   This is a provision frequently inserted in a bond indenture for the protection or benefit of the corporation issuing the bonds. It permits the corporation to redeem the entire bond issue by paying the call price, which usually is set somewhat above par. For example, if the bonds have a face value of $1,000, the corporation may be permitted to call (redeem) them at $1,050. The time at which the bonds may be called may begin either immediately or after a certain number of years. A callability provision has a disadvantage from the borrower's point of view since it puts a limit on the price potential of the bond. If interest rates decline, the bond price will rise as a consequence and, apart from the call price, may reach a level substantially above par. However, if the corporation has the call privilege, it will probably exercise it when bond prices begin to rise, because this means the corporation can refinance by issuing a new bond issue at lower interest rates.

TERM LOANS BY BANKS AND INSURANCE COMPANIES

Term loans are a common way of providing intermediate financing, i.e., from one to five years and sometimes up to ten years. The parties frequently proceed on the assumption that a term loan will be renewed each time it becomes due, provided of course that the financial condition of the business warrants such renewals. While such debt may therefore remain on the company's books for very long periods of time, it is nevertheless classified as intermediate because the lender has the option at relatively frequent intervals to terminate the loan.

There are numerous purposes for intermediate borrowing. One of the most common is to provide adequate working capital. A company may be under-capitalized from the start, or it may find that in times of prosperity more capital than anticipated is tied up in inventory and accounts receivables. In such a case, a term loan can supplement the firm's own equity investment. Another common use of the term loan is to acquire equipment with relatively short lives. Depreciation of the equipment affords tax-free cash which is available to pay off the loans; when new equipment is again required, the loan can be renewed. Finally, a term loan is often used when the company is actually seeking long-term funds but decides that the time is not propitious for floating long-term debt or for a public issue of stock. Typically, companies are reluctant to issue long-term debt when interest rates are very high, or to issue common stock when the market is quite weak.

Interest rates on term loans will, as befits their intermediate status, fall somewhere between the extremes of the maturity yield curve. They will tend to rise during periods of business expansion as the commercial banks are called upon to increase their business loans, and conversely term loans will be in less demand during times of economic recession. Commonly, the interest is in the form of a discount, whereby the bank deducts annual interest at the inception of the loan. This will make the actual interest rate higher than the nominal (contract) rate.

As regards repayment of principal, a term loan may be a standing loan, a fully amortized loan or a partially amortized loan. In the last case, the loan is called a balloon loan since a portion of the principal will remain due at maturity despite regular payments of principal. Generally, unsecured term loans will require some amortization, particularly if they run for more than one year. On the other hand, if the loan is secured by stocks or bonds or by other assets of the borrower, no or very little amortization may be required even though the loan is for a longer term.

Restriction in Term Loan Agreements

A term lender will be particularly interested in the borrower's cash flow rather than net income after taxes. The reason is that over a relatively short period, a company may be fully capable of paying off a term loan out of its cash flow, even though it may go through a temporary period of declining or nonexistent earnings. Or under opposite circumstances, a company may anticipate a large net income but may have a very small cash flow due to the need to purchase new equipment, pay off other loans, etc. Important provisions in the term loan agreement which act to restrict the borrower include the following:

Additional debt. The lender may impose restrictions on the borrower's right to incur additional debt. This is more likely where the term debt is unsecured and new debt, by virtue of security provisions, may place the term loan in a subordinated position.

Restriction on dividends.   A common provision is one forbidding dividends unless net profits and/or cash flow and/or working capital reach designated amounts.

Restrictions of cash payments.   In addition to limiting dividend payments, the loan agreement may limit other cash payments. For example, surplus may not be used to retire existing stock or for investment in foreign subsidiaries.

Restrictions on salaries.   In the case of smaller companies, a lender may insist that salaries, bonuses and other compensation be restricted to stated amounts.

Minimum working capital.   The effect of the preceding restrictions is to insure that the company has sufficient working capital for its needs. In addition, the loan agreement may specifically provide for a minimum working capital position.

Barring merger or consolidation.   Finally, the lender may insist that no merger or consolidation take place while the term loan is outstanding. The reason is that such a combination may deprive the borrower of necessary cash or may place the term loan in a very subordinated position.

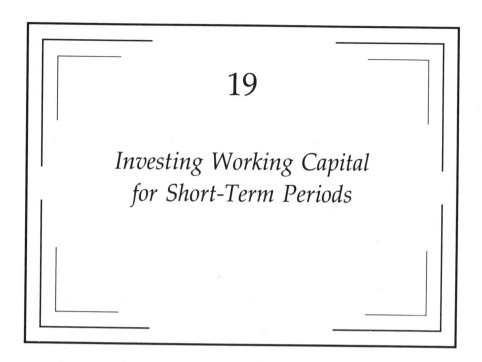

19

Investing Working Capital for Short-Term Periods

CONSERVING CASH

The amount of current assets which must be maintained by the business to sustain its working capital needs will vary, depending on such matters as the rapidity of inventory turnover, the length of the collection period, and the extent to which current assets are reduced by capital replacement, dividends and similar needs of the business.

Regardless of the absolute amounts needed by a particular business, it is a general principle of business finance that cash should be conserved whenever possible. In other words, the amount of inventory should be no higher than needed to sustain the normal sales volume of the business and every effort should be made to collect receivables as soon as possible.

Until quite recently, this principle of conserving cash led most financial officers to favor large cash balances in corporate checking accounts, since this represented 100% liquidity. The view was taken that any type of investment represented an unnecessary business risk. But this is now regarded as too conservative and, since it denies the business any return on its cash, too costly a practice to follow.

The Minimum Need for Cash

There are at least five reasons why a minimum cash balance must be maintained:

(1) Immediate liabilities.   The company must have cash for its payroll and for other liabilities, such as tax payments or trade accounts which must be paid in the next few weeks.

(2) Emergencies.   It is possible that the business will need a sum of cash for some emergency purpose, or perhaps even to make a highly advantageous purchase which must be consummated at once.

(3) Purchase discount.   Companies like to have sufficient cash on hand to take advantage of all purchase discounts. While, today, many companies look upon the cost of merchandise or other items purchased as the net cost after discount, nevertheless, failure to pay a bill within a discount period can be quite expensive. For example, merchandise purchased on a 2%/ten; net/30-basis will, in effect, pay 2% interest for the use of the money for 20 days if the bill is not paid within the 10-day period. This is the equivalent of a 36% annual interest rate. Hence it becomes important to pay all bills within the discount period, so it is important to have sufficient cash on hand to take advantage of the discounts.

(4) Compensating bank balances.   Most commercial banks require that borrowers maintain a compensating deposit with them. For example, a company borrowing $100,000 may be required to maintain a continuing deposit of $20,000. This increases the actual interest cost because the borrower has the use of $80,000 instead of $100,000.

(5) "Window-dressing."   This is a purely psychological factor but one which should not be overlooked. Even though a company has excellent reasons for maintaining an extremely low cash balance, such a figure on its balance sheet may prove disconcerting to stockholders and creditors, who may feel that the business is short of working capital, one of the most common reasons for business failure.

Nature of Risks in Investing Cash

In theory, conversion of cash into any other form of investment creates three possible kinds of risks: credit, money, and liquidity.

(1) Credit risk.   This is the risk that the organization which issues the investment obligation will fail or will otherwise be unable to honor its obligation. Where the organization is the U.S. Government, this risk is almost nonexistent. The risk is small also for all practical purposes when the organization is a state, municipality or private organization which is insured by an agency of the government. Investors now, however, are more cautious of municipal obligations, after the experience of New York City. On the other hand, investing in common stock of a small enterprise obviously involves a high degree of risk.

(2) Money risk.   This refers to the risk of loss due to changes in interest rates. For example, the price of a U.S. Government bond may fall (even though no credit risk is involved) because interest rates rise, which in turn reflects changes in the supply and demand for money. The existence of money risk precludes any investment of cash in long-term obligations. However, there are forms of short-term investments (Government bills and certificates and time deposits, called "near-money") which involve such a minimum degree of money risk that it can be ignored.

(3) Liquidity risk.   This refers to the absence of a market for the investment. For example, a real estate mortgage may suffer no decline in price due to money risk or credit risk, but nevertheless may have no market at the time the holder wishes to sell it. To insure liquidity, corporate cash should be invested in obligations having an extremely active market, the most typical of which are U.S. Government securities.

Types of Investments for Corporate Cash

Having defined the basic type of risk, we may briefly indicate the types of investments which may be appropriate for the investment of corporate cash balances:

(1) Ninety-day treasury bills.   Treasury bills are the shortest term obligation issued by the Federal Government and represent an obligation almost equal to actual cash in terms of the various risks outlined above. Treasury bills are issued for 91 or 182 days (there is normally a new issue every week), and their interest rate will vary depending on the degree of monetary ease which prevails. They are completely liquid, are sold by the government on a discount basis rather than on the basis of a face value plus accrued interest, and can be purchased only in minimum amounts.

(2) Other federal obligations.   There are three other classes of Federal obligations: Treasury certificates (maturity of 6 to 12 months), Treasury notes (maturity of 1 to 5 years), and Treasury bonds (maturity of over 5 years). While these involve little credit risk or liquidity risk, they do involve a money risk as their prices will fluctuate in relation to the movement of interest rates.

(3) Certificates of deposit.   The institutions which were hurt most by the transfer of corporate funds from demand deposits to income-bearing investments have been the commercial banks. In an attempt to win back some of the lost funds, commercial banks now offer certificates of deposit. These are issued to a corporation on deposit of a minimum amount of funds (e.g., $15,000-$100,000) for a minimum period of time (e.g., six months) and carry an interest rate which substantially exceeds the current rate on savings accounts. Although the money deposited must remain for the minimum period in order to earn interest, the certificates themselves are negotiable in the money market so that from the point of view of the corporation, there is no problem as to liquidity. Because of the short-term nature of the deposit, there is similarly less risk of loss from changes in interest rates.

(4) Savings and loan association deposits.   Until commercial banks began issuing certificates of deposits, much of the corporate funds which were not invested in securities were placed in savings and loan associations. Here, they could earn high interest and normally could be withdrawn upon 30-days' notice. While such deposits normally create little money risks or credit risks (since deposits are insured by an agency of the Federal Government), there is some possibility of nonliquidity in the event of a severe economic downturn which could result in a high foreclosure rate, which in turn might mean that some savings and loan associations (which invest primarily in mortgages) might not be in a position to pay their depositors upon demand.

(5) Short-term commercial notes.   Finance companies and other monied corporations whose main assets are cash are constantly offering short-term notes to investors for the purpose of raising working capital. These notes, with maturities of from 90 days upwards, are suitable for many corporations since they provide a return slightly higher than that on Treasury obligations and, in the case of the largest finance companies, there is little risk.

(6) Short-term corporate bonds.   One type of investment that is used by corporate treasurers is corporate bonds which have only a short time until maturity. In the case of our largest and strongest corporations, their bonds involve small risk. If their bonds are bought at a discount a short time prior to maturity, this also reduces the money risk since even if money rates rise (causing a decline in bond prices generally), the investor knows he must receive at least par at the maturity of the bonds.

(7) Municipal bonds.   This type of investment may yield slightly less than some others, but income is exempt from tax at the corporate level. Such income cannot be distributed as a tax-free dividend.

(8) Commercial paper.   This is a short-term investment that usually pays interest at a rate higher than government obligations. The larger corporations borrow short-term funds in this manner with a 30-day maturity. If they are bought with discretion, the risk factor is moderate.

(9) Repurchase agreements.   Many financial institutions now offer to sell investors a package of government securities at a discount, with an agreement to repurchase the package at some later date, 30 days to 89 days, at a specified price. The risk factor is small if purchased from solid institutions.

(10) Money market funds.   Money-market funds are simply portfolios of money-market instruments put together by a manager and made available to investors. Such funds are highly liquid and can be bought and sold daily. In some cases the funds are set up so that you may withdraw funds by merely writing a check. Risk can be minimized by buying funds which hold only government securities.

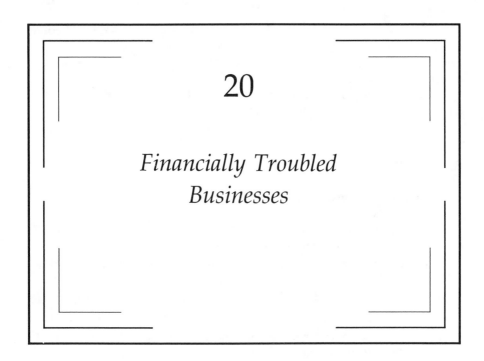

20

Financially Troubled Businesses

HANDLING A COMPANY IN FINANCIAL DIFFICULTY

The corporate accountant's need for handling a company in financial difficulty can arise when his own company is in trouble, or when a debtor of his company is the one that has the financial problems. In either case, he might, for example, be concerned with preparing or evaluating a statement of affairs. And he might be concerned with the rules of bankruptcy when his company or the debtor might be thrown into, or voluntarily go into, bankruptcy. More often, rather than outright bankruptcy, he might be involved in working out an arrangement for rehabilitating or reorganizing the company either as debtor or creditor.

Statement of Affairs

The purpose of the statement of affairs is to determine how much the unsecured creditors can hope to get from the business if it is liquidated. The statement may be prepared by a trustee in bankruptcy to determine whether the business would be better off being dissolved or continued. It may also be prepared anywhere along the line where a business is in trouble (perhaps in trying to work something out with creditors) to determine the status of the unsecured creditors. (Note that we are referring here to an accounting statement of affairs as distinguished from a statement of affairs prescribed under the Bankruptcy Act, which is a comprehensive debtor's questionnaire.)

Included here is an illustration of a statement of affairs with a statement of the estimated deficiency to unsecured creditors.

BANKRUPTCY

You may have contact with the Bankruptcy Reform Act of 1978 when:

1. You want to obtain for your company the status of a secured creditor in anticipation of the possible bankruptcy of the debtor.
2. You want to protect your company as creditor by putting the debtor in bankruptcy.
3. You want to press a claim against or recover an asset from a bankrupt estate.
4. Your company is the harassed debtor seeking to be discharged of its debt.
5. You want the protection of the court and an appointed trustee to rehabilitate your financially embarrassed business.

Chapter 11 of the Bankruptcy Code replaces Chapters X, XI, and XII of the Bankruptcy Act that applied to cases filed before October, 1, 1979.* Chapter 11 can be used as the means of working out an arrangement with creditors, with the debtor continuing or for a complete reorganization with the debtor or a trustee in charge of the business.

Avoidance of Preferences

The trustee or debtor in possession can avoid transfers that are considered preferences including the recovery of payments so considered. The elements of a preference are:

1. A transfer of the debtor's property,
2. To or for the benefit of a creditor,
3. For or on account of an antecedent debt,
4. While the debtor is insolvent,
5. Within 90 days before the petition (one year for insiders),
6. The creditor receiving the transfer receives more than he would have in a liquidation case without the transfer.

---

*Prior law (Bankruptcy Act) used roman numerals for chapter identification while the new law (Bankruptcy Code) uses arabic numbers. There are eight chapters in the new law (all odd numbers) contained in Title 11 U.S. Code.

X CORPORATION
Statement of Affairs
. . . . , 19 . . . .

Assets

Book Value	Assets	Appraised Value	Available to Unsecured Creditors	Estimated Shrinkage
$250,000	Fully Pledged Assets: Land & Building	$180,000		$70,000
	Less: Mortgage Payable (deducted contra)	150,000		
	Partly Pledged Assets: Bonds of Y, Inc.	$32,000		
30,000	(deducted contra)		$30,000	
	Unpledged Assets:			
5,000	Cash	$5,000	5,000	
100,000	Accounts Receivable (less bad debts)	80,000	80,000	20,000
200,000	Inventories	120,000	120,000	80,000
1,000	Goodwill			1,000
$586,000	TOTALS		$235,000	$171,000
	Preferred Creditors (see contra)		55,000	
	Balance Available to Unsecured Creditors		$180,000	

Liabilities and Stockholder's Equity

Book Value	Liabilities and Stockholder's Equity	Unsecured Claims
	Preferred Creditors	
$10,000	Wages Payable	$10,000
40,000	Taxes Payable	40,000
5,000	Estimated Administration Costs	5,000
	Deducted contra	55,000
	Fully Secured Creditors:	
150,000	First Mortgage Bonds and Accrued Interest (deducted contra)	
	Partially Secured Creditors:	
40,000	Notes Payable and Accrued Interest	40,000
	Less: Appraised value of Y, Inc., Bonds	32,000
		$8,000
	Unsecured Creditors:	
300,000	Accounts Payable	300,000
	Stockholders' Equity:	
200,000	Capital Stock	
(159,000)	Deficits	
$586,000	TOTALS	$308,000
	Available to Unsecured Creditors Contra	180,000
	Estimated Deficiency to Unsecured Creditors	$128,000

Making Claims Against a Bankrupt

A creditor establishes a claim in bankruptcy by filing what is known as a "proof of claim." You can go into almost any legal stationery store and buy appropriate forms. A creditor is not required to file a proof of claim if it agrees with the debt listed in the schedule submitted by the debtor to the court. However, creditors, who for any reason, disagree with the amount admitted on the debtor's schedules, or creditors desiring to give a power of attorney should prepare and file a complete proof of claim.

Putting a Debtor in Involuntary Bankruptcy

Three or more creditors (if there are 11 or fewer creditors, only one creditor is necessary) with unsecured claims of at least $5,000 can file to force a debtor into involuntary bankruptcy. Under prior law, before proceedings could commence, it was necessary for the debtor to have committed one of the acts of bankruptcy. The new law eliminates the acts of bankruptcy and permits the court to allow a case to proceed only (1) if the debtor generally fails to pay its debts as they become due, or (2) within 120 days prior to the petition a custodian was appointed or took possession (such as often happens with an assignment for the benefit of creditors). The latter excludes the taking of possession of less than substantially all property to enforce a lien.

Governmental units, estates, trusts, farmers and non-profit corporations cannot have an involuntary petition filed against them.

The petition can be filed under Chapter 7 (Liquidation) or under Chapter 11 (Reorganization).

There are several reasons why a creditor might want to force a debtor into bankruptcy:

1. There is a segregation of assets immediately without the risk of having the bankrupt dissipate or conceal the property available to pay his debts.
2. There is an orderly administration of the bankrupt's estate as well as a procedure under which claims against it can be expeditiously established.
3. If the bankrupt has made any substantial preferences—that is to say, if it has favored certain creditors—they can be required to return property to the estate for ratable distribution among all claims.
4. There is a provision for the examination of the bankrupt and witnesses to determine the nature of the acts, conduct and property of the bankrupt whose estate is in the process of administration.

Procedure Steps in Bankruptcy Proceedings

The steps in a bankruptcy proceeding are these:

1. Filing of petition—a voluntary petition constitutes an adjudication; an involuntary petition may be contested. An answer to an involuntary petition would

deny the allegations contained in the petition, generally the allegation that debts are not being paid when due.

2. The court will issue an order for relief which creates an automatic stay of the actions of creditors. As a result of the stay, no party, with minor exceptions, having a security or adverse interest in the debtor's property can take any action that will interfere with the debtor or his property until the stay is modified or removed.

3. A committee of creditors will be appointed as soon as practicable by the court in Chapter 11 proceedings. In Chapter 7 proceedings a trustee will be appointed by the court who may then appoint a committee of creditors. A meeting of the creditors committee can require the bankrupt to submit to a broad examination covering every phase of his operations.

4. The debtor must file an inventory of all his property and a list of all his creditors, secured and unsecured, showing the amount owed each. He must also file a "statement of affairs" giving information as to his financial history, the volume of business, his income and other pertinent information. The schedule must claim any exemptions the debtor believes he's entitled to, otherwise the exemption may be lost.

5. A trustee in bankruptcy may be elected at the first meeting of creditors by 20% of the unsecured creditors, both as to number and amount of claims, in a Chapter 7 proceeding. In a Chapter 11 proceeding, the appointment of a trustee is made only by petition to the court.

6. The trustee, if any, has a key role in bankruptcy proceedings. He must take over and gather together all the bankrupt's assets. To this end, he has the job of uncovering fraud and concealment and recovering preferences and fraudulent transfers. In Chapter 11 cases where the debtor is left in control of the business, the court may appoint an examiner to investigate if there has been fraud or concealment.

How the Assets of the Bankrupt Are Distributed

The Bankruptcy Code of 1978 modifies to a limited extent the order of payment of the expenses of administration and other unsecured claims. The Code provides the following priorities:

1. Administrative expenses.

2. Unsecured claims in an involuntary case arising after commencement of the proceedings but before an order of relief is granted.

3. Wages earned within ninety days prior to filing the petition (or the cessation of the business) to the extent of $2,000 per individual.

4. Unsecured claims to employees' benefit plans arising within 180 days prior to filing petition limited to $2,000 times the number of employees less the amount paid in (3) above.

5. Unsecured claims of individuals to the extent of $900 from deposits of money to purchase, lease, or rental of property or purchase of services not delivered or provided.

6. Unsecured tax claims of governmental units:

a) Income or gross receipts tax provided tax return due (including extension) within three years prior to filing petition.

b) Property tax last payable without penalty within one year prior to filing petition.

c) Withholding taxes.

d) Employment tax on wages, etc., due within three years prior to the filing of the petition.

e) Excise tax due within three years prior to filing of the petition.

f) Customs duty on merchandise imported within one year prior to the filing of the petition.

g) Penalties related to a type of claim above in compensation for actual pecuniary loss.

Getting Debts Discharged

From the bankrupt's viewpoint, the discharge of his debts is the most important feature of the entire proceedings. He's entitled to a discharge as a matter of right unless proper objections are made and sustained. For everyone but a corporation, adjudication operates as an automatic application for discharge. A corporation may not obtain a discharge under Chapter 7 of the Code. This prevents the previous practice of maintaining the shell of a bankrupt corporation for latter use.

Grounds for Objecting to or Denying Discharge

There are ten statutory conditions that will deny the debtor a discharge:

1. Is not an individual.

2. Within one year prior to the filing of the petition, or after filing, transferred, destroyed, or concealed, or permitted to be transferred, destroyed, or concealed, any of his property with the intent to hinder, delay, or defraud his creditors.

3. Failed to keep or preserve adequate books or accounts or financial records.

4. Knowingly and fraudulently made a false oath or claim, offered or received a bribe, or withheld information in connection with the case.

5. Failed to explain satisfactorily any losses of assets or deficiency of assets to meet his liabilities.

6. Refused to obey any lawful order or to answer any material questions in the course of the proceedings after being granted immunity from self incrimination.

7. Within one year prior to the filing of the petition, committed any of the above acts in connection with another case concerning an insider.

8. Within the past six years received a discharge in bankruptcy under Chapters 7 or 11 of the Code or under the Bankruptcy Act.

9. Within the past six years received a discharge under Chapter 13 of the Code or Chapter XIII of prior law unless payments under the plan totaled 100 percent of the allowed unsecured claims or at least 70 percent of such claims under a plan proposed in good faith and determined to have been performed according to the debtor's best effort.

10. In addition, the discharge will be denied if, after the order for relief, the debtor submits a written waiver of discharge and the court approves.

It is interesting to note that the issuance of false financial statements to obtain credit, which was grounds for denial of discharge under the old law, will only prevent discharge for that particular debt rather than bar a discharge from all debts.

We can sum up these ten grounds by saying that a discharge in bankruptcy is available only to an honest debtor who has kept adequate records, cooperated in the bankruptcy proceedings, and hasn't been through bankruptcy proceedings for more than six years.

REHABILITATION

The financially embarrassed business can get relief under the Bankruptcy Code or by voluntary agreement with creditors.

Voluntary Agreements

We talk here about composition and extensions outside bankruptcy. In this connection, an arrangement under which the debtor is to pay a percentage of his debts is called a "composition." The main idea of an "extension" is that it gives the debtor more time to pay.

Either a composition or an extension involves two agreements: (1) one among two or more creditors and the debtor, and (2) one among the creditors themselves.

Why should the creditors want to approach the matter as a group rather than deal with the debtor on an individual basis? There may be a number of reasons, but certainly one of the more important is that, if a single creditor undertakes to collect the full amount owing him, he may precipitate bankruptcy proceedings either by the debtor or the other creditors. In those proceedings, he may have to return to the bankrupt's trustee any payment made by the debtor as an unlawful preference. And if no payment had been made but he had started legal proceedings which gave him sort of a lien, he would find that his lien was of no value to him, having been dissolved by the bankruptcy proceedings. Hence, a creditor might conclude that it would be better for him to try to work out some arrangement with the debtor and the other creditors rather than to engage in a race to collect his individual debt, especially since he could "win" the race in the first instance only to find himself disqualified in the end.

You can't have an effective composition or extension outside bankruptcy proceedings, however, unless all the creditors (or the great majority of creditors) are willing to go along with it and to overlook favored treatment to one or more creditors who won't go along. This is because the dissenting creditors won't be bound by the agreement and can proceed to the recovery of the amount due them by legal process. If you want a composition or extension that will bind the dissenters, the only way to get it is through bankruptcy proceedings or special local proceedings.

Effect of agreement.   A voluntary agreement will generally operate to discharge the debtor only when its terms have been carried out. Thus, a failure to pay notes given under the agreement may operate to revive the original debt even though the agreement doesn't expressly provide for its revival.

Care must be exercised to avoid discharging parties secondarily liable with the debtor. An extension of time of payment may, for example, discharge a surety unless he's agreed in advance to permit the extension.

Preferring creditors.   In a composition there's nothing wrong in "preferring" some types of creditors, where the preference has some rational or legal basis—e.g., the creditors "preferred" hold security or are entitled to some type of priority. Also, all the creditors who are parties to the composition should be told about the preference. A secret promise of a preference or other advantage made to one or more creditors will render the agreement fraudulent and void or voidable.

State insolvency laws.   Before resorting to a composition outside bankruptcy, be sure to check the insolvency laws of your own state. They may operate as a limiting factor in the use of these agreements.

Assignment for the Benefit of Creditors

The distinction between compositions and assignments for the benefit of creditors is not always clear. One distinction has been said to be that a composition requires the consent of the creditors while an assignment does not. However, as a practical matter you can't have an effective assignment for the benefit of creditors unless the creditors at least passively acquiesce. If the creditors don't go along with the idea, they may be able to treat the assignment as an act of bankruptcy and throw the debtor into bankruptcy proceedings.

There's another big difference between a composition and an assignment. In a composition, the debtor holds on to his business and works out a readjustment of his debts with his creditors. In an assignment, he turns over his business and all his property to an assignee or trustee to be distributed in payment of his debts. Also, a composition contemplates release of the debtor from further liability; not so in the ordinary assignment, although the creditors can, of course, consent to a release or discharge.

In an assignment, the debtor has what is called "a resulting trust in any assets." This may remain after the creditors have been paid. But the debtor has no equity of redemption; that is, he can't come in at any stage after he's made the assignment and get his property back by paying off his creditors, unless, of course, all of them consent.

Local variations in law. Local variations in the law governing assignments must be checked out. Here are the main areas to be watched:

(1) Assignment of part of property. (In some states, a partial assignment is void; in others, it is valid if the part not assigned is open to the remedies of all of the creditors.)

(2) What property passes under a general assignment. [Generally, all property, real or personal, tangible or intangible, including goodwill, trademarks (not personal), patents, interest in insurance policies or assignor's life, and rights under trust; but property held in trust and property fraudulently obtained will not pass.]

(3) Necessity of acknowledging, filing or recording assignment. (Many states have provisions.)

(4) Inventory of property assigned and schedule of creditors who are to participate. (These will usually be included in assignment as a matter of course, but state law requirements should be checked for formal requirements.)

(5) Notice to creditors. (Statutes may prescribe time and form.)

(6) Reservation of control by debtor. (Assignment will be invalid if there is reservation of any degree of control. Debtor cannot reserve right to revoke or declare future uses or trusts to which assignment is to be subject.)

(7) Reservation of possession. (Some authorities hold that debtor's reservation of possession will invalidate an assignment.)

(8) Intent to hinder or delay creditors. (Assignment made with a view to debtor's own advantage and to hinder and delay creditors in the just enforcement of their claims is vulnerable to attack as fraudulent.)

(9) Preferential treatment of creditors. (While there is nothing wrong with favoring creditors having recognized priorities, do not include a provision that those creditors will be first paid who will accept their pro rata share on condition that receipt constitutes a full release).

CORPORATE REORGANIZATION

Under the Bankruptcy Reform Act, Chapter 11 is designed to replace Chapters VIII, X, XI, and XII of prior law. Agreements under this Chapter can affect unsecured creditors, secured creditors, and stockholders. It is designed to provide the debtor with court protection while a plan is developed to rehabilitate the business and to minimize the substantial economic losses associated with liquidation (Chapter 7).

The new act favors the debtor in possession and will only appoint a trustee if requested by the party in interest and for cause. The term "cause" includes fraud, dishonesty or incompetence, or gross mis-management of affairs.

Who Can Start Reorganization Proceedings?

Reorganization proceedings can be instituted by the corporation (voluntary), or against it (involuntary) (1) by three or more creditors whose claims total $5,000 or more, are liquidated as to amount, and are not contingent as to liability, or (2) by an indenture trustee acting on behalf of the bondholders. If the corporation is to take the initiative, it can only do so with proper corporate authorization—usually a resolution of the board of directors.

Reclamation Proceedings

Reclamation proceedings are a quick way for a third party to get hold of property which belongs to him which is in possession of the trustee. Of course, in many situations where it is clear that the third party is entitled to property in possession of the trustee, he's not going to have to start a reclamation proceeding to get it; but if there's any doubt about the matter, chances are he'll resort to reclamation proceedings. He will not have to if he's the absolute owner of the property, because he'll win out as against a purchaser from the trustee if it comes to that unless, of course, the property in question is an intangible and negotiable. If the claimant holds a security interest only, the trustee will not hand it over if the property is worth more than the claim it secures. In that case he'll ask the court either to permit the secured creditor to sell the property outside bankruptcy and pay over the excess or to permit sale by the trustee, free and clear, and give the creditor an interest in the proceeds. The first course is likely to be followed only where the property in question is at some distant point and can't be conveniently sold with the other assets.

Allowance of Claims

At the first meeting of creditors, a provisional allowance of claims will be made for voting purposes, but this is not an allowance for purposes of dividend participation. However, as a general rule, claims filed at or before the first meeting will be allowed at that time if no objection is raised. If an objection is raised by either the trustee or one or more creditors, the referee will fix a date to hear and determine the points raised. There's no time limit on filing objections, but the referee may in his discretion refuse to entertain objections filed too late. Secured and priority claims will be allowed only to the extent they're unsecured. If a creditor has received a transfer, lien or preference which is voidable, his claim will not be allowed until he surrenders it to the trustee.

7

Budgeting for Profits

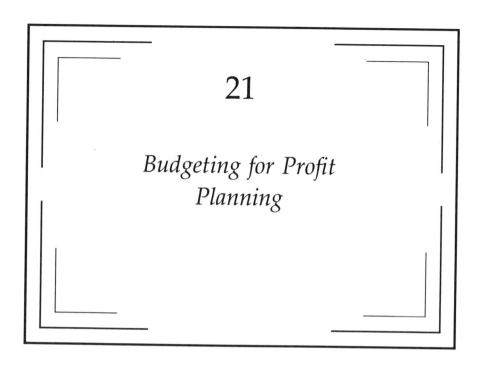

21

Budgeting for Profit Planning

BUDGETARY CONTROL

A budget in its simplest terms is an estimate of future events. This is not a purely random guess, but a forecast which is computed from historical data that has been verified and assumed with some degree of credibility. The volume of sales for the following year, for example, may be estimated by using data from past experience, present-day market conditions, buying power of the consumer and other related factors.

Merely preparing the annual budget, then leaving it unaltered for the remainder of the budget period, is not the purpose. Preparation is only the first step. The second step is for management to control the operations of the firm and to adhere to the budget. Budgetary control is the tool of management for carrying out and controlling business operations. It establishes predetermined objectives and provides bases for measuring performance against these objectives. If variations between performance and objective arise, management alters the situation by either correcting the weakness in performance or modifying the budget. Firms that adopt budgetary control have a better control of operations and are better able to modify them to meet expectations.

Types of Budgets

There are two principal types of annual profit budgets: the operating or earnings budget, and the financial or cash budget. The earnings budget, as its name implies, is an attempt to forecast the earnings of a company for a future period. To make such forecast, other estimates have to be made. Consequently, we have sales budgets, production budgets (which include labor budgets, materials budgets, purchases budgets, capital expenditure budgets, manufacturing expense budgets), administrative expense budgets, distribution expense budgets and appropriation-type budgets (e.g., advertising, research). The accuracy of each of these budgets determines the accuracy of the earnings forecast.

The cash budget, on the other hand, tries to forecast the utilization of the company's cash resources. It estimates the company's anticipated cash expenditures and resources for a period of operation. Cash budget forecasts, like the earnings forecast, depend heavily on sales forecasts. The amount of sales determines the amount of cash the company has for purposes of its operation.

THE SALES BUDGET

The foundation of the entire budget program is the sales budget. If anticipated sales of a particular product (or project) do not exceed the cost to produce and market it by an amount sufficient to reward the investors and to compensate for the risks involved, the product (project) should not be undertaken. Sales forecasting must be continuous. Conditions change rapidly; in order to direct one's efforts into the most profitable channels, there must be a continuous review and revision of the methods employed.

Forecasting Sales

A sales forecast represents the revenue side of the earnings forecast. It is a prediction as to the sales quantity and sales revenue. Sales forecasts are made for both short and long periods.

Forecasting sales with any degree of accuracy is not an easy task. For example, a firm which estimates sales with the expectation that a patent which it holds will not become obsolete may be disappointed.

In general, the business forecaster has two situations: (1) those which he can to some extent control, and (2) those where conditions created by others can only be observed, recorded, interpreted and applied to his own situation. A firm that has a monopoly due to an important patent which it owns is an example of a company which controls the situation. Forecasts made by such a company may be very accurate. In most cases, however, a company has no such control. It must attempt to interpret general conditions, the situation in its own industry, and future sales of its particular company before making forecasts.

Making the forecast is the responsibility of the sales manager, who, with the help of the district managers and the individual salesmen, determines the primary sales objectives for the year. Corrections of the forecast are made by the heads of the firm so that sales estimates will better reflect expected economic conditions. Before an estimate of sales is made, you must be reasonably sure that it is attainable. It must be based on the best evidence available. As conditions change, the forecast is revised.

If a firm desires to sell more than in the past, an analysis of past sales performances must be supplemented by other analyses. Consideration must be given to general business conditions. The effects of political and economic changes throughout the world are quickly reflected on individual business communities. Some of these factors which affect sales are wars, government regulations, and technological developments. This information should be used in appraising the probable effect of these changes on the sales of the firm for the budget period.

Market analysis.   A sales manager needs to know if his firm is getting its full share of potential customer demand as indicated by a market analysis.

The questionnaire is a popular method of reaching consumers, retailers and jobbers. Data collected gives the firm valuable information, essential in arriving at a forecast of sales possibilities.

A market analysis at a given time gives a picture of the present and potential consumption of a product. This picture provides only half the significant information. The other half can be obtained by continuing the survey over a period of time to discover market trends.

Pricing policy.   The sales budget is not complete until the firm decides on a practical policy as to what price can be secured for its product(s). Generally, estimates should be made to conform with the market prices during the budget period.

The next step is to formulate the sales policies of the firm. These policies should be established relative to such considerations as territorial expansion and selection, customer selection, types and quality of products and service, prices, terms of sales and sales organization and responsibility.

Only after a firm has thoroughly analyzed past sales experience, general business conditions, market potentials, the product to be sold and prices and has formulated its sales policies is it ready to develop the sales program.

Measuring individual performance.   As a basis for measuring individual performance, a rewarding-merit sales standard could be established. A sales standard is an opinion of the best qualified judgment of performance which may reasonably be achieved under ideal conditions. By comparing this standard with the budget estimate (the figure expected) under normal conditions, management has provided the most important tool of sales control.

An example of how a comparison between the standard and budget estimate may serve as a basis for reward is the following: A salesman may be told to produce sales of

$150,000 (standard), but the firm may expect him to produce sales of only $125,000 (budget estimate). The salesman does not have to be told what the firm's budget figures are. In his endeavor to reach $150,000, he is trying to better what he believes is the budget figure. Depending on how close he comes to the $150,000, the firm may devise a method of rewarding him. It should be kept in mind, however, that the standard should not be set too high, since it may have a reverse effect if the salesman feels it is unreachable.

THE PRODUCTION BUDGET

After the sales budget has been prepared, the next step is to prepare the production budget which specifies the quantity and timing of production requirements.

While the sales budget is prepared in anticipation of seasonal fluctuations, the production budget endeavors to smooth out the fluctuations and thus make most effective use of productive capacity. This is accomplished by manufacturing for stock over the slow periods and using the stock to cover sales during busy periods.

There are different problems for a firm that sells stock products and one that produces special-order goods. The objective for a stock-order-type firm is to coordinate sales and production to prevent excessive inventories, but at the same time to have enough stock to meet sales. A forecast of production in such a firm should enable the executive to arrange to lay out the factory so as to handle the anticipated volume most conveniently. Production in such a firm must be as evenly distributed as possible over the year. It is uneconomical to manufacture the whole period's requirements within a relatively short period at the beginning of the budget period. This involves unduly heavy capital costs of carrying the large inventory. Also, distributing the work over the entire period spreads the labor costs.

With special-order items, the production department has to be prepared at all times to manufacture the goods as soon as possible after receiving the order. Production in this case has to be arranged for the best possible utilization of equipment and labor, so that idle time is reduced to a minimum.

Budgeting Production Costs

Production budgets should be rigid as long as conditions remain the same, but they should be capable of prompt adjustment when circumstances change. For example, if a company operates at 70% of capacity in a period and the budget was based on a production volume of 80%, the budget is of little use. The budget will have to be altered to show what production costs will be at the 70% level. It is prudent when planning production at a particular anticipated percentage level to indicate in the budget the estimates of possible production costs at different levels.

Preparing the Production Budget

The production budget period may vary in length. However, it is common practice among large corporations to use what is known as a "product year." As an example, the automobile industry will usually start with the introduction of new models. The budget year should include at least one complete cycle of operations so that money tied up in raw materials and work-in-process materials may undergo one complete liquidation. Another factor influencing the budget period is the stability of general business conditions. It is more difficult to budget operations during an unstable period, and it is advisable at these times to shorten the budget period.

The production budget should be expressed in terms of physical units. To compute the physical quantities is simple. For example, a simple computation to estimate production required is:

	Units
Estimated sales	250,000
Less opening inventory	150,000
Total requirements	100,000
Add: Closing inventory	100,000
Production required	200,000

Before computing the quantity to be produced, it is necessary to decide quantities to be in the inventory at the end of the period. This decision should be based on factors such as:

(a) Adequate inventory to meet sales demands

(b) Evenly distributed production to prevent shortage of material and labor

(c) Danger of obsolescence

(d) High costs of storing large inventories.

Available facilities.   The production program must conform with the plant facilities available and should determine the most economical use of these facilities. The capacity of the plant is measured in two ways: maximum plant capacity and normal plant capacity. All other measurements are in percentages of maximum or normal capacity. Maximum capacity, of course, can never actually be attained. There are many unavoidable interruptions, such as waiting for setup of machines; time to repair machines; lack of help, tools, materials; holidays; inefficiency; etc. However, these interruptions should be looked into to determine how they can be minimized.

Management should also consider whether additional equipment is needed just to meet temporary sales demands. Later, such equipment may be idle. The replacement of old machinery with new high-speed equipment should also be considered. A careful study should help determine which step would be more profitable in the long run.

Records for each product showing the manufacturing operations necessary and a record of each machine, showing the operations capable of being performed by the machine together with its capacity, should be kept. Estimates must be made of material to be used, number of labor hours and quantities of service (power) required for each product. These estimates are called ''standards of production performance.'' The establishment of these standards is an engineering rather than an accounting task. In this respect, these standards are similar to those used in standard cost accounting.

Cost of production. The following is an illustration of how cost of production is determined: Assume a concern has a normal capacity of 100 units of product. Current production budget calls for 80 units. Only one product is made; and its production requires two operations, A and B. The standard costs are: variable costs per unit of product, one unit of direct material, $2; operation A (direct labor and overhead), $3; operation B (direct labor and overhead), $5; total $10. Fixed production costs for the budget period are $500, or $5 per unit based on normal capacity. This production cost budget would then be expressed as follows:

Variable cost (80 units @ $10)	$ 800
Fixed costs (80 units @ $5)	400
Costs chargeable to production	1,200
Cost of idle capacity (500 less 400)	100
Total budgeted costs	$1,300

There is a tie-in here between estimated costs, standard costs, and production budgets.

Materials Budget

The purpose of the materials budget is to be sure that there are sufficient materials to meet the requirements of the production budget. This budget deals with the materials for the purchase of raw materials and finished parts and controls the inventory. How to estimate the material required depends on the nature of the individual company. A company manufacturing standard articles can estimate fairly accurately the amount of raw materials and the purchases required for the production program. Even where the articles are not standard, there is usually a reliable relationship between the volume of business handled and the requirements for the principal raw materials.

Tie-in to standard costs. In the preparation of the material budget, there is a tie-in to standard costs. Here is an example of how purchase requirements are computed:

Quantity required for production	300,000 units
Desired inventory at end of budget period	75,000 units
Total requirements	375,000 units
Less: Inventory at beginning of period	80,000 units
Purchase requirements	295,000 units

The next step is to express material requirements in terms of prices. Some firms establish standard prices based on what are considered normal prices. Differences between standard and actual purchase prices are recorded as a price variance.

Factors affecting policy.   These are:

(1) The time it takes the material to be delivered after the purchase order is issued.

(2) The rate of consumption of material as indicated by the production budget.

(3) The amount of stock that should be on hand to cover possible delays in inventory of raw materials.

On the basis of these factors, the purchasing department working with the production department can establish figures of minimum stocks and order quantities of raw materials and parts for each product handled. Purchases in large quantities are advisable if price advantages can be obtained. Bulk purchases are advisable during periods of rising prices but not during periods of declining prices. The unavoidable time lag between order and delivery of the material is also a reason to buy in advance.

Buying in advance does not necessarily involve immediate delivery. The deliveries may be spread over the budget period in order to coordinate purchases with production and to control inventory. To control inventory, it is desirable to establish minimum and maximum quantities for each material to be carried. The lower limit is the smallest amount which can be carried without risk of production delays. If materials can be obtained quickly, the inventory can be held near the lower limit. The advantage of keeping inventory at this lower limit is that it minimizes the cost of storage and possible obsolescence. If materials cannot be obtained quickly, there is the possibility of a rise in prices, and so it is advisable to carry more than minimum inventory.

Goods in process.   The time it takes for material to enter the factory and emerge as a finished product is frequently much longer than necessary for efficient production. Comparisons with other companies may reveal that a firm allows its goods to remain in process much longer than other firms. Investigations should be made to determine the causes of such delays and formulate remedies. These investigations are usually made in connection with the production budget.

Finished goods.   The budget of finished goods inventory is based on the sales budget. For example, if 100 units of an item are expected to be sold during the budget period, the problem is to determine how much must be kept in stock to support such a sales program. Since it is difficult to determine the exact quantity customers will demand each day, the finished goods inventory must maintain a margin of safety so that satisfactory deliveries can be made. Once this margin is established, the production and purchasing programs can be developed to replenish the stock as needed.

THE LABOR BUDGET

The labor budget deals only with direct labor. Indirect labor is included in the manufacturing expense budget. (The manufacturing expense budget includes the group of expenses in addition to indirect labor, expenses such as indirect material, repairs and maintenance, depreciation and insurance.)

The purpose of the labor budget is to ascertain the number and kind of workers needed to execute the production program during the budget period. The labor budget should indicate the necessary man-hours and the cost of labor required for the manufacture of the products in the quantities shown by the production budget.

Preparation of the Labor Budget

The preparation of a labor budget begins with an estimate of the number of labor hours required for the anticipated quantity of products. Before this can be done, it is necessary to know the quantity of items that are going to be produced. This information comes from the production budget. If the products are uniform and standard labor time allowances have been established, it is just a matter of multiplying the production called for by the standards to determine the labor hours required. If the products are not uniform but there is uniformity of operations, it is first necessary to translate production into operation requirements. Operation standards then should be established in terms of man- or machine-hours. The quantity of labor required may then be ascertained.

The next step in preparing the labor budget is to estimate the cost of direct labor. These estimates are computed by multiplying the number of units to be produced by the labor costs per unit. The problem then is to predetermine the unit labor costs. Some of the methods of determining these costs are:

(1) Day rate system
(2) Piece rate system.
(3) Bonus system.

In firms where standard labor costs have been established for the products manufactured, it is necessary only to multiply the units of the product called for in the production budget by the standard labor costs.

A detailed analysis should frequently be made of the differences between actual and estimated labor costs. These should be investigated to determine whether they are justified. An investigation may reveal inefficient workers, wasted time, defective materials, idle time, poor working conditions, high-priced workers, etc. Responsibility must be definitely placed and immediate action taken to correct those factors which are capable of being controlled.

The budgets for direct labor and manufacturing expenses are not complete until schedules of the final estimates are prepared. The form will vary, depending on the needs of the firm. The following is an example of a schedule of estimated direct labor costs where estimates are shown for each department of the firm:

X Corporation

Estimated Direct Labor Costs
for the Period 1/1/xx to 12/31/xx

Dept.	Quantity to Be Produced	Standard Labor Cost Per Unit	Total Estimated Labor Cost
1	127,600	$ .90	$115,000
2	127,600	1.60	204,000
3	127,600	1.12	143,000
		$3.62	$462,000

CAPITAL EXPENDITURES BUDGET

Since capital expenditures represent a large part of the total investment of a manufacturing concern, the capital expense budget is of great importance. Unwise capital expenditures can seldom be corrected without serious loss to stockholders. The purpose of the capital expenditures budget is to subject such expenditures to careful examination and so avoid mistakes that cannot easily be corrected.

A carefully prepared capital expenditures budget should point out the effect of such expenditures on the cash position of the company and on future earnings. For example, too large a portion of total assets invested in fixed plant and equipment sooner or later may result in an unhealthy financial condition because of the lack of necessary working capital.

Preparation of Capital Expenditures Budget

In preparing the capital expenditures budget, the following information is recorded:

(1) The amount of machinery, equipment, etc., on hand at the beginning of the budget period;

(2) Additions planned for the period;

(3) Withdrawals expected for the period;

(4) The amount of machinery, equipment, etc., expected at the end of the budget period.

Consideration should be given to estimates of additions planned for the period. Additions will be justified if they increase the volume of production and earnings, will reduce unit costs, and the money needed can be spared. Consideration should also be given to the percentage investment for fixed assets as compared with net worth of the firm for a number of years. Various business authorities have realized that an active business enterprise with a tangible net worth between $50,000 and $250,000 should have as a maximum not more than two-thirds of its tangible net worth in fixed assets. Where the tangible net worth is in excess of $250,000, not more than 75% of the tangible net worth should be represented by fixed assets. When these percentages are greatly exceeded, annual depreciation charges tend to be too heavy, the net working capital too moderate, and liabilities expand too rapidly for the good health of the business, alternative leasing should be considered.

The capital expenditures budget should include estimates not only for the budget period, but long-range estimates covering a period of many years. The ideal situation is where machinery is purchased at a time when prices are low. A long-range capital expenditures budget will indicate what machinery will be of use in the future. Then, machinery may be acquired when prices are considered low. Inefficient or obsolete machines can sometimes be made into satisfactory units by rebuilding them. If it is estimated that gains derived from rebuilding machinery will exceed the costs, then provision should be made in the capital expenditures budget to incur these expenses. Such expenditures are frequently called betterments and prolong the useful life of the machines. The preparation of detailed and accurate records is an essential part of the capital expenditures budget. The following information should be included in such a record:

(1) Description of machines;
(2) Date of requisition;
(3) Cost for depreciation rate.

From the above information, it is a simple matter to complete the depreciation for the budget period.

As with other budgets, actual expenditures should be compared with the estimates, and any variation should be analyzed. In addition, a statement should be prepared showing the extent to which actual results obtained from the use of certain capital expenditures are in line with expectations. This is particularly important where substantial investments are made in labor-saving equipment, new processes or new machines.

THE CASH BUDGET

The cash budget is a composite reflection of all the operating budgets in terms of cash receipts and disbursements. Its purpose is to determine the cash resources that will be available during the entire budget program so that the company will know in advance whether it can carry out its program without borrowing or obtaining new capital or whether it will need to obtain additional capital from these sources. Thus, the company can arrange in advance for any necessary borrowing, avoiding emergencies and, more importantly, a cash crisis caused by a shortage.

A knowledgeable financial man goes into the market to borrow money when he can get the cheapest rate. The cash budget will tell the manager when he will need to borrow so he can plan accordingly. In a like manner, he can foresee when he will have sufficient funds to repay loans.

A cash budget is very important to a firm which does installment selling. Installment selling ties up cash resources, and a careful analysis of estimated future collections is needed to forecast the cash position of the company.

Other purposes of the cash budget are: (1) to provide for seasonal fluctuations in business which make heavy demands on funds to carry large inventories and receivables; (2) to assist the financial executive in having funds available to meet maturing obligations; (3) to aid in securing credit from commercial banks; the bank is more likely to lend funds for a definite plan that has been prepared, indicating when and how the funds will be repaid; and (4) to indicate the amount of funds available for investments, when available and for what duration.

Preparation of the Cash Budget

The main difference between a cash budget and other budgets is that in the cash budget all estimates are based on the dates when it is expected cash will be received or paid. Other budgets are prepared on the basis of the accrual of the different items (for accrual-basis companies). Therefore, in the cash budget, the budget executive cannot base the estimate of cash receipts directly on the sales budget for the obvious reason that all the cash will not be received from such sales in the same month in which they are billed. This is not true in the case of a business on a strictly cash basis. Depreciation is another item handled differently in the cash budget. Depreciation is a cost of doing business, and increases expenses and reduces net income for financial reporting purposes. It is not, however, a cash item and is ignored in preparing the cash budget, but the amount paid for a new plant or equipment in a single year or budget period is included in full in the cash budget.

Cash receipts of a typical firm come from cash sales, collections on accounts and notes receivable, interest, dividends, rent, sale of capital assets and loans. The cash sale estimate is taken from the sales budget. The estimate of collections on accounts should be based on the sales budget and company experience in making collections. With concerns whose sales are made largely on account, the collection experience should be ascertained with considerable care. As an illustration, assume the March account sales have actually been collected as follows:

Month	%
March	6.4
April	80.1
May	8.5
June	3.6
Cash Discount Taken	1.1
Bad Debts Loss	.3
Total	100.00

If the same experience is recorded for each month of the year, it is possible to resolve the sales estimates into a collection budget. It is sometimes desirable to develop the experience separately for different classes of customers for different geographical areas. Once these figures are ascertained, they should be tested from time to time.

Cash disbursements in a typical firm are made for payroll, materials, operating expenses, taxes, interest, purchases of equipment, repayment of loans, payment of dividends, etc. With a complete operating budget on hand, there is little difficulty in estimating the amount of cash that will be required and when it will be required. Wages and salaries are usually paid in cash and on definite dates. For purchases of material (from the materials budget), the purchasing department can readily indicate the time allowed for payments. Operating expenses must be considered individually. Some items, such as insurance, are prepaid. Others, such as commissions, are accrued. So, cash payments may not coincide with charges on the operating budget.

MANUFACTURING EXPENSE BUDGET

In preparing the manufacturing expense budget, estimates and probable expenses should be prepared by persons responsible to authorize expenditures. The general responsibility for variable expenses lies with the production manager. But the immediate responsibility for many of these expenses lies with the foremen of the several departments. Generally, expenses are estimated by those who control them. Each person who prepares a portion of the manufacturing expense budget is furnished with data of prior periods and any plans for the budget period which may affect the amount of expenses. With these data we can decide:

(1) Which, if any, of present expenses can be eliminated.

(2) Probable effect of the sales and production forecasts on those expenses which must be incurred.

No plans for the elimination or reduction of variable expenses should be made unless it is certain that the plan can be enforced.

The responsibility for many fixed manufacturing expenses is with the general executives. Such fixed expenses include long-term leases, pension plans, patents, amortization, salaries of major production executives, etc.

In preparing the budget estimates of manufacturing expenses, a common practice is to use percentages. Each expense is taken as a percent of sales or production costs. For example, if a certain expense is estimated to be 5% of sales, this percentage is applied to the sales estimate to obtain the amount of this expense. The fallacy with this method is that all expenses do not vary proportionately with sales or production. A sounder method of estimating manufacturing expenses is to give individual expenses separate treatment. In estimating the indirect labor expense, it is important to first analyze the expense for the period preceding the budget period. The requirements for additional help, or the possibility of eliminating some of the help, should be considered along with plans for increasing or decreasing any rates of compensation. Detailed schedules should be prepared, showing the nature of each job and the amount to be paid. By summarizing these schedules, an aggregate estimate can be determined. Indirect materials expense should be estimated by first analyzing the amount consumed in prior periods. This, together with the production budget showing the proposed volume for the budget period, serves as a basis for estimating the quantities of the indirect material requirements. The probable cost of such requirements estimated by the purchasing department is the amount to be shown in the manufacturing expense budget. Repairs and maintenance estimates are based on past experience data, supplemented by a report on the condition of the present equipment. If any additional equipment is to be installed during the budget period, recognition must be given to the prospect of additional repairs and maintenance charges. Electric power expense is in direct proportion to the production volume. The charges for depreciation of equipment can be estimated with considerable accuracy. Insurance expense for the budget period is estimated on the basis of the insurance in force charged to production with adjustments made for contemplated changes in equipment, inventories, or coverage of hazard incident to manufacturing.

To budget manufacturing expenses effectively it is important to establish standard overhead rates.

At frequent intervals during the budget period, comparison should be made between the actual expenses in each department and the amount estimated to be spent for actual production during the period. Variations should be investigated and steps taken to correct weaknesses in the production program.

A distinction should be made between controllable and uncontrollable expenses so that the responsibility of individuals can be more closely determined. To facilitate the estimating of expenses, a further distinction is made between fixed and variable expenses. Fixed expenses are those which remain the same regardless of the variations in sales or production. Variable expenses are those which increase or decrease proportionally with changes in volume, sales or production. Maintenance is seldom treated in a separate budget. It is usually regarded as part of the manufacturing expense budget.

Here is an example of a Schedule of Estimated Manufacturing Expenses for each operation of a particular product:

Y Corporation
for the Year Ended 12/31/xx

	Total	Operation 1	Operation 2	Operation 3
Variable expenses:				
Indirect materials	$ 20,000	$ 5,000	$ 10,000	$ 5,000
Indirect labor	100,000	10,000	15,000	75,000
Light and power	30,000	5,000	13,000	12,000
Telephone	5,000	3,000	—0—	2,000
	Total	Operation 1	Operation 2	Operation 3
Fixed and semi-variable:				
Factory rent	50,000	14,000	18,000	18,000
Superintendence	100,000	30,000	35,000	35,000
Depreciation	100,000	20,000	60,000	20,000
General and administrative expense	50,000	12,000	17,000	21,000
Total	$455,000	$ 99,000	$168,000	$188,000

After estimates of materials, direct labor and manufacturing expenses have been prepared, a Schedule of Estimated Cost of Production may be prepared as follows:

Z Corporation
for the Year Ended 12/31/xx

	Total	Product A	Product B	Product C
Cost Element:				
Materials	$200,000	$ 80,000	$ 50,000	$ 70,000
Labor	340,000	100,000	80,000	160,000
Manufacturing expenses	70,000	30,000	30,000	10,000
Total	$610,000	$210,000	$160,000	$240,000

8

Financial Statement Analysis and Interpretation

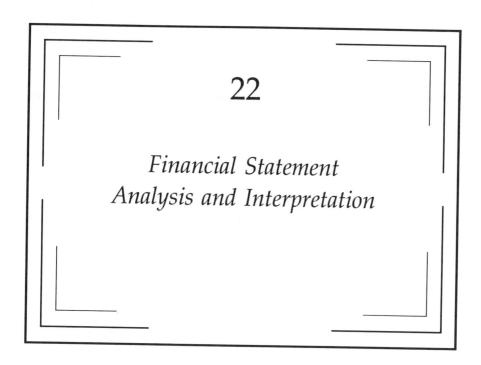

22

Financial Statement Analysis and Interpretation

THE PURPOSE OF FINANCIAL STATEMENTS

Analysis techniques applied to financial statements are of interest to the corporate financial officer in a number of instances. For one thing, his own company's financial statements will be subject to analysis by creditors, credit grantors, and investors. Furthermore, he will want to analyze his own company's statements for internal management use. Also, he may be called upon to analyze other companies' financial statements for credit purposes and perhaps for investment purposes (where an acquisition is being considered).

The financial statements are a systematic and convenient presentation of the financial position and operating performance of a business entity. The question is: What can be learned by analyzing and interpreting the information available in the statements?

There is much valuable information to be learned, as ratio analysis answers questions concerning the financial facts of a business; e.g.,:

- GAAP permits a variety of accounting procedures and practices that significantly affect the results of operation reported in the statements. Statement analysis helps to evaluate the choices of alternative accounting decisions.

- The statements for a number of successive years can be compared by the use of ratios and unusual trends and changes can be noted.
- A company's statements can be compared with those of other similar companies in the same industry.
- Statement analysis is the basis for estimating, or projecting, potential operating results by the development of *pro forma* statements.
- The effects of external economic developments on a company's business can be applied to results as shown in the statements.
- The balance sheet valuations can be related to the operating results disclosed in the income statement, since the balance sheet is the link between successive income statements.
- Since ratios are *index numbers* obtained by relating data to each other, they make comparisons more meaningful than using the raw numbers without relating an absolute dollar figure to another statement item.

Four Groups of Ratios

Ratios are usually classified into four groups:

1. *Liquidity Ratios*: Measures of the ability of the enterprise to pay its short-term obligations.
2. *Profitability Ratios*: Measures of the profits (losses) over a specified period of time.
3. *Coverage Ratios*: Measures the protection for the interest and principal payments to long-term creditors and investors.
4. *Activity Ratios*: Measures of how efficiently the company is employing its assets.

The ratios in the following discussion are those most commonly applied to measure the operating efficiency and profitability of a company. (There are hundreds of possible relationships that can be computed and trends identified.) The discussion includes an explanation of the answers that each ratio provides; each ratio's application to a specific area of a business will be noted.

Accountant's Responsibility

In evaluating the ratios, the accountant must be mindful that the ratios are simply a measuring tool, not the final answers nor the end in themselves. They are one of the tools for evaluating the *past* performance and providing an indication of the future performance of the company. Ratios are a *control* technique and should be thought of as furnishing management with a "red flag" when a ratio has deviated from an established norm, or average, or predetermined standard.

Accordingly, ratio analysis is meaningless without an adequate *feedback* system by which management is promptly informed of a problem demanding immediate attention and correction.

While accountants are concerned primarily with the *construction* of the financial statements, particularly their technical accuracy and validity, the accountant is also relied upon by the many different users of the statements for assistance in the interpretation of the financial information. The accountant must use his experience and technical skill to evaluate information and to contribute to management decisions that will maximize the optimum allocation of an organization's economic resources.

BASIC ANALYSIS TECHNIQUES

Much of the analytical data obtained from the statements are expressed in terms of ratios and percentages. (Carrying calculations to one decimal place is sufficient for most analysis purposes.) The basic analysis technique is to use these ratios and percentages in either a *horizontal* or *vertical* analysis, or both.

Horizontal analysis.   Here, we compare similar figures from several years' financial statements. For example, we can run down two years' balance sheets and compare the current assets, plant assets, current liabilities, long-term liabilities, etc., on one balance sheet with the similar items on the other and note the amount and percentage increases or decreases for each item. Of course, the comparison can be for more than two years. A number of years may be used, each year being compared with the base year or the immediate preceding year.

Vertical analysis.   Here, we compare component parts to the totals in a single statement. For example, we can determine what percentage each item of expense on the income statement is of the total net sales. Or, we can determine what percentage of the total assets the current assets comprise.

Ratios.   Customarily, the *numerator* of the equation is expressed first, then the denominator. For example, fixed assets to equity means fixed assets *divided by* equity. Also, whenever the numerator is the larger figure, there is a tendency to use the word "turnover" for the result.

As indicated above, these techniques are widely used, generally in the course of one analysis.

BALANCE SHEET ANALYSIS

The significance of the balance sheet is that it shows relationships between classes of assets and liabilities. From long experience, businessmen have learned that certain relationships indicate the company is in actual or potential trouble or is in good financial shape. For example, they may indicate that the business is short of working capital, is undercapitalized generally, or has a bad balance between short- and long-term debt.

It must be emphasized that there are no fixed rules concerning the relationships. There are wide variations between industries and even within a single industry. It is often more valuable to measure these relationships against the past history of the same company than to use them in comparison with other businesses. If sharp disparities do show, however, it is usually wise not to ignore them. Many of the so-called "excesses" that in the past have led to recessions often show up in the balance sheets of individual companies. The most important balance sheet ratios and their implications for the business are discussed below.

Ratio of Current Assets to Current Liabilities

The *current ratio* is probably the most widely-used measure of liquidity, i.e., a company's ability to pay its bills. It measures the ability of the business to meet its current liabilities. The current ratio indicates the extent to which the current liabilities are covered. For example, if current assets total $400,000 and current liabilities are $100,000, the current ratio is 4 to 1.

Good current ratios will range from about 2 to almost 4 to 1. However, the ratio will vary widely in different industries. For example, companies which collect quickly on their accounts and do not have to carry very large inventories can usually operate with a smaller current ratio than those companies whose collections are slower and inventories larger.

If current liabilities are subtracted from current assets, the resulting figure is the *working capital* of the company—in other words, the amount of free capital which is immediately available for use in the business. One of the most significant reasons for the failure of small businesses is the lack of working capital, which makes it difficult or impossible for the business to cope with sudden changes in economic conditions.

The details of working capital flow are presented in the two-year comparative Statement of Changes in Financial Position which is now a mandatory part of the financial statements.

An important feature of the ratios to remember is:

When you *decrease* both factors by the *same* amount, you *increase* the ratio:

	Old	Change	New
Current Assets	$100,000	$(25,000)	75,000
Current Liabilities	50,000	(25,000)	25,000
Working Capital	50,000	—0—	50,000
Ratio	2 to 1		3 to 1

By paying off $25,000 worth of liabilities (depleting Cash), you have increased the ratio to *3 to 1* from *2 to 1*. Note that the *dollar* amount of *working capital* remains the same $50,000.

Conversely, should you borrow $50,000 on short-terms (increasing Cash and Current Liabilities), you would *reduce* the ratio to *1½ to 1* ($150,000/100,000), again with the dollar amount of working capital remaining at $50,000.

A variation of the current ratio is the *acid test*. This is the ratio of *quick assets* (cash, marketable securities, and accounts receivable) to *current liabilities*. This ratio eliminates the inventory from the calculation, since inventory may not be readily convertible to cash.

Ratio of Current Liabilities to Stockholders' Equity

This ratio measures the relationship between the short-term creditors of the business and the owners. Excessive short-term debt is frequently a danger sign, since it means that the short-term creditors are providing much or all of the company's working capital. If anything happens to concern the sort-term creditors, they will demand immediate repayment and create the risk of insolvency. Short-term creditors are most often suppliers of the business, and the company's obligation to them is listed under accounts payable. However, short-term creditors may also include short-term lenders.

A general rule occasionally cited for this ratio is that for a business with a tangible capital and earnings (net worth) of less than $250,000, current liabilities should not exceed two-thirds of this tangible net worth. For companies having a tangible net worth over $250,000, current liabilities should not exceed three-fourths of tangible net worth.

Tangible net worth is used instead of total net worth because intangible assets (such as patents and copyrights) may have no actual market value if the company is forced to offer them in distress selling.

Ratio of Total Liabilities to Stockholders' Equity

The ratio differs from the preceding one in that it includes only long-term liabilities. Since the long-term creditors of a company are normally not in a position to demand immediate payment, as are short-term creditors, this ratio may be moderately greater than the preceding one without creating any danger for the company. However, the ratio should never exceed 100%. If it did, this would mean that the company's creditors have a larger stake in the enterprise than the owners themselves. Under such circumstances, it is very likely that credit would not be renewed when the existing debts matured.

Ratio of Fixed Assets to Stockholders' Equity

The purpose of this ratio is to measure the relationship between fixed and current assets. The ratio is obtained by dividing the book value of the fixed assets by the tangible value of stockholders' equity. A rule sometimes used is that if tangible net worth is under $250,000, fixed assets should not exceed two-thirds of tangible net worth. If tangible net worth is over $250,000, fixed assets should not exceed three-fourths of tangible net worth.

Ratio of Fixed Assets to Long-Term Liabilities

Since long-term notes and bonds are often secured by mortgages on fixed assets, a comparison of the fixed assets with the long-term liabilities reveals what "coverage" the note or bondholders have—i.e., how much protection they have for their loans by way of security. Furthermore, where the fixed assets exceed the long-term liabilities by a substantial margin, there is room for borrowing additional long-term funds on the strength of the fixed asset position.

Ratio of Cost of Goods Sold to Inventory—Inventory Turnover

One of the most frequent causes of business failure is lack of inventory control. A firm that is optimistic about future business may build up its inventory to greater than usual amounts. Then, if the expected business does not materialize, the company will be forced to stop further buying and may also have difficulty paying its creditors. In addition, if a company is not selling off its inventory regularly, that item, or part of it, is not really a *current* asset. Also, there may be a considerable amount of unsalable inventory included in the total. For all these reasons, a business is interested in knowing how often the inventory "turns over" during the year. In other words, how long will the current inventory be on the shelves, and how soon will it be turned into money?

To find out how often inventory turns over, we compare the average inventory to the cost of goods sold shown on the income statement. (Typically, average is computed by adding opening and closing inventories and dividing the total by two.) For example, if average inventory is $2,000,000 and cost of goods sold adds up to $6,000,000, we have in the course of the year paid for three times the average inventory. So we can say the inventory turned over three times, and at year-end we had about a four months' supply of inventory on hand.

Another way to measure the same results is by using the ratio of net sales to inventory. In this ratio, net sales is substituted for cost of goods sold. Since net sales will always be a larger figure (because it includes the business's profit margin), the resulting inventory turnover will be a higher figure.

Ratio of Inventory to Working Capital

This is another ratio to measure over- or under-inventory. Working capital is current assets minus current liabilities. If inventory is too high a proportion of working capital, the business is short on quick assets—cash and accounts receivable. A general rule for this ratio is that businesses of tangible net worth of less than $250,000 should not have an inventory which is more than three-fourths of net working capital. For a business with tangible net worth in excess of $250,000, inventory should not exceed net working capital. The larger-size business can tolerate a condition where there are no quick assets because its larger inventory can be borrowed against; in addition, it presumably has fixed assets which can be mortgaged if necessary.

Average Collection Period

An important consideration for any business is the length of time it takes to collect its accounts receivable. The longer accounts receivable are outstanding, the greater the need for the business to raise working capital from other sources. In addition, a longer collection period increases the risk of bad debts. A general rule for measuring the collection period is that it should not be more than one-third greater than the net selling terms offered by the company. For example, if goods are sold on terms of 30 days net, the average collection period should be about 40 days, though this varies from industry to industry. Special rules apply in the case of installment selling.

Another way of measuring the collection rate of accounts receivable is to divide the net sales by the average accounts receivable. This gives us the accounts receivable turnover; i.e., how many times during the year the average accounts receivable were collected. A comparison with prior years reveals whether the company's collection experience is getting better or worse.

Ratio of Net Sales to Stockholders' Equity

A company acquires assets in order to produce sales which yield a profit. If tangible assets yield too few sales, the company is suffering from underselling: i.e., the under-utilization of its assets. On the other hand, the company may suffer from overtrading; i.e., too many sales in proportion to its tangible net worth. In other words, there is too heavy a reliance on borrowed funds to generate sales.

Another way of measuring the effective utilization of assets is to determine the ratio of net sales to total assets (excluding long-term investments).

In either case, comparisons of these ratios with similar ratios of other companies in the same industry can indicate the relative efficiency in utilization of assets of the company being analyzed.

Ratio of Net Sales to Working Capital

This is similar to the preceding ratio, since it measures the relationship between sales and assets. In this case, the ratio measures whether the company has sufficient net current assets to support the volume of its sales or, on the other hand, if the capital invested in working capital is working hard enough to produce sales.

Book Value of the Securities

This figure represents the value of the outstanding securities according to the values shown on the company's books. This may have little relationship to market value—especially in the case of common stock. Nevertheless, book value is an important test of financial strength. It is computed by simply subtracting all liabilities from total assets. The remaining sum represents the book value of the equity interest in the business. In computing this figure, it is a good idea to include only tangible assets—land, machinery, inventory, etc. A patent right or other tangible may be given a large dollar value on the balance sheet, but in the event of liquidation may not be salable at all. The theory underlying the measurement of book value is that it is a good measure of how much cash and credit the company may be able to raise if it comes upon bad times. Book value is usually expressed per share outstanding.

Book value is also an important measure for the bondholders of the company. For them, the value has the significance of telling them how many dollars per bond outstanding the company has in available assets. Since they have a call on the company's assets before either the preferred stockholders or the common stockholders, a substantial book value per bond in excess of the face amount of the bond offers relative assurance of the safety of the bond—assurance that funds will be available to pay off the bonds when they become due. To find the book value of the bonds, add together the total stockholders' equity and the amount of the bonds outstanding.

For example, stockholders' equity totals $5 million. Bonded indebtedness is $2 million. From this $7 million total we subtract $1 million of intangibles. That leaves $6 million. This represents a coverage of three times the total bond indebtedness, usually a fairly substantial coverage.

Ratio of Long-Term Debt to Equity

This ratio measures the leverage potential of the business; that is, the varying effects which changes in operating profits will have on net profits. The rule is that the higher the debt ratio, the greater will be the effect on the common stock of changes in earnings because of increased interest expenses.

Many security analysts feel that in an industrial company equity should equal at least half the total of all equity and debt outstanding. Railroads and utilities, however, are likely to have more debt (and preferred stock) than common stock because of the heavy investments in fixed assets, much of which is financed by the use of debt and preferred stock.

Earnings Per Share (EPS)

Probably, the most important ratio used today is the earnings per share (EPS) figure. It is a *mandatory* disclosure on all annual financial (income) statements (for public companies) and mandatory for all interim statements (though unaudited) for public companies. Moreover, the EPS must be broken out separately for extraordinary items. The standards of calculation are quite complex where preferred stock, options and convertibility are involved.

The factors involved in the computation and disclosure of a complex stock structure are discussed in Section One of this book.

Basically, the EPS is the net income divided by the number of outstanding shares (including equivalent shares which are treated on an "as-if-issued" basis).

Investor reaction to the EPS figure—how it compares with other companies, with its own prior history, with the other investment choices (bonds, commodities, bank accounts, treasury notes, etc.)—is considered to be one of the significant factors in setting the market price of the stock, second only to dividends actually paid.

Return on Equity

This ratio is another method of determining earning power. Here, the opening Equity (Capital Stock plus Retained Earnings, plus or minus any other equity-section items) is divided into the net income for the year to give the percentage earned on that year's investment.

Return to Investors

This is a relatively new ratio used mostly by financial publications, primarily for comparison of many companies in similar industries. The opening equity is divided into the sum of the dividends paid plus the market price appreciation of the period. In addition, the ratio is sometimes extended to cover five years, ten years or more.

INCOME STATEMENT ANALYSIS

Just as with the balance sheet, most of the figures obtained from the income statement acquire real meaning only by comparison with other figures—either with similar figures of previous years of the same company or with the corresponding figures of other companies in the same or similar business.

For example, we could compare each significant item of expense and cost with net sales and get a percentage of net sales (vertical analysis) which we could then compare with other companies. Percentages are more meaningful to compare than absolute dollar amounts since the volume of business done by other companies in the same industry may vary substantially from the volume of our company.

We could also compare each of the significant figures on the income statement with the same figures for prior years (horizontal analysis). Here, too, comparisons of percentages rather than absolute dollar amounts might be more meaningful if the volume of sales has varied substantially from year to year.

Other significant comparisons are covered in the following paragraphs.

Sales Growth

The raw element of profit growth is an increase in sales (or revenues when the company's business is services). While merely increasing sales is no guarantee that higher profits will follow, it is usually the first vital step, so in analyzing a company, check the sales figures for the past four or five years. If they have been rising and there is no reason to believe the company's markets are near the saturation point, it is reasonable to assume that the rise will continue.

When a company's sales have jumped by the acquisition of another firm, it is important to find out if the acquisition was accomplished by the issuance of additional common stock, by the assumption of additional debt, or for cash. If the company paid by common stock and if the acquired firm's earnings are the same on a per-share basis as those of the acquiring firm, the profit picture remains exactly as it was before. The additional sales growth is balanced by the *dilution of the equity*— that is, the larger number of shares now sharing in the earnings.

The situation is quite different if the purchase was for cash or in exchange of bonds or preferred stock. Here, no dilution of the common stock has occurred. The entire profits of the new firm (minus the interest which must be paid on the new debt or the interest formerly earned on the cash) benefit the existing shareholders.

In any event, acquisitions of new companies often require a period of consolidation and adjustment and frequently are followed by a decreased rate of sales growth.

Consideration should be given to the effect of inflation on sales. A situation can exist where the increase in sales may be caused by the increase in prices. The result may be that unit sales have dropped in relation to the previous year's, but the dollar sales have increased. Comparing unit sales may be a better method of ascertaining the sales increase under certain circumstances.

Computing Operating Profit

A company's costs of operations fall into two groups: *cost of goods sold* and *cost of operations*. The first relates to all the costs of producing the goods or services matched to the revenues produced by those costs. The second includes all other costs not directly associated with the production costs, such as selling and administrative costs (usually called period expenses).

Subtracting both of these groups of costs from sales leaves *operating profit*.

Various special costs and special forms of income are then added or subtracted from operating income to get *net income before taxes*. After deducting state and federal income taxes, the final figure (which is commonly used for computing the profit per share) is *net income*. When analyzing a company, however, you will often be most interested in the operating profit figure, since this reflects the real earning capacity of the company.

The best way to look at cost figures is as a percentage of sales. Thus, a company may spend 90 cents out of every dollar in operating costs. We say its cost percentage is 90% or, more commonly, its operating profit margin is 10%. Profit margins vary a great deal among industries, running anywhere from 1% to 20% of sales, so don't compare companies in different industries. The trend of the operating profit margin for a particular company, however, will give an excellent picture of how well management is able to control costs. If sales increases are obtained only by cutting prices, this will immediately show as a decrease in the margin of profit. In introducing a new product it is sometimes necessary to incur special costs to make initial market penetration, but this should be only temporary.

The most used, examined and discussed ratio within a company is the Gross Profit Ratio. More significance is probably attached to this ratio than to any other, because increases usually indicate improved performance (more sales, more efficient production) and decreases indicate weaknesses (poor selling effort, waste in production, weak inventory controls).

The terminology in the gross profit percentages is sometimes confusing and misinterpreted, especially when the word "markup" is used. As an example:

	$	%
Sales	$ 100	100%
Cost of Sales	80	80%
Gross Profit	$ 20	20%

In conventional usage, there is a 20% Gross Profit or Margin on the sale (20/100).

However, if we were to determine the *markup*, the Cost of Sales is the denominator and the Gross Profit is the numerator (20/80 equals a 25% markup).

Sometimes, we start with Gross Profit *percentage desired*; we want to gross 20%, so what should the selling price be? (The only known factor is Cost.)

	%	Known	As calculated
Selling price	100%	?	$ 150
Cost	80%	$ 120	120
Gross Profit	20%	?	$ 30

Selling price is always 100%. If cost is $120 and is equal to 80% of the selling price (it must be 80% because we've set a gross of 20%), divide $120 *by* 80% to get the 100% selling price of $150.

EVALUATION OF FINANCIAL RATIOS

While most ratios are valuable in measuring the financial excellence of a business, certain ratios will be emphasized for particular purposes. The more common purposes for which ratios are used are the following:

Management Evaluation

Management's primary interest is efficient use of the company's assets. Management will be particularly interested in the turnover ratios, such as the inventory turnover and the relationship of working capital to total sales. To the extent that assets are not being used efficiently, the company is overinvesting and consequently is realizing a smaller return than possible on its equity. On the other hand, excessive turnover is dangerous because it puts the company in an extremely vulnerable position. Management will also be particularly interested in trend relationships shown in the income statement for the past few years. Excessive selling expenses may indicate that commissions or other payments are out of line with the market. Management will also make a comparison between the company and its competitors in all areas to indicate where improvement in operations should be expected.

Short-Term Creditors

A lender from whom short-term loans are sought will be particularly interested in the current ratio, since this is a measure of the borrower's ability to meet current debt and his margin of working capital. Also important is the net-worth-to-debt ratio, which shows the relationship of the stockholders' investments to funds contributed by trade creditors and others. It shows ability to stand up under pressure of debt. The sales-to-receivables ratio (net annual sales divided by outstanding trade receivables) shows the relationship of sales volume to uncollected receivables and indicates the liquidity of the receivables on the balance sheet. Another important ratio to the short-term lender is cost of sales to inventory, which shows how many times the company turns over its inventory. Among other things, this shows whether inventories are fresh and salable and helps evaluate the liquidation value of such inventory.

Long-Term Creditors

Since the long-term lender is looking some periods ahead, he wants to be convinced, above all, that the company's earnings will continue at least at the same level. In addition, he will study the various working capital ratios to determine if the company will have sufficient cash when needed to amortize the debt. The ratio of total liabilities to the stockholders' equity is important because the long-term lender wants to be sure that the shareholder has a sufficient stake in the business. One ratio which is used almost solely by the long-term lender is the number of times fixed charges are earned. Fixed charges represent the interest payments on the lender's debt as well as any debt which has priority over it. When total earnings of the company are divided by total fixed charges (including preferred stock dividends, if any), the resulting figure represents the number of times fixed charges are earned.

Stockholders

While stockholders are interested in the excellence of the company as a whole, they will tend to think in terms of per-share figures. Of these, probably the most important is the dividend return, since this represents the actual income which the stockholder will receive. For many years now, there has been greater emphasis on growth companies and capital appreciation, and far less emphasis on dividends. Consequently, to a stockholder in a growth company, earnings per share is a far more important figure than dividends. Investors who seek "bargain" situations will be on the lookout for stocks which sell at a price equal to or lower than book value per share. In theory, the liquidating value of such a company is at least equal to the price paid for the stock. An even more restrictive test is a stock which is selling at a price equal to net working capital per share. In such a company, the liquid assets alone are equal to the market value of the shares.

CASH FLOW

The term "cash flow" refers to a variety of concepts, but its most common meaning in financial literature is the same as "funds derived from operations." The *concept* of cash flow can be used effectively as one of the major factors in judging the ability to meet debt retirement requirements, to maintain regular dividends, to finance replacement and expansion costs, etc.

In no sense, however, can the amount of cash flow be considered to be a substitute for, or an improvement upon, the net income as an indication of the results of operations or the change in financial position.

Importance of Cash Flow

The concept of cash flow has been originated by security analysts. It has been stated that in evaluating the investment value of a company, cash flow is frequently regarded as more meaningful than net income as a measure of a company's ability to finance expansion without undue borrowing or holding back payment of dividends.

In using cash flow as an analytic tool, care is required. For example, Corporation X has been capitalized with straight common stock. Corporation Y, the same size as Corporation X and comparable in other respects, has been capitalized 25% with common stock and 75% with debt. A cash flow equivalent to, say, 20% of each corporation's gross sales will seem to be four times as large in relation to Corporation Y's stock when compared with the common stock of Corporation X. Cash flow as a meaningful tool, therefore, will have more significance when related to industries and companies in which long-term debt is limited.

One valid point in using cash flow is to put the profit margin squeeze into proper perspective. One of the most rapidly increasing costs is the depreciation charged against newly acquired plants and equipment. The use of accelerated methods of depreciation has created huge depreciation deductions which reduce profits. At the same time, accelerated depreciation creates additional cash flow and encourages further spending for facilities. In the opinion of some financial authorities, a showing of relatively high cash flow per dollar of capitalization is some compensation for a poor showing of net income per dollar of capitalization.

High cash flow is also the reason that some companies with relatively poor earnings per share are able to continue paying cash dividends per share; sometimes in excess of earnings. In addition to profits, the extractive industries get cash flow through depletion allowances, drilling writeoffs and amortization of development costs and depreciation.

Cash flow also helps analysts judge whether debt commitments can be met without refinancing, whether the regular cash dividend can be maintained despite ailing earnings, whether the extractive industries (i.e., oils and mining) will be able to continue exploration without raising additional capital, or whether additional facilities can be acquired without increasing debt or present capital.

Relative cash flow is an important factor in deciding whether to buy or lease. But it's not necessarily true that owning property creates funds for use in expansion. The cash made available to a corporation through operations will be similar whether the business property is owned or leased. Owned property acquired by borrowed capital will require periodic payments on the debt which will have to be met before funds are available for expansion.

9

Securities and Exchange Commission Organization and Filing Requirements

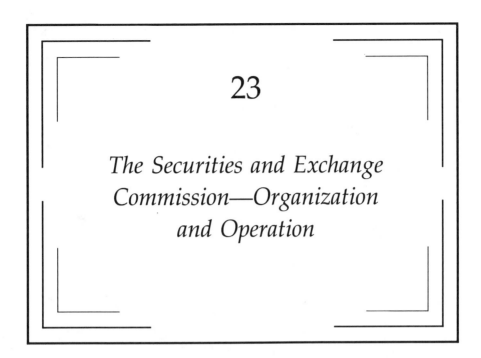

23

The Securities and Exchange
Commission—Organization
and Operation

In today's world of regulated business, it is important for accountants to have a working knowledge of the rules and regulations influencing SEC accounting.

In the late 1920s there was widespread speculation in the stock market. When the market crashed in 1929, the public demanded protective action from their legislators. Congressional committees held hearings into all phases of the securities industry, investment banking, and commercial banking activities prior to the market crash. As a result of these hearings, eight Federal statutes were enacted between 1933 and 1940 (with a ninth in 1970), bringing the securities markets and the securities business under federal jurisdiction. These laws are referenced as the "truth in securities" statutes. They include the Securities Act of 1933, the Securities Exchange Act of 1934, the Public Utility Holding Company Act of 1935, the Maloney Amendment to the Securities Exchange Act of 1934, and the Federal Bankruptcy Code. Also included are the Trustee Indenture Act of 1939, the Investment Company Act of 1940, the Investment Advisers Act of 1940, the Securities Investor Protection Act (SPIC) of 1970, and the Securities Act Amendments of 1975.

EXHIBIT 1–4   The Organization of the SEC

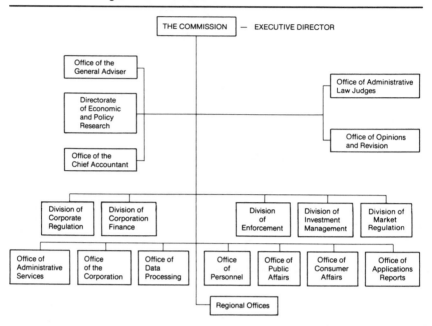

EXHIBIT 1–3   Regional Offices of the SEC

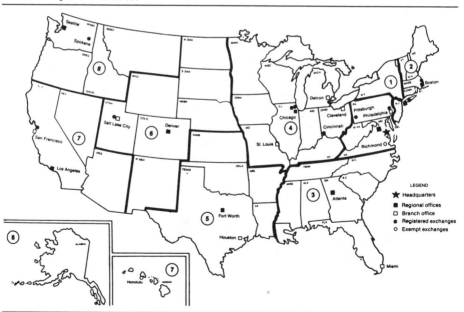

SOURCE: Securities and Exchange Commission. *The Work of the Securities and Exchange Commission* (Washington, D.C.: U.S. Government Printing Office, 1978).

SECURITIES AND EXCHANGE COMMISSION TERMINOLOGY

The Securities and Exchange Commission in Article 1, Rule 1-02, Title 17, Code of Federal Regulations (which is Accounting Regulation S-X), defines the meaning of terms used by the SEC in its Accounting Rules and Regulations. Also, many of the terms are defined as they appear in the Securities Act of 1933, the Securities and Exchange Act of 1934, in Regulations S-K and D, and in the various Forms that publicly-held corporations must file periodically with the SEC.

Occasionally, the Commission will use a term in a rule which, in context, will have a meaning somewhat different from its defined meaning. In these instances, the SEC explicitly clarifies departures from that term's listed definition.

Many of the definitions as they are written in the statutes and accounting regulations often are lengthy and legalistic in style. The objective here is to "delegalize" the "legaleze" in the interests both of clarity and brevity. The definitions are not, therefore, verbatim as developed by the Commission.

AFFILIATE.   An affiliate of or with a person (*see Person*) is one that directly or indirectly, through one or more intermediaries, controls or is controlled by, or is under common control with, the person specified.

AMICUS CURIAE.   "Friend of the Court." An SEC advisory upon request of a court which assists a court in the interpretation of some matter concerning a securities law or accounting regulation.

AMOUNT.   When used to reference securities means:
  a. The principal amount of a debt obligation if "amount" relates to evidence of indebtedness.
  b. The number of shares if "amount" relates to shares.
  c. The number of units if "amount" relates to any other type of securities.

APPLICATION FOR LISTING.   A detailed questionnaire filed with a national securities exchange providing information concerning the corporation's history and current status.

BROKER.   A person in the business of buying and selling securities, for a commission, on behalf of other parties.

CENSURE.   A formal reprimand by the SEC for improper professional behavior by a party to a filing.

CERTIORARI, WRIT OF.   An order issued by a superior court directing an inferior court to deliver its record for review.

CHAPTER 11 BANKRUPTCY.   Deals with individuals, partnerships, and corporations whose securities are not publicly held. Affects only voluntary arrangements of unsecured debts.

CIVIL ACTION. Involves the private rights and remedies of the parties to a suit; that is, actions arising out of a contract.

CLASS OF SECURITIES. A group of similar securities that give shareholders similar rights.

CLOSED-END INVESTMENT COMPANY. A corporation in the business of investing its funds in securities of other corporations for income and profit. Investors wishing to ''cash out'' of the investment company do so by selling their shares on the open market, as with any other stock.

CLOSING DATE. Effective date (*see Effective date*) of a registration statement.

COMMENT LETTER. (*see Deficiency letter*).

COMPENSATING BALANCE. Restricted deposits of a borrower required by banks to be maintained against short-term loans.

CONSENT ACTION. Issued when a person agrees to the terms of an SEC disciplinary action without admitting to the allegations in the complaint.

CONSOLIDATED STATEMENTS. Includes the operating results of a corporation's subsidiary(ies) with intercompany transactions eliminated.

COOLING-OFF PERIOD. The period between the filing and effective dates (*see Effective date*) of a registration statement.

CRIMINAL ACTION. Suits initiated for the alleged violation of a public law.

DEALER. A person in the business of buying and selling securities for his own account.

DEFICIENCY LETTER. A letter from the SEC to the registrant setting forth needed corrections and amendments to the issuing corporation's registration statement. Also termed a *Comment Letter* (defined below).

DELISTING. Permanent removal of a listed security from a national securities exchange.

DISBARMENT. Permanent removal of a professional's privilege to represent clients before the SEC.

DISCLOSURE. The identification of accounting policies and principles that materially affect the determination of financial position, changes in financial position, and results of operations.

DOMICILED CORPORATION. A corporation doing business in the state in which its corporate charter was granted.

DUE DILIGENCE MEETING. A meeting of all parties to the preparation of a registration statement to assure that a high degree of care in investigation and independent verification of the company's representations has been made.

EFFECTIVE DATE. The twentieth (20th) day after the filing date of a registration statement or amendment thereto, unless the Commission shortens or extends that time period.

EXCHANGE. An organized association providing a market place for bringing together (through brokers) buyers and sellers of securities.

EXEMPT SECURITY. A security that does not have to be registered with the SEC.

EXEMPT TRANSACTION. A transaction in securities that does not require registration with the SEC.

EXPERT. Any specialist (accountant, attorney, engineer, appraiser, etc.) who participates in the preparation of a registration statement. Broadly, *any* signatory to the registration statement is assumed to be an *expert*.

FIFTY-PERCENT-OWNED-PERSON. A person whose outstanding voting shares are approximately 50 percent owned by another specified person directly, or indirectly through one or more intermediaries.

FILING. The process of completing and submitting a registration statement to the SEC.

FILING DATE. The date a registration statement is received by the SEC.

FOOTNOTE. Appended to financial statements as supplemental information for specific items in a statement.

FOREIGN CURRENCY. Any currency other than the currency used by the enterprise in its financial statements.

INDEMNIFICATION PROVISION. An agreement protecting one party from liability arising from the occurrence of an unforeseeable event.

INFORMATION STATEMENT. A statement on any pending corporate matters furnished by the registrant to every shareholder who is entitled to vote when a proxy is not solicited.

INITIAL MARGIN PERCENTAGE. The percentage of the purchase price (or the percentage of a short sale; *see Short sale*), that an investor must deposit with his broker in compliance with Federal Reserve Board margin requirements.

INVESTMENT BANKER (UNDERWRITER). A person in the business of financing (underwriting) and selling new issues of corporate securities. The underwriter purchases from the issuing corporation the entire issue of securities for resale to the public.

INJUNCTION. A court order directing a person to stop alleged violations of a securities law or regulation.

ISSUER. Any corporation that sells a security in a public offering.

LETTER OF CONSENT. Written permission from participating experts to include their names and signatures in a registration statement.

LISTED STATUS. Condition under which a security has been accepted by an exchange for full trading privileges.

MARGIN CALL. The demand by a broker that an investor deposit additional cash (or acceptable collateral) for securities purchased on credit when the price of the securities declines to a value below the minimum shareholder's equity required by the stock exchange.

MATERIAL. Pertains to information regarding any subject limiting the information required to those matters about which an average prudent investor ought reasonably to be informed.

NATIONAL ASSOCIATION OF SECURITIES DEALERS, INC. (NASD). An association of brokers/dealers who are in the business of trading over-the-counter securities.

NEW YORK STOCK EXCHANGE (AND REGIONAL EXCHANGES). An association organized to provide physical, mechanical, and logistical facilities for the purchase and sale of securities by investors through brokers and dealers.

NO-ACTION LETTER. The SEC's written reply to a corporate issuer of securities stating its position regarding a specific filing matter.

NOTIFICATION. Filing the terms of an offering of securities that are exempt from registration with the SEC.

OFFERING DATE. The date a new security issue can be sold to the public.

OPEN-END INVESTMENT COMPANY (MUTUAL FUND). A corporation in the business of investing its funds in securities of other corporations for income and profit. An open-end company continuously offers new shares for sale and "redeems" shares previously issued to investors who want to "cash out." (Note: *mutual fund* is not legal terminology; it's a financial term commonly used in street jargon to mean an open-end investment company as defined in the Investment Company Act of 1940.)

OPTION. The contractual privilege of purchasing a security (*a call*) for a specified price, or delivering a security (*a put*) at a specified price.

OVER-THE-COUNTER SECURITIES. Corporate and government securities that are not listed for trading on a national stock exchange.

PARENT. An affiliate that controls another specified person directly, or indirectly through one or more intermediaries.

PENSION PLAN. An arrangement whereby a company undertakes to provide its retired employees with benefits that can be determined or estimated in advance.

PERSON. An individual, a corporation, a partnership, an association, a joint-stock company, a business trust, or an unincorporated organization.

PREFILING CONFERENCE. A meeting of corporate officers and experts outlining the SEC requirements for the filing of a registration statement. Occasionally an SEC staff member will attend.

PROSPECTUS. Document consisting of Part I of the registration statement filed with the SEC by the issuing corporation that must be delivered to all purchasers of newly issued securities.

PROXY. A power of attorney whereby a stockholder authorizes another person or group of persons to act (vote) for that stockholder at a shareholders' meeting.

PROXY STATEMENT. Information furnished in conjunction with a formal solicitation in the proxy for the power to vote a stockholder's shares.

RED HERRING PROSPECTUS. Preliminary prospectus with a statement (in red ink) on each page indicating that the security described has not become effective, that the information is subject to correction and change without notice, and is not an offer to buy or sell that security.

REFUSAL. SEC action prohibiting a filing (*see Filing*) from becoming effective.

REGISTRANT. A corporation that has filed a registration statement with the SEC.

REGISTRATION. Act of filing with the SEC the required information concerning the issuing corporation and the security to be issued.

REGISTRATION STATEMENT. The document filed with the SEC containing legal, commercial, technical, and financial information concerning a new security issue.

REPLACEMENT COST. The lowest amount that would have to be paid in the normal course of business to obtain a *new* asset of equivalent operating or productive capability.

RESTRICTED SECURITY. "Private Offering" of an issue that cannot be resold to the public without prior registration. Also called "investment letter" securities for the letter that the *purchaser* of such securities must submit to the SEC stating that the securities are being acquired for investment purposes, not for immediate resale.

RIGHT.   Provides current security holders the privilege of participating on a *pro rata* basis in a new offering of securities.

SALE.   Every contract of sale, disposition, or offer of a security for value.

SCHEDULE.   Detailed financial information presented in a form prescribed by the SEC in Regulation S-X, Article 12.

SCIENTER.   Intent to deceive, manipulate, or defraud. Requires proof that defendant *knew* of material misstatements or omissions; that defendant acted willfully and knowingly.

SECURITY.   Any instrument representing a debt obligation or an equity interest in a corporation, or any instrument "commonly known as a *security* as defined in Section 2(1) of the Securities Act of 1933."

SELLING GROUP.   Several broker/dealers who distribute a new issue of securities at retail.

SHORT-SELLING.   Selling a security that is not owned with the expectation of buying that specific security later at a lower market price.

SOLICITATION.   Any request for a proxy or other similar communication to security holders.

SPREAD.   The difference between the price paid for a security by the underwriter and the selling price of that security.

STOP ORDER.   SEC order stopping the issue or listing of a security on a stock exchange.

SUBSIDIARY.   An affiliate controlled by a specified person directly, or indirectly through one or more intermediaries.

SUBSTANTIAL AUTHORITATIVE SUPPORT.   FASB principles, standards and practices (found in Statements and Interpretations), AICPA Accounting Research Bulletins, and AICPA Opinions, except to the extent altered, amended, supplemented, revoked, or superseded by an FASB Statement.

SUSPENSION.   SEC order temporarily prohibiting the trading of a security on the stock exchange, usually invoked by the SEC when a news release is pending which may cause a "disorderly market" in that security. Trading is usually resumed shortly after the information has been publicly disseminated.

SYNOPSIS: THE SECURITIES ACT OF 1933

In 1933, the first Federal legislative act designed to regulate the securities business on an interstate basis was passed. Its expressed purpose was:
   "To provide full and fair disclosure of the character of securities . . . and to

prevent frauds in the sale thereof, and for other purposes.'' There are four things to note:

1. It related to newly-issued securities, not to those already in the hands of the public.
2. It called for full and fair disclosure of all the facts necessary for an intelligent appraisal of the value of a security.
3. It was designed to prevent fraud in the sale of securities.
4. This legislation led to the Securities Exchange Act of 1934 establishing the Securities and Exchange Commission which would administer both acts.

There are 26 sections to the Act:

Section 1.   ''This title may be cited as the Securities Act of 1933.'' Various court decisions have very liberally interpreted the meaning of ''securities'' as covered by the Act. One decision contains the following: ''. . . that this statute was not a penal statute but was a remedial enactment . . . A remedial enactment is one that seeks to give a remedy for an ill. It is to be liberally construed so that its purpose may be realized.'' (SEC v Starmont, (1940) 31 F. Supp. 264.)

Section 2.   Definitions. This section defines many of the terms used throughout the other sections of the Act. Importantly, it contains definitions of ''security,'' ''person,'' ''sale,'' ''offer to sell,'' and ''prospectus,'' among many others. Several important Rules of the SEC are directly derived from this section, including Rule 134 (discussed in Section 15).

Section 3.   Exempted Securities. Some securities, such as those issued or guaranteed by the United States, are exempted from the provisions of the Act.

Section 4.   Exempted Transactions. Describes the transactions for which Section 5 does not apply.

Section 5.   Prohibitions Relating to Interstate Commerce and the Mails. It is unlawful to offer any security for sale ''by any means or instruments of transportation or communication in interstate commerce or of the mails,'' unless a registration statement is in effect as to that security. It also prohibits the transportation by any means of interstate commerce or the mails of such a security for the purpose of sale or delivery after sale.

This Section further requires that any security that is registered cannot be sold without prior or concurrent delivery of an effective prospectus that meets the requirements of Section 10(a) of the Act.

There have been two important Rules promulgated by the SEC under this Section. The first, Rule 134, defines the types of advertising and of letters or other communications that can be used without prior or concurrent delivery of a prospectus. This Rule is frequently violated in letter form and also in telephone conversations. SEC Release 3844 of October 8, 1957, shows the importance of delivering a prospectus either before or at the same time that an attempt to sell is made. This Release states that a prospectus is defined to include any notice, circular, advertisement, letter, or communication, written or by radio or by television, which offers any security for sale except that any communication sent or given after the effective date of a registration statement shall not be deemed a prospectus if, prior to or at the same time with such a communication, a written prospectus meeting the requirements of Section 10 of the Act was sent or given.

Thus, any letter that gives more information than that allowed by Rule 134 becomes itself a prospectus, unless it is preceded or accompanied by the actual prospectus. A letter prospectus is in violation of Section 5 since it could not possibly comply with the requirements of Section 10.

The second, Rule 433 deals with the so-called "red-herring" prospectus which cannot be used as an offer to sell, but merely to disseminate information prior to the delivery of a regular prospectus which does offer the security for sale.

Section 6.   Registration of Securities and Signing of Registration Statement. This Section details what securities may be registered and how such registration is to be done.

Section 7.   Information Required on Registration Statement. This Section gives the SEC broad powers in regulating what must appear in a registration statement. In part, the section reads:

"Any such registration statement shall contain such other information, and be accompanied by such other documents, as the Commission may by rules or regulations require as being necessary or appropriate in the public interest or for the protection of investors."

Section 8.   Taking Effect of Registration Statements and Amendments Thereto. Registration statements normally become effective on the twentieth day after filing, under this section. However, the SEC is empowered to determine whether or not the statement complies with the Act as to completeness and may refuse to allow the statement to become effective unless amended. If it appears to the SEC that untrue statements have been included, the Commission may issue a stop order.

Section 9.   Court Review of Orders. As with any other act of Congress, provision is made so that any person who is aggrieved by an order of the administrative body (in this case the SEC) may obtain a review of the order in the Federal courts.

Section 10.   Information Required in Prospectus. A prospectus must contain the same information as that contained in the registration statement. In addition, the SEC is given the authority to define the requirements for any additional material which that body considers necessary in the public interest. "Red herring" requirements and the manner of use of this type of preliminary prospectus are also detailed in this Section.

Note the application of Rule 134, discussed under Section 5, with respect to an "incomplete" prospectus.

One part of the Section, 10(3), relates to the length of time a prospectus may be used (that is, be considered an effective prospectus).

Under this Section of the Act, the SEC issued Rule 425, which requires the statement at the bottom of the first page of all prospectuses "These securities have not been approved or disapproved by the Securities and Exchange Commission nor has the commission passed upon the accuracy or adequacy of this prospectus. Any representation to the contrary is a criminal offense."

Section 11. Civil Liabilities on Account of False Registration Statement. Anyone directly connected with a company or signing the registration statement is subject to suit at law or in equity should the registration statement contain an untrue statement or fail to include a material fact necessary to make the statement not misleading.

Section 12. Civil Liabilities. If any person offers to sell or does sell a security in violation of Section 5, or uses any fraudulent means to sell a security, he is liable to civil suit for damages. This liability is in addition to any criminal liability arising under the Act.

Section 13. Limitation of Actions. Specified are the time limits within which civil suits may be instituted under Sections 11 and 12.

Section 14. Contrary Stipulations Void. Any provision in the sale of a security that binds the purchaser to waive the provisions of this Act or of the rules and regulations of the SEC is void. In other words, no one buying a security can relieve the seller from complying with the Act and with the rules issued under the Act.

Section 15. Liability of Controlling Persons. A dealer or broker is liable under Section 11 or 12.

Section 16. Additional Remedies. "The rights and remedies provided by this title (the Act) shall be in addition to any and all other rights and remedies that may exist at law or in equity."

Section 17. Fraudulent Interstate Transactions. As interpreted by the SEC, this section might be referred to as a "catch-all" section.

(a) "It shall be unlawful for any person in the offer or sale of any securities by the use of any means or instruments of transportation or communication in interstate commerce or by the use of the mails, directly or indirectly.

(1) to employ any device, scheme or artifice to defraud, or

(2) to obtain money or property by means of any untrue statement of a material fact or any omission to state a material fact necessary in order to make the statements made, in the light of the circumstances under which they were made, not misleading, or

(3) to engage in any transaction, practice or course of business that operates or would operate as a fraud or deceit upon the purchaser."

Both TV and radio have been included by the SEC as "communication in interstate commerce" because it is impossible to control their area of reception.

While Section 17(a) refers only to the criminal courts in the term "unlawful," a court decision makes it clear that civil liability is incurred by violation of the section, in addition to criminal liability.

Court decisions also implement and amplify the language of the Act itself, with respect to the phrase "or by use of the mails." It would appear that Section 17 only applied to interstate mailings. However, the courts have ruled that if one used the mails *within one State* on an *intrastate* offering, and violated any provision in Section 17(a), he is as guilty as if he had mailed across a state line.

Subparagraph (b) of Section 17 makes it illegal for anyone to publish descriptions of securities when the publisher is paid for such publicity, without his also publishing the fact that compensation has been, or will be, received for the publishing.

Section 17(c) makes the Section applicable to those securities exempted under Section 3. In other words, fraud is fraud whether in connection with exempt or other securities.

Section 18.   State Control of Securities. "Nothing in this title (the Act) shall affect the jurisdiction of the Securities Commission . . . of any State. . . ." In other words, all the provisions of the Federal act *and* all the laws of the State in which business is being conducted must be complied with.

Section 19.   Special Powers of Commission. The Commission has the authority to make, amend, and rescind such rules and regulations as may be necessary to carry out the provisions of the Act. Commissioners or their representatives are also empowered to subpoena witnesses and to administer oaths.

Section 20.   Injunctions and Prosecution of Offenses. The SEC is empowered to make investigations and to bring criminal actions at law against persons deemed to have violated the Act. The wording of the section is interesting in that it gives the Commission power to act "whenever it shall appear . . . that the provisions of this title (the Act) . . . have been *or are about to be* violated. . . ."

Section 21.   Hearings by Commission. "All hearings shall be public and may be held before the Commission or an officer or officers of the Commission designated by it, and appropriate records shall be kept."

Section 22.   Jurisdiction of Offenses and Suits. Jurisdiction of offenses and violations and certain rules in connection with them, are defined in this section. Jurisdiction is given to the District Courts of the United States, the U.S. Court of any Territory, and the U.S. District Court of the District of Columbia.

Section 23.   Unlawful Representations. The fact that the registration statement for a security has been filed or is in effect does not mean that the statement is true and accurate, or that the Commission has in any way passed upon the merits of the security. It is unlawful to make any representations to the contrary.

In short, the words in the registration statement (*and* the prospectus) have been made under the penalties of fraud. The registrants are liable, even though the Commission has not certified the truth and accuracy of the statements or of the worth of the security.

Section 24.   Penalties. "Any person who willfully violates any of the provisions of this title (the Act), or the rules and regulations promulgated by the Commission under authority thereof . . . shall upon conviction be fined not more than $10,000.00 or imprisoned not more than five years, or both."

Section 25.   Jurisdiction of Other Government Agencies Over Securities. Nothing in the Act shall relieve any person from submitting to other U.S. Government supervisory units information required by any provision of law.

Section 26.   Separability of Provisions. If any one section of the Act is invalidated, such findings will not affect other sections.

Schedule A.   Sets forth the requirements for the registration of securities.

Schedule B.   Sets forth the registration requirements for securities issued by a foreign government or political subdivision thereof.

SYNOPSIS: THE SECURITIES EXCHANGE ACT OF 1934

The Securities Act of 1933 protects investors in the purchase of newly-issued securities. The Securities Exchange Act of 1934 concerns the regulation of trading in already issued securities.

The stated purpose of the 1934 Act is "to provide for the regulation of securities exchanges and of over-the-counter markets operating in interstate and foreign commerce and through the mails, to prevent inequitable and unfair practices on such exchanges and markets, and for other purposes."

The Act has been of importance in prohibiting abuses and manipulations through its creation of the SEC and later of the self-regulatory National Association of Securities Dealers, Inc.

The Act has 35 sections:

Section 1.   Short Title. "This Act may be cited as the Securities Exchange Act of 1934."

Section 2.   Necessity of Regulation. Citing that transactions in securities are affected with a national public interest, this section states that it is necessary to regulate and control such transactions and other matters in order to protect interstate commerce, the national credit, the Federal taxing power, to protect and make more effective the national banking system and Federal Reserve System, and to insure the maintenance of fair and honest markets in such transactions.

Parts of Sections 2(3) and 2(4) explain the effects of "rigged" markets and manipulative practices:

Section 2(3).   Frequently, the prices of securities on such exchanges and markets are susceptible to manipulation and control, and the dissemination of such prices gives rise to excessive speculation, resulting in sudden and unreasonable fluctuations in the prices of securities which (a) cause alternately unreasonable expansion and unreasonable contraction of the volume of credit available for trade, transportation, and industry in interstate commerce . . . (c) prevent the fair valuation of collateral for bank loans and/or obstruct the effective operation of the national banking system and Federal Reserve System.

Section 2(4).   "National emergencies, which produce widespread unemployment and the dislocation of trade, transportation, and industry, and which burden interstate commerce and adversely affect the general welfare, are precipitated, intensified, and prolonged by manipulation and sudden and unreasonable fluctuations of security prices and by excessive speculation on such exchanges and markets, and to meet such emergencies the Federal Government is put to such great expense as to burden the national credit."

Section 3.   Definitions. In addition to defining 38 technical terms used in the Act, this Section gave the Securities Exchange Commission and the Federal Reserve System the authority to define technical, trade, and accounting terms so long as such definitions are not inconsistent with the provisions of the Act itself.

Section 4.   This Section established the Securities and Exchange Commission. Prior to the Commissioner's taking office, the Securities Act of 1933 was administered by the Federal Trade Commission.

Section 5.   Transactions on Unregistered Exchanges. Under this Section, it became illegal for transactions to be effected by brokers, dealers, or exchanges on an exchange unless the exchange was registered under Section 6 of the Act.

Section 6.   Registration of Exchanges. Combined with Section 5, this Section sets forth the requirements for exchanges to be registered and the method of registration. Exchanges file their rules and regulations with the SEC and must agree to take disciplinary action against any member who violates the Act or violates any of the rules and regulations issued by the SEC under the Act.

Section 7.   Margin Requirements. The Board of Governors of the Federal Reserve System is given the power to set margin requirements for any securities, which requirements may be changed from time to time at the discretion of the Board. Under this authority, the Board issued Regulation T and Regulation U. Regulation T governs the extension and maintenance of credit by brokers, dealers, and members of national securities exchanges. Regulation U governs loans by banks for the purpose of purchasing or carrying stocks registered on a national securities exchange.

Section 8.   Restrictions on Borrowing. In four parts, this Section (a) details from whom brokers or dealers may borrow money on listed securities, (b) lays the foundation for the SEC's "net capital rule," (c) deals with pledging and comingling of customers' securities, and (d) states no broker or dealer may lend or arrange for the lending of any securities carried for the account of a customer without the written consent of the customer.

Section 9.   Prohibition Against Manipulation. Both this Section and Section 10 deal with manipulative practices that are intended to make money for those in the securities business at the expense of the general public.

Section 9 makes it unlawful to do certain things that constitute manipulation, such as: (a) creating a false or misleading appearance of active trading in a security, (b) giving of information to potential investors as to the likelihood of a rise or fall in price solely for the purpose of causing the market price to react to purchases or sales by such potential investors, (c) making false or misleading statements about a security, (d) "pegging" or "fixing" prices, (e) improper use of puts, calls, straddles, or other options to buy or sell. Transactions in which there is no real change in ownership are also specifically prohibited.

Section 10.   Regulation of Manipulative and Deceptive Devices. Section 10 first forbids the use of short sales or stop-loss orders that violate any rules or regulations the Commission may set to protect investors. Its wording, then, becomes much more inclusive than Section 9 or the first part of Section 10, since it forbids in general "any manipulative or deceptive device or contrivance. . . ."

Section 11.   Trading by Members of Exchanges, Brokers, and Dealers. Authority is given to the Commission to set rules and regulations as to floor trading by members, brokers, or dealers for their own accounts and to prevent excessive trading off the floor of the exchanges. A part of this Section deals with the roles of the odd-lot dealers and the specialist on the floor of the exchange. Further, the section places a limitation on certain customer credit extension in connection with underwritings.

Section 11A.   National Market System for Securities; Securities Information Processors. Concerns the planning, developing, operating, or regulating of a national market system.

Section 12.   Registration Requirements for Securities. It is unlawful for any broker or dealer to effect transactions in a security or a national securities exchange unless a registration statement is effective for that security. Information stating how such registration is to be accomplished is given here. The SEC is given authority to allow trading on one exchange in securities that are listed on another exchange (such securities are said to have "unlisted trading privileges").

Section 13.   Reports. All companies whose securities are listed on a national securities exchange must file reports at such intervals and in such form as the SEC may require. The purpose of requiring such reports was to ensure that enough information was available on any company to enable an investor to make an intelligent decision concerning the worth of its securities.

Section 14.   Proxies. Paragraph (a) of this Section gives the SEC the authority to make rules and regulations as to the solicitation of proxies and makes it illegal to solicit proxies other than in accord with such rules and regulations. Several rules have been issued under this Section which detail the manner in which proxies may be solicited and the information that must be given to shareholders whose proxies are being solicited. All of these rules are designated to ensure that the recipient of a proxy solicitation will understand what it is that he is being asked to sign and to give enough background on the matter in question so that the shareholder can make an intelligent decision as to how he should vote.

Subparagraph (b) relates to the giving of proxies by brokers or dealers in connection with securities held for the accounts of customers. It is standard practice for broker/dealers to vote proxies for shares held in their names for customers directly in accord with the wishes of the customers themselves.

Section 15.   Over-The-Counter Markets. It is mandatory that all brokers and dealers who deal in the over-the-counter market (on other than an intrastate basis) be registered with the SEC. Further, the Section states that registration will be in accord with rules and regulations issued by the Commission. "Intrastate" means that the broker or dealer deals only in intrastate securities as well as doing business only within his state. Here, as elsewhere in the Act, the "use of the mails," even if within one State, places the user under the Act.

Section 15 also defines the grounds for denial of registration, for suspension, or for revocation of registration. Basically, these grounds are:

1. Making false or misleading statements in the application for registration.
2. Having been convicted within the last ten years of a felony or misdemeanor involving the purchase or sale of any security or arising out of the business of a broker or dealer.
3. Being enjoined by a court from engaging in the securities business.
4. Having willfully violated any of the provisions of the 1933 Act or of the 1934 Act. (After passage of the Investment Advisers Act of 1940 and the Investment Company Act of 1940, violation of those Acts also became grounds for suspension or revocation.)

Sections 9 and 10 dealt with manipulation with respect to securities listed on a national exchange. Section 15 adds a prohibition against over-the-counter manipulation as defined by the Commission. Some of the practices that have been so defined are:

1. Excessive prices that are not fairly related to the market.
2. False representations to customers.
3. Taking of secret profits.
4. Failure to disclose control of a market.
5. Creating false impression of activity by dummy sales.
6. "Churning," or unnecessary purchases and sales in a customer's account.

Another important rule of the SEC under Section 15 seeks to protect investors by forbidding certain practices in connection with pledging or comingling of securities held for the accounts of customers. This rule specifically applies to over-the-counter broker/dealers; a similar rule, under Section 8, applies to broker/dealers who are members of or do business through members of a national exchange.

Section 15(c)(3) requires financial responsibility on the part of broker/dealers.

Sections 12 and 13 deal with registration and report requirements for listed securities. Section 15(d) is a corresponding list of requirements with respect to unlisted securities.

Section 15A.   Registration of National Securities Associations. Aided by the Maloney Act of 1938, which amended the original Act by adding this Section, the formation of associations, such as the National Association of Securities Dealers, was authorized.

Section 15B. Concerns municipal securities dealers and transactions in municipal securities.

Section 16. Directors, Officers, and Principal Stockholders. Requires statements of ownership of stocks by "insiders" and other related information.

Section 17. Accounts and Records. Not only does this section require that all brokers and dealers maintain records in accord with such rules and regulations as the SEC may set forth, but it also authorizes the SEC to make examinations of any broker's or dealer's accounts, correspondence, memoranda, papers, books, and other records whenever the Commission deems it in the public interest. Rules and regulations issued by the SEC under this Section state the types of records that must be kept. In practice, an SEC examiner may walk into a broker/dealer's office and ask that all files and books be opened for his inspection. Under the law, no broker/dealer may refuse the examiner access to any and all correspondence and records. A broker/dealer can have his registration suspended or revoked by failure to keep copies of all correspondence or to keep books and records as required by the SEC.

Section 17A. Settlement of Securities Transactions. Concerns the clearance and settlement of securities transactions, transfer of ownership, and safeguarding of securities and funds. Congress directed the SEC to facilitate the establishment of a national system for securities clearings.

Section 18. Liability for Misleading Statements. In a rather unusual statement of law, this Section makes a person both criminally and civilly liable for any misleading statements made in connection with the requirements of Section 15 of this Act.

Section 19. Registration, Responsibilities, and Oversight of Self-Regulatory Organizations. The SEC has the power to suspend for 12 months or revoke the registration of any national securities exchange or of any security, if the Commission is of the opinion that such action is necessary or appropriate for the protection of investors. Further, authority is granted the SEC to suspend or expel from an exchange any member or officer who has violated any of the provisions of this Act.

Other provisions of this Section give the SEC broad powers in supervising the rules of national securities exchanges, which the Commission may require to be changed or amended. In other words, the SEC supervises the members of an exchange through the exchange itself as well as on an individual basis.

Section 20. Liabilities of Controlling Persons. In effect, this Section states that if A commits an illegal act under the direction of B, who controls A, then both A and B are equally liable under the law. Section 20 also makes it illegal for any "controlling person" to "hinder, delay, or obstruct" the filing of any information required by the SEC under this Act.

Section 21. Investigations; Injunctions and Prosecution. In the Securities Act of 1933, Sections 19 and 20 gave the SEC special powers in the areas of investigation, subpoenaing of witnesses, prosecutions of offenses and the like. Section 21 of this Act is similar in its provisions.

Section 22. Hearings. It is interesting to note the difference in wording with respect to hearings in the 1933 Act and in this Act. Section 21 of the 1933 Act states that "All hearings *shall* be public. . . ." Section 22 of the 1934 Act states "Hearings *may* be public. . . ."

Section 23. Rules and Regulations. Power to make rules and regulations under this Act is specifically given the SEC and the Board of Governors of the Federal Reserve System by this Section. Both bodies are required to make annual reports to Congress.

Section 24. Public Availability of Information. To protect those required to file under this Act, this Section makes it possible for certain information, such as trade secrets, to be made confidential and not a matter of public record. This Section also forbids any member or employee of the Commission to use information that is not public for his own benefit.

Section 25. Court Review of Orders and Rules. Like Section 9 of the 1933 Act, this Section reserves final judgment on any issue to the courts, rather than to the Commission itself.

Section 26. Unlawful Representations. It is unlawful to make any representation to the effect that the SEC or the Federal Reserve Board has passed on the merits of any issue. Also, the failure of either body to take action against any person cannot be construed to mean that that person is not in violation of the law.

Section 27. Jurisdiction of Offenses and Suits. Jurisdiction of violations of this Act is given to the district courts of the United States.

Section 28. Effect on Existing Law. "The rights and remedies provided by this title (the Act) shall be in addition to any and all other rights and remedies that may exist in law or at equity. . . ." The Section also leaves jurisdiction of offenses against a State law with the State.

Section 29. Validity of Contracts. No one can avoid compliance with the provisions of this Act by getting someone else to waive the requirements in any contract. Any contract that seeks to avoid the provisions of this Act are automatically void.

Section 30. Foreign Securities Exchange. It is unlawful to deal in securities whose issuers are within the jurisdiction of the United States on a foreign exchange in any manner other than that in which dealing in such securities would have to be handled in this country. In other words, the laws of the U.S. exchanges cannot be circumvented by placing business through a foreign exchange.

Section 31. Transaction Fees. Each national securities exchange is required to pay an annual fee to the Commission.

Section 32. Penalties. Individuals may be fined a maximum of $10,000.00 or sentenced to a maximum term of imprisonment of five years, or both, for violations of the Act. An exchange may be fined a maximum of $500,000.00.

Section 33. Separability of Provisions. An escape section that states that if any one section of the Act is found to be invalid, such findings shall have no effect on the other sections.

Section 34. Effective Date. July 1, 1934.

Section 35. Authorization of Appropriations. Such sums as the Congress may authorize by law, not to exceed $55,000.00 for fiscal year ending September 30, 1977.

Truth in Securities Laws

The objectives of the laws are twofold. First is the protection of investors and the public against fraudulent acts and practices in the purchase and sale of securities. The second objective is to regulate trading in the national securities markets. For example:

1. "To provide full and fair disclosure of the character of securities sold in interstate and foreign commerce and through the mails, and to prevent fraud in the sale thereof, and for other purposes." (Securities Act of 1933.)
2. "To provide for the regulation of securities exchanges and the over-the-counter markets operating in interstate and foreign commerce and through the mails, to prevent inequitable and unfair practices on such exchanges and markets, and for other purposes." (Securities Exchange Act of 1934.)
3. "To provide for the registration and regulation of investment companies and investment advisers, and for other purposes." (Investment Company Act of 1940 and the Investment Advisers Act of 1940.)

SEC REPORTING: THE INTEGRATED DISCLOSURE SYSTEM

Overview: In September, 1980, the SEC adopted rules implementing an Integrated Disclosure System (hereinafter "IDS"). SEC registrants must follow the new rules in their Form 10-K report, certain other SEC filings, and in their annual reports to shareholders (hereinafter "annual report").

The new rules are lengthy and involved an extensive revision of Regulation S-X and commonly used SEC formats. The result is symmetry and consistency of financial statements and other disclosures among many public reports and filings.

A Historical Note: For years, the SEC researched and studied ways by which a single comprehensive financial reporting system could be achieved, not only between the 1933 and 1934 Securities Act, but also between these Acts and the annual shareholder report. It is this effort which led to the IDS.

To understand why the need developed for an IDS, an understanding of SEC registration and reporting form genesis may be helpful. Many 1933 Act registration forms were spawned in response either to the nature of the offering (e.g., stock option plans on Form S-8), or by virtue of the status of the offeror (e.g., Form S-7). Financial statement periods and content varied considerably among the many filings (forms). These differences developed over a long period of time by an evolutionary process as different perceived needs arose, even though the 1933 Act relates simplistically to the same transaction—the public sale of securities. With the passage of time since the enactment of the 1933 Act, a proliferation of SEC regulations, rules, reports, registration statement forms, and amendments to the Act occurred.

In the first 30 years of the SEC's existence annual reports were exclusively a product of management decision. Until the early 1970's, the shareholder report financial statements were governed by Generally Accepted Accounting Principles (GAAP).

In the 1970s, however, the SEC added significantly to the shareholder report content by requiring disclosures such as a five-year summary of earnings and Management's Discussion and Analysis. Financial statements were expanded to include additional information such as quarterly operating data. Notwithstanding, the annual report to shareholders and the Form 10-K were typified as much by differences as by similarities. Since the differences were expanding and increasingly confusing, as well as compliance becoming increasingly expensive, an evaluation by the SEC of over 40 years of diverse rulemaking became necessary. The new IDS attempts to minimize these differences by achieving an interrelation among public financial reports.

For the SEC to achieve its goal of symmetry, a central framework of disclosure was necessary. SEC developed this framework only after evaluation of all elements of mandatory reporting (e.g., Regulation S-X, periodic filings, and shareholder reports) together with disclosures required by GAAP. This framework had to be adequate not only for annual reports, but also to meet the diverse disclosure requirements of the SEC—whether for the public sale of securities (1933 Act require-ments) or for the Form 10-K annual report (1934 Act requirements).

Briefly, the IDS is based upon a "Basic Information Package" consisting of:

- Audited financial statements.
- Management's Discussion and Analysis.
- Selected income and balance sheet data.

This *Package* is common to the annual report, Form 10-K, and most 1933 Act filings.

Changes Affecting Independent Auditors

The significant changes affecting the independent auditor concern the financial statements appearing in the annual report to shareholders. Formerly, the SEC had no authority over the annual report; the statements in the annual report, therefore, did not have to conform to Regulation S-X (but, of course, had to comply with GAAP). The new S-K requirements now govern the annual report. This was accomplished by the requirement that all financial statements presented in annual reports must conform to the S-X accounting and disclosure requirements.

For example, and among other major changes, a shareholder report:

- Must contain three-year comparative financial statements prepared in con-formity with Regulation S-X.
- A majority of the Board of Directors must sign the Form 10-K.
- Management's Discussion and Analysis is expanded, materially.

There are two significant consequences resulting from the requirements of the IDS. *First*, the SEC financial statement disclosure requirements will in many instances add considerable volume and detail to the filings. *Second*, the prior distinction be-tween GAAP and S-X compliance disclosures will be thoroughly submerged. His-torically, GAAP has been conceptually oriented, and the SEC often applied GAAP concepts as a springboard to specific S-X disclosures by applying rigid materiality criteria (most of which have been retained). Formerly, any audited financial state-ment disclosures appearing only in an SEC filing presumptively were an S-X com-pliance disclosure and not a GAAP requirement. This distinction disappears. GAAP no longer will be pristinely visible.

The S-X Revisions

In order to reach the objective of uniformity of financial statements content, the SEC significantly revised S-X to bring the S-X requirements into conformity and consistency with GAAP.

- Transferring some of the information formerly required in the financial reports into schedules, which are not included in the annual report (but are included in the 10-K).
- Rules that duplicated GAAP have been deleted from the SEC rules.
- Obsolete S-X rules have been deleted.
- New disclosure rules have been added because of their informational value to the investing public, irrespective of the fact they may exceed GAAP requirements.
- Existing rules have been clarified, modified, and condensed.

A significant revision of the rules relates to the standardization of the financial statements in the individual forms. Article 3 of S-X are the general instructions for financial statement presentation in all disclosure documents. These uniform instructions require:

- Audited balance sheets as of the end of each of the *two* most recent fiscal years.
- Audited statements of income and changes in financial position for each of the *three* most recent fiscal years preceding the date of the *most recent* audited balance sheet being filed.

(NOTE: These requirements do not apply to Form S-18 which has been developed for "small business" offerings.)

Aging

The new aging requirements synchronize with the time frame for a 10-K filing (within 90 days after the end of the registrant's fiscal year). Continuous updating synchronizes with the quarterly report Form 10-Q, which must be filed with the SEC within 45 days after the end of each of the first three (but not the fourth) fiscal quarters.

Interim statement requirements closely follow 10-Q requirements.

For registration statements, the SEC adopted 135 days as the critical date for determining the aging of financial statements at the expected effective date of the registration statement, or proposed mailing date of a proxy statement, which includes financial statements. Registration statements which are filed and are to become effective 90 days after the end of the fiscal year, but *before* the 135th day, must include audited balance sheets for the last two fiscal years and the three-year income and changes in financial position statements. If the filing or expected effective date is 135 days *or more* after the end of the fiscal year, they must be updated with an unaudited interim balance sheet as of a date within 135 days of filing, and expected effective date and unaudited income and changes in financial condition statements for the interim period, and for the corresponding period of the preceding year must be included.

The Basic Information Package (BIP)

The new financial disclosure rule is termed the Basic Information Package (hereinafter BIP). The requirements of the BIP are common to Forms S-1, S-2, S-3, 10-K, and to the annual report to shareholders. The few differences are in the presentation of the financial information on the registration forms, i.e.:

Form S-1. The Form requires complete disclosure to be set forth in the prospectus, and permits *no* incorporation by reference. Form S-1 is to be used by registrant in the Exchange Act reporting system for less than three years.

Form S-2. Information can either be presented in the prospectus or in the most recent annual report, with the annual report delivered with the prospectus to shareholders. In the latter option, information is incorporated by reference *from* the annual report *into* the prospectus.

Form S-3. Information can be incorporated by reference *from* the 10-K.

What Does the BIP Include?

Broadly, the Package requires information that the SEC considers to be essential for user decision making. Specifically, the following items constitute the substance of the BIP:

- Five years of comparative financial information.
- Management's Discussion and Analysis (MD&A) of the company's financial condition and results of operations.
- Information explaining the circumstances associated with a change in the registrant's independent auditor during the prior two fiscal years, if the change resulted from a disagreement on accounting practices and disclosure matters, or auditing scope or procedures.
- A description of the registrant's business and specified segmental information.
- Market and dividend record.
- Any material information necessary for a prudent investor to make an investment decision. Particularly, emphasis must be placed upon adverse information. "The SEC, in accord with the congressional purposes, specifically requires *prominent* emphasis be given in filed registration statements and prospectuses to *material adverse* contingencies." (Italics provided).

Projections and Forward-Looking Information

Historically, the SEC has been opposed to projections and forecasts by registrants in their filings and annual reports. Over the years, however, there has been an increasingly widespread use of projections, estimates, forecasts, and other forward-looking information by private securities research organizations, with the projections based upon information originated with management in the first place.

Starting in 1963 with a *Special Study* reported to Congress, there have been a number of studies of this issue by various committees. Finally, in 1978, the SEC decided that as a practical matter the Commission should approve forward looking information because such information had become widely used. Accordingly, Securities Act Release No. 5992 and Securities Exchange Act Release No. 15305, both dated November 7, 1978, read:

> "In light of the significance attached to projection information and the prevalence of projections in the corporate and investment community, the Commission has determined to follow the recommendation of the Advisory Committee and wishes to encourage companies to disclose management projections both in their filings with the Commission and in general."

The Safe Harbor Rule

Concurrently, with the adoption of the forward looking rule, the Commission adopted a "safe harbor" rule which protects the registrant and independent auditor from lawsuits for a subsequently proved inaccurate projection *if* the projection was made in a:

> "good faith assessment of a registrant's performance" and that management "must have a reasonable basis for such assessment."

What is the significance of the safe harbor rule? It means that the plaintiff must carry the burden of proof to establish that the forecasts and projections did *not* have a reasonable basis, or were *not* disclosed in good faith. Heretofore, for the most part, the burden of proof was upon the defendants (the registrant, accountants, attorneys, and other signatories) to prove that they had, in fact, a reasonable basis for the projections, and had disclosed them in good faith.

The Information Covered By The Financial Forecasts Safe Harbor Rule

- Projections of revenues.
- Projections of earnings (losses).
- Projections of capital expenditures.
- Projections of dividend payments.
- Projections of capital structure and other financial items.
- Statements of management's plans and objectives.
- Statements of future economic performance in the MD&A.
- Disclosed assumptions underlying or relating to any of the projected financial information.

NOTE: It should be clear that the Commission "encourages" forward-looking information; it is not required in either an SEC filing nor in the registrant's annual report.

Also, the independent auditor does not have to certify the forward-looking information as presented by the management. However, the auditor must be mindful that many of the projections will be based upon certified information in the statements. Therefore, the auditor should take care to review management's forward-looking statements for consistency with the financial information in the certified statements.

The pages of SEC Release No. 33-6383, the Integrated Disclosure System, as appears in the Federal Register follow. Only the rules relevant to the independent accountant's responsibilities are reprinted here. The balance of the Release concern attorneys and legal matters only.

The information should be rigorously reviewed by the accountant because the new rules determine the accountant's preparation and presentation of the registrant's financial data.

SEC Forms

The forms specify the financial and other information to be included in a filing and how the forms are to be prepared. The most frequently used forms are:

1. Form 10-K, the annual report structured as follows:
   a) Part I—Business, properties, legal proceedings, security ownership of certain beneficial owners and management.
   b) Part II—Market for the registrant's common stock and related security holders matters; selected financial data; management's discussion and analysis; financial statements and supplementary data.
   c) Part III—Directors and executive officers of the company; management remuneration and transactions.
   d) Part IV—Exhibits, financial statement schedules and reports on Form 8-K.
2. Forms S-1, S-2, S-3. Required for new securities issues.
3. Form S-8. For employee benefit plans.
4. Form S-15. For certain business combinations.
5. Form S-16. For certain primary and secondary offerings.
6. Form S-18. For certain smaller offerings.
7. Form 10. For registration of securities traded over the counter.
8. Form 8-K. A current report to be filed after the occurrence of events expected to affect the company's operating results.
9. Form 10-Q. Quarterly report to the SEC.

Forms S-1, S-2, S-3

A significant part of the Integrated Disclosure System and revision of the rules was the adoption by the Commission of three new registration forms. These new Forms S-1, S-2, S-3 replace forms S-1, S-7 and S-16. The differences in the new forms related primarily to the extent that required information is actually delivered to potential investors.

New Form S-3.   An abbreviated form relies on the "efficient market theory"—information about companies using this form is already known or is so readily available it need not be repeated in a prospectus. The criteria for its use are designed to be indicative of a company's following in the market. The form allows maximum use of incorporation by reference of 1934 Act reports (contains minimal prospectus disclosure requirements). The qualifications for use of Form S-3 are:

- A registrant must have $150 million in *voting* stock held by holders not affiliated with the company.
- Or, registrant's having $100 million in voting stock and an annual trading volume in the stock market of 3 million, or more, shares.

The aggregate market value of the registrant's outstanding voting stock is computed by use of the price at which the stock was last sold, or the average of the bid and asked prices of the stock, as of a date within 60 days prior to the date of filing. Annual trading volume is the volume of shares traded in any continuous twelve-month period ended within 60 days prior to the date of filing.

Form S-3 also may be used for certain primary offerings of investment grade nonconvertible debt securities, secondary offerings other than by the issuer, offerings for dividend and interest reinvestment plans, and for exercise of certain conversions and warrants.

New Form S-2.   This form is available for the registration of securities to be offered to a "middle range" of public companies. The qualifications for the use of Form S-2 are:

- The registrant has filed reports with the Commission for at least 36 calendar months immediately preceding the filing of the registrations statement (yet whose securities are not actively followed in the market to meet the test of Form S-3).
- The registrant has filed in a timely manner all reports required to be filed during the 12 calendar months immediately preceding the filing of the registration statement.
- Neither the registrant nor any of its consolidated or unconsolidated subsidiar-

ies have, since the end of their last fiscal year for which certified financial statements of the registrant and its consolidated subsidiaries were included in a report: a) failed to pay any dividend or sinking fund installment on preferred stock; b) defaulted on any rental installment or installments on indebtedness for borrowed money; c) defaulted on any rental on one or more long-term leases, which defaults in the aggregate are material to the financial position of the registrant and its consolidated and unconsolidated subsidiaries, taken as a whole.

Form S-2 combines incorporation by reference of 1934 Act reports and delivery of the annual report to shareholders with the prospectus.

New Form S-1.   This form is used for registration of securities of all issuers "for which no other form is authorized or prescribed, except that the form is not used for securities of foreign governments or political subdivisions thereof."

New Form S-1 is very similar to old Form S-1. New Form S-1 must be used by registrants in the 1934 Act reporting system for less than three years, and also may be used by any registrants who choose to do so, or for whom no other form in the reporting system is available. This Form requires complete disclosure to be set forth in the Prospectus and permits *no incorporation by reference.*

New Form S-1 is governed entirely by Regulation S-K for its nonfinancial substantive disclosure provisions. The Prospectus must include information about the registrant as is required to be reported in an annual report on Form 10-K. This information includes:

- The basic information package.
- The full Regulation S-K descriptions of business, properties, and legal proceedings.
- S-K disclosures with respect to management and security holders.
- All other S-K items where appropriate.

Regulation S-X.   This regulation covers the form and content of financial statements filed with the SEC. Regulation S-X also covers the qualifications of accountants who report on financial statements and schedules filed with SEC.

Financial Reporting Releases.   FRR's are a part of Regulation S-X which are issued periodically by the SEC. These releases cover individual topics concerning accounting requirements and reporting practices. The releases also give guidelines and examples of situations involving the independence of accountants.

The SEC has also developed a new release: Accounting and Auditing Enforcement Releases (AAER's) which are related to Commission enforcement actions.

GOING PUBLIC

"Going Public" is a significant step in the business life of any company. It is a step which should be taken only after a rigorous appraisal of the advantages, disadvantages, consequences, and other sources of financing. Going public is an expensive means of raising capital, so the benefits must more than outweigh the disadvantages.

When considering a public offering, planning should begin long in advance. Many of the decisions associated with a first stock offering require a long period of time to implement. A well-planned public offering, therefore, requires the preliminary studies and implementing procedures to begin sometimes years before the securities are offered to the investing public.

The listing that follows are some of the more common advantages and disadvantages of going public. Following the listing are brief generalizations of the requirements and procedures in a public offering of securities.

Advantages

1. Funds are obtained from the offering. When the securities are sold by the company, the money can be used for working capital, research and development of new products, plant and equipment expansion, retiring existing indebtedness, and for diversifying the company's operations.
2. Through public ownership of its securities, the company may gain prestige, become better known, and improve the business's operating results.
3. A company's customers and suppliers may become shareholders resulting in increased sales of the company's products or services.
4. Companies often consider expansion by the acquisition of other businesses. A company with publicly-traded stock is in a position to finance acquisitions with its own securities, instead of investing cash.
5. The business may be better able to attract and retain key personnel if it can offer stock having a public market (or options to purchase such stock).
6. A public offering of equity securities will usually improve a company's net worth, enabling the company to borrow capital on more favorable terms.
7. Once a public market is created for a stock and its price performs favorably, additional equity capital can be raised from the public, as well as privately from institutional investors on favorable terms.
8. Private ownership by one or a few persons of a fractional or even all of a closely-held business is an asset with no ready market, usually no market at all. Once the company becomes publicly owned and the after-market becomes well developed, there will be a ready market for even a small number of the majority owners' shares.

Disadvantages

1. Public offerings are expensive, as registration with the SEC requires the retention of various professionals, i.e., investment bankers (underwriters), attorneys, accountants, and perhaps engineers, actuarials, and other experts.

2. Because of their responsibility to the public, the owners of a business lose some flexibility in management. There are practical, if not legal, limitations on salaries, fringe benefits, relatives on the payroll, and on operating procedures and policies. The authority to make decisions quickly may be lost, as many policies require prior approval by a board of directors, and in some instances by a majority of the shareholders.

3. There are many additional expenses and administrative problems for a publicly-owned company. Routine legal and accounting fees can increase materially. Recurring additional expenses include the preparation and distribution of proxy material and annual reports to shareholders, the preparation and filing with the Securities and Exchange Commission of reports required by the Securities Exchange Act of 1934, and the expenditure of fees for a transfer agent, registrar, and usually a public relations consultant. Added to the out-of-pocket costs is the cost in terms of executive time allocated to shareholder relations and public disclosures.

4. The owners of a privately-held business are often in so high a tax bracket that they prefer their company to pay either small dividends, or no dividends at all. The underwriters of an issue will usually require otherwise in order to increase the marketability and distribution of the first-time issue.

5. Once a company is publicly owned, research has demonstrated that management, some to a greater some to a lesser extent, tends to consider the effect on the market price of its stock when considering major decisions that will affect the profits. While it is generally acknowledged that management's preoccupation with day-to-day stock price fluctuations should be avoided, there are undoubtedly situations where a conscientious concern about the shareholders' investment quite properly should limit the decision-making alternatives for the management of a publicly-held company.

6. The one or few owners of a business possibly could be faced with a loss of control of the company if a sufficiently large proportion of the shares are sold to the public. Also, once a company's stock becomes publicly held, dilution of the prior owners' equity interest by subsequent public offerings, secondary financing, and acquisitions must be anticipated.

Evaluating a Company for Public Financing

In evaluating the advisability of going public, as well as pricing the company's stock, the underwriters will consider:

1. The amount and trend of sales and earnings.
2. Present and projected working capital and cash flow.
3. The experience, integrity and quality of the company's management.
4. The growth potential of the business.
5. The nature and number of the customers.
6. The company's suppliers.
7. The company's competitive position in the industry.

Selecting an Underwriter

Once the decision has been made to go public, one of the most important decisions to be made is the selection of an underwriter. Investment banking firms vary widely in prestige, financial strength, and ability to provide various services which the company needs. Some underwriters are not interested in first offerings; others specialize in that phase of the underwriting business. Some underwriters specialize in certain industries; the large investment banking firms will usually accept business in all of the major industries. The company's attorneys, auditors, and bankers can be helpful in selecting the underwriter.

The Underwriting Agreement

It is customary for the company going public to sign a "letter of intent" for the underwriter. If used, the letter outlines the details and proposed terms of the offering and the underwriter's compensation. It is explicitly written into the agreement that it is not binding upon either party, except there usually is a binding provision spelling out the payment of expenses if one party withdraws from the offering.

What Securities to Offer

Once a company has decided to go public, it must determine with the advice of the underwriter what class of securities to offer. Most first offerings are common stock issues. A first offering can consist of a package including other securities, such as debenture bonds which may or may not be convertible into common stock; warrants to purchase common stock can be "attached" to the new offering; preferred stock with a conversion privilege can be included in the package.

The Registration Statement

The registration statement is the disclosure document filed with the SEC that must accompany a registered offering of securities for sale to the public. This "filing" consists of two parts: Part I of the registration statement is the *prospectus*, which is the information that must be distributed to the offerees (the investors) of the securities. Part II contains supplemental information about the company of specific interest to the SEC, but which is available for public inspection at the office of the Commission.

Liabilities

It should be emphasized that management is responsible to determine that the factual information in the registration statement is accurate and complete. Management cannot assume a passive interest by relying entirely upon the attorneys and accountants to determine the information to be furnished, verify the information, and prepare the registration statement properly. It is reasonable, however, for management to rely upon counsel, accountants, and other experts associated with the registration for accuracy and completeness of the material in the statement, *assuming* management has properly disclosed factual information to the experts.

Under the Securities Act of 1933 (the governing statute for new security issues) and related statutes and regulations, civil and criminal liability can arise:

1. From material misstatements or omissions in a registration statement, including the final prospectus.
2. From failure to comply with applicable registration requirements.
3. From failing to supply a prospectus in connection with specified activities.
4. From engaging in fraudulent transactions.

Under various provisions of the Securities Act, company officers, directors, underwriters, controlling persons and experts who sign the registration statement are jointly and severally liable, and their civil liability can extend to the full sales price of the security; a criminal offense (fraud) can result in imprisonment for the signatory.

Preparation and Filing of a Registration Statement

Once it has been determined that a public offering of securities will take place, a corporate meeting involving the following parties is generally arranged:

1. A financial officer of the company (registrant).
2. Counsel for the issuer.
3. A representative of the underwriters.
4. Counsel for the underwriters.
5. The independent public accountant.

This group generally constitutes the *registration team.*

Responsibilities of the Registration Team Members	
Member	*Responsibility*
Issuing company financial officer	Primary responsibility for all aspects of the offering. The SEC considers the registration statement to be the property of the issuing company.
Counsel for the issuer	Provides expert advice on compliance with state and federal securities laws. Helps issuer prepare the registration statement.
Underwriter	Also provides expert advice on financial matters. Manages the underwriting group composed of participating underwriters and distributes securities to retailers.
Independent accountant	Provides expert advice on accounting matters. Audits the financial statements of the issuer and provides an opinion as required by the SEC.

Annual Report Requirements of Rule 14a-3

Summary of operations and management's discussion and analysis
Description of business
Identity of directors and executive officers
Identity of principal market where voting securities are traded and high/low sales prices and dividends paid for past eight quarters
Statement that Form 10-K is provided without charge
Balance sheet
Income statement
Statement of security holders' equity
Footnote disclosure required by Regulation S-X
Reconciliation of differences between 10-K and financial statements
Schedule XVI, Supplementary Earnings Statement Information
Opinion letter
Other voluntarily disclosed information (including letter to shareholders; announcement of annual meeting and the year in brief)

Contents of Regulation S-X		
Article	*Subject*	*Explanation*
1	Application of Regulation S-X	Regulation S-X applies to filings of the 1933 act, the 1934 act, the 1935 act, and the 1940 act. Article 1 also defines the terms used throughout the regulation.
2	Qualifications and Reports of Accountants	Sets out the SEC's professional standards for the auditor, including independence, conditions under which an accountant can be suspended or disbarred, and the types of auditor's opinions accepted by the SEC.
3	Rules of General Application	Explains the SEC's general requirements

Contents of Regulation S-X (*Continued*)

		for financial statements in regard to form, order, terminology, material items succinctness, and completeness. Defines specific current assets, current liabilities, owners' equity, revenue, and expense.
4	Consolidated and Combined Financial Statements	Presents the SEC standards for consolidating financial statements in order to clearly exhibit the financial position and results of operations of the registrant and its subsidiaries.
5	Commercial and Industrial Companies	Provides specific accounting requirements for all companies not included in one of the special categories in Articles 5A through 10.
5A	Companies in the Development Stage	Provides specific reporting requirements.
6	Management Investment Companies	Provides specific reporting requirements.
6A	Unit Investment Trusts	Provides specific reporting requirements.
6B	Face-Amount Certificate Investment Companies	Provides specific reporting requirements.
6C	Employee Stock Purchase, Savings, and Similar Plans	Provides specific reporting requirements.
7	Insurance Companies Other than Life Insurance Companies	Provides specific reporting requirements.
7A	Life Insurance Companies	Provides specific reporting requirements.
8	Committees Issuing Certificates of Deposit	Provides specific reporting requirements.
9	Bank Holding Companies and Banks	Provides specific reporting requirements.
10	National Persons	Provides specific reporting requirements.
11	Content of Other Stockholders' Equity	Specifies the content of other stockholders' equity required by Articles 5, 6, 7, and 7A.
11A	Statement of Changes in Financial Position	Specifies the content of the statement of changes in financial position.
12	Form and Content of Supporting Schedules	Sets forth the form and content of certain schedules, when and if they are required in support of balance sheets and income statements.

Some Footnote Items Generally Required for SEC Reports by Regulation S-X

Rule	*Item*
Rule 3-07	Changes in accounting principles and practices and retroactive adjustments of accounts.

Some Footnote Items Generally Required for SEC Reports by Regulation S-X (*Continued*)

Rule 3-08	Encourages registrants to summarize their accounting principles and practices under one footnote.
Rule 3-16	(a) Principles of consolidation or combination
	(b) Principles of translation of items in foreign currency
	(c) Assets subject to lien
	(d) Intercompany profits and losses
	(e) Defaults
	(f) Preferred shares
	(g) Pension and retirement plans
	(h) Restrictions limiting the availability of retained earnings for dividend purposes
	(i) Commitments and contingent liabilities
	(j) Bonus, profit sharing, and other similar plans
	(k) Significant changes in bonds, mortgages, and similar debt
	(l) Basis of revenue recognition
	(m) Depreciation, depletion, obsolescence, and amortization
	(n) Capital stock optioned, sold, or offered for sale to directors, officers, or key employees
	(o) Income tax expense
	(p) Warrants or rights outstanding
	(q) Leased assets and lease commitments
	(r) Interest capitalized
	(s) Disagreements on accounting and financial disclosure matters
	(t) Disclosure of selected quarterly financial data in roles to financial statements
Rule 3-17	(This requirement for replacement cost information was deleted for fiscal years ending after December 31, 1979.)
Rule 3-18	Oil and gas reserves

Timetable for Preparation of Registration Statement

Date	Description of Procedure	General Responsibility
Jan. 20	Hold board of directors meeting to authorize: issuance of additional amount of stock to be offered, preparation of registration statement for filing with SEC, negotiation of underwriting agreement.	Registrant
Jan. 25	Hold organizational meeting to discuss preparation of registration statement.	All parties
Jan. 26	Begin drafting registration statement.	Registrant and counsel
Jan. 30	Complete and distribute timetable for registration process.	Registrant's counsel
Feb. 10	Distribute first draft of underwriting agreement for review.	Underwriter counsel
Feb. 15	Distribute questionnaires to directors and	Registrant's counsel

Timetable for Preparation of Registration Statement (*Continued*)

	officers covering matters relating to registration requirements.	
Feb. 20	Distribute first draft of textual portion of registration statement of review.	Registrant and counsel
Feb. 25	Submit draft of financial statements to be included in registration statement.	Registrant and independent accountant
Feb. 27	Review draft of registration statement.	All parties
March 1	Send complete draft of registration statement to printer.	Registrant or counsel
March 10	Approve and submit final audited financial statements and related report for inclusion in registration statement.	Independent accountant
March 22	Receive and correct first printed proofs of registration statement.	All parties
	Distribute proof of registration statement to directors and officers.	Registrant or counsel
	Send revised draft of registration statement to printer.	Registrant or counsel
March 23	Hold board of directors meeting to approve and sign registration statement.	Registrant
March 24	File registration statement with SEC.	Registrant's counsel
	File listing application with stock exchange for common stock to be offered.	Registrant and counsel
	Distribute preliminary (red herring) prospectus.	Underwriters
April 15	Receive letter of comment from SEC regarding registration statement.	Registrant and counsel
April 16	Hold meeting to discuss letter of comment.	All parties
April 19	Complete draft of first amendment of registration statement and send to printer.	Registrant and counsel
April 20–21	Review printer's proof of amendment to registration statement.	All parties
	Send corrected proof to printer.	Registrant's counsel
April 22	File amendment to registration statement to cover SEC comments and to reflect any material developments since initial filing on March 24.	Registrant and counsel
	Notify SEC in writing that a final (price) amendment will be filed on May 2 and that the company requests "acceleration" in order that the registration statement may become effective as of the close of business on that date.	Registrant or counsel
	Receive approval from stock exchange of listing application subject to official notice of issuance and subject to effectiveness of registration statement.	Registrant and counsel
April 27	Resolve any final comments and changes with	Registrant and counsel

Timetable for Preparation of Registration Statement (*Continued*)

	SEC by telephone.	
April 29	Hold due diligence meeting.	All parties
May 1	Finalize offering price.	Registrant and under-writers
May 2	Deliver first comfort letter to underwriters.	Independent accountant
	Sign underwriting agreement.	Registrant and under-writers
	File amendment to registration statement identifying price.	Registrant and counsel
	Receive notification that registration statement has become effective.	Registrant and counsel
	Notify stock exchange of effectiveness.	Registrant or counsel
May 7	Deliver second comfort letter to underwriters.	Independent account-ants
	Complete settlement with underwriters—closing date.	Registrant, registrant's counsel, underwriters, and underwriter's counsel

REGULATION D

Small Business Can Now Go Public

One of the primary sources of financing for small business public securities offerings is venture capital organizations. New venture capital investments have increased significantly in recent years, and the reduction in the capital gains rate in the Economic Recovery Tax Act of 1981 to 20% maximum tax on capital gains encourages risk-taking by venture capital firms. Small business enterprises are a significant investment for venture capital risk-takers. Access to venture capital financing, as well as to the money markets generally through investment bankers, has been made easier for the small enterprèneur by the *Small Business Issues' Simplification Act* passed by Congress in 1980. The objective of this legislation is to enable small business enterprises to raise funds in the public market, with reduced registration and reporting requirements of the SEC.

In response to the small business legislation, the SEC adopted new rules effective April 15, 1982, which significantly reduces the time and expense for small and new "start-up" enterprises to raise capital. Regulation D was promulgated by the SEC to simplify the procedures for small business enterprises to enter the capital markets.

The SEC points out in Release No. 33-6389:

Regulation D is the product of the Commission's evaluation of the impact of its rules and regulations on the ability of small businesses to raise capital. This study has revealed a particular concern that the registration requirements and the exemptive scheme of the Securities Act impose disproportionate restraints on small issuers.

The important aspect of Regulation D concerns exemption from registration for small offerings and private placements. The Regulation is implemented by Rules 501-506.

Rule 501. Defines 8 terms used in Regulation D.

1. Accredited investor.
2. Affiliate.
3. Aggregate offering price.
4. Business combination.
5. Calculation of number of purchasers.
6. Executive officer.
7. Issuer.
8. Purchaser representative.

Rule 502. Sets forth the general conditions which apply to the three exemptions under Regulation D. The conditions relate to integration, information requirements, limitation on manner of offerings and limitations on resale.

Rule 503. A uniform notice of sales form, designated Form D, is provided for in this rule. It is available for all offerings exempted by Regulation D. (Form D is reproduced immediately following the reprint of Regulation D.)

Rule 504. Permits any issuer, other than an investment company or an Exchange Act reporting company, to offer and sell a maximum of $500,000 of its securities to an unlimited number of persons during a twelve-month period.

Rule 505. Provides a registration exemption for any noninvestment company issuer, *whether or not* a reporting company under the Exchange Act. An eligible issuer can offer and sell up to $7,500,000 during a twelve-month period without general advertising or general solicitation. An offering under this rule can be made to an unlimited number of accredited investors, and to a maximum of 35 nonaccredited investors.

Rule 506. The transactional exemption provided by this rule does not restrict the dollar amount of securities offered. It is available to any issuer, whether or not a reporting company. A Rule 506 offering can be made to an unlimited number of accredited investors and to a maximum of 35 nonaccredited investors, but where the offering is to nonaccredited investors, the issuer must *reasonably* believe, *prior* to the sale, that each nonaccredited investor, either alone or with a purchaser representative, understands the merits and risks of the offering.

Definition of Small Business

In Release 33-6380 (January 28, 1982), the SEC defined the term "small business" or "small organization" as:

> . . . an issuer whose total assets on the last day of its most recent fiscal year were $3,000,000 or less, and that is engaged or proposing to engage in small business financing . . . if it is conducting or proposes to conduct an offering of securities which does not exceed the dollar limitation prescribed by Section 3(b) of the Securities Act.

Form S-18

The qualified start-up company can register on Form S-18 when the total offering is not more than $7,500,000. This form can also be used for the registration of securities of any person other than the issuer (secondary offerings), provided the total offering price of the securities does not exceed $1,500,000, and the total offering price of the securities together with the total offering price of any securities to be sold by the issuer does not exceed $7,500,000.

Accountants Form S-18 Responsibilities

Financial Statement Requirements:

- An audited balance sheet for one year. (S-1 requires two years.)
- An audited income statement for two years. (S-1 requires three years.)
- An audited changes in financial position statement for two years. (S-1 requires three years.)
- Financial statements must be as of 90 days of the filing date.
- If a "stub" period (since the end of the last fiscal year) must be used to bring the financial statements into conformity with the 90-day requirement, the stub period can be unaudited, *but* must be presented on a comparative basis with the *same* stub period for the prior year.
- A consolidated balance sheet must be filed as of a date within 90 days prior to the date of filing the registration statement. This balance sheet need not be audited if it is not as of the latest fiscal year. If the balance sheet is not audited, an audited balance sheet must be filed as of a date within one year, unless the fiscal year of the registrant has ended within 90 days prior to the date of the filing, in which case the audited balance sheet may be as of the end of the preceding fiscal year.
- A consolidated balance sheet must be filed as of a date within 90 days prior to the date of filing of the registration statement. This balance sheet need not be audited if it is not as of the latest fiscal year. If the balance sheet is not audited, an audited balance sheet must be filed as of a date within one year, unless the fiscal year of the registrant has ended within 90 days prior to the

date of the filing, in which case the audited balance sheet may be as of the end of the preceding fiscal year.

- Consolidated statements must be filed of income, statement of changes in financial condition, and statements of other stockholders' equity for each of the two fiscal years preceding the date of the most recent balance sheet being filed and for the interim period, if any, between the end of the most recent of such fiscal years and the date of the most recent balance sheet being filed. These statements shall be audited to the date of the most recent audited balance sheet being filed.
- Aging requirements. Same as those applicable to the financial statements in other registration statements.

Information not required:

- No financial schedules to the financial statements are required.
- Management's Discussion and Analysis is not required because start-up companies have little or no financial history.
- Separate statements of unconsolidated subsidiaries and investees can be omitted.
- An index of financial statements and schedules need not be furnished.
- In general, Form S-18 departs from Regulation S-K requirements by requiring somewhat less detailed disclosures than Form S-1 concerning description of business, properties, officers and directors, legal proceedings, and management remuneration.

The significant differences of the reduced requirements of Form S-18 compared to Form S-1 can be summarized:

- The time factor. The S-18 is filed in an SEC regional office, instead of in Washington, D.C. This considerably reduces the time the SEC takes to review the filing.
- Proximity to the regional SEC office expedites assistance from the SEC staff in that office in the preparation of the S-18 filing.
- The S-18 does not require a number of detailed disclosures required by the S-1; e.g., less detail with respect to pension funds; no computation of the ratio of earnings to fixed charges; no management's discussion and analysis; less detailed narratives of segment information, foreign operations, and order backlogs; less discussion of a number of other business activities required in an S-1 filing.
- The most recent year of an audited balance sheet and most recent two fiscal years of audited income, changes in financial position, and changes in stockholders' equity statements. Form S-1 requires one additional year of these statements.

- A particularly economical change for small business allows the application of GAAP in the S-18 filing, instead of the SEC's Regulation S-X accounting requirements, which are very extensive in the disclosure information required and, therefore, more costly for the registrant's accounting and legal expenses.
- The regulations give the small business three years to complete the transition for the application of S-X accounting requirements to the Form 10-K (annual report) filing and the Form 10-Q (the quarterly filing).

SHELF REGISTRATION

Historically, every new security issue by a corporation had to undergo the complete registration process, regardless of how short or long the intervening time period between issues, including new issues of the same security.

The registration and marketing of a new issue is expensive; for a large company the cost of a new issue runs into seven figures.

On March 3, 1982, the SEC issued ASR 306 announcing a temporary rule—Rule 415—which established a procedure permitting "delayed or continuous offerings." The procedure is termed "shelf registration." The essential element in the self-registration process gives public corporations permission to register a security whether or not the new issue is to be sold immediately. Subsequent issues of the *same* security can be sold without a new registration for each issue.

The Requirements

- Shelf registrations are limited to primary distributions made at the current market price of the security. Secondary issues do not qualify for shelf registration.
- Forms S-1-2-3- and S-8 (for employee benefit plans) can be shelf-registered, except that primary distribution "at the market" can be made only by S-3 qualified corporations.

(Note: At-the-market is defined by the SEC: "An offering into an existing trading market other than at a fixed price or through the facilities of a national securities exchange or to a market-maker otherwise than on an exchange.")

- There must be a reasonable expectation of selling shelf-registered shares within a two-year period. (The shares do not have to ever be sold, however.)
- The number of shares self-registered cannot exceed 10% of the float (outstanding Stock) in the class of securities being shelf-registered.
- An underwriter(s) must be involved: 1) to provide an orderly distribution of the issue; 2) to ensure the accuracy of the Prospectus: 3) to assure compliance with the Prospectus delivery requirements.

Purpose

As noted, the registration process is expensive for the issuer. By permitting continuous registration, a corporation will incur the expense of only one registration for several new issues of the *same* class of security.

Formerly, corporations sold a new issue on the effective date of the registration, which involved an unknown price for the security until (literally) a few hours before the sale. With shelf registration the issuer can take advantage of favorable changes in the market price of the security, and withhold an issue if market conditions have turned unfavorable.

Updating the Shelf Registration

When necessary, a shelf registration is updated either by a supplement or amendment to the original registration. A supplement is simply a sticker attached to the Prospectus; it contains information relevant to the issue considered sufficiently material in nature by the issuer to be communicated to the public. Supplemental information is not passed upon by the SEC, nor is a part of the registration statement.

A post-effective amendment usually involves a revision of the original Prospectus. It is reviewed by the SEC, becomes a part of the registration statement, and must be declared effective by the SEC.

Rule 512 (a) (2) of regulation S-K:

". . . each such post-effective amendment shall be deemed to be a new registration statement relating to the securities offered therein . . ."

Amendments are required:

- When anytime after nine months after the effective date of the registration statement the Prospectus contains information *more than* 16 months old.
- The Rule provides that anytime after nine months subsequent to the effective date of a registration statement, a Prospectus can no longer be used if any information in the Prospectus is over 16 months old. This requirement is usually triggered by the age of the certified financial statements. Assume year-end (any year) certified financial statements and assume a registration statement became effective on June 1. An updated Prospectus would have to be filed and become effective prior to April 30 of the following year.
- When any "facts or events arising after the effective date of the registration statement which, individually or in the aggregate, represent a fundamental change in the information set forth in the registration statement."
- When there is a material change in the original distribution plan of the issue.
- When there is a change in the managing underwriter.

- When false or misleading information is discovered after the effective date of the original registration statement.

The shelf-registration procedure is an experiment for which the SEC has set a time limit of two years ending December 31, 1983. The Commission will, during that time period, continuously appraise the results of the application of the shelf-registration approach before making a final determination with respect to its use.

The proponents of the Rule believe that it makes it easier for companies trying to deal with volatile markets to seize advantageous moments in the market to sell new security issues.

The opponents of the process believe the procedure can disrupt the stock market, after underwriting techniques, and is contrary to the interests of the investing public.

GOING PRIVATE

Going Private is a term applied to transactions that result in a reduction (or complete elimination) in the number of shareholders of a publicly-held corporation. In recent years there has been increasing activity in returning publicly-held corporations to private ownership.

The transactions are accomplished by open market purchases, cash tender offers, some type of exchange offer of one type of security for the outstanding securities, merger of the existing company with another company controlled by the issuer's principal shareholders, by reverse stock splits, and other types of transactions that alter the ownership of equity securities to a private ownership status.

Why go private?

While the stocks of many publicly-held corporations have increased greatly in value the past several years, the stocks of many companies, nevertheless, have continued to sell significantly below liquidating values. It is these companies that have been subject to corporate raiders, to shareholder pressures on management, have low returns on investment, have substantial cash positions, have consistently increased costs of public ownership and listing expenses on national securities exchanges, and have changed management attitudes toward the tangible and intangible benefits of public ownership.

Accountant's Participation

The accountant should know that the Securities and Exchange Commission requires valid reasons for "taking a company private," as current public shareholders must be dealt with fairly. The Exchange Act prohibits fraudulent, deceptive and manipulative acts or practices with respect to going private transactions. Rule 13e3, the controlling SEC rule governing going private transactions by public companies or their affiliates, requires filing with the SEC the disclosures and dissemination requirements to prevent unfair treatment of existing shareholders.

The primary question the accountant must ask is: Why go private? The answer includes such factors as reviewing the participation of the majority stockholders, the minority stockholders, management, directors, as well as the historic and recent financial and operating performance of the company.

The accountant must also consider whether private ownership will continue to manage the corporation on a "going concern" basis. This appraisal consists primarily first of considering the various methods of going private and then developing *pro forma* projections of financial statements to determine which of the methods best protects the rights of the public shareholders.

Other considerations are an understanding of the company's industry and the company's position in that industry, the risk factors, the prospects of the company, the effects of the going private transaction on the current shareholders, comprehensive financial information, a history of the company, history of the prior price performance of the stock, and a detailed disclosure of the majority and minority interests. These and other factors that may be uniquely relevant to the corporation must be considered to ensure that a fair price is paid to the shareholders by the issuer.

One of the most significant problems that has developed in going private transactions is the interests of minority stockholders. Primarily, what is a fair price for their stock? The stockholders will lose the liquidity of a public marketplace and their investment position. For their protection, the regulations prohibit any sort of pressure, or coercion, to force minority stockholders to give up their investment.

The following is a list of the information required by Exchange Rule 13E-3 that must be disclosed to the shareholders on schedule 13E-3 of the corporation when they are solicited to approve a going private transaction.

The Income Statement:

- Net sales, operating revenues, and other revenues.
- Income before extraordinary items.
- Net income.

Balance Sheet:

- Working capital.
- Total assets.
- Stockholders' equity.

Per share Disclosure:

- Income per common share (before extraordinary items).
- Extraordinary items.

- Net income per common share, *and* per common share equivalents, if applicable.
- Net income per share on a *fully diluted* basis.
- Average number of shares of common stock outstanding for the two most recent fiscal years and adjusted for stock dividends or stock splits.
- Ratio of earnings to fixed charges for the two most recent fiscal years.
- Book value per share of the most recent fiscal year.
- *Pro Forma* data for the financial information that will disclose the effect of the method selected to complete the going private transaction.
- Audited financial statements for the past two years.
- Unaudited interim financial statements for the latest year-to-date interim period and corresponding interim period of the preceding year.

Additional information required:

1. The issuer must explicitly state the belief that the transaction is fair (or unfair) to unaffiliated security holders. The reasons for stating the belief that the offer is fair must be discussed.
2. Identity and background of the persons filing the controlling Schedule 13E3.
3. Past contracts, transactions or negotiations.
4. Terms of the transaction.
5. Plans or proposals of the issuer or affiliate.
6. Source and amounts of funds to finance the transaction.
7. Purpose, alternatives, reasons, and effects of the going private transaction.

(The relevant Rules and Schedules that should be referenced if responsible for a going private transaction are: Rule 13e3, *Going Private Transactions by Certain Issuers or their Affiliates*; Schedule 13E-3, *Transactions Statement*; Rule 13e4, *Tender Offers by Issuers*; Schedule 13E-4, *Issuer Tender Offer Statement*.)

10

Materiality
and Financial
Statement Disclosure

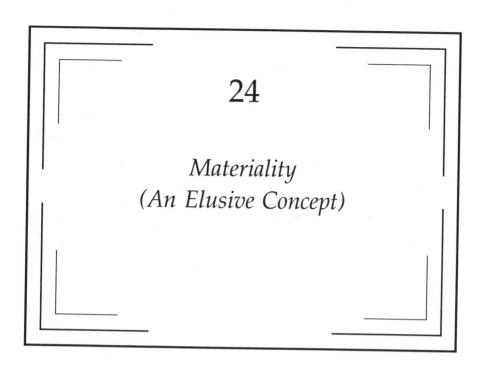

24

Materiality
(An Elusive Concept)

There have been attempts by authoritative rule-making bodies, scholars of accounting, users of financial statements, and others to develop quantitative criteria for determining the materiality of items in the financial statements. If Item A is x percent of a total, Item A is material. If Item B is y percent of a total, then Item B is material, etc. All efforts have proved fruitless, and there are no accepted quantitative standards that can be wholly relied upon for an unquestioned determination of whether an item is material or immaterial (and can be omitted from the statements or notes thereto).

The courts to some extent have helped. However, it should be cautioned that different jurisdictions in different geographic areas of the country have established many different opinions and definitions of materiality. For example, the Tenth Circuit Court of Appeals ruled that information is material if ". . . the trading judgment of reasonable investors would not have been left untouched upon receipt of such information." (Mitchell vs. Texas Gulf Sulphur Co.) In the "landmark" *Bar Chris* case the judge said that a material fact is one ". . . which if it had been correctly stated or disclosed would have deterred or tended to deter the average prudent investor from purchasing the securities in question" (*Escott et al v. Bar Chris Construction Corporation et al.*)

Principally because the U.S. Supreme Court defined materiality in the *TSC Industries Inc. v. Northway Inc.*, case, the following statement of the Court is considered to be a recent (1976) and authoritative basis upon which to render a judgment of materiality:

> "An omitted fact is material if there is a substantial likelihood that a reasonable shareholder would consider it important in deciding how to vote. This standard is fully consistent with the general description of materiality as a requirement that the defect have a significant *propensity* to affect the voting process."

(Note: This decision dealt with *omissions* of material information.)

> "The Securities and Exchange Commission in Regulation S-X, Rule 1-02, defines *material* information: 'The term *material* when used to qualify a requirement for the furnishing of information as to any subject, limits the information required to those matters as to which an average prudent investor ought reasonably to be informed.' "

WHAT'S MATERIAL?

Precisely what information requiring disclosure is for the accountant to decide. The accountant must exercise judgment according to the circumstances and facts concerning material matters and their conformity with Generally Accepted Accounting Principles. A few examples of material matters are:

- The form and content of financial statements.
- Notes to the statements.
- The terminology used in the statements.
- The classification of items in the statements.
- Amount of detail furnished.
- The bases of the amounts presented, i.e., for inventories, plants, liabilities, etc.
- The existence of affiliated or controlling interests.

(Note: Statement on Auditing Standard No. 32 *Adequacy of Disclosure in Financial Statements* should be reviewed for more details related to this topic).

A clear distinction between materiality and disclosure should be noted. Material information involves both quantitative (data) and qualitative information. Additionally, the information must be disclosed in a manner that enables a person of "average" comprehension and experience to understand and apply it to an investment decision. Contra speaking, information disclosed in a manner that only an "expert" can evaluate is not considered within the meaning and intent of disclosure requirements.

Materiality should be thought of as an abstract concept. While many efforts to define the term can be found in the literature, e.g., accounting and auditing books, law books, and Regulation S-X, nevertheless, in the final analysis, judgments with respect to what is material as found in court decisions, SEC actions, accountants' interpretations, and corporate and financial officers' judgments have evolved into the subjective judgment of individuals (accountants and management) responsible for deciding what is and is not material.

(Statement of Financial Accounting Concepts No. 2. "Qualitative Characteristics of Accounting Information" provides excellent guidance for the decision: "What is material?")

DISCLOSURES REQUIRED IN FINANCIAL STATEMENTS

Below is an outline of the most important disclosures required in financial statements with a brief comment of the substance of each requirement.

Accounting Policies. APB Opinion No. 22 "Disclosure of Accounting Policies" is the applicable GAAP. The disclosure should set forth the accounting principles underlying the statements that materially affect the determination of financial position, changes in financial position, and results of operations. Also included are the accounting principles relating to recognition of revenue, allocation of asset costs to current and future periods, the selection from existing acceptable alternatives, such as the inventory method chosen, and any accounting principles and methods unique to the industry of the reporting entity.

As a general rule, the preferred position of the review of accounting policies is footnote No. 1, but a section summarizing the policies preceding the footnotes is acceptable.

Who decides what information is material? This decision is the responsibility of management working with the company's accountant. Listed below are a few items considered material that must be recognized. As a generalization, the *causes* for material changes in financial statement items must be noted to the extent necessary for users to understand the business as a whole. This requirement applies to all financial statements, not just to the income statement.

1. Sales and revenues. Increases or decreases in sales and revenues that are temporary or nonrecurring and their causes.
2. Unusually increased costs.
3. Informative generalizations with respect to each important expense category.
4. Financial expenses. Changes in interest expenses (and interest income); changes in the company's cost of borrowing; changes in the borrowing mix, e.g., long-term vs. short-term.
5. Other income and expense items. These may include dividend income from investees; the equity in the income or losses of investees or of unconsolidated subsidiaries.
6. Income taxes. The effective tax rate paid by corporations should be reconciled to the statutory rates. The reconciliation provides the basis for a description of

the reasons for year-to-year variations in the effective tax rate to which a business is subject. Changes caused by the adoption of new or altered policies of tax-deferred accounting are considered material.

7. Material changes in the relative profitability of lines of business.

8. Material changes in advertising, research and development, new services, or other discretionary costs.

9. The acquisition or disposition of a material asset.

10. Material and unusual charges or gains, including credits or charges associated with discontinuance of operations.

11. Material changes in assumptions underlying deferred costs and the plan for the amortization of such costs.

12. The cost of goods sold, where applicable. The gross margin of an enterprise can be affected by important changes in sales volume, price, unit costs, mix of products or services sold, and inventory profits and losses. The composition of cost among fixed, semi-variable and variable elements influence profitability. Changes in gross margins by an analysis of the interplay between selling prices, costs, and volume should be explained.

13. Cash flow information.

14. Dilution of earnings per share.

15. Segmental reporting.

16. Rental expense under leases.

17. Receivables from officers and stockholders.

CONCEPTUAL FRAMEWORK

The Financial Accounting Standards Board has developed six Statements of Financial Accounting Concepts. The Concepts constitute a foundation of financial accounting standards focusing upon the nature, function, and limits of financial accounting and are to be used as guidelines for consistent reporting. The structure of the framework for financial accounting and reporting as set forth in the Concepts follows.

The six FASB Concepts Statements:

1. *Objectives of Financial Reporting by Business Enterprises*: This Statement is concerned primarily with information that is useful to creditors, investors, and other users of financial statements. ''The objectives are those of general purpose external financial reporting by business enterprises . . . the needs of internal users who lack authority to prescribe information they want and must rely on information management communicates to them.''

2. *Qualitative Characteristics of Accounting Information*: ''The purpose of this Statement is to examine the characteristics that make accounting information

useful." The Statement provides the guidelines for acceptable accounting methods, the amount and types of information to be disclosed, and the form in which the information should be presented. The Board has determined that *relevance and reliability* are the primary attributes of useful accounting information, followed by verifiability, comparability, and consistency as secondary qualities.

3. *Elements of Financial Statements of Business Enterprises.* (Superseded by Concept No. 6.)

4. *Objectives of Financial Reporting by Nonbusiness Organizations*: "This Statement focuses on organizations that have predominantly nonbusiness characteristics that heavily influence the operations of the organizations." The Statement covers external financial reporting by non-business organizations, which includes governmental units and government sponsored entities, such as hospitals, universities, utilities, etc.

5. *Recognition and Measurement in Financial Statements of Business Enterprises*: This Statement sets forth recognition criteria and guidance on *what* information should be incorporated into financial statements and *when*. The Statement discusses four basic assumptions that are the foundation of the structure of financial accounting: 1) A going concern, 2) A monetary unit, 3) An economic entity, and 4) Periodicity.

6. *Elements of Financial Statements*: This Statement gives a number of basic definitions of ten elements of the financial statements and a number of other attributes of each element. "The definitions in this Statement are of economic things and events that are relevant to investment, credit, and other resource-allocation decisions and thus are relevent to financial reporting." The ten basic elements that are the components of financial statements are considered to be interrelated. The ten elements are:
   1. Assets.
   2. Liabilities.
   3. Equity.
   4. Investments by Owners.
   5. Distributions to Owners.
   6. Comprehensive Income.
   7. Revenues.
   8. Expenses.
   9. Gains.
   10. Losses.

(It should be understood that the Concepts are *not* standards for specific accounting procedures or disclosure practices for specific items that are required by GAAP. The six Concepts concern relations that underlie financial accounting standards and practices and are intended ultimately to be the basis for evaluating existing standards and practices.)

FULL DISCLOSURE

Full Disclosure is an attempt to present all essential information about a company in a:

- Balance Sheet
- Income Statement
- Statement of Stockholders' Equity
- Statement of Changes in Financial Position

The objectives of financial reporting are set forth in *FASB Concepts Statement No. 1* outlined earlier. The financial statements, notes to the financial statements, and necessary supplementary information are governed by FASB standards. Financial reporting includes other types of information, such as *Management's Discussion and Analysis*, letters to stockholders, order backlogs, statistical data, and the like, commonly included in reports to shareholders.

The Full Disclosure Principle

Financial facts significant enough to influence the judgment of an informed person should be disclosed. The financial statements, notes to the financial statements, summary of accounting policies, should disclose the information necessary to prevent the statements from being *misleading*. The information in the statements should be disclosed in a manner that the intended meaning of the information is apparent to a reasonably informed user of the statements.

DISCLOSURE IN FINANCIAL REPORTING

Disclosure. The heart of the compilation and disclosure of financial information is *accounting*. Yet, the idea of "adequate disclosure" stands alone as the one concept in accounting that involves all of the good things and all of the dangers inherent in the professional practice of accounting and auditing. Probably the use of the colloquism "disclosure" best describes the all-embracing nature of the concept. That is to say, *disclosure is the name of the financial reporting game*.

For decades the profession has been inundated with disclosure literature, rules, regulations, statements, government agencies' accounting regulations, court decisions, tax decisions, intellectualizing by academics, books and seminars, all concerning what disclosure is all about.

Yet, nobody has precisely answered what continues to remain the essential question: Disclosure of *what*, by *whom*, for *whom*?

The lack of definitive qualitative and quantitative criteria for what information must or need not be disclosed forces upon the independent accountant the responsibility to decide what constitutes a matter requiring disclosure, requiring him to exercise his judgment in light of the circumstances and facts of which he is aware at the time. The accountant's responsibility is confined to the expression of his opinion based upon his examination. The representations made through the statements are *management's* responsibility.

What is a material fact, and for whom does a disclosed fact have material significance? What substantive standards of disclosure must the accountant maintain? Who is to promulgate these standards? The profession? One or all of the governmental regulatory agencies? A federal board of accounting? The courts? The Congress?

One conclusion is clear, however. There is an unmistakable trend toward increasing demands upon the accounting profession for more financial information. What better evidence can be cited than the conclusion of the AICPA Study Group on the Objectives of Financial Statements? The group's report said that ". . . financial statements should meet the needs of those with *LEAST* ability to obtain information."

The confusion between what is and is not material is caused by a widely held concept—different facts have different meanings for the individual user of financial information. Information that is important to one user may be insignificant to another.

> "All information must adapt *itself* to the perception of those towards whom the information is intended."
>
> Anonymous

It is neither possible nor economically feasible, however, for an accountant to cover in the statements every single small detail concerning a client's business. Where should the accountant draw the line? (Not many years ago, a large accounting firm had to defend a lawsuit up to the U.S. Supreme Court at a cost of several million dollars because the accountant did not question the company's chief executive officer's policy that he, alone, open the company's mail.)

Recent trends in financial reporting reflect an increase in the amount of disclosure found in financial statements. The information is communicated in the footnotes, which are an integral part of the financial statements. Although the footnotes are usually drafted in somewhat technical language, they are the accountant's means of amplifying or explaining the items present in the main body of the statements. Footnote information can generally be classified as follows:

- *Disclosure of Accounting Policies Applied.* This information is required in order to inform the user of the statements of the accounting methods used in preparing the information that appears in statements.
- *Disclosure of Gain or Loss Contingencies.* Because many contingent gains or losses are not properly included in the accounts, their disclosure in the footnotes provides relevant information to financial statement users.

- *Examination of Credit Claims.* A liability, such as a bank loan, may have numerous covenants that are not conveniently disclosed in the liability section of the balance sheet.
- *Claims of Equity Holders.* The rights of various equity security issues along with certain unique features that may apply to certain issues are commonly disclosed in footnotes to the statements.
- *Executory Commitments.* These refer to contract obligations undertaken by the company that have not been performed, or have been only partially performed at the statement date.

In some cases a company is faced with a sensitive issue that requires disclosure in a footnote. Some examples are: 1) related party transactions, 2) errors, 3) irregularities, and 4) illegal acts.

DISCLOSURES ITEMIZED

Here is an alphabetic listing of items *requiring disclosure* with short comments thereon, if applicable.

Accelerated Depreciation Methods—when methods are adopted.

Accounting Policies—see prior "Summary of Significant Accounting Policies."

Allowances (depreciation, depletion, bad debts)—deduct from asset with disclosure.

Amortization of Intangibles—disclose method and period.

Amounts Available for Distributions—note the needs for any hold-back retention of earnings.

Arrangements with Reorganized Debtor—disclose if a subsequent event.

Arrears on Cumulative Preferred Stock—the rights of senior securities must be disclosed on the face of balance sheet or in the notes.

Assets (interim changes in)—only significant changes required for interims.

Business Segments.

Cash-Basis Statements—fact must be disclosed in the opinion with delineation of what would have been had accrual basis been used, if significant variance.

Change in Stockholders' Equity Accounts—in a separate schedule. This is not the changes in retained earnings statement, which is one of the basic required statements.

Change to Declining Balance Method—disclose change in method and effect of it.

Changes, Accounting—see text.

Commitments, Long-Term—disclose unused letters of credit, assets pledged as security for loans, pension plans, plant expansion or acquisition; obligations to reduce debt, maintain working capital or restrict dividend.

Commitments to Complete Contracts—only extraordinary ones.

Consolidation Policy—method used.

Construction Type Contracts—method used.

Contingencies—disclose when reasonable possibility of a loss, the nature of, and estimated loss. Threats of expropriation, debtor bankruptcy if actual. Those contingencies which might result in gains, but not misleading as to realization. Disclosure of uninsured risks is advised, but not required. Gain contingencies should be disclosed, but not reflected in the accounts.

Contingencies in Business Combinations—disclose escrow items for contingencies in the notes.

Control of Board of Directors—disclose any stock options existing.

Corporate Officer Importance—disclose if a major sales or income factor to the company.

Current Liabilities—disclose why, if any, omitted (in notes).

Dating (Readjusted) Earned Surplus— no more than 10 years is the term now required.

Deferred Taxes—disclose and also see Timing Differences in this text.

Depreciation and Depreciable Assets—disclose the following:
Depreciation expense for the period
Balances of major classes of depreciable assets by nature or function
Accumulated depreciation by classes, or in total
A general description of the methods used in computing depreciation.

Development Stage Enterprises—are required to use the same basic financial statements as other enterprises, with certain additional disclosures required. Special type statements are not permissible.

Discontinued Operations—disclose separately below continuing-operating income, net of tax, but before extraordinary items. Show separate EPS.

Diversified Company's Foreign Operations.

Dividends per Share—desirable, but not required.

Earnings per share—see prior section for presentation, but the following is also required in addition to the data stated there (does not apply to non-public enterprises):
1. Restatement for a prior period adjustment.
2. Dividend preference
3. Liquidation preference
4. Participation rights
5. Call prices and dates
6. Conversion rates and dates

7. Exercise prices and dates
8. Sinking fund requirements
9. Unusual voting rights
10. Bases upon which primary and fully diluted earnings per share were calculated
11. Issues which are common stock equivalents
12. Issues which are potentially dilutive securities
13. Assumptions and adjustments made for earnings per share data
14. Shares issued upon conversion, exercise, and conditions met for contingent issuances
15. Recapitalization occurring during the period or before the statements are issued
16. Stock dividends, stock splits or reverse splits occurring after the close of the period before the statements are issued
17. Claims of senior securities entering earnings per share computations
18. Dividends declared by the constituents in a pooling
19. Basis of presentation of dividends in a pooling on other than a historical basis
20. Per share and aggregate amount of cumulative preferred dividends in arrears.

Equity Method—as follows:
1. Financial statements of the investor should disclose in the notes, separate statements or schedules, or parenthetically;
   The name of each investee and % of ownership
   The accounting policies of the investor, disclosing if, and why, any over 20% holdings are not under the equity method
   Any difference between the carrying value and the underlying equity of the investment, and the accounting treatment thereof;
2. Disclose any investments which have quoted market prices (common stocks) showing same—do not write down;
3. Present summary balance sheet and operating information when equity investments are material;
4. Same as above for any unconsolidated subsidiaries where ownership is majority;
5. Disclose material effects of contingent issuances.

Extinguishment (Early) of Debt—gains or losses should be described, telling source of funds for payoff, income tax effect, per share amount.

Extraordinary Items—describe on face of income statement (or in notes), show effect net of tax after income from continuing operations, also after business disposals if any, show EPS separately for extraordinary item. May aggregate immaterial items.

Fiscal Period Differences (in Consolidating)—disclose intervening material events.

Fiscal Year Change—disclose effect only.

Foreign Items—Assets, must disclose any significant ones included in U.S. statements; gains or losses shown in body of U.S. statement; disclose significant "subsequent event" rate changes; operations, adequate disclosure to be made of all pertinent dollar information, regardless of whether consolidating or not (for foreign subsidiaries).

Headings and Captions—may be necessary to explain.

Income Taxes (and Deferred Taxes)—(see Timing Differences in this text.)

Income Taxes of Sole Proprietor or Partnership—may be necessary to disclose personal taxes to be paid if the money will come from and put a drain on the firm's cash position.

Infrequent Events—show as separate component of income and disclose nature of them.

Interim Statements—(see separate chapter in this text.)

Inventories—disclose pricing policies and flow of cost assumption in "Summary of Significant Accounting Policies"; disclose changes in method and effect on income. Dollar effect based upon a change should be shown separately from ordinary cost of sales items.

Investment Tax Credits–disclose method used, with amounts if material. Also, disclose substantial carryback or carryforward credits.

Leases—See Non-current Assets in this text.

Legal Restrictions on Dividend Payments—put in notes.

Liability for Tax Penalties—if significant, disclose in notes. May have to take exception in opinion.

Market Value of Investments in Marketable Securities—should be written down to market value and up again, but not to exceed cost for entire portfolio per classification—

Non-Cumulative Preferred Stock—should disclose that no provision has been made because it is non-cumulative.

Obligations (Short-Term)—disclose in notes reason any short-term obligations not displayed as current liabilities.

Partnerships, Limited—disclose fact that it's a limited partnership.

Patent Income—disclose if income is ending.

Pension Plans—must disclose the following:
1. Describe and identify employee groups covered by plan
2. The accounting and funding policy
3. The provision for pension cost for the period
4. Excess, if any, of vested benefits over fund-total; any balance sheet deferrals, accruals, prepays
5. Any significant matters affecting comparability of periods presented.

Pension Reform Act of 1974—must disclose the effect of future compliance for vesting in the first year *prior* to the date the plan is afffected by the law's provisions.

Political Contributions—must disclose if material or not deductible for taxes, or if they are beneficial to an officer.

Pooling of Interests.

Price-level Restatements.

Prior Period Adjustments—must disclose with tax effects. Must disclose in interim reports.

Purchase Commit Losses—should be separately disclosed in dollars in income statement.

Purchase Method. (See Business Combinations.)

Purchase Option Cancellation Costs—yes, disclose.

Real and Personal Property Taxes—disclose if using estimates, and if substantial. All adjustments for prior year estimates should be made through the current income statement.

Real Estate Appraisal Value—for Development Companies, footnote disclosure might be useful.

Receivables, Affiliated Companies, Officers and Employees—should be segregated and shown separately from trade receivables.

Redemption Call of Preferred Stock—disclose in the equity section.

Renegotiation Possibilities—use dollars if estimable or disclose inability to estimate.

Research and Development Costs—"disclosure shall be made in the financial statements of the total research and development costs charged to expenses in each period for which an income statement is presented." Government regulated enterprises should disclose the accounting policy for amortization and the totals expensed and deferred. But do not disclose the confidential details of specific projects, patents, new products, processes or company research philosophy. Applies the above provision for disclosure to business combinations.

Restricted Stock Issued to Employee—disclose circumstance and the restrictions.

Retained Earnings Transferred to Capital Stock—arises usually with "split-ups effected as dividends" and with stock dividends; must disclose and include schedule showing transfers from retained earnings to capital stock. Also, must disclose number of shares, etc., for EPS; must show subsequent event effects.

Sale and Leaseback

Seasonal Business (Interim Statements)—must disclose, and advisable to include 12-month period, present and past.

Stock Dividends, Split-up, etc.—must disclose even if a subsequent event and use as if made for and during all periods presented.

Stock Options—disclose status—(See Equity chapter in this text.) Has effect on EPS.

Stockholders Buy/Sell Stock Agreements—disclose.

Subleases—(See Leases in Non-Current Assets chapter in this text.)

Termination Claims (War & Defense Contracts)—shown as current receivable, unless extended delay indicated; usually shown separately and disclosed if material, in income statement.

Treasury Stock—(See Equity chapter in this text.) Shown in body of balance sheet (equity section ordinarily); should, in notes, indicate any legal restrictions.

Unconsolidated Subsidiaries—if using cost method, should also give independent summary information about position and operations.

Undistributed Earnings of Subsidiaries—(See disclosures required when not accruing deferred taxes under Indefinite Reversal Criteria in this text.)

Unearned Compensation—(See Stock Options in this text.)

Unremitted Taxes—disclose only if going concern concept is no longer valid.

(See next section for those disclosures which require *Restatement*.)

(Also, see sections on *Timing Differences and Taxes*, and *Permanent Differences*.)

RESTATEMENTS

The following alphabetic listing indicates those areas which *require* a restatement (with disclosure) for all prior periods presented in the comparative financial statements:

Appropriations of Retained Earnings—any change made to conform with Section 4311 for the reporting of contingencies requires retroactive adjustment.

Changes in Accounting Principle Requiring Restatement

1. Change *from* LIFO to another method.

2. Change in long-term construction method.

3. Change to or from "full cost" method in the extractive industries.

Must show effect on both net income and EPS for all periods presented.

Change in Reporting Entity—must restate.

Contingencies—restate for the cumulative effect applying the rules for contingencies.

Earnings Per Share—the effect of all restatements must be shown on EPS, separating as to EPS from continuing operations, EPS from disposals, EPS from extraordinary items and EPS from net income.

Equity Method—restatement required when first applying the method, even though it was not required before.

Extraordinary Items—if a similar one in prior period was not classified as extraordinary, but is now, reclassify now for comparison.

Foreign Currency Translations—restate to conform with adoption of standards; if indeterminable, use the cumulative method. Disclose nature of restatement and effect (or cumulative effect) on income before extraordinary items, on net income, and on related per share amounts.

Income Taxes (Equity Method)—restate to comply.

Interim Financial Statements—restate for changes in accounting principle and for prior period adjustments. If it's a cumulative type change, the first interim period should show the entire effect; if in later period, full effect should be applied to the first period and restated for other periods.

Leases—see Non-Current Assets chapter in this text.

Oil and Gas Producing Companies—in conforming with standards, restatement is not required, but it is permissible.

Pooling of Interests—A change in accounting method for pooled unit should be applied retroactively.

In initial pooling, combine year to date, restate prior periods presented, show separate information for independent operations and positions. Purchase method shows pro forma combine.

Until pooling is consummated, include the proportion of earnings in ordinary financials; *but* also present statements (retroactively applied) as if pooling had occurred.

Prior Period Adjustments—must restate the details affected for all periods presented, disclose and adjust opening retained earnings. Must also do it for interim reports.

Refinancing Short-Term Obligations—restatement is permitted, but not required.

Research and Development Costs—In conforming with standards, apply retroactively as a prior period adjustment.

No retroactive recapitalization of costs is permissible. Applies to *purchase* combinations also. Basic rule; expense as incurred.

Statistical Summaries (5 years, 10 years, etc.)—Restate all prior years involved in prior period adjustments.

Stock Dividends and Splits—Must restate earnings per share figures and number of shares to give effect to stock dividends and splits *including* those occurring *after* close of period being reported on (for all periods presented).

Revision based on FASB Opinions—retroactive restatement is not required *unless* the new standard *specifically* states that it is required.

Note that restatements are *not* required for a change from FIFO to LIFO, nor for a change in the method of handling investment tax credits.

TIMING AND PERMANENT DIFFERENCES—INCOME TAXES

Those which will not reverse or "turn around" in other periods:

1. Specific *revenues exempt* from taxability (examples):
    Dividend exclusions
    Interest on tax exempt securities
    Life insurance proceeds
    Negative goodwill amortization
    Unrealized gains on marketable securities
    Unrealized gains on foreign currency translations
    Tax benefits arising from stock-option compensatory plans (when booked as income)
2. Expenses which are *not* tax deductible:
    Depreciation taken on appraisal increases or donated property
    Goodwill amortization
    Premiums on officer life insurance
    Tax penalties and fines
    Unrealized losses on securities or currency translations
3. Those expenses which are predicated upon different bases for financial and tax purposes:
    Depreciation on trade-ins
    Statutory depletion vs. cost depletion
    Business combinations which treat purchase as "pooling for tax return or pooling as purchase."

TIMING DIFFERENCES

Those which *will* turn around or reverse in one or more subsequent periods. Four broad categories:

1. Income—for Accounting NOW—for Taxes LATER
2. Expenses—for Accounting NOW—for Taxes LATER
3. Income—for Accounting LATER—for Taxes NOW
4. Expenses—for Accounting LATER—for Taxes NOW

1. Items of *income* included for accounting financial statement purposes NOW—not taken on the tax return until a LATER time (examples):

> Gross profit on installment method date of sale/when collected on tax return.
> Percentage of completion method on books/completed contract method for tax return.
> Leasing rentals on books under financing method/actual rent less depreciation for tax return.
> Subsidiary earnings reported now/as received for tax return.

2. Items of *expense* taken on financial statements NOW, not taken on tax returns until LATER (examples):

> Accelerated depreciation used for financials/not for tax return.
> Contributions on financials over 5% limit/carried over for taxes.
> Deferred compensation accruals/taken when paid on tax return.
> Estimated costs of various kinds/taken when cost or loss becomes actual and known, such as: guarantees, product warranties, inventory losses, legal settlements, segment disposals, major repairs.
> Depreciation based on shorter life for books than for tax return.
> Organization costs taken now/amortized for tax return.

3. Items of *income* taken into financial books LATER, but reported as income NOW on tax returns:

> Rents and royalties deferred until earned/reported when collected for tax return.
> Deferred fees, dues, services contracts/reported when collected for tax returns.
> Intercompany consolidation gains and losses/taxed now if filing separate return.
> Leaseback gains amortized gains over lease-term/date of sale for tax return.

4. Items of *expense* taken into financial books LATER, but taken NOW on tax returns.

> Depreciation; shorter lives used for tax purposes accelerated rates on tax return/straight-line on books certain emergency facility amortization taken on tax returns/later on books.
> Bond discount, premium costs taken on return/amortized on books.
> Certain costs which are taken for tax purposes/but deferred for financial purposes, as;

Incidental costs of property acquisitions

Preoperating costs

Certain research and development costs (deferred for financial purposes only those approved exceptions to those which must be expensed).

Other Considerations Regarding Income Taxes:

Interperiod tax allocation should be followed under the deferred method. Timing differences may be considered individually or grouped by similarity.

Tax carryback losses (including investment tax credit carrybacks should be recognized in the loss period in which the carryback originated). Carryforwards should not be recognized until realized (then show as *extraordinary* item) unless there is no doubt of realization (then show as part of operating profit or loss).

Balance Sheet Presentation of Income Taxes:

Tax accounts on the balance sheet should be separately classified so as to show:

1. Taxes estimated to be paid currently.
2. *Net* amount of current deferred charges and deferred credits related to timing differences.
3. *Net* amount of noncurrent deferred taxes related to timing differences.
4. Receivables for carryback losses.
5. When realization is beyond doubt, show an asset for the benefit to be derived from a carryforward of losses.
6. Deferred investment credits, when this method is employed.

Income Statement Presentation of Income Taxes

All taxes based on income, including foreign, federal, state and local should be reflected in income tax expense in the income statement.

The following components should be disclosed separately and put on the income statement before extraordinary items and prior period adjustments:

1. Taxes estimated to be payable.
2. Tax effects of timing differences.
3. Tax effects of operating losses.

In addition, the following general disclosures are required:

1. Amounts of any operating loss carryforwards not recognized in the loss period, with expiration dates and effect on deferred tax accounts;
2. Significant amounts of any other unused tax deductions or credits, with expiration dates;
3. Any reasons for significant differences between taxable income and pretax accounting income.
4. Deferred income taxes related to an asset or liability are classified the same as the related asset or liability. A deferred tax charge or credit is related to an asset or liability if reduction of the asset or liability would cause the underlying timing difference to reverse. Deferred income taxes that are not related to an asset or liability are classified according to the expected reversal date of the timing difference.

THE PRINCIPLES OF FINANCIAL STATEMENT PRESENTATION

The general objective is to provide reliable information on resources, obligations and progress. The information should be useful for comparability, completeness and understandability. The basic features involved in financial accounting are: the individual accounting entity, the use of approximation and the preparation of fundamentally related financial statements.

"Fair Presentation in Conformity with GAAP"

1. GAAP applicable in the circumstances have been applied in accumulating and processing the accounting information; and
2. Changes from period to period in GAAP have been properly disclosed; and
3. The information in the *underlying* records is properly *reflected* and *described* in the financial statements in conformity with GAAP; and
4. A proper balance has been achieved between:
   A. The conflicting needs to disclose the importance aspects of financial position and results of operation in conformance with conventional concepts, and to
   B. Summarize the voluminous underlying data with a limited number of financial statement captions and supporting notes.

There are 12 Principles of Financial Statement Presentation

1. Basic Financial Statements—minimum requirements:
   A. Balance Sheet
   B. Statement of Income

C. Statement of Changes in Retained Earnings
D. Statement of Changes in Financial Position
E. Disclosure of Accounting Policies
F. Disclosure of Related Notes
Usually presented for two or more periods.
Other information may be presented, and in some cases required as supplemental information; Price-level statements; information about operations in different industries; foreign operations and export sales; major customers (segment reporting).

2. A Complete Balance Sheet (or "Statement of Financial Position")
   A. All Assets
   B. All Liabilities
   C. All classes of Owners' Equity.

3. A Complete Income Statement
   A. All Revenues
   B. All Expenses.

4. A Complete Statement of Changes in Financial Position
   Includes and describes all important aspects of the company's financing and investing activities.

5. Accounting Period
   Basic time period in one year
   An interim statement is for less than one year.

6. Consolidated Financial Statements
   They are presumed to be more meaningful than separate statements of the component legal entities
   They are *usually* necessary when one of the group owns (directly or indirectly) *over 50%* of the outstanding voting stock
   The information is presented as if it were a *single enterprise*.

7. The Equity Basis
   For unconsolidated subsidiaries (where over 50% is owned) *and for investments in 50% or less* of the voting stock of companies in which the investor has significant influence over investees, 20% or more ownership presumes this influence, unless proved otherwise.
   The investor's share of the net income reported by the investee is picked up and shown as income and an adjustment of the investment account—for all earnings subsequent to the acquisition. Dividends are treated as an adjustment of the investment account.

8. Translation of Foreign Branches
   Translated into U.S. Dollars by conventional translation procedures involving foreign exchange rates.

9. Classification and Segregation:
   (Must separately disclose these important components)

A. *Income Statement*—Sale (or other source of revenue); Cost of Sales; Depreciation; Selling Administration Expenses; Interest Expense; Income Taxes.

B. *Balance Sheet*—Cash; Receivables; Inventories; Plant and Equipment; Payables; and Categories of Owners' Equity:

Par or stated amount of capital stock; Additional paid-in capital

Retained earnings: (affected by—

Net income or loss

Prior period adjustments

Dividends

Transfers to other categories of equity).

Working Capital—current assets and current liabilities should be classified as such to be able to determine working capital—useful for enterprises in: manufacturing, trading, some service enterprises.

Current assets—include cash and other that can reasonably be expected to be realized in cash in one year or a shorter business cycle.

Current liabilities—include those that are expected to be satisfied by the use of those assets shown as current; or the creation of other current liabilities; or expected to be satisfied in one year.

Assets and liabilities should *not* be offset against each other unless a legal right to do so exists, which is a rare exception.

Gains and Losses—arise from other than products or services, may be combined and shown as one item. Examples: write-downs of inventories, receivables, capitalized research and development costs, *all sizable*. Also, gains and losses on: temporary investments, non-monetary transactions, currency devaluations are a few typical items.

Extraordinary items or gain or loss—should be shown separately under its own title, distinguished by unusual nature and infrequent occurrence—should be shown net of taxes.

Net Income—should be separately disclosed and clearly identified on the income statement.

10. Other disclosures: (Accounting policies and notes)

    A. Customary or routine disclosures:

        1. Measurement bases of important assets

        2. Restrictions on assets

        3. Restriction on owners' equity

        4. Contingent liabilities

        5. Contingent assets

        6. Important long-term commitments not in the body of the statements

        7. Information on terms of equity of owners

        8. Information on terms of long-term debt

        9. Other disclosures required by AICPA

B. Disclosure of changes in accounting policies.

C. Disclosure of important subsequent events—between balance sheet date and date of the opinion.

D. Disclosure of accounting policies ("Summary of Significant . . .").

11. Form of Financial Statement Presentation:

No particular form is presumed better than all others for all purposes. Several are used.

12. Earnings Per Share:

Must be disclosed on the *face of the Income Statement*. Should be disclosed for:

A. Income before extraordinary items

B. Net Income.

Should consider:

A. Changes in number of shares outstanding

B. Contingent changes

C. Possible dilution from potential conversion of:

Convertible debentures

Preferred stock

Options

Warrants

AUDITING STANDARDS

GENERALLY ACCEPTED AUDITING STANDARDS (GAAS): The authoritative rules for measuring the quality of auditor performance. The second sentence in the scope paragraph of an auditor's report indicates whether the examination was made in accordance with generally accepted auditing standards and includes all auditing procedures that the auditor considered to be necessary. The AICPA Committee on Auditing Procedure set forth the following requirements of the 10 standards.

General Standards

1. The examination is to be performed by a person or persons having adequate technical training and proficiency as an auditor.

2. In all matters relating to the assignment an independence in mental attitude is to be maintained by the auditor or auditors.

3. Due professional care is to be exercised in the performance of the examination and the preparation of the report.

Standards of Field Work

1. The work is to be adequately planned and assistants, if any, are to be properly supervised.
2. There is to be a proper study and evaluation of the existing internal control as a basis for reliance thereon and for the determination of the resultant extent of the tests to which auditing procedures are to be restricted.
3. Sufficient competent evidential matter is to be obtained through inspection, observation, inquiries, and confirmations to afford a reasonable basis for an opinion regarding the financial statements under examination.

Standards of Reporting

1. The report shall state whether the financial statements are presented in accordance with generally accepted principles of accounting.
2. The report shall state whether such principles have been consistently observed in the current period in relation to the preceding period.
3. Informative disclosures in the financial statements are to be regarded as reasonably adequate unless otherwise stated in the report.
4. The report shall either contain an expression of opinion regarding the financial statements, taken as a whole, or an assertion to the effect that an opinion cannot be expressed. When an overall opinion cannot be expressed the reasons therefore should be stated. In all cases where an auditor's name is associated with financial statements the report should contain a clear-cut indication of the character of the auditor's examination, if any, and the degree of responsibility he is taking.

(Note: See Au Sections 150, 320, and 321 in the AICPA Codification of Statements on Auditing Standards.)

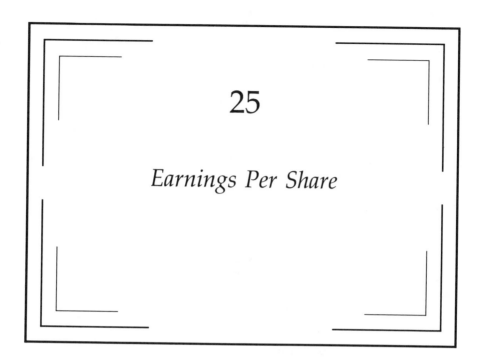

25

Earnings Per Share

REPORTING EARNINGS PER SHARE

It is mandatory that earnings per share (EPS) data be shown in conjunction with the presentation of financial statements, annual or interim, and that such data be shown on the face of the income statement. However, these requirements no longer apply to non-public enterprises. A non-public enterprise, as defined in FASB #21, is an enterprise other than one (a) whose debt or equity securities trade in a public market, on a foreign or domestic stock exchange, or in the over-the-counter market (including securities quoted only locally or regionally), or (b) that is required to file financial statements with the SEC.

When reporting for companies that are considered to be public enterprises, such amounts should be presented for:

1. Income before extraordinary items, and
2. Net income.

It is customary to show the earnings per share for the extraordinary items also.

There are basically two types of capital structure involved in the calculation of EPS:

1. A simple capital structure, or

2. A complex capital structure.

Corporations with complex capital structures should present two types of earnings per share data:

1. Primary earnings per share, based on outstanding common shares and those securities that are in substance equivalent to common shares; and

2. Fully diluted earnings per share which reflect the dilution of earnings per share that would have occurred if all contingent issuances of stock had taken place. (Reduction of less than 3% is not deemed sufficient to cause dilution)

Earnings per share should be presented for all periods covered by the income statement. If a prior period has been restated, the earnings per share should also be restated for that period.

The underlying simple basic formula for calculating EPS is:

Net income (earnings) *divided by* number of shares outstanding (common only)

$$\frac{\text{Earnings (net income)}}{\text{Number of common shares outstanding}} = \text{EPS}$$

The *dollars* are always the numerator; the *number* of shares the *denominator*.

The complexity of determining either factor in the formula increases as the corporate's capital structure expands into more exotic types of equity security and potential types of equity security.

Refer now to the *Fact Sheet* presented next and to the illustrations which follow based on that fact sheet:

FACT SHEET FOR EARNINGS PER SHARE ILLUSTRATIONS

	(in thousands of dollars)		
INCOME STATEMENT	1987	1986	1985
Income before extraordinary item	$12,900	$ 9,150	$7,650
Extraordinary item—net of tax	900	900	—
Net Income	$13,800	$10,050	$7,650
SHARE INFORMATION			
Common stock outstanding:	(in thousands of shares)		
Beginning of year	3,300	3,000	3,000*
Issued during year	—	300(3)	—
Conversion of preferred stock(1)	500	—	—
Conversion of debentures(2)	200	—	—
End of year	4,000	3,300	3,000

	(in thousands of dollars)		
INCOME STATEMENT (*Continued*)	1987	1986	1985
Common stock reserved under employee stock options granted	7	7	—
Weighted average number of shares (see calculations):			
1985—3,000,000 shares weighted average			
1986—3,150,000 shares weighted average			
1987—4,183,333 shares weighted average			

*issued at 1/1/85.

(3) issued at 7/1/86.

1. *Convertible preferred stock*: 600,000 shares issued at the beginning of the second quarter of 1986. Dividend rate is 20¢ per share. Market value was $53 at time of issue with a cash yield of 0.4% as opposed to bank prime rate of 18%. Warrants to buy 500,000 shares of common stock at $60 per share for a period of five years were, in addition, issued along with this convertible preferred. Each share of the convertible stock was convertible into one common share (exclusive of the warrants).

   During 1987, 500,000 shares of the preferred stock were converted because the common dividend exceeded the preferred. But, *no warrants were exercised* during the year.

2. *Convertible debentures*: 10% with a principal amount of $10,000,000 (due 2000) were sold at 100 in the last quarter of 1985. Each $100 debenture was convertible into *two* shares of common stock. The entire issue was converted at the beginning of the *third* quarter of 1987, when called by the company. (None were converted in 1985 or 1986).

   The prime rate at issue in 1985 was 12%. The coupon face rate of the bonds was 10%. The bonds had a market value of $100 when issued.

Additional information:

Market price of the common stock: (average prices)

	1987	1986	1985
1st quarter	50	45	40
2nd quarter	60	52	41
3rd quarter	70	50	40
4th quarter	70	50	45
Dec 31 closing price	72	51	44
Cash dividends on common stock:			
Declared and paid *each* quarter	$1.25	$ .25	$ .25

ILLUSTRATIONS (Based on the Fact Sheet)

1985—SIMPLE CAPITAL STRUCTURE
The simplest computation involves those companies with:

1. Only common stock issued, and
2. No change in outstanding number during the year, and
3. Net income arising without any extraordinary items.

For 1985, the first year of the company's operation on the fact sheet, the EPS would be:

$$\frac{\text{Income}}{\text{\# shares outstanding}} \text{ or } \frac{\$7,650,000}{3,000,000} \text{ or } \$2.55 \text{ per share.}$$

1986—EXPANDED SIMPLE CAPITAL STRUCTURE
The significant changes in 1986 affecting EPS:

1. The extraordinary item of income of $900M, requiring separate disclosure; and
2. The 300,000 shares issued during the year, requiring the computation of a weighted average.

Computing the weighted average—determine the number of shares outstanding at the end of each quarter and divide by four:

1st quarter	3,000,000
2nd quarter	3,000,000
3rd quarter	3,300,000
4th quarter	3,300,000
	12,600,000 divided by 4, or 3,150,000 shares

The employee stock options are *under* 3% of the aggregate outstanding, so they are not considered dilutive and are ignored in the EPS calculation.

Proper *disclosure* for the 1986 EPS would be:

Earnings per common share:	1986	1985
Income before extraordinary items	$2.90(4)	$2.55
Extraordinary item	.29(5)	—
Net Income	$3.19	$2.55
$9,150,000 divided by 3,150,000		
900,000 divided by 3,150,000		

(In the above example, the dilution factors used *below* are not applicable, appearing on the fact sheet merely for use in the complex structure example next.)

1987—COMPLEX CAPITAL STRUCTURE
The significant changes in 1987 affecting EPS:

1. The number of common shares (equivalents) represented by the warrants; and
2. The number of common share equivalents represented by the 600,000 shares of convertible preferred stock, issued in 1984; and
3. The additional EPS computation required for the full dilution assumption.

1. The number of common shares (equivalents) represented by the warrants.

$60 exercise price × 500,000 warrants of $30,000,000	
$30,000,000 divided by $70 share market price	428,572
	(shares)
500,000 shares minus 428,572	71,428
	(shares)

Weighted average of the warrant shares: Not applicable for any quarter prior to the third quarter of 1985 because the market price did not exceed the exercise price:

First quarter 1987	—
Second quarter 1987	—
Third quarter 1987	71,428
Fourth quarter 1987	71,428
	142,856 divided by 4
Warrant share equivalents—or 35,714 shares	

2. The number of common share equivalents represented by the convertible preferred stock:

	1987	1986
Number of shares of preferred stock issued in 1981	600,000	450,000*
Less the number of shares of common stock issued on conversion in 1987 (500,000). But, these shares were issued at various times during the year. Based on even issuance, the weighted average is ½ or	(250,000)	—
The equivalent shares with potential issue factor	350,000	450,000

	1982	1981
The weighted average number of common shares and equivalents is therefore:		
Shares outstanding at beginning (incl. 7/1/86 issue)	3,300,000	3,150,000
Shares issued on conversion of preferred stock (as above)	250,000	—

*Based on weighted average from start of second quarter

	1982	1981
Shares issued on conversion of the debentures—200,000 at 7/1/87 weighted average is 100,000	100,000	
Equivalents for the warrants (as prior)	35,714	
Equivalents for the convertible preferred stock above	350,000	450,000
Total weighted average (primary)	4,035,714	3,600,000

3. Additional share calculation to determine full dilution:

	1982	1981
Remaining shares applicable to convertible debentures	100,000	200,000
Shares applicable to warrants	(35,714)	—
Shares applicable to warrants based on yearend price of $72—$60 × 500,000 divided by $72, with result subtracted from 500,000	83,333	
Add primary weighted shares above	4,035,714	3,600,000
Shares for full-dilution EPS	4,183,333	3,800,000

Proper disclosure of EPS for 1987 would then be:

	1987	1986
Primary earnings per common share and common equivalent shares (Note __):		
Income before extraordinary item	$ 3.20(1)	$ 2.54(1A)
Extraordinary item	.22(2)	.25(2A)
Net Income	$ 3.42(3)	$ 2.79(3A)

	1987	1986
Fully diluted earnings per common share (Note __):		
Income before extraordinary item	$ 3.11(4)	$ 2.46(7)
Extraordinary item	.21(5)	.24(8)
Net income	$ 3.32(6)	$ 2.70(9)

(1) $12,900,000 divided by 4,035,714 or $3.20

(2)   900,000 divided by 4,035,714 or   .22

(3)   13,800,000 divided by 4,035,714 or $ 3.42

(1A)   9,150,000 divided by 3,600,000 or $ 2.54

(2A)   900,000 divided by 3,600,000 or   .25

(3A)   10,050,000 divided by 3,600,000 or $ 2.79

(4)   13,004,000 divided by 4,183,333 or $ 3.11

(above includes $104,000 addback for debenture interest)

(5)   900,000 divided by 4,183,333 or   .21

(6)	13,904,000 divided by 4,183,333 or	$ 3.32
(7)	9,358,000 divided by 3,800,000 or	$ 2.46
	(includes $208,000 for interest or debentures)	
(8)	900,000 divided by 3,800,000 or	.24
(9)	$10,258,000 divided by 3,800,000 or	$ 2.70

The illustrations here do *not* cover the following topics:

1. Disclosure requirements for financial notes.
2. Handling of dividends paid or unpaid on convertible stocks.
3. Subsequent events which require supplemental calculations.
4. Anti-dilution.
5. The test for common stock equivalent status (including the treasury stock method).
6. Details of calculating dilution under the treasury stock method.
7. Effect of stock splits or stock dividends on number of shares.
8. EPS in business combinations.
9. Discussion of the "if converted" method of computation.
10. Discussion of the "cash-yield" test for the consideration of equivalents.
11. Effect of contingencies involved in share issuance.
12. Securities of subsidiaries.

Some of the above topics may be illustrated best in financial statements issued by prominent public corporations.

SEGMENT REPORTING

As a result primarily of the conglomerate movement, which is essentially an approach to corporate diversification, the users of financial statements (particularly financial analysts), needed more detailed information about the financial condition of affiliated companies underlying consolidated reports, as well as for business activities in foreign countries. Accordingly, in 1976 the FASB issued Statement No. 14, *Financial Reporting for Segments of a Business Enterprise*. The purpose of the Statement is to provide revenue and income data and additional significant information about the individual subsidiaries, divisions, affiliates, etc., which contribute to the total income results that reported on the consolidated statements.

(Statement No. 14, has also since been amended by Statements Nos. 18, 21, 24, and 30)

It should be noted that Statement No. 21 eliminates the original requirement that *all* companies, large and small, nonpublic or public, had to disclose segment information. Now, only publicly-held corporations must comply with Statement No. 14.

Definitions

IDENTIFIABLE ASSETS: Tangible and intangible assets used by a segment.

INDUSTRY SEGMENT: A component of a business that provides a product or service or a group of related products or services, primarily to unaffiliated customers, for a profit.

REPORTABLE SEGMENT: An industry segment, or a group of related segments for which information is required to be disclosed by Statement 14, and amendments.

REVENUE: Revenue both from sales to unaffiliated customers and intersegment sales or transfers.

The following are the essential requirements for reporting by segments. *(Any user of this book who may have to comply with the segment rules should have access to the above Statements, as they are technically complex rules and long in substance.)*

- *Segment information* (termed *disaggregated information*) must be disclosed using the same accounting principles as those applied to the consolidated statements.
- The revenues, operating profits (or losses), and identifiable assets of each segment (or related segments) must be reconciled to the consolidated statements.
- Depreciation, depletion, and amortization expense must be reported by segment.
- Capital expenditures must be disclosed by segment.
- Transactions between segments must be included in segment information, even though eliminated in the preparation of consolidated statements.
- The effect on operating profits of a segment resulting from a change in an accounting principle must be disclosed.
- When prior information about a segment is reported in the *current* period, the *prior* period information must be retroactively restated.
- *What is a segment?* A segment must be determined by management; it is a judgment decision. The FASB *suggests* three broad factors to be considered in identifying a segment: 1) The type of product or service. Principally, this means products that are similar in character with reasonably comparable rates of profitability. 2) The production process, which means products or services that share the same production facilities, sales efforts, equipment, labor, etc. 3) Markets and/or marketing policies and methods, which mean similar geographic markets, types of customers, and other marketing factors common to the enterprise's products or services.

The Statement suggests the following *quantitative* guidelines for disclosure:

- If the revenue generated by a segment (or related segments) is 10 percent or more of the enterprise's total revenue, the product or service should be considered a segment.
- The operating profit (or loss) is 10 percent or more of the greater of 1) the combined operating profit of all the segments in the enterprise that did not have an operating *loss*, or 2) the operating loss of all industry segments that *did* have an operating loss. (Operating profit, or loss, excludes general corporate revenue, expenses, interest expense, and income taxes.)
- The identifiable assets of a segment (or related segments) are 10 percent or more of the combined identifiable assets of all of the enterprise's segments.

There is an additional percentage to be applied; i.e., the segmented results must be 75 percent or more of the combined sales of the enterprise to unaffiliated customers. This requirement prevents a company from reporting on only a few segments and combining the results of a large number of segments, defeating the objective of Statement 14. However, the FASB recognized there should be a reasonable limit to the number of segments that should be reported to avoid what might result in excessive accounting costs. The Statement suggests (but does not offer a precise definition) a guideline limit of 10 reportable segments (or a few more if necessary to comply with the 75 percent test).

The statement sets forth three broad bases for reporting segmented results: 1) service or product line in different industries, 2) foreign operations and export sales by absolute amounts and significant geographic areas, and 3) major customers' classifications.

- Foreign operating income, revenues, and identifiable assets are reported when sales of this type are 10 percent or more of consolidated revenues, or identifiable assets are 10 percent or more of the total assets of the business.
- Export sales must be reported when a company gets 10 percent or more of its revenues from sales from this source.
- A "major" customer is one that accounts for 10 percent or more of a company's total sales and requires separate disclosure.

Segment Presentation

Segment information can be included in the financial statements in any of the following ways:

- Included directly in the statements with explanatory footnotes.
- All of the information can be presented in footnotes.
- The information can be disclosed in separate Schedules.

FASB STATEMENT NO. 95

Statement of Cash Flows, Financial Accounting Statement No. 95, was issued in November, 1987. The Statement establishes the standards for reporting cash flows in the financial statements. It supersedes APB Opinion No. 19, *Reporting Changes in Financial Position*, and supersedes or amends prior pronouncements (listed in Appendix D of the manual).

The Statement is effective for annual financial statements for fiscal years ending *after* July 15, 1988. Restatement of financial reports for prior years is encouraged but not required.

Specifically, the Statement requires disclosure of cash flows to be included in the full set of financial statements, replacing the *Statement of Changes in Financial Position*.

Business enterprises are encouraged to report cash flows from operating activities *directly* by disclosing the major sources of operating cash receipts and disbursements (the *direct* method). Enterprises can elect not to show operating cash receipts and disbursements, but will be required to disclose the same amount of net cash flow from operating activities *indirectly* by adjusting net income to reconcile the net cash flow from operating activities (the *indirect* reconciliation method) by eliminating the effects of:

- all deferrals of past operating cash receipts and payments.
- all accruals of expected future operating cash receipts and payments.
- all items that are included in net income that do *not* affect operating cash receipts and payments.

It should be noted that if the direct method is applied, a reconciliation of net income and net cash flow from operating activities is required to be provided in a separate schedule.

If a reporting company has foreign business operations, the cash flows statement must disclose the currency equivalent of foreign currency cash flows, applying the current exchange rate at the time of the cash flow. The effect of changes in the exchange rates is disclosed as a separate item in the reconciliation of beginning and ending balances of cash and cash equivalents.

Information about investing and financing activities not resulting in cash receipts or payments is to be disclosed separately.

TERMINOLOGY

Precise definitions to clarify the meaning of the terms related specifically to the new rule can be helpful to an understanding of the new requirements.

CASH. Includes currency on hand, demand deposits with banks, and accounts with financial institutions that have the general characteristics of demand deposits; e.g., a depository that accepts deposits and permits withdrawals without prior notice or penalty.

CASH EQUIVALENT.   Short-term, highly liquid investments that are 1) readily convertible into known amounts of cash, and 2) near enough to maturity (*see Original Maturity*) that a change in the interest rate structure presents an insignificant risk of changes in the value of the investment.

CASH FLOW.   Cash receipts and cash payments resulting from investing, financing, or operating activities.

DIRECT METHOD.   Shows the principal components to be operating cash receipts and payments; e.g., cash received from accounts receivable; cash paid to suppliers.

FINANCING ACTIVITIES.   Borrowing money; paying borrowings; long-term credit. In general, transactions to acquire and repay capital.

INDIRECT METHOD.   Computation starts with net income that is adjusted for revenue and expense items *not* resulting from operating cash transactions (e.g., noncash transactions) to reconcile to net cash flow from operating activities. This method does not disclose operating cash receipts and payments.

INVESTING ACTIVITIES.   Making loans; collecting loans; acquiring and disposing of debt; acquiring and disposing of equity; acquiring and disposing of productive assets; e.g., plant and equipment.

NET CASH FLOW.   The arithmetic sum of gross cash receipts and gross cash payments which results in the net cash flow from operating activities.

NONCASH AND INVESTING ACTIVITIES.   Investing and financing activities which affect assets or liabilities, but do not result in cash receipts or cash payments.

OPERATING ACTIVITIES.   All transactions and other events that are *not* defined as investing or financing activities. Cash flows from activities which generally result from transactions and other events that enter into the determination of net income.

ORIGINAL MATURITY.   An investment *purchased* three months from the maturity date. (NOTE: An investment *purchased more than three months from maturity* is not a cash equivalent, even though its remaining maturity on financial statement date is within the three months' rule.)

SUMMARY

The summary that follows brings together in columnar format the significant requirements of the Statement that are scattered throughout the FASB manual.

- The objective of the Rule is to provide information about the cash receipts and cash payments of an enterprise during an accounting period.
- The statement of cash flows reports the cash effects of any enterprise's operations, investing transactions and financing transactions.
- Related disclosures should report the effects of investing and financing transactions that affect an enterprise's financial position, but do not directly affect cash flows.
- A reconciliation of net income and net cash flow from operating activities to provide information about the *net* effects of operating transactions and other events.
- The cash flows statement should explain the change during an accounting period in cash and cash equivalents.
- The Rule requires enterprises with foreign currency transactions (e.g., cash receipts and payments) to report the currency equivalent of foreign currency cash flows applying the exchange rates in effect at the time of the cash flows. (A weighted average exchange rate for the period for translation is permissible as specified in FASB No. 52, Para. 12.)
- Noncash transactions have a significant effect on the cash flows of a company and should be disclosed. (Reference APB Opinion No. 29, *Accounting for Nonmonetary Transactions.*)

CLASSIFICATION OF CASH RECEIPTS AND CASH PAYMENTS

From Operating Activities

Cash Inflows	Cash Outflows
Receipts from sales of goods or services.	Payments to suppliers for materials for manufacture or for resale.
Collections on accounts.	Payments on account.
Collections on short- and long-term notes receivable arising from sales.	Principal payments on short- and long-term notes payable to suppliers
Interest and dividend receipts.	Interest payments.
All other cash receipts that do not originate from investing or financing activities.	All other cash payments that do not originate from investing or financing activities.
Generally, the cash effects of transactions and other events that enter into the determination of net income.	Payments to employees. Tax Payments.

From Investing Activities

Cash Inflows	Cash Outflows
Loan collections of *principal* amount that were purchased by the enterprise.	Loans made. Payments for debt instruments of other entities.
Sale of equity securities of other enterprises.	Purchase of equity of securities of other enterprises.
Sale of plant, equipment, property, productive assets.	Purchase of plant, equipment, productive assets
Proceeds from equity security issues.	Repurchase of enterprise's equity securities.
Bond, mortgages, notes, and other borrowings.	Repayments of borrowings. Dividend payments.

Computational Procedures

The Statement requires determination of the amount of taxes payable or refundable in each future year as if a tax return were prepared for the net amount of temporary differences that will result in taxable or deductible amounts in each of those years. If alternative tax systems exist, those procedures are applied in a manner consistent with the tax laws. The procedures are applied separately for each tax jurisdiction.

The following is the procedure, step-by-step, for computing the tax in the reversal year (which is the deferred tax). It is essential to understand the concept underlying the approach to the calculations. Zero income or losses from all other sources in future years is assumed, as the future periods are the reversal periods.

- Estimate the specific future years in which temporary differences will result either in taxable or in deductible amounts.
- Compute the net taxable or deductible amount for each future year.
- Deduct operating loss carryforwards from net taxable amounts scheduled to occur in the future years that are included in the loss carryforward period.
- Carry back or carry forward net deductible amounts occurring in particular years to offset net taxable amounts scheduled to occur in subsequent years.
- Recognize a deferred tax asset for the tax benefit of net deductible amounts that could be realized by loss carryback from future years (1) to reduce a current deferred tax liability, and (2) to reduce taxes paid in the current or a prior year. No asset is recognized for any additional net deductible amounts in future years.
- Calculate the amount of tax for the remaining net taxable amounts scheduled to occur in each future year by applying current tax rates for each of those

years to the type and amount of net taxable amounts scheduled for those years.

- Deduct tax credit carryforwards from the amount as calculated above for future years that are included in the carryforward periods. No asset is recognized for any additional amount of tax credit carryforward.
- Recognize a deferred tax liability for the remaining amount of taxes payable for each future year.

DIRECT METHOD—DISCUSSION AND ILLUSTRATION

The direct method requires reporting the three major classes of gross cash receipts and gross cash payments, as well as their arithmetic sum (see earlier definition) to disclose the *net cash flow* from operating activities.

The Rule allows reporting entities to detail cash receipts and payments to any extent considered to be meaningful. For example, payments to suppliers might be divided between raw material purchases and other major supplies used in the business. Wage and salary payments might be divided between manufacturing, selling, and administrative expenses. Sales receipts could be divided among different sources, with an "other" operating cash receipts, if any.

The reconciliation of net income to net cash flow from operating activities must be provided in a separate schedule.

Statement of Cash Flows
Increase (Decrease) in Cash and Cash Equivalents

(Direct Method)
Year Ended December 31, 19xx

Cash flows from *operating* activities:		
Cash received from customers	$435,000	
Interest received	5,000	
Cash provided by operations		440,000
Cash paid to employees and suppliers	(382,000)	
Interest paid	(13,000)	
Taxes paid	(20,000)	
Cash disbursed by operations		(415,000)
Net cash flow from operations		$ 25,000
Cash flows from *investing* activities:		
Marketable securities purchases	$(32,500)	
Proceeds-marketable securities sales	20,000	
Loans made	(8,500)	
Loan collections	6,000	
Plant purchase	(80,000)	
Proceeds-sale of plant assets	37,500	
Net cash used in investing activities		$(57,500)

(Direct Method), *Con't*
Year Ended December 31, 19xx

Cash flows from *financing* activities:		
Loan proceeds	$ 22,500	
Debt repayment	(27,500)	
Proceeds-Bond issue	50,000	
Proceeds-Common Stock issue	25,000	
Dividends paid	(20,000)	
Net cash provided by financing activities		$50,000
Net increase (decrease) in cash		$17,500

The following is a more comprehensive Statement of Cash Flow from operations applying the *direct* method. This approach includes the disclosure of noncash transactions in a separate schedule formatted beneath the statement.

Statement of Cash Flows
Increase (Decrease) in Cash and Cash Equivalents

(Direct Method)
Year Ended December 31, 1988

Cash flow from operations:		
Cash from receivables	$10,000,000	
Dividend receipts	700,000	
Cash provided		10,700,000
Cash paid to suppliers	2,000,000	
Wage and salary payments	4,000,000	
Interest payments	750,000	
Taxes	1,000,000	
Cash disbursed		7,750,000
Net cash flow from operations		$2,950,000
Cash flow from investing activities:		
Property and plant purchases	(4,000,000)	
Proceeds from sale of equipment	2,500,000	
Acquisition of Corporation X	(900,000)	
Securities purchases	(4,700,000)	
Securities sales	5,000,000	
Borrowings	(7,500,000)	
Collections on notes receivable	5,800,000	
Net cash outflow from investments		$(3,800,000)
Cash flow from financing activities:		
Increase in customer deposits	1,100,000	
Short-term borrowings (increase)	75,000	
Short-term debt payments	(300,000)	
Long-term debt proceeds	1,250,000	
Lease payments	(125,000)	
Common stock issue	500,000	
Dividends to shareholders	(450,000)	

(Direct Method), *Con't*
Year Ended December 31, 1988

Net cash provided by financing	$2,050,000
Foreign exchange rate change	100,000
Net increase (decrease) in cash	$1,300,000

Schedule—Noncash Investing and Financing Activities:

Incurred lease obligation	$ 750,000
Acquisition of Corporation X:	
Working capital acquired (except cash)	(100,000)
Property and plant acquired	3,000,000
Assumed long-term debt	(2,000,000)
Cash paid for acquisition	$ 900,000
Common stock issued in payment	
of long-term debt	$ 250,000

Indirect Method—Discussion and Illustration

The indirect method (also termed the *reconciliation method*) requires *net cash flow* to be reported indirectly with an adjustment of net income to reconcile it to net cash flow from operating activities. The adjustment requires:

- The removal from net income of the effects of all deferrals of past operating cash receipts and payments.
- The removal from net income of the effects of all accruals of expected future operating cash receipts and payments.
- The removal from net income of the effects of all items of investing and financing cash flows.

The reconciliation can be reported *either* within the statement of cash flows *or* in a separate schedule, with the statement of cash flows reporting only the net cash flow from operating activities. However, if the reconciliation is disclosed in the cash flow statement, the adjustments to net income must be identified as reconciling items.

Statement of Cash Flows
Increase (Decrease) in Cash and Cash Equivalents

(Indirect Method)
Year Ended December 31, 19xx

Cash flows from *operating* activities:		
Net cash flow from operating activities*		$ 25,000
Cash flows from *investing* activities:		
Marketable securities purchases	$(32,500)	
Proceeds-marketable securities sales	20,000	
Loans made	(8,500)	
Loan collections	6,000	
Plant purchase**	(80,000)	
Proceeds-sale of plant assets	37,500	

(Indirect Method), *Con't*
Year Ended December 31, 19xx

Net cash used in investing activities		$(57,500)
Cash flows from *financing* activities:		
Loan proceeds	$ 22,500	
Debt repayment	(27,500)	
Proceeds-Bond issue	50,000	
Proceeds-Common Stock issue	25,000	
Dividends paid	(20,000)	
Net cash provided by financing activities		$50,000
Net increase (decrease) in cash		$17,500

*See supplemental schedule A. (Details operating activity.)
**See supplemental schedule B. (Details investing and financing activity.)

The following is a more comprehensive Statement of Cash Flow from operations applying the *indirect* method. This approach includes the disclosure of noncash transactions in a separate schedule formatted beneath the statement.

Statement of Cash Flows

(Indirect Method)
Year Ended December 31, 1988

Net cash flow from operations		$2,950,000
Cash flow from investing activities:		
Property and plant purchases	(4,000,000)	
Proceeds from sale of equipment	2,500,000	
Acquisition of Corporation X	(900,000)	
Securities purchases	(4,700,000)	
Securities sales	5,000,000	
Borrowings	(7,500,000)	
Collections on notes receivable	5,800,000	
Net cash outflow from investments		$(3,800,000)
Cash flow from financing activities:		
Increase in customer deposits	1,100,000	
Short-term borrowings (increase)	75,000	
Short-term debt payments	(300,000)	
Long-term debt proceeds	1,250,000	
Lease payments	(125,000)	
Common stock issue	500,000)	
Dividends to shareholders	(450,000)	
Net cash provided by financing		$2,050,000
Foreign exchange rate change		100,000
Net increase (decrease) in cash		$1,300,000
Schedule—Earnings to net cash flow reconciliation from operations:		
Net income	$3,000,000	
Noncash expenses, revenues, losses, and gains included in income:		
Depreciation and amortization	1,500,000	

(Indirect Method), *Con't*
Year Ended December 31, 1988

Deferred taxes	150,000	
Net increase in receivables	(350,000)	
Net increase in payables	(200,000)	
Net increase in inventory	(300,000)	
Accrued interest earned	(350,000)	
Accrued interest payable	100,000	
Gain on sale of equipment	(600,000)	
Net cash flow from operations		$2,950,000

Schedule of noncash investing and financing
  activities:

Incurred lease obligation	$ 750,000

Acquisition of Corporation X:

Working capital acquired (except cash)	$(100,000)
Property and plant acquired	3,000,000
Assumed long-term debt	(2,000,000)
Cash paid for acquisition	$ 900,000

Common stock issued in payment of long-
  term debt $ 250,000

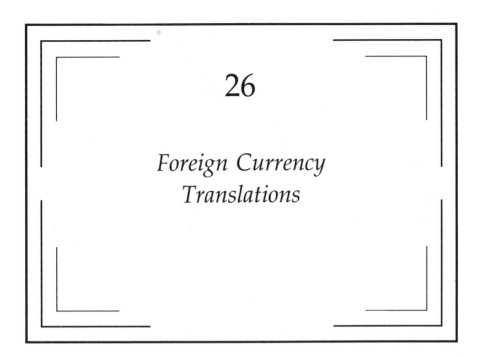

26

Foreign Currency Translations

FOREIGN CURRENCY TRANSLATIONS FOR FINANCIAL STATEMENTS

The principle of conservatism *generally* requires the use of historical cost, and increases or decreases in assets or liabilities brought about by market conditions are not recorded until actual transfer or exchange occurs.

However, there are two exceptions, now accepted as standard procedure, which require the consideration of the *market price*, matching it to historical cost, and recording the *unrealized* loss or gain for the period, to reflect the market price of the asset (or liability), generally at balance sheet date.

This chapter is concerned with one of those exceptions—*foreign currency translations*. It reviews FASB Statement No. 52, *Foreign Currency Translation*, issued in December, 1981, effective for fiscal years beginning after December 15, 1982. Statement No. 52 replaces FASB Statement No. 8, *Accounting for the Translation of Foreign Currency* And Foreign Currency Financial Statements, dated October 1975. The other exception is in the handling of marketable securities, covered separately in the "Current Assets" portion of this section on accounting.

Why is translation necessary? It is not arithmetically possible to combine, add, or subtract measurements expressed in different currencies. It is necessary, therefore, to translate assets, liabilities, revenues, expenses, gains, and losses that are measured or denominated in a foreign currency.

There are two steps in the translation procedure:

1. Translate from the foreign currency to U.S. dollars.
2. Bring the foreign subsidiary's statements into conformity with U.S. GAAP requirements.

Definitions

EXCHANGE RATE. The *ratio* between a unit of one currency (A) and the amount of another currency (B) for which currency A can be exchanged at a particular time.

FOREIGN CURRENCY TRANSACTIONS. Transactions whose terms are denominated in a currency other than the entity's functional currency.

FOREIGN CURRENCY TRANSLATION. Disclosing in the reporting currency of the enterprise the amounts that are denominated in a different currency.

FOREIGN ENTITY. An operation whose financial statements are prepared in a currency other than the reporting currency, and accounted for on the equity basis in the financial statements of the reporting enterprise.

FUNCTIONAL CURRENCY. The currency of the primary environment in which the entity operates, which in turn is considered to be the environment in which the entity primarily generates and expends cash.

REPORTING ENTERPRISE. An entity or group whose financial statements reflect 1) the financial statements of one or more foreign operations; 2) foreign currency transactions; 3) both.

TRANSACTION GAIN OR LOSS. Gains or losses from a change in exchange rates between the functional currency and the currency in which a foreign transaction is denominated.

TRANSLATION ADJUSTMENTS. The translation of financial statements from the entity's functional currency into the reporting currency. (See para. 13 of FASB No. 52.)

REPORTING CURRENCY. The currency in which the reporting enterprise prepares its financial statements.

The application of Statement No. 52 (the "Statement") is to the financial reports of most companies with foreign operations. The essential requirements of the Statements are:

1. Transaction adjustments arising from consolidating a foreign operation which do not affect cash flows are *not* included in net income. Adjustments should be disclosed separately and accumulated in a separate classification of the equity section of the balance sheet.

2. Exchange rate changes on a foreign operation which directly affect the parent's cash flows *must* be included in net income.

3. Hedges of foreign exchange risks are accounted for as hedges without regard to their form.

4. Transaction gains and losses result from exchange rate changes on transactions denominated in currencies other than the functional currency.

5. The balance sheet translation uses the exchange rate prevailing as of the date of the balance sheet.

6. The exchange rate used for revenues, expenses, gains and losses is the rate on the date those items are recognized.

7. Upon sale (or liquidation) of an investment in a foreign entity, the amount accumulated in the equity component is removed and reported as a gain (or loss) on the disposal of the entity.

8. Intercompany transactions of a long-term investment nature are not included in net income.

9. Financial statements for fiscal years before the effective date of this Statement may be restated. If restatements are provided, they must conform to requirements of the Statement.

10. The financial statements of a foreign entity in a highly inflationary economy must be remeasured as if the functional currency were the reporting currency. A "highly inflationary economy" is defined in the Statement to be an economy that has had a cumulative inflation rate of 100%, or more, over a three-year period.

11. If material change in an exchange rate has occurred between year-end and the audit report date, the change should be reported as a subsequent event.

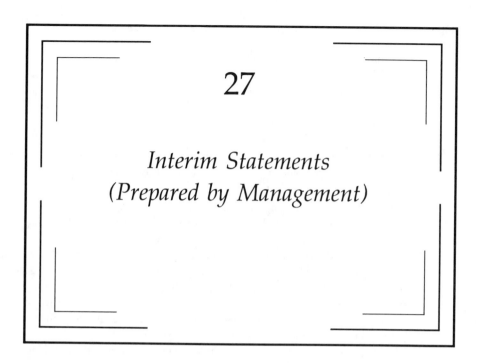

27

Interim Statements
(Prepared by Management)

GUIDELINES FOR INTERIM REPORTING

Guidelines for interim reporting by publicly traded companies have been established by the AICPA (and the SEC).

For those private companies which do not bear the same responsibility for full and adequate disclosure to public shareholders, the guideline for public disclosure should be studied and followed, where feasible and relevant, for possible self-protection against insurgent parties, since adherence to standards would probably be more defensible than non-adherence.

The following standards for determining information and the guidelines indicated for minimum disclosure have prevailed since December 31, 1973.

1. Results should be based on the same principles and practices used for the latest annual statements (subject to the modifications below).
2. Revenue should be recognized as earned for the interim on the same basis as for the full year. Losses should be recognized as incurred or when becoming evident.
3. Costs may be classified as:
   A. Those associated with revenue (cost of goods sold);

    B. All other costs—expenses based on;

        1) Those actually incurred, or

        2) Those allocated, based on:

            a) Time expired, or

            b) Benefits received, or

            c) Other period activity.

4. Costs or losses (including extraordinary items) should not be deferred or apportioned unless they would at year end. Advertised costs may be apportioned in relation to sales for interims.

5. With respect to inventory and cost of sales:

    A. LIFO basis should not be liquidated if expected to be replaced later, but should be based on expected replacement factor;

    B. Do not defer inventory losses because of cost or market rule; and conversely, later periods should then reflect gains on market price recoveries. Inventory losses should be reflected if resulting from permanent declines in market value in the interim period in which they occur; recoveries of such losses would be gains in a later interim period. If a change in inventory value is temporary, no recognition is given.

    C. With standard costs, variances which are expected to be absorbed by year-end should be deferred for the interim, not expensed. Unplanned purchase price or volume variance, not expected to turn around, are to be absorbed during the period;

    D. The estimated gross profit method may be used, but must be disclosed.

6. The seasonal nature of activities should be disclosed, preferably including additional 12-month-to-date information with prior comparative figures.

7. Income taxes:

    A. Effective yearly tax rate (including year-end applicable tax-planned advantages) should be applied to interim taxable income;

    B. Extraordinary items applicable to the interim period should be shown separately net of applicable tax and the effect of the tax not applied to the tax on ordinary net income.

8. Extraordinary and unusual items including the effects of segment disposals should be disclosed separately, net of tax, for the interim period in which they occur, and they should not be apportioned over the year.

9. Contingencies should be disclosed the same as for the annual report.

10. Changes in accounting practices or principles from those followed in prior periods should be disclosed and, where possible, those changes should be made in the first period of the year.

11. Retroactive restatement and/or prior period adjustments are required under the same rules applying to annual statements.

12. The effect of a change in an accounting estimate, including a change in the estimated effective annual tax rate, should be accounted for in the period in which the change in estimate is made. No restatement of previously reported interim information should be made for changes in estimates, but the effect on earnings of a change in estimate made in a current interim period should be reported in the current and subsequent interim periods, if material in relation to any period presented, and should continue to be reported in interim financial information of the subsequent year, for as many periods as necessary to avoid misleading comparisons.

Minimum Data to be Reported on Interim Statements is as Follows:

1. Sales or gross revenues, provisions for income taxes, extraordinary items (including related tax), cumulative effect of changes in accounting principles or practices, and net income;
2. Primary and fully diluted earnings per share data for each period presented;
3. Seasonal revenue, costs and expenses;
4. Disposal of business segments and extraordinary items, as well as unusual or infrequent items;
5. Contingencies;
6. Changes in estimates, changes in accounting principles or practices;
7. Significant changes in balance sheet items;
8. Significant changes in tax provisions;
9. Current year-to-date, or the last 12 months, with comparative data for prior periods;
10. In the absence of a separate fourth-quarter report, special fourth-quarter adjustments and extraordinary, infrequent or unusual items which occurred during that fourth quarter should be disclosed in a note to the annual financial statement;
11. Though not required, condensed balance sheet data and funds flow data are suggested to provide better understanding of the interim report.
12. If a fourth quarter is not presented, any material adjustment to that quarter must be commented upon in the annual report.

Interim reports are usually prepared by management and issued with that clear stipulation.

Accounting firms which issue reports for interim periods are to be guided by auditing standards set for ''Reports on a Limited Review of Interim Financial Information'' in Section 722 of Statements on Auditing Standards, April, 1981.

ACCOUNTING CHANGES IN INTERIM STATEMENTS

FASB No. 3, *Reporting Accounting Changes in Interim Financial Statements* amended APB Opinion No. 28, *Interim Financial Reporting* with respect to reporting an accounting change in interim financial reports that have a *cumulative effect*.

The following disclosures of accounting changes that have cumulative effects on income from continuing operations, net income, and related per share amounts for the interim period in which the change is made must be included in interim reports:

- In the interim period in which the new accounting principle is adopted, disclosure should explain the nature and justification for the change.
- Disclosure should be made of the effect of the change in the interim period in which the change is made.
- The effect of the change for each pre-change interim period of that fiscal year should be disclosed.
- The cumulative effect of the change should be shown on retained earnings at the beginning of that fiscal year, if the change is made in other than the first interim period of the company's fiscal year.
- In the interim period in which a change is made, disclosure must include amounts computed on a *pro forma* basis for the interim period in which the change is made and for any interim periods of prior fiscal years for which financial information is being presented.
- In financial reports for a subsequent interim period of the fiscal year in which a new principle is adopted, disclosure must include the effect of the change on income from continuing operations, net income, and related per share amounts for the post-change interim period.

84 ACCOUNTING AND FINANCIAL STATEMENTS DISCLOSURE DEFICIENCIES

The Securities and Exchange Commission has issued a list of 86 accounting and disclosure deficiencies commonly found by the Commission in the financial statements of corporations. The errors usually occur in the accountant's opinion, consolidated financial statements, balance sheet, liabilities, capital stock, surplus, profit and loss statement, and in various notes and schedules that supplement the statements.

The deficiencies that recur involve, for the most part, errors resulting from oversights in following accounting disclosure principles and presentation of financial data required in the financial statements.

It is the Commission's view that if accountants give careful attention to the requirements for completing the reports, corporations will avoid considerable expense and inconvenience to themselves. Properly completed statements (and annual reports to shareholders, where applicable), will facilitate user analysis of the statements, a factor to the reporting entity's interest from the point of view of prompt acceptance by users of the information in the financial reports.

The 84 Deficiencies

1. Failure to state clearly an opinion with respect to the accounting principles and practices followed by the reporting entity.

2. Frequent use of equivocal phrases; i.e., "subject to the foregoing," "subject to comments and explanations in exhibits," "subject to accompanying comments," etc.

3. Failure to include in the opinion a comprehensive statement regarding the scope (the "scope paragraph") of the audit; i.e., restrictions by the company because of expense placed on the scope of the accountant's examination.

4. The accountant's failure to make a complete examination. The rules require that accountants must not omit any procedure that independent public accountants would ordinarily employ in the course of a regular annual examination.

5. Failure to certify *all* financial statements. For example, failure to certify the balance sheet and the income statements. Also, failure to certify the statements of the parent and subsidiaries consolidated.

6. Failure to identify clearly all supporting schedules, if any.

7. Certifying without explicit indication that the accounting practices of the company are in accordance with generally accepted accounting principles and procedures.

8. Failure either to comment upon or to clearly disclose the effect upon the financial statements of significant changes in accounting policies and practices.

9. Inadequate comment on the effect on the financial statements of the company's failure to follow GAAP.

10. Disclaiming responsibility for matters clearly within the certifying accountant's examination responsibilities.

11. Written reservation by the accountant with respect to matters not necessarily within his province, but in which the accountant was not satisfied.

12. Certificate undated. Certificate not manually signed.

13. Failure to footnote the accounting methods followed, clarifying the difference between the investment in subsidiaries on the parent's books, and the parent's equity in the net assets of the subsidiaries on the subsidiaries' books, as well as omitting the amount of the difference.

14. Failure to show in the balance sheet the amount of minority interest in the capital and surplus of the subsidiaries consolidated.

15. Failure to disclose the accounting principles followed for the inclusion and exclusion of subsidiaries in each consolidated balance sheet.

16. Improper treatment (in consolidation) of surpluses of subsidiary companies existing at the date of acquisition by the parent company.

17. Preparation of consolidated profit and loss statement on a basis different from the consolidated balance sheet. For example, including income and expenses in the consolidated profit and loss statement of subsidiaries whose assets and liabilities are not reflected in the consolidated balance sheet, but for which separate balance sheets are furnished.

18. A failure to eliminate intercompany items, or to explain satisfactorily the reasons for not eliminating the items.

19. Failure to total current assets and to label the total.

20. Classification as current assets not realizable within one year. If recognized trade practices permit this procedure, an explanation should be footnoted.

21. Classifying receivables from subsidiaries as current assets in the parent's balance sheet, but classifying as noncurrent the subsidiary's obligations to the parent.

22. Failure to identify hypothecated (pledged) assets.

23. Failure to disclose or clearly explain conditionally held assets.

24. Classifying securities as "marketable" that are not in fact readily marketable.

25. Failure to disclose the basis for determining the balance sheet amounts of marketable securities and investments.

26. Failure to disclose the aggregate quoted value of investments and marketable securities when not shown on a current market basis.

27. Failure to reduce the carrying value of investments in subsidiaries by the amount of any dividends received out of the surplus of the subsidiaries.

28. Inclusion of improper accounts under trade receivables category.

29. Failure to disclose separately in the balance sheet, or to reference a schedule, the major classes of inventory; i.e., raw materials, work-in-process, finished goods, supplies, etc.

30. Failure to show the basis for determining the amount of the inventories on the balance sheet.

31. Failure to provide a reserve for depreciation on the appreciated value of fixed assets.

32. Improper inclusion of expenditures in carrying value of fixed assets.

33. Failure to disclose the method used for amortizing debt discount and expense.

34. Failure to explain the method for writing off discounts and commissions on capital stock.

35. Failure to state the reasons for carrying treasury stock as an asset.

36. Failure to disclosure separately the amount of reacquired debts.

37. Unexplained absence of an allowance for doubtful accounts.

38. Failure to total current liabilities and to label the total.

39. Inclusion in general reserves tax accruals that are actual liabilities.

40. Failure to segregate accounts and notes payable and accruals.

41. Deferred income not classified separately.

42. Failure to fully disclose all contingent liabilities.

43. Failure to disclose separately the aggregate capital stock liability of each class of stock.

44. Failure to show separately the number of authorized, treasury, and outstanding shares.

45. Failure to disclose in the balance sheet the division of retained earnings into various classes, if applicable.

46. Failure to disclose the par value, or a failure to show the assigned stated value of no par value stock.

47. Use of capital surplus to absorb writedowns in plant and equipment that should have been charged to retained earnings.

48. Failure to date earned surplus account after eliminating a deficit by a charge to capital surplus.

49. Failure to state the amount of retained earnings restricted because of the acquisition of company's own stock. Also, failure to state amount of surplus restricted for the difference between par or stated value of preferred stock and the liquidating value of that class of stock.

50. Deficit not clearly designated in the balance sheet.

51. Treatment of surplus of subsidiary at date of acquisition of earned surplus.

52. Charges to surplus, rather than to profit and loss, for expenses or losses properly identified with current operations.

53. Crediting profit and loss instead of retained earnings for the proceeds of sale of assets previously written off by a charge to retained earnings.

54. Failure to disclose the basis for determining inventories when opening and closing inventories are used to determine the cost of goods sold.

55. Failure to indicate the omission of provisions for depreciation or depletion, and the effect on the profit and loss statement.

56. Failure to disclose the basis of conversion of all items in foreign currencies. Also, failure to state the amount and disposition of unrealized profits or losses in foreign currencies.

57. Failure to show gross sales net of discounts, and returns and allowances.

58. Failure to disclose gross sales and operating revenues separately, when the lesser of the two amounts exceeds 10 percent of the total of the two amounts.

59. Failure to segregate selling, general, and administrative expenses.

60. Failure to explain in footnotes the effect of changes in accounting practices in the compilation of the profit and loss statement.

61. Failure to disclose separately from other taxes a surtax on undistributed profits, or a failure to state explicitly that no liability for a surtax exists.

62. Failure to explain the method used to determine the cost of securities sold; i.e., average cost, first-in, first-out, specific certificate or bond or type of security.

63. Failure to show the basis for the recognition of profits on installment or other deferred sales.

64. Failure to reference appropriate schedules to the profit and loss statement when expense details are presented in supporting schedules.

65. Failure to list property by major classification; i.e., land, buildings, equipment, machinery, leaseholds, etc.

66. Failure to explain the nature of changes in property, plant, and equipment accounts.

67. Failure to disclose accounting policies with respect to amortization and/or depreciation of property, plant, and equipment when credited directly to asset accounts.

68. Failure to state accounting policies with respect to the provisions for depreciation, depletion, and amortization, or reserves created in lieu of appropriate provisions.

69. Failure to comply with the requirement that reserves should be disclosed to correspond with the classification of property in separating depreciation, depletion, and amortization.

70. Failure to explain charges to reserves, other than retirement, renewals, and replacements.

71. Failure to identify intangible assets by major classes.

72. Failure to state policy with respect to provisions for the amortization of intangible assets in cases where a clarifying schedule is not provided.

73. Failure to state the accounting policy with respect to the provisions for amortization of intangible assets, or reserves created in lieu of appropriate provisions.

74. Failure to explain all changes in reserves during the accounting period.

75. Failure to list each issue of capital stock of all the corporations in a consolidated group, whether or not eliminated in consolidation.

76. Improperly identifying unissued stock as treasury stock.

77. Failure to disclose division of retained earnings into classes; i.e., paid-in capital, capital surplus, earned surplus, appraisal surplus.

78. Failure to include an analysis of the retained earnings account, either in the balance sheet, or in a continuation of the profit and loss statement, or in a schedule referenced in the balance sheet.

79. Failure to describe precisely all miscellaneous retained earnings additions and deductions.

80. Failure to segregate amounts charged to costs, and amounts charged to other profit and loss items not segregated.

81. Failure to report all maintenance and repair expenses.
82. Failure to show items in schedules which are at variance or inconsistent with other statements or schedules.
83. Failure to disclose the amount of equity in net profit and loss for the fiscal year of affiliates, if dividends were received during the year from affiliates.
84. Failure to disclose separately for each affiliate the amount of dividends and the amount of equity in net profit and loss for the fiscal year. Corporations may report these items in total only when substantially all the stock and funded debt of the subsidiaries are held within the affiliated group.

11

Taxes—The Tax Reform Act of 1986

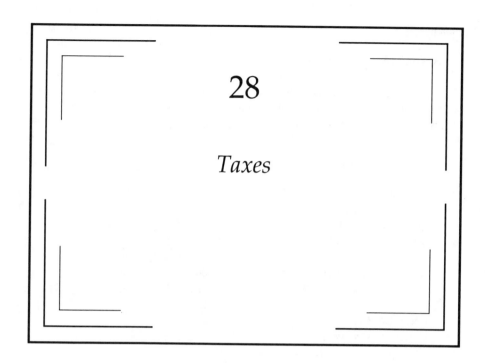

28

Taxes

"The art of taxation consists in so plucking the goose as to obtain the largest amount of feathers with the least amount of hissing."

—Jean Baptiste Colbert (1693-1783)

THE TAX REFORM ACT OF 1986 (Redesignated: *Internal Revenue Code of 1986*)

On October 22, 1986, the President signed into law the most extensive tax legislation in the history of the country. The new law affects every individual, business, nonprofit organization, and all other sectors of the economy to a significant extent, as the New Law repeals, changes, or adds sections to the 1954 Code.

Our concern in this tax section is with the Act's changes that affect business entities. In Section Three that follows, *Tax Accounting* provisions will be covered.

(Note: Appendix B is a reprint of an abridgement of the 1986 Act, furnished by KMG Main Hurdman. The users of this desk manual will note frequent references to Appendix B in parenthesis at the end of many of the topics covered in Sections Two and Three. The reprint furnishes additional detail for topics of specific interest to the user.)

CORPORATE TAX PROVISIONS

The following is a synopsis of the corporate tax provisions of the New Law that will also furnish a topical outline of the detailed explanations and clarifications in the pages that follow of Title VI Corporate Taxation.

The New Law

Tax Rates	Three Graduated Brackets
Capital Gain Rate	34%
Investment Tax Credit	None effective 1986.
Depreciation	New Rules.
Expensing Allowance	Increased with limitations.
Business Meals & Entertainment	Deductions reduced.
Minimum Tax	Alternative Minimum Tax (AMT) 20–25%.
R&D Tax Credit	Reduced and extended.
Dividends Received	Reduced.
Net Operating Losses	Still allowed, difficult to claim: restrictions.
Completed Contracts	Method application curtailed.
Cash Method	Restricted.
Installment Sales	Method restricted.
Bad Debt Reserve	Eliminated (except for financial institutions).
Taxable Years	S Corps, personal service corps use calendar year; partnerships use partner year-end.
Foreign Taxes	Very complex and restrictive.

Title VIII Accounting Provisions—A Synopsis

LIFO	A "simplified" method.
Production Cost Rules	Uniform Rules.
Cash Method	Limited to "small business," S Corps, personal service corps.
Installment Sales	Deferral disallowed for revolving credit sales.
Bad Debt Reserve	Specific charge-off method required.
Construction Period	Interest included in property basis.
Completed Contracts	Method subject to AMT. Restrictive capitalization rules.

Corporate tax rates. The corporate tax rates table is a three-bracket graduated rate structure:

Taxable Income	Tax Rate
Not over $50,000	15%
Over $50,000 but not over $75,000	25%
Over $75,000	34%

There is a 5 percent surcharge up to a maximum of $11,750 on corporate taxable income over $100,000 up to $335,000, which results in a marginal tax rate of 39 percent for income within this range. Corporations with income in excess of $335,000 will pay the flat 34 percent rate. A "controlled" group of corporations must aggregate the group's income to avoid phaseout of the lower graduated rates. (App. B)

The new rates are effective for taxable years beginning on or after July 1, 1987. Income in taxable years that straddle July 1, 1987, will pay a blended rate in order to reflect the reduced rates for the part of the year that falls after June 30, 1987. A corporation with a calendar year, for example, will have a top rate of 40 percent for 1987. The computation is not difficult:

1. Compute the tax for the entire straddle year applying the old rate and the new rate.
2. Compute the proportionate part of each of the results of Step 1 with the proportions based upon the number of days that each of the two rates was in effect during the taxable year.
3. Add the results to obtain the tax for the year.

Capital Gains. The long-term capital gains provisions of the old law is abolished with the alternative tax on capital gains recognized after 1986 increased from 28 percent to 34 percent. Capital losses can be deducted only against capital gains, not applied to reduce the corporation's taxable income. However, as under the old law, capital losses are allowed to be netted in full against capital gains.

Recapture of depreciation on the sale of both residential and nonresidential real property has been eliminated. Because net capital gains are subject to the 34 percent rate applicable to ordinary income, this provision is of little importance.

An *alternative minimum tax* replaces the old law add-on tax. The rate is 20 percent and there is a $40,000 exemption phased out at the rate of 25 cents on the dollar (not below zero) for alternative minimum taxable income in excess of $150,000. (App. B)

Form 1120

Department of the Treasury
Internal Revenue Service

U.S. Corporation Income Tax Return

For calendar 1986 or tax year beginning _____, 1986, ending _____, 19 ____
▶ For Paperwork Reduction Act Notice, see page 1 of the instructions.

OMB No. 1545-0123

1986

Check if a—
A Consolidated return ☐
B Personal Holding Co. ☐
C Business Code No. (See the list in the instructions)

Use IRS label. Otherwise please print or type.

Name

Number and street

City or town, state, and ZIP code

D Employer identification number

E Date incorporated

F Total assets (see Specific Instructions)
     Dollars   Cents

G Check box if there has been a change in address from the previous year . . . . ▶ ☐ $

Income

1a	Gross receipts or sales _____ b Less returns and allowances _____ Balance ▶	1c
2	Cost of goods sold and/or operations (Schedule A)	2
3	Gross profit (line 1c less line 2)	3
4	Dividends (Schedule C)	4
5	Interest	5
6	Gross rents	6
7	Gross royalties	7
8	Capital gain net income (attach separate Schedule D)	8
9	Net gain or (loss) from Form 4797, line 17, Part II (attach Form 4797)	9
10	Other income (see instructions—attach schedule)	10
11	TOTAL income—Add lines 3 through 10 and enter here . . . . ▶	11

Deductions

12	Compensation of officers (Schedule E)	12
13a	Salaries and wages _____ b Less jobs credit _____ Balance ▶	13c
14	Repairs	14
15	Bad debts (Schedule F if reserve method is used)	15
16	Rents	16
17	Taxes	17
18	Interest	18
19	Contributions (**see instructions for 10% limitation**)	19
20	Depreciation (attach Form 4562) 20	
21	Less depreciation claimed in Schedule A and elsewhere on return . 21a	21b
22	Depletion	22
23	Advertising	23
24	Pension, profit-sharing, etc., plans	24
25	Employee benefit programs	25
26	Other deductions (attach schedule)	26
27	TOTAL deductions—Add lines 12 through 26 and enter here . . . . . . ▶	27
28	Taxable income before net operating loss deduction and special deductions (line 11 less line 27) .	28
29	**Less: a** Net operating loss deduction (see instructions) 29a	
	b Special deductions (Schedule C) 29b	29c

Tax and Payments

30	Taxable income (line 28 less line 29c)	30
31	TOTAL TAX (Schedule J)	31
32	**Payments: a** 1985 overpayment credited to 1986	
b	1986 estimated tax payments	
c	Less 1986 refund applied for on Form 4466 . . ( )	
d	Tax deposited with Form 7004	
e	Credit from regulated investment companies (attach Form 2439) . .	
f	Credit for Federal tax on gasoline and special fuels (attach Form 4136) .	32
33	Enter any **PENALTY** for underpayment of estimated tax—check ▶ ☐ if Form 2220 is attached .	33
34	**TAX DUE**—If the total of lines 31 and 33 is larger than line 32, enter AMOUNT OWED	34
35	**OVERPAYMENT**—If line 32 is larger than the total of lines 31 and 33, enter AMOUNT OVERPAID	35
36	Enter amount of line 35 you want: **Credited to 1987 estimated tax** ▶ Refunded ▶	36

Please Sign Here

Under penalties of perjury, I declare that I have examined this return, including accompanying schedules and statements, and to the best of my knowledge and belief, it is true, correct, and complete. Declaration of preparer (other than taxpayer) is based on all information of which preparer has any knowledge.

▶ _____   ▶ _____
Signature of officer   Date   Title

Paid Preparer's Use Only

Preparer's signature ▶	Date	Check if self-employed ☐	Preparer's social security number
Firm's name (or yours, if self-employed) and address ▶		E.I. No. ▶	
		ZIP code ▶	

Form 1120 (1986)

Schedule A — Cost of Goods Sold and/or Operations (See instructions for line 2, page 1)

1 Inventory at beginning of year.	1	
2 Purchases .	2	
3 Cost of labor	3	
4 Other costs (attach schedule).	4	
5 Total—Add lines 1 through 4 .	5	
6 Inventory at end of year.	6	
7 Cost of goods sold and/or operations—Line 5 less line 6. Enter here and on line 2, page 1	7	

8a Check all methods used for valuing closing inventory:

   (i) ☐ Cost   *(ii)* ☐ Lower of cost or market as described in Regulations section 1.471-4 (see instructions)

   (iii) ☐ Writedown of "subnormal" goods as described in Regulations section 1.471-2(c) (see instructions)

   (iv) ☐ Other (Specify method used and attach explanation) ▶ _____

  b Check if the LIFO inventory method was adopted this tax year for any goods (if checked, attach Form 970) . . . . ☐

  c If the LIFO inventory method was used for this tax year, enter percentage (or amounts) of closing inventory computed under LIFO . . . . | 8c |

  d If you are engaged in manufacturing, did you value your inventory using the full absorption method (Regulations section 1.471-11)? . . . . ☐ Yes ☐ No

  e Was there any change in determining quantities, cost, or valuations between opening and closing inventory? . . . ☐ Yes ☐ No
If "Yes," attach explanation.

Schedule C — Dividends and Special Deductions (See Schedule C instructions)

	(a) Dividends received	(b) %	(c) Special deductions: multiply (a) X (b)
Domestic corporations subject to section 243(a) deduction (other than debt-financed stock).		see instructions	
Debt-financed stock of domestic and foreign corporations (section 246A)		see instructions	
Certain preferred stock of public utilities		see instructions	
Foreign corporations and certain FSCs subject to section 245 deduction		see instructions	
Wholly-owned foreign subsidiaries and FSCs subject to 100% deduction (sections 245(b) and (c)) . .		100	
Total—Add lines 1 through 5. See instructions for limitation	░░░░░░		
Affiliated groups subject to the 100% deduction (section 243(a)(3))		100	
Other dividends from foreign corporations not included in lines 4 and 5			
Income from controlled foreign corporations under subpart F (attach Forms 5471) .			
Foreign dividend gross-up (section 78)			
IC–DISC or former DISC dividends not included in lines 1 and/or 2 (section 246(d)) .			
Other dividends			░░░░░░
Deduction for dividends paid on certain preferred stock of public utilities (see instructions)	░░░░░░	░░░░░░	░░░░░░
Total dividends—Add lines 1 through 12. Enter here and on line 4, page 1 . . . ▶		░░░░░░	░░░░░░
Total deductions—Add lines 6, 7, and 13. Enter here and on line 29b, page 1 . . . . ▶			

Schedule E — Compensation of Officers (See instructions for line 12, page 1)

Complete Schedule E only if total receipts (line 1a, plus lines 4 through 10, of page 1, Form 1120) are $150,000 or more.

(a) Name of officer	(b) Social security number	(c) Percent of time devoted to business	Percent of corporation stock owned (d) Common	(e) Preferred	(f) Amount of compensation
		%	%	%	
		%	%	%	
		%	%	%	
		%	%	%	
		%	%	%	
		%	%	%	
		%	%	%	

Total compensation of officers—Enter here and on line 12, page 1. . . . .

Schedule F — Bad Debts—Reserve Method (See instructions for line 15, page 1)

Year	(b) Trade notes and accounts receivable outstanding at end of year	(c) Sales on account	Amount added to reserve (d) Current year's provision	(e) Recoveries	(f) Amount charged against reserve	(g) Reserve for bad debts at end of year
31						
32						
33						
34						
35						
36						

Form 1120 (1986)   Page **3**

Schedule J | **Tax Computation** (See instructions) (Fiscal year corporations see page 12 of instructions before completing Schedule J)

1 Check if you are a member of a controlled group (see sections 1561 and 1563) . . . . ▶ ☐

2a If line 1 is checked, see instructions. Enter your portion of each $25,000 taxable income bracket amount:

   (i) $ _____ (ii) $ _____ (iii) $ _____ (iv) $ _____

   b If your tax year includes July 1, 1987, see instructions and enter share of tax bracket amounts

   (i) _____ (ii) _____

3 Income tax (see instructions) to figure the tax; enter this tax or alternative tax, whichever is less). Check if alternative tax is used ▶ ☐ . . . . | **3** |

4a Foreign tax credit (attach Form 1118) . . . . | **4a** |

   b Possessions tax credit (attach Form 5735) . . . . . . | **b** |

   c Orphan drug credit (attach Form 6765) . . . . | **c** |

   d Credit for fuel produced from a nonconventional source (see instructions) . . . . | **d** |

   e General business credit. Enter here and check which forms are attached ☐ Form 3800 ☐ Form 3468 ☐ Form 5884 ☐ Form 6478 ☐ Form 8007 ☐ Form 6765 ☐ Form 8586 . | **e** |

5 Total—Add lines 4a through 4e . . . . | **5** |

6 Line 3 less line 5 . . . . | **6** |

7 Personal holding company tax (attach Schedule PH (Form 1120)) . . . . | **7** |

8 Tax from recomputing prior-year investment credit (attach Form 4255) . . . | **8** |

9 Minimum tax on tax preference items (see instructions—attach Form 4626) . . | **9** |

10 Total tax—Add lines 6 through 9. Enter here and on line 31, page 1 . . . . . | **10** |

Additional Information (See instruction F)   Yes | No

H Did the corporation claim a deduction for expenses connected with:

   (1) Entertainment facility (boat, resort, ranch, etc.)? . .

   (2) Living accommodations (except employees on business)? . .

   (3) Employees attending conventions or meetings outside the North American area? (See section 274(h).) . . . .

   (4) Employees' families at conventions or meetings? . .

   If "Yes," were any of these conventions or meetings outside the North American area? (See section 274(h).) . . . .

   (5) Employee or family vacations not reported on Form W-2? . .

I (1) Did the corporation at the end of the tax year own, directly or indirectly, 50% or more of the voting stock of a domestic corporation? (For rules of attribution, see section 267(c).) . .

   If "Yes," attach a schedule showing: (a) name, address, and identifying number; (b) percentage owned; (c) taxable income or (loss) before NOL and special deductions (e.g., if a Form 1120: from Form 1120, line 28, page 1) of such corporation for the tax year ending with or within your tax year; (d) highest amount owed by the corporation to such corporation during the year; and (e) highest amount owed to the corporation by such corporation during the year.

   (2) Did any individual, partnership, corporation, estate, or trust at the end of the tax year own, directly or indirectly, 50% or more of the corporation's voting stock? (For rules of attribution, see section 267(c).) If "Yes," complete (a) through (e). . . .

   (a) Attach a schedule showing name, address, and identifying number.

   (b) Enter percentage owned ▶ _____

   (c) Was the owner of such voting stock a person other than a U.S. person? (See instructions.) **Note:** If "Yes," the corporation may have to file Form 5472. . . . .

   If "Yes," enter owner's country ▶ _____

   (d) Enter highest amount owed by the corporation to such owner during the year ▶ _____

(e) Enter highest amount owed to the corporation by such owner during the year ▶ _____   Yes | No

Note: For purposes of I(1) and I(2), "highest amount owed" includes loans and accounts receivable/payable.

J Refer to the list in the instructions and state the principal:

   Business activity ▶ _____

   Product or service ▶ _____

K Was the corporation a U.S. shareholder of any controlled foreign corporation? (See sections 951 and 957.) . . . .

   If "Yes," attach Form 5471 for each such corporation.

L At any time during the tax year, did the corporation have an interest in or a signature or other authority over a financial account in a foreign country (such as a bank account, securities account, or other financial account)? . . . .

   (See instruction F and filing requirements for form TD F 90-22.1.)

   If "Yes," enter name of foreign country ▶ _____

M Was the corporation the grantor of, or transferor to, a foreign trust which existed during the current tax year, whether or not the corporation has any beneficial interest in it? . . . .

   If "Yes," the corporation may have to file Forms 3520, 3520-A, or 926.

N During this tax year, did the corporation pay dividends (other than stock dividends and distributions in exchange for stock) in excess of the corporation's current and accumulated earnings and profits? (See sections 301 and 316.) . . . .

   If "Yes," file Form 5452. If this is a consolidated return, answer here for parent corporation and on Form 851, Affiliations Schedule, for each subsidiary.

O During this tax year did the corporation maintain any part of its accounting/tax records on a computerized system? . . . .

P Check method of accounting:

   (1) ☐ Cash

   (2) ☐ Accrual

   (3) ☐ Other (specify) ▶ _____

Q Check this box if the corporation issued publicly offered debt instruments with original issue discount . . . . . ☐

   If so, the corporation may have to file Form 8281.

hedule L **Balance Sheets**		Beginning of tax year		End of tax year	
Assets	**(a)**	**(b)**	**(c)**	**(d)**	
Cash					
Trade notes and accounts receivable . . .					
a Less allowance for bad debts					
Inventories.					
Federal and state government obligations . .					
Other current assets (attach schedule). . .					
Loans to stockholders					
Mortgage and real estate loans					
Other investments (attach schedule) . . .					
Buildings and other depreciable assets . . .					
a Less accumulated depreciation					
Depletable assets					
a Less accumulated depletion					
Land (net of any amortization)					
Intangible assets (amortizable only)					
a Less accumulated amortization					
Other assets (attach schedule)					
Total assets					
Liabilities and Stockholders' Equity					
Accounts payable					
Mortgages, notes, bonds payable in less than 1 year					
Other current liabilities (attach schedule) . .					
Loans from stockholders					
Mortgages, notes, bonds payable in 1 year or more					
Other liabilities (attach schedule)					
Capital stock: a Preferred stock					
b Common stock					
Paid-in or capital surplus					
Retained earnings—Appropriated (attach schedule)					
Retained earnings—Unappropriated . . .					
Less cost of treasury stock.		( )		( )	
Total liabilities and stockholders' equity . .					

hedule M-1 **Reconciliation of Income per Books With Income per Return**
Do not complete this schedule if the total assets on line 14, column (d), of Schedule L are less than $25,000.

		7 Income recorded on books this year not
Net income per books		included in this return (itemize)
Federal income tax		a Tax-exempt interest $_____
Excess of capital losses over capital gains . .		_____
Income subject to tax not recorded on books		_____
this year (itemize) _____		8 Deductions in this tax return not charged
		against book income this year (itemize)
Expenses recorded on books this year not		a Depreciation $_____
deducted in this return (itemize)		b Contributions carryover $_____
a Depreciation $_____		_____
b Contributions carryover $_____		_____
_____		9 Total of lines 7 and 8 . . . . .
Total of lines 1 through 5		10 Income (line 28, page 1)—line 6 less line 9 .

hedule M-2 **Analysis of Unappropriated Retained Earnings per Books (line 24, Schedule L)**
Do not complete this schedule if the total assets on line 14, column (d), of Schedule L are less than $25,000.

		5 Distributions: a Cash . . . . .
Balance at beginning of year		b Stock . . . .
Net income per books		c Property . . . .
Other increases (itemize) _____		6 Other decreases (itemize)_____
_____		_____
_____		_____
_____		7 Total of lines 5 and 6 . . . . .
Total of lines 1, 2, and 3		8 Balance at end of year (line 4 less line 7)

Effective July 1, 1987, the tax rates for corporations were reduced. The new rates of tax are:

15% on the first $50,000 of income;

25% on the next $25,000 of income; and

34% on any amount over $75,000.

Also, an additional tax of 5% is applied against income in excess of $100,000. The maximum amount of this additional tax is $11,750. In addition, different rules apply for computing the alternative tax on net capital gains for fiscal year corporations that ha a tax year that includes January 1, 1987. These rules are explained in the instructions that follow Schedule B. If the corporation's fiscal tax year includes July 1, 1987, the tax liability shall be computed by completing Schedules A and B of the worksheet below. I the corporation's tax year ends on or before June 30, 1987, only Schedule A must be completed. Supplemental Instructions for completing Schedules A and B follow Schedule B.

Fiscal year corporations complete the following schedules to determine tax liability.

Schedule A   **Tax Computed for Period Before July 1, 1987**

1	Taxable income (line 30, Form 1120, or line 26, Form 1120-A).
2	Net capital gain income from line 10a, Schedule D (Form 1120), if applicable (see instructions)
3	Subtract line 2 from line 1.
4	Enter the lesser of line 3 or $25,000 (members of a controlled group, see instructions)
5	Subtract line 4 from line 3.
6	Enter the lesser of line 5 or $25,000 (members of a controlled group, see instructions)
7	Subtract line 6 from line 5.
8	Enter the lesser of line 7 or $25,000 (members of a controlled group, see instructions)
9	Subtract line 8 from line 7.
10	Enter the lesser of line 9 or $25,000 (members of a controlled group, see instructions)
11	Subtract line 10 from line 9
12	Multiply line 4 times 15%.
13	Multiply line 6 times 18%.
14	Multiply line 8 times 30%.
15	Multiply line 10 times 40%.
16	Multiply line 11 times 46%
17	If line 3 is greater than $1,000,000, enter the lesser of: (a) 5% of the excess of line 3 over $1,000,000 or (b) $20,250 (members of a controlled group, see instructions). Fiscal year corporations whose tax years end after June 30, 1987, skip lines 18 and 19, and complete Schedule B of this worksheet
18	Alternative tax on net capital gain from the worksheet on page 13
19	Add amounts on lines 12 through 18
	Fiscal year corporations whose tax years end before July 1, 1987, enter the tax liability before credits (line 19) on line 1, Part I, Form 1120-A, or line 3, Schedule J, Form 1120. Do **Not** complete Schedule B.

Schedule B   **Tax Computed for Period After June 30, 1987**

20	Enter amount from line 3, Schedule A.
21	Enter the lesser of line 20 or $50,000 (members of a controlled group, see instructions)
22	Subtract line 21 from line 20.
23	Enter the lesser of line 22 or $25,000 (members of a controlled group, see instructions)
24	Subtract line 23 from line 22.
25	Multiply line 21 times 15%
26	Multiply line 23 times 25%
27	Multiply line 24 times 34%
28	Additional tax. If line 20 is more than $100,000, enter the lesser of: (a) 5% of the excess of line 20 over $100,000 or (b) $11,750.
29	Add lines 25 through 28
30	Add lines 12 through 17, Schedule A
31	Line 30 × $\dfrac{\text{number of days in tax year before 7-1-87}}{\text{number of days in tax year}}$
32	Line 29 × $\dfrac{\text{number of days in tax year after 6-30-87}}{\text{number of days in tax year}}$
33	Alternative tax on net capital gain from the worksheet on page 13
34	Tax liability before credits. Add amounts on lines 31, 32, and 33. Enter here and on line 3, Schedule J, Form 1120, or on line 1, Part I, Form 1120-A

"At Risk" Rules To Apply to Real Property.—The "at risk" rules of section 465 apply to real property acquired after 1986. For more information, see section 465 and **Form 6198**, Computation of Deductible Loss From an Activity Described in Section 465(c).

New Low-Income Housing Credit.—A new low-income housing credit applies to certain buildings placed in service after 1986. See Form 8586 and section 42 for rules and computations.

Investment Tax Credit for Rehabilitation Expenditures.—An investment tax credit will be allowed for qualified rehabilitation expenditures made to property placed in service after 1986. See Form 3468.

Repeal of ESOP Credit.—The credit for contributions to an employee stock ownership plan (ESOP) has been repealed for compensation paid or accrued after December 31, 1986.

Information Reporting on Royalties.—Reporting requirements for payers of royalties have been changed for payments made after December 31, 1986. Information reporting is required on a royalty payment of $10 or more to a payee. See new section 6050N.

Alternative Tax for Fiscal Year Corporation.—Generally, the alternative tax has been repealed for tax years beginning after 1986. However, transitional rules allow fiscal year corporations to compute the alternative tax. The alternative tax computation for fiscal year corporations is (a) 28% of the lesser of: the net capital gain determined by taking into account only gain and loss for the portion of the tax year before January 1, 1987, or the net capital gain for the tax year, plus (b) 34% of the excess of the net capital gain for the tax year over the amount of net capital gain taken into account in (a) above. See section 1201.

The following provisions begin in 1987 and affect calendar year 1987 tax returns.

Revolving Credit Sales.—For tax years beginning after 1986, corporations that sell personal property on a revolving credit plan will not be permitted to account for such sales on the installment method. Any adjustment resulting from the corporation's not being able to use the installment method will be treated as a change in method of accounting for the first tax year beginning after December 31, 1986, and the period for taking into account adjustments under section 481 shall not exceed 4 years. This change in method of accounting will be treated as initiated by the corporation and as having been made with the consent of the Secretary. See sections 453 and 453A for more information.

Reserve Method for Bad Debts.—For tax years beginning after 1986 only certain financial institutions will be able to use the reserve method of computing bad debts. All other taxpayers must use the specific charge-off method for computing bad debts. Corporations not entitled to use the reserve method must include in income any amount remaining in the reserve as income ratably over a 4 year period.

For additional information, see sections 166, 585, and 593.

Also, for tax years beginning after 1986, section 586, reserve for losses on loans of small business corporations, etc., has been repealed.

Limitation on Net Operating Loss Carryovers.—The amount of net operating loss carryovers is limited when there has been a change in ownership or equity for net operating losses incurred after 1986. The limitation is described in section 382(b) and applies generally when a 5% shareholder or group of 5% shareholders increases its or their ownership in a corporation by more than 50 percentage points, or when there has been a change in equity. See section 382 for rules and definitions.

Limitation on Certain Excess Credits.—For certain ownership changes occurring after 1986, a change in ownership of a corporation will result in the amount of the following excess credits being limited for subsequent years: the unused general business credit, any unused minimum tax credit, and any capital loss carryover. The foreign tax credit carryover is also limited. See section 383 for more information.

Meals, Travel, and Entertainment Expenses.—For tax years beginning after 1986, many of the rules on what are allowable expenses for meals, entertainment, travel, and certain other business expenses have been changed. See section 274.

Meals and entertainment. The amount deductible for meals and entertainment expenses is generally limited to 80% of the amount otherwise allowable. In addition, meals must not be lavish or extravagant; a bona fide business discussion must precede or directly follow the meal; and your employee must be present at the meal. If the corporation claims a deduction for unallowable meal expenses, it may have to pay a penalty.

Limits on Losses and Credits From Passive Activities of Personal Service Corporations and Closely Held Corporations.—For tax years beginning after 1986, losses from passive trade or business activities generally may not offset active business income. Credits from passive activities generally are limited to tax allocable to the passive activities. See section 469 for more detailed information.

Reporting of Tax-Exempt Interest.—For tax years beginning after 1986, any taxpayer required to file a tax return must report, as an item of information, on that return the amount of the tax-exempt interest received or accrued during the tax year.

Taxable Year of Personal Service Corporations.—For tax years beginning after 1986, all personal service corporations are generally required to adopt the calendar year. See section 441.

Real Estate Mortgage Investment Conduits.—For tax years beginning after 1986, new code section 860A requires that real estate mortgage investment conduits (REMICs) allocate their income to their interest holders. REMICs may take the form of a corporation, partnership, or trust. See section 860A through 860G for rules, definitions, and other information.

Regulated Investment Companies.—Regulated investment companies are subject to a 4% excise tax for tax years beginning after 1986. For more information, see new code section 4982.

Cooperative Housing Corporations.—For tax years beginning after 1986, corporations, trusts, and other nonindividual persons may be tenant-stockholders in a cooperative housing corporation. Additionally, the method for computing the tenant-stockholder's interest and taxes is changed for tax years beginning after 1986. See section 216 for more information.

Minimum Tax.—For tax years beginning after 1986, the add-on minimum tax will be replaced by an alternative minimum tax based on alternative minimum taxable income. A corporation will have to compute its tax under the regular system and under the minimum tax provisions. See sections 55 through 59 for more information. For tax years beginning after 1986, corporations must take minimum tax into account when computing estimated tax. See 1987 Form 1120W for more information.

Certain Entities Required To Use the Accrual Method of Accounting.—Generally, C corporations, partnerships with C corporations as partners, tax-exempt entities with unrelated business income, and tax shelters are prohibited from using the cash method of accounting for tax years beginning after 1986. See new section 448.

Special Rule for Dividends Received From Foreign Corporation (Section 245).—For tax years beginning after 1986, only corporations that own at least 10% of stock (by vote and value) of a foreign corporation are entitled to claim the section 245 dividends-received deductions. To obtain the proper amount of deduction, the 10% owner should see section 245.

For additional information on these changes, see **Publication 553**, Highlights of 1986 Tax Changes.

Form **1120-A**	**U.S. Corporation Short-Form Income Tax Return** To see if you qualify to file Form 1120-A, see instructions.	1235

Department of the Treasury
Internal Revenue Service

For calendar 1986 or tax year beginning _____, 1986, ending _____, 19____
▶ **Fiscal Year Corporations See Instructions Before Computing Tax.**

OMB No. 1545-0890

1986

	A Activity	Use IRS label. Other-wise, please type or machine print	Name		D Employer identification number (EIN)
See Instruc-tions for list of principal business:	B Product or service		Number and street		E Date incorporated
	C Code		City or town, state, and ZIP code		F Total assets (see Specific Instructions)

			Dollars	Cents
			$	

G Check method of accounting: **(1)** ☐ Cash **(2)** ☐ Accrual **(3)** ☐ Other (specify) ▶ _____ ▶

H Check box if there has been a change in address from the previous year . . . . ▶

Income

1a	Gross receipts or sales _____ **b** Less returns and allowances _____ Balance ▶	1c
2	Cost of goods sold and/or operations (see instructions)	2
3	Gross profit (line 1c less line 2)	3
4	Domestic corporation dividends subject to the Section 243(a)(1) deduction	4
5	Interest	5
6	Gross rents	6
7	Gross royalties	7
8	Capital gain net income (attach separate Schedule D (Form 1120))	8
9	Net gain or (loss) from Form 4797, line 17, Part II (attach Form 4797)	9
10	Other income (see instructions)	10
11	TOTAL income—Add lines 3 through 10	11

Deductions

12	Compensation of officers (see instructions)	12
13a	Salaries and wages _____ **b** Less jobs credit _____ Balance ▶	13c
14	Repairs	14
15	Bad debts (if reserve method is used, answer Question K on page 2)	15
16	Rents	16
17	Taxes	17
18	Interest	18
19	Contributions **(see instructions for 10% limitation)**	19
20	Depreciation (attach Form 4562)	20	
21	Less depreciation claimed elsewhere on return	21a	21b
22	Other deductions (attach schedule)	22
23	TOTAL deductions—Add lines 12 through 22	23
24	Taxable income before net operating loss deduction and special deductions (line 11 less line 23) . . .	24
25	**Less: a** Net operating loss deduction (see instructions)	25a	
	b Special deductions (see instructions)	25b	25c

26	Taxable income (line 24 less line 25c)	26
27	TOTAL TAX (from Part I, line 6 on page 2)	27

Tax and Payments

28 **Payments:**

a	1985 overpayment allowed as a credit		
b	1986 estimated tax payments		
c	Less 1986 refund applied for on Form 4466 . . . ( )		
d	Tax deposited with Form 7004		
e	Credit from regulated investment companies (attach Form 2439)		
f	Credit for Federal tax on gasoline and special fuels (attach Form 4136) . . .		28
29	Enter any **PENALTY** for underpayment of estimated tax—Check ▶ ☐ if Form 2220 is attached . .		29
30	**TAX DUE**—If the total of lines 27 and 29 is larger than line 28, enter AMOUNT OWED		30
31	**OVERPAYMENT**—If line 28 is larger than the total of lines 27 and 29, enter AMOUNT OVERPAID . . .		31
32	Enter amount of line 31 you want: **Credited to 1987 estimated tax** ▶ _____ Refunded ▶		32

Please Sign Here

Under penalties of perjury, I declare that I have examined this return, including accompanying schedules and statements, and to the best of my knowledge and belief, it is true, correct, and complete. Declaration of preparer (other than taxpayer) is based on all information of which preparer has any knowledge.

▶ _____   ▶
Signature of officer   Date   Title

Paid Preparer's Use Only

Preparer's signature ▶	Date	Check if self-employed ▶ ☐	Preparer's social security number
Firm's name (or yours, if self-employed) and address ▶		E.I. No. ▶ ZIP code ▶	

For Paperwork Reduction Act Notice, see page 1 of the instructions.   Form **1120-A** (1986) m 1120-A (1986)   **Part I**   **Tax Computation (See Instructions)** Page 2   Enter EIN ▶

Income tax (See instructions to figure the tax. Enter lesser of this tax or alternative tax.) Check if alternative tax was used ▶ ☐	1
Credits. Check if from ☐ Form 3800 ☐ Form 3468 ☐ Form 5884 ☐ Form 6478 ☐ Form 8007 ☐ Form 6765 ☐ Form 8586	2
Line 1 less line 2	3
Tax from recomputing prior-year investment credit (attach Form 4255)	4
Minimum tax on tax preference items (see instructions—attach Form 4626)	5
Total tax—Add lines 3 through 5. Enter here and on line 27, page 1	6

Additional Information (See instruction F)

Was a deduction taken for expenses connected with:

(1) An entertainment facility (boat, resort, ranch, etc.)? Yes ☐   No ☐

(2) Employees' families at conventions or meetings?   Yes ☐ No ☐

Did any individual, partnership, estate, or trust at the end of the tax year own, directly or indirectly, 50% or more of the corporation's voting stock? (For rules of attribution, see section 267(c).) If "Yes," complete (1) and (2)   Yes ☐ No ☐

(1) Attach a schedule showing name, address, and identifying number.

(2) Enter "highest amount owed;" include loans and accounts receivable/payable:

  (a) Enter highest amount owed by the corporation to such owner during the year ▶

  (b) Enter highest amount owed to the corporation by such owner during the year ▶

If the reserve method is used for bad debts, complete (1) and (2) for the current year:

(1) Amount added to the reserve account:

  (a) Current year's provision ▶

(b) Recoveries ▶

(2) Amount charged against the reserve account ▶

L If an amount for cost of goods sold and/or operations is entered on line 2, page 1, complete (1) and (2):

(1) Purchases ▶

(2) Other costs (attach schedule) ▶

M At any time during the tax year, did you have an interest in or a signature or other authority over a financial account in a foreign country (such as a bank account, securities account, or other financial account)? (See instruction F for filing requirements for Form TD F 90-22.1.)   Yes ☐ No ☐

If "Yes," write in the name of the foreign country

▶

N During this tax year was any part of your accounting/tax records maintained on a computerized system?   Yes ☐ No ☐

O Enter amount of cash distributions and the book value of property (other than cash) distributions made in this tax year ▶

Part II   **Balance Sheets**

		(a) Beginning of tax year	(b) End of tax year
Assets			
1	Cash		
2	Trade notes and accounts receivable		
a	Less: allowance for bad debts	( )	( )
3	Inventories		
4	Federal and State government obligations		
5	Other current assets (attach schedule)		
6	Loans to stockholders		
7	Mortgage and real estate loans		
8	Depreciable, depletable, and intangible assets		
a	Less: accumulated depreciation, depletion, and amortization	( )	( )
9	Land (net of any amortization)		
10	Other assets (attach schedule)		
11	Total assets		
Stockholders' Equity			
12	Accounts payable		
13	Other current liabilities (attach schedule)		
14	Loans from stockholders		
15	Mortgages, notes, bonds payable		
16	Other liabilities (attach schedule)		
17	Capital stock (Preferred and Common stock)		
18	Paid-in or capital surplus		
19	Retained earnings		
20	Less cost of treasury stock	( )	( )
21	Total liabilities and stockholders' equity		

Part III   **Reconciliation of Income Per Books With Income Per Return (See Instructions)**

Enter net income per books		5 Income recorded on books this year not included in this return (itemize)	
Federal income tax			
Income subject to tax not recorded on books this year (itemize)		6 Deductions in this tax return not charged against book income this year (itemize)	
Expenses recorded on books this year not deducted in this return (itemize)		7 Income (line 24, page 1). Enter the sum of lines 1, 2, 3, and 4 less the sum of lines 5 and 6	

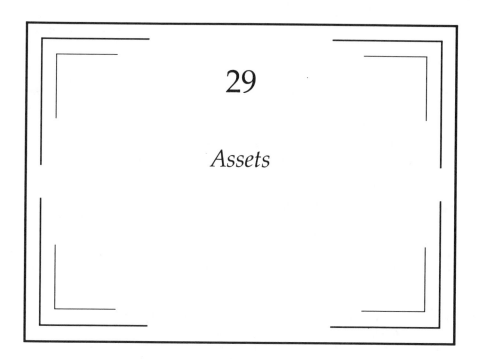

29

Assets

CASH

Where the corporation has accumulated large amounts of cash, the possibility of the imposition of the accumulated earnings penalty should be checked. The penalty may be avoided if this situation can be corrected in time.

The penalty is not imposed if the accumulation is reasonable for purposes of carrying out the financial needs of the business. Also, the penalty may be avoided by a timely distribution of dividends or by a timely Subchapter S election.

Note that the accumulation problem can not be avoided by the investment of excess cash in tax-exempt bonds. Although the tax-exempt interest is not subject to the penalty, its accumulation may cause the imposition of the penalty.

Where the corporation's cash position is meager, the company might consider the use of a sale-leaseback of its plant or other real estate. This may produce additional funds from two sources: (1) from the sale of proceeds, and (2) from the tax benefits that may be derived from rental payments. There would be a tax benefit to the extent that the rental payments exceed the depreciation that the company was taking on the fixed assets.

Note that for cash basis taxpayers, certain types of income are considered to be constructively received for tax purposes, such as; interest credited on bank accounts, and matured interest coupons.

ACCUMULATED EARNINGS TAX

An accumulated earnings tax is imposed on corporations that are formed for the purpose of avoiding the income tax with respect to shareholders, by permitting earnings and profits of the corporation to accumulate instead of being distributed. Where applicable, the tax is 27½ percent of the first $100,000 of accumulated taxable income for the taxable year and a rate of 38½ percent on accumulated taxable income in excess of $100,000.

The term "accumulated taxable income" means taxable income, with certain adjustments, less the accumulated earnings credit, reduced by a deduction for dividends paid. The accumulated earnings credit allowed is the *greater* of (1) Earnings and profits of the tax year retained for the reasonable needs of the business *minus* net capital gains (reduced by the tax on such gains); or (2) $250,000 ($150,000 for certain personal service corporations) *minus* (accumulated earnings and profits at the end of preceding tax year reduced by dividends paid during the first 2½ months of the tax year). In determining accumulated taxable income, a corporation is permitted a deduction for net capital losses during the year in question. A corporation is also permitted a deduction for net capital gains during the year determined without regard to capital loss carryover or carrybacks, less certain taxes.

Whether or not a widely held corporation is subject to the accumulated earnings tax has been an unresolved issue, because no individual or small group of individuals was considered by the courts to have effective control of a widely held company, in contrast to one controlled by a few shareholders.

Under the new law, the fact that a corporation is widely held will not exempt it from the accumulated earnings tax.

The Act changes the determination of accumulated taxable income. The deduction from accumulated taxable income for net capital gains, less certain taxes, remains the same. However, in determining net capital gains for this purpose, net capital losses for any taxable year are treated as short-term capital losses during the next taxable year. The deduction for net capital losses also generally remains, but the deduction is reduced by any deduction from adjusted taxable income for net capital gains, less certain taxes, for preceding years beginning after July 18, 1984. No such net capital gains, less certain taxes, are to be used to reduce the deduction for net capital losses more than once. In the case of corporations other than mere holding or investment companies, net capital loss carryovers are to be used only once in determining accumulated taxable income.*

ACCOUNTS RECEIVABLE

Here tax savings may be realized by switching to a more advantageous method of reporting income. A change to the installment method of reporting sales may defer

Interest on accumulated earnings tax underpayments will be charged from the date of the return, instead of from the date the IRS demanded payment of the tax.

taxes for a company that sells its products on an installment basis. This option is available under either cash or accrual method.**

An installment sale is defined by the regulations as a "disposition of property where at least one payment is to be received after the close of the year in which the disposition occurs." The installment method permits the taxpayer to spread the income over the time-period of the installment contract. The logic underlying the regulation is that a taxpayer should not be expected to remit tax payments before receiving payment for the income on which the tax liability is based.

UNIFORM CAPITALIZATION RULE

Beginning after December 31, 1986, taxpayers must include in inventory both direct and indirect costs that are allocable to inventory valuation. While the IRS has required the full-absorption method since 1973, the capitalization rule will become, essentially, obsolete effective January 1, 1987. Primarily, the ending inventory computations will become more complicated.

A few of the items that will have to be factored into inventory costs are:

* Personnel costs associated with the purchasing function.
* Rent for warehousing and other off-site storage facilities.
* Personnel costs associated with invoice processing for purchases.
* Indirect materials and supplies, tools and equipment, quality control and inspection costs.
* Repairs.
* Maintenance.
* Utilities.
* Financial statement depreciation.
* Current costs of Pension and Profit Sharing Plans.
* Factory administrative expenses.
* Executive officers' salaries related to production.
* Direct and indirect service functions; i.e., payroll, accounting, purchasing, etc.

Under the old law, many of the above could be either expensed or capitalized, as long as the taxpayer used a consistent basis and in conformance with GAAP. Under the New Law, the items must be capitalized regardless of financial statement treatment.

In addition to the new rules to be applied for costs in taxable years beginning after December 31, 1986, ending inventory (which is the new beginning inventory)

**See App. B, p. xx for the changes in installment sales reporting.

in the last tax return to be filed under the old rules must be restated to apply the new capitalization rules retroactively. If, for example, a taxpayer adopted the dollar-value LIFO method ten years ago, then inventories will have to be recomputed for those ten years.

The effect of the retroactive adjustment will be to increase inventory and increase taxable income. The adjustment must be taken into income over a period not to exceed four years.

The simplified method. The New Law provides a simplified method for applying the uniform capitalization rules in the case of taxpayers acquiring property for resale. Taxpayers not electing to use the simplified method are required to apply the new rules to property acquired for resale under the same methods applicable to manufacturers. Once a taxpayer has chosen either the simplified method or the capitalization methods applicable to manufacturers, the method cannot be changed without obtaining the permission of the Treasury Department.

When applying the simplified method, taxpayers should initially calculate their inventory balances without regard to the new capitalization rules. Next, determine the amounts of additional costs that must be capitalized under the new rules and add the amounts, along with amounts of additional costs contained in beginning inventory balances where appropriate to the preliminary inventory balances to determine their final balances. With respect to a taxpayer using LIFO, the calculation of a particular year's LIFO index will be made without regard to the new rules. Costs capitalized under the new rules will then be added to the LIFO layers applicable to the various years for which the costs were accumulated. Likewise, if the FIFO method is used and the taxpayer does not sell the entire beginning inventory during the year, a proportionate part of the additional costs capitalized into the beginning inventory will be included in ending inventory.

An example of the arithmetic involved is illustrated using storage costs. Storage costs are included in inventory based on a ratio of total storage costs for the year to the sum of the beginning inventory balance and gross purchases during the year. Assume that a FIFO taxpayer incurred $1,000,000 of storage costs during the year, had a beginning inventory of $2,000,000, gross purchases of $8,000,000, and an ending inventory of $3,000,000.

$1,000,000/$10,000,000 = 0.10 so the taxpayer for each dollar of ending inventory must capitalize 10.0 of storage costs.

Ending inventory for the year is increased by $300,000, with the balance of the storage costs ($700,000) included in cost of goods sold.

If LIFO method is being used, to the extent that ending inventory exceeds beginning inventory additional capitalized storage costs would be calculated by multiplying the increase in inventory for the year by the applicable ratio. In the above example and under the LIFO method, an additional $100,000 (0.10 × $1,000,000) of storage costs would be included in ending inventory. Any storage costs that were included in the beginning balance would remain in the ending inventory balance and would therefore not be included in cost of goods sold for the year.

The uniform capitalization rules do not affect the valuation of inventories on a basis other than cost. The rules will not affect the valuation of inventories at market by a taxpayer using the lower of cost or market method, or by a dealer in securities or commodities using the market method. However, the rules will apply to inventories valued at cost using the lower of cost or market method.

Manufacturers must accumulate costs of producing inventory goods in an inventory account. Accumulated inventory costs may be deducted as the goods to which they relate are sold. Tax regulations provide for use of the "full absorption method" in determining which costs must be included in inventory; i.e., all direct production costs and labor directly contributing to the products manufacture must be inventoried, as well as the costs of materials incorporated into the product or consumed during production. The treatment of indirect production costs varies according to the nature of the costs, with some costs currently deductible, others are inventoriable, and others ("financial conformity" costs) are deductible only if deducted by the taxpayer for financial reporting purposes. Wholesalers and retailers must include in inventory the invoice price of the purchased goods plus transportation and other necessary costs incurred in acquiring possession. (The uniform capitalization rules do not apply to purchasers of goods for resale having average annual gross receipts not in excess of $10,000,000.)

INVENTORIES—NEW LAW

In an inflationary economy, a company will want to consider changing the method of valuation of inventories from FIFO to LIFO. The change, however, would affect the company's earnings for financial purposes because, if the company chooses to use LIFO for tax purposes, it *must* use the same method for financial reporting.

In the past, businesses were reluctant to adopt LIFO because of the complicated nature of the tax regulations associated with this method. The new tax law simplifies the requirements.

Particularly troublesome to small business was the IRS requirement that wholesalers, retailers, jobbers and distributors keep separate LIFO inventory accounts (termed "pools") for each product. After December 31, 1986, qualifying "small businesses," (defined as those with average annual gross receipts for the next preceding three years of $10 million or less), can elect the new "simplified method" of dollar value LIFO. In addition, a small business can use governmental indexes (under regulations yet to be issued) in pricing its inventory. (Note: The Treasury will issue appropriate governmental indexes to be applied. Formerly, businesses had to construct their own indices.) (App. B, p. xx.)

A taxpayer who uses inventories must use the accrual method of accounting.

Supplies are not, in themselves, inventoriable. They become so only when acquired for sale or to be physically a part of merchandise intended for sale.

If you use the lower of cost or market for valuing inventory, the tax rule is that each item must be taken into consideration separately—i.e., the cost and market of each item must be compared. The Treasury does not recognize the right to value aggregates of similar inventory items on a total cost or market, whichever is lower, basis.

Taxpayer can elect in the first return the method of valuing inventory which conforms to the best accounting practice in the trade or business and which clearly reflects taxable income. The usual methods are: (1) cost, and (2) cost or market, whichever is less.

Taxpayer can elect, in the first return, the method of measuring cost [by specific identification, first-in-first-out (FIFO), LIFO, etc.]. Elections can be changed only with Commissioner's permission.

The Treasury does *not* for manufacturers, allow the use of ''Prime Costing'' (no overhead in inventory) or ''Direct Costing'' (the inclusion of only variable overhead).

Retailers can elect to use the retail inventory method. Other options are available in certain specialized fields (farming, security dealers).

The last-in-first-out method (LIFO) can be elected by making application on Form 970, filed with the return for the first year the method is to be used.

Change of Inventory Method

Except for LIFO, which the taxpayer adopts by election, change in inventory method for tax purposes is treated as a change of accounting method, and the Commissioner's consent must be obtained. Since tax saving is not sufficient to justify a change, state in your request the business objective you seek to accomplish.

Recomputation of the opening inventory according to your new method will ordinarily be required.

Businesses that use LIFO must value their inventory at cost:

1. Any reductions of inventories, for whatever reason, must be restored to original cost.

2. Under the former rules, taxpayers had to report any adjustments as taxable income in the year prior to the election of LIFO. Under the Act, adjustments must be taken into income over a 3-year period beginning with the year LIFO is adopted.

3. The ''financial conformity'' rule was not repealed. This means the LIFO-FIFO earnings comparisons are prohibited.

Statements of an inventory valuation basis in the first return is a binding election, even if there is no difference at that time between this method and some other method you try to use later. If permission to change is granted, but you fail to make the change for the year approved, you must request permission again if you want to make the change in a later year. However, the Commissioner cannot take advantage of an oversight to force the use of an inconsistent method.

LIFO

For tax purposes, when LIFO is used, only cost—not the lower of cost or market—may be used.

The following LIFO rules pertain to the tax-law requirements. Since LIFO may be used for tax purposes only if also used in financial reports, the tax rules for LIFO influence the use of LIFO for financial reporting purposes, too.

How goods on LIFO are to be valued.

Goods comprising the beginning inventory of the first year on LIFO must be valued at average cost. The average cost of units in each inventory class is obtained by dividing the aggregate cost of this inventory class, computed according to the inventory method previously employed by the taxpayer, by the number of units on hand. In effect, each unit is considered to have been acquired at the same time.

Goods of a specified type on hand at the close of a taxable year are treated as being, first, those included in the opening inventory of the taxable year in the order of acquisition and, second, those acquired in the taxable year. The taxpayer is given permission to value any physical increment of goods of a specified type at costs determined in one of the following ways:

(a) By reference to the actual cost of the goods most recently purchased or produced;

(b) By reference to the actual cost of the goods purchased or produced during the taxable year in the order of acquisition;

(c) By application of an average unit cost equal to the aggregate cost of all of the goods purchased throughout the taxable year divided by the total number of units so purchased or produced, the goods reflected in such inventory increase being considered for the purposes of the LIFO rules as having all been acquired at the same time.

Retail LIFO for Department Stores

The Regulations permit department stores to use LIFO in connection with the retail method of inventory, on the basis of the semiannual price indices prepared by the Department of Labor.

The retail method of inventory valuation is suitable for retail establishments and businesses where selling prices are very closely related to cost. It isn't suitable to a manufacturing concern. It has found favor because it is relatively easy to use in the control of merchandise inventories, especially those that involve numerous items. For example, an average-sized supermarket has over 14,000 items on the shelves.

Where records of cost and selling prices are kept, this method permits a sound valuation for inventories. Compared with other methods, it is simple and inexpen-

Form **970** (Rev. April 1987) Department of the Treasury Internal Revenue Service	**Application To Use LIFO Inventory Method** ▶ **Attach to your tax return.** ▶ **For Paperwork Reduction Act Notice, see instructions on back.**	OMB No. 1545-0042 Expires 3-31-90

Name _____   Identifying number (See instructions) _____

Address (Number, street, city, state and ZIP code) _____

CHECK ONE:
☐ Initial Election
☐ Subsequent Election

Statement of Election and Other Information:

A The taxpayer applies to adopt and use the LIFO inventory method provided by section 472. The taxpayer will use this method for the first time (or modify this method) as of (date tax year ends) _____, for the following goods (give details as explained in instructions; use more sheets if necessary): _____

B The taxpayer agrees to make any adjustments that the District Director of Internal Revenue may require, on examination of the taxpayer's return, to reflect income clearly for the years involved in changing to or from the LIFO method or in using it.

1 Nature of business _____

2 a	Inventory method used until now		
b	Will inventory be taken at actual cost regardless of market value? If "No," attach explanation	☐ Yes	☐ No
3 a	Was the inventory of the specified goods valued at cost as of the beginning of the first tax year to which this application refers, as required by section 472(d)? If "No," attach explanation	☐ Yes	☐ No
b	Will you include in income over 3 tax years any adjustments that resulted from changing to LIFO? If "No," attach explanation	☐ Yes	☐ No
4 a	List goods subject to inventory that are not to be inventoried under the LIFO method.		
b	Were the goods of the specified type included in opening inventory counted as acquired at the same time and at a unit cost equal to the actual cost of the total divided by the number of units on hand? If "No," attach explanation	☐ Yes	☐ No
5 a	Did you issue credit statements, or reports to shareholders, partners, other proprietors, or beneficiaries covering the first tax year to which this application refers?	☐ Yes	☐ No
b	If "Yes," state to whom, and on what dates.		
c	Show the inventory method used in determining income, profit, or loss in those statements.		

6 a Check method used to figure the cost of the goods in the closing inventory over those in the opening inventory. (See instructions.)
☐ Most recent purchases   ☐ Earliest acquisitions during the year
☐ Average cost of purchases during the year   ☐ Other—Attach explanation

b The taxpayer selects the month of _____ as the appropriate representative month to be used in selecting the index or indexes to be used in determining the current-year cost of the taxpayer's inventory pool(s) under regulations section 1.472-8(e)(2)(ii) (see instructions).

7 Method used in valuing LIFO inventories: ☐ Unit method   ☐ Dollar-value method

8 a If you use pools, list and describe contents of each pool and, if applicable, the consumer or producer price index or indexes selected for each pool.

b ☐ As an eligible small business, the taxpayer has elected under section 474 to use the Simplified Dollar-Value LIFO Method.

c ☐ As a retailer, wholesaler, jobber, or distributor, the taxpayer selects the pooling method authorized by regulations section 1.472-8(e)(3)(iv).

d Describe briefly the cost system used.

e Method used in computing LIFO value of dollar-value pools (see instructions and attach required information):
☐ Double extension method   ☐ Published price index (describe)
☐ Other method (describe and justify)

9 Did you change your method of valuing inventories for this tax year with the Commissioner's permission?   ☐ Yes   ☐ No
If "Yes," attach a copy of the National Office's "grant letter" to this Form 970.

10 Were you ever on LIFO before?   ☐ Yes   ☐ No
If "Yes," attach a statement to list the tax years you used LIFO and to explain why you discontinued it.

Under penalties of perjury, I declare that I have examined this application, including any accompanying schedules and statements, and to the best of my knowledge and belief, it is true, correct, and complete.

_____   _____
Date   Signature of taxpayer

_____   _____   _____
Date   Signature of officer   Title

Form **970** (Rev. 4-87)

Form 970. Application to Use LIFO Inventory Method.

eneral Instructions

*ection references are to the Internal Revenue Code
nless otherwise noted.)*

aperwork Reduction Act Notice. — We ask for this
formation to carry out the Internal Revenue laws of the
nited States. We need it to ensure that taxpayers are
mplying with these laws and to allow us to figure and
llect the right amount of tax. You are required to give us
is information.

urpose of Form. — Form 970 is an optional form that you
n file with your income tax return to adopt or expand the
FO inventory method described in section 472. If you
refer, you can file a statement that gives the information
sked for on Form 970. (See regulations section 1.472-
(a).) File the application with your return for the first tax
ar for which you intend to use or expand the LIFO
ethod.

**ew Simplified Dollar-Value LIFO Method Available to
ertain Small Businesses (item 8b).** — The Tax Reform
ct of 1986 added a new category to the LIFO inventory
ethod, Simplified Dollar-Value LIFO method. Only small
usinesses whose average annual gross receipts for the
ree preceding tax years did not exceed $5,000,000 may
ect to use this method. If the taxpayer is a member of a
ontrolled group, the gross receipts of the group are used to
etermine if the taxpayer qualifies. The new method
quires that the taxpayer maintain a separate inventory
ool for items in each major category in the applicable
overnment price index, and that the taxpayer make
djustments to each separate pool based on changes from
e preceding tax year in the component of such index for
e major category. The qualified taxpayer does not need
e consent of the Secretary to elect these provisions. The
ection is in effect for the first year the election is made
nd for each succeeding year the taxpayer qualifies as an
igible small business. The election may be revoked only
ith the consent of the Secretary. The Simplified Dollar-
alue LIFO method applies for tax years beginning after
986.

rotective Election. — A protective election in connection
ith section 95 of the Tax Reform Act of 1984 (P.L. 98-
69) may be made by completing and filing Form 970 as
ecified in temporary regulations section 5h.4(g). Write
Protective Election Under Regulations 5h.4(g)" at the top
f the Form 970 you file to make this election. This election
ust be made for your first tax year beginning after July
8, 1984.

hange from LIFO Method. — Once you adopt the LIFO
ethod, it is irrevocable unless the Commissioner allows
ou to change to another method.

pecific Instructions

dentifying Number. — An individual's identifying number
the social security number. For all others it is the
mployer identification number.

Initial Election or Subsequent Election. — If this is your
first election to use the LIFO method, check the box for
Initial Election. If you are expanding a prior LIFO election,
check the box for Subsequent Election.

Statement of Election and Other Information. — If this is
an initial election, enter the tax year you will first use the
LIFO method and specify the goods to which you will apply
it. If this is a subsequent election, enter the tax year you will
expand the LIFO method and specify the goods to which
the LIFO method is being expanded.

Attach a detailed analysis of all your inventories as of the
beginning and end of the first tax year for which you will use
the LIFO method (tax year for which the LIFO method is
being expanded if this is a subsequent election) and as of
the beginning of the preceding tax year. Also, include the
ending inventory reported on your return for the preceding
tax year. Regulations sections 1.472-2 and 1.472-3 give
more information about preparing this analysis.

Item 6a. — See regulations sections 1.472-2 and
1.472-8(e) for more information.

Item 6b. — See regulations section
1.472-8(e)(3)(iii)(C) before completing item 6b.

Item 8a. — To adopt and use the inventory price index
computation method provided by regulations section
1.472-8(e)(3), you must enter in item 8a a list of each
inventory pool, the type of goods included in each pool, and
the consumer or producer price index or indexes selected
for each inventory pool. If more space is needed, attach a
schedule showing the information.

Item 8b. — Check item 8b if you have made the section
474 election to use the Simplified Dollar-Value LIFO
method. See section 474 for additional details.

Item 8c. — Check item 8c to select the pooling method
authorized by regulations section 1.472-8(e)(3)(iv). See the
regulations for additional details.

Item 8e. — You may use the "dollar-value" LIFO method to
determine the cost of your LIFO inventories as long as you
use it consistently and it clearly reflects income.
Regulations section 1.472-8 gives details about this
method.

If you are a wholesaler, retailer, jobber, or distributor,
see regulations section 1.472-8(c) for guidelines on
establishing dollar-value LIFO pools.

To figure the LIFO value of a dollar-value pool, use a
method described in regulations section 1.472-8(e). If you
do not use the "double-extension" or "index" method,
attach a detailed statement to explain the method you do
use and how it is justified under regulations section 1.472-
8(e)(1). For example, if you use a "link-chain" method,
your statement should explain why the nature of the pool
makes the other two methods impractical or unsuitable.

Signature. — Form 970 must be signed. If you are filing for
a corporation, the form must be signed by the president,
vice president, treasurer, assistant treasurer, chief
accounting officer, or other corporate officer (such as tax
officer) authorized to sign.

☆ U.S. Government Printing Office: 1987—181-447/40141

sive. Valuation is made by converting the current indicated retail value of an inventory into its related costs. Advantages are: (1) inventory for statement purposes can be obtained without a physical count; (2) the cost of each item of purchase is avoided; (3) ratios for merchandise turnover are more dependable because more inventory figures are available for ascertainment of average inventory methods.

LIFO for Subsidiary Using FIFO

IRS says that an affiliated group may use the FIFO method of valuing the inventory of one of its members in preparing *consolidated financial statements* for credit purposes and for the purpose of reporting to stockholders even though the member corporation uses the LIFO method for tax purposes. While the rule requires the sub to use the LIFO method *in its financial statements* used for purposes of credit or stockholders, it does not require that the *consolidated statements* of the affiliated group be restricted in this same manner. The requirements of the statute are satisfied as long as the subsidiary uses a consistent method for valuing its inventory.

Changes in LIFO Reserves

A corporation's earnings and profits are to be increased by the amount of any increase in the corporation's LIFO reserve for a taxable year. In addition, earnings and profits are to be decreased by the amount of any decrease in the corporation's LIFO reserve for a taxable year. However, decreases in reserve amounts below the LIFO reserve as of the beginning of the taxable year, beginning after the date of enactment of the new law, will not—except as provided by regulations—reduce earnings and profits.

In general, earnings and profits are to be increased or decreased by the amount of any increase or decrease in the LIFO recapture amount. This provision is designed to eliminate the impact of LIFO on earnings and profits.

An exception is provided, under regulations, for decreases below the amount of the reserve as of the close of the taxable year of the taxpayer, preceding the first taxable year to which the provision applies. Since the cumulative effect of the LIFO reserve has been to keep earnings and profits lower than they otherwise would have been, it is contemplated that the regulations will provide that in the event of a reduction in the LIFO reserve below its level as of the close of such taxable year (the pre-enactment reserve), earnings and profits will be increased as under present law without any offsetting reduction under the new rules. However, because a reduction in the reserve below the pre-enactment results in an increase in taxable income and earnings and profits, any subsequent restoration of the reserve up to the level of the pre-enactment reserve should result in an adjustment under the new rules.

SECURITIES AND OTHER INTANGIBLES

Account for all on hand at beginning of year. Analyze acquisitions and dispositions during the year for gain or loss, long-term or short-term (depending on holding period). Determine whether any securities were written off as worthless during the year.

Income from investments may be increased by switching from taxable bonds paying ordinary interest to tax-exempt bonds. Also, switching from interest-bearing securities to dividend-paying stocks may boost income because of the special 80 percent dividend-received deduction. When the switch produces a capital loss, the loss may be carried back for a quick carryback refund (not, however, to increase a net operating loss of a carryback year).

Owning less than 80% of another company may provide tax savings through dividend deductions. But owning at least 80% of a company provides the special privilege of filing consolidated returns. Affiliated corporations which do not file consolidated returns are allowed a 100% deduction for "qualifying" dividends (as defined in the regulations) received from affiliates.

PROPERTY, PLANT, AND EQUIPMENT

Accelerated Cost Recovery System (ACRS)

Congress recognized, when passing the Tax Act of 1981, that the useful-life depreciation rules developed over the past 50 years had become obsolete and very complex in their application. They, therefore, replaced the old system with a new one called the "accelerated cost recovery system" (ACRS).

Depreciation and Investment Credit

The *Capital Recovery* requirements of the New Law includes a number of significant changes for the calculation of depreciation under the Accelerated Cost Recovery System (ACRS) for buildings, machinery, and equipment. There is also a change in the availability of the Investment Tax Credit (ITC) for the acquisition of business machinery and equipment. The new rules are generally effective for property (buildings, machinery, and equipment) placed in service after 1986. (App. B, p. 596.)

SUMMARY

- The New Law assigns property classes, using the Asset Depreciation Range (ADR). Deductions for depreciation are calculated by writing off the basis of the asset over specified recovery periods for each property class, instead of by statutory percentages or by using conventions.
- For three-, five-, and ten-year recovery classes, the depreciation schedules have been shortened.
- Seven- and twenty-year property classes have been added.

- Real property *must* be calculated under the straight-method over extended recovery periods.
- Deductions can also be computed applying the straightline method over the applicable recovery period.
- The election to expense depreciable assets has been modified.
- ACRS method can be applied to used property. The recovery methods and periods the same as for new property.
- Salvage value is not included in the ACRS computation.
- The ten percent investment tax credit (ITC) is generally repealed for property placed in service beginning January 1, 1986.

THE NEW RULES

Property Classes:

3-year property.   Defined to be property with an ADR midpoint class life of four years or less. Depreciated applying the 200 percent DDB method, switching to the straight-line (SL) method when the cost recovery deduction is maximized.

5-year property.   Property with an ADR midpoint class life of more than four years and less than ten years. Depreciated applying the 200 percent DDB method, switching to the SL method when the cost recovery deduction is maximized.

7-year property.   Property with an ADR midpoint class life of ten years or more but less than sixteen years. Depreciated applying the 200 percent DDB method, switching to the SL method when the cost recovery deduction is maximized.

10-year property.   Property with an ADR midpoint class life of sixteen years or more and less than twenty years. Depreciated applying the 200 percent DDB method, switching to the SL method when the cost recovery deduction is maximized.

15-year property.   Property with an ADR midpoint class life of twenty years or more but less than twenty-five years. Depreciated applying the 150 percent declining balance method, switching to the SL method when the cost recovery deduction is maximized.

20-year property.   Property with an ADR midpoint class life of twenty-five years and more, other than Code Section 1250 real property, with an ADR midpoint of 27.5 years or more. Depreciated applying the 150 percent declining balance method, switching to the SL method when the cost recovery deduction is maximized.

27.5-year residential rental property. Includes rental property that generates 80 percent or more of the gross rental income from dwelling units and low-income housing. The straight-line method must be applied.

31.5-year nonresidential real property. Section 1250 real property that is not residential rental property, nor property with a class life of less than 27.5 years. This class also includes property that has no ADR class life. The straight-line method must be applied.

All property placed in service during the taxable year can apply the straight-line method over the assigned recovery periods (no optional recovery periods) at the election of the taxpayer. The election, however, is irrevocable.

As under the Old Law, averaging conventions are applied, labeled:

Half-year convention.

Mid-month convention.

Mid-quarter convention.

(See Appendix B.)

Gains. All gains on the disposition of tangible personal property is recaptured as ordinary income to the extent of previously allowed ACRS deductions, including the expensing deduction. An exception is the disposition of post-1986 residential rental property and nonresidential real property for which recapture is not required.

Expensing rule. A limit of $10,000 can be expensed in the year property is placed in service; if the cost of the property exceeds $200,000, the $10,000 ceiling is reduced by the amount of the excess. The expensed amount is also limited to an amount that does not exceed the total taxable income of the taxpayer during the tax year the property is placed in service. *Qualified Expense Property* is defined to be recovery property bought for use in the active conduct of a trade or business.

Automobiles. Depreciation for passenger cars placed in service after 1986 has been reduced to $2560 for the first year (formerly $3,200), $4,100 for the second year (formerly $4,800), $1,475 for the third and all following years (formerly $4,800). If the car is used 50 percent or less for business purposes, straight-line depreciation must be applied over a life of five years, pro rated by applying the percentage of business usage to the new annual dollar limits.

Investment tax credit repealed. For Section 38 property, the *regular* 10 percent Investment Tax Credit (ITC) is repealed for property placed in service after December 31, 1985. (Section 38 property is defined to be: "Generally depreciable or ACRS cost recovery property used in a trade or business or for the production of income.") The ITC carryover rules will continue to apply for property placed in service before 1986. The repeal does not apply to certain *transition property* and qualified progress expenditures. However, for post-1985 credits and carryovers to post-1985 taxable years, the allowable credit must be reduced by 35 percent for taxable years starting July 1, 1987.

Transition property is defined to be:

- Property constructed, reconstructed, or acquired under a *legally binding written* contract as of December 31, 1985.
- Property constructed or reconstructed that was started by December 31, 1985, and the lesser of $1,000,000 or 5 percent of the contract cost either was incurred or committed by December 31, 1985.
- If construction of a building or plant facility was started by December 31, 1985, and *more than* one-half of the cost was incurred or committed by December 31, 1985.
- Property that is clearly identifiable and used to carry out a written supply or service contract or lease agreement that was binding on December 31, 1985.

With respect to qualified progress expenditures, under the Old Act, an election was permitted to claim advance ITC over a period of two or more years. If property qualifies as transition property under a binding contract, advance credits can be claimed for post-1985 progress expenditures on the property. These expenditures will not qualify for the regular ITC, however, if it is not reasonable to expect that the property will qualify as transition property when placed in service.

(NOTE: *It is important to know that Section 46a(1) of the Old Law continues to apply to exempt Section 38 property. Essentially, the Congress repealed the ITC by prohibiting Section 46a(1) of the Old Law to apply to non-transition Section 38 property. Accordingly, Code Section 46 AMOUNT OF CREDIT starts in the New Law with subsection (b). Section 46a(1) of the Old Law should, therefore, be referenced when dealing with qualified transition property.*) The New Law requires a full-basis adjustment, effective for periods after December 31, 1985, for ITC transition property to be reduced by the full amount of allowable credits, regardless of the election to claim a reduced ITC instead of the basis adjustment. The basis must be reduced by the full amount of credits earned after application of the 35 percent reduction. The full-basis adjustment rule also applies to credits on qualified progress expenditures, as well as to all depreciable property, irrespective of whether the property qualifies for ACRS. The reduced basis must be used to compute depreciation and to compute a gain or loss on the disposition of the property.

With respect to *recapture* provisions, the New Law allows current depreciation recapture rules to apply to sales made in 1987. Subsequently, all or part of the ITC is recaptured if the property is prematurely disposed of or changed to an unqualified use. If recapture occurs in the first year the property is placed in service,

100 percent of the credit is recaptured. The percentage decreases by 20 percent in each succeeding year after the first year. Accordingly, a 3-year class property will pay no recapture if held for three years (and in a qualified activity). For all other class property, no recapture is paid if held and used in a qualified activity for five years.

The full amount of depreciation taken on *personal* property will be subject to recapture, regardless of whether straight-line or accelerated depreciation is applied. The elimination starting in 1988 of capital gains makes recapture insignificant because all gains from property sales will be ordinary income after 1986. There is no recapture for *real* property because real property is now limited to straight-line depreciation.

The *at-risk* rule now applies under the New Law to real estate. Formerly, investors in real estate were exempt from the at-risk rules that applied to other investments. *At-risk* is defined to mean that unless the investor has an economic investment in real estate (the amount at-risk) and is obligated to make the mortgage payments, any depreciation loss deductions on that portion of the investment will be nondepreciable.

The new at-risk rules apply to losses from the holding of real property placed in service after 1986. The rule also applies for losses to S corporation stock and partnership interests, if the real property is owned by the S corporation or partnership and acquired after 1986.

The date of the investment must be considered. Investments in a real estate venture made before 1987 are not subject to the at-risk rules. But if the venture started before 1987, and the investor acquired the interest in 1987, or later, the at-risk rules under the New Law will apply to that specific investor.

Safe Harbor

ERTA established "safe harbor" leasing provisions which stipulated that a lease of qualified property placed in service after 1980 would be considered as a bona fide lease for Federal income tax purposes, even though the lease had no non-tax economic substance. The lessor was treated as the owner of the property and was entitled to the ACRS deduction and, if applicable, any investment tax credit associated with the property. The provision also gave owners of property who could not use the tax benefits to sell those benefits.

The provision permitting the sale of the tax benefits resulted in a loss of periods or amortized over the remaining period of the lease, whichever is shorter. In some cases, however, improvements made by a tenant may be deducted, if they are made in lieu of rent.

If you are a lessee with an option to renew, the question arises as to whether the renewal period should be included.

For tax purposes, to avoid controversies as to probability of renewal, specific rules have been set down. Renewal periods are to be taken into account in determining the period over which amortization is to take place if the initial term of the lease remaining upon the completion of the improvements is less than 60% of the recovery period of the improvements. Even if you do not meet the 60% rule, you can still amortize over the initial term if you can establish that, as of the taxable year of the improvements, it is more probable that the lease will not be renewed than that it will be renewed.

THE COST OF ACQUIRING A LEASE

The cost of acquiring a lease is amortized over the life of the lease. If less than 75% of the cost is attributable to the remaining term of the lease, you must take into account the renewal period as well as the remaining initial period for the purposes of amortization.

LEASEHOLD IMPROVEMENTS

The costs of leasehold improvements are capital expenditures which are not currently deductible. For tax purposes, they are depreciated over their recovery periods or amortized over the remaining period of the lease, whichever is shorter. In some cases, however, improvements made by a tenant may be deducted, if they are made in lieu of rent.

If you are a lessee with an option to renew, the question arises as to whether the renewal period should be included.

For tax purposes, to avoid controversies as to probability of renewal, specific rules have been set down. Renewal periods are to be taken into account in determining the period over which amortization is to take place if the initial term of the lease remaining upon the completion of the improvements is less than 60% of the recovery period of the improvements. Even if you do not meet the 60% rule, you can still amortize over the initial term if you can establish that, as of the taxable year of the improvements, it is more probable that the lease will not be renewed than that it will be renewed.

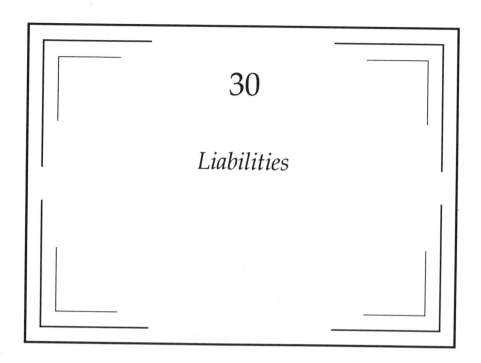

30

Liabilities

TYPES OF LIABILITIES

Liabilities to stockholders. Interest, rent and salary owned by an accrual basis corporation to related parties (stockholders) should be given special attention. The payment cannot be deducted until the year it is actually paid out.

Deferred income. Where income is received in advance of a sale or services to be rendered, the special election to defer sales should be considered.

Notes and bonds payable. Tax incentives favoring debt over stock capitalization should be considered.

Accrued liabilities. A company on the accrual basis should consider the advantages of accruing employee bonuses in the current year and paying them in the next year. But the bonus must be paid within 2½ months after the close of the year (otherwise, the corporation loses its current deduction).

Reserves for Estimated Costs and Expenses

The general rule is that an expense is deductible by a cash-basis taxpayer when he pays it, and by an accrual-basis taxpayer when his liability is fixed.

Where a taxpayer receives income for services he is to perform in the future, the question arises as to when he may deduct the expenses attributable to such income.

If a liability is certain and all events to fix the fact have occurred, it may be accrued. Where uncertainty, or contingency exists, no liability may be accrued until the debt is certain. When a liability is fixed, with the amount uncertain, reasonable estimates may be used and the difference to actual accounted for in the year of exact determination.

How should you treat an expense which you pay in full but continue to contest because you believe you have no obligation to make payment?

The Supreme Court in *Consolidated Edison*, 366 U.S. 380, held that a contested property tax was not deductible until the contest was finally terminated, despite the fact that payment of the tax was made in a prior year. The Court stated that the tax could not be accrued because the payment was in the nature of a "deposit."

The Revenue Act of 1964 revised this rule by *requiring* the taxpayer to deduct the contest liability in the year it is paid, even though the contest is resolved finally in a later year.

As an example of how this provision works, assume the following situation: An accrual-basis taxpayer has a $100 liability asserted against it. It pays the $100, but later contests the liability in a court action. The court action is settled for $80. The law requires the taxpayer to deduct $100 initially, then pick up $20 in income in the later year of court decision.

When law doesn't apply.   Where payment is not made until after the contest is settled, an accrual-basis taxpayer may accrue the deduction in the year in which the contest is settled, although the actual payment is made in a later year.

Example: An accrual-basis corporation has a $100 liability asserted against it. The corporation contests it. The contest is settled for $80. In the succeeding year it pays the $80. The company has to accrue the $80 in the year of settlement and deduct it then. If any portion of the contested amount is refunded, such refund must be included in income unless it comes within the "tax benefit" rule (§111). Under the tax benefit rule, to the extent a prior deduction did not result in a tax benefit, the recovery of that deduction item is not taxable.

Liabilities are included.   Generally, the rule applies to contested local or state taxes. But it is equally applicable to any other contested liability.

Transfer of funds requirement.   One of the requirements necessary for the deduction is that taxpayer transfer money or "other property" to satisfy the liability. When money is transferred to a bona fide escrow agent, you can usually take the deduction as long as the funds are no longer within your control.

Contingent items.   Reserves for contingent expenses, though used for financial reporting, are not usually deductible for tax purposes (except for bad debt reserve additions). Some may be deductible if the liability is fixed. An analysis must therefore be made concerning such items. Estimates of *amounts* may be used and deducted, so long as the fact of liability is fixed.

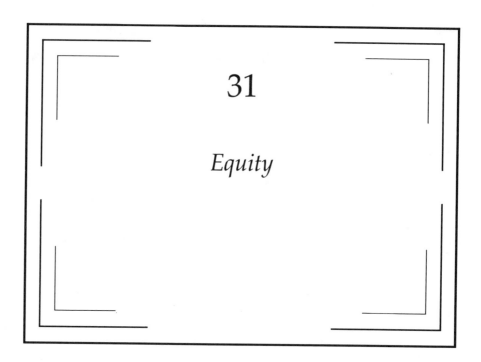

31

Equity

CAPITAL

Dividend payments should be timed to suit the *stockholders'* tax situation whenever possible. Tax savings may be realized by having the corporation defer payment of split payment over two or more years.

Using appreciated property for dividends should be considered. A corporation realizes a taxable gain when it distributes appreciated property to redeem its stock. But this is not true when it distributes certain appreciated property used in the company's business as a dividend.

TAX BENEFITS IN CAPITALIZATION

In financing business operations we have these broad objectives, each of which has tax prospects, as follows:

(1) *Minimize the Risk*: This means cushioning against loss by getting the maximum charge-off against fully taxable income.

(2) *Maximize the Gain*: This means setting the stage for the best possible conversion of income into capital gain and for getting as much of the money back tax free as possible by way of a recovery of the investment.

(3) *Minimize the Cost of Capital*: This means making the carrying charges tax deductible: fully deductible interest or rent rather than nondeductible dividends.

Tax Guidelines in Capitalization

Tax factors have vastly increased the costs and the risks of financing. In shaping the form and the capital structure of a business, we must consider:

(1) Dividends are paid out of after-tax earnings.

(2) Interest paid on debt is tax deductible.

(3) From the investor's viewpoint (and this becomes important in close corporations), losses on stock are subject to capital loss restrictions and can be used to offset ordinary income to only a limited extent. However, there is a special exception for small business stock (§ 1244) which allows ordinary losses on the worthlessness of the stock (see discussion below).

(4) Individual losses on debt are usually subject to the same restriction. Bad debts from nonbusiness operations will be short-term losses and thus will first offset short-term gains. (And losses on advances to a closely held business generally are treated as nonbusiness bad debts.)

(5) Worthless securities (stock, bonds, debentures, or notes with coupons or in registered form) owned by a domestic corporation in an affiliated corporation may be fully deductible as ordinary losses.

(6) When a corporation starts to earn income, an investor will have to pay tax on the return he receives on his investment in stock. Even if part of the stock is redeemed, he is likely to be charged with having received a taxable dividend to the extent of the corporation's accumulated earnings.

On the other hand, corporate funds may be used to repay debt without tax to the investor. Thus an investor stands to recover the money he advances for bonds or notes without having taxes eat into his capital.

(7) A corporation can borrow money at a much lower net cost than it can take money for stock. The cost of servicing debt is tax deductible, while the cost of servicing equity money must come out of net after-tax money.

Special Treatment for Small Business Stock ("1244 stock")

One problem with stock is that, should there be a decline in value and the investors realize a loss, normally the loss will be a capital loss. This form of loss, of course, has a limited tax value. However, it is possible to issue stock (within certain limits) so that it qualifies under § 1244 of the Internal Revenue Code. When this is done, losses realized may be deducted by the investor as ordinary losses.

The ordinary-loss rule of § 1244 applies whether the loss was incurred on sale of the stock or on its becoming worthless. It can be used only by the original purchaser of the stock. In order to qualify for this special treatment, the following requisites have to be met:

(1) Such stock cannot be issued in a total amount of more than $1,000,000. The one million dollar limit is determined by the total of the amount of money and the value of other property to be received by the corporation for stock, as a contribution to capital, and as paid in surplus at the time the stock is issued. For this purpose, the value of the property is the corporation's adjusted basis for determining gain, less any liabilities assumed or taken subject to.

(2) The stock must be issued for money or property and not for stock or securities.

(3) The corporation issuing the stock must be an operating company.

(4) If § 1244 stock was issued for property in a tax-free exchange and the basis for the property was higher than its fair market value, the deductible loss on the § 1244 stock is limited to that fair market value.

(5) Ordinary losses on small business stock are limited to the basis originally acquired on its issuance. Such losses cannot be increased by increasing basis as a result of subsequent capital contributions. Any such increase must be applied to other stock.

The loss that an investor can take in any one year under § 1244 is limited to $50,000. (Where a joint return is filed, the maximum is $100,000.)

S CORPORATIONS

Background. The S Corporation election was first legislated in 1958 under the Code title *Subchapter S Corporation*. There have been several modifications of the applicable Code Section over the years, culminating in the Subchapter S Revision Act of 1982, which essentially set forth an entire new set of rules and requirements effective for taxable years beginning after 1982. Subsequently the title was changed simply to *S Corporations*.

The original intent of Congress was to allow small corporations to have the advantage of the avoidance of double taxation by structuring the tax status of S Corporations in a manner similar to partnerships. Subsequent developments demonstrated that the legislation not only failed to achieve its original purpose, but also created tax "traps" that were not intended by the Congress. The three main traps were:

1. Unintentional violations of the eligibility rules resulting in retroactive termination of the S election.
2. Declaring taxable distributions that were thought to be tax-free distributions of previously taxed income.
3. Shareholders having an insufficient basis to absorb their share of the corporation's losses resulting in the permanent disallowance of that loss.

SUBCHAPTER S REVISION ACT OF 1982

The following is a listing of the significant provisions of the 1982 Act (the current applicable section of the Code). A listing follows of the essential tax and legal differences between S Corporations, C Corporations, and Partnerships. The Section concludes with a synopsis of the significant changes in the 1986 Act.

- *Definitions.* An S Corporation is a corporation which has elected to be taxed under Sec. 1362(a). A C Corporation is any corporation that is not an S Corporation.
- *Qualified shareholders.* Limited to a maximum of 35. Husband and wife are treated as one shareholder.
- *Nonqualified shareholders.* Nonresident aliens. Foreign trusts. Corporations. Members of an affiliated group. Holding a subsidiary other than a DISC.
- *Outstanding stock.* More than one class of common stock allowed if the only difference is in voting rights. Sec. 1361 (c)(4).
- *Income disqualification.* Not more than 25 percent of gross receipts from passive income. If no accumulated earnings and profits, passive income may be taxed at corporate rate without terminating election. Passive income test modified to exclude interest in deferred payment sales of property to customers. Sec. 1221(1).
- *Election period.* Any time during the preceding year. On or before the 15th day of third month of the taxable year.
- *Electing shareholders.* All shareholders must elect Sec. 1362(a)(2).
- *Election form.* Form 2553. Requires the names, addresses, Social Security number of all shareholders, shares of stock owned, and dates acquired. All shareholders must sign the Form 2553.
- *Revocation period.* On or before the 15th day of third month of the taxable year.
- *Revocating shareholders.* Shareholders holding more than one-half of the shares on the day when revocation is made. Sec. 1362(d)(1)(B).
- *Inadvertent termination.* If the IRS determines event was inadvertent and the corporation timely corrects the event, and if the shareholders agree to be treated as though election remained in effect, the IRS will be reasonable in granting waivers. Sec. 1362(f).
- *Computation of corporations' taxable income.* The taxable income of an S Corporation is computed in the same manner as in the case of an *individual* except that all items will be distributed on a pro rata basis. (Sec. 1366), and items not deductible in computing partnership income will also not be deductible. Sec. 703(a)(2). The provisions for personal exemptions, deductions for foreign taxes, charitable contributions, NOLs, additional itemized deduc-

tions, deduction for depletion on oil and gas wells are covered under Sections 611 and 1363(b).

- *Pass through of income to shareholders.* The shareholders will realize a pro rata share of nonseparately computed income or loss. Shareholder receives items of income (including tax-exempt income), loss, deductions or credits, the separate treatment of which could affect the tax liability of any shareholder. In other words, the conduit approach is applied for income that is used in partnership reporting, as in Sec. 702(a), which requires each partner to take into account separately his distributive share of the partnership. The items of income, deductions, and credits are divided on a daily basis to shareholders. Sec. 1377(a)(1).

- *Distribution by an electing corporation.* Post-1982 earnings of an S Corporation are not considered earnings and profits. Income is categorized as "accumulated adjustments account" and adjusts the basis. Sec. 1368(e)(1). If there are no prior earnings and profits, distributions are made against the basis (whenever made) to the extent of the basis. Subsequent distributions are treated as proceeds from sale of stock.

- *Tax on capital gains.* If the net capital gain exceeds $25,000 and exceeds 50 percent of taxable income for the year, and the taxable income of the corporation exceeds $25,000, there is a corporate tax on the gain in excess of $25,000. Sec. 1374.

- *Exceptions.* The tax is not imposed if the corporation had been an S Corporation for the current year and three preceding years. Sec. 1362(a).

- *Net operating losses.* Losses and deductions are deductible by the shareholders. Any loss or deduction, which is disallowed because shareholder does not have sufficient basis or loans, can be carried over to next succeeding year when the shareholder has sufficient basis. Sec. 1366(d)(2). The carryover term is indefinite, as long as the corporation is an S Corporation.

- *Net operating losses deducted against shareholder.* Gross income reported by a shareholder restores basis to loans prior to increasing basis in stock. Sec. 1367(a)(2)(B).

- *Tax year of corporation.* Permitted year is a taxable year which (1) is a year ending December 31 and (2) is any other accounting period for which the corporation establishes a business purpose to the satisfaction of the IRS.

- *Fiscal year.* Corporations that are electing corporations for the year which included December 31, 1982, are not required to change until they have a change of stock ownership of more than 50 percent (Sec. 1378), excluding stock ownership changed by reason of death.

- *Coordination with partnership and individual rules.* S Corporations are treated like partnerships for purposes of certain provisions. Sections 613(c)(13), 4996(a)(1)(C), 194(b)(2), 48(c), 108(d), 267(b).

- *Family corporations.* If an individual who is a member of the family of one or more of the shareholders of an S Corporation renders services to the corporation or furnishes capital to the corporation without receiving reasonable compensation, an adjustment will be made to give the individual income to reflect the value of compensation or capital. Sections 1366(e) and 704(e)(3).

Summary
Tax and Legal Differences
S Corporations, C Corporations, Partnerships

Points to Consider	S Corporations	C Corporations	Partnerships
Separate Entity or Aggregation	An entity apart from the shareholders.		Sometimes treated as separate entity; generally considered an aggregation of members among partners.
Period of Existence	Continues until dissolution; not affected by disaffiliation of shareholders, or sale of their shares, unless sale is to ineligible shareholder.	Same as S Corporation except period of existence not affected by share transfers.	Termination by agreement, or on partner's death, retirement or other disaffiliation.
Transfers of Interest	Readily and easily marketable by transfer of certificate of stock. Sale of shares to partnership, corporation, certain trusts, or nonresident alien terminates election.	Same as S Corporation with no restriction on eligibility to own shares.	Addition of new partner or transfer of partner's interest often requires consent of other partners
Non-Loan Capital Sources	Sale of only one class of stock to no more than 35 eligible shareholders. Differences in voting rights permitted.	Sale of multiple classes of stock or other securities to unlimited number of individuals, corporations, or partnerships.	Contributions by general or limited partners with unlimited number of partners permitted.
Ownership Limitations	35 shareholder limit and qualification requirements to be shareholders.	No limit on number or class of shareholders.	No limit on number of partners.
Liability Exposure	Except in rare circumstances, shareholders are only liable for capital contributions.		General partners are personally,

Points to Consider	S Corporations	C Corporations	Partnerships
			jointly and severally liable for partnership obligations. Limited partner liable for capital contributions only.
Loan Collateralization	Shares may be used as loan collateral.		Partnership interests cannot serve as loan collateral.
Ownership/Management Responsibility	No requirement for shareholder participation in management.		All general partners participate in management and share joint responsibility. Limited partners do not participate in management.
Organizational Expenditures	Option to amortize over at least 60 months or capitalize.		
Tax Year	S Corporation must use a calendar year unless business purpose shown for fiscal year.	Calendar or fiscal year permitted. Tax year does not have to match shareholders' tax years.	Same restrictions as S Corporations.
Federal Tax Return	Form 1120-S Information return.	Form 1120, Corporate income tax return. May have to file estimated tax returns.	Form 1065, Information return.
Treatment of Income and Losses	Corporate income determined at entity level and passed through to each shareholder and taxed at individual rates. Some S Corporations pay capital gains tax and tax on "excess net passive income." Income loss items that affect a shareholder's tax liability are separately stated-e.g. charitable contributions, depletion.	All corporate income taxed at corporate level and again taxed at shareholder level when distributed as dividends. Some C corporations taxed as personal holding companies and can be taxed on excess accumulate income.	Same as S Corporation except no partnership capital gains tax nor tax on passive income.

Points to Consider	S Corporations	C Corporations	Partnerships
Net Operating Losses	Losses pass through to shareholders and are deductible to the extent of their stock and debt basis. Losses may be carried back or forward.	Deductible only by the corporation in a year which it has offsetting income. Losses may be carried back or forward.	Same passthrough rules as S Corporation.
Tax-Exempt Income	Tax-exempt income earned by the corporation retains its character when passed through to the shareholders. It increases shareholders' stock bases.	Tax-exempt income increase corporate earnings and profits and is not taxed at corporate level. If distributed to shareholders as dividends, it is subject to tax.	Same passthrough rule as S Corporation
Foreign Income	No restrictions.	No restrictions.	No restrictions.
Capital Gains	Capital and Sec. 1231 gains pass through to shareholders and retain their character at shareholder level. 60% of long-term gains are excluded from gross income but are subject to the alternative minimum tax. *Some* S Corporations subject to tax on capital gains in excess of $25,000.	Capital and Sec. 1231 gains taxed at regular corporate rate or the alternative 28% rate.	Same rule as for S Corporation except no tax at partnership level on capital gains.
Capital Losses	Capital losses pass through to shareholders and retain their character at the shareholder level. Losses offset capital gains and then up to $3,000 ordinary income. May be carried forward indefinitely.	Capital losses deducted at corporate level only to the extent of capital gains. Losses may be carried back three years or forward 15 years.	Same rule as S Corporations.
Accumulated Earnings	After 1982, all income is passed through and taxed at shareholder level. S Corpora-	C corporations may accumulate income for reasonable business needs. Up to $150,000 for	All income taxed to partners whether distributed or not.

Points to Consider	S Corporations	C Corporations	Partnerships
	tions with carryover C corporation earnings and profits are subject to 46% tax on excess passive income and distributions of accumulated earnings and profits taxed as dividend income.	personal service corporations and $250,000 for other C Corporations may be accumulated without question. Unreasonable accumulations subject to tax.	
Distributions and Income Allocations	Distributions are taxed to the extent they exceed a shareholder's basis in stock and debts. Corporation recognizes gain on distribution of appreciated property. Income may only be allocated in proportion to shareholdings.	Distributions taxed as ordinary income and allocated on basis of shareholders. C corporation does not recognize gain on distribution of appreciated property.	Distributions taxed to the extent they exceed partner's basis in stock and partnership debt. Distributive income shares may be allocated by agreement of the partners. Partnership does not recognize gain on distribution of appreciated property.
Fringe Benefits	Owner of 2% or more of S Corporation shares cannot receive tax-free most fringe benefits including, employer-provided health care, meals and lodging and life insurance.	Shareholder employees may receive tax qualified fringe benefits without restriction.	All partners not eligible for tax-free fringes.
Retirement Plans	Through 1983, S Corporations can only contribute $15,000 a year to a shareholder-employee's retirement plan. After 1983, S Corporations, C corporations and partnerships are governed by the same retirement plan rules.	C Corporations can provide a broad variety of defined benefit and defined-contribution plans. After 1983, all corporations and partnerships governed by the same rules.	Through 1983, partners' Keogh, plan contribution limits were less than limits for C Corp. employees. After 1983, partnerships and corporations governed by the same rules.

Points to Consider	S Corporations	C Corporations	Partnerships
Investment Interest Deduction	Shareholder deducts his share of the S Corporation's investment interest as if the $10,000 plus net investment income limit applied at the corporate level.	No Limitation.	Partner may deduct his share of partnership's interest up to $10,000 plus his net investment income.
Dividends Received	Income passes through to shareholders and is subject to the $100 dividend exclusion. Corporation does not get exclusion for dividends it receives.	C Corporation can exclude 85% of dividends received from domestic corporations.	Same rule as S Corporations.
FICA Taxes	Tax payable by the corporation and the employees.		Self employment tax applies to salary and drawings.

1986 CODE CHANGES

The New Law makes only minor modifications in the S Corporation section of the Code.

- S Corporations, partnerships, and personal service corporations *must* use a taxable year that generally conforms to the taxable year of the owners. A partnership must use in order of priority: 1) the taxable year of the partners owning the majority of partnership profits and capital; 2) the taxable year of all of its principal partners; 3) a calendar year. S Corporations and personal service corporations must use the calendar year. If, to the satisfaction of the Secretary of the Treasury, it can be established that there is a business purpose for having a different taxable year, these three entities may be permitted by IRS to have a different taxable year. (See Appendix B.)
- The alternative minimum tax law does not apply to S Corporations.
- S Corporations can continue to use the cash method of accounting.
- The new tax law requires most corporations to recognize gains or losses on *liquidating* sales and distributions as if the assets were sold at fair market value. S Corporations are exempt from this requirement.

Form **1120S**	**U.S. Income Tax Return for an S Corporation**	OMB No. 1545-0130

Form **1120S**

Department of the Treasury
Internal Revenue Service

U.S. Income Tax Return for an S Corporation

For the calendar year 1986 or tax year beginning _____, 1986, ending _____, 19 _____

▶ **For Paperwork Reduction Act Notice, see page 1 of the instructions.**

OMB No. 1545-0130

1986

A Date of election as an S corporation	Use IRS label. Other-wise, please print or type.	Name	C Employer identification number
B Business Code No. (see Specific Instructions)		Number and street	D Date incorporated
		City or town, state, and ZIP code	E Total assets (see Specific Instructions) Dollars Cents

F. Check applicable boxes: (1) ☐ Final return   (2) ☐ Change in address   (3) ☐ Amended return $

1986-87 fiscal year corporations see Specific Instructions before completing page 1.

Income

1a Gross receipts or sales _____ b Less returns and allowances _____ Balance ▶		1c	
2 Cost of goods sold and/or operations (Schedule A, line 7).		2	
3 Gross profit (subtract line 2 from line 1c)		3	
4 Taxable interest and nonqualifying dividends		4	
5 Gross rents		5	
6 Gross royalties		6	
7 Net gain or (loss) from Form 4797, line 17, Part II		7	
8 Other income (see instructions—attach schedule).		8	
9 TOTAL income (loss)—Combine lines 3 through 8 and enter here . . . . . . ▶		9	

Deductions

10 Compensation of officers		10	
11a Salaries and wages _____ b Less jobs credit _____ Balance ▶		11c	
12 Repairs		12	
13 Bad debts (see instructions)		13	
14 Rents		14	
15 Taxes		15	
16a Total deductible interest expense not claimed elsewhere on return (see instructions)	16a		
b Interest expense required to be passed through to shareholders on Schedule K-1, lines 9, 13a(2), and 13a(3).	16b		
c Subtract line 16b from line 16a		16c	
17a Depreciation from Form 4562 (attach Form 4562)	17a		
b Depreciation claimed on Schedule A and elsewhere on return . .	17b		
c Subtract line 17b from line 17a		17c	
18 Depletion (**Do not deduct oil and gas depletion. See instructions**)		18	
19 Advertising		19	
20 Pension, profit-sharing, etc. plans		20	
21 Employee benefit programs		21	
22 Other deductions (attach schedule)		22	
23 TOTAL deductions—Add lines 10 through 22 and enter here . . . . ▶		23	
24 Ordinary income (loss)—Subtract line 23 from line 9		24	

Tax and Payments

25 Tax:			
a Excess net passive income tax (attach schedule)	25a		
b Tax from Schedule D (Form 1120S), Part IV	25b		
c Add lines 25a and 25b		25c	
26 Payments:			
a Tax deposited with Form 7004	26a		
b Credit for Federal tax on gasoline and special fuels (attach Form 4136)	26b		
c Add lines 26a and 26b		26c	
27 **TAX DUE** (subtract line 26c from line 25c). See instructions for Paying the Tax . . . . . ▶		27	
28 **OVERPAYMENT** (subtract line 25c from line 26c). . . . . ▶		28	

Please Sign Here

Under penalties of perjury, I declare that I have examined this return, including accompanying schedules and statements, and to the best of my knowledge and belief, it is true, correct, and complete. Declaration of preparer (other than taxpayer) is based on all information of which preparer has any knowledge.

▶ _____   _____   ▶ _____
Signature of officer   Date   Title

Paid Preparer's Use Only

Preparer's signature ▶	Date	Check if self-employed ▶ ☐	Preparer's social security number
Firm's name (or yours, if self-employed) and address ▶		E.I. No. ▶	
		ZIP code ▶	

Form **1120S** (1986)

Form 1120S (1986)   Page

Schedule A   **Cost of Goods Sold and/or Operations**   (See instructions for Schedule A)

1 Inventory at beginning of year	**1**	
2 Purchases	**2**	
3 Cost of labor	**3**	
4 Other costs (attach schedule)	**4**	
5 Total—Add lines 1 through 4	**5**	
6 Inventory at end of year	**6**	
7 Cost of goods sold and/or operations—Subtract line 6 from line 5. Enter here and on line 2, page 1	**7**	

8a Check all methods used for valuing closing inventory:

    (i)   ☐   Cost

    (ii)   ☐   Lower of cost or market as described in Regulations section 1.471-4 (see instructions)

    (iii)   ☐   Writedown of "subnormal" goods as described in Regulations section 1.471-2(c) (see instructions)

    (iv)   ☐   Other (Specify method used and attach explanation) ▶ _____

  b Check this box if the LIFO inventory method was adopted this tax year for any goods (if checked, attach Form 970)   . . . . ☐

  c If the LIFO inventory method was used for this tax year, enter percentage (or amounts) of closing

    inventory computed under LIFO **8c**

  d If you are engaged in manufacturing, did you value your inventory using the full absorption method (Regulations

    section 1.471-11)?   . . . . ☐ Yes   ☐ N◖

  e Was there any change in determining quantities, cost, or valuations between opening and closing inventory?   . . . . ☐ Yes   ☐ N◖

    If "Yes," attach explanation.

Additional Information Required

	Yes	No
G Did you at the end of the tax year own, directly or indirectly, 50% or more of the voting stock of a domestic corporation?		

    (For rules of attribution, see section 267(c).)

    If "Yes," attach a schedule showing:

    (1) Name, address, and employer identification number;

    (2) Percentage owned;

    (3) Highest amount owed by you to such corporation during the year; and

    (4) Highest amount owed to you by such corporation during the year.

      (Note: *For purposes of G(3) and G(4), "highest amount owed" includes loans and accounts receivable/payable.)*

H Refer to the listing of Business Activity Codes at the end of the Instructions for Form 1120S and state your principal:

    Business activity ▶ _____; Product or service ▶ _____

I   Were you a member of a controlled group subject to the provisions of section 1561?   . . . .

J   Did you claim a deduction for expenses connected with:

    (1) Entertainment facilities (boat, resort, ranch, etc.)? . . . .

    (2) Living accommodations (except for employees on business)? . . . .

    (3) Employees attending conventions or meetings outside the North American area? (See section 274(h).) . . .

    (4) Employees' families at conventions or meetings? . . . .

      If "Yes," were any of these conventions or meetings outside the North American area? (See section 274(h).) . . .

    (5) Employee or family vacations not reported on Form W-2? . . . .

K At any time during the tax year, did you have an interest in or a signature or other authority over a financial account in a

    foreign country (such as a bank account, securities account, or other financial account)? (See instructions for exceptions

    and filing requirements for form TD F 90-22.1.) . . . .

    If "Yes," write the name of the foreign country ▶ _____

L   Were you the grantor of, or transferor to, a foreign trust which existed during the current tax year, whether or not you

    have any beneficial interest in it? If "Yes," you may have to file Forms 3520, 3520-A, or 926 . . . .

M During this tax year did you maintain any part of your accounting/tax records on a computerized system? . . . . .

N Check method of accounting: **(1)**☐ Cash   **(2)**☐ Accrual   **(3)**☐ Other (specify) ▶ _____

O Check this box if the S corporation has filed or is required to file Form 8264, Application for Registration of a Tax

    Shelter . . . . ▶☐

P Check this box if the corporation issued publicly offered debt instruments with original issue discount   . . . . . ▶☐

    If so, the corporation may have to file Form 8281.

Form 1120S (1986)

Schedule K	Shareholders' Share of Income, Credits, Deductions, etc. (See Instructions.)	Page 3

(a) Distributive share items		(b) Total amount
Income (Losses) and Deductions		
1a Ordinary income (loss) (page 1, line 24) * .	1a	
b Income (loss) from rental real estate activity(ies) (FY corporations only) .	1b	
c Income (loss) from other rental activity(ies) (FY corporations only) .	1c	
d Portfolio income not reported elsewhere on Schedule K (FY corporations only) .	1d	
2 Dividends qualifying for the exclusion .	2	
3 Net short-term capital gain (loss) (Schedule D (Form 1120S)) * .	3	
4 Net long-term capital gain (loss) (Schedule D (Form 1120S)) * .	4	
5 Net gain (loss) under section 1231 (other than due to casualty or theft) * .	5	
6 Other income (loss) (attach schedule) .	6	
7 Charitable contributions .	7	
8 Section 179 expense deduction (FY corporations attach schedule) .	8	
9 Other deductions (attach schedule) .	9	
Credits		
10a Jobs credit * .	10a	
b Low-income housing credit (FY corporations only) .	10b	
c Qualified rehabilitation expenditures related to rental real estate activity(ies) (FY corporations only) (attach schedule)		
d Other credits related to rental real estate activity(ies) other than on line 10b and 10c (FY corporations only) (attach schedule) .	10d	
11 Other credits (attach schedule) * .	11	
Tax Preference and Adjustment Items		
12a Accelerated depreciation on nonrecovery real property or 15, 18, or 19-year real property placed in service before 1-1-87 .	12a	
b Accelerated depreciation on leased personal property or leased recovery property, other than 15, 18, or 19-year real property, placed in service before 1-1-87 .	12b	
c Accelerated depreciation on property placed in service after 12-31-86 (FY corporations only) .	12c	
d Depletion (other than oil and gas) .	12d	
e (1) Gross income from oil, gas, or geothermal properties .	12e(1)	
(2) Gross deductions allocable to oil, gas, or geothermal properties .	12e(2)	
f (1) Qualified investment income included on page 1, Form 1120S .	12f(1)	
(2) Qualified investment expenses included on page 1, Form 1120S .	12f(2)	
g Other items (attach schedule) .	12g	
Investment Interest		
13a Interest expense on: (1) Investment debts incurred before 12-17-69 .	13a(1)	
(2) Investment debts incurred before 9-11-75 but after 12-16-69 .	13a(2)	
(3) Investment debts incurred after 9-10-75 .	13a(3)	
b (1) Investment income included on page 1, Form 1120S .	13b(1)	
(2) Investment expenses included on page 1, Form 1120S .	13b(2)	
c (1) Income from "net lease property" .	13c(1)	
(2) Expenses from "net lease property" .	13c(2)	
d Excess of net long-term capital gain over net short-term capital loss from investment property .	13d	
Foreign Taxes		
14a Type of income .		
b Name of foreign country or U.S. possession .		
c Total gross income from sources outside the U.S. (attach schedule) .	14c	
d Total applicable deductions and losses (attach schedule) .	14d	
e Total foreign taxes (check one): ▶ ☐ Paid ☐ Accrued .	14e	
f Reduction in taxes available for credit (attach schedule) .	14f	
g Other (attach schedule) .	14g	
Other Items		
15 Total property distributions (including cash) other than dividend distributions reported on line 17	15	
16 Other items and amounts not included in lines 1 through 15 that are required to be reported separately to shareholders (attach schedule).		
17 Total dividend distributions paid from accumulated earnings and profits contained in other retained earnings (line 26 of Schedule L) .	17	

* Calendar year filers are not required to complete lines 1a, 10a, and 11. Completion of these lines is optional because the amounts which would appear in column (b) appear elsewhere on Form 1120S or on other IRS forms or schedules which are attached to Form 1120S. See Specific Instructions for Schedules K and K-1.

Form 1120S (1986)   Page **4**

Schedule L   Balance Sheets

Assets	Beginning of tax year		End of tax year	
	(a)	(b)	(c)	(d)
1 Cash.				
2 Trade notes and accounts receivable				
a Less allowance for bad debts				
3 Inventories.				
4 Federal and state government obligations				
5 Other current assets (attach schedule).				
6 Loans to shareholders				
7 Mortgage and real estate loans				
8 Other investments (attach schedule)				
9 Buildings and other depreciable assets.				
a Less accumulated depreciation				
10 Depletable assets				
a Less accumulated depletion				
11 Land (net of any amortization)				
12 Intangible assets (amortizable only).				
a Less accumulated amortization				
13 Other assets (attach schedule)				
14 Total assets				
Liabilities and Shareholders' Equity				
15 Accounts payable				
16 Mortgages, notes, bonds payable in less than 1 year				
17 Other current liabilities (attach schedule)				
18 Loans from shareholders				
19 Mortgages, notes, bonds payable in 1 year or more				
20 Other liabilities (attach schedule)				
21 Capital stock				
22 Paid-in or capital surplus				
23 Accumulated adjustments account				
24 Other adjustments account				
25 Shareholders' undistributed taxable income previously taxed				
26 Other retained earnings (see instructions). Check this box if the corporation has subchapter C earnings and profits at the close of the tax year ▶ ☐ (see instructions)				
27 Total retained earnings per books—Combine amounts on lines 23 through 26, columns (a) and (c) (see instructions)		( )		( )
28 Less cost of treasury stock.				
29 Total liabilities and shareholders' equity				

Schedule M   Analysis of Accumulated Adjustments Account, Other Adjustments Account, and Shareholders' Undistributed Taxable Income Previously Taxed (If Schedule L, column (c), amounts for lines 23, 24, or 25 are not the same as corresponding amounts on line 9 of Schedule M, attach a schedule explaining any differences. See instructions.)

	Accumulated adjustments account	Other adjustments account	Shareholders' undistributed taxable income previously taxed
1 Balance at beginning of year			
2 Ordinary income from page 1, line 24			
3 Other additions			
4 Total of lines 1, 2, and 3			
5 Distributions other than dividend distributions			
6 Loss from page 1, line 24			
7 Other reductions			
8 Add lines 5, 6, and 7			
9 Balance at end of tax year—Subtract line 8 from line 4			

SCHEDULE K-1	**Shareholder's Share of Income, Credits, Deductions, etc.**	OMB No. 1545-0130
(Form 1120S)	For calendar year 1986 or tax year	
Department of the Treasury Internal Revenue Service	beginning _____, 1986, and ending _____, 19 ____. **(Complete a separate Schedule K-1 for each shareholder—see Instructions)**	19**86**

Shareholder's identifying number ▶	Corporation's identifying number ▶
Shareholder's name, address, and ZIP code	Corporation's name, address, and ZIP code

A Shareholder's percentage of stock ownership for tax year . . . . ▶   %

B Internal Revenue Service Center where corporation filed its return ▶

C Tax shelter registration number (see Instructions) . . . . ▶

D Did the shareholder materially participate in the trade or business activity(ies) for which income or loss (or credit(s)) is reported on line 1a, 6, or 9 or line 11 below? . . . . ☐ Yes ☐ No

E Did the shareholder actively participate in the rental real estate activity(ies) for which income or loss (or credit(s)) is reported on line 1b, 6, or 9 or line 10b, c, or d below? . . . . ☐ Yes ☐ No

F If (1) question D is checked "No" or income or loss is reported on line 1b or 1c and (2) the shareholder had acquisition(s) of corporate stock after 10/22/86, check here ▶ ☐ and enter the shareholder's weighted percentage increase in stock ownership after 10/22/86 (see instructions for Schedule K-1) . . . . . . ▶   %

G If question D is checked "No" and any activity referred to in question D was started or acquired by the corporation after 10/22/86, check here ▶ ☐ and enter the date of start-up or acquisition in the date space on line 1a. Also, if an activity for which income or loss is reported on line 1b or 1c was started after 10/22/86, check the box and enter the start-up date in the date space on line 1b or 1c.

Caution: *Refer to attached Instructions for Schedule K-1 before entering information from Schedule K-1 on your tax return.*

	(a) Distributive share items	(b) Amount	(c) 1986 1040 filers enter the amount in column (b) on:
Income (Losses) and Deductions	**1a** Ordinary income (loss). Date: _____		Sch. E, Part II, col. (e) or (f)
	b Income or loss from rental real estate activity(ies). Date: ____		See Shareholder's Instructions for Schedule K-1 (Form 1120S)
	c Income or loss from rental activity(ies) other than line 1b above. Date: ____		
	d Portfolio income not reported elsewhere on Schedule K-1		
	2 Dividends qualifying for the exclusion		Sch. B, Part II, line 4
	3 Net short-term capital gain (loss)		Sch. D, line 5, col. (f) or (g)
	4 Net long-term capital gain (loss)		Sch. D, line 12, col. (f) or (g)
	5 Net gain (loss) under section 1231 (other than due to casualty or theft) .		Form 4797, line 1
	6 Other income (loss) (attach schedule)		(Enter on applicable line of your return)
	7 Charitable contributions		See Form 1040 Instructions
	8 Section 179 expense deduction (attach schedule). . . .		See Shareholder's Instructions for Schedule K-1 (Form 1120S)
	9 Other deductions (attach schedule)		(Enter on applicable line of your return)
Credits	**10a** Jobs credit		Form 5884
	b Low-income housing credit		
	c Qualified rehabilitation expenditures related to rental real estate activity(ies) (attach schedule)		See Shareholder's Instructions for Schedule K-1 (Form 1120S)
	d Other credits related to rental real estate activity(ies) other than on line 10b and 10c (attach schedule)		
	11 Other credits (attach schedule).		
Tax Preference and Adjustment Items	**12a** Accelerated depreciation on nonrecovery real property or 15, 18, or 19-year real property placed in service before 1/1/87 . . .		Form 6251, line 4c
	b Accelerated depreciation on leased personal property or leased recovery property, other than 15, 18, 19-year real property, placed in service before 1/1/87.		Form 6251, line 4d
	c Accelerated depreciation on property placed in service after 12/31/86 .		See Form 6251 Instructions
	d Depletion (other than oil and gas)		Form 6251, line 4i
	e (1) Gross income from oil, gas, or geothermal properties . .		See Form 6251 Instructions
	(2) Gross deductions allocable to oil, gas, or geothermal properties . .		
	f (1) Qualified investment income included on page 1, Form 1120S . .		See Shareholder's Instructions for Schedule K-1 (Form 1120S)
	(2) Qualified investment expenses included on page 1, Form 1120S . .		
	g Other items (attach schedule)		

For Paperwork Reduction Act Notice, see page 1 of Instructions for Form 1120S.   **Schedule K-1 (Form 1120S) 1986**

Schedule K-1 (Form 1120S) (1986)   Page **2**

	(a) Distributive share items	(b) Amount	(c) 1986 1040 filers enter the amount in column (b) on:
Investment Interest	**13a** Interest expense on:		
	(1) Investment debts incurred before 12/17/69		Form 4952, line 1
	(2) Investment debts incurred before 9/11/75 but after 12/16/69 . .		Form 4952, line 15
	(3) Investment debts incurred after 9/10/75		Form 4952, line 5
	b (1) Investment income included on page 1, Form 1120S		
	(2) Investment expenses included on page 1, Form 1120S		See Shareholder's Instructions for Schedule K-1 (Form 1120S)
	c (1) Income from "net lease property"		
	(2) Expenses from "net lease property"		
	d Excess of net long-term capital gain over net short-term capital loss from investment property		Form 4952, line 20
Foreign Taxes	**14** Type of income ▶		Form 1116, Check boxes
	b Name of foreign country or U.S. possession ▶		Form 1116, Part I
	c Total gross income from sources outside the U.S. (attach schedule) . .		Form 1116, Part I
	d Total applicable deductions and losses (attach schedule)		Form 1116, Part I
	e Total foreign taxes (check one): ▶ ☐ Paid ☐ Accrued		Form 1116, Part II
	f Reduction in taxes available for credit (attach schedule)		Form 1116, Part III
	g Other (attach schedule)		See Form 1116 Instructions
Other Items	**15** Property distributions (including cash) other than dividend distributions reported to you on Form 1099-DIV		See Shareholder's Instructions for Schedule K-1 (Form 1120S)
	16 Amount of loan repayments for "Loans from Shareholders"		
	17 Property eligible for investment credit (attach schedule)		

		A	B	C	
Property Subject to Recapture of Investment Credit	**18** Properties:				
	a Description of property (State whether recovery or non-recovery property. If recovery property, state whether regular percentage method or section 48(q) election used.)				Form 4255, top
	b Date placed in service				Form 4255, line 2
	c Cost or other basis . .				Form 4255, line 3
	d Class of recovery property or original estimated useful life .				Form 4255, line 4
	e Date item ceased to be investment credit property				Form 4255, line 8

19 Supplemental information for lines 6, 8, 9, 10c, 10d, 11, 12g, 14c, 14d, 14f, 14g, 17, or other items and amounts not included in lines 1a through 18 that are required to be reported separately to each shareholder (attach additional schedules if more space is needed):

Supplemental Schedules

Loss Passthroughs

The law limits the deduction an S corporation shareholder can claim for losses passed through to the shareholder. The limit is the basis of the stock investment of the shareholder, plus any debt of the corporation owed to the shareholder. The shareholder can carry losses forward indefinitely, and the law allows a deduction in any future year(s) up to the stockholder's aggregate stock and debt basis.

Can a deduction be bought? Yes, it can. Assume a shareholder with a loss in excess of his basis. All the shareholder has to do is contribute to the corporation an amount in stock or debt, or both, equal to the loss, or any part of it. Further, the stockholder can borrow the money for this purpose. There is no limitation on the number of years the stockholder can take to buy an excess loss that is outstanding.

Passive Investment Income

Under the New Law, passive activities are defined to include trade or business activities in which the taxpayer does not *materially* participate, such as a limited partner in an activity, and rental activities.

Deductions from passive activities, to the extent that they exceed income from all such activities (exclusive of portfolio income) generally may not be deducted from other income of the taxpayer. Similarly, credits from passive activities generally are limited to the tax allocable to the passive activities. Suspended losses and credits are carried forward and treated as deductions and credits from passive activities in the next taxable year. When the taxpayer disposes of his entire interest in an activity, any remaining suspended loss incurred in connection with that activity is allowed in full.

Under the old Act, gross receipts included the *entire amount* of the proceeds from the disposition of capital assets other than stock or securities, but *no* part of those proceeds was passive income. While proceeds from the sale of capital assets still are not included in passive income, the amount of the gross receipts is limited to realized gain.

Inadvertent Terminations

In view of Congress' intent to remove the traps which under the old Act caused inadvertent noncompliance with the requirements for Sub S continuance, the IRS is authorized by the new Act to waive the termination penalty under certain circumstances, which are:

- a violation of the passive income requirement, if the Commissioner determines the violation was inadvertent.
- whatever the inadvertent event might have been, if the corporation has taken steps to correct the event.

- the corporation's shareholders agree to make whatever corrections the Commissioner requires.

The Ways and Means Committee explained: "The committee intends that the Internal Revenue Service be reasonable in granting the waivers, so that corporations whose S eligibility requirements have been inadvertently violated do not suffer the tax consequences of a termination if no tax avoidance would result from the continued S treatment. In granting waivers, it is hoped that taxpayers and the government will work out agreements that protect the revenues without undue hardships to taxpayers. For example, if a corporation, in good faith, determined that it had no earnings and profits, but it is later determined on audit that its election terminated by reason of violating the passive income test because the corporation in fact did have accumulated earnings, if the shareholders were to agree to treat the earnings as distributed and include the dividends in income, it may be appropriate to waive the terminating events, so that the election is treated as never terminated. Likewise, it may be appropriate to waive the terminating event when the one class of stock requirement was inadvertently breached, but no tax avoidance had resulted. It is expected that the waiver may be made retroactive for all years, or retroactive for the period in which the corporation again became eligible for S treatment, depending on the facts."

Safe-Harbor Rule—A Trap Eliminated

Under the prior law, the Internal Revenue Service ruled that debt of an S corporation that resulted in an obviously thinly capitalized company (very highly leveraged) was a tax avoidance scheme, because interest on a heavy debt structure could add to the corporation's losses and deduction from the shareholders' other sources of income. This created the problem of tax avoidance *intent*, and whether or not tax avoidance was, in fact, present in a given situation. To correct the problem, in order to prevent the corporation's S status from being terminated because a debt instrument could be classified as a separate class of stock, the 1982 Act's revision includes a "safe harbor" for *straight debt* obligations.

What is straight debt?

- The debt is a written unconditional demand to pay a fixed amount on demand on a specified date.
- The interest rate and the interest payment dates are not contingent on profits, nor at the corporation's discretion. However, a rate tied to the prime rate is an exception, because the prime rate is an external factor outside of the corporation's discretion.
- The debt cannot be convertible into stock.
- The creditor must be an individual (including an estate or trust) who is an eligible person to own stock (but does not have to) in the corporation.

In clarifying the safe-harbor rule, the Ways and Means Committee said:

> "It is intended that these rules will treat the instrument in such a way as to prevent tax avoidance, on the one hand, and also to prevent unfair, harsh results to the taxpayer. It is anticipated that these safe-harbor instruments will be treated as debt under S, so that no corporate income or loss will be allocated to the instruments. Payments on the instruments shall be includible in the income of the holder and deductible by the corporation (subject to the rules of the bill relating to the accrual of unpaid amounts). Payments on these instruments may be examined to determine whether the payments represent interest or other income in any situation where the treatment as interest might give the taxpayer an unwarranted tax advantage, such as under the net interest exclusion.
>
> "In the case of a regular corporation (with a straight debt instrument outstanding, which is treated as stock under corporate tax law principles) that elects S, it is intended that the election not be treated as an exchange of debt for stock, but a later redemption of the instrument may be treated as a dividend if the corporation had remaining accumulated earnings and profits. Prior to the issuance of final regulations, it is intended that these general principles will apply to straight debt instruments.
>
> "The classification of an instrument outside the safe-harbor rules as stock or debt will be made under the usual tax laws classification principals."

A Trust as a Shareholder

A "qualified S trust" can be a shareholder of an S corporation. *Definition*: A qualified S trust is a trust which owns stock in one or more electing small business corporations; all of the income is distributed to *one* individual; the *one* individual must be a citizen or resident of the United States (cannot be a nonresident alien); the corpus of the trust is distributable only to the income beneficiary; the beneficiary's interest terminates upon death or the termination of the trust; if the corporation is terminated before the death of the beneficiary, all assets of the trust must be distributable to the beneficiary.

If a qualified trust fails to meet any of these requirements, it will lose its qualified status.

Technical Corrections

The 1984 law incorporated a number of technical corrections to the S Revision Act of 1982.

- Gain is recognized to an S corporation that makes a distribution of appreciated property with respect to its stock, as if the S corporation had sold the property to the distributee at its fair market value. The new law makes this rule inapplicable to distributions in complete liquidation of S corporations and of stock by an S corporation in a reorganization, where the receipt of such stock is tax free to the shareholder.

- If a shareholder contributed a debt to an S corporation as a contribution to capital after December 31, 1980, corporate income will not result to the extent that the debt had previously been reduced by the passthrough of losses from the corporation.

- Under the prior law, an S corporation could not own a subsidiary other than an inactive subsidiary, which was defined as a corporation which had no *taxable* income. The new law substitutes a *gross* income test for the *taxable* income test. Now an S corporation's election will terminate on the first day during the corporation's taxable year that the subsidiary has gross income.

- Under the prior law, passed-through S corporation losses were taken into account before any deductions for worthless stock. The new law extends this rule to situations where the shareholder's debt in the corporation becomes worthless. This means that if a shareholder has no basis in his S corporation stock, but does have a basis in debt owed by the corporation and that debt becomes worthless, corporate losses for the year will be allowed to the shareholder to the extent of the shareholder's basis in the debt. This in turn will reduce the amount of the short-term capital loss for the worthless debt.

- Under the prior law, the recapture of investment tax credits claimed in pre-S years is to be made at the corporate level. No adjustments to E & P were allowed for any investment credit recapture. Now, an S corporation can reduce accumulated E & P by the investment credit recaptured.

- Certain trusts that distributed income currently can qualify as shareholders in S corporations. Under prior law, the election could be retroactive for up to 60 days. Under the new law, the election may be retroactive for up to 2 months and 15 days, which conforms to the time provided the corporation to make an S election. In addition, under the new law, the disqualification of a "qualified S trust" because of the failure to meet the distribution requirements is effective on the first day of the first taxable year after the distribution requirements are not met.

- The law amended the passive income rules to prevent the termination of an S corporation because of excess passive income. Now, an S corporation with excess passive income can elect to terminate rather than paying both a corporate and shareholder tax on that income. If the S corporation does elect to terminate, it cannot reelect S corporation status within 5 years without the consent of IRS.

- Cash distributions by an S corporation during the one-year post-termination transition period are tax free. The new Act permits an S corporation to elect to treat such distributions as dividends, provided all shareholders agree. This enables the corporation to avoid the accumulated earnings and personal holding company tax.

- The corporate preference rules generally have not applied to S corporations. Now the corporate preference rules apply to the first 3 taxable years after a C corporation elects S status. This prevents a C corporation from electing S status to avoid the preference rules.

- Under the law, interest and expenses owed by an accrual basis S corporation to a cash-basis related taxpayer are allowable deductions to the corporation no earlier than the day such amounts are includible in the gross income of the payee.
- Present law imposes a tax on S corporations with passive income and C corporation's earnings and profits. Under the new law, IRS can waive this tax if the corporation has in good faith determined that it had no such E & P, and the earnings are distributed after discovery.
- Present law requires the basis of debt that is reduced by losses to be restored to subsequent income. The new law clarifies that this applies only to the extent the basis in the debt was reduced in taxable years beginning after 1982.

PROFESSIONAL CORPORATIONS

Organizations of doctors, lawyers, accountants and other professionals duly organized under state laws as professional associations or corporations are now generally recognized by the IRS as corporate entities.

They now have the choice of being taxed as:

1. Corporations, or
2. S Corporations.

In the past, combinations of professional persons were considered to be partnerships for tax purposes with all income earned, whether distributed or not, flowing through to the individual returns. In addition, deferment of income for flowing through to the individual returns, and, deferment of income for retirement purposes and later taxation was extremely limited in comparison with what could be deferred for corporate officials.

If they exercise the *S option*, professional corporations will:

1. Eliminate the corporate form of double taxation (on dividends) by being taxed on all earnings, whether distributed or not, effectively (with exceptions) being taxed as if it were a partnership, yet having some of the corporation-type benefits:
2. *Not be able to obtain key corporate fringe benefits:* In general, the following fringe benefits are taxable to S shareholder-employees who own more than 2% of the stock; employer-funded medical reimbursement plan; employer-paid accident, health, and group-term life insurance. On the plus side, in tax years beginning after 1984, deductible contributions to a S Corp. retirement plan are the same as for a C Corp. retirement plan.

In other-than-tax considerations, and excluding the factor of personal liability for professional malpractice, the corporate structure for the professional group offers the same advantages and disadvantages of a regular corporation.

RECAPITALIZATIONS

A recapitalization may be tax free or taxable, depending on how it is accomplished. An exchange of stock for stock—i.e., common for common or preferred for preferred—is tax free regardless of whether or not a reorganization or recapitalization is involved. In other cases, to get freedom from taxes, you need to meet the reorganization rules.

Tax-Free Recapitalizations

Tax-free recapitalization should have a proper plan of reorganization and a "good business purpose" (other than just for a tax-saving purpose). In determining whether an exchange is tax free, you'll have to rely on your interpretation of the law and regulations; there is no complete listing of exchanges that are tax free or not tax free. Here is a brief summary of the types of changes and their tax results.

Stock for stock.   The following exchanges have been held to be tax free:

(1) A surrender to the corporation for cancellation of a portion of its preferred stock in exchange for no-par value common stock.

(2) A surrender of common stock for preferred stock previously authorized, but unissued.

(3) An exchange of outstanding preferred stock, having priorities as to the amount and time of payment of dividends and the distribution of the corporate assets upon liquidation, for a new issue of common stock having no such rights.

(4) An exchange of common for common or preferred for preferred could also qualify as a recapitalization with no gain or loss resulting.

(5) An exchange of outstanding preferred stock with dividend arrearages, for a similar amount of preferred stock plus an amount of stock (preferred or common) applicable to the amount of the arrearages. But this exchange cannot be made solely for the purpose of effecting the payment of dividends for current and immediately preceding taxable years on the preferred stock exchanged. If it is, an amount equal to the value of stock issued in lieu of such dividends can become taxable.

Bonds for bonds.   An exchange of bonds for bonds in equal principal amounts is tax free. However, the fair market value of the excess of principal amount of bonds received over those surrendered is taxable as "boot," and if the securities are capital assets to the holder, this excess is taxed as capital gain.

Bonds for stock. A discharge of outstanding bonds for preferred stock instead of cash is tax free. (The same result could probably be achieved with any type of security.) The entire exchange is tax free with no allocation as to the interest on the arrearages. Further, stock worth less than the principal amount of bonds surrendered may be distributed to creditors with no taxable result.

Stock for bonds. A distribution of bonds or other securities in exchange for the surrender of stock is taxable. In addition, if the corporation has substantial earnings on hand, a distribution of bonds to the common stockholders (whether or not pro rata) is likely to be taxed as a dividend. But where the distribution of bonds is to preferred stockholders (rather than pro rata to common stockholders) on a non-pro rata basis, capital gain or loss may result.

Recapitalization Exchanges Taxed as Dividends

There are four reasons why a recapitalization exchange may be taxed as a dividend. It is important to avoid having your exchange fall into any one of these danger zones. The four possibilities are:

(1) *Distribution of "boot" where there are corporate earnings available for distribution.* Distribution of "boot" automatically means a tax of some sort; and if the corporation has undistributed earnings, the Treasury will be tempted to charge that distribution of the "boot" was a distribution of earnings.

(2) *Redemption of stock treated as a dividend.* To avoid this, the redemption must be one of the following: (a) not essentially equivalent to a dividend; (b) substantially disproportionate; (c) a complete termination of stockholder's interest.

(3) *Failure to meet "net effect" test.* Regardless of technical compliance with the law, a recapitalization can be taxed if it fails to meet the "business purpose" test. The "net effect" test is a refinement of the "business purpose" test. It means that the recapitalization will be taxed if its net effect is to accomplish a distribution of earnings.

(4) *Preferred stock bailout.* A preferred stock dividend followed by sale or redemption of the preferred stock is taxable as a dividend to the extent the corporation had earnings and profits.

Elimination of Arrearages in Dividends or Interest

A recapitalization is often used as a means of eliminating back dividends on a preferred stock or back interest on bonds. Generally, the investor will be given a new security to replace the defaulted one plus something to take the place of the arrearage. Only some exchanges for this purpose will be tax free.

Dividend or interest arrearages could be eliminated tax free only by replacing them with new stock. In the case of dividend arrearages on preferred stock, the arrearage might be eliminated by issuance of new preferred in exchange for the old preferred, the amount issued being sufficient to cover both the old preferred and the back dividends. In the case of bond interest, the back interest might be eliminated by issuance of new bonds in the same amount as the old bonds, plus preferred stock to cover the back interest. However, there are exceptions if the arrearage pertains to the current or preceding taxable years.

When to Use a Taxable Recapitalization

In most discussions of the tax effects of recapitalizations, the stress is placed upon avoiding taxability. This doesn't always produce the best result. For example, in the usual bonds for preferred stock recapitalization, there is no spread between the basis of the old securities and the value of the new ones. In this case, since there is no gain, it makes no particular difference whether the recapitalization is taxed. And where basis exceeds value, it will be desirable to have the exchange taxed in order to realize a loss.

Even where there is a tax, it will be at the capital gain rate unless the corporation has earnings and the recapitalization is equivalent to the payment of a dividend. Depending upon the circumstances, it may be advantageous to effect a taxable recapitalization, rather than a nontaxable one.

DIVIDENDS

Cash dividends, stock dividends, rights and split-ups.   In making distributions to shareholders, corporations should be aware of the possible tax effect to the distributee (shareholder).

Cash dividends are taxable at ordinary rates to the recipient in the year of receipt, if the distribution is out of current profits or accumulated retained earnings. Portions of the dividend may be capital gain distributions; portions may be non-taxable distributions. Distinctions must be indicated on the 1099-DIV sent to the recipient ($10 or more).

Stock dividends are ordinarily non-taxable to the recipient at the time of distribution, merely adjusting his basis by changing the number of shares owned at the same prior total cost. Stock rights usually increase the cost-basis and the number of shares. However, there are some circumstances under which stock dividends/rights *may* be taxable in the year of issue, such as distributions when the recipient has an alternative option of receiving cash or property from the corporation, or in disproportionate distributions, or distributions involving preferred or convertible stocks— these instances may involve a pickup of income at the *market price* at the time of distribution.

''Stock Split-ups'' and ''Stock Splits Effected in the Form of a Dividend'' (to conform with State laws) change the holding basis of the stock to the recipient. The corporation may have to make Schedule M adjustments on its Form 1120, if the stock distribution entailed an adjustment of retained earnings, because such earnings, if not taxable upon distribution, may still be considered available for cash dividend distribution by the IRS and, therefore, at some future day, taxable at regular individual rates when and if distributed in cash.

OTHER EQUITY CONSIDERATIONS

Net operating loss carryover.   Determine the availability of carryover losses from prior years for possible reduction of current year's taxes.

Retained earnings.   Federal and many state returns require an analysis of the retained-earnings account.

"Schedule M" adjustments.   Gather the data needed to prepare Schedule M—the schedule that reconciles the company's income per its books with the income according to the tax return. Items involved may include losses (e.g., net capital losses); items not allowed as tax deductions; income items picked up in prior years for book purposes but for the current year for tax purposes, or vice versa; or deductions picked up currently for tax purposes but not for book purposes, or vice versa.

☐ CORRECTED

PAYER'S name, street address, city, state, and ZIP code	1 Gross dividends and other distributions on stock	OMB No. 1545-0110	Dividends and Distributions
	2 Dividends qualifying for exclusion	19**86** Statement for Recipients of	
PAYER'S Federal identification number · RECIPIENT'S identification number	3 Dividends not qualifying for exclusion	4 Federal income tax withheld	**Copy B For Recipient**
RECIPIENT'S name (first, middle, last)	5 Capital gain distributions	6 Nontaxable distributions (if determinable)	This is important tax information and is being furnished to the Internal Revenue Service. If you are required to file a return, a negligence penalty or other sanction will be imposed on you if this dividend income is taxable and the IRS determines that it has not been reported.
Street address	7 Foreign tax paid	8 Foreign country or U.S. possession	
City, state, and ZIP code	**Liquidation Distributions**		
	9 Cash	10 Noncash (Fair market value)	
Account number (optional)			

Form **1099-DIV**

Department of the Treasury · Internal Revenue Service

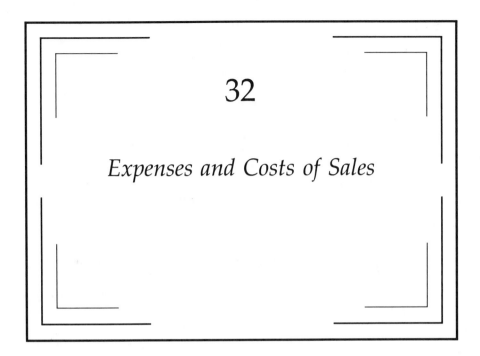

32

Expenses and Costs of Sales

CONFLICTS BETWEEN TAX AND BUSINESS ACCOUNTING FOR EXPENSES

As there are conflicts in the timing of entering and recognizing income, as indicated in the prior chapter, so too are there divergencies in the recognition of deductions. The following list of expense-timing differences was also included in the submission by the AICPA to the House Committee on Ways and Means during the 1954 Code Hearings:

Divergencies Involving the Time of Allowance of Deductions:

(A) Costs and expenses, recognized for general accounting purposes, on basis of reasonable estimates, in period of related revenues; but not deductible for tax purposes until established with certainty by specific transactions:

    (1) Sales returns and allowances.

    (2) Freight allowances.

    (3) Quantity discounts.

    (4) Cash discounts allowable to customers.

    (5) Allowances for customers' advertising.

(6) Provision for return of commissions resulting from cancellations of related contracts.

(7) Costs of product guarantees.

(8) Deferred management compensation and incentive bonuses.

(9) Vacation pay.

(10) Pending injury and damage claims.

(11) Rentals on percentage lease with minimum.

(12) Provisions for major repairs and maintenance regularly done at intervals of more than a year.

(13) Professional services rendered but unbilled.

(14) Social Security taxes on unpaid wages.

(15) Retailers' occupation taxes on credit sales.

(16) Costs of restoration of property by lessee at termination of lease.

(17) Contractors' provisions for restoration of property damaged during construction.

(18) Costs of handling, packing, shipping, installing, etc., of merchandise already sold.

(19) Provisions for future costs to be incurred in collection of accounts receivable arising from installment sales, where profit is reported in the year of sale.

(20) Provisions for losses on foreign exchange.

(21) Allowances for perpetual care of cemetery (where not actually segregated from receipts).

(B) Expenses, deferred for general accounting purposes to period of related benefit, but deducted for tax purposes in year of payment or incurrence of liability:

    (1) Advertising expenses from which benefit has not yet been obtained, including costs of preparation of catalogs not yet put into use.

(C) Property taxes recognized for general accounting purposes ratably over the year for which they are levied, but deductible in total tax purposes on a certain critical date.

The foregoing differences do not include conflicts which result from Congressional policy decisions. These include, on the *income side*: tax-exempt interest, tax-free exchanges, exemption of life insurance proceeds, capital gains, etc.; and, on the *deduction side*: percentage depletion, amortization of emergency facilities, loss carryovers and the disallowance of excess charitable contribution, losses on wash sales, losses on sales between certain relatives or related business interests, capital losses, etc.

The special treatment accorded these items originates from social, economic, and revenue considerations which, in the main, are unrelated to accounting principles.

BAD DEBT METHOD CHANGE

The New Act repeals the reserve method of computing deductions for bad debts by disallowing the deduction until the debt becomes partially or totally worthless. Any reserve balance in a bad debt account may be taken into income in equal amounts over four years, or 25 percent a year.

The deduction for a partially worthless debt is allowable only in the year in which the partial amount of the debt is charged off the books. Totally worthless debts need not be charged off the books to be deductible: such debt can be deductible in full in the year that it becomes worthless. (See Appendix B.)

DEPRECIATION METHODS

Note: This section applies to depreciable assets acquired *before* January 1, 1981.

Depreciation methods permitted by the tax law include: (1) straight-line method (equal annual installments), (2) declining-balance method (up to double the straight-line rate), (3) sum-of-the-years-digits method (rate is a fraction, the numerator being the property's remaining useful life at the start of the tax year and the denominator being the sum of all the years' digits corresponding to the estimated useful life at acquisition), and (4) any other consistent method which during the first two-thirds of the property's useful life does not give greater depreciation than under the declining-balance method.

Method number (4) embraces use of a sinking fund, writeoffs on the basis of periodic appraisal, unit of production, etc. However, most taxpayers who do not use the classic straight-line method employ instead one of the acceleration methods, either the 200%-declining-balance method of the sum-of-the-years-digits methods.

Another possibility that should be mentioned is a combination of the straight-line method and the 200%-declining-balance method. With this method, you use the 200%-declining-balance method, which gives you extra large deduction in the early years. At this point where this starts to peter out, you switch to straight-line which can be accomplished without consent of the Commissioner.

A good deal of what you do here will depend on prior years' actions. But you will want to analyze the existing situation to see if special, quick writeoffs are justified as to special assets; whether it's time to switch from double-declining-balance to straight-line on certain assets. Where new assets were acquired during the year, whether accelerated depreciation should be used as to them even though you use straight-line as to your other assets; whether you are using adequate salvage provisions; and whether you are taking advantage of the right to disregard salvage where permissible.

The 1969 Tax Reform Act restricted the use of accelerated depreciation for real property to 150% and also tightened the recapture rules. It also provided quicker writeoffs for certain types of properties and improvements. Low-income housing rehabilitation may be depreciated over a 60-month period. Pollution control facilities which are certified by governmental authorities may also be amortized over a 60-month period and so may railroad rolling stock, child-care facility and on-the-job training facility expenditures.

The applicable allowable depreciation (or amortization in lieu of depreciation) methods and rates may be summarized as follows:

Declining-balance method, 200% rate is allowed for new tangible personal property with a useful life of three years or more; all types of newly constructed real estate structures acquired before July 25, 1969; only on new residential rental property where 80% or more of gross rentals are from dwelling units.

Declining-balance method, 150% rate is allowed for used tangible personal property and for new real estate bought or constructed after July 24, 1969. No accelerated depreciation is allowed for used realty bought after that same date, unless it is used residential rental property (see next paragraph).

Declining-balance method, 125% rate is allowed only for used residential rental property acquired after July 24, 1969, and having a useful life of 20 years or more, or if the Commissioner permits it on application for other types.

Sum-of-the-years-digits method is allowed only for new tangible personal property and new residential rental property.

Straight-line (useful life) method is allowed for all depreciable property, new or used, personal or real.

Straight-line method (no salvage value), 60 months applies to low-income rental housing rehabilitation expenditures; certified pollution control facilities; certain railroad rolling stock.

Additional first-year 20% depreciation write-off is also permitted (regardless of which method above is used) to the maximum extent of $2,000 depreciation (the same maximum applies to an *entire* affiliated group).

The taxpayer has a further election:

For assets placed in service after 1970, depreciation rates used may be based on either:

1) Estimated Useful Life, generally based on guidelines in Rev. Proc. 62–21 or prior IRS Bulletin F; or

2) The Class Life Asset Depreciation Range System (ADR).

Regulations regarding the use of ADR are quite extensive and detailed. Taxpayers should study this election further. It offers many taxable advantages.

OTHER ELECTIONS

Leasehold amortization.   Improvement costs on leaseholds are recovered by one of two methods. You will need information about cost of improvement, useful life, remaining term of the lease, renewal options available. For example, if remaining life of lease is less than 60% of useful life of improvement, amortization must be over remaining lease life *plus* renewal periods, but not longer than useful life of improvement. Or, if lessor is an affiliate, shortest available life over which amortization may be taken is useful life of improvement. Location of lease property is also useful information for state allocation purposes.

Under ACRS, leasehold costs are recovered in about the same way, except instead of comparing the remaining years of the lease to the useful life, the remaining lease term is compared to the recovery period. This results in improvement costs being recovered either by straight-line amortization, or through ACRS recovery, whichever is shorter.

Trademark and trade name amortization. Examine costs of trademarks or trade names incurred during the year (including cost of acquisition other than purchase), protection, expansion, registration (federal, state, or foreign), or defense of trademark or trade name; cost can be written off over at least a 60-month period rather than capitalized.

Patent amortization. Examine patent data to determine whether there is any basis to increase deduction—e.g., patent has become worthless.

Bond premiums. The bondholder can elect to amortize bond premium on wholly taxable obligations to maturity or to the date on which the bond is first callable if the deduction is smaller. The bond premium, which is deductible, reduces the basis of the bond. Taxpayer makes the election by claiming the deduction in the first taxable year for which he wishes it to apply. It applies to all bonds and can be revoked only with Commissioner's permission.

Every taxpayer must amortize premium on wholly-tax-exempt bonds, even though no tax deduction results, thus reducing the basis annually.

Carrying charges. There is an election to deduct or capitalize taxes, interest and other carrying charges in connection with the following kinds of property:

(1) Unimproved and unproductive real property. The election is to deduct or capitalize taxes, interest and other carrying charges.

(2) Real property being developed or improved. The election is to deduct or capitalize costs up to the time construction or development has been completed. For instance: Social Security taxes on own employees, sale or use taxes on materials used in development or improvement of property, and other necessary expenditures paid or incurred in connection with this work.

(3) Personal property. The election is to deduct or capitalize interest on loans to purchase the property or to pay for transporting or installing, sales and use taxes paid on the property, Social Security taxes on own employees used in transporting and installing the property, paid or incurred up to the date installed or first put into use, whichever date is later.

Election to capitalize any item is made by filing a statement with the return, stating the items being charged to capital. Commissioner's consent is not required.

Circulation expenditures. Publisher can elect to capitalize rather than deduct expenditures made to establish or increase circulation. Year-to-year expenditures to maintain circulation cannot be capitalized but must be deducted currently.

The election, if made, must be applied to all expenditures to increase circulation in the present or later years, except where the Commissioner permits change on written application.

The election is made by a statement attached to the first tax return to which it is applicable.

Depletion. Bear in mind that a taxpayer has no election, in the true sense of that word, in selecting a depletion method. What actually happens is that he must make a computation for depletion based on both the cost and percentage methods and then select the method which results in the greatest deduction, regardless of whether it will be a disadvantage to the taxpayer. This computation is to be made each year.

Cost depletion formula:

$$\frac{\text{Original Cost } + \text{ Development Expense}}{\text{Estimated Units of Recovery}} = \text{Unit Depletion}$$

$$\text{Unit Depletion} \times \text{Units Extracted and Sold} = \text{Cost Depletion Allowed}$$

Percentage depletion is the lesser of the statutory percentage of gross income (varies from 22% on down, depending upon the statutory classification, with gas and oil also having additional limitations) from the property, or 50% of the net computed without the depletion deduction.

Foreign taxes. With respect to income, war profits and excess profits taxes paid or accrued to a foreign country, a taxpayer has the option to take credit against income taxes or a reduction from gross income.

Involuntary conversion. Taxpayer can use recovery to either replace or restore property and avoid tax or pay the tax and step up the basis of newly acquired property.

To avoid the tax, the taxpayer must replace or restore the property within the time beginning with first date of known imminence of condemnation or the actual date of destruction and ending two years after the end of the first taxable year, or a later approved IRS date (three years for real property).

Mining—development expenses (excluding oil or gas well). Taxpayer can either deduct these in the year they were incurred or capitalize them and deduct them ratably over units of ore as produced or minerals as benefited.

These expenses do not include exploration expenses or expenditures for depreciable property. For a mine in the development stage, the election applies only to the excess of expenditures over the net receipts from ores or minerals produced during the year. Election, if made, applies to all development expenditures. It is made by a written statement, filed with the Director of Internal Revenue with whom the return is filed, or by a rider attached to the return. A new election is made each year.

Mining—exploration expenses. All such expenditures paid or incurred after 1969 are deductible. Such expenditures made for the discovery of a new mine are subject to recapture when the mine begins producing, with some exceptions.

Rent expenses. Examine rent agreements in first year of agreement to see if there are any purchase options that might warrant IRS treating the rental as a purchase. In this connection, compare the rent called for where there is an option with what the rent would have been without an option. Rents paid may also be needed for state allocation formulas.

EMPLOYEE BENEFITS

"Reasonable" Compensation

All payments to compensate an employee for services which are ordinary and necessary to the operation of the business are deductible *provided* they are "reasonable."

What Is Reasonable? Determining reasonable compensation is not an easy task. The courts themselves have a hard time determining what is reasonable under certain facts. Nevertheless, here is a list of the several factors usually considered by the courts in dealing with this problem: (1) The employee's special qualifications; (2) the nature, extent and scope of work; (3) the size and complexities of the business; (4) the prevailing general economic conditions; (5) comparison of salaries to dividends; (6) rates of compensation for comparable positions in comparable concerns; (7) the "arm's length" element in the compensation deal; (8) consideration for past services and compensation in prior years; (9) comparison of salaries paid with employee's stock ownership.

Cash and Stock Bonuses

The cash bonus is used to assure the employee of an immediate share of the company's profits over and above his regular compensation. In a noncontractual plan, the amount of the bonus, who is to get it, and, in what proportions, are usually determined on a year-by-year basis—depending on the amount of profits.

Under a formal contractual basis, the employee knows before-hand exactly what to expect. If a certain profit is reached, he gets a definite amount as his share.

The stock bonus plan is exactly like the cash bonus except, of course, that the payment is made in company stock. The big advantage of paying employee's bonuses in stock rather than cash is that the company can retain the cash to be used in the business. Furthermore, the corporation gets a compensation deduction for the market value of the stock.

Stock Options

The requirement that incentive stock options must be exercised in the order granted is repealed beginnng after December 31, 1986. The $100,000 limit on the amount of options that may be granted in any year is modified, i.e., an employer cannot grant options that are first exercisable during any one calander year, if the aggregate fair market value of the stock exceeds $100,000. (See Appendix B.)

An employee does not recognize any income upon the granting or exercise of an incentive stock option provided that the option is exercised no later than three months after termination of employment and the employee does not dispose of the acquired shares within two years after the date of grant and one year after the date of exercise. Any gain realized upon disposition thereafter is treated as long-term capital gain. (A similar provision that applied to qualified stock options required a holding period of three years after the date of exercise.)

These are the requirements for an incentive stock option.

(1) The option must be granted in connection with employment and pursuant to a plan that includes (a) the aggregate number of shares that may be issued under the options and (b) the employees or class of employees eligible to receive options. The plan must be approved by the stockholders of the granting corporation within 12 months before or after the plan is adopted. (An identical requirement applied to qualified stock options.)

(2) The option must be granted within 10 years after the plan is adopted or approved by the stockholders, whichever is earlier. (The same provision applied to qualified options.)

(3) The option cannot be exercisable more than 10 years after the date of grant. See, however, Special Rule (5) on the following page. (Qualified options had a 5-year limit.)

(4) The option price cannot be less than the fair market value of the stock at the time of grant* (The same provision applied to qualified options.) However, see Special Rule (1) on the following page.

(5) The option is nontransferable except by will or the laws of descent and distribution, and is exercisable only by the employee during his lifetime. (Same as qualified option.) Under the 1984 Tax Act, a change in the terms of an option to

---

*The 1984 Tax Act makes the determination of a stock's fair market value for both income and minimum tax purposes without regard to any restriction other than one which, by its terms, won't lapse.

make it nontransferable (and thereby qualify as an ISO), will be treated as a new option. As a result, the option must be adjusted to meet ISO requirements.

(6) The employee does not own more than 10% of the voting stock of the employer corporation or of its parent or subsidiary. See, however, Special Rule (5). (For a qualified option, ownership could not exceed 5% of the voting stock if the corporation's equity capital was $2 million or more.)

(7) An option may not be exercisable while an incentive stock option that was granted earlier remains outstanding. (A similar restriction applied to qualified options.)

(8) No more than $100,000 worth of stock can be optioned to an individual in any one year. However, if less than $100,000 is granted in any year, one-half of the ungranted amount may be carried over to three succeeding years. (Qualified options had no such limitations.)

Special Rules

(1) There is *no penalty* if the option price is less than the fair market value of the stock on the date of grant, as long as there was an attempt, "made in good faith," to meet the requirement that the price be no less than the market value. (Qualified stock options had a similar "good faith" provision, but required the lucky optionee to include in income either 1½ times the difference between the option price and the value at the time of grant or the difference between the option price and the value at the time of exercise, whichever was less.)

(2) If an employee sells acquired stock within two years after the option is granted, the employee's gain will be included in his gross income and deductible by the corporation as compensation.

(3) A transfer by an insolvent individual to a trustee, receiver, or other fiduciary in a bankruptcy proceeding or other similar proceeding for the benefit of creditors will not be subject to the two-year or one-year holding period.

(4) An option may be treated as an incentive stock option if:

a) The employee may pay for the stock with stock of the corporation granting the option;

b) The employee has a right to receive property when the option is exercised;

c) The option is subject to any condition that is not inconsistent with the requirements for an incentive stock option.

(5) An incentive stock option may be granted to an individual who owns more than 10% of the voting stock of the corporation or its parent or subsidiary if the option price is at least 110% of the fair market value of the stock at the time of grant and the option is not exercisable after five years.

(6) If an individual who received an incentive stock option is disabled, the

option may be exercised as late as one year after employment is terminated because of disability.

Deferred Compensation Arrangements

With the fantastic growth of business over the years, the arrival of high corporate and individual tax rates, and the increased public interest in retirement planning, there has been evolved a mass of intricate and involved deferred compensation plans to attract new employees or retain old employees.

Under a deferred compensation plan, payment of compensation presently earned is postponed to a future period. If the plan qualifies as an exempt trust, the employer gets an immediate deduction for a contribution—even though the employee does not receive the sum until a later time. However, under a non-qualified deferred compensation contract, the employer gets a deduction only when he actually pays the deferred compensation to the employee (who is taxed at that time).

Under a nonqualified plan, the employer can pick and choose who will benefit; he is not committed to a class of employees or any other rigid requirement as provided for qualified deferred compensation plans. Generally, this arrangement is less ambitious than qualified plans and therefore more attractive to smaller organizations.

Most often the nonqualified deferred compensation plan is used for a key executive. The ordinary plan is to have the company accumulate funds for the benefit of the executive and then pay them out when the executive reaches post-retirement years and is in a lower tax bracket.

The maximum amount that an employee can elect to defer for any taxable year under all cash or deferred arrangements in which the employee participates is limited to $7,000, adjusted for inflation by reference to percentage increases in the dollar limit under a defined benefit plan. (Effective beginning after December 31, 1986.)

Elective deferrals under a Simplified Employee Pension Plan (SEPs) are to be treated like elective deferrals under a qualified cash or deferred arrangement and are subject to the $7,000 (indexed) cap on elective deferrals.

The maximum amount that an employee can elect to defer for any taxable year under all tax-sheltered annuities in which the employee participates is limited to $9,500, adjusted for inflation when the $7,000 cap on elective deferrals under a qualified cash or deferred arrangement reaches $9,500. (See Appendix B.)

Insurance Plans

Key-person insurance.   This is insurance on a key-person's life. It is deductible only if the *employer* is not directly or indirectly the beneficiary, and if the premiums are in the nature of compensation and are not unreasonable.

Split-dollar insurance.   The employee pays a portion of the premium to the employer under this plan (life insurance), and that portion reduces the amount included in income (the includable amount would be, in effect, the employer's share of the premium). Any policy dividends received by the employee are also included in his income.

Group term life insurance.   This arrangement offers an employee an opportunity to acquire low-cost life insurance because it's purchased for a "group." Under a "group term" plan the employee can get up to $50,000 of insurance protection tax free; that is, all premiums paid on over that amount of insurance must be included in income. But the plan has to be a group *term* plan. Permanent insurance (whole life policies) does not qualify under this provision.

Group health.   This plan provides for the reimbursement of medical and hospitalization expenses incurred by an employee. Premiums are tax deductible by the employer and not taxable to the employee—even though the plan provides for the protection of the employee's family. This plan is widely used by many employers to provide their employees with at least the basic health and accident protection. Of course, individual health plans for particular employees are also used.

Tax Advantages of Qualified Plans

(1) *Employer*: The employer gets a current deduction for amounts contributed to the plan, within specified limits, although no benefits may have been actually distributed to the participating employees that year. This permits an employer to accumulate a trust fund for his employees with 100-cent, before-tax dollars which, in effect, represent 54-cent after-tax dollars to the employer in the 46% tax surtax bracket. The employer expense for the contribution to a qualified plan may be accrued at year-end, but it must be paid no later than the legal time of filing the return (including extensions).

(2) *Employees*: The tax to the employee is deferred until the benefits under the plan are actually distributed or made available to him. If the employee receives a lump-sum distribution, a portion of it may be capital gains (based on years of participation prior to 1974) and the remaining taxable portion is subject to ordinary income rates, but there is a special 10-year averaging option available.

(3) *Trust Fund*: The income and gains on the sale of trust property of the trust fund are exempt from tax, in effect, being postponed until distribution. Funds, which are compounded tax free under a qualified plan, increase at a much greater rate than if such funds were currently distributed to employees and personally invested by them. In the latter case, the amount received by the employees is subject to two tax bites—when he receives the benefits and again on the investment income earned on what is left.

CHOOSING BETWEEN PENSION AND PROFIT SHARING

Profit Sharing	*Pension*
(1) Generally favors younger employees.	(1) Generally favors older employees.
(2) Need not provide retirement benefits.	(2) Must provide retirement benefits.
(3) Contribution can be made only if profits exist.	(3) Contributions must be made for profitable as well as for loss years.
(4) Even in profitable years the amount of contributions, if any, can be left to discretion of management.	(4) Amount of contribution is not discretionary; it must be actuarially justifiable and tied to definitely determinable benefits.
(5) Contributed amounts generally cannot exceed 15% of year's payroll for participants.	(5) No maximum limit on contributions as long as they are actuarially justifiable and total compensation is within IRS 162 limitations.
(6) Forfeitures may be allocated in favor of remaining participants.	(6) Forfeitures must be used to decrease future cost to employer.
(7) No more than 50% of participant's account may be invested in life insurance.	(7) May be completely funded by investment in life insurance.
(8) Broad fringe benefits can be included (incidental accident and health insurance).	(8) Limited fringe benefits can be included (disability pension).
(9) Employer may never recover any part of contribution or income therefrom.	(9) Employer on termination of plan may recover excess funds which arose as a result of actuarial error.

ERISA

The Employee Retirement Income Security Act of 1974, commonly called ERISA, substantially changed the rules and set new minimum standards for employees' trusts, most notably in the following areas:

1) Participation rules.
2) Vesting rights.
3) Funding requirements.

In addition, the tax and information forms which are required to be filed with the IRS (and in some cases with the Department of Labor) were changed and are constantly being revamped.

Arguments both for and against the new law are being debated, and much confusion still surrounds its administration, regulation, interpretation and effect. Professional advice should be sought for updating old plans and for instituting new plans, as well as for assuring conformance with the required new regulations and reporting.

Non-corporate entities and individuals should also pursue the tax deferral opportunities now expanded for them under the new law.

HOW TO SHIFT BUSINESS EXPENSES

Here is how to shift expenses, depending on whether you want to boost the current year's or the following year's deductions:

(1) *A cash-basis taxpayer can pay all bills by December 31.* If it wants to defer expenses, it will hold off payment until January. You can't get a deduction for certain prepayments—even if you are on the cash basis (e.g., insurance premiums, rents)—especially if they cover more than one year's period.

(2) *Rush through repairs,* buy office supplies, pay research and experimental costs if you want the deduction this year. Hold off if you want it next year.

(3) *Accrual-basis taxpayers can pick up sales returns and allowances* by December 31, to get a deduction this year—after December 31, for a deduction next year.

(4) *Have your lawyer and accountant bill you* before year-end if you want to accrue or pay the bill for the taxable year.

(5) *Junk or abandon equipment, etc.,* before the year's end for deduction this year—next year for a deduction next year.

(6) *Switching from bad debt writeoffs to reserve* method brings more deduction into this year. Theoretically, this switch can double up your bad debt deduction. But, as a practical matter, since you need IRS' permission to switch, IRS will make you spread the additional deduction over a ten-year period. So you can only increase your deduction by 10% this year.

(7) *Corporate contribution deductions can be accrued* this year if paid within 2½ months after the end of the tax year. So, where the corporation is short of cash now but wants the deduction this year, make sure you pass the appropriate corporate resolution making the contribution and calling for payment no later than 2½ months after the end of your tax year. (*Caution:* The new premature accrual rules may affect this strategy.)

(8) *Items in dispute—contested taxes or other liabilities—*must be deducted when they are paid, even though a contest which finally determines the liability is resolved in a later year. This applies to accrual as well as cash-basis taxpayers. So, if you are anxious to get the deduction this year, pay the liability by year-end.

(9) *Losses on worthless assets* have to be shown by an identifiable event in the year the loss is taken. Where worthlessness may be difficult to prove, dispose of the asset in the year you want the loss.

Here are some other considerations that you should have at the end of the year.

Business Gifts at Year-End

Since year-end is often the season of making business gifts, it's important to check your lists carefully to be aware whether or not you are making total gifts to one person or more than $25—the deductible ceiling on a business gift. In addition, you ought to be aware of the definition of business gifts and where you can avoid falling within the definitions.

Maybe your "gift" can qualify as entertainment.   There's no ceiling on entertainment costs; but you have to have full substantiation.

Generally, says IRS, where an item might be either entertainment, on the one hand, or a gift or travel cost, on the other, it will be considered entertainment. But packaged food and beverages given to a customer, for example, for use at some other time are gifts.

As for theater and similar tickets of admission, if you go along, it's entertainment, even if you give the tickets to your guest. If you don't go along, you can treat the expense either as entertainment or a business gift.

Audit Your Pay Setup at Year-End

Wages and salaries are by far the most compelling income and expense factor in many a business. The final months of the year provide the last opportunity to arrange compensation policies for minimum tax cost—both for employer and for employees.

Here are some important points you will want to watch:

Are office-stockholders getting the best "tax" salary?   That's the amount at which any increase will cost the employee-stockholder more in taxes than the corporation will save by the increase and at which any decrease would cost the corporation more than the employee saves.

Bonus declarations.   Year-end bonus declarations and payments boost this year's compensation deductions. But you always have to be concerned with the problem of reasonableness. Suppose part of the compensation is disallowed as being unreasonable. The corporation loses the deduction and the employee still has income for what he received—so we have a double tax. If the corporation can use more deductions now but doesn't have the cash, it can accrue them (assuming, of course, the corporation uses the accrual method of accounting). It gets the deduction now, and the employee has income when he receives it.

But keep in mind the special rules; if the employee is a more-than-50% stockholder, the corporation has to pay the accrued salaries or bonuses within 2½ months after the end of the year. Otherwise, it loses its deduction altogether.

Unusual transactions.   Check all transactions during the year of an unusual nature—outside the scope of what the corporation normally does—to determine whether any special tax problems exist as to any of these transactions.

Compensation.   Details of officers' compensation are required for tax returns—name, Social Security number, address, title, time devoted to business, percentage of stock owned (common and preferred), amount of compensation and expense account allowances. As to other compensation, it's a good idea to reconcile the total compensation claimed on the tax return with the amounts shown on the payroll tax reports. Note that the compensation shown on the payroll tax reports is on a cash basis, so a reconciliation to the amounts of compensation claimed as deductions on the tax return which is on the accrual basis is necessary. This reconciliation will help justify your deduction if your tax return is audited.

Information on interest, rents and other payments to officers and stockholders may also be required for state tax returns.

Note the statutory definition of what must be included as "expense account allowance."

OTHER TAX-EXPENSE CONSIDERATIONS

Charitable contributions.   Examine charitable contributions in the form of donations of the company's own product. Deduction is based on market value plus ½ of appreciated value (not to exceed twice basis), since it is considered ordinary income property. Where deduction is based on accrual to be paid within two and a half months after close of taxable year, make sure the proper corporate resolution was passed before year end. The annual limit on a company's charitable contributions is 10% of taxable income.

Payroll taxes.   As in the case of compensation, the payroll taxes paid by the employer and deductible as expenses should be reconciled with the payroll taxes shown on the payroll tax returns, since the taxes on the payroll returns were computed on a cash basis and your deduction for income tax purposes may be deducted on the accrual basis.

Interest expense.   Examine basis for write-downs and keep sufficient backup information to support the write-down (or merchandise destruction), in the event of an examination.

Inventory write-downs.   Examine basis for write-downs and keep sufficient backup information to support the write-down (or merchandise destruction), in the event of an examination.

Repairs.   An analysis of the amounts expensed as repairs during the year should be made to see if all pass as repairs and are not likely to be held to be improvements. Where the items are very numerous, it is likely that a revenue agent will test the account. An analysis of the larger items—e.g., those costing $1,000 or more—made in advance, with sufficient data to back up the deduction of each of these items as a repair, may be very helpful if the return is audited.

Reimbursed travel and entertainment expenses.   The laws applicable to other entertainment expenses now apply to deductions for food and beverage expenses. No deduction is allowed unless business is actually discussed during, before or after the meal. The New Law reduces to 80 percent the amount of any deduction otherwise allowable for business meals and entertainment expenses. This requirement includes meals while away from home and meals furnished on an employer's premises to its employees. (Transportation costs for business travel remain fully deductible.) (See Appendix B.)

State income and franchise taxes.   These should be accrued on the federal tax return for the current year although not yet paid. Also check to see whether taxes that have been prepaid, and therefore deferred on the books, are nevertheless deductible for federal income taxes (as is allowed in many situations— e.g., property taxes may be deducted in the year they accrue even if the period of the tax extends beyond the taxable year). However, a few state franchise taxes specifically pertain to ensuing years and are not deductible until then (California).

Sales and use taxes.   Where a company has a number of locations, it may be advantageous to review the policies at each location and make sure that only those sales and use taxes to which a particular location is subject and being paid or allocated.

Also, be informed as to the possibility of being liable for the sales tax in situations where "location" may not be a factor, such as direct mail sales or shipments.

INFORMATION FOR STATE ALLOCATIONS

Types of locations.   Determine whether the sales in any particular state are subject to any tax at all by the state. For example, where no offices are maintained within the state and orders are subject to acceptance outside the state and goods are shipped from outside the state, it may be that no franchise/income tax is due on sales made in that state. If you are subject to tax, however, consider the following data for the purpose of allocation under each state's own allocation formula.

Sales data.   For each state, you will want to know how much sales were billed to customers within that state, totals of sales reflected by shipments to all customers (wherever located) from points within the state, total sales reflected by shipments from within the state to customers within the state, total sales credited to a sales office within that state (a salesman who lives within the state and works out of his home, there being no "formal" office within the state, does not usually count as a sales office within the state).

Average fixed assets.   For each physical location of the company, determine the balances at the beginning and end of the year (and the average by adding and dividing by two) of the net book values of the fixed assets—e.g., land, buildings, furniture and fixtures, equipment. Some states require the use of cost (California).

Inventories.   For each physical location get the values of all inventories at beginning and end of year and average.

Payroll.   For each state, determine the total payroll actually paid out during the year to employees in that state.

Officer/stockholders.   Determine if information is needed for separate disclosure of sums paid or accrued to officer/stockholders—salaries, rent interest—and the extent of loans to or from officers.

Taxes.   Some states require separate itemization of all taxes by type paid everywhere and specifically within the state.

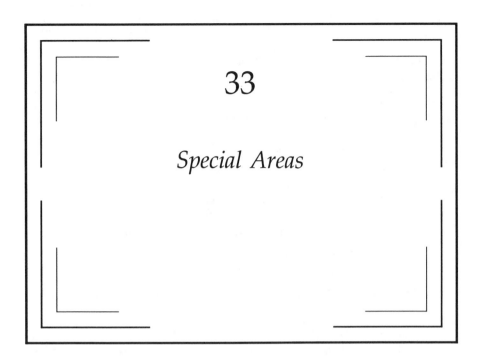

33

Special Areas

RESEARCH AND DEVELOPMENT

The New Law extends the incremental tax credit for an additional three years for qualified research and development expenditures paid or incurred through December 31, 1988. The extension provisions are effective for taxable years beginning after December 31, 1985, and apply to expenditures prior to January 1, 1989. The provisions modifying the credit for university basic research credits are effective for taxable years beginning after December 31, 1986.

A significant change is a reduction in the credit from 25 percent to 20 percent for "qualified" research expenditures as defined in Code Section 174. The Code sets forth in detail three tests to determine if an R & D expenditure qualifies for the credit, and also provides an extensive discussion of a list of research expenditures that do not qualify.

The general limitation on the use of business credits is applied to the research credit; e.g., the credit can offset only 75 percent of tax liability in excess of $25,000.

There are increased tax incentives provided for corporate cash expenditures and donations for basic research payments to universities or certain scientific research organizations. The term *"basic research payments"* is defined in the Code to mean "any amount paid in *cash* during the taxable year by a corporation, other than an S Corporation, a personal holding company, or a service organization as defined in Code Section 414(m)(3).'' (See Appendix B.)

ALTERNATIVE MINIMUM TAX (AMT)

(NOTE: The following discussion is an abridgement of Section 701 of the Code. The AMT rules are very complex; in any application of these rules, the practitioner should carefully reference Section 701.)

The AMT rules use terminology that makes it difficult to understand and apply the AMT requirements without clear definitions of the terms. The following ten terms are defined in the Code in order to better understand their meaning.

ADJUSTED NET BOOK INCOME. The net income or loss of the taxpayer set forth on the taxpayer's applicable financial statement.

ALTERNATIVE MINIMUM TAX. The tentative minimum tax less the regular tax.

ALTERNATIVE MINIMUM TAXABLE INCOME (AMTI). Taxable income for the year, modified by certain adjustments and increased by preference items.

ALTERNATIVE TAX NET OPERATING LOSS DEDUCTION. The net operating loss deduction allowable for the taxable year.

CIRCULATION EXPENDITURES. All expenditures to establish, maintain, or increase the circulation of a newspaper, magazine, or other periodical.

AMT FOREIGN TAX CREDIT. The portion of foreign taxes paid during the taxable year that is attributable to foreign-source income included in AMTI.

REGULAR TAX LIABILITY. The tax computed on regular taxable income.

REGULAR TAX. The regular tax liability less the regular foreign tax credit.

TENTATIVE MINIMUM TAX (TMT). 20 percent of AMTI reduced by a specific exemption less the AMT foreign tax credit.

AMTI is offset by a $40,000 exemption; however, the exemption is reduced by 25% of AMTI over $150,000. The effect is to completely phase out the exemption once AMTI reaches $310,000.

In determining AMTI, taxable income must be calculated making the following adjustments:

- Real property placed in service after 1986 (with a few exceptions), and property placed in service in 1986 for which the new depreciation rules are elected, must be depreciated using the straight-line method over 40 years.
- Personal property placed in service after 1986 (with a few exceptions), and

property placed in service in 1986 for which the new depreciation rules are elected, must be depreciated using the 150 percent declining balance method, switching to straight-line when necessary to maximize the deduction.

- For personal holding companies, circulation expenditures must be amortized ratably over three years, beginning with the year in which the expenditures are made.

- The percentage-of-completed method of accounting must be used to compute income from long-term contracts entered into on or after March 1, 1986.

- Income deferred for regular tax purposes on post-March 1, 1986, installment sales of inventory, and on other installment sales subject to the new proportionate disallowance rules, must be included in AMTI.

- No deduction is allowed for amounts deposited in a capital construction fund, and earnings of the fund may be included in AMTI.

- The alternative net operating loss must be deducted instead of the regular NOL.

- For 1987 through 1989 a book income adjustment must be made, except for S corporations, regulated investment companies, real estate investment trusts, or real estate mortgage investment conduits. In computing AMTI, taxable income must be increased by one-half of the excess of adjusted net book income over AMTI before the adjustment and before deduction of any alternative tax net operating loss. Adjusted book income is the net income (or loss) on the taxpayer's applicable financial statement (AFS). The AFS required to be used for this purpose, in order of priority, is:

1) A financial statement required to be filed with the SEC.

2) An audited financial statement used for credit purposes, shareholder reporting, or some other substantial nontax purpose.

3) An income statement required to be provided to the Federal government or an agency other than the SEC, to a state government or agency, or to a political subdivision.

4) An income statement used for credit purposes, shareholder reporting or some other substantial nontax purpose.

In computing *adjusted* net book income, the following modifications to *net* book income are required:

1) All Federal income tax expense must be added back to net book income. State, local, and foreign income taxes that are deducted in arriving at regular taxable income need not, however, be added back.

2) If different companies are consolidated for financial statement purposes instead of for tax return purposes, net book income must be adjusted so as to reflect only the income (or loss) of those companies that are consolidated for Federal income tax purposes. Example: If a subsidiary is included in the parent's consolidated financial statement but not in the consolidated tax return, the parent's adjusted net book income should only include dividends received from the subsidiary.

3) Net book income must be adjusted if different year-ends are used for tax and financial reporting purposes.

4) Extraordinary items are included in adjusted net book income unless they represent items of tax benefit or expense, such as the use of a net operating loss carryforward.

(For a more detailed analysis of AMTI, see Appendix B.)

Illustration—Net Book Income calculation.

For fiscal year ending June 30, 1987. Corporation X shows net book income of $3,060,000, computed as follows:

Gross Sales		$20,000,000
Cost of Sales		(12,000,000)
Gross Profit		$ 8,000,000
Tax Exempt Interest	100,000	
Domestic Dividends	400,000	500,000
Total Income		$8,500,000
Depreciation		(800,000)
Other Deductions		(3,080,000)
Pretax Income		$ 4,620,000
Tax Expense:		
Federal Income Tax	$1,360,000	
State Income Tax	200,000	(1,560,000)
Net Book Income		$3,060,000

AMT COMPUTATIONAL ILLUSTRATIONS

For year ending 1987 Corporation A has no taxable income, but owes an AMT of $64,000 because of various preferences and adjustments. The minimum tax credit to be carried to future tax years is $59,400 because $4,600 of the AMT is attributable to an exclusion preference.

	Total AMT Paid	Exclusion Items	Deferral Items
Taxable income	$ 0	---	---
Book income adj.	150,000	---	$150,000
Preference item	63,000	63,000	---
Excess depreciation	87,000	---	87,000
IDC preference	20,000	---	20,000
AMTI	$320,000	$ 63,000	$257,000
Exemption	0*	(40,000)	40,000
Net AMTI	$320,000	$ 23,000	$297,000
	× .20	× .20	× .20
AMT	64,000	$ 4,600	$ 59,400

*Phased out.

Assumptions: In the following example Corporation X (for tax purposes) uses the installment method of reporting gains from sales. After application of the proportionate disallowance rule. Corporation X reported:

Sales	$15,000,000	
Cost of Sales	9,000,000	
ACRS	1,500,000	(On pre-1987 real property, and which was $500,000 in excess of straight-line.)
ACRS	300,000	(On post-1986 property; $150,000 would have been allowable under the alternative system.)

All tax-exempt interest is on bonds issued before 1986.

There are no available credits.

	Regular Tax	*AMT*
Gross Sales	$15,000,000	$20,000,000
Cost of Sales	(9,000,000)	(12,000,000)
Dividends ($400,000 less 80% deduction)	80,000	80,000
Depreciation on pre-1987 property:		
ACRS	(1,500,000)	(1,500,000)
Preference	---	500,000
Depreciation on post-1986 property:		
ACRS	(300,000)	---
Alternative depreciation	---	(150,000)
State income taxes	(200,000)	(200,000)
Other deductions	(3,080,000)	(3,080,000)
Taxable income/Pre-book AMTI	$ 1,000,000	$ 3,650,000
Book income adjustment	---	385,000(1)
AMTI before exemption		$ 4,035,000
Less: Exemption	---	0 (2)
Net AMTI		$ 4,035,000
AMT Rate		× .20
TMT		$ 807,000
Less: Regular tax		(340,000)(3)
AMT		$ 467,000(4)

(1)	Net book income	$ 3,060,000
	Add: Federal income tax expense	1,360,000
	Adjusted net book income	$ 4,420,000
	Less: Pre-book AMTI	(3,650,000)
	Excess adjusted net book income	$ 770,000
		× .5
	Book income adjustment	$ 385,000

(2) Exemption phased out since AMTI exceeds $310,000.

(3) $1,000,000 × 34% = $340,000. Since there is no foreign tax credit, the regular tax is the same as the regular tax liability.

(4) This amount can be carried forward as credit against the regular tax liability to the extent that it exceeds TMT for a particular year.

Form **6251**	**Alternative Minimum Tax Computation**	OMB No. 1545-0227
Department of the Treasury Internal Revenue Service	▶ Attach to Forms 1040, 1040NR, 1041 or 990-T (Trust).	1986 Attachment Sequence No. **32**

Name(s) as shown on tax return   Identifying number

1 Adjusted gross income (see instructions) **1**

2 Deductions (Individuals, attach Schedule A (Form 1040))(see instructions):

   a (1) Medical and dental expense from Schedule A, line 5 . . .   **2a(1)**

     (2) Multiply Form 1040, line 33, by 5% (.05) . . . .   **2a(2)**

     (3) Subtract line 2a(2) from line 2a(1). (If zero or less, enter zero.) . . . . . . **2a(3)**

   b Contributions from Schedule A, line 18, **OR** Form 1040, line 34d **2b**

   c Casualty and theft losses from Schedule A, line 19 . . . . **2c**

   d Qualified interest on property used as a residence (see instructions) **2d**

   e (1) Interest, other than line 2d above, from Schedule A, line 14   **2e(1)**

     (2) Net investment income (If zero or less, enter zero) . . . .   **2e(2)**

     (3) Enter the smaller of line 2e(1) or line 2e(2) . . . . **2e(3)**

   f Gambling losses to the extent of gambling winnings from Schedule A, line 22 . . . **2f**

   g Estate tax allowable under section 691(c) from Schedule A **2g**

   h Estates and trusts only: Charitable deduction and income distribution deduction . . **2h**

   i Add lines 2a(3), b, c, d, e(3), f, g, and h **2i**

3 Subtract line 2i from line 1. **3**

4 Tax preference items:

   a Dividend exclusion **4a**

   b 60% capital gain deduction **4b**

   c Accelerated depreciation on nonrecovery real property or 15-, 18-, or 19-year real property **4c**

   d Accelerated depreciation on leased personal property or leased recovery property other than 15-, 18-, or 19-year real property. **4d**

   e Amortization of certified pollution control facilities **4e**

   f Mining exploration and development costs **4f**

   g Circulation and research and experimental expenditures **4g**

   h Reserves for losses on bad debts of financial institutions **4h**

   i Depletion **4i**

   j Incentive stock options **4j**

   k Intangible drilling costs **4k**

   l Add lines 4a through 4k. **4l**

5 Alternative minimum taxable income (add lines 3 and 4(l)) (short period returns, see instructions) **5**

6 Enter: $40,000, if married filing joint return or Qualifying widow(er). . . . . . .

       $30,000, if single or head of household   }   **6**

       $20,000, if married filing separate return or estate or trust

7 Subtract line 6 from line 5. If zero or less, do not complete the rest of this form **7**

8 Enter 20% of line 7 . . . . **8**

9 Amount from Form 1040, line 49, or Form 1040NR, line 49. (Do not include Form 1040, line 39, or Form 1040NR, line 40.) (Estates and trusts, see instructions.). **9**

10 Subtract line 9 from line 8. If zero or less, enter zero **10**

11 Foreign tax credit **11**

12 ALTERNATIVE minimum tax (subtract line 11 from line 10). Enter on your tax return, on the line identified as alternative minimum tax **12**

Instructions

(Section references are to the Internal Revenue Code)

Paperwork Reduction Notice.— We ask for this information to carry out the Internal Revenue laws of the United States. We need it to ensure that taxpayers are complying with these laws and to allow us to figure and collect the right amount of tax. You are required to give us this information.

Who Must File.—File this form if : (a) You are liable for the alternative minimum tax; **or** (b) you have one or more tax preference items on lines 4c through 4k; **or** (c) your adjusted gross income is more than line 6 and you have an amount on line 2e(3), and line 2e(2) includes income other than interest and dividend income.

Individuals, estates or trusts may be liable if their adjusted gross income plus tax preference items listed on line 4 total more than line 6.

For more information, see **Publication 909,** Alternative Minimum Tax.

Minimum Tax Deferred From Earlier Year(s).—If a net operating loss carryover from an earlier year(s) reduces taxable income for 1986 and the net operating loss giving rise to the carryover resulted in the deferral of minimum tax in that earlier year(s), all or part of the deferred minimum tax may be includible as tax liability for 1986. Figure the deferred minimum tax in the worksheet in Publication 909 and enter it on Form 1040, line 51, or Form 1041, line 31. Write "Deferred Minimum Tax."

Partners, Beneficiaries, etc.—If you are a:

(1) Partner or shareholder of an S corporation, take into account separately your distributive share of items of income and deductions that enter into the computation of tax preference items.

(2) Beneficiary of an estate or trust, see section 58(c) and the line 4(1) instructions.

(3) Participant in a common trust fund, see section 58(e).

(4) Shareholder or holder of beneficial interest in a regulated investment company or a real estate investment trust, see section 58(f).

Carryback and Carryover of Unused Credits.— It may be necessary to figure the carryback or carryover of certain unused credits. See section 55(c)(3).

Note : *If you have an earned income credit, you must reduce that credit by any alternative minimum tax.*

Line-by-Line Instructions

Line 1, Estates and Trusts.—Adjusted gross income is figured in the same way as for an

Form **6251** (1986)

individual except that the costs of the administration of the estate or trust are allowed in figuring adjusted gross income.

All taxpayers.—Do not deduct any interest expense incurred to purchase or carry a limited business interest in a partnership or S corporation, in figuring adjusted gross income. Instead, include in line 2(e)(1).

Do not include in line 1 any alcohol fuel credit included in income.

Add to adjusted gross income any net operating loss deduction taken, and reduce the result by any alternative tax net operating loss deduction. See **Publication 909,** Alternative Minimum Tax, for details and attach a computation.

Lines 2(a) through 2(h).—Do not include on these lines any deduction that can be carried back or forward as a net operating loss or forward as a charitable contribution.

Individuals.—Complete and attach Schedule A (Form 1040) for any deduction listed on these lines, whether or not you completed it in figuring Form 1040, line 34. If you did not use Schedule A to figure Form 1040, line 34, write **"Alt Min Tax"** in the top margin of Schedule A.

Estates and Trusts.—Enter on the applicable line any deduction listed on these lines allowable to the estate or trust. Include on line 2h, any itemized deduction not allowable on lines 2a to 2g, and allocated to the beneficiaries of the estate or trust.

Line 2(d).—Enter on line 2(d) your qualified interest from Schedule A, line 11. Include allowable points from line 13.Enter the part of the interest that is from debts you incurred in acquiring, constructing, or substantially rehabilitating property, other than a houseboat, which you, or certain family members listed in section 267(c)(4), use as a residence.

If the interest expense is on debts incurred before July 1, 1982, the following applies. At the time you incurred the debt, it must have been secured by property which you, or certain family members listed in section 267(c)(4), used as a residence.

Line 2(e)(2).—Enter your investment income minus investment expenses.

Investment income is your gross income from interest, dividends, rents, and royalties, and any amount treated as ordinary income under sections 1245, 1250, and 1254. Do not include income from a trade or business. Include as investment income, your capital gain net income from the sale or exchange of property held for investment, and the amount to be entered on line 4(a). Add or subtract from investment income, any income or loss from a limited business interest.

Investment expenses are those expenses allowable against the production of investment income provided they are allowed in figuring adjusted gross income and not includible in line 4.

Line 4(a), 60% Capital gain deduction.—

Individuals.—Enter your 60% capital gain deduction from your Schedule D (Form 1040), line 20, or Form 4798, line 9. If you had an entry on Form 1040, line 14, enter 60% of your capital gain distributions. Do not include the capital gain deduction attributable to a sale or exchange of a principal residence.

Certain insolvent farmers may reduce their capital gain tax preference item on a farm insolvency transaction. See Publication 909 for more information. Indicate any reduction on the dotted portion of line 4(b), and write "Section 13208 Relief."

Estates and Trusts.—Enter the capital gain deduction taken into account on Forms 1041 or 990-T. However, an amount paid or permanently set aside for a charitable purpose is not a tax preference item.

Lines 4(c) and 4(d), Accelerated depreciation on real property; Accelerated depreciation on leased personal property or leased recovery property other than 15, 18, or 19-year real property.—If you use the Class Life Asset

Depreciation Range (CLADR) System, use the asset guideline period as the straight-line useful life to figure lines 4(c) and (d).

For (c) but not (d), use any variance in useful life under section 167(m)(1) as the straight-line useful life.

Line 4(c).—For property other than recovery property, enter the amount you get (never less than zero) by subtracting the depreciation that would have been allowable for the year if you had used the straight-line method, from the depreciation or amortization actually allowable. Figure this amount separately for each property.

For 15, 18, or 19-year real property, or low income housing, enter the amount by which the deduction allowed under section 168(a) (or section 167 for section 167(k) property) is more than the deduction which would have been allowable had the property been depreciated using a 15, 18, or 19-year period and the straight-line method without salvage value.

Line 4(d).—For leased property other than recovery property, enter the amount you get (never less than zero) by subtracting the depreciation that would have been allowable for the year if you had used the straight-line method, from the depreciation or amortization actually allowable. Figure this amount separately for each property.

For leased recovery property other than 15,18, or 19-year real property, or low income housing, enter the amount by which your deduction under section 168(a) is more than the deduction allowable using the straight-line method with a half-year convention, no salvage value, and the following recovery period:

3 year property	5 years
5 year property	8 years
10 year property	15 years
15 year public utility property	22 years

Note: *If the recovery period actually used is longer than the recovery period in 4(c) or 4(d), do not complete lines 4(c) or 4(d).*

Line 4(e), Amortization of certified pollution control facilities.—Enter the amount by which the amortization allowable under section 169 is more than the depreciation deduction otherwise allowable.

Line 4(f), Mining exploration and development costs.—For each mine or other natural deposit (other than an oil or gas well), enter the amount by which the deductions allowable under section 616(a) or 617 are more than the amount that would have been allowable if you had amortized the expenses over a 10-year period.

Line 4(g), Circulation and research and experimental expenditures.—Enter the amount by which the deductions allowable for circulation and research and experimental expenditures under sections 173 or 174(a) are more than the amount that would have been allowable if you had amortized the circulation expenses over a 3-year period and the research and experimental expenditures over a 10-year period.

Line 4(h), Reserves for losses on bad debts of financial institutions.—Enter your share of the excess of the addition to the reserve for bad debts over the reasonable addition to the reserve for bad debts that would have been allowable if you had maintained the bad debt reserve for all tax years based on actual experience.

Line 4(i), Depletion.—In the case of mines, wells, and other natural deposits, enter the amount by which the deduction for depletion under section 611 (including percentage depletion for geothermal deposits), is more than the adjusted basis of such property at the end of the tax year. Figure the adjusted basis without regard to the depletion deduction and figure the excess separately for each property.

Line 4(j), Incentive stock options.—If you received stock through the exercise of an incentive stock option, enter the amount by which the fair market value of the shares at the time of exercise was more than the option price. See sections 57(a)(10) and 422A.

Line 4(k), Intangible drilling costs.—Intangible drilling costs are a tax preference item to the extent that the excess intangible drilling costs are more than your net income from oil, gas, and geothermal properties.

Figure excess intangible drilling costs as follows: from the allowable intangible drilling and development costs (except for costs in drilling a non-productive well), subtract the amount that would have been allowable if you had capitalized these costs and either amortized them over the 120 months that started when production began, or treated them according to any election you made under section 57(d)(2).

Your net income from oil, gas, and geothermal properties is your gross income from them, minus the deductions allocable to them, except for excess intangible drilling costs and nonproductive well costs.

Figure the line 4(k) amount separately for oil and gas properties which are not geothermal deposits and for all properties which are geothermal deposits.

Line 4(1), Special Tax Preference Item for Estate and Trust Beneficiaries. Some itemized deductions of the estate or trust (such as state and local taxes) are deducted by the estate or trust in figuring the income passed through to you, but are not allowed as itemized deductions on this form. These amounts must be treated as a tax preference item allocated to you. The estate or trust should separately show these amounts on the Schedule K-1 it sends you. Add any such amounts to the total of your other tax preference items on line 4(1). Also, on the dotted line to the left of the entry space for line 4(1), write "Section 58(c)" and indicate the amount.

Lines 5 and 8.—If this is a short period return, use the formula in section 443(d)(1) to determine the amount to enter on these lines.

Nonresident Alien Individuals.—If you disposed of U.S. real property interests at a gain, see Form 1040NR instructions for a special rule in figuring line 8.

Line 9, Estates and trusts.—Enter your tax after credits. Do not include any tax from Forms 4970, 4972 or 5544.

Line 11, Foreign Tax Credit.—If line 10 is more than zero, and you incurred foreign taxes and elect to take them as a credit, enter on line 11 the foreign tax credit allowed against the alternative minimum tax. Figure this credit as follows:

(1) Use and attach a separate Form 1116 for each type of income specified at the top of Form 1116.

(2) Print across the top of each Form 1116 used: "ALT MIN TAX."

(3) Part I.—Fill in a new Part I using that portion of your income, deductions and tax preference items from Form 6251, attributable to sources outside the U.S.

(4) Part III.—Complete only the following lines:

(a) Insert on line 5 the result of the following:

   (i) the amount from Part III, line 5 of the Form 1116 used to figure the credit allowed against your regular tax, minus

   (ii) the amount from Part III, line 15 of that Form 1116, plus

   (iii) the smaller of (A) the amount from Part III, line 15 of that Form 1116, or (B) Form 6251, line 10 (or if more than one Form 1116 is being used, an allocable portion of Form 6251, line 10).

(b) Complete lines 6 through 8, using the result of step 3 for line 6.

(c) Line 11.—Enter Form 6251, line 5.

(d) Complete line 12 as indicated in Part III.

(e) Line 13.—Enter Form 6251, line 8.

(f) Complete lines 14 and 15 as indicated in Part III.

(5) Part IV.—Enter on line 1, Form 6251, the amount from line 7, Part IV of this Form 1116 (but not more than the amount on Form 6251, line 10).

AMT WORKSHEET

Because the AMT rules require a set of calculations different from the computations for the regular tax liability, a worksheet can be helpful in determining if the AMT applies to the corporate taxpayer.

TAXABLE INCOME

Adjustments: $

Alternative depreciation (post-1986 property).(1)
Percentage-of-completion method for long-term contracts.
Full reporting of certain installment sales.
Alternative recovery of pollution control facilities (post-1986 property).
Alternative tax net operating loss.
Capital construction fund deposits and earnings.
One-half of excess book income.(2)
Taxable income as adjusted. $

Add Preferences: $

Excess charitable contribution deduction.
Tax exempt interest on certain bonds.
Excess depreciation and amortization of pollution control facilities
(pre-1987 property).
Alternative minimum taxable income.

Less Exemption: (   )

Net alternative minimum taxable income.
Rate   × 20%
Tentative minimum tax before credits.
Less: AMT foreign tax credit.   (   )
Tentative minimum tax (TMT)
Less: Regular Tax.(3)   (   )
Alternative minimum tax.(4) $

---

(1) Regular tax election is available to avoid adjustment or preference.
(2) Does not apply to S corporations, regulated investment companies, real estate investment trusts, and real estate mortage investment conduits.
(3) Regular tax liability less foreign tax credit.
(4) Pay in addition to regular tax. However, corporations are permitted generally to use ITC carryovers to offset up to 25% of the TMT.

BUSINESS ACQUISITIONS—SALES AND PURCHASES

Tax Considerations

Much of the planning of the purchase or sale of a business is influenced by the tax consequences. What follows is a summary of the major tax considerations and the alternatives available to bring about the desired results.

How to Maximize Tax Benefits

If business assets are sold as a unit for a lump-sum consideration, the sales proceeds must be allocated among the individual assets of the business, and the gain or loss computed accordingly. The owner is not permitted to treat the sale of his business as the sale of a single capital asset. Moreover, the burden of proving that any portion of the sale proceeds is attributable to the goodwill and other capital assets of the business is on the vendor. The problem may be eased by drafting the contract or bill of sale to provide for specific prices for each individual asset in the business. The buyer will want to allocate as much of the purchase price as possible to depreciable assets. He may prefer to rely on an appraisal if he can't get a favorable allocation agreed to in the contract.

No gain is recognized to the corporation if it sells its assets and liquidates (except for §1245 and 1250 property).

The following chart illustrates the tax effects and the conflicting desires of buyer and seller involved in allocating the purchase price of the business:

Asset	Price Benefiting Buyer	Price Benefiting Seller
(1) *Capital* (Goodwill, trade name, covenant not to compete ancillary to sale of goodwill)	Low (not depreciable)	High (capital gain)
(2) *Property used in the trade or business:*		
(a) Machinery, fixtures, etc.	Medium (recoup cost via depreciation)	Medium (ordinary loss)
(b) Land	Low (not depreciable)	High (capital gain or ordinary loss)
(c) Copyright (purchased for use in the business)	Medium (recoup cost via amortization)	High (capital gain or ordinary loss)
(d) Patents	Medium (recoup cost via amortization)	High
(3) *Noncapital:*		
(a) Inventory and stock in trade	High (recoup via cost of goods sold)	Low (ordinary income)
(b) Accounts receivable	High (recoverable as collected)	Low (ordinary income)
(c) Copyrights and intellectual property sold by the creator	Medium (recoup cost via amortization)	Low (ordinary income)
(d) Covenant not to compete	Medium (usually recoup cost via amortization)	Low (ordinary income)
(e) Interest on deferred payment of purchase price	Medium (deduct as ordinary business expense)	Low (ordinary income)

Sale of Stock vs. Sale of Assets

Here are the opposing considerations of the seller and buyer on the sale of a corporate business.

The seller wants to sell stock because:

(1) He has a *clean* deal, realizing capital gains (unless he has a collapsible corporation).

(2) There is no problem of depreciation recapture at ordinary income rates.

(3) There is no problem of recapture of any investment credit.

(4) It is easier to set up an installment sale; if the corporation makes the sale of assets, it can't then distribute the installment obligations to the stockholders without tax consequences.

The buyer wants to buy assets, because:

(1) He need not worry about any *hidden* or contingent corporate liabilities.

(2) He gets a basis for the assets acquired equal to their market values—i.e., what he paid for them. If he acquires stock, the corporation's basis for the assets does not change even if the assets have appreciated considerably. A corporation can, however, within 75 days of purchasing at least 80% of the stock of the corporation, make an election to have the purchase price of the stock assigned to the assets. The seller in this case may be stuck with recapture of depreciation (income).

Goodwill vs. Covenant Not to Compete

The buyer writes off the noncompete agreement over the period of its restriction. He gets no tax writeoff for goodwill. The seller, on the other hand, gets capital gain on the sale of his goodwill, but ordinary income for the covenant. The agreement should be as explicit as possible regarding the intent of the parties respecting either or both goodwill and a covenant not to compete. Courts will not usually set aside executed agreements.

Bird's-Eye View of Tax Rules

The following table sets forth the various ways in which a corporate business can be sold and the tax consequences to the buyer and seller in each case.

Type of Transaction	Tax Consequence to Seller	Tax Consequence
Sale of assets by the corporation.	Corporation realizes gain or loss in same manner as proprietorship. If proceeds are then distributed to the stockholders in liquidation, a second tax (capital gain) is paid by them. *But the tax at the corporate level can be avoided by a statutory liquidation.*	Purchase price is allocated in same manner as in purchase of sole proprietorship.
Sale by corporation after adopting a liquidation resolution and distribution within 12 months.	Corporation pays no tax on its gain—stockholders pay a tax on liquidation. (But corporation can have income if depreciation or investment credit recapture is involved.) This method is not available if corporations is collapsible.	Same as above.
Liquidation and distribution of assets to stockholders and subsequent sale of the assets by them.	Stockholders pay a capital gains tax on liquidation (unless corporation is collapsible). Corporation has no taxable income on liquidation unless there's depreciation or investment credit recapture. They get a stepped-up basis for assets received; so they have no gain or loss on the resale. But must make sure corporation didn't enter into sales negotiations before liquidations; otherwise the double tax will not be avoided.	Buyer's basis is what he pays for the assets—allocated in same manner as on purchase of sole proprietorship.
Liquidation by corporation within one month.	No gain or loss recognized on liquidation, but corporation can have income if depreciation or investment credit recapture is involved. Basis for assets received is basis for stock. Gain is then recognized on subsequent resale—with nature of the gain on each item depending on the nature of the asset in the hands of the selling stockholder.	Same as above.

Con't.

Type of Transaction	Tax Consequence to Seller	Tax Consequence
	Warning: If corporation has earnings and profits, there is a dividend on liquidation. Cash and securities distributed are immediately taxable, too.	
Sale of stock in the corporation.	Seller generally gets capital gain—unless the corporation is collapsible. *Warning:* Depreciation and ITC recapture can result.	Buyer has a basis for his stock equal to what he paid for it; the corporation retains the same basis for its assets as before the sale. But if the assets have appreciated in value and 80% or more of the stock was purchased by a corporation within a 12-month period, the buyer can elect to have the basis stepped up to the purchase price of the stock, if such election is made within 75 days.
Tax-free acquisitions via one of several types of reorganizations.	Seller usually acquires stock in the buying corporation; there is no gain or loss on the transaction recognized for tax purposes. In some types of reorganization transactions, *boot* (cash or other property other than the permitted stock) is received. Then, to extent the boot does not exceed to gain, it is taxable (usually as capital gain; where shown to be such, it may be a dividend). Seller's basis for his new stock is same as his basis for his old, increased by any recognized gain and decreased by boot received.	The buyer's basis for the property acquired is generally the same as the basis of the property to the transferor prior to the transfer. But if there was any recognized gain to the transferor on the exchange, then the buyer's basis is increased by that gain.

ACQUIRING COMPANIES WITH TAX LOSSES

At one time there was a considerable traffic in loss companies—a profitable operation would acquire a loss company in order to use the acquired company's carryover loss to offset its own income. A number of restrictions in the Code, plus IRS's strict interpretations in its regulations, make the acquisition of loss companies today very difficult.

Net operating losses.   (Note: The treatment of NOLs under the New Law is exceedingly complex. Accordingly, Sections 382 and 383 of the new Code should be referenced when applying the new requirements.)

The limitations on the use of net operating losses (NOLs) and other carryforwards is modified by the New Law, principally the carryover limitations dating back to 1976, which have been repealed (retroactively) beginning January 1, 1986.

The highlights of the provisions of the New Law follow:

- If within a 3-year period there is larger than a 50 percent change in ownership in a *loss* corporation, the amount of an NOL that can be used to offset earnings is limited.
- Capital contributions made within two years preceding an ownership change are presumed by the New Law to have a tax avoidance purpose.
- NOL carryovers are prohibited for a loss corporation in tax-free reorganizations or taxable purchases unless the corporation continues in the same business for at least two years following the change in ownership.
- Net capital losses, excess credits, and foreign tax credits cannot be carried forward.
- The use of "related parties, pass-thru entities, or other intermediaries" for tax avoidance purposes is prohibited.
- NOL carryforwards are reduced if one-third of the loss corporation's *assets* are passive.
- There are special rules in the Code for unrealized built-in gains or losses (explicitly defined in the Code).

The new requirements become effective after the occurrence of one of two types of ownership changes in the corporation possessing the tax-beneficial items.

- More than a 50 percent ownership change.
- More than a "50% equity structure" change.

Unlike the old law, the new provisions ordinarily do not permanently extinguish tax beneficial items in whole or in part. Instead, they impose an annual limit (the Section 382 limitations) on the extent to which such items can be used after an ownership change. (See Appendix B.)

CONSOLIDATED TAX RETURNS

Consolidated returns can be filed by affiliated groups of corporations. Basically, an affiliated group is one where there is a common parent and 80% control at each level of the chain of corporations. Thus, losses of one company can be set off against the income of another. In effect, all the corporations are being taxed as a single economic unit. Tax accounting with reference to *intercompany transactions* conforms closely to general consolidation accounting principles for financial statements.

Certain corporations are excluded from the affiliated group for this purpose and are thus ineligible to participate in the filing of a consolidated return. These corporations are: (1) corporations exempt; (2) insurance companies; (3) foreign corporations; (4) possessions corporations; (5) China Trade Act corporations; (6) regulated investment companies and real estate investment trusts; (7) unincorporated businesses which have elected to be taxed as corporations.

One hundred-percent-owned Canadian or Mexican corporations can be treated as domestic corporations and thus be eligible to participate in the filing of a consolidated return, at the election of the domestic parent, if the corporations were organized and maintained solely for the purpose of complying with the laws of such country as to the title and operation of property.

Where consolidated returns are filed, the affiliated group is deemed by law to have consented to all the consolidated return regulations prescribed by the Internal Revenue Service. These regulations are extremely complex and in some cases, have been deemed a sufficient reason by affiliated groups for not filing consolidated returns.

Once consolidated returns are filed, they must be continued to be filed in succeeding years, unless IRS gives its permission to change. Note that some states (like New Jersey) do not permit the filing of consolidated returns for franchise/income taxes.

Includable corporations which are members of an affiliated group of corporations are generally entitled (or required) to file consolidated Federal income tax returns. The Code defines an ''includible corporation'' to mean any corporation. An affiliated group means one or more chains of includible corporations connected through stock ownership with a common parent for an affiliated group. There are two requirements: (1) At least 80% of all classes of voting stock, and at least 80% of each class of nonvoting stock of each includible corporation (except the common parent) must be owned directly by one or more of the other includible corporations; (2) The common parent must own at least 80 percent of the voting power of all classes of stock, and at least 80 percent of each class of the nonvoting stock of at least one of the other includible corporations.

For purposes of the definition, nonvoting stock which is limited and preferred as to dividends is disregarded, as is certain stock held under employee stock ownership plans. Once the stock ownership requirements cease to be met with respect to any one corporation, it can no longer be included in the consolidated return of its former affiliated group.

The new law adds a significant requirement. In addition to the 80 percent of voting power rule, one corporation is not an affiliate of another corporation unless one owns stock having a value equal to at least 80 percent of the total fair market value of the stock (disregarding certain preferred stock) of the other.

The Act specifies the kind of stock that can be ignored in testing for affiliated group status:

- Stock which is not entitled to vote.
- Stock limited and preferred as to dividends.
- Stock with redemption and liquidation rights that do not exceed the stock's paid-in capital or par value.
- Stock that is not convertible into any other stock.

With respect to consolidation after deconsolidation, the law reads that if a corporation is included in a consolidated return filed by an affiliated group for a taxable year which includes any period after December 31, 1984, and such corporation ceases to be a member of such group for a taxable year beginning after December 31, 1984, then such corporation (and any successor) may not be included in any consolidated return filed by that group or any other group having the same common parent (or a successor) before the 61st month after the cessation.

MULTIPLE CORPORATIONS/CONTROLLED GROUPS

For tax purposes, "controlled" groups are of two kinds:

(1) Parent-subsidiary type, or
(2) Brother-sister type.

In the latter type, the rules of attribution pertain and should be thoroughly examined for pertinence and applicability.

All individual members of controlled groups are, for the purposes of certain statutory tax advantage provisions, considered to be one aggregate unit, entitled to only *one* benefit in the following areas:

(1) *Surtax Exemption*—for 1979 and later, a total of only $25,000 in each of the rate brackets, for the first $100,000, is permitted by the entire group. The exemption may be divided in any fashion by consent (attached to the returns).

(2) *20% Additional First-Year Depreciation*—is limited to one maximum for the entire affiliated group.

(3) *Accumulated Earnings Credit*—for 1982 and later, only one $250,000 accumulated earnings credit is permitted to a controlled group, with the single credit divided *equally* unless approval is obtained from the Commissioner for unequal allocation.

(4) *Investment Tax Credit*—the credit must be apportioned among all members of the group.

Each member of the controlled group is still allowed separate and individual 100%-dividends-received deductions for dividends from affiliates.

GOLDEN PARACHUTE CONTRACTS

The present law allows a corporation a deduction for all the ordinary and necessary expenses paid or incurred during the taxable year in carrying on a trade or business. Reasonable allowances for salaries or other compensation for personal services qualify as ordinary and necessary trade or business expenses.

A golden parachute contract generally is any contract entered into by a corporation with an officer, shareholder, or highly compensated individual, including any independent contractor—providing at the time of execution for contingent payment of cash (or property) which is to be made in the event of a change (or threatened change) in ownership or control of the corporation (or of a significant portion of its assets).

No deduction is allowable for "excess parachute payments" paid or accrued. A nondeductible 20 percent excise tax is imposed on the recipient of any excess parachute payments, in addition to income taxes and FICA withholding.

An excess parachute payment is an amount equal to the excess of the parachute payment over the portion of the base amount allocable to the payment. "Base amount" is an individual's annualized income for a base period, which is the most recent five taxable years ending before the date on which the ownership or control of the corporation changed, or the portion of the five years that the person was an employee of the corporation. Excess payment is quantified to be the aggregate present value of the payments that equal or exceed three times the base amount.

Example: Assume that an individual's base amount is $100,000. Assume also that a payment totalling $400,000 is made on the date of a change in control, which is four times the base amount. The excess payment amount is $300,000. The provision, therefore, applies. Further, assume that the taxpayer establishes by clear and convincing evidence that reasonable compensation for services compensated for by the parachute payments totals $150,000. Excess parachute payments equal $250,000—$300,000 less ($150,000—$100,000).

If in the example parachute payments totalled $290,000, the provision would not apply because the payments would not equal or exceed three times the base amount.

For agreements entered into after June 14, 1984, the New Law excludes from treatment as "parachute payments" those payments relating to small business corporations (definition similar to the definition of an S Corporation) whose stock was not readily marketable on an established securities market, or otherwise not saleable. Also excluded is any part of a payment that the taxpayer establishes to be reasonable compensation for services to be rendered on or after the change of control. Parachute payments are also reduced by amounts that the taxpayer proves to be reasonable compensation for services actually rendered before the change in control. Payments to or from qualified retirement plan trusts, annuities, or SEPs are excluded from treatment as parachute payments.

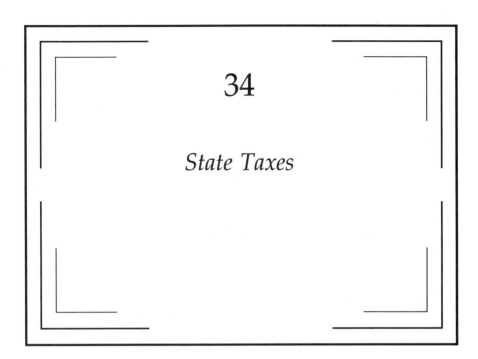

34

State Taxes

VARIOUS FORMS OF STATE TAXATION

Virtually all states impose some form of franchise and/or income tax on corporations. The basis for either or both taxes varies from state to state, as does the definition of the terminology. For the corporation involved in interstate commerce, these state taxes can present some onerous burdens. You need detailed records in order to work out the various allocation or apportionment formulas called for by the states involved (so as to avoid imposing a tax on more than what is applicable to that state). Sometimes with proper planning, taking into account the needs of the business, it is possible to avoid altogether the taxes of some of the states with which your company has contact.

In addition to an income or franchise tax, some states impose a capital values tax, and a large number have a sales and use tax. This can become a burden when the states insist that you collect the use tax from customers to whom you sell in that state, even though you have no office or other permanent contact within that state. In the paragraphs that follow, we consider these taxes, when they apply, and what you can do about them in some situations.

CORPORATE INCOME TAXES

There are three basic types of state corporate income taxes:

(1) A state may impose a tax on all income arising out of, or derived from, property located within the state. Often these taxes will be imposed without regard to whether business is conducted within the geographical confines of the state. Where a company has a manufacturing plant or real property located in a state which imposes taxes upon income from property located within the geographical confines of the state, it will be subject to the tax on the income which can be traced to that property.

(2) Some states which impose a corporation income tax, base it on income from business conducted in the state. If the state basis was restricted to business conducted within the state, it might be that investment-type income derived from property in the state would not be reached. The applicability of a tax imposed upon income from a business conducted within a state to income from real estate or other tangible property located within the state would generally depend upon the use to which the property is put, the language of the particular statute, and its administration.

(3) Some states impose a tax upon income attributable to, or derived from, sources within the state. This probably affords the widest possible tax base for a state attempting to tax foreign corporations.

Some states do not permit the filing of consolidated returns.

Apportionment of Tax

Normally the federal taxable income is a starting point for determining the state income tax. The federal income is usually then modified by eliminating the deduction for local and state franchise and income taxes. There are other adjustments according to the state laws that are made to the federal income before allocating a portion of that income to the state. The most commonly used apportionment formula (or a variant of such), is:

$$\frac{\text{Receipts in taxing state}}{\text{Receipts everywhere}} + \frac{\text{Payroll in taxing state}}{\text{Payroll everywhere}} + \frac{\text{Property in taxing state}}{\text{Property everywhere}} \div 3$$

Often the formula will provide for a separate allocation of items like capital gains income, rents, royalties, and dividends. Income of this type may be allocated to the situs of the property, the place of its use, the domicile of the owner, or the source of the income.

Unitary and separate businesses.

Some states which impose an apportioned corporate income tax on foreign corporations apply the apportionment formulas only to unitary businesses. A unitary business is one which has basically one income-producing activity and its separate divisions are connected with, and directed toward, this activity. Thus, a company which both manufactured and sold its products, even though it operated through separate departments or divisions, would be a unitary business. Where two or more businesses of different types are conducted independently of each other, they are sometimes entitled to use their own separate accounting for purposes of apportioning income under state apportionment formulas.

What Is a Sufficient "Nexus"?

A foreign corporation will have sufficient nexus or connection with the taxing state where it has assets or property within the borders of the taxing state. Similarly, where a foreign corporation qualifies to do business within a particular state by complying with the provisions of the state "qualification" statute, the corporation will be deemed to have established a domicile or residence within the state, giving that state a sufficient nexus for taxing that corporation.

Merely deriving income from within a state may be a sufficient nexus, unless:

(1) The corporation is engaged in truly minimal operations within the taxing state.

(2) The state's tax statute is not sufficiently broad to reach, in whole or in part, the particular type of activity which the foreign corporation is engaged in.

(3) The tax, although described as a corporate income tax, is not really a corporate income tax but essentially a privilege tax, so it may not be imposed upon a corporation which is engaged solely in interstate commerce as to the taxing state.

HOW TO AVOID A STATE'S INCOME TAX

There are situations when a corporation can plan its operations so as to avoid all or part of the taxes imposed in one or more states from which it derives income.

Planning Activities Within a State

Where a state taxes only companies doing business within the geographical confines of a state, the state's taxing authority may be avoided if you avoid activities which will bring your corporation within the definitions of the state tax law. Often this will mean that you cannot maintain an office in the state, maintain servicemen in the state, sell on consignment to in-state agents, and execute or perform contracts.

Withdrawing from a State

Where your contacts with a state are reduced to the point that qualification is no longer required under the state's corporate statutes, you should consider withdrawing from the state. Most state corporate statutes have provisions whereby companies which have qualified under the laws of the state can subsequently withdraw.

Taking Advantage of Apportionment Formulas

Often by carefully planning your activities and locating property, payroll, or other factors which enter into apportionment formulas in states which do not consider those factors in apportioning income, or minimize those factors in their allocation formulas, you can reduce the over-all tax bite.

CAPITAL VALUES TAX

Many states impose a tax upon the capital value of corporations. A capital values tax imposed on domestic corporations will generally tax the entire capital value of the corporation. However, apportionment is required when a capital values tax is imposed upon the property of a foreign corporation doing business in the state. The capital values taxes are generally based on the following factors: (a) actual value, (b) debt capital, and (c) capital stock.

Actual value.   A foreign corporation may be taxed on the entire property which it employs in a particular state. This would include physical property located in the state even though it is used primarily in interstate commerce. However, a state's authority to tax the intangible property of a foreign corporation is restricted. A state may tax the entire property—tangible and intangible—of a domestic corporation.

In some states credits are given in calculating the actual value on which the capital values tax is imposed for property which is reached by the state's property tax.

Debt capital.   In some states the amount of debt can be a factor in determining the basis for the capital values tax. Where a state seeks to use "debt capital" as a basis for a tax imposed upon foreign corporations, it must apportion the debt capital. A foreign corporation's tax liability will be limited to the proportion of the debt capital which may be apportioned to the state.

Capital stock.   A capital values tax can be based upon the capital stock of the corporation. Most states levy a tax of this form on domestic corporations (in the form of a franchise tax) and on foreign corporations which are qualified to do business within the state. Where a tax or fee based on the capital stock of the corporation is levied upon the stock of a foreign corporation, there is generally either a reasonable floor or minimum or provision whereby it is apportioned—i.e., a foreign corporation is required to pay the tax on only that portion of its authorized capital stock which would be apportioned to the activities or capital employed within the geographic confines of the state.

Apportioning Intangible Property for Capital Values Tax

Intangible property presents a special problem for a capital values tax. Where a capital values tax on foreign corporations must be apportioned, it is necessary to establish a situs of the intangible property owned by a foreign corporation. Several basic theories have arisen as to the situs of intangible property:

Domicile. The traditional theory is that corporate intangible property has a situs in the state where the corporation is incorporated. This is known as the domicile theory of situs. A few states have provided by statute that intangible property has a situs in the state where the principal office of the corporation is located, rather than the state of incorporation. Tangible property would have a situs where it is physically located.

Business situs. In some states a doctrine of "business situs" for intangible property has developed. Under the business situs theory, intangible property may be taxed in the state where it has its situs or the intangible property came into existence. For example, an account receivable—a typical example of business intangible property—would have a situs in the state where the account arose. Other forms of business intangible property would have a situs where the business out of which they arose was conducted.

SALES AND USE TAXES

Where a corporation makes sales to consumers within a state (i.e., not for resale) from goods located within the state, or it otherwise retains places of business within the state from which the sales are made, it is required to collect sales taxes in those states which impose this tax.

The big problem arises for companies engaged in interstate commerce which make interstate sales to customers in states imposing a sales tax. Usually, there is no basis for the state to impose a sales tax. But to "protect" the sales tax, the state imposes a "compensating use" tax. The tax is imposed on the buyer located in the state, on goods acquired from without the state and not subject to the sales tax, but which would have been subject to the sales tax had it been purchased within the state. Although the tax is imposed on the user within the state, the state in most cases would have difficulty enforcing the tax. The state attempts to find some basis for having the *seller* (who is located outside the state) collect the use tax from the buyer and remit it to the buyer's state.

It is very important that the corporation obtain and preserve the documentation where it is not required to collect sales tax. For example, if the buyer has an exemption certification because it resells the goods, the corporation should have a copy of the exemption certificate in its files.

12

Tax Accounting

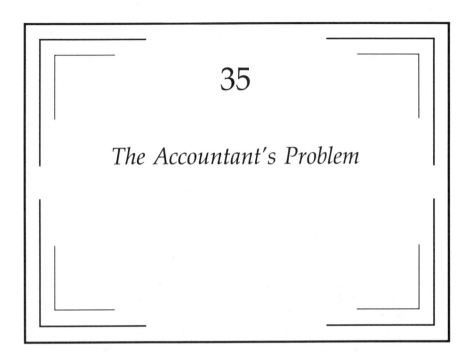

35

The Accountant's Problem

In a landmark case, the court ruled:

> "The essence of any effective system of taxation is the production of revenue ascertainable and payable to the Government at regular intervals. Only a system of ascertaining income and tax at regular intervals, i.e., years, could produce a regular flow of income to the Treasury and permit the application of methods of accounting, assessment and collection capable of practical application by both the government and the taxpayer."

The determination of the proper timing for reporting income and deductions for tax purposes is considered to be the most important function of accounting. The timing of income and deductions involves determining the proper year in which each item of income and each deductible item should be reported. In a Tax Court case, the court ruled:

> "The annual reporting period is a necessity in administering the tax law, and the cornerstone of our tax structure."

There is not complete conformity between tax accounting and financial accounting, primarily because many financial accounting decisions are based upon estimates and opinions, while tax accounting decisions are based upon completed transactions and clearly identifiable events. For example, it is proper financial accounting practice to establish a reserve for a contingent warranty expense, based upon a manufacturer's experience for the estimate of future warranty expense. This approach complies with the matching principle, i.e., the income from the sale of the product is matched with one of the expenses of making the sale—the expense of fulfilling the warranty obligation. However, no tax deduction is allowed for tax accounting purposes until the estimated expense is actually incurred under the terms of the warranty.

Therefore, the main problem in tax accounting is the allocation of income and expense deductions to the maximum benefit to the taxpayer.

ACCOUNTANT'S RESPONSIBILITY

Most everyone knows *something* about taxes. However, no one knows *everything* about taxes. Nonetheless, accountants are *presumed* to know taxes. Generally speaking, they probably are familiar with most of the overall, basic, more prominent features of the tax law—those sections which have been thoroughly tested in the courts and resolved into the traditional body of the law.

However, because of the intricate provisions and the relief loopholes provided and adjudicated, because of the often ambiguous legal wording and the necessity for interpretive regulations and further testing in the Tax Court, because of the very nature of the taxpayer/IRS adversary relationship, accountants, as well as others, merely serve as perhaps better-informed, but still "opinion-only" experts. Formerly, it was only the taxpayer who had to bear the burden—and the cost and the responsibility.

Now, the Tax Reform Act of 1976, and subsequent amendments, subject preparers of tax returns to incur penalties if they do not comply with new standards and procedures. Accountants, and others, who prepare tax returns or give tax advice, should be familiar with the preparer's liabilities for penalties. These penalties are incurred for the following simple omissions:

1. The failure to sign a tax return for which they were paid;
2. The failure to give a copy of the tax return to the taxpayer;
3. Failure to maintain a list of tax returns prepared.

A more serious problem has been created by subjecting a preparer to a penalty for other negligence or the willful understatement of income tax. This has been interpreted by some Districts of the Internal Revenue Service to mean the failure to follow all the rules and regulations of the Service. The highlights of tax methods, procedures and considerations presented in this section are timely reminders of certain features of the tax law to be considered when advising a client. In no way should they be considered all-inclusive or all-instructive.

Further research into the tax law, the regulations, the interpretations and the court decisions is advised. Extensive tax publication services are available, constantly updating the ever-changing features of Federal and State tax laws and regulations.

Tax *evasion* is illegal.

Tax *avoidance* is legal. It is statutory.

Tax avoidance is on the books, in the courts—for you to find.

Research all pertinent topics.

Tax Return Preparation

For many corporations, assembling and analyzing the information needed to prepare the corporate tax returns can be a considerable task. Most, if not all, of the company's accounts have to be analyzed; provision often must be made for various types of allocations for state tax purposes; in the case of a corporation the activities of many branches, subsidiaries, or affiliates have to be coordinated (and the accounting records may be dispersed over many locations). In addition, the accounting personnel responsible for keeping the corporate books are not likely to be tax men, and the tax department may have to review the accounts with an eye to the tax significance of the various transactions.

How the tax return information will be assembled will depend in large part on the organization of the company. In a small company with few employees, the "tax man" may also be the one in charge of the books and may do all the analysis himself by direct examination of the company's books and records. In larger companies, the task of gathering the tax information may be more or less systematized, depending on the size of the company; the number and geographic location of the divisions, subsidiaries, or affiliates; the location and responsibilities for the accounting record; and the existence of a separate tax department.

In any event, however, the information is put together whether by direct examination of the books and records by the tax man, direct interviews of various accounting personnel by the tax department representatives, use of questionnaires (completed by the accounting personnel or by the tax department personnel after discussion with accounting personnel) some system should be developed to make sure all the pertinent information is gathered and analyzed in some systematic and usable form.

The accountant's task in finding tax opportunities (or pitfalls) may be greatly simplified by the use of a tax-planning checklist which points out some of the planning possibilities. The items on the checklist should be set up in financial audit format and suggest the action to be taken which would bring the desired tax results.

Accountant performing preparer services must require a written statement from a client that the client has adequate records to support claimed travel and entertainment deductions.

A tax preparer who colludes with a client in a willful misstatement of the client's tax liability is liable to a $1,000 fine, and loss of the privilege to practice before the Internal Revenue Service. A taxpayer can be assessed a 5% penalty for poor record keeping of deductions.

While it may not be necessary to analyze in detail each account for routine items, it probably is necessary to have some formal procedure for analyzing all items that have special tax significance. The checklists enumerate many of the items you may want to check (if they apply) and the reasons for wanting a special analysis of each. With these as starting points, you may readily find other areas of special significance that could be added.

The tax consequences of business transactions are usually determined by their legal status, the accounting treatment of such items, or both. It therefore becomes imperative to plan accounting techniques and legal opinions based upon legal requirements and generally accepted accounting principles and practices *before* entering into any transactions.

Once the transaction has occurred and the book entry has been made, it is usually too late to worry about the tax consequences. Even minor issues should be worked out in advance using proper procedures. For example, careful wording of purchase orders will often insure proper description on invoices, so that portions of work done that are deductible as repairs are properly described and billed separately from work done on permanent installations and improvements, that are required to be capitalized.

In order to plan properly, you must know the accounting techniques available to you. Here are the choices:

(1) Taxable year.

(2) Cash, accrual, or an approved hybrid accounting method.

(3) Last-in-first-out (LIFO) or first-in-first-out (FIFO) inventory method.

(4) Cost, or lower-of-cost-or-market, as method of evaluation of inventory.

(5) Method of handling time sales.

(6) Method of handling long-term contracts.

What the Tax Law Requires

Definitions

GROSS INCOME: All income from whatever source derived, unless excluded by law. Includes income realized in any form whether in money, property, or services.

INCOME TAXES: Taxes based on income determined under the provisions of the U.S. Internal Revenue Code.

TAXABLE INCOME: For business, gross income reduced by all allowable deductions.

INCOME TAX EXPENSE: The amount of income taxes (whether or not currently payable or refundable) allocable to a period in the determination of net income.

The law specifies only that you compute taxable income in accordance with the method of accounting you regularly employ in keeping your books; however, such method must clearly reflect your income.

Each taxpayer is authorized to adopt such forms and systems of accounting as, in his judgment, are best suited to his purpose. No uniform method is prescribed for all taxpayers. Nevertheless, the Regulations provide that:

(1) All items of gross income and deductions must be treated with reasonable consistency;

(2) In all cases in which the production, purchase, or sale of merchandise is an income-producing factor, the accrual method of accounting must be used. Inventories of merchandise on hand (including finished goods, work in process, raw materials and supplies) must be taken at the beginning and end of the accounting period and used in computing taxable income of the period;

(3) Expenditures made during the fiscal year should be properly classified as between capital and expense. Expenditures for items such as plant and equipment which have a useful life extending over a number of years must be charged to capital expenditures rather than to expense;

(4) Where capital costs are being recovered through deductions for wear and tear, depletion, or obsolescence, expenditures (other than ordinary repairs) made to restore the property or prolong its useful life should be added to the property account or charged against the appropriate reserve, not to current expense;

Those who neither produce nor sell goods and consequently have no inventories can use either of the two regular methods of accounting, the cash or accrual. This includes artists; authors; artisans, such as carpenters and masons who either use their customers' materials or buy materials for specific jobs only; professionals, such as accountants, architects, attorneys, dentists, physicians and engineers; and brokers and agents rendering services of various kinds;

(5) Special methods of accounting are also prescribed in the Code. Such methods include the crop method, the installment method and the long-term contract method. There are also special methods of accounting for particular items of income and expense;

(6) A combination of methods (hybrid system) of accounting may also be used in connection with a trade or business, if consistently used;

(7) The fact that books are kept in accordance with the requirements of a supervisory agency does not mean that income for tax purposes is computed in the same manner.

CHOOSING A TAXABLE YEAR

Taxable year.   The taxpayer's annual accounting period (including a 52- or 53-week year) which is the basis for which the taxpayer regularly computes his income in keeping the books.

The initial choice of an accounting period is generally within the control of the taxpayer. However, many taxpayers forfeit this right by giving the matter haphazard, last-minute consideration. The result is that they adopt an annual accounting period ill-suited to their business needs.

Four Possible Choices

There are four types of taxable years recognized by the Code. They are:

(1) *Calendar Year.* A 12-month period ending on December 31;

(2) *Fiscal Year.* A 12-month period ending on the last day of any month of the year other than December.

(3) *52-53 Week Year.* This is a fiscal year, varying from 52 to 53 weeks in duration, which ends always on the same day of the week, which (a) occurs for the last time in a calendar month, or (b) falls nearest the end of the calendar month.

(4) *Short Period.* A period of less than 12 months (allowed only in certain special situations such as initial return, final return, change in accounting period, and termination of taxable year by reason of jeopardy assessment).

Partnerships, S Corporations, and personal service corporations must use a taxable year that generally conforms to the taxable year of the owners. A partnership must use in order of priority: 1) the taxable year of the partners owning the majority of partnership profits and capital; 2) the taxable year of all of its principal partners; 3) a calendar year. S Corporations and personal service corporations must use the calendar year. If to the satisfaction of the Secretary of the Treasury it can be established that there is a business purpose for having a different taxable year, these three entities may be permitted a different taxable year.

Shift of Tax Year With Permission

In his first return a new taxpayer can select any taxable year permitted by the code. However, a taxpayer whose taxable year is a calendar year cannot adopt a fiscal year without the prior approval of IRS.

If a taxpayer does receive permission to change his accounting period, a return should be made for the short period beginning on the day after the close of the old taxable year and ending at the end of the day before the day designated as the first day of the new taxable year. Generally, if a return is made for a short period, it is necessary that the income for the period be annualized and then divided by the number of months in the short period. The tax is then computed on that amount.

To prevent inequities, the law provides that on the taxpayer's establishing the amount of his taxable income for the 12-month period, computed as if the period were a taxable year, the tax for the short period shall be reduced to the greater of the following;

(1) An amount which bears the same ratio to the tax computed on the taxable income for the 12-month period, as the taxable income computed on the basis of the short period bears to the taxable income for the 12-month period; or

(2) The tax computed on the taxable income for the short period without placing the taxable income on an annual basis.

How to get permission: Application for permission to change must be made on Form 1128 by the 15th day of the second month following the short period needed to effect the change. The motive for the change must be a business reason and not one of tax avoidance.

CHANGE OF ACCOUNTING METHOD

What is a change in accounting method? A change in accounting method occurs when an accounting principle is used that is different from the principle used previously for reporting purposes. The term "accounting principle" includes not only accounting principles and practices, but also the methods of applying them. For example, a change in inventory valuation from LIFO to FIFO is a change in method.

It should be noted that the correction of an error in previously issued financial statements (computational errors, oversights, misapplication of an accounting principle) is not an accounting change or change in method.

A change in accounting method can be required either by IRS or initiated by the taxpayer. If the former, the change must conform to the method required by the law. If the latter, the taxpayer, with a few exceptions, must obtain IRS approval, irrespective of whether the changes conform to GAAP, or the tax law.

Changes requiring IRS approval:

• A change from cash to the accrual method for gross income and expenses.
• A change in depreciation method.
• A change in the basis for inventory valuation method.
• Changes in the reporting entity; e.g., a change in the subsidiary-parent organization because the statements are considered to be those of a different entity.

- Changes in the method for a material item. (A material item is defined in the Code to be "any item that involves the proper time for inclusion of an item in income or the taking of a deduction.")

Changes in method do not include:

- Correction of arithmetic errors.
- Correction of improper postings.
- Adjustments to the depreciation schedule.
- Changes made necessary by changes in the circumstances and facts governing the current method.

A special rule applies to dealers in personal property. A dealer can adopt at the time of a transaction (or a change *to*) the installment method of accounting without IRS consent. But a dealer cannot change *from* the installment method *to* any other method without IRS consent.

Under present procedure application for permission to change an accounting method or practice is filed on Form 3115 within the first 180 days of the year to which the change is to apply. Adjustments resulting from the change are taken ratably "over an approximate period, prescribed by the Commissioner, generally ten years," beginning with the year of change. Applications usually receive favorable consideration if the taxpayer agrees to the ten year spread or any other approach suggested by IRS.

In the case of the taxpayer wanting to discontinue the LIFO method of inventory valuation, the readjustment period of ten years will usually be allowed; however, the taxpayer cannot apply LIFO again during the 10-year allocation period without IRS consent.

Income for tax purposes must be computed under the same method of accounting regularly used by you in keeping your books. If you have not used a method regularly or if the method regularly used does not clearly reflect income, the Commissioner can compute your income under a method which he considers clearly reflects your income.

Except for some special situations, you may not change your method of accounting without the prior consent of the Commissioner.

It becomes important, therefore, to know whether a change constitutes a change in accounting method or merely a correction of an error (not requiring consent).

Consent is *required* for the following changes:

(1) From the cash to the accrual basis;

(2) Method of valuing inventory;

(3) From/to completed contract method, from/to percentage-of-completion method, or a change from/to any other method to the contract method;

(4) Those involving special methods, such as the installment method or crop method;

(5) Those specifically enumerated in the Code.

Consent is *not* required for the following changes:

(1) Correction of mathematical, posting or timing errors;

(2) Correction of bad debt reserves;

(3) Changes in estimated useful lives of depreciable assets.

The 1984 tax bill clarified the Code with respect to changes in an accounting method. In the past, some taxpayers contended that there is no requirement to obtain IRS's permission to change from an *improper* to a proper accounting method; that a failure of IRS to consent to a change in this circumstance is a defense against an IRS charge of negligence and penalty assessment.

Congress in the new law has specifically provided that when a taxpayer fails to file a request to change its accounting method, the absence of IRS consent cannot be a defense to any penalty assessed by the taxpayer's failure to request a consent to the change.

Normally, a corporation is likely to use the accrual method of accounting. But some service companies will use the cash method. And in special types of businesses, specialized methods may be desirable. Appendix D summarizes the workings of the various accounting methods available for tax purposes and the advantages and disadvantages of each.

(Note: APB Opinion No. 20, *Accounting Changes*, is the GAAP covering accounting changes.)

Form **3115** (Rev. April 1986)	**Application for Change in Accounting Method**	OMB No. 1545-0152 Expires 12-31-88

Note: *If you are applying for a change in accounting period, use Form 1128.*

Department of the Treasury
Internal Revenue Service

▶ **See separate instructions.**

Name of applicant (if joint return is filed, show names of you and your spouse)	Identifying Number (See instructions)
Address (Number and street)	Applicant's area code and telephone number
City or town, state, and ZIP code	District Director's office having jurisdiction
Name of person to contact (Please type or print)	Telephone number of contact person

Check one: ☐ Individual ☐ Partnership; No. of Partners _____ ☐ Corporation ☐ S Corporation; No. of Shareholders _____
☐ Cooperative (Section 1381(a))   ☐ Ins. Co. (Sec. 801)   ☐ Ins. Co. (Sec. 821)   ☐ Ins. Co. (Sec. 831)
☐ Exempt organization; Enter code section _____
☐ Other (specify) ▶ _____

NOTE: *Are you making an election under section 458 or 466?* . . . . ☐ **Yes** ☐ **No**
If "Yes," see Specific Instructions for Section J. Do not fill in Section A. If "No", you must complete Section A.

Section A. Applicable to All Filers Other Than Those Answering "Yes" to "Note" Above

1 a   Tax year of change begins (mo., day, yr.) ▶ _____ and ends (mo., day, yr.) ▶ _____

   b   Enter the 180th day of your tax year ▶ _____ If this date is earlier than date you signed this Form 3115 on page 6, see
       General Instruction for "Late Applications" before proceeding any further.

2   Nature of business and principal source of income (including type of business designated on your latest income tax return) ▶ _____

   _____

3   The following change in accounting method is requested (check and complete appropriate spaces):

   a   ☐ Overall method of accounting : from ▶ _____ to _____

   b   ☐ The accounting treatment of (identify item) ▶_____
       from (present method) ▶_____ to (new method) ▶_____
       Attach a separate statement providing all relevant facts, including a detailed description of your present and proposed methods.
       See also item 14 of Section A on page 2 regarding the "legal basis" for the proposed change.

   c   If a change is requested under 3b above, check the present overall method of accounting:
       ☐ Accrual   ☐ Cash   ☐ Hybrid (if a hybrid method is used, explain the overall hybrid method in detail in a
       separate statement)

   d   Is your use of your present method specifically not permitted by the Internal Revenue Code, the Income Tax Regula-
       tions, or by a decision of the U.S. Supreme Court? See sections 4, 5, and 6 of Rev. Proc. 84-74 . . . . . .

   e   Are you currently under examination, or were you or any member of the affiliated group contacted in any manner by a
       representative of the Internal Revenue Service for the purpose of scheduling an examination of your Federal tax
       return(s) prior to the filing of this application, or do you have an examination under consideration by an appeals officer
       or before any Federal court, or is any criminal investigation pending? See sections 4 and 6 of Rev. Proc. 84-74. . . .

   f   Are you a manufacturer to whom Regulations section 1.471-11 applies? If "Yes," complete Section E-2 on page 4

4   In the last 10 years have you requested permission to change your accounting period, your overall method of accounting,
    or the accounting treatment of any item? (Members of an affiliated group of corporations filing a consolidated return, see
    item 7d on page 2.) . . . .

   a   If "Yes," was a ruling letter granting permission to make the change issued? If "Yes," attach a copy of the letter. If
       "No," attach an explanation . . . .

   b   Regardless of your response to 4a, do you or an affiliated corporation have pending any accounting method or period
       ruling or technical advice request in the National Office? . . . .

   c   If 4b is "Yes," indicate the type of request (method, period, etc.) and the specific issue involved in each request ▶ _____

   _____

5   If engaged in a business or profession: **a** Enter your taxable income or (loss)* from operations for tax purposes for the five (5) tax years
    preceding the year of change: (See Specific Instructions for Section A.)

1st preceding year ended: mo. yr.	2nd preceding year ended: mo. yr.	3rd preceding year ended: mo. yr.	4th preceding year ended: mo. yr.	5th preceding year ended: mo. yr.
$	$	$	$	$

   b   Enter the amount of net operating loss to be carried over to the year of change, if any . . . . $
   c   Amount of investment credit carryover to year of change, if any . . . . $
   d   Other credit carryover, if any. (Identify) ▶ _____ $

*Individuals enter net profit or (loss) from business; partnerships enter ordinary income or (loss); members of an affiliated group filing a consolidated
return, see item 7a on page 2.

For Paperwork Reduction Act Notice, see separate instructions.   Form **3115** (Rev. 4-86)

Form 3115 (Rev. 4-86)   Page **2**

	Yes	No

6 Do you have more than one trade or business? . . . .

   a If "Yes," do you account for each trade or business separately? . . . .

   b If "Yes," see Specific Instructions for Section A.

7 Is applicant a member of an affiliated group filing a consolidated return for the tax year of change? . . . .

   a If 7 is "Yes," state parent corporation's name, identifying number, address, tax year, and Service Center where return is filed and provide the information requested in item 5 on a consolidated basis ▶ ----------------------------

----

   b If 7 is "Yes," do all other members of the affiliated group employ the method of accounting for which the change is requested? If "No," explain ▶ --

   c If 7 is "Yes," are any of the items involved in the calculation of the net section 481(a) adjustment attributable to transactions between members of the affiliated group?. . . . . If "Yes," attach explanation.

   d If 7 is "Yes," provide the information requested in items 4a, 4b, and 4c for each member of the affiliated group. Also, see General Instructions for "Signature."

8 Is applicant a member of an affiliated group not filing a consolidated return for the tax year of change? . . . . If "Yes," are any of the items involved in the calculation of the net section 481(a) adjustment attributable to transactions between members of the affiliated group or other related parties? (If "Yes," attach explanation.) . . . .

9 If change is granted, will the new method be used for financial reporting purposes? . . . . If "No," attach an explanation. Such explanation should include a discussion of whether your new method of accounting conforms to generally accepted accounting principles and why it will clearly reflect income.

10 Enter the net section 481(a) adjustment for the year of change, and the net section 481(a) adjustment that would have been required if the requested change had been made for each of the 3 preceding tax years preceding the year of change. (See Specific Instructions for Section A.)	At the beginning of the year of change ending, enter: mo. yr.	At the beginning of the 1st preceding year ended, enter: mo. yr.	At the beginning of the 2nd preceding year ended, enter: mo. yr.	At the beginning of the 3rd preceding year ended, enter: mo. yr.
	$	$	$	$

11 Has net adjustment under section 481(a) for the year of change been reduced in any way by a pre-1954 amount?

12 Number of tax years present method has been used for which the change is requested in item 3a or 3b. (See Specific Instructions for Section A.) ▶ --

13 Has your present method been designated by Rev. Rul. or Rev. Proc. more than 2 years before filing this Form 3115 as a change in method of accounting to which section 5.12(2) of Rev. Proc. 84-74 applies? . . . .

14 State the reason(s) including the legal basis (statutes, regulation, published rulings, etc.) why you believe approval to make this change should be granted. See section 7 of Rev. Proc. 84-74. --
----

Section B. Change in Overall Method of Accounting

1 The following amounts should be stated as of the end of the tax year **preceding** the year of change. If none, state "None." (Although some of the items listed below may not have been required in the computation of your taxable income due to your present method of accounting, it is necessary that they be entered here for this form to be complete. Show amounts attributable to long-term contracts on page 4, Section G-1.) Provide on a schedule the breakdown of the individual items which make up the "Amount" for lines 1a through 1h. See Rev. Proc. 85-36 and Rev. Proc. 85-37 for rules to make this change expeditiously.

	Amount	Show by (✓) how treated on last year's return	
		Included in income or deducted as expense	Excluded from income or not deducted as expense
a Income accrued but not received	$		
b Income received before the date on which it was earned. State nature of income. If discount on installment loans, see Section C below. For advance payments for goods and services, see Specific Instructions for Section B. ▶ ----------------			
c Expenses accrued but not paid			
d Other (specify) ▶ ----------------			
e Prepaid expense previously deducted			
f Supplies on hand previously deducted			
g Inventory on hand . . . . . $_____ Inventory reported on your return $_____ Difference.			
h Reserve for bad debts (See instructions)			
i **Net adjustment** (combine lines 1a through 1h)		$	

Form 3115 (Rev. 4-86)   Page **3**

2   Nature of inventory ▶ _____

3   Method used to value inventory ☐ Cost   ☐ Cost or market, whichever is lower   ☐ Other (attach explanation)

4   Method of identifying costs in inventory   ☐ Specific identification   ☐ FIFO   ☐ LIFO

5 Have any receivables been sold in the past three years? . . . . ☐ Yes ☐ No	1st preceding year ended, enter: mo. yr	2nd preceding year ended, enter: mo. yr.	3rd preceding year ended, enter: mo. yr.
If "Yes," enter the amounts sold for each of the three years	$	$	$

6   Attach copies of Profit And Loss Statement (Schedule F (Form 1040) in the case of farmers) and Balance Sheet, if applicable, as of the close of the tax year preceding the year of change. State accounting method used when preparing balance sheet. If books of account are not kept, attach copy of the business schedule provided with your Federal income tax return or return of income for that period. If amounts in 1 above do not agree with those shown on profit and loss statement and balance sheet, explain on separate page.

Section C. Change in Method of Reporting Interest (Discount) on Installment and Other Loans

1   Change with respect to interest on ☐ Installment loans,   ☐ Commercial loans, and ☐ Other loans (explain) ▶ _____

2   Do any of these loans cover a period in excess of 60 months? . . . . ☐ Yes   ☐ No
If "Yes," please attach an explanation. (See Rev. Rul. 83-84 and Rev. Proc. 83-40.)
If you wish to change from the sum of the months digits method (rule of 78's) to the economic accrual of interest method for reporting interest (discount) under Rev. Rul. 83-84, see Rev. Procs. 84-27, 84-28, 84-29, and 84-30.

3   Amount of earned or realized interest that has not been reported on your return as of the end of the tax year
preceding the year of change . . . . |$

4   Amount of unearned or unrealized interest that has been reported on your return as of the end of the tax year
preceding the year of change . . . . |$

5   Method of rebating in event of prepayment of loans ▶

Section D. Change in Method of Reporting Bad Debts
(See Specific Instructions for Section D before completing item 2.)

1   If a change to the Reserve Method is requested and applicant has installment sales, are such sales reported on the installment method?   ☐ Yes   ☐ No
If "Yes," show whether change relates to: ☐ Installment sales,   ☐ Sales other than installment sales, or ☐ Both.

2   If a change to the Reserve Method is requested, provide the following information for the five tax years preceding the year of change:

	1st preceding year	2nd preceding year	3rd preceding year	4th preceding year	5th preceding year
Total sales					
Deductions for specific bad debts charged off [1] . .					
Recoveries of bad debts deducted in prior years					
Year-end balances:					
Trade accounts receivable					
Trade notes receivable [2].					
Installment accounts receivable [3] . .					
Other receivables (explain in detail) . .					

3   If a change to the method of deducting specific bad debt items is requested, enter the amount in reserve for
bad debts at end of the year preceding the year of change . . . . |$

[1] If your return was examined, enter amount allowed as a result of the examination.
[2] If loan company, enter only capital portion.
[3] Applicable only to receivables attributable to sales reported on installment method. Enter only the capital portion of such receivables.

Section E-1. Change in Method of Valuing Inventories. *(See Specific Instructions for Section E-1.)*

1   Nature of all inventories ▶ _____

2   Method of identifying costs in inventory . . . . ☐ Specific identification   ☐ FIFO   ☐ LIFO
If "LIFO," attach copy of Form 970 adopting that method and copies of any Forms 970 filed to extend the use of the method.

3   Method used to value inventory: ☐ Cost ☐ Cost or market, whichever is lower ☐ Retail cost ☐ Retail lower cost or market
☐ Other (attach explanation)

4   Method of allocating indirect production costs: ☐ Standard cost method ☐ Burden method ☐ Other (attach explanation)

5   Show method and value of all inventories at the end of the tax year preceding the year of change under:
   a   Present method ▶ _____ |$
   b   New method ▶ _____ |$
   c   If changing to cost method, are you going to elect LIFO for identifying costs? . . . . ☐ Yes   ☐ No

Form 3115 (Rev. 4-86)   Page **4**

Section E-2. Change in Method of Inventory Costing by Manufacturers and Processors.
(See Specific Instructions for Section E-2.)

Please check (✓) the appropriate boxes showing which costs are included in inventoriable costs, under both the present and proposed methods, of all costs listed in Regulations sections 1.471-11(b)(2), (c)(2)(i), and (c)(2)(ii) for Federal income tax purposes, and all costs listed in or subject to Regulations section 1.471-11(c)(2)(iii) for tax and financial statement reporting purposes. If any boxes are not checked, it is assumed that these costs are excluded from inventoriable costs. If certain costs are not incurred, please mark "N/A" in the appropriate box.

		Federal income tax purposes	
		Present method	Proposed method
Part I Direct Production Costs (Regulations section 1.471-11(b)(2))		Included (✓)	Included (✓)
1	Material.		
2	Labor.		
Part II Indirect Production Costs:			
1	Category One Costs (Regulations section 1.471-11(c)(2)(i))		
a	Repairs		
b	Maintenance		
c	Utilities		
d	Rent		
e	Indirect labor and production supervisory wages		
f	Indirect materials and supplies		
g	Small tools and equipment		
h	Quality control and inspection		
2	Category Two Costs (Regulations section 1.471-11(c)(2)(ii) (See also Rev. Rul. 79-25))		
a	Marketing		
b	Advertising		
c	Selling		
d	Other distribution expenses		
e	Interest		
f	Research and experimental		
g	Section 165 losses		
h	Percentage depletion in excess of cost depletion		
i	Depreciation and amortization for Federal tax purposes in excess of financial report depreciation and amortization		
j	Local and foreign income taxes		
k	Past service costs of pensions		
l	Administrative (general)		
m	Other salaries (general)		

		Federal Income Tax Purposes		Financial Statements	
		Present method	Proposed method	Present method	Proposed method
3	Category Three Costs (Regulations section 1.471-11(c)(2)(iii)). (See also Rev. Proc. 75-40 and attach the data required by either section 5.02 or 5.03 of Rev. Proc. 75-40.)	Included (✓)	Included (✓)	Included (✓)	Included (✓)
a	Taxes under section 164 (other than local and foreign income taxes).				
b	Financial statement depreciation and cost depletion				
c	Employee benefits				
d	Costs of strikes, rework labor, scrap, and spoilage				
e	Factory administrative expenses				
f	Officers' salaries (manufacturing)				
g	Insurance costs (manufacturing)				

Section F. Change in Method of Treating Vacation Pay

1 Is the plan(s) fully vested as of the end of the tax year preceding the year of the change? . . . . ☐ Yes ☐ No
2 If "Yes," enter the amount of accrued vacation pay as of the end of the tax year preceding the year of change . . . . . $ . . . .
3 Number of tax years plan(s) has been vested ▶

Section G-1. Change in Method of Reporting Income from Contracts

1 Are your contracts long-term contracts as defined in Regulations section 1.451-3? . . . . ☐ Yes ☐ No
2 Is the same method used for reporting all long-term contracts regardless of duration? If "No," explain . . . . ☐ Yes ☐ No
3 Do you have extended period long-term contracts as defined in Regulations section 1.451-3(b)(3)? . . . . ☐ Yes ☐ No
4 Net adjustment required under section 481(a) . . . . $

Form 3115 (Rev. 4-86)   Page 5

Section G-2. Change to the Completed Contract Method or Change in Allocation of Costs

Please check (✓) the appropriate boxes showing which costs are allocable to long-term contracts to the extent required by Regulations sections 1.451-3(d)(5) and (6) for Federal income tax purposes. Please mark "N/A" in boxes for costs that do not apply to the taxpayer.

	Tax Purposes			
	Non-Extended Period		Extended Period	
	Present Method	Proposed Method	Present Method	Proposed Method
	Included (✓)	Included (✓)	Included (✓)	Included (✓)
Direct Material				
Direct Labor				
Repairs				
Maintenance				
Utilities				
Rent				
Indirect labor and contract supervisory wages				
Indirect material and supplies				
Tools and equipment				
Quality control and inspection				
Taxes under section 164 (other than local and foreign income taxes)				
Financial statement depreciation and cost depletion				
Percentage depletion in excess of cost depletion				
Depreciation and amortization for Federal tax purposes in excess of financial report depreciation and amortization for equipment and facilities in use				
Administrative costs				
Other administrative, service, or support costs				
Officers' salaries attributable to long-term contract activities				
Insurance				
Employee benefits				
Research and experimental expenses attributable to extended period long-term contracts	▨	▨		
Other research and experimental expenses				
Rework labor, scrap, and spoilage				
Bidding expenses incurred in the solicitation of extended period long-term contracts	▨	▨		
Other bidding expenses				
Marketing, selling, and advertising				
Interest				
Other general and administrative costs				
Section 165 losses				
Income taxes				
Cost of strikes				

Section H. Change in Overall Method of Reporting Income of Farmers to Cash Receipts and Disbursements Method

Note: *Also complete Section B.*

1. Is the taxpayer a corporation? . . . . ☐ Yes ☐ No
2. Is the taxpayer a partnership with a corporation as a partner? . . . . ☐ Yes ☐ No
3. If either 1 or 2 is "Yes," has the taxpayer had gross receipts of $1,000,000 or less in each of its tax years beginning after 1975? . . . . ☐ Yes ☐ No
   If "No," attach a schedule showing which years the taxpayer's receipts were more than $1,000,000.
4. Provide the following information for the five tax years before the year of change:

	1st preceding yr.	2nd preceding yr.	3rd preceding yr.	4th preceding yr.	5th preceding yr.
a Gross receipts from farming					
b Inventory: Crops, etc.					
Livestock held for sale:					
Purchased					
Raised					
Livestock held for draft breeding, sport, or dairy purposes:					
Purchased					
Raised					
Total inventory					

5 Method used to value inventory *(check appropriate block):*

☐ Cost ☐ Cost or market, whichever is lower ☐ Farm price ☐ Unit livestock price ☐ Other (explain on separate page)

Section I. Change in Method of Accounting for Depreciation

Applicants desiring to change their method of accounting for depreciation must complete this section. This information must be supplied for each account for which a change is requested. **Note:** *Certain changes in methods of accounting for depreciation may be filed with the Service Center where your return will be filed. See Rev. Proc. 74-11 for the methods covered.*

1 Date of acquisition ▶ ....

2 a Are you the original owner or the first user of the property? . . . . ☐ Yes ☐ No

   b If residential property, did you live in the home before renting it? . . . . ☐ Yes ☐ No

3 Is depreciation claimed under Regulations section 1.167(a)-11 (CLADR)? . . . . ☐ Yes ☐ No

   If "Yes," the only changes permitted are under Regulations section 1.167(a)-11(c)(1)(iii). Identify these changes on the tax return for the year of change.

4 Is the property public utility property? . . . . ☐ Yes ☐ No

5 Location of the property (city and state) ▶ ....

6 Type or character of the property ▶ ....

7 Cost or other basis of the property and adjustments thereto (exclude land) . . . . | $

8 Depreciation claimed in prior tax years (depreciation reserve) . . . . | $

9 Estimated salvage value . . . . | $

10 Estimated remaining useful life of the property ▶ ....

11 If the declining balance method is requested, show percentage of straight-line rate ▶ ....

12 Other information, if any ▶ ....

Section J. Change in Method of Accounting Not Listed Above *(See Specific Instructions for Section J.)*

Signature—All Filers *(See instructions.)*

Under penalties of perjury, I declare that I have examined this application, including accompanying schedules and statements, and to the best of my knowledge and belief, it is true, correct and complete. Declaration of preparer (other than applicant) is based on all information of which preparer has any knowledge.

Applicant's name	Signature and title	Date

Signing official's name (Please print or type)	Signature and title of officer of the parent corporation, if applicable	Date

Signature of individual or firm preparing the application		Date

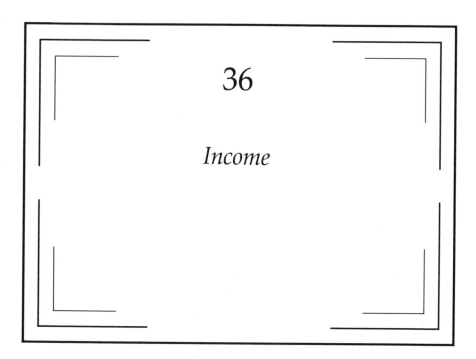

36

Income

The conflicts between tax accounting and generally accepted business accounting center around the questions: (1) *when* is it income? and (2) *when* is it deductible? To illustrate the differences that have existed in these two areas, we include the following list which was submitted by the American Institute of Certified Public Accountants to the House Committee on Ways and Means.

Divergences Involving the Time of Recognition of Revenues

(A) Revenues, deferred for general accounting purposes until earned, but reportable for tax purposes when received:

  (1) Revenues susceptible of proration on a fixed-time basis or on a service-rendered basis:

    Rentals.

    Commissions.

    Revenues from maintenance and similar service contracts covering a specified period.

    Warehousing and trucking fees.

    Advertising revenues.

    Advance royalties on patents or copyrights.

    Transportation ticket and token sales.

    Sales of coupon books entitling purchaser to services.

    Theatre ticket sales.

Membership fees.

Tuition fees.

Laboratory fees.

(2) Revenues susceptible of proration over average duration of demand:

Life memberships.

Revenues from service contracts extending over life of article serviced or period of ownership by original owner.

(B) Revenues deferred for general accounting purposes until right to retain them is substantially assured, but reportable for tax purposes when received:

(1) Receipts under claim of right.

(C) Revenues accrued for general accounting purposes, but not reportable for tax purposes until collected:

(1) Dividends declared.

(2) Increase in withdrawal value of savings and loan shares.

Income Received in Advance

Frequently, a taxpayer receives payment for services he has not yet performed (e.g., club membership dues, magazine subscriptions). The question then is, in what year does the taxpayer have to report these payments as income?

Accounting rule.   The accountant says that you have no income until it is actually *earned*; that the mere receipt of cash or property does not result in a realization of income. The accountant treats the prepayment as a liability which obligates the recipient to perform services before he can be said to have *earned* the payment. (This problem applies to accrual-basis taxpayers; cash-basis taxpayers are considered to have *earned* a prepayment when it is received.)

Tax rule.   You have income when you have the *right to receive* it, even though it is not earned. Thus, cash payments received in advance, negotiable notes received as advance payments, and contract installments due and payable are taxable to the recipient as advance income, even though these payments are for services to be provided by the taxpayer in a subsequent tax year. Here is a composite tax picture.

Type of Income	Basis	Extent Taxable	Authority
Cash receipts	Cash or accrual	Full amount	*American Automobile Association*, 367 US 687; *Schlude*, 372 US 128.

Cont.

Type of Income	Basis	Extent Taxable	Authority
Negotiable notes	Cash	Fair market value	*Pinellas Ice Co.*, 287 US 462; Reg. §1.61—2(d)(4).
	Accrual	Face Value	*Schedule*, 372 US 128; *Schedule*, TC Memo 1963-307; *Spring City* *Foundry Co.*, 292 US 182.
Unpaid contractual payments due and payable un- der terms of the contract	Cash	None—no fair mar- ket value	Est. of *Ennis*, 23 TC 799; *nonacq.*, 1956-2 CB 10; *Ennis*, 17 TC 465.
	Accrual	Face Value	*Schedule*, 32 TC 1271.
Unpaid contractual installments not due under the contract nor evi- denced by notes	Cash	None	*Schedule*, 372 US 128.
	Accrual	None	*Schedule*, 372 US 128.

The tendency of the courts seems to be to require reporting prepaid receipts.

(1) *Accrual-basis taxpayers* may defer prepaid income from service contracts or from the sale of goods.

(2) *Publishers* may elect to spread prepaid subscription income.

(3) *Membership organizations* organized without capital stock which do not distribute earnings to any members and do not report income by the cash receipts and disbursements method may spread their prepaid dues income ratably over the period (not to exceed 36 months) during which they are under a liability to render services.

Repayment of Income Received Under Claim of Right

Since the tax law requires the accrual-basis taxpayer to include payments received (although not yet earned) in taxable income when received, it obviously disagrees with good accounting practice on how to treat such payments if they must be repaid.

If you are required to repay money received under a claim of right, the tax law says you can deduct it in the year of repayment.

Premature Accruals—New Law*

Under the accrual method of accounting, an expense is generally deductible in the taxable year in which all the events have occurred that determine the fact of the liability, and the amount of the liability can be determined with reasonable accuracy (the so-called "all events test"). Whether an expense involving a future obligation can satisfy the all-events test in a year significantly earlier than the year in which the taxpayer must fulfill the obligation, has been the subject of controversy under present law. In general, the new law provides that in determining whether an accrual method taxpayer has incurred an amount during the taxable year, all the events which establish the taxpayer's liability for such amount will not be deemed to have occurred any earlier than the time when economic performance occurs. If economic performance has occurred, the amount will be treated as incurred for purposes of the Code. Amounts incurred are deductible currently only if they are not properly chargeable to a capital account, and are not subject to any other provision of the Code that requires the deduction to be taken in a taxable year later than the year when economic performance occurs. Effective date: Accruals after July 18, 1984.

The new law provides criteria for determining when economic performance occurs in the case of two categories of liabilities: 1) liabilities arising from another person providing goods or services or the use of property to the taxpayer; 2) liabilities of the taxpayer to provide property or services. Economic performance occurs with respect to the first category as the property or services are provided to the taxpayer. Economic performance occurs with respect to the second category as the taxpayer provides the property or service.

In the case of interest, economic performance occurs with the passage of time; that is, it occurs as the borrower uses, and lender foregoes use of, the lender's money—rather than as payments are made. Interest incurred by accrual method taxpayers, with respect to debts incurred after June 8, 1984, will be deductible only on a constant interest basis.

INCOME TAXES—TIMING INCOME AND EXPENSES

There can be many reasons for shifting income and expenses. One year may have so many deductions already that additional income can be picked up tax free. True, if the income were not picked up, the current year's loss could be carried back three years and forward 15 years. But, perhaps the prior years were also loss years and no immediate benefit can be realized from the current year's loss (or if refunds will be available, the years may be subject to tax audit). On the other hand, the current

*The use of the cash method of accounting by any C corporation, partnership that has a C corporation as a partner, tax-exempt trust with unrelated business income, or a tax shelter, is not allowable. The accrual method of accounting must be used. Qualified personal service corporations and entities, other than tax shelters, with average annual gross receipts of $5 million or less, are exempted from this requirement. (App. B, p. xx.)

year's deductions may be "light" but the following years' deductions are expected to be "heavy." Shifting income forward can match up the deductions with the income.

Similar results can be achieved by shifting expenses from one year to another. In a year when additional income is desirable, the same effect may be achieved by shifting expenses out of that year.

Where we have installment sales—whether the company is an installment dealer or makes a so-called casual sale of substantial property calling for payment over a number of years—the total tax paid on the income realized from the sale may be the same whether we use installment sale or accrual accounting. We may prefer to use the installment method of reporting the sale for tax purposes so as to match the actual tax payments with the receipt of income.

HOW TO HANDLE SALES

Gross sales are a decisive factor in determining the income level for a given year. The method of selling and the timing of shipments can control the tax year. In a cash-basis business, it is relatively simple to control the time of payment. Income can be increased for the year by accelerating collections; it can be reduced by either allowing payments to take their normal course or by a delay in billing. For accrual-basis businesses, a sale is taken into income when completed, which is when title has passed. As a general rule, title passes when delivery has been made, usually determined by reference to the invoice or bill of lading. Thus, an accrual-basis taxpayer can accelerate income by speeding up deliveries. Similarly, income can be reduced by holding off deliveries in the closing weeks of the year.

Long-term contracts.   Taxpayer has the option of reporting on the percentage-completion method or the completed-contract basis.

Both the percentage-of-completion and the completed-contract methods of accounting are permitted for income tax purposes as long as more than one year elapses from the date of execution to the date of completion and acceptance of the contract.

Use of either of these methods is optional; the taxpayer may use the cash or accrual method for other operations although using the percentage-of-completion or completed-contract method for long-term contracts. But once the method of accounting is originally adopted, a change requires IRS approval.

Completed Contract Method of Accounting

A corporation that accounts for income and expenses attributable to a long-term contract on the completed contract method of accounting generally recognizes income and expense in the year in which the contract is completed. Under the new law, a corporation that accounts for income and expense on this method is required to compute earnings and profits as if it were accounting for income and expense attributable to long-term contracts on a percentage of completion basis.

This provision is effective for contracts entered into after September 30, 1984, other than for binding contracts entered into on or prior to that date.

Construction Period Interest, Taxes, and Carrying Charges

For purposes of computing a corporation's earnings and profits, construction period interest, taxes, and carrying charges are required to be capitalized as a part of the asset to which they relate, and written off as is the asset itself. This rule applies to all corporations. Further, it applies with respect to both residential and nonresidential real property, and to personal property.

"Construction period interest and taxes" include: property taxes (real and personal); interest paid or accrued on debt incurred or continued, to acquire, construct, or carry property; and other carrying charges, but only to the extent such taxes, interest, and carrying charges are attributable to the construction period for such property.

This provision is applicable to the effect on earnings and profits of amounts paid or accrued in taxable years beginning after September 30, 1984.

INSTALLMENT SALES

Under prior laws a gain or loss from a sale of property generally is recognized in the taxable year in which the property is sold. Gain from certain sales of property in exchange for which the seller receives deferred payments is reported on the installment method, unless the taxpayer elects otherwise. Eligible sales include dispositions of personal property on the installment plan by a person who regularly sells or otherwise disposes of personal property on the installment plan and other dispositions of property, including publicly-traded property, where at least one payment is to be received after the close of the taxable year in which the disposition occurs. The installment method cannot be used where a sale results in a loss.

Under the installment method, a taxpayer recognizes income resulting from a disposition of property equal to an amount that bears the same ratio to the payments received in that year that the gross profit under the contract bears to the total contract price. Payments taken into account for this purpose generally include cash or other property, marketable securities, certain assumptions of liabilities, and evidences of indebtedness of the purchaser that are payable on demand or are readily tradable.

A portion of the receivables from sales of property sold under a revolving credit plan can be treated as installment receivables, and report any income there from on the installment method. A revolving credit plan is an arrangement under which the customer agrees to pay a part of the outstanding balance of the customer's account during each period of time for which a periodic statement of charges and credits is rendered.

If an obligation is disposed of, a gain or loss is recognized equal to the difference between the amount realized and the basis of the obligation in the case of disposition at other than face value, or sale or exchange of the obligation. In the case of any other disposition, the difference is recognized between the fair market value of the obligation at the time of disposition and the basis of the obligation in the case of any other disposition.

For tax purposes, the books of account needn't be kept on the installment basis; they can be kept regularly on the cash or accrual basis. But adequate records must be kept to provide the necessary information for computing the profit portion of the different installments.

The installment method applies only to *gains* from the sale of property. If the installment sale resulted in a *loss*, the loss must be deducted in the year of sale.

Expenses.   A *dealer* must deduct the expenses in the year when paid (on the cash basis) or when incurred (on the accrual basis). He cannot apportion or spread the expenses over the years when the income from the installment sale is reported as collected.

Choice of Installment Method by a Dealer

What is meant by "installment method?" This method allows the taxpayer to report gains over the entire time period of the installment sales contract. This enables the taxpayer to avoid the burden of paying the tax before receiving the cash. The essential element of this method is for each dollar collected to be partly recovery of costs and partly taxable profit. (This method does not apply to losses; losses on an installment sale must be deducted in the taxable year of the sale.)

For tax purposes, a dealer can switch to installment reporting without prior approval. All he needs to do is reflect the proper figures, with appropriate supporting schedules, in his return. A dealer can use the installment method for reporting installment sales and the accrual method for reporting sales on open account.

Change of method.   Once the taxpayer begins installment reporting, he needs the Commissioner's approval to switch to accrual reporting. (If changed within the first three years, the taxpayer can revoke his election automatically by filing amended returns for those years.) A dealer switching from accrual to installment reporting must report, when collected, the unrealized profit on receivables outstanding at the time of the switch. The fact that the entire profit was accrued and reported in the period the receivable arose doesn't change this.

The law largely eliminates the double tax that arises from reporting the same income twice. You take the gross profit in the current year attributable to collections of items accrued in a previous year and divide it by the total gross profits of the year

Form **6252**	**Computation of Installment Sale Income**	OMB No. 1545-0228
Department of the Treasury Internal Revenue Service	▶ See instructions on back. ▶ Attach to your tax return. Use a separate form for each sale or other disposition of property on the installment method.	19**86** Attachment Sequence No. **79**

Name(s) as shown on tax return	Identifying number

A Description of property ▶ _____

B Date acquired (month, day, and year) ▶ _____ **C** Date sold (month, day, and year) ▶ _____

D Was property sold to a related party after May 14, 1980? (See instructions.) . . . . ☐ Yes ☐ No

E If the answer to D is "Yes," was the property a marketable security? . . . . ☐ Yes ☐ No

If you checked "Yes" to question E, complete Part III.
If you checked "No" to question E, complete Part III for the year of sale and for 2 years after the year of sale.

Part I **Computation of Gross Profit and Contract Price** *(Complete this part for the year of sale only.)*

1 Selling price including mortgages and other indebtedness. (Do not include stated or unstated interest.)		**1**	
2 Mortgages and other indebtedness buyer assumed or took the property subject to, but not new mortgages the buyer got from a bank or other source . . .	**2**		
3 Subtract line 2 from line 1	**3**		
4 Cost or other basis of property sold	**4**		
5 Depreciation allowed or allowable.	**5**		
6 Adjusted basis (subtract line 5 from line 4)	**6**		
7 Commissions and other expenses of sale	**7**		
8 Income recapture from Form 4797, Part III. (See instructions.)	**8**		
9 Add lines 6, 7, and 8.		**9**	
10 Subtract line 9 from line 1. If zero or less, do not complete rest of form		**10**	
11 If question A above, is a principal residence, enter the sum of lines 7 and 13 of Form 2119		**11**	
12 Gross profit (subtract line 11 from line 10)		**12**	
13 Subtract line 9 from line 2. If line 9 is more than line 2, enter zero		**13**	
14 Contract price (add line 3 and line 13)		**14**	

Part II **Computation of Taxable Part of Installment Sale** *(Complete this part for the year of sale and any year you receive a payment.)*

15 Gross profit percentage (divide line 12 by line 14) (for years after the year of sale, see instructions) . .	**15**	
16 For year of sale only—enter amount from line 13 above; otherwise enter zero	**16**	
17 Payments received during year. (Do not include stated or unstated interest.)	**17**	
18 Add lines 16 and 17	**18**	
19 Payments received in prior years. (Do not include stated or unstated interest.). **19**	**20**	
20 Taxable part of installment sale (multiply line 18 by line 15)	**20**	
21 Part of line 20 that is ordinary income under recapture rules. (See instructions.).	**21**	
22 Subtract line 21 from line 20. Enter on Schedule D or Form 4797	**22**	

Part III **Information and Computation for Related Party Installment Sale** *(Do not complete this part if you received the final installment payment this tax year.)*

F Name, address, and taxpayer identifying number of related party _____

_____

G Did the related party, during this tax year, resell or dispose of the property? . . . . ☐ Yes ☐ No

H If the answer to question G is "Yes," complete lines 23 through 30 below unless one of the following conditions is met (check only the box that applies).

☐ The first disposition was a sale or exchange of stock to the issuing corporation.

☐ The second disposition was an involuntary conversion where the threat of conversion occurred after the first disposition.

☐ The second disposition occurred after the death of the original seller or purchaser.

☐ It can be established to the satisfaction of the Internal Revenue Service that tax avoidance was not a principal purpose for either of the dispositions. If this box is checked, attach an explanation. (See instructions.)

23 Selling price of property sold by related party	**23**	
24 Enter contract price from line 14 for year of first sale	**24**	
25 Enter the smaller of line 23 or line 24	**25**	
26 Total payments received by the end of your 1986 tax year. Add lines 18 and 19	**26**	
27 Subtract line 26 from line 25. If line 26 is more than line 25, enter zero	**27**	
28 Multiply line 27 by the gross profit percentage on line 15 for year of first sale	**28**	
29 Part of line 28 that is ordinary income under recapture rules. (See instructions.)	**29**	
30 Subtract line 29 from line 28. Enter on Schedule D or Form 4797	**30**	

For Paperwork Reduction Act Notice, see back of form.   Form **6252** (198

General Instructions

(Section references are to the Internal Revenue Code, unless otherwise noted.)

Paperwork Reduction Act Notice

We ask for this information to carry out the Internal Revenue laws of the United States. We need it to ensure that taxpayers are complying with these laws and to allow us to figure and collect the right amount of tax. You are required to give us this information.

A Change You Should Note

The Tax Reform Act of 1986 provides new rules that apply to certain sales you make after August 16, 1986 if your tax year ends after December 31, 1986 and you use the installment method to report the following:

   a. Real property used in your trade or business and sold for more than $150,000.

   b. Real property you held for the production of rental income and sold for more than $150,000.

For more information on figuring the amount of gain to report under the new law, see section 453C.

Purpose of Form

Form 6252 is used to report income from sales of real property and casual sales of personal property other than inventory if you will receive any payments (including payments from sales reported on the installment method prior to 1980) in a tax year after the year of sale.

Use Form 6252 unless you elect not to report the sale on the installment method. If you want to elect out, see the instructions for **Schedule D,** Capital Gains and Losses and Reconciliation of Forms 1099-B, or **Form 4797,** Gains and Losses From Sales or Exchanges of Assets Used in a Trade or Business and Involuntary Conversions. If you do not use the installment method, report the sale on your Schedule D or Form 4797.

You need not use this form for year-end stock sales where payment is received in the following year. Instead, report the sale directly on your Schedule D for the year of payment unless you elect out of the installment method by reporting it on Schedule D in the year of sale.

Report the ordinary income from sections 1245, 1250, 179, and 291 in full in the year of the sale even if no payments were received. Figure the ordinary income to be recaptured on Form 4797, Part III.

What Parts To Complete

For the Year of Sale—Complete questions A through E, Part I, and Part II.

For Years After the Year of Sale—Complete questions A through E, and Part II, for any year you receive a payment from an installment sale.

Related Party Sales—If you sold marketable securities to a related party, complete Form 6252 for each year of the installment agreement, even if you did not receive a payment. See **Installment Sales to Related Party** for the definition of a related party. For a year after the year of sale, complete questions A through E, and Part III. (If you received a payment, also complete Part II.) If you sold property other than marketable securities to a related party, complete the form for the year of sale and for 2 years after the year of sale, regardless of whether you received any payments. If during this 2-year period you did not receive a payment, complete questions A through E, and Part III. After this 2-year period, see "For Years After the Year of Sale" above.

Installment Sales to Related Party

A related party is your spouse, child, grandchild, parent, or a related corporation, S corporation,

partnership, estate, or trust. See **Publication 537,** Installment Sales, for related party rules which are in effect for sales after October 22, 1986.

If one of the exceptions in Part III applies, check the appropriate box and do not complete lines 23 through 30. If you can establish that tax avoidance was not a principal purpose for either disposition, attach an explanation. The following are some examples that are not tax avoidance:

● The second disposition is also an installment sale and the payment terms are equal to or longer than the first installment sale.

● The property sold is not real property or real property improvements, and it is used by the related purchaser as inventory for sale in the ordinary course of conducting a trade or business.

● The second disposition is a charitable contribution but not a bargain sale, and the property is capital-gain type property for which an election under section 170(b)(1)(C)(iii) is not in effect.

● Certain tax-free transfers, certain like-kind exchanges, and in some cases bankruptcy of the related buyer.

Sale of Depreciable Property to Related Party

If you sell depreciable property to a related party as defined in section 1239, installment sale rules do not apply, unless it is established to the satisfaction of the Internal Revenue Service that tax avoidance was not a principal purpose for the sale.

Get Publication 537 and the regulations under section 453 for more information, including single sales of several assets, disposition of installment obligations, like-kind exchanges, and change in selling price. Also see section 453(g) for new rules which apply to sales after October 22, 1986 if any of the payments are contingent as to amount and the FMV cannot be readily ascertained.

Specific Instructions

Do not include interest received, carrying charges received, or unstated interest on this form. Get Publication 537 for information on unstated interest.

Partnerships and S corporations that pass through a section 179 expense to their partners or shareholders should not include this amount on lines 5 and 8.

For the Year of Sale.—If this is the year of sale and you sold section 1245, 1250, 1252, 1254, or 1255 property, you may have ordinary income. Complete Part III of Form 4797 to figure the ordinary income and see Part IV of the Form 4797 instructions before starting Part I of Form 6252.

Line 1—Selling price.—Enter the sum of the money, face amount of the installment obligation, and the fair market value of other property, such as the buyer's note, that you received or will receive in exchange for the property sold. Include in line 1 any existing mortgage or other debt the buyer assumed or took the property subject to.

If there is no stated maximum selling price, such as in a contingent sale, attach a schedule showing the computation of gain, and enter the taxable part on lines 20 and 28, if Part III applies. See the regulations under section 453.

Line 2—Mortgage and other indebtedness.—Enter only mortgages (or other indebtedness) the buyer assumed from the seller or took the property subject to. Do not include new mortgages the buyer gets from a bank, the seller, or other source.

For information on wraparound mortgages, see regulations section 15A.453-1(b)(3)(ii).

Line 4—Cost or other basis of property sold.—Enter the original cost and other expenses you incurred in buying the property. Add the cost of improvements, etc., and subtract any casualty losses previously allowed. For more information, get **Publication 551,** Basis of Assets.

Line 5—Depreciation allowed or allowable.—Enter all depreciation or amortization you deducted or should have deducted from the date of purchase until the date of sale. Add any deduction you took under section 179 and the section 48(q)(1) downward basis adjustment, if any. Subtract 50% of any investment tax credit recaptured if the basis of the property was reduced under section 48(q)(1) and any section 179 or 280F recapture amount included in gross income in a prior tax year.

Line 7—Commissions and other expenses of sale.—Enter sales commissions, advertising expenses, attorney and legal fees, etc., you incurred in selling the property.

Line 8—Ordinary income recapture.— See Form 4797, Part III and Part IV of the instructions, to figure the recapture. Enter the part of the gain from the sale of depreciable property recaptured under sections 1245 and 1250 (including sections 179 and 291) here and on line 12 of Form 4797.

Line 15—Gross profit percentage.—Enter the gross profit percentage determined for the year of sale even if you did not file Form 6252 for that year.

Line 17—Payments received during the year.—Enter all money you received and the fair market value of any property you received in 1986. Include as payments any amount withheld to pay off a mortgage or other debt, such as broker and legal fees. Do not include the buyer's note or any mortgage or other liability assumed by the buyer. If you did not receive any payments in 1986, enter zero.

If in prior years, an amount was entered on the equivalent of line 25 of the 1986 form, do not include it on this line. Include it, however, on line 19.

Line 19—Payments received in prior years.— Enter all money and the fair market value of property you received before 1986 from the sale.

Lines 21 and 29.—Report on line(s) 21 and/or 29, any ordinary income recapture remaining from prior years on section 1245 and 1250 property sold before 6/7/84. Also report on these lines any ordinary income recapture on section 1252, 1254, and 1255 property regardless of when it was sold (that is, ordinary income recapture in the year of sale or any remaining recapture from a prior year sale). Do not enter ordinary income from the section 179 deduction. If this is the year of sale, see the instructions for Part IV of Form 4797.

The amount on these lines should not exceed the amount shown on line(s) 20 and/or 28.

Lines 22 and 30—Trade or business property.—Enter this amount on Form 4797, line 3 if the property was held more than 6 months. If the property was held 6 months or less or, if you have an ordinary gain from a noncapital asset (even if the holding period is more than 6 months), enter the amount on Form 4797, line 9 and write "From Form 6252."

Capital assets—Enter this amount on Schedule D as short-term or long-term gain. Use the lines identified as from Form 6252.

Line 23.—If in 1986 the related party sold part of the property from the original sale, enter the selling price of the part resold. If part was sold in an earlier year and part was sold this year, enter the cumulative selling price.

of collection. You then apply that fraction to the year's tax to find what percentage of the current tax is attributable to that collection. Next, take that same gross profit attributable to the prior year's collection and divide it by the total gross profit of the year of accrual. This results in the percentage of the prior year's tax that was attributable to the amount accrued then but collected now. The lesser of the two figures is then applied to reduce the current year's tax.

(1) Adjustments in Tax on Change to Installment Method

	Taxable Years Prior to Change		Adjustment Years After Change	
	Year 1	Year 2	Year 3	Year 4
Gross profit from installment sales (receivable in periodic payments over 5 years)	$100,000	$ 50,000	$ 20,000[1] $ 10,000[2] 80,000[3]	$ 12,000[4] 8,000[5] 40,000[6] 90,000[7]
Other income	80,000	200,000	90,000	90,000
Gross income	$180,000	$250,000	$200,000	$240,000
Deductions	60,000	50,000	50,000	60,000
Taxable income	120,000	200,000	150,000	180,000
Tax rate assumed	30%	50%	40%	40%
Tax would be	$ 36,000	$100,000	$ 60,000	$ 72,000

	Computation of Adjustment in Year 3 Year 1 Items	Lesser Tax Portion
In Year 3 Portion of tax	$20,000/200,000 \times 60,000 = \$6,000$	
In Year 1 Portion of tax	$20,000/180,000 \times 36,000 = 4,000$	$4,000
	Year 2 Items	
In Year 3 Portion of tax	$10,000/200,000 \times 60,000 = 3,000$	3,000
In Year 2	$10,000/250,000 \times 100,000 = 4,000$	
Adjustment to tax of Year 3		$7,000
	Computation of Adjustment in Year 4 Year 1 Items	
In Year 4 Portion of tax	$12,000/240,000 \times 72,000 = \$3,600$	
In Year 1 Portion of tax	$12,000/180,000 \times 36,000 = 2,400$	$2,400

Cont.

	Taxable Years Prior to Change		Adjustment Years After Change	
	Year 1	Year 2	Year 3	Year 4
	Year 2 Items			
In Year 3				
Portion of tax	8,000/240,000 × 72,000 = 2,400			2,400
In Year 2				
Portion of tax	8,000/250,000 × 100,000 = 3,200			
Adjustment to tax of Year 4				$4,800

[2] and [4] from Year 1 Sales
[5] and [6] from Year 2 Sales
[8] and [9] from Year 3 Sales
[7] from Year 4 Sales

(2) Computation by Dealer Under Installment Method

	First Year		Second Year		Third Year	
	(a)	(b)	(a)	(b)	(a)	(b)
	Cash Sales	Installment Sales	Cash Sales	Installment Sales	Cash Sales	Installment Sales
(1) Unit sales	40	80	60	100	70	120
(2) Gross sales	$16,000	$40,000	$24,000	$50,000	$28,000	$60,000
(3) Cost of goods	12,000	24,000	18,900	31,500	20,300	34,800
(4) Gross profit	$ 4,000	$16,000	$ 5,100	$18,500	$ 7,700	$25,200
(5) Gross profit accrual basis	$20,000		$23,600		$32,900	
(6) Rate of gross profit		40%		37%		42%
(7) Receipts from installment sales:						
First year	$15,000		$24,000		$ 1,000	
Second year			15,000		27,500	
Third year					22,500	
(8) Gross profit from installment sales:						
First year 40%	$ 6,000		$ 9,600		$ 400	
Second year 37%			$ 5,550		10,175	
Third year 42%					9,450	
Total	$ 6,000		$15,150		$20,025	
Gross profit from cash and installment sales (4a) plus (9b)	$10,000		$20,250		$27,725	

(3) Uncollected Installments and Unrealized Gross Profits

An example showing how the dealer computes his profit if he uses the installment method follows. Our dealer runs an appliance store and has been selling refrigerators on the installment plan. The price is $400 cash or $500 on an 18-month installment basis, $50 down and $25 a month thereafter. Average cost per unit sold is $300 for the first year, $315 for the second, and $290 for the third.

If an installment account becomes uncollectible, there is no deduction for uncollected gross profit; but the portion of the uncollected balance that represents unrecovered cost is a bad debt. To use an extreme case, suppose the entire $45,000 in the example below became uncollectible. There would be no deduction for the $18,525 of unrealized gross profit; however, the balance of $26,475 would be deductible as a bad debt. Repossessions would reduce the deduction by an amount equal to the fair market value of the repossessed items. If the value of the repossessions exceeds the basis for the installment obligation, the difference, in the case of a dealer, is ordinary income.

Here are the uncollected installments and unrealized gross profits at the end of the third year:

	Uncollected Installments	Rate	Unrealized Gross Profit
2nd year's sales	$ 7,500	37%	$ 2,775
3rd year's sales	37,500	42%	15,750
Total	$45,000		$18,525

Discounting Installment Receivables

There are two types of arrangements a dealer can make with banks or factors to obtain advances on his installment receivables. He can: (1) pledge them; that is, borrow against the receivables as collateral, or (2) discount them; that is, sell them at less than face value.

Proportionate disallowance rule. The New Law provides that if an installment obligation is pledged as collateral for a loan, the proceeds of the loan are treated as a payment on the obligation, and a proportionate amount of the gain that was deferred under the installment method must be recognized. The bill makes an exception with no payments treated as having been received on a portion of an installment obligation due within nine months of the receipt of the obligation, regardless of the maturity of any other payments on the obligation. If property is sold on a revolving credit plan, the amount eligible for the exception is that portion the receivable balance that is determined to be paid within nine months of the related sale. Another exception to the new rule exempts pledges of obligations for debt that by its terms is payable within 90 days, provided that the debt is not renewed or otherwise continued, and provided that the taxpayer does not issue additional debt within 45 days.

Use of the installment method is limited based on the amount of the outstanding indebtedness of the taxpayer. The limitation generally is applied by determining the amount of the taxpayer's "allocable installment indebtedness" (AII) for each taxable year and treating such amount as a payment immediately before the close of the taxable year on "applicable installment obligations" of the taxpayer that arose in that taxable year and are outstanding as of the end of the year. Applicable installment obligations are any installment obligations that arise from the sale after February, 1986, of (1) certain property held for sale to customers, and (2) real property used in the taxpayer's trade or business or held for the production of rental income, provided that the selling price of the property exceeds $150,000.

The AII for any taxable year is determined by dividing the face amount of the taxpayer's applicable installment obligations that are outstanding at the end of the year by the sum of the face amount of all installment obligations and the adjusted basis of all other assets of the taxpayer. The resulting quotient is multiplied by the taxpayer's average quarterly indebtedness, with any AII subtracted that is attributable to applicable installment obligations arising in previous years. (Depreciation can be deducted for purposes of computing the adjusted basis of the assets.)

In subsequent taxable years, the taxpayer is not required to recognize gain attributable to applicable installment obligations arising in prior years to the extent that any actual payments on the obligations do not exceed the amount of AII attributable to those obligations. On the receipt of the payments, the AII attributable to the obligation on which the payment is received is reduced by the amount of such payments. Payments on an applicable installment obligation in excess of the AII allocable to such obligations are accounted for under the ordinary rules for applying the installment method.

The taxpayer must compute average indebtedness for the year in order to calculate the amount of AII. The computation is made on a quarterly basis; all indebtedness of the taxpayer outstanding at the end of each quarter is taken into account. Indebtedness includes accounts payable and accrued expenses, as well as other amounts commonly considered as indebtedness, such as loans from banks and indebtedness in connection with the purchase of property by the taxpayer. If the taxpayer is a member of an affiliated group or a group under common control, all the members are treated as one taxpayer when making the calculations.

With respect to the installment method, the use of the method is disallowed in whole or in part for transactions in which the effect of the proportionate disallowance rule would be avoided through the use of related parties, pass-through entities, or intermediaries. Any corporation, partnership, or trust can be considered related to shareholders, partners, or beneficiaries.

The proportionate disallowance rule is effective for taxable years ending after December 31, 1986. Sales on a revolving credit plan are effective beginning after December 31, 1986. Any adjustment resulting from the change in accounting method must be taken into account over a period not exceeding four years; if a four year period is used, 15 percent of the adjustment is taken into account the first year, 25 percent the second year, and 30 percent in each of the following two years.

CONSIGNMENT SALES

Selling on consignment will defer income until sale by the consignee. Thus, delivery to distributors on consignment postpones income. Instead of taking sales into account upon delivery, as where sales are made on open account, income on consignment sales is deferred while the goods are held on the distributor's floor.

Thus, a manufacturer can defer income by placing his sales on a consignment basis. And, conversely, he can accelerate income by shifting to an open-account basis. He might do this, for example, in order to use up an operating loss which is about to expire. Consigned goods (out) remain part of the manufacturer's inventory until sold.

Approval and return sales.   Sales on approval aren't reflected in income until the buyer decides to take the goods. The parties agree the buyer is to take possession of the goods temporarily, with the understanding that if the goods aren't satisfactory, he owes nothing to the seller except their return. New and perishable products are frequently sold this way. Title does not pass until buyer approves.

Substantially the same business result, but different tax consequences can be achieved by a transaction known as "a sale or return." Seller and buyer agree that the goods will pass to the buyer on delivery but that he may return them if they prove unsatisfactory. The income must be taken up immediately, even though the buyer may subsequently return the goods. Here, title passes on delivery. The form of the contract determines whether the transaction is a sale on approval or a sale with return privileges.

Application.   If you have been using a contract which provides for sale with the privilege of return, you can defer a large slice of income simply by changing the contract to one for sale on approval. Or, if you have been selling on approval, you can bring a lot of additional sales into a given year by changing your contract to one providing for sale on delivery with the privilege of return.

Consignment and approval sales under the uniform commercial code.   Where the term *consignment sale* or its equivalent is used but nothing else is said, the UCC says the transaction is treated as a sale or return. Thus, if the parties want the income postponed until the buyer resells the goods, merely using the *consignment sale* designation is probably not enough; the contract should spell out the details of when the title is to pass. Whether this is desirable in view of other consequences under the UCC—e.g., rights in the goods of the buyer's creditors—is something to be decided by the parties.

OTHER FACTORS AFFECTING SALES

Here are some other areas involving sales where timing techniques may be employed for tax purposes.

Conditional sales.   In a conditional sale, the seller delivers merchandise to a buyer who contracts to pay for it over a period of time. The seller stipulates that title is not to pass until the price has been fully paid.

The sale is not legally complete until final payment is made and title has passed to the buyer. Nevertheless, for tax purposes, the sale price must be taken into income when the property has been transferred to the buyer.

Sales of specific goods on which work must be done.   When a contract for the sale of specific goods calls for the seller to do something to the goods to put them into a deliverable state, the property does not pass to the purchaser until such things are done unless the parties agree otherwise. Thus, the accrual seller will realize no taxable income until he places the goods in a deliverable state or title passes to the buyer, and to this extent he can control his receipt of taxable income.

Sales on open account.   Where such goods, in a deliverable state, are "unconditionally appropriated" (i.e., "identified to," under the UCC) to the contract by either the buyer or seller with the consent of the other, the title in the goods passes to the buyer. Delivery of the goods to a *carrier* for shipment to the purchaser, even if such shipment is made C.O.D., constitutes an "unconditional appropriation." If the seller wants a larger taxable income in a particular year, he can realize it by simply increasing the rate of shipments. If, on the other hand, he wants to postpone taxable income, he can slow up on the shipments or other acts of "unconditional appropriation."

Sales returns and allowances.   Where credits or refunds are made for damaged or unsatisfactory merchandise, the deduction becomes available when the liability is admitted.

OTHER ORDINARY INCOME

Dividend income.   Breakdown between foreign and domestic payors of dividends is necessary for federal tax purposes—e.g., domestic dividends are generally subject to an 80% dividend deduction; foreign dividends may be subject to credit for foreign taxes paid. Intercorporate dividends of affiliated corporations should be earmarked for elimination on consolidated returns. 100% deduction is now allowed for qualifying dividends received by affiliated corporations from other affiliates in the group, as long as consolidated returns are *not* filed.

Royalty and license income.   Allocation between foreign and domestic royalty or license income may be required for federal tax purposes (including foreign tax credit). It is important to have details about possible withholding of tax at the source. State allocations may also depend on source of the income.

Rental income.   It is very important to keep location information of properties throwing off the rental income for state allocation purposes. In addition, rent paid by related taxpayers (e.g., subsidiaries) may be subject to reallocation by IRS on audit unless they have good substantiation for amounts paid.

Interest income.   Source of payments is necessary for possible exemption of some of the income from either or both federal and state taxes.

Foreign income, blocked.   In regard to income received or accrued in foreign currency which is not convertible into United States currency, a taxpayer has the election of deferring reporting the income until the restrictions are lifted or including it in his present year's income.

IMPUTED INTEREST

Seller-held financing is often a key ingredient in real estate deals. Taking back a note for part of the sales price helps the seller get top dollar for his property. From the buyer's viewpoint, seller financing is an attractive alternative to often hard-to-get bank financing.

Tax angle.   The seller pays tax in the year of sale on the profit paid to him in the year of sale. Assuming there is no recapture of depreciation, the balance of his profit is taxed in later years when he receives payments on the note from the buyer. The interest payments the seller receives on the note are fully taxable ordinary income. Generally, the buyer's tax basis in the property—for all purposes, including depreciation—is his cost, including the seller-held mortgage. The interest he pays on the note is deductible and not included in basis.

The 1984 Tax Law may have absolutely no effect on a seller-held financing deal. On the other hand, if a transaction is affected by the New Law, a seller may be required to pay more tax dollars sooner.

Background: Before 1985, a seller must charge at least 9% interest on his note. If he doesn't, the transaction is refigured as if 10% interest had been charged. Result: A portion of the note principal is transformed into interest. For the seller, that results in a reduced sales price—and less low-taxed profit and more high-taxed ordinary income. For the buyer, it means a lower cost basis and bigger interest deductions.

Beginning in 1985, there is a higher minimum interest rate. It's set at 110% of the rate paid on Treasury obligations with maturities similar to the seller-held note. If the seller charges a lower rate on his note, the transaction is refigured at a new, higher "imputed" interest rate—120% of the Treasury rate.

While these rates change every six months, the rate in effect when a transaction is closed governs the interest rate for the life of the note.

Still another change: In general, if the sales price exceeds $250,000 and the minimum rate isn't met, the transaction is covered by the complex original issue discount (OID) rules. And even if the stated note interest equals or exceeds the minimum rate, the OID rules apply if payment of part or all of the note interest payments is deferred. Here, the results are especially harsh: The seller is taxed on interest income each year even though he may not receive a penny in interest for years. The buyer, on the other hand, can take current deductions for interest he hasn't yet paid.

Congress passed a measure that modifies the imputed-interest rules described above. Here are the highlights of the law: (1) For sales of real property and used personal property before July 1, 1985, involving seller financing of $2 million of principal or less, no interest will be imputed if the parties state at least 9% compound interest. If the parties fail to state an adequate interest, interest will be imputed at a 10% compound rate; (2) Transactions involving seller financing of more than $2 million will be subject to a blended interest rate, based on a weighted average between 9% and 10%, and 110% and 120% of the Treasury borrowing rate; (3) Assumptions of loans in connection with sales of principle residences, vacation homes, farms, ranches and small business property will be permanently exempt from '84 TRA provisions applying imputed interest rules to assumptions. And assumptions made before October 16, 1984 will be permanently exempt from new assumption rules, except for assumptions in connection with transactions involving a purchase price of $100 million or more; (4) For sales before July 1, 1985, of real property and used personal property used in the active business of farming or ranching, with seller financing of $2 million or less of principal, interest income and deductions will be accounted for by both the buyer and seller on the cash method; (5) Under the permanent rules of '84 TRA, sales of all principal residences, and farms or ranches costing $1 million or less, will be permanently exempt from original issue discount rules. The sale of a principal residence to the extent the cost is less than $250,000, and the sale of land in connection with the sale of a farm or ranch costing $1 million or less, will be permanently exempt from the requirement to state interest at 110% of the Treasury borrowing rate. These transactions will be subject to interest rates established by the IRS.

FASB STATEMENT NO. 96

Accounting for Income Taxes, Financial Accounting Statement No. 96, was issued on December 30, 1987. The New Rule virtually supersedes all existing authoritative accounting rules for income tax accounting, principally APB Opinion No. 11, *Ac-*

counting for Income Taxes. The Statement also supersedes or amends other pronouncements associated with accounting for income taxes. Adoption is required for fiscal years beginning after December 15, 1988. (Earlier adoption is permissible and is encouraged.)

Statement No. 96 requires determination of the amount of taxes payable or refundable in each future year as if a tax return were prepared for the net amount of temporary differences that will result in taxable or deductible amounts in each of those years. If alternative tax systems exist, those procedures are applied in a manner consistent with the tax laws. The procedures are applied separately for each tax jurisdiction.

SUMMARY

The Significant Differences Between The "Old Rule" and "New Rule"

Significant points in the New Rule are scattered throughout the 126 page manual. The summary that follows organizes in columnar format the salient requirements of the New Rule, as well as compares the new requirements with those of the Old Rule.

Old Rule	*New Rule*
Purpose was to match tax expense with the related revenues and expenses recognized in pre-tax financial income.	Purpose is to recognize a tax liability or asset for the tax effects of amounts taxable or deductible in future years.
Deferred method of accounting was permissible.	Liability *only* method allowable.
Balance sheet disclosure related deferred taxes to the related asset or liability.	Classification is related to the expected reversal date of the temporary difference.
Flow-through or deferral method was applied for the investment tax credit.	No change in this requirement.
Tax expense for interim periods was computed by estimating an effective tax rate for the fiscal year and the resulting estimated tax expense for the year.	"Old Rule" unchanged.
Deferred taxes not adjusted for tax rate changes.	Deferred taxes are adjusted for rate changes.
Deferred tax debits recognized as an asset based on the results of the deferred tax computation.	Deferred tax debits recognized as assets only for the tax benefit of future net tax deductions that can be

Cont.

Old Rule	New Rule
	realized by NOL carryback from the future year.
Alternative Minimum Tax included in "with-and-without" calculation.	AMT in the computation of current and deferred tax liability.
The effects of timing differences are computed using incremental rates that applied to the year the differences originated.	The tax liability is computed using the tax rates applicable in *future* years.
Net deferred charges recognized as assets.	Deferred tax asset allowable only for the benefit of future tax deductions arising from a loss carryback from a future year.
NOL carryforwards recognized as an asset if realization is reasonably expected in the year the loss occurs.	NOL carryforwards cannot be recognized as an asset, but can offset deferred tax liabilities.
The gross change method applied to changes in the tax law. The effect was to recognize the changes in the years when the timing differences reversed.	The effect of tax law or rate changes is recognized as of the date of the change.
Deferred taxes required for all timing differences (exceptions allowed in Opinion 23), including differences that may not reverse until an indefinite number of years in the future.	No change in requirements, except no analogies to the exceptions in Opinion 23. (If the item is *not* specified in Opinion 23, the deferred method is to be applied.)
Computes the added effect of timing differences on income tax expense for the year in which timing differences originate.	Computes the future tax to be given up that result from differences between the tax basis and the reported assets and liabilities.
Covered timing differences between the year in which reported transactions affects taxable income and the year in which it is disclosed in financial income.	Discloses the difference between the reported amount of an asset (or liability) and its tax basis.

TERMINOLOGY

As with so many of the accounting rules, Statement 96 contains a number of terms relevant only to that specific rule. The succinct definitions that follow will be helpful to the reader in understanding the Statement.

ASSUMPTION.   Reported amount of assets and liabilities that will be recovered and settled, respectively.

CURRENT TAX EXPENSE OR BENEFIT.   The amount of income taxes paid or payable (or refundable) for a year determined by applying the tax law to taxable income or excess of deductions over revenues for that year.

DEFERRED TAX ASSET.   The amount of deferred tax consequences attributable to temporary differences that will result in net tax deductions in future years that could be recovered (based on loss carryback provisions in the tax law) by refund of taxes paid in the current or a prior year. Recognition and measurement of a deferred tax asset does not anticipate tax consequences of financial income that might be earned in future years.

DEFERRED TAX CONSEQUENCES.   The future effects on income taxes as measured by the provisions of enacted tax laws resulting from temporary differences at the end of the current year without regard to the effects of events not yet recognized or inherently assumed in the financial statements.

DEFERRED TAX EXPENSE OR BENEFIT.   The net change during the year in an enterprise's deferred tax liability or asset.

DEFERRED TAX LIABILITY.   The amount of deferred tax consequences attributable to temporary differences that will result in net taxable amounts in future years. The liability is the amount of taxes that would be payable on those net taxable amounts in future years based on the provisions of the tax law. Recognition and measurement of a deferred tax liability does not anticipate the tax consequences of losses or expenses that might be incurred in future years.

EVENT.   A happening of consequence to an enterprise. The term encompasses both transactions and other events affecting an enterprise.

GAINS AND LOSSES INCLUDED IN COMPREHENSIVE INCOME BUT EXCLUDED FROM NET INCOME.   Under present practice, this category includes certain changes in market value of investments in marketable equity securities classified as noncurrent assets, certain changes in market values of investments in industries having specialized accounting practices for marketable securities, adjustments from recognizing certain additional pension liabilities, and foreign currency translation adjustments. Future changes to Generally Accepted Accounting Principles may change what is included in this category.

INCOME TAXES.   Domestic and foreign federal (national), state, and local (including franchise) taxes based on income.

INCOME TAXES CURRENTLY PAYABLE (REFUNDABLE).   (See *Current Tax Expense or Benefit.*)

INCOME TAX EXPENSE (BENEFIT). The sum of current tax expense (benefit) and deferred tax expense (benefit).

NONPUBLIC ENTERPRISE. An enterprise other than one (a) whose debt or equity securities are traded in a public market, including those traded on a stock exchange or in the over-the-counter market (including securities quoted only locally or regionally), or (b) whose financial statements are filed with a regulatory agency in preparation for the sale of any class of securities.

OPERATING LOSS CARRYBACK OR CARRYFORWARD FOR TAX PURPOSES. An excess of tax deductions over gross income during a year that may be carried back or forward to reduce taxable income in other years. Different tax jurisdictions have different rules about whether an operating loss may be carried back or forward and the length of the carryback or carryforward period. This term also includes carrybacks or carryforwards for individual deductions that exceed statutory limitations.

OPERATING LOSS CARRYFORWARD FOR FINANCIAL REPORTING. The amount of an operating loss carryforward for tax purposes (a) reduced by the amount that offsets temporary differences that will result in net taxable amounts during the carryforward period and (b) increased by the amount of temporary differences that will result in net tax deductions for which a tax benefit has not been recognized in the financial statements.

OPERATING LOSS CARRYFORWARD FOR FINANCIAL REPORTING. The amount of an operating loss carryforward for tax purposes (a) reduced by the amount that offsets temporary differences that will result in net taxable amounts during the carryforward period and (b) increased by the amount of temporary differences that will result in net tax deductions for which a tax benefit has not been recognized in the financial statements.

PUBLIC ENTERPRISE. An enterprise (a) whose debt or equity securities are traded in a public market, including those traded on a stock exchange or in the over-the-counter market (including securities quoted only locally or regionally), or (b) whose financial statements are filed with a regulatory agency in preparation for the sale of any class of securities.

STATUTORY LIMITATIONS. Provisions in the tax law that limit the amount by which certain deductions or tax credits are applied to reduce taxable income or income taxes payable.

TAXABLE INCOME. The excess of taxable revenues over tax deductible expenses and exemptions for the year as defined by the governmental taxing authority.

TAX CONSEQUENCES. The effects on income, current or deferred, of an event.

TAX CREDIT CARRYBACK OR CARRYFORWARD FOR TAX PUR-POSES. Tax credits that exceed statutory limitations that may be carried back or forward to reduce taxes payable in other years. Different tax jurisdictions have different rules regarding whether a tax credit may be carried back or forward and the length of the carryback or carryforward period.

TAX CREDIT CARRYFORWARD FOR FINANCIAL REPORTING. The amount of a tax credit carryforward for tax purposes reduced by the amount recognized as a reduction of a deferred tax liability for temporary differences that will result in net taxable amounts during the tax credit carryforward period.

TAX PLANNING STRATEGY. A transaction or series of transactions that meet certain criteria set forth in paragraph 19 of the Statement. If implemented the transactions would affect the particular future years in which temporary differences result in taxable or deductible amounts. A tax planning strategy either reduces the amount of a deferred tax liability or increases the amount of a deferred tax asset that would otherwise be recognized.

TEMPORARY DIFFERENCE. A difference between the tax basis of an asset or liability and its reported amount in the financial statements that will result in taxable or deductible amounts in future years when the reported amount of the asset or liability is recovered or settled, respectively. (Paragraph 10 of the Statement cites nine examples of temporary differences.)

LIABILITY METHOD REQUIRED

The most significant change from the Old Rule is from the deferred method to the liability method of computing deferred taxes. Also, taxpayers can change deferred taxes when there are changes in the tax rates.

The New Rule requires deferred taxes for transactions occurring in different years for financial reporting and tax purposes. Statement No. 96 revises the calculation to adjust the amount of deferred taxes for changes in tax rates (or changes in other provisions of the tax law which may apply). This approach is commonly referenced as the *liability method* of accounting for income taxes, and is significant because formerly the Old Rule did not permit adjustments for tax law changes. The liability method, therefore, will give different results when tax rates change, as in the 1986 Tax Reform Bill.

The New Rule limits the recognition of net deferred tax assets, which is the deferred tax effects of expenses or losses reported later for tax purposes than for financial reporting purposes.

The application of Statement No. 96 can be one of two methods. 1) There can be a retroactive restatement of prior financial statements, which assumes that the new Rule has been effective in prior years. This method is applied by adjusting income as of the beginning of the earliest year restated, or to the beginning of the retained earnings amount, if the earliest year restated is not available. 2) There can be an adjustment as of the *beginning* of the year in which No. 96 is adopted. This method if applied is disclosed in the current year's statement as an entry after income from operations but before net income.

ACCOUNTING METHODOLOGY

The accounting procedures are changes from the deferred method (formerly governed by Opinion No. 11) to the liability method. The liability method requires deferred tax assets (or liabilities) to be recognized at the tax rates prevailing at the time and, therefore, assumes such rates will be effective when the temporary differences turn around. Also, deferred tax balances must be adjusted whenever tax rates change.

The requirement of the New Rule to recognize changes in tax rates is considered to be one of the significant changes from the deferred method (which provides for the tax effect of a temporary difference to be recognized in the year it arises, and is not adjusted until the difference reverses. Therefore, deferred tax balances under the Old Rule were not adjusted when new tax rates were legislated.)

There are other modifications of the Old Rule that must be considered:

1. The gross and net change methods of accounting for deferred taxes are no longer allowable.
2. Deferred tax balances must be adjusted both for expired tax credits and for changes in statutory limits on unexpired tax credits that were previously recognized for *financial* reporting purposes as reductions of deferred tax credits.
3. Preference taxes paid that cannot be carried forward to offset future tax liabilities must now be charged to expense, instead of applied to reduce deferred tax credits on the balance sheet.
4. On the balance sheet deferred taxes (under the deferred method) were classified according to a related asset or liability. The Statement now requires the balance sheet classification to be determined by the scheduled reversals of book and tax differences. Reversals scheduled to occur within one year are classified as current, all other reversals are to be classified as long-term. (The best example of the application of the new requirement is accelerated depreciation methods for plant and equipment.)
5. The liability method requires the tracking of cumulative differences between financial reporting and tax basis amounts. It will be necessary to develop a tax basis balance sheet for each tax jurisdiction—the deferred method usually did not require keeping track of cumulative differences.

COMPUTATION OF DEFERRED TAX LIABILITIES OR ASSETS

The new rule eliminates the ''with and without'' method of computing deferred tax balances and the deferred tax provision. The following outlines the required computations:

1. Identify all existing differences between the financial reporting basis and tax basis of assets and liabilities. These are the temporary differences.
2. Estimate the specific future years in which temporary differences will result in taxable or deductible amounts.
3. Calculate the net taxable or deductible amount in each future year.
4. Deduct operating loss carryforwards for tax purposes allowable by the law from net taxable amounts that are scheduled for future years included in the loss carryforward period.
5. Carry back or carry forward, as allowed by law, the net deductible amounts occurring in particular years to offset net taxable amounts that are scheduled for prior or subsequent years.
6. Schedule the expected reversal of existing temporary differences.
7. Calculate the tax effects of reversals based on existing tax laws and rates.
8. Recognize a deferred tax asset for the tax benefit of net deductible amounts that could be realized by loss carryback from future years (1) to reduce a current deferred tax liability and (2) to reduce taxes paid in the current or a prior year.
9. Calculate the amount of tax for the remaining net taxable amounts that are scheduled to occur in each future year by applying current tax rates for each of those years to the type and amount of net taxable amounts scheduled for those years.
10. Deduct tax credit carryforwards for tax purposes from the amount of tax calculated for future years that are included in the carryforward periods.
11. Recognize a deferred tax liability for the remaining amount of taxes payable for each future year.
12. Record the effects on deferred taxes of changes in tax rates and laws when the changes occur. Report the effects as a component of tax expense for the period of the change. For accounting purposes, the change occurs the day the new law is enacted (the date the President signs a new tax law).

LIABILITY METHOD ILLUSTRATED

The liability method measures the future tax effects of existing timing differences awaiting reversal. In the balance sheet, deferred taxes are assets and liabilities in the usual sense, presenting the estimated effects on taxes receivable or payable for the period in which timing differences will reverse. Deferred tax expense for a period is derived from the change for the period in the balance sheet deferred tax receivables or payables.

Deferred taxes on existing timing differences are computed using tax rates expected to be in effect when the timing differences reverse. Existing deferred taxes are adjusted when tax rates change or future rate changes become known. If there are no legislative changes in the tax law or rates, current rates are used—no estimate or prediction of rate changes is made; current rates are applied.

The liability method is not too involved as the cumulative timing differences are simply multiplied by the current tax rate. The result is a deferred tax liability or asset, and the change in that amount for a year is the deferred tax expense for the year. The total tax currently payable and deferred tax expense is the income tax expense for the year.

Assume a taxpayer has a deferred tax liability of $50,000 on a cumulative timing difference of $100,000 at the beginning of the year. Taxable income for the year is $200,000; the only timing difference is ACRS tax deductions over book depreciation. At year-end the net book value of depreciable assets is $500,000. The tax basis is $350,000. Pre-tax book income is $250,000.

Taxable Income	$200,000
Tax Rate	50%
Tax Currently Payable	$100,000
Book basis of depreciable assets	$500,000
Tax Basis of depreciable assets	350,000
Cumulative timing differences	150,000
Tax Rate	50%
Deferred tax liability at end of year	$75,000
Deferred tax liability at beginning of year	50,000
Deferred Tax Expense	25,000
Tax Currently Payable	100,000
Tax Expense	$125,000

Another illustration: This illustration compares the computations for the deferred method with the liability method, including a change in the tax rate in 1988.

Deferred Method

	1987	1988
Pre-tax Book Income	$1,000,000	$1,000,000
Taxable Income	200,000	200,000
Tax Rate	40%	50%
Taxes Payable	$320,000	$400,000
Deferred Tax		
($200,000 × 40%)	80,000	
($200,000 × 50%)		100,000
Tax Expense	$400,000	$500,000
Cumulative Deferred		
Tax Credit	$80,000	180,000

Liability Method

Applying the liability method and using the same data, the tax provisions and balance sheet amounts for the two years are calculated as follows:

	1987	1988
Taxes Payable........................	$320,000	$400,000
Tax Effects of Timing Differences ($200,000 × 50%)................	100,000	100,000
Tax Expense..........................	$420,000	$500,000
Cumulative liability for future taxes	$100,000	$200,000

The illustrations above show the usual models that are generally applicable to accounting for income taxes.

Appendix A in the Statement manual presents 43 pages of examples (41 models) and discussions that illustrate the application of the New Rule to specific aspects of accounting for income taxes.

The 41 models for specific situations are listed here, with a brief description of the particular application to enable the user to identify the illustration of the standard requiring compliance.

It can be seen that practitioners who have the responsibility to apply Statement No. 96 have access to a model appropriate to their specialized problems. Especially helpful is the detailed presentation of the computations. In many instances one has only to substitute in a model the data applicable to a specialized problem to comply with the requirements of the New Rule.

(*The titles of the models are noted in italics.*)

Deferred Tax Liability. Recognizes the deferred tax consequences of temporary differences that will result in *net* taxable amounts in future years.

Deferred Tax Asset. Tax deductions provide a tax benefit only by offsetting amounts that are taxable. Temporary differences sometimes will result in deductible amounts that either exceed or cannot offset taxable amounts in past or future years.

Offset of Taxable and Deductible Amounts. The tax law determines whether temporary differences that will result in taxable and deductible amounts in future years may be offset against each other.

Pattern of Taxable or Deductible Amounts. The particular years in which most temporary differences will result in taxable or deductible amounts is determined by reference to the timing of the recovery of the related asset or settlement of the related liability and may require estimates.

Temporary Differences for Foreign Assets and Liabilities. After a change in exchange rates, temporary differences attributable to an enterprise's foreign assets and liabilities can result.

Measurement of a Deferred Tax Liability or Asset. A deferred tax liability or asset is computed at the date of the financial statements by applying the provisions in the tax law to measure the deferred tax consequences of temporary differences that will result in net taxable or deductible amounts in each future year.

Comprehensive Alternative Tax Systems. A tax law may require that more than one comprehensive method or system be used to determine an enterprise's potential tax liability. The higher (possibly, lower) outcome of the calculations determine the actual tax liability. (The best example is the Code requires a corporation to calculate its potential federal income tax liability using both the "regular tax" system and an "alternative minimum tax" system. The corporation's actual income tax liability for the year is the greater of the two.)

Recognition of a Tax Benefit for Carrybacks. An operating loss and some tax credits arising but not utilized in the current year may be carried back or carried forward.

Recognition of a Tax Benefit for Carryforwards. An operating loss or tax credit carryforward is recognized as a reduction of a deferred tax liability for temporary differences that will result in taxable amounts during the operating loss or tax credit carryforward period.

Reporting the Tax Benefit of Operating Loss Carryforwards or Carrybacks. The manner of reporting the tax benefit of an operating loss carryforward or carryback is determined by the source of the income or loss in the current year, and not by the source of the operating loss carryforward or taxes paid in a prior year.

Carryforwards for Tax Purposes and for Financial Reporting. An operating loss carryforward for tax purposes is an excess of tax deductions over gross income during a year that may be carried forward to reduce taxable income in future years. If there is an operating loss carryforward for tax purposes, an operating loss carryforward for financial reporting is the amount for tax purposes.

Quasi Reorganizations. The tax benefit of an operating loss or tax credit carryforward for financial reporting as of the date of a quasi reorganization is reported as a direct addition to contributed capital, if the tax benefits are recognized in subsequent years.

Tax Planning Strategies. Tax-planning strategies apply exclusively to the recovery of assets and settlement of liabilities in future years. Tax-planning strategies that anticipate the tax consequences of earning income or incurring losses in future years are prohibited for purposes of recognition or measurement of a tax liability or asset.

Aggregate Calculation of a Deferred Tax Liability or Asset. Calculation of the deferred tax consequences of temporary differences will require information about the particular future years in which temporary differences will result in taxable or deductible amounts because of several factors (enumerated and described under this item).

Regulated Enterprises. A regulated enterprise is required to capitalize an incurred cost that would otherwise be charged to expense if certain criteria are met (listed under this item).

Leveraged Leases. The New Rule does not change (a) the pattern of recognition for the after-tax income for leveraged leases as required by FASB Statement No. 13 or (b) the allocation of the purchase price in a purchase business combination to acquired leveraged leases as required by *Interpretation 21*.

Nontaxable Business Combinations. A liability or an asset must be recognized for the deferred tax consequences of differences between the assigned values and the tax bases of the assets and liabilities recognized in a business combination accounted for as a purchase.

Taxable Business Combinations. The purchase price is assigned to the assets and liabilities recognized for tax purposes as well as for financial reporting. The amounts assigned to particular assets and liabilities may differ for financial reporting and tax purposes. A liability or asset is recognized for the deferred tax consequences of those temporary differences in accordance with the recognition and measurement requirements as required by the New Rule.

Carryforwards—Purchase Method. Accounting for a business combination should reflect any provisions in the tax law that permit or restrict the use of either of the combining enterprises' operating loss or tax credit carryforwards to reduce taxable income or taxes payable attributable to the other enterprise subsequent to the business combination.

Carryforwards—Pooling-of-Interest Method. The separate financial statements of combining enterprises for prior periods are restated on a combined basis when a business combination is accounted for by the pooling-of-interests method. For restatement of periods prior to the combination date, a combining enterprise's operating loss carryforward does not offset the other enterprise's taxable income because consolidated tax returns cannot be filed for those periods.

Subsequent Recognition of Carryforward Benefits. If not recognized at the acquisition date, the tax benefits of an acquired enterprise's operating loss or tax credit carryforward for financial reporting are recognized in financial statements for the subsequent year(s) when those carryforward amounts reduce either a deferred tax liability or taxes payable on the tax return.

The Tax Basis of the Stock of an Acquired Enterprise. An acquiring enterprise's tax basis of the stock of an acquired enterprise may exceed the tax basis of the net assets of the acquired enterprise.

Classification in a Statement of Financial Position. A deferred tax liability or asset is classified in two categories—the current amount and the noncurrent amount—in a classified statement of financial position.

Allocation of Income Tax Expense between Pre-tax Income from Continuing Operations and Other Items. The amount of income tax expense or benefit allocated to continuing operations (in addition to adjustments for changes in tax status and tax laws or rates) is the tax consequences of the pre-tax income or loss from continuing operations exclusive of any other category of items that occurred during the year. The amount allocated to a category of items other than continuing operations is the incremental effect on income taxes that results from that category of items.

DISCLOSURE REQUIREMENTS

- Statement 96 requires the deferred tax consequences of temporary differences scheduled to reverse during the next year to be disclosed as current. The tax effects scheduled to reverse beyond the following year are classified as noncurrent.

- On the income statement, the amount of income tax expense (or benefit) from continuing operations is computed separate from any other category of earnings. Income taxes are allocated among other categories, such as the cumulative effect of accounting changes, discontinued operations, extraordinary items, and the taxes are based on the incremental effect that each category has on income tax expense.

- The tax benefits arising from operating loss and tax credit carryforwards are classified based on the type of income that gives rise to their realization in the current period.

- Adoption of the Statement will result in a cumulative catch-up adjustment that can be disclosed by either 1) retroactively restating financial statements for prior years or 2) including the adjustment in net income as of the beginning of the year in which the Statement is adopted.

- Taxpayers must continue to disclose amounts of refundable income taxes, income taxes currently payable, and deferred taxes.

- Deferred taxes continue to be classified as current and noncurrent amounts. The method of computing current and noncurrent amounts must be consistent with the liability method.

- The current amount is the net deferred tax asset or deferred tax liability caused by timing differences reversing in the year following the balance sheet date. Remaining net deferred taxes would be the noncurrent amounts. This results in a change from the Old Rule, which required the current or noncurrent classification of most deferred taxes to follow the classification of the related asset or liability, if any. An example of the application of this requirement follows:

Assume a taxpayer's deferred tax liability of $750,000 resulting from 10-year straight-line depreciation for accounting purposes and 5-year ACRS deductions for tax purposes. Original cost of the equipment was $3,000,000. The net book value on statement date is $1,500,000. The tax basis is zero. Timing difference reversals the following year will be $300,000. The current portion of the deferred tax liability would be $150,000 ($300,000 × 50%) and the $600,000 balance is classified as noncurrent. Under the Old Rule the entire $750,000 would be noncurrent because it relates to the equipment, a noncurrent asset.

- A change caused by the liability method disallows deferred tax liabilities and assets attributable to different tax jurisdictions to be offset.
- For interim reporting the entire effect of a change in tax rates is reported in the interim period a change is enacted. It should not be allocated over prior or future interim periods.
- The components of income tax expense or benefit resulting from continuing operations must be disclosed in the financial statements, or in footnotes. These include:
  1) Current tax expense or benefit.
  2) Deferred tax expense or benefit.
  3) Investment tax credits and grants.
  4) The benefit of operating loss carryforwards, which result in a reduction of income tax expense.
  5) Adjustments of a deferred tax liability or asset for changes in the tax laws, or rates, or a change in the tax status of the taxpayer.
  Similar to SEC requirements for publicly-held corporations, taxpayers must reconcile income tax expense on continuing operations with the amount that results from applying current tax rates to pre-tax income from current operations. (Note: SEC Regulations S-X requirements are *not* affected by the New Rule.)
- Disclosure is required for the amounts and expiration dates of operating loss and tax credit carryforwards for financial reporting purposes and for tax purposes.
- Taxpayers must disclose the amount of income tax expense or benefit allocated to other than continuing operations, such as extraordinary items and the foreign currency translation component of equity.
- APB Opinion No. 4, which requires disclosure of the method of accounting for ITC—the flow-through or deferral method—continues to apply.

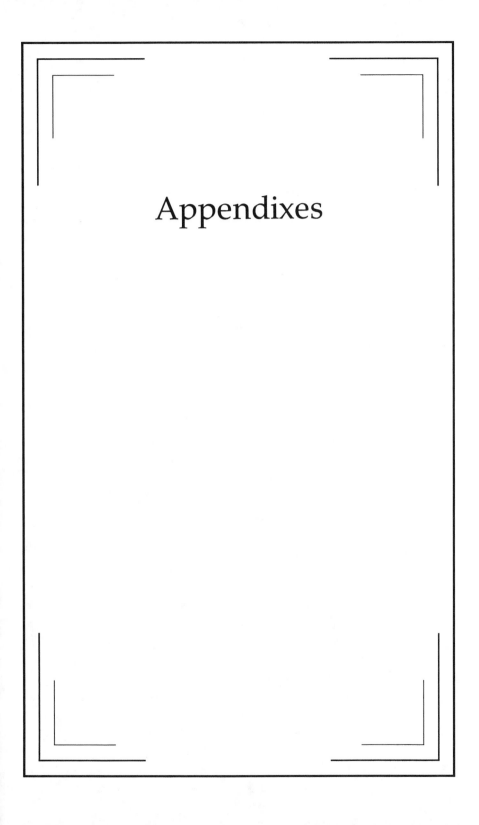

Appendixes

Appendix A

INDEX TO JOURNAL ENTRIES EXAMPLES

References Are To Journal Entry Numbers

SAMPLE JOURNAL ENTRIES

OPENING INVESTMENT — Sole Proprietorship:
[1]

Cash	5,000	
Building (fair value)	45,000	
A. Able, Net Worth		50,000

OPENING INVESTMENT — Partnership:
[2]

Cash	30,000	
Inventory	30,000	
B. Baker (50%), Capital		30,000
C. Charles (50%), Capital		30,000

PARTNERSHIP INVESTMENT — with Goodwill:
[3]

Building (fair value)	45,000	
Goodwill	15,000	
A. Able (50%), Capital		60,000

Able contributes building for
½ share of partnership.

PARTNERSHIP INVESTMENT — Skill, no funds:
[4]

A. Able, Capital	3,000	
B. Baker, Capital	3,000	
C. Charles, Capital	6,000	
D. Dog, Capital		12,000

Dog gets 10% of partnership
for the skill he'll contribute.
Ratios will now be:

Able	(25% less 10%)	22.5%
Baker	(same)	22.5%
Charles	(50% less 10%)	45.0%
Dog	(as granted)	10.0%
		100.0%

PARTNERSHIP INCORPORATES:
[5]

Cash	30,000	
Inventory — Raw Material	30,000	
Building (fair value)	45,000	
Capital Stock (par $10; 10,000 shares issued; 100,000 auth.)		100,000
Additional Paid-in Capital		5,000

Shares issued: A. 2250; B. 2250;
C. 4500; D. 1,000. Note that
partnership goodwill is not carried
over to corporation.

CORPORATE INVESTMENT — with Goodwill:
[6]

Machinery & Equipment (fair value)	9,000	
Goodwill	1,000	
Capital Stock (1,000 shares)		10,000

Issuing 1,000 shares to E. Easy
@ $10 par for machinery contributed.

CORPORATION MONTHLY ENTRIES — The corporation

records all entries into the general ledger *through* summary entries
made in the general journal from the books and sources of original
entry:

[7] *Summary of Purchase Journal,* where all vendor invoices
are entered:

Purchases — Raw Material	10,000	
Shop Supplies	2,000	
Office Supplies	1,000	
Office Equipment	3,000	
Utilities	1,000	
Freight Out	2,000	
Advertising	1,000	
Accounts Payable		20,000

[8] *Summary of Cash Disbursement, Regular Cash A/C:*

Cash — Payroll A/C	13,000	
Petty Cash	200	
Accounts Payable	14,500	
Federal Tax Deposits Made	5,100	
Bank Charges	2	
Cash — Regular A/C		32,602
Cash Discounts Taken		200

[9] *Summary of Cash Disbursements, Payroll A/C:*

Direct Labor — Shop	12,500	
Indirect Labor — Shop	1.500	
Salaries — Sales Dept.	2,000	
Salaries — G & A	4,000	
Cash — Payroll A/C (net pay)		13,000
W/H Tax Pay — Federal		4,400
FICA Tax Withheld		1,200
SUI & Disability W/H		300
State Income Taxes W/H		600
Savings Bonds W/H		500

[10] *Summary of Sales Book:*

Accounts Receivable	35,000	
Sales Returns & Allowances	500	
Sales — Product L		18,000
Sales — Product M		16,600
Sales Taxes Payable		900

[11] *Summary of Cash Receipts Book:*

Cash — Regular A/C	30,500	
Cash Discounts Allowed	500	
Accounts Receivable		30,000
Machinery and Equipment		1,000

[12] *Summary of Petty Cash Box:*

Postage	40	
Entertainment	60	
Travel Expense	30	
Misc. Expense	20	
Petty Cash		150

[13] *General Journal Entries during month:*

Depreciation — M & E	10	
Machinery and Equipment	400	
Gain on Sale of Machinery		410

To correct entry from cash receipts:

Basis	$ 600	
Deprec.	10 (1/60th)	
	590	
S.P.	1000	
Gain	$ 410	

[14]

Depr.— Bldg (1/40x45,000x1/12)	94	
Depr.— M&E (1/5 x 8,400x1/12)	140	
Depr.— OE (1/5 x 3,000x1/12)	50	
Amortization (1/40x1,000x1/12)	2	
Accum Depr.— Bldg		94
Accum Depr.— M&E		140
Accum Depr.— OE		50
Goodwill		2

[15]

Real Estate Taxes	300	
Accrued Taxes — RE		300
1/12th of estimated $3,600 for yr		

[16]

Direct Labor (3125)	2,500	
Indirect Labor (375)	300	
Salaries — Selling (500)	400	
Salaries — G & A (1000)	800	
Accrued Salaries (5000)		4,000
To accrue 4/5 of last payroll in month.		

[17]

W/H Tax Payable — Federal	3,300	
FICA Tax Withheld	900	
FICA Tax Expense — employer	900	
Federal Tax Deposits Made		5,100
FICA Tax Expense — employer	300	
SUI & DISAB Expense	600	
FUI Expense	100	
Accrued Taxes — Payroll		1,000

To zero deposit account against
withholding accounts and to book
employer FICA expense and estimated
unemployment tax for month.

[18]

Overhead	6,106	
Depr.— Bldg (60% of 94)		56
Depr.— M&E (all)		140
Indirect Labor (all)		1,800
Payroll Tax Exp (70% of 1900)		1,330
Shop supplies (all considered used)		2,000

Utilities (60% of 1000)   600
Taxes — RE (60% of 300)   180
To allocate expenses to overhead.
Taxes based on payroll proportion.
Other allocations based on space occupied.

[19]

Inventory — Raw Materials   (15,000)
Inventory — Work in Process   none
Inventory — Finished Goods   15,369
    Cost of Production — Inventory Change   369
To increase or (decrease) inventory
accounts to reflect new month-end
inventory as follows:

Raw Material:

Opening Inventory	$ 30,000
Purchases	10,000
Less used in production	(25,000)
Closing inventory	15,000
To adjust opening	$ (15,000)

Finished Goods:

Materials used (above)	$ 25,000
Direct labor costs	15,000
Overhead costs	6,106
3 units produced	46,106
1 unit unsold (⅓)	$ 15,369

(none at hand at beginning)
No work in process this month.

(The entries through here are all related with respect to the dollars shown. From here on, they are independent with respect to each CAPITAL HEADING, but related within the headed area.)

CUSTOMER'S CHECK BOUNCES
[20]

Accounts Receivable (Mr. A.)   100
    Cash (Disbursements)   100
To record bank charge for
Mr. A's check return — insufficient
funds.

[21]

Cash (Receipts)   100
    Accounts Receivable (Mr. A.)   100
For re-deposit of above, per
customer's instructions.

NOTES RECEIVABLE DISCOUNTED

[22]

Cash   9,900
Interest Expense   250

Notes receivable Discounted		10,000
Interest Income		150

For proceeds from customer note discounted,
due 90 days @ 6%, discount rate 10%.

[23]

Notes Receivable Discounted	10,000	
Notes Receivable		10,000

To offset. Customer note paid,
per bank notice.

FIRST-YEAR DEPRECIATION

[24]

Depreciation Expense — M & E	2,000	
Accumulated Depr — M & E		2,000

For maximum first-year depreciation
taken on 6/30 purchase of extruder.
See next entry for regular deprec.

[25]

Depreciation — M & E	400	
Accumulated Depr — M & E		400

To take straight-line on above:

Cost	$	10,000
Less 1st yr. Depr		(2,000)
S/L basis		8,000
Over 10 yrs — per yr	$	800
Six months this yr (no salvage value).	$	400

TAX LOSS CARRYBACK

[26]

FIT Refund and Interest Receivable	106,000	
Income Tax (Current Yr. Income Statement)		100,000
Interest Income		6,000

To set up receivable for carryback tax
refund due, plus interest.

SUB-CHAPTER S EQUITY ENTRIES

End of Year 1:

[27]

Net income for Current Year	30,000	
Undistributed Earnings — Post-Election		30,000

To close year's net income into
new Sub-S undistributed earnings
Equity account.

[28]

Retained Earnings	55,000	
Retained Earnings — Pre-Election		55,000

To retitle opening retained earnings
account and keep it separate from
earnings after Sub-S election.

[29]

Post-Election Dividends	10,000	
Cash		10,000

For cash distributions made of current earnings. (NOTE: State law may require a *formal* declaration of a dividend for corporations. If this is true, and there is no such declaration, this must be treated as a *loan receivable* from stockholders.)

INSTALLMENT SALES METHOD

[30]

Accounts Receivable	1,000	
Cost of Installment Sale		700
Deferred Gross Profit on Installment Sales		300

For original sale. (GP% is 30%)

[31]

Cash	300	
Accounts Receivable		300

For payment on account.

[32]

Deferred Gross Profit on Installment Sales	90	
Realized Gross Profit		90

To amortize 30% of above collection
to realized income.

VOIDING YOUR OWN CHECK (Issued in a prior period)

[33]

Cash (Ck # 1601)	1,500	
Rent Expense		1,500

To void check #1601 (last month).
Check reported lost. Payment
stopped. Replaced with this month's
check #1752. (See CD book)

INVESTMENT TAX CREDIT — THE DEFERRAL METHOD

[34]

Taxes Payable	7,000	
Deferred Investment Tax Credits		7,000

To set up investment tax credit under
the deferred method. *Note:* The tax
expense for this year on the income
statement does *not* reflect the use
of this credit.

Year 2:

[35]

Deferred Investment Tax Credits	700	
Income Tax Expense		700

To amortize 1/10th, based on 10-year
life of asset to which applicable.

ACCUMULATED PREFERRED STOCK DIVIDENDS
[36]

Dividends (Income Statement)	30,000	
Dividends Payable (Liability)		30,000

To accrue this year's commitment,
6% of $500,000. *Note:* There was
no "only as earned" provision attached
to this issue.

DIVIDEND DECLARATION — COMMON STOCK
[37]

Retained Earnings	100,000	
Common Stock Extra Dividend		
Declared — (show in Equity Section)		100,000

To segregate common stock extra dividend
from accumulated earnings (until paid),
10¢ per share, 1,000,000 shares.

PAYMENT OF ABOVE TWO DIVIDENDS
[38]

Dividends Payable	30,000	
Common Stock Extra Dividend Declared	100,000	
Cash		130,000

For payment of dividends.

APPROPRIATION OF RETAINED EARNINGS
[39]

Retained Earnings	50,000	
Reserve Appropriation for Inventory		
Declines (Equity Section)		50,000

To set aside retained earnings for possible
inventory losses — per Board resolution.

[40]

Retained Earnings — (1/1 opening)	150,000	
Accounts Payable (XYZ Co.)		150,000

To record prior year billing error made
by supplier, XYZ Co., on invoice #____,
dated 12/10. Error not discovered by
XYZ until after closing of our books and
issuance of statements. Error is considered
material enough to treat as prior period
adjustment. Item was not in inventory
at 12/31.

STOCK DIVIDEND
Usually:
[41]

Retained Earnings (at market)	45,000	
Common Stock (par $10, 3,000 shares)		30,000
Additional Paid-in Capital		15,000

For 3% stock dividend distributed on
100,000 shares — 3,000 shares issued.
Market value $15 at dividend date.

Sometimes:

[42]

Additional Paid-in Capital	30,000	
Common Stock (par $10, 3,000 shares)		30,000
For non-taxable distribution out of		
Paid-in Capital.		

SPLIT-UP EFFECTED IN THE FORM OF A STOCK DIVIDEND

[43]

Retained Earnings (at par)	1,000,000	
Common Stock (par $10, 100,000 shs)		1,000,000
For split in the form of a stock dividend		
(to conform with state law). One share		
issued for each share outstanding.		
100,000 shares at par of $10.		

STOCK SPLIT-UP

[44]

Common Stock (100,000 shares @ $10.)	memo	
Common Stock (200,000 shares @ $5.)		memo
Memo entry only. To record stock split-up		
by showing change in par value and in		
number of shares outstanding. One share		
issued for each outstanding. Par changed		
from $10 to $5.		

STOCK OPTIONS FOR EMPLOYEES AS COMPENSATION

PARTNERSHIP WITHDRAWALS

[45]

S. Stone, Withdrawals	15,000	
T. Times, Withdrawals	5,000	
Cash		20,000
For cash withdrawals.		

PARTNERSHIP PROFIT ENTRY

[46]

Net Income — P & L a/c		100,000	
S. Stone, Capital (50%)			50,000
T. Times, Capital (50%)			50,000
To split profit as follows:			
Per P & L closing account	$ 80,000		
Add back above included			
in P & L account	20,000		
Profit to distribute	$100,000		

[47]

S. Stone, Capital	15,000	
T. Times, Capital	5,000	
S. Stone, Withdrawals		15,000
T. Times, Withdrawals		5,000
To close withdrawal accounts		
to capital accounts.		

IMPUTED INTEREST (ON NOTES RECEIVABLE)

[48]

Notes Receivable (Supplier A — 6 yrs)	1,000,000	
Cash		1,000,000

For loan made to supplier. Received
non-interest bearing note, due 6 yrs.

[49]

Cost of Merchandise (from supplier A)	370,000	
Unamortized Discount on Notes Receiv.		370,000

To charge imputed interest of 8% on
above note, due in 6 years, to cost
of merchandise bought from A.

Year 2:

[50]

Unamortized Discount on Notes Receiv.	50,000	
Interest Income		50,000

To amortize this year's applicable
imputed interest on note.

BOND DISCOUNT, PREMIUM AND ISSUE COSTS

[51]

Cash	2,025,000	
Unamortized Bond Issue Costs	15,000	
Bonds Payable (8%, 10 yrs)		2,000,000
Unamortized Premium on Bonds		40,000

To set up face value of bonds, issue
costs and net cash proceeds received.

Year 2:

[52]

Unamortized Premium on Bonds	4,000*	
Unamortized Bond Issue Cost		1,500*
Interest Expense (difference)		2,500

To set up approximate amortization.
(*Should actually be based on present
values.)

[53]

Interest Expense	160,000	
Cash		160,000

To record actual payment of bond
interest. 8% of $2,000,000.

FEDERAL INCOME TAX — INTERIMS — AND EXTRAORDINARY ITEM

[54]

Income Tax (on continuing operations)	350,000	
Extraordinary Loss (tax effect)		50,000
Taxes Payable		300,000

To set up FIT at end of First Quarter
based on full year's 50% rate and
to segregate tax applicable to
extraordinary item.

Statement should show:

Net from continuing operations	$700,000
Less FIT	(350,000)
	350,000

Extraordinary loss (net of $50,000 tax effect)	50,000
Net Income	$300,000

CAPITALIZING A LEASE (LESSEE)

At contracting:

[55]

Capitalized Leases	1,920,000	
Long-Term Lease Liability		3,600,000
Unamortized Discount on Lease		(1,680,000)

To capitalize lease of $25,000 per
month for 12 years @ 12% imputed
interest rate. Estimated life of asset
is 15 years. Present value used, since
fair value is higher at $2,000,000.

(Note: The two credit items shown are
netted and shown as *one net liability*
on the balance sheet. The liability
(at present value) should always equal
the asset value, also at present value.
Future lease payments are broken out,
effectively, into principal and interest.)

Month-end 1:

[56]

Long-Term Lease Liability	25,000	
Cash		25,000

First payment on lease.

[57]

Interest Expense	18,950	
Unamortized Discount on Lease		18,950

For one month's interest.
1% of $3,600,000 less $1,680,000,
less initial payment on signing of
contract of $25,000 *(entry not shown)* or
$1,895,000.

[58]

Depreciation Expense	10,667	
Accumulated Depr of Capitalized Lease		10,667

One month:
$1,920,000 x 1/5 x 1/12

CASH SURRENDER VALUE — OFFICER LIFE INSURANCE

[59]

Officer Life Insurance — expense	1,500	
Cash		1,500

For payment of premium. *Note:* Expense

is not deductible for tax purpose and
is a *permanent* difference.

[60]

Cash Surrender Value-Officer Life Ins.	1,045	
Officer Life Ins. expense		1,045

To reflect increase in C.S.V. for year

[61]

Cash	5,000	
Loans Against Officer Life Insurance		5,000
(Displayed against the asset "C.S.V.")		

To record loan against life policy. No intent
to repay within the next year.

STANDARD COST VARIANCES

[62]

Purchases — Raw Mat (at stand)	200	
Accounts Payable — actual		188
Variance — material price		12

[63]

Direct Labor — at standard	50	
Variance — Direct Labor rate	10	
Payroll — actual direct labor		58
Variance — Labor Time		2

[64]

Overhead — at Standard	75	
Variance — overhead	15	
Overhead itemized actual accounts		90

Adjusting Inventories:

[65]

Inventory — Raw Materials at standard	100	
Finished Goods — at standard	75	
Cost of Production — at standard		175

To adjust inventory accounts to reflect
end-of-month on-hand figures at standards.

[66]

Variance — material price	xx	
Variance — labor time	xx	
Variance — direct labor rate		xx
Variance — overhead		xx
Contra Inventory Asset a/c (variances		
to offset standard and reflect cost)		xx

To pull out of variance accounts that
portion which is applicable to inventory,
in order to keep an isolated contra account,
which in offset to the "standard" asset
account, reflects approximate cost.
The portion is based on an overall ratio
of variances to production and inventory
figures (at standard). (If normal, apply
to cost of sales for interims.)

ADJUSTING INVENTORY FOR SAMPLING RESULTS

[67]

Cost of Sales	50,000	

Inventory		50,000

To reduce inventory by $50,000 based
on sampling results:

Inventory per computer run	$ 1,000,000	
Estimated calculated		
inventory per sample	950,000	
Reduction this year	$ 50,000	

Year 2:

[68]

Inventory	10,000	
Cost of Sales		10,000

To adjust inventory to actual
based on actual physical count
of entire inventory. Last year-end
sample error proved to be 4%,
not 5%.

ADJUSTING CLOSING INVENTORY FROM CLIENT'S STANDARD COST TO
AUDITOR'S DETERMINED (AND CLIENT AGREED) ACTUAL COST, AND TO
REFLECT PHYSICAL INVENTORY VS. BOOK INVENTORY DIFFERENCES

[69]

Inventory — Finished Goods (Standard)	25,000	
Cost of Sales		25,000

To adjust general ledger inventory
(at standard) to actual physical
inventory count, priced out at
standard. Actual is $25,000 more.

[70]

Cost of Sales	80,000	
Inventory — Finished Goods		
(Asset Contra Cost account)		80,000

To set up a contra account reducing
asset account, which is at standard
costs, effectively to audited actual
cost or market, whichever lower.

Year 2: (End of Year)

[71]

Inventory — Finished Goods (Asset		
Contra Cost account)	50,000	
Cost of Sales		50,000

To reduce the contra account to
the new year-end difference between
the "standard" asset account and the
actual cost determined for this new
year-end inventory.

PARTNERSHIP DISSOLUTION:

Balance Sheet

Cash	$ 20,000
Assets other	35,000

Liabilities	(25,000)
A Capital (50%)	(20,000)
B Capital (30%)	(14,000)
C Capital (20%)	4,000
	-0-

[72]

Cash	15,000	
Assets other		15,000

For sale of some assets at book value.

[73]

A Capital (⅝)	2,500	
B Capital (⅜)	1,500	
C Capital		4,000

C cannot put in his overdraw —
to apportion his deficit.

[74]

Liabilities	25,000	
Cash		25,000

To pay liabilities

[75]

Cash	10,000	
Loss on Sale of Assets other	10,000	
Assets other		20,000
A Capital (⅝)	6,250	
B Capital (⅜)	3,750	
Loss on Sale of Assets other		10,000

Selling remaining assets and apportioning loss

[76]

A Capital (remaining balance)	11,250	
B Capital (remaining balance)	8,750	
Cash		20,000

To distribute remaining cash
and zero capital accounts.

NOTE THE SHARING OF C'S DEFICIT
AND OF THE LOSS ON ASSET SALE
BEFORE DISTRIBUTING REMAINING
CASH.

MARKETABLE SECURITIES

Shown as Current Assets:
[77]

Unrealized Loss — to P & L	1,500	
Valuation Allowance — Current		1,500

To write down 100 U.S. Steel:

Cost 1/1	$10,000
Market 12/31	8,500
Unrealized Loss	$ 1,500

Year 2:
[78]

Cash	4,500	
Realized Loss — P & L	500	

Marketable Securities — Current			5,000
Sold 50 @ 90	$ 4,500		
Cost 50 @ 90	5,000		
Realized Loss	$ 500		

[79]

Valuation Allowance — Current		1,250	
Valuation Adjustment — Current (P&L Gain)			1,250*

To adjust valuation allowance a/c
(current) for remaining securities
left in portfolio:

50 US Steel — cost 100	$ 5,000
Market, this year end — 95	4,750
Bal. should be	250 Cr.
Balance in valuation a/c	1,500 Cr.
Debit valuation a/c	$ 1,250 Dr.

*Note: Unrealized *gains* are called
"valuation adjustments." Unrealized
losses are called "unrealized losses."

Shown as Noncurrent Asset:

[80]

Unrealized Noncurrent Loss (Equity section)	1,000	
Valuation Allowance — Noncurrent		1,000

To write down 100 shares GM
from cost of 60 to market
value at 12/31 of 50.

Year 2:

[81]

Cash		2,900	
Realized Loss — P & L		100	
Marketable Securities — Noncurrent			3,000
Sold 50 GM @ 58	$ 2,900		
Cost 50 GM @ 60	3,000		
Realized loss	$ 100		

[82]

Valuation Allowance — Noncurrent	1,000	
Unrealized Noncurrent Loss (Equity Section)		1,000

To adjust valuation allowance a/c
(Noncurrent) as follows:

Cost 50 GM @ 60	$ 3,000
Market now @ 65	N/A
(Higher than cost)	
Valuation a/c should be	-0-
(Because market is higher	
than cost)	
Balance in valuation a/c	1,000 Cr.
Debit to correct	$ 1,000 Dr.

TREASURY STOCK

Purchase of:

[83]

Treasury Stock — at Cost	125,000	
Cash		125,000

Purchase of 1,000 shares @ 125
market. Par value $50.
No intent to cancel the stock.

Sale of:

[84]

Cash	140,000	
Treasury Stock — at Cost		125,000
Additional Paid — in Capital		15,000

For sale of treasury stock @ 140.

APPRAISAL WRITE-UPS
[85]

Building	350,000	
Appraisal Capital (Equity Section)		350,000

To raise building from cost of $400,000 to
appraised value of $750,000 per require-
ment of the lending institution.

Year 2:

[86]

Depreciation — Building	21,667	
Accumulated Depreciation — Building		21,667

To depreciate based on appraised value:
(400,000 for 40 years; 350,000 for 30 yrs)
Building was 10 years old at appraisal.

FOREIGN CURRENCY EXCHANGE
[87]

Unrealized Loss (balance sheet)	10,000	
Accts Payable — Foreign		10,000

To adjust liabilities payable in
Swiss Francs to US Dollars at 12/31:

Exchange rate at 12/31 .40	$40,000
Booked at (100,000 frs) .30	30,000
More dollars owed	$10,000

[88]

Deferred Taxes	5,000*	
Unrealized Loss		5,000*

To show deferred tax effect (50% rate
times $10,000 above)
*Less Foreign or Domestic Dividend
Credits, if Applicable

Year 2:

[89]

Accounts Payable — Foreign	20,000	
Cash		19,000
Realized gain (Books, not Tax)		1,000

For payment of 50,000 Swiss Francs at exchange rate of .38

[90]

Accounts Payable — Foreign	500	
Balance Sheet		500

To restate liability at year-end:

50,000 Frs @ .39	$ 19,500	
Booked to last yr.	20,000	
(Gain)	$ (500)	

[91]

Taxes Payable	2,000	
Income Tax Expense	500	
Deferred Taxes		2,500

To transfer to actual taxes payable (from
deferred) that portion applying to the payment of $19,000. Original debt in dollars
was $15,000. 50% tax rate on $4,000 or
$2,000, plus $500 — to offset 2,500
booked to last 12/31.

[92]

Income Tax Expenses	250	
Deferred Taxes		250

To adjust deferred taxes to equal ½ of
4,500 (19,500 liability now, less original
liability of 15,000) for $2,250 tax deferral.

THE EQUITY METHOD
[93]

Investment — Oleo Co.	275,000	
Cash		275,000

Purchase of 25% of Oleo's stock,
at cost (25,000 shares @ $11).

[94]

Investment — Oleo Co.	40,000	
Deferred Good Will in Oleo		40,000

To set up additional underlying equity in
Oleo Co. at date of acquisition — to
write-off over 40 years.

[95]

Cash	5,000	
Investment — Oleo Co.		5,000

For receipt of 20¢ per share cash dividend
from Oleo.

[96]

Investment — Oleo Co.	27,500	
Income from Equity Share of Undistributed Earnings of Oleo continuing operations		25,000
Income from Equity Share of Undistributed Extraordinary Item of Oleo		2,500

To pick up 25% of the following
reported Oleo annual figures:

Net income after taxes, but before Extraordinary item	$100,000	
Extraordinary Income (net)	10,000	
Total net income reported	$110,000	

[97]

Income Tax Expense — Regular	12,500*	
Income Tax Expense — Extra Item	1,250*	

Deferred Taxes   13,750*
To set up 50% of above income as accrued
taxes. Expectation is that Oleo will
continue paying dividends.

*Dividend Tax Credit, if any, should reduce
these Amounts

[98]

Deferred Taxes   2,500*
    Income Taxes Payable   2,500*
To set up actual liability for tax on cash
dividends received.

*Dividend Tax Credit, if any, should reduce
these Amounts

CONSOLIDATION

Trial Balances
Now-at
*12/31-*End of Year

	A Co.	B Co.	Fair Value Excess at Acquisition
Cash	10,000	6,000	
A/R	20,000	10,000	
Inventory	30,000	5,000	
Equip	50,000	30,000	5,000
Investment Cost	40,000		
Liabilities	(30,000)	(5,000)	(1,000)
Common Stock	(20,000)	(10,000)*	
Retained Earnings	(50,000)	(20,000)*	
Sales	(80,000)	(40,000)	
Costs of Sale	20,000	14,000	
Expenses	10,000	10,000	
	-0-	-0-	
	(Parent)	(Sub)	

*Unchanged from opening balances.

*At year-end there were $5,000 intercom-
pany receivables/*payables. The parent had
sold $5,000 worth of product to the sub-
sidiary. The inventory of the subsidiary was
$1,000 over the parent's cost.

Consolidating
Entries:

[99]

Excess Paid over Book Value   10,000
    Investment Cost   10,000

To reduce investment cost to that of the
subsidiary's equity at time of purchase (unchanged at 12/31).

[100]

Equipment	5,000	
Liabilities		1,000
Excess Paid over Book Value		4,000

To reflect fair value corrections at time of
consolidation for the combination of current year-end trial balances.

[101]

B Co. Equity	30,000	
Investment Cost		30,000
Sales	5,000	
Costs of Sale		5,000
Costs of Sale	1,000	
Inventory		1,000
Liabilities	5,000	
Accounts Receivable		5,000
Excess paid over book value (expense)	150	
Goodwill		150

To eliminate intercompany dealings, debt,
investment, and to amortize goodwill.

Consolidated figures will then be:

Cash	16,000	
A/R	25,000	
Inventories	34,000	
Equipment	85,000	
Investment cost	—	
Goodwill	5,850	
Liabilities	(31,000)	
Common Stock	(20,000)	(Opening)
Ret. Earnings	(50,000)	(Opening)
Sales	(115,000)	
Cost of sales	30,000	
Expenses	20,150	
	-0-	

The year's consolidated net income (before
provision for income taxes) is $64,850.

PURCHASE METHOD OF BUSINESS COMBINATION

[102]

Accounts Receivable (present value)	50,000	
Inventory (current cost or market, lowest)	40,000	
Building (fair value)	110,000	
Equipment (fair value)	30,000	
Investments, non-current securities-market	5,000	
Goodwill	16,200	
Accounts Payable — (present value)		25,000
Long-term Debt — (face value)		30,000
Unamortized discount on long-term debt		

(to reflect present value)		(3,800)
Common Stock (Par $10; 10,000 shares)		100,000
Additional Paid-in Capital		100,000

To reflect, by the purchase method, the
purchase of Diablo Company assets and
liabilities for 10,000 shares of common
stock; total purchase price of contract
$200,000 based on market price of stock at
date of consummation of $20 per share
(1/1).

[103]

Amortization of Goodwill (1/40)	405	
Goodwill		405
Unamortized discount on long-term debt	760	
Discount Income (approx 1/5th)		760*

To amortize pertinent Diablo items, first
yearend. Goodwill on straight-line basis —
40 years. *Should be calculated present
value computation.

POOLING METHOD OF BUSINESS
COMBINATION
[104]

Inventory	43,000	
Cash	5,000	
Accounts Receivable	60,000	
Reserve for Doubtful Accounts		7,000
Building	75,000	
Accumulated Depreciation — Building		15,000
Equipment	100,000	
Accumulated Depreciation — Building		60,000
Investments — non-current securities	4,000	
Accounts Payable		25,500
Long-Term Debt		30,000
Common Stock (10,000 shs @ par $10)		100,000
Additional Paid-in Capital		49,500

To reflect the pooling of Diablo items, per
their book value on date of consummation.

FUND ACCOUNTING

Initial transactions:
[105]

Cash	100,000	
Dues Income		100,000

For initial membership dues received.

[106]

Building	50,000	
Mortgage Payable		40,000
Cash		10,000

Purchase of building for cash and mortgage.

[107]

Interest Expense	2,400	
Mortgage Payable	2,000	

Cash		4,400

For first payment on mortgage.

[108]

| Net income (100,000 less 2,400) | 97,600 | |
| Current Fund Balance | | 97,600 |

To close year's income

[109]

Mortgage Payable	38,000	
Current Fund Balance	12,000	
Building		50,000

To transfer building and mortgage to plant fund.

Plant Fund Entry:

[110]

Building	50,000	
Mortgage Payable		38,000
Plant Fund Balance		12,000

To set up building in plant fund.

Note that interest expense is to be borne by the current fund every year as a current operating expense used in the calculation of required dues from members. Also, the principal sum-payments against mortgage are to come out of current fund assets, with no interfund debt to be set up, until such time as a special drive is held for plant fund donations for improvements and expansion.

MUNICIPAL ACCOUNTING — CURRENT OPERATING FUND

To book the budget:

[111]

Estimated Revenues	600,000	
Appropriations		590,000
Fund Balance		10,000

Actual year's transactions:

[112]

| Encumbrances | 575,000 | |
| Reserve for Encumbrances | | 575,000 |

To enter contracts and purchase orders issued.

[113]

Expenditures — itemized (not here)	515,000	
Vouchers Payable		515,000
Reserve for Encumbrances	503,000	
Encumbrances		503,000

To enter actual invoices for deliveries received and service contracts performed and to reverse applicable encumbrances.

[114]

Taxes Receivable — Current	570,000	
Revenues		541,500
Estimated Current Uncollectible Taxes		28,500

To enter actual tax levy and to estimate uncollectibles at 5%.

[115]

Cash	55,000	
Revenues		55,000

For cash received from licenses, fees,
fines and other sources.

[116]

Cash	549,500	
Estimated Current Uncollectible Taxes	8,000	
Taxes Receivable		549,500
Revenues		8,000

For actual taxes collected for this year.

To close out budget accounts:

[117]

Revenues	604,500	
Appropriations	590,000	
Estimated Revenue		600,000
Expenditures		515,000
Encumbrances		72,000
Fund Balance		7,500

To zero budget accounts and adjust
fund balance.

DISCS — DEEMED DISTRIBUTIONS (Parent's Books)

1975 — under old law

[118]

DISC Dividends Receivable (previously taxed)	110,000	
Deemed Distribution from DISC (income)		110,000

To pick up ½ of DISC's net of $220,000.

1976 — under the new law.

[119]

DISC Dividends Receivable (previously taxed)	189,375	
Deemed Distribution from DISC (income)		189,375

As follows:

Facts:

Gross export receipts average for 1972-1975	$1,100,000
Gross export receipts - 1976	$1,300,000
Net DISC income - 1976 only	$ 250,000

Since the 1976 net income is over
$150,000, the graduated relief in the 1976
law does not apply, and the calculation is:

67% of 1,100,000 = 670,000

670,000 ÷ 1,300,000 = 51.5%

51.5% × 250,000 = $ 128,750

250,000 − 128,750 = 121,250

121,250 × 50% =   60,625

       Total Deemed Distribution $ 189,375

[120]

Capitalization of Interest Costs
Qualifying Asset   10,000
    Accrued Interest   10,000

[121]

Employee Compensation   50,000
    Accrued Vacation   50,000

Appendix B
Concise Guide to the
Tax Reform Act of 1986*

Introduction

When the Senate and House of Representatives agreed on the Tax Reform Act of 1986, a major step was taken in U.S. tax history. This Act, which, as we go to press, is awaiting President Reagan's signature, is the most comprehensive tax legislation enacted since 1954. In addition to removing millions of low-income Americans from the tax rolls, it simplifies the reporting burdens of millions of other Americans.

For the remaining taxpayers, the Act should not be thought of as simplifying the tax law. Rather, it imposes new and, in many cases, more complex rules. Among its many changes the Act:

- Reduces all tax rates
- Restructures itemized deductions
- Alters the taxation of minor children's unearned income
- Expands the alternative minimum tax
- Restructures the income taxation of estates and trusts
- Alters the deductibility of business meals and entertainment
- Revises the capital cost recovery system
- Expands the corporation minimum tax
- Severely limits the use of cash-method accounting
- Modifies the reporting of installment sales income
- Creates a new structure for foreign exchange transactions and translations
- Restricts the availability of IRAs
- Imposes new rules on qualified retirement plans
- Expands information reporting requirements

These and other provisions of the Act are discussed on the following pages.

Another historic step taken by the Tax Reform Act of 1986 was to rename the tax law *The Internal Revenue Code of 1986.*

The material contained in this book is general information and should not be acted on or used without professional advice.

October 1, 1986

---

*Reproduced with permission of KMG Main Hurdman, © Copyright 1986 by KMG Main Hurdman, New York, NY 10055.

Provisions Affecting Individuals

Rate Structure

Blended tax rate schedules reflecting a mixture of the 1986 rates and the new Act rates with a maximum 38.5% rate will apply to calendar year 1987 returns. Depending on filing status and taxable income, the brackets and rates for 1987 are:

	Single	Married/ Joint	Married/ Separate	Head of Household
11%	not over $1,800	not over $3,000	not over $1,500	not over $2,500
15%	1,800 - 16,800	3,000 - 28,000	1,500 - 14,000	2,500 - 23,000
28%	16,800 - 27,000	28,000 - 45,000	14,000 - 22,500	23,000 - 38,000
35%	27,000 - 54,000	45,000 - 90,000	22,500 - 45,000	38,000 - 80,000
38.5%	over 54,000	over 90,000	over 45,000	over 80,000

For 1988 and later years, the Act provides for a reduction in the top marginal rate from 50% to 28% and replaces the 14 or 15 brackets of 1986 law with just two brackets. Depending on filing status and taxable income, the 1988 brackets and rates are:

	Single	Married/ Joint	Married/ Separate	Head of Household
15%	not over $17,850	not over $29,750	not over $14,875	not over $23,900
28%	over 17,850	over 29,750	over 14,875	over 23,900

Beginning in 1988, the benefit of the 15% bracket is phased out for taxpayers above certain income levels through a rate adjustment resulting in additional tax liability. This adjustment is computed as 5% of the excess of a taxpayer's taxable income over the amount specified for their filing status.

For each filing status, the minimum and maximum taxable income level at which the adjustment would apply and the maximum possible adjustment are as follows:

	Single	Married/ Joint	Married/ Separate	Head of Household
Minimum Taxable Income	$43,150	$ 71,900	$ 35,950	$ 61,650
Maximum Taxable Income	89,560	149,250	113,300	123,790
Maximum Adjustment	2,321	3,868	3,868	3,107

The dollar amounts listed for the tax rate brackets and for the phase out of the 15% bracket will be adjusted for inflation starting in 1989.

Standard Deduction

Under prior law, a zero bracket amount (ZBA) was built into the tax rate schedules and tax tables. The ZBA gives all taxpayers a flat reduction of taxable income (depending on their filing status) whether they itemize deductions or not. Because the benefit of the ZBA is built into the rate schedules or tax tables, taxpayers who itemize deductions must reduce their total itemized deductions by the ZBA amount.

Under the Act, the ZBA, starting in 1987, will be replaced by a standard deduction. The amounts by filing status are as follows:

| | | Standard Deduction | |
	1986 (ZBA)	1987	1988
Single	$2,480	$2,540	$3,000
Married/Joint	3,670	3,760	5,000
Married/Separate	1,835	1,880	2,500
Head of Household	2,480	2,540	4,400

Beginning with 1989, the standard deduction will be adjusted for inflation.

The standard deduction of any dependent claimed as a personal exemption by another taxpayer is limited to the greater of earned income or $500.

The Internal Revenue Service (IRS) will continue to prepare tax tables reflecting the tax liability of individuals who use the standard deduction. It may prepare tax tables for taxpayers who itemize, but these tables will not incorporate the standard deduction.

For calendar years 1987 and 1988, an additional standard deduction of $600 is allowed for a married elderly or blind individual ($1,200 for a married individual who is both). An equal amount is available for an elderly or blind spouse. Single taxpayers who are elderly or blind would receive an additional standard deduction of $750 ($1,500 for a single individual who is both). The $600 or $750 additional standard deduction will be indexed for inflation beginning in 1989.

Personal Exemption

Under prior law, taxpayers reduced their adjusted gross income by the sum of the personal exemptions for themselves, their spouses and dependents. For 1986, the personal exemption amount is $1,080.

The Act increases the personal exemption amount to $1,900 in 1987, $1,950 in 1988 and $2,000 in 1989. Beginning in 1990, the $2,000 personal exemption will be indexed for inflation.

Starting in 1987, the currently available additional personal exemptions for the elderly and for the blind will no longer be available. It will be replaced with an additional standard deduction.

Persons eligible to be claimed as dependents on another's return are not allowed a personal exemption on their own returns.

Beginning with tax year 1988, the personal exemption benefit is phased out for taxpayers with taxable income in excess of:

Single	Married/Joint	Married/Separate	Head of Household
$89,560	$149,250	$113,300	$123,790

These amounts are the taxable income levels at which the benefit of the 15% tax rate is fully phased out. As the 15% and 28% brackets are adjusted for inflation, these amounts will change.

The income tax liability of taxpayers is increased by 5% of taxable income in excess of these amounts. Therefore, taxpayers with taxable incomes above the threshold amounts will pay a marginal tax rate of 33% on each dollar of additional income until all of the benefit of their personal exemptions is lost.

In 1988, the tax benefit of one personal exemption ($546 in reduced tax liability) will be completely lost for each $10,920 in taxable income above the threshold amounts. In 1989, each $11,200 of additional income will completely offset the benefit of one exemption.

Dependents' Taxpayer Identification Numbers

Every taxpayer claiming a dependent who is at least five years old must obtain a Social Security number for that dependent. That number must be reported on the tax return on which a personal exemption for the dependent is claimed. To obtain a Social Security number for a dependent minor child, a parent must submit Form SS-5 with a copy of the child's birth certificate.

Effective Date

This provision applies to tax returns due on or after January 1, 1988 (without regard to extensions).

Income of Children Under Age 14

Under prior law, the income of a child, regardless of age, was generally taxed in the same manner as an adult's. The major difference being that if the child was claimed as a dependent on another's return, the child's zero bracket amount (ZBA) could only be used to offset the child's earned income.

The Act radically alters this historic pattern. For taxable years starting after December 31, 1986, *all* net unearned income of a child under age 14 that exceeds $1,000 ($500 exclusion plus $500 allowable standard deduction) will be taxed at the parent's top marginal rate.

Children subject to the new tax on net unearned income must include their specified parent's tax identification number on their returns.

Comment

This radical change in the pattern of taxing the unearned income of children under age 14 when combined with other changes, such as the compressed trust tax rates and new tax structure for grantor trusts (both discussed below), necessitates the rethinking of classic tax-planning techniques and the creation of new ones. Because there will be no tax saving on a young child's unearned income over $1,000, the primary motive for giving income producing property to children —

the accumulation of wealth at a lower tax cost—has been removed. The shift in planning motivation will now be towards overall family wealth accumulation and its related estate (both tax and legal) consequences.

Warning

This new provision will necessitate the review of all financial and estate plans of parents of children under age 14 before year end to assure that the tax erosion beginning in 1987 will not radically alter the plan's goals or the ability of the plan to attain the goals.

Planning Points

Consider the following when reviewing the options available for shifting income to children under age 14:

- The tax deferral built into Series EE bonds could shelter income until a child reaches age 14.
- The tax-free feature of municipal bonds could be used to avoid current tax to a child under 14.
- When appropriate, the purchase or gift of single premium life insurance or a deferred annuity could effectively shelter the built in income from current taxation.
- In appropriate situations, consideration should be given to using an accumulation trust, notwithstanding the new compressed rate structure (see below).
- Giving investments that have growth rather than current income potential could defer taxation at least until the child reaches 14 years and becomes taxable as an independent individual.
- Do not lose sight of the important estate planning considerations of giving property, whether income producing or not, to young children. The estate tax savings could well be sufficient reason to transfer the property even though the net income tax result of the transfer is neutral.

Dividend Exclusion

Under prior law, individuals could exclude the first $100 ($200 for married couples filing joint returns) of qualifying dividends received. The Act repeals the exclusion for dividends received in taxable years beginning after December 31, 1986.

Capital Gain and Loss

Under prior law, individuals and other noncorporate taxpayers could deduct from gross income 60% of any net capital gain for the taxable year, i.e., 60% of the excess of net long-term capital gain over net short-term capital loss. Therefore, the highest effective rate on capital gain was 20% (50% maximum rate × the 40% net capital gain included in adjusted gross income). The capital-gain deduction, however, was included in the minimum tax base as a preference item.

The capital loss of an individual was fully deductible from capital gain. In addition, a maximum of $3,000 of capital loss was deductible against ordinary income. However, only 50% of net long-term capital loss in excess of net short-term capital gain was deductible from ordinary income.

The Act repeals the net capital gain deduction. In 1987, even though the top individual rate is 38.5%, the highest long-term capital gain rate will be 28%. In 1988, capital gain will be taxed at the same rate as ordinary income—15% or 28%, depending on the applicable tax bracket.

Because of the repeal of the 60% capital gain deduction, capital gain will no longer be a preference under the individual alternative minimum tax. The Act also retains the $3,000 limit on the deductibility of capital loss against ordinary income. However, capital loss will now be deductible dollar for dollar.

Effective Date
This provision applies to taxable years beginning after December 31, 1986.

Planning Point
Because the highest effective rate on capital gain will jump from 20% to 28%, investors should consider selling long-term capital gain property before 1987.

Example: Under prior law, when Mr. Gold, who was in the 50% bracket, sold long-term capital gain property, with an adjusted basis of $50,000, for $100,000, he would pay a tax of $10,000 ($50,000 gain $\times$ 20%). Under the Act, he would pay a tax of $14,000 ($50,000 $\times$ 28%).

Planning Point
Because the top individual rate will be lower under the Act, investors should consider delaying, when economically feasible, the sale of otherwise short-term capital gain assets until 1987 or 1988 to avoid their current taxation at higher ordinary income rates.

Estimated Tax

Waiver of Penalties
The Act makes several changes that increase tax liabilities retroactively to the beginning of 1986. Consequently, the Act allows individual taxpayers until April 15, 1987, (the final filing date for calendar year returns) to pay their full 1986 income tax liabilities without incurring any additions to tax on account of the underpayments of estimated tax attributable to retroactive changes in the law.

Minimum Payments
Under prior law, individuals who underpaid their quarterly estimated taxes were subject to a penalty unless their quarterly payments equalled or exceeded the lesser of 100% of the prior year's tax liability or 80% of the current years' liability.

Under the Act the 80% requirement is increased to 90%. The change is effective for the first quarterly estimated tax payment due for 1987, i.e., the payment due April 15, 1987.

Limitation on the Deduction of Nonbusiness Interest
Under prior law, interest on debt relating to a trade or business or to rental property was fully deductible. In addition, individuals who itemized their deductions generally were allowed to deduct the full amount of interest paid on

consumer debt and other nonbusiness indebtedness The only exception was the limitation on interest paid on indebtedness incurred to purchase or carry property that was held for investment. The deduction for investment interest was limited to $10,000 per year ($5,000 for a married person filing a separate return) plus the amount of the taxpayer's net investment income. Any amount in excess of the limitation was carried forward indefinitely to subsequent taxable years.

For noncorporate taxpayers, the Act radically changes the rules governing the deduction of *nonbusiness* interest. Its effect could have a profound impact on future consumer debt.

Business Interest

Under the Act, interest on business indebtedness remains fully deductible. Business indebtedness includes both debt incurred in the *operation* of the taxpayer's trade or business and, in certain circumstances, debt incurred to *acquire an interest* in a trade or business the taxpayer materially participates in.

To the extent that a loan finances an asset used partially for business and partially for personal purposes, it appears that interest would have to be prorated between the two uses and treated accordingly.

Example (1): Ms. Green, a self-employed consultant, finances a new automobile used 80% for business and 20% for personal purposes. She would treat 80% of the interest as deductible business interest and 20% as nondeductible consumer interest.

Consumer Interest

Under the Act, no deduction is allowed for consumer interest other than *qualified residence interest*. Accordingly, interest on personal loans, personal credit card charges, automobile loans (except business automobiles), and similar types of *consumer debt* are nondeductible. As explained below, the disallowance of consumer interest is phased in over a five-year period.

Consumer debt includes all debt other than debt incurred or continued in connection with either a trade or business (except the trade or business of performing services as an employee) or property held for the production of income. The specific inclusion of debt incurred by an employee as consumer debt appears to mean that interest on any amount borrowed to finance an employment-related expense is treated as nondeductible consumer interest rather than deductible business interest.

Example (2): In Example (1), if Ms. Green was an employee rather than a self-employed individual, it appears that all of the interest that she pays on her automobile loan would be treated as consumer interest—and not deductible—even if she uses the automobile 80% of the time in her employer's business.

Planning Point

The new limitations on deductions for consumer interest and employee business expenses (see page 19) call for new tax strategies for automobiles used for business by employees. Under the Act, it is generally more advantageous to have a business-use vehicle owned by the employer rather than by the employee, even though the employee must include the value of any personal use as compensation income.

Type of Expense	Employer-Owned	Employee-Owned
Interest expense	Fully deductible	Fully nondeductible
Depreciation, insurance and operating expenses	Fully deductible	Cents-per-business-mile or business percentage of depreciation, insurance and operating expenses deductible, subject to 2%-of-AGI deduction floor

Interest on underpayments of tax (other than certain deferred estate taxes) is treated as consumer interest. This applies to interest paid to state and local taxing authorities as well as interest paid to the IRS.

Qualified Residence Interest

The disallowance of consumer interest does not apply to interest paid or accrued on debt secured by a security interest perfected under local law on the taxpayer's principal residence or a second residence owned by the taxpayer. However, under the qualified residence exception, interest is deductible only on the portion of the debt that does not exceed the total of:
- The purchase price of the residences,
- The cost of any capital improvements, and
- An additional amount, up to the fair market value (FMV) of the residences, if incurred after August 16, 1986, for educational or medical purposes.

Example: Mr. and Mrs. Blue's principal residence has an FMV of $250,000. They purchased it 10 years ago for $110,000 and have made $20,000 of improvements. In 1987, they refinance the residence for $200,000 (including the payoff of the original mortgage). Interest on $130,000 ($110,000 cost plus $20,000 improvements) of the new loan would be deductible as qualified residence interest. The balance would be nondeductible consumer interest (subject to the five-year phase-in of the disallowance).

If the Blues use an additional $40,000 of the mortgage proceeds to pay for their child's education, interest on that amount would also be deductible as qualified residence interest.

The requirement that the indebtedness be *secured* by the residence appears to disqualify interest paid on an unsecured home improvement loan.

The qualified residence exception contains a special relief provision for any taxpayers who refinanced their homes before August 17, 1986, at an amount that exceeded their cost basis. Those taxpayers are allowed to deduct interest on the amount of the secured debt as of August 16, 1986, plus any secured amount incurred after August 16, 1986, for qualified medical and educational expenses.

A husband and wife who file separate returns may each deduct interest on debt secured by one of the residences they own. Or, they may consent in writing to allow one spouse to deduct interest on two residences, one of which must be a principal residence. In that event, the other spouse would not be allowed to deduct any qualified residence interest.

A taxpayer who owns more than two residences may elect each year which of the nonprincipal residences will be treated as the second residence. A new choice of second residence may be made each year.

Comment
If a taxpayer owns a residence located on substantial acreage, which is subject to a single mortgage, the Act does not clarify whether and under what circumstances the interest on the surrounding acreage is deductible under the qualified residence interest exception. Under appropriate circumstances the IRS might take the position that a portion of the acreage is held primarily for investment and that the interest on that portion is subject to the investment interest limitation explained below.

Boat Owners
The term *residence* as used in the qualified residence interest exception, includes, in addition to houses, condominium units and cooperative housing units, any other property that the taxpayer uses for personal purposes as a dwelling unit. The term *dwelling unit* generally includes a mobile home, motor home or a boat with living accomodations. Accordingly, although the Act is not clear on this point, it appears that a taxpayer who owns a boat that is large enough to live aboard for short periods may be able to treat it as a second residence for purposes of the residential interest deduction.

The requirement that the indebtedness be secured by the residential property also applies to boats, trailers and motor homes.

Investment Interest
The Act limits the deduction for investment interest to the amount of the taxpayer's net investment income.

Investment interest includes all interest except:
- Business interest
- Consumer interest
- Qualified residence interest

Any investment interest disallowed because of the limitation is carried over indefinitely to subsequent taxable years.

For purposes of the deduction limitation, *net investment income* includes:
- Interest, dividends, rents and royalties in excess of any related expenses (using the actual amount of depreciation or depletion allowable)
- Any amount of recaptured depreciation or amortization on the disposition of depreciable property
- Capital-gain net income from the disposition of property held for investment

Interaction of Interest Limitation and Passive-Activity Loss Limitation
Interest expense and income from activities that are subject to the passive-activity loss limitation rules (described on page 46) generally are *not* treated as investment interest expense or investment income. Thus, interest allocable to a rental real estate activity is not treated as investment interest regardless of the taxpayer's active participation. However, during the five-year phase in of the

passive-activity loss limitation, the deductible portion of any passive-activity losses will be subtracted in computing net investment income. Presumably, this means that the IRS will revise the partnership tax return (Form 1065 and Schedule K-1) so that interest expense will be included in a passive partner's share of partnership income or loss, rather than reported as a separate item on Schedule K-1.

Example: In 1987, Mr. Black has a $15,000 loss from a limited partnership in which he is a limited partner. The amount of the loss includes $5,000 of partnership interest expense. Since his share of the partnership loss, which includes the interest expense, is subject to the limitation on passive-activity losses, the interest element will *not* be subject to a second-level interest deduction limitation. However, the 65% of the loss that is deductible in 1987 under the phase-in rule is taken into account in computing 1987 net investment income for purposes of the interest deduction limitation.

Interest on Vacation Rental Property

Interest related to property that is used for rental purposes at least 15 days per year and is also used partly for personal purposes, such as a beach house or a condominium unit at a resort area, must first be allocated between rental use and personal use. The interest is allocated to rental use in the ratio of the number of days during the year that the property was rented at fair rental value to the total number of days the property was used during the year. The remaining interest is allocated to personal use.

If the property is a principal or second residence for purposes of the qualified residence interest exception, the personal use portion of the interest is deductible. Otherwise, the personal use portion would be nondeductible consumer interest.

The rental portion of the interest is deductible against rental income. However, if there is a net rental loss from the property the passive-activity rules (including the residential rental exception explained on page 50) apply.

Effective Date

The interest deduction limitations apply to interest paid or incurred in taxable years beginning after 1986, *regardless of when the obligation was incurred.* However, the limitation is phased in over a five-year period. For any taxable year beginning in calendar years 1987 through 1990 the portion of the interest disallowed is determined in accordance with the following table.

Taxable Year Beginning In	Percentage Disallowed
1987	35%
1988	60%
1989	80%
1990	90%

For *investment interest*, the amount disallowed under the phase-in rule is the amount that would have been disallowed under prior law plus the applicable percentage of the amount that would have been allowed under prior law taking into consideration the $10,000 allowance ($5,000 for a separate return).

Planning Points

- Beginning in 1987, the tax subsidy for consumer borrowing will gradually be eliminated. Careful management of consumer credit will become even more important since interest will no longer be fully deductible.

- Many financial institutions have begun to offer home equity lines of credit secured by a recorded lien against the borrower's residence. Home equity borrowing for educational or medical expenses will enable the borrower to deduct interest paid on the amount borrowed. No interest would be deductible on a loan for educational or medical purposes that is not secured by the borrower's principal or second residence. However, interest on a home equity loan for other purposes, such as a vacation or the purchase of an automobile, generally, is *not* deductible to the extent that the amount of the loan exceeds the cost of the home plus the cost of capital improvements.

  Prospective borrowers should compare the closing costs of a home equity loan to the potential tax savings of the interest deduction to determine whether the savings justify the cost. They should also be aware that the loan may have to be repaid in full if the residence is sold.

- The Act reverses some of the tax planning techniques used in seller-financed sales of property. Under prior law, *sellers* of property generally preferred to increase the sales price and lower the interest rate because gain on the sale was generally taxed at favorable capital-gain rates, while interest income was taxed as ordinary income. Conversely, *purchasers* frequently preferred lowering the price and increasing the interest rate because interest was fully deductible and the purchase price may have been nondepreciable, e.g., unimproved land or a personal residence. Now, with capital gains taxed at the same rates as ordinary income and with limitations on the deductibility of consumer interest and investment interest, the classic patterns will have to be reconsidered.

  For *business* real estate, it will frequently be advantageous for the purchaser to minimize the purchase price and to maximize the interest rate. This is primarily attributable to the Act's lengthening of the depreciation period of real estate from 19 years to 27½ years and 31½ years. Generally, the seller's tax consequences would be either neutral or favorable.

  Similarly, for seller-financed residential real estate, both purchaser and seller will generally obtain a tax advantage by minimizing the sales price and maximizing the interest rate. This will allow the seller to increase investment income against which otherwise nondeductible investment interest expense can be deducted, and the purchaser will have fully deductible interest provided the property qualifies as a principal or second residence.

  For investment property, the seller will be in the same tax position either way. Both interest income and capital gain on the sale of investment property are treated as investment income for purposes of the investment interest deduction limitation. However, a purchaser who has substantial investment income would generally be better off with a lower purchase price and higher interest since the investment interest expense could be deducted against the investment income from other sources.

- Maintaining records of business automobile use will be increasingly important to self-employed individuals. Not only will the records support the deduction of operating expenses for the business use of the automobile, they will also show the percentage of automobile interest expense that will be deductible as business interest.

- After 1986, a self-employed individual who has a choice of paying cash for either a business purchase or a consumer purchase and financing the other, generally should pay cash for the consumer purchase and finance the business purchase.

- Taxpayers who owe interest to the IRS for previous underpayments of tax should consider paying the interest before January 1, 1987, or they will lose the interest deduction (subject to the phase-in rule).

- Prepayment in 1986 of one or more 1987 installments on nonresidential consumer loans will preserve (and accelerate) the full interest deduction.

- Even though interest on a principal residence remains fully deductible, taxpayers planning to purchase or refinance a residence should still investigate the substantial interest-saving advantage of a 15-year mortgage over a 30-year mortgage.

- A taxpayer who is planning to purchase a new home that is likely to be sold within a few years should investigate having appliances and options, e.g., deck, fencing, landscaping, installed by the builder and included in the sales price. Interest on all of these items would then qualify as fully deductible residential interest. If they are separately acquired with financing that is not secured by the residence, the interest will be treated as nondeductible consumer financing (subject to the phase-in rule).

- When refinancing a residence, remember that interest is only fully deductible on the portion of the loan that equals the sum of:
  — The original purchase price
  — The cost of any improvements
  — Any amount incurred for educational or medical purposes, up to the FMV of the residence.

This limitation reinforces the importance of maintaining records of the costs of improvements to the property, which also affect the amount of gain on the sale.

- The interest deduction limitation affects the use of interest-free and other below-market rate loans. An individual borrower's imputed interest deduction will no longer fully offset the imputed interest income. Taxpayers who are either borrowers or lenders under employment-related or gift-type interest-free loans should review the arrangement to determine whether any modifications are advisable.

- A taxpayer with otherwise nondeductible investment interest expense should consider recognizing a capital gain by selling property held for investment. No tax will be due on the gain to the extent that it is offset by the investment interest expense.

Itemized Deductions

Charitable Contributions
Charitable contributions remain fully deductible for taxpayers who itemize their deductions. The Act eliminates the charitable deduction for nonitemizers.

Under the Act, if travel expenses incurred in performing services away from home for a charitable organization involve a significant element of personal pleasure, recreation or vacation, a charitable deduction is denied.

Effective Date
These changes are effective for taxable years beginning after December 31, 1986.

Sales Tax Deduction
Under the Act, individuals will no longer be able to deduct state and local sales taxes that are not incurred in a trade or business.

Sales taxes incurred on the acquisition or disposition of property will be treated as part of the cost of the acquired property or as a reduction in the amount realized on the disposition.

Effective Date
The changes are effective for sales taxes incurred after December 31, 1986.

Medical Expense Deduction
Under prior law, individuals who itemized deductions could deduct amounts paid for medical care during the taxable year to the extent the total expenses exceed 5% of adjusted gross income.

The Act increases the 5% floor to 7.5% effective for taxable years beginning after December 31, 1986.

In addition, the Conference Committee report directs the IRS to allow expenses incurred by physically handicapped individuals for removal of structural barriers in their residences to accommodate their handicapped condition to be treated as medical expenses.

Adoption Expenses
The Act repeals the deduction currently allowed to individuals who legally adopt a child with special needs. The change is effective for expenses incurred after December 31, 1986. An exception is provided for expenses paid in 1987 for an adoption for which the taxpayer paid deductible expenses during 1986. The Act also amends the Social Security law to provide assistance for these adoption expenses.

Ministers and Military Personnel: Mortgage Interest and Taxes
Under prior law, it is the IRS's position that ministers who receive a nontaxable rental allowance cannot deduct mortgage interest and real estate taxes on their residences to the extent that the expenses are allocable to the tax-free allowance. The IRS has been considering a similar policy for military personnel who receive tax-free housing allowances.

The Act makes mortgage interest and real estate taxes on the home of a taxpayer deductible even if the taxpayer receives a tax-free housing or parsonage allowance. The change is effective for all years not closed by the statute of limitations.

Planning Point
All taxpayers who have received tax free housing or parsonage allowances should consider filing an amended return or refund claim for any open years.

Miscellaneous Deductions

Limitation on Employee Business Expenses

Under prior law, certain types of employee business expenses were deductible whether or not the employee itemized deductions. The employee business expenses deductible by nonitemizers were:

- Expenses reimbursed by the employer.
- Travel expenses incurred while away from home.
- Transportation expenses incurred while on business.
- Business expenses of outside salespersons.

Other types of employee business expenses were deductible only as itemized deductions.

The Act allows nonitemizers to deduct those expenses they pay that are reimbursed by their employers. All other employee business expenses will be deductible only as miscellaneous itemized deductions. See below for a discussion of the limits the Act places on the deductibility of miscellaneous itemized deductions.

Effective Date

Applicable for expenses incurred in taxable years beginning after December 31, 1986.

Other Miscellaneous Itemized Deductions

In addition to reclassifying almost all employee business expenses as miscellaneous itemized deductions, the Act limits their deductibility as well as that of certain other miscellaneous expenses. The following miscellaneous expenses will continue to be deductible in full:

- Moving expenses.
- Impairment related work expenses for handicapped employees.
- Estate tax related to income in respect of a decedent.
- The adjustment required when a taxpayer restores amounts held under claim of right.
- Amortization of bond premium.
- Certain costs of cooperative housing corporations.
- Short sale expenses in the nature of interest.
- Certain terminated annuity payments.
- Gambling losses to the extent of gambling winnings.

All other miscellaneous deductions (including employee business expenses) will continue to be deductible only to the extent that they exceed 2% of adjusted gross income. The floor is to apply to indirect deductions from pass-through entities—including mutual funds—other than estates, trusts, cooperatives and Real Estate Investment Trusts (REITS).

Effective Date

The changes are effective for taxable years beginning after December 31, 1986.

Alternative Minimum Tax (AMT)

Under prior law, individuals were subject to an alternative minimum tax (AMT) that was payable, in addition to all other tax liabilities, to the extent that it exceeded the individual's regular tax. The tax was imposed at a flat rate of 20% on alternative minimum taxable income in excess of an exemption amount. The resulting tax was reduced by foreign tax credits.

Alternative minimum taxable income (AMTI) was generally equal to adjusted gross income, as increased by certain tax preferences and decreased by the alternative tax itemized deductions. The exemption amount, which was subtracted from AMTI before applying the 20% rate, was $40,000 for joint returns, $20,000 for married individuals filing separately, and $30,000 for single returns.

Some of the more common items of tax preference included:

- Dividends excluded from gross income
- The excess of accelerated depreciation over straight-line depreciation on real property and leased personal property
- The excess of percentage depletion over the adjusted basis of property
- The portion, i.e., 60%, of net capital gain deducted from gross income
- The excess of deducted intangible drilling costs (IDCs) over the amount of net oil and gas income

AMTI deductions included:

- Casualty or theft losses, and gambling losses not in excess of gambling gains
- Charitable deductions
- Medical expenses in excess of 10% of adjusted gross income
- Qualified interest expenses
- Deductions for estate taxes

Under the Act, the individual AMT is retained with structural modifications that include:

- A flat 21% tax rate.
- Retention of exemption amounts for individuals. However, the exemption amounts are reduced by 25 cents for each dollar of alternative minimum taxable income that exceeds $150,000 for married taxpayers filing jointly ($112,500 for single taxpayers and $75,000 for married taxpayers filing separately).

The adjustments and preferences under the Act include:

- Accelerated depreciation is a preference item for individuals. For *personal* property placed in service after December 31, 1986, the amount of the preference is the excess of regular ACRS depreciation over the depreciation calculated using the 150% declining-balance method and the appropriate ADR period (see page 33). For *real* property, the excess of regular ACRS depreciation over depreciation calculated using the straight-line method over 40 years is a preference item.
- Regular ACRS depreciation on property placed in service before 1987 continues to be a preference item to the extent that it constituted a preference under prior law.
- The excess of IDCs over 65% of the income from oil, gas, and geothermal properties is treated as a preference. Excess IDCs are the excess of

regularly deducted IDCs over the amount that would have been deducted on a 10-year straight-line basis.

- Mining exploration and development costs that are expensed for regular tax purposes are required to be recovered through 10-year, straight-line amortization for AMT purposes.
- Except for bonds issued on behalf of Code section 501(c)(3) charitable organizations, interest on most private purpose tax-exempt bonds issued on or after August 8, 1986 is treated as a preference.
- As under prior law, the excess of the fair market value of stock acquired through an incentive stock option (ISO) over the exercise price is treated as a preference. However, for AMT purposes, the stock acquired through the exercise of an ISO after 1986 equals the fair market value taken into account in determining the amount of the preference.
- As under prior law, the excess of percentage depletion over the adjusted basis of the property is a preference.
- In computing AMTI, there is a limitation on the ability to offset losses from passive business activities against other income. The rule is identical to the new rule in the Act for regular tax purposes which is phased in over five years (see page 46) except it is fully effective in 1987 for minimum tax purposes. Thus, the amount of the passive-activity loss deducted for regular tax purposes is treated as a preference. The loss subject to the limitation is reduced by the amount, if any, of the taxpayer's insolvency.
- The amount of any passive loss that is subject to the limitation is determined after computing all preferences and making all other adjustments to income that apply for minimum tax purposes.
- An individual's passive loss from farming is not allowed as a deduction in computing AMTI. The loss is reduced by the amount, if any, of the taxpayer's insolvency—subject to the limitation.
- The untaxed appreciation on charitable contributions of appreciated capital-gain property is a preference. The preference does not apply to carryovers of the deduction for charitable contributions made before August 16, 1986.
- Net operating losses and foreign tax credits cannot offset more than 90% of the minimum tax liability, but can be carried over to subsequent taxable years.
- Because of the elimination of the capital-gain exclusion (see page 10), there is no longer a capital-gain preference.
- For long-term contracts entered into after March 1, 1986, any items related to a contract that were computed under the completed- contract method of accounting for regular tax purposes must be recomputed under the percentage of completion method and included in AMTI as recomputed.
- With certain exceptions, all gains subject to the proportionate disallowance rule, i.e., dealer sales and sales of trade or business or rental property when the purchase price exceeds $150,000, after March 1, 1986, are treated as a preference by not permitting the use of the installment method for the AMT.
- Post-1986 circulation or research and experimentation expenses are not deductible expenditures for minimum tax purposes. Instead, in computing

AMTI, the individual is required to amortize the expenditures ratably over a three-year (circulation expenses) or ten-year (research expenses) period.

Planning Point

To avoid preference treatment for research and experimentation expenditures, IDCs, circulation expenditures, and mining exploration and development expenses, taxpayers should consider electing to spread the deduction over longer periods for regular tax purposes.

AMT Itemized Deductions

In general, AMT itemized deductions are the same as under prior law. However, in determining qualified interest expenses, interest related to limited business interests is included in the calculation of qualified investment income and qualified investment expenses. Disallowed investment interest deductions can be carried over. A minimum tax itemized deduction is not allowed for consumer interest.

Minimum Tax Credit

The amount of the AMT net of exclusion preferences, e.g., the percentage depletion preference, paid after 1986 is allowed as a credit against regular tax liability in future years. This credit can be carried forward indefinitely. However, the minimum tax credit cannot be used to reduce minimum tax liability in subsequent years.

Effective Date

Generally, these provisions apply to taxable years beginning after December 31, 1986.

Planning Point

Because deductions for losses from passive business investments will be limited for AMT purposes starting January 1, 1987, taxpayers should consider accelerating these losses into 1986. Additionally, because regular tax depreciation on property placed in service before 1987 is treated as a preference only to the extent it constitutes a preference under prior law, consideration should be given to investing in depreciable property in 1986.

Income Taxation of Estates and Trusts

Compressed Rate Schedule

Under prior law, estates and trusts paid tax on their accumulated income at the same rates as a married individual filing a separate return. For taxable years beginning after December 31, 1986, a trust's accumulated income will be taxed on a new compressed rate schedule. The first $5,000 of taxable income will be taxed at 15% with the excess taxed at 28%. The benefit of the 15% bracket will be phased out between $13,000 and $26,000 of taxable income.

Comment

The new compressed tax rates will have a greater impact on trusts than on estates, since the latter either do not accumulate income or are wound up relatively quickly. It will, however, have a profound effect on taxpayers' use of accumulation trusts to shift the income tax burden on investment income into lower brackets, while benefitting family members.

The compressed rate schedule could make the use of separately taxed multiple trusts less attractive for larger trusts because the net saving of $650 (28% less 15% = 13% × $5,000) starts to disappear when the trust's income exceeds $13,000.

Planning Points

Depending on the size of the estate, it may be more advantageous to deduct estate administrative expenses on the estate tax return than on the estate's income tax return.

Grantor Trusts

Under prior law, trusts created with a term of more than 10 years—the so-called Clifford trusts—allowed a grantor to shift the tax burden generated by the trust corpus to the trust or the income beneficiary while regaining the property when the trust term ended. This made the Clifford trust a popular financial planning tool for purposes such as creating an education fund for a minor child.

Under the Act, any transfer in trust after March 1, 1986, in which the grantor retains (or gives a spouse living with the grantor at the time of the gift) a power or a reversionary interest of more than 5% of the value of the transferred property will be taxed to the grantor. This effectively does away with the income shifting benefits of the Clifford trust. There is an exception for a reversion following the death of a lineal descendant of the grantor.

Planning Points

- Although the planning opportunities of the use of grantor trusts have been severely restricted, they can still prove effective in providing care and financial independence for a chronically ill family member.
- Consider having a family member other than the grantor or spouse receive the trust corpus at the end of the term.
- Consider using a charitable remainder trust as an alternative.

Example: Grandpa Magnate's widowed daughter Amy Jo's daughter Jo Jo is entering medical school. Amy Jo , who has been living on a modest income since her ne'er do well husband died, does not personally have sufficient income or capital to see Jo Jo through her medical school program. To solve this problem, and as part of his new estate plan, Grandpa Magnate creates a $300,000 trust with a five-year term providing that the income is to be paid to cover the cost of Jo Jo's schooling. At the end of the trust's term, the corpus will go to Amy Jo to make her financially independent. In addition, to solving a family financial problem, Grandpa Magnate has shifted the income tax burden to Jo Jo during her school years and then to Amy Jo.

Taxable Years

For taxable years beginning after December 31, 1986, all trusts must adopt the calendar year. To ease any potential income bunching, beneficiaries can spread the income resulting from any short period over four years beginning in 1987.

Planning Points

- Complex Trusts—Complex trusts should consider delaying any distributions until the short taxable year beginning in 1987, to allow the beneficiary the opportunity of the four-year spread forward. Also, consideration should be given to increasing the income of the beneficiary during the short year through the use of the "65-day" rule.

- Simple Trusts—Consideration should be given to shifting income from the current trust year into the short 1987 taxable year. In addition, trustees should also consider shifting income to 1988 from 1987 to avoid bunching too much income into 1987 with its short taxable year and higher tax rates. Additional savings might be possible by paying expenses prior to the short year's end or deferring trust expenses until 1988 to increase the amount of the spread forward.

Estimated Tax Payments

For taxable years beginning after December 31, 1986, all trusts, and those estates that are in existence for more than two years, must pay estimated taxes in the same manner as individuals. This new rule applies to existing estates that are open for more than two years on the effective date. In addition, estates will no longer be able to pay tax in four equal installments after the estate's year end.

Planning Points

- Care must be taken to ensure that adequate estimates are made to avoid the imposition of the under-estimation penalty.
- Fiduciaries should ensure that their trusts or estates have sufficient liquidity to meet the new estimated tax requirements. This is especially important because the penalty for underpayment will increase for amounts assessed after December 31, 1986.
- Because estates will not have to pay estimated taxes during their first two years, consideration should be given to avoiding a short first year. This would, if the estate is wound up within two years, avoid the necessity of paying any estimated taxes.

Generation Skipping Transfer Tax (GST)

The Act repeals retroactively to June 11, 1976, the current law generation skipping transfer tax (GST). A new GST, applicable to transfers after the date of enactment, will be imposed on terminations, distributions and direct transfers to persons more than one generation below that of the grantor who have an interest in a trust or similar arrangement.

A general exclusion of $1 million would be allowed each transferor, and an additional exclusion of $2 million per grandchild would be allowed to grandparents (the grandparental exclusion would end for transfers subject to the GST on or after January 1, 1990). Transfers subject to the GST would be taxable at the maximum federal estate tax rate of 55% (50% for 1988 and later years). In addition, there would be a credit for state taxes of up to 5% of the GST.

Planning point

With the retroactive repeal of the old GST, any payments of tax previously made are available for credit or refund. Under the Act, claims for refund can be filed within one year of the date of enactment. Taxpayers who paid the old GST should not hesitate before filing for their refund.

Effective Date

The GST applies to transfers made after the date of enactment. Inter-vivos transfers made after September 25, 1985, are to be treated as if they were made after the date of enactment. Irrevocable trusts in existence on September 25, 1985, benefit from several special transition rules:

- Transfers to a qualifying trust are exempted from GST to the extent the transfer was not made from the corpus of the trust added after that date.
- Transfers to or reinvestments in a qualified trust are exempt to the extent the trust consists of property included in the decedent's gross estate (other than inter-vivos property transfers by the decedent after the date of enactment).
- Transfers that result from the death of the decedent are exempt provided the decedent was incompetent on the date of enactment and at all times thereafter.

Losses on Deposits in Insolvent Financial Institutions

For taxable years beginning after December 31, 1982, the Act provides that qualified individuals can elect to deduct losses on deposits in any commercial bank, thrift institution, insured credit union, or similar institution chartered and supervised under Federal or state law, as casualty losses (subject to the casualty loss rules) in the year in which the amount of the loss could have been reasonably estimated. A qualified individual is any individual other than an owner of 1% or more of the value of the stock of the institution sustaining the loss, an officer of the institution, and certain relatives and related persons of these owners and officers.

Additionally, accrued but unpaid interest on a deposit in a financial institution for a taxable year beginning before 1987 is not includible in the depositor's taxable income for that taxable year if the interest is not subject to withdrawal at the end of that taxable year. This interest income is includible in gross income in the taxable year in which it is withdrawable.

Planning Point

Because both of these provisions possibly make prior law more favorable for affected taxpayers, all affected taxpayers should, in the near future, investigate the possibility of taking advantage of the changes to obtain refunds.

Prizes and Awards

Generally under prior law, prizes and awards were considered taxable income. Under certain circumstances, a special exclusion was provided for prizes and awards received for achievements in fields such as charity, the sciences and the arts. Under other circumstances, an exclusion was provided for an award of tangible personal property to an employee for length of service, safety achievement or productivity.

Under the Act, prizes and awards received for achievements in fields such as charity, the sciences and the arts are fully taxable unless the recipient designates that the prize or award is to be transferred by the payer to a government unit or a tax-exempt charitable, educational or religious organization. No charitable deduction is allowed for the transferred amount.

Subject to certain dollar limitations, the Act allows an employee to exclude the value of specified employee achievement awards from gross income. To qualify, the award must be in the form of tangible personal property—cash does not qualify. The award must be made by an employer to an employee for length of service or safety achievement. It must be given during a meaningful presentation ceremony and under conditions and circumstances that do not create a significant likelihood of the payment of disguised compensation. Any amount of an employee award that is excluded from gross income for income tax purposes is also excluded from wages or compensation for employment tax, e.g., FICA, purposes.

Effective Date
Applies to prizes and awards received after December 31, 1986.

Scholarships and Fellowships

Under prior law, degree candidates at a college or university could exclude from taxable income the total amount received as a scholarship or fellowship grant. Nondegree students could exclude a maximum of $3,600 per year for three years.

The Act limits the amount excludable by a degree candidate to the amount of the scholarship or fellowship that is used for tuition, fees, books, supplies and equipment. Amounts in excess of these qualified expenses are included in taxable income. Nondegree students may not exclude from taxable income any part of a scholarship or fellowship grant.

Under the Act, amounts received for performing services, such as teaching or research, are not excludable under any circumstances.

Effective Date
Applies to scholarships and fellowship grants awarded after August 16, 1986. Amounts received after August 16, 1986, under a scholarship or fellowship that was awarded on or before that date are not affected by the changes.

Business Use of Home

Under prior law, the business use of a taxpayer's home could have given rise to a deduction for the business portion of the expenses related to operating the home, e.g., rent, utilities, insurance, repairs and depreciation. However, deductions were allowed only for the part of the home used exclusively and regularly either as the taxpayer's principal place of business or as a place of business to meet patients, clients or customers. A separate structure used for business purposes would also qualify. For employees, a further requirement for a deduction was that the business use of a home must be for the employers' convenience.

However, in a 1985 decision, the Tax Court held that these rules did not apply when an employee had leased a portion of his home to his employer. The Court stated that the taxpayer did not have to meet any of the above rules to deduct a portion of his home operating expenses.

In response to this ruling, the Act provides that no home office deduction is allowable for the business use of a portion of the taxpayer's home solely because the employee leases a part of a home to an employer.

Under prior law, IRS regulations defined gross income derived from the business use of the home as total income less the expenditures required to operate the business other than those associated with operating the home. This definition of gross income made it impossible to create or increase an operating loss with the business portion of home operating expenses. However, a 1985 Tax Court decision disagreed with the IRS's definition and said it is possible for home operating expenses to create or increase an operating loss that could be used to offset income from other sources.

In response to this ruling, the Act adopts the IRS's definition of gross income. Thus, the business portion of home operating expenses (other than expenses that are deductible without regard to business use) are deductible only to the extent they do not exceed the gross income of the business reduced by all other deductible expenses attributable to the activity. The home office expenses that are disallowed due to the income limit can be carried forward and deducted in future years subject to the same income limit rules.

Effective Date
The changes in the deductibility of home office expenses are effective for taxable years beginning after December 31, 1986.

Hobby Losses
A facts and circumstances test is generally used to determine whether a particular activity is actually a business being pursued for profit or is recreationally motivated. If the activity is recreationally motivated, it is a hobby and expenses incurred are deductible only to the extent of income produced by the activity. To avoid the uncertainty of the facts and circumstances test, the law presumes the activity to be a business if it is profitable for any two out of five consecutive years, or if the activity consists of breeding, training, showing or racing horses, two out of seven consecutive years.

The Act changes the test so that if an activity is profitable in any three out of five consecutive years, it is presumed to be a business rather than a hobby. The Act does not change the test for horse related activities.

Effective Date
The change is effective for taxable years beginning after December 31, 1986.

Miscellaneous Deductions

Moving Expenses
Under the Act, only taxpayers who itemize their deductions will be able to deduct moving expenses incurred after December 31, 1986.

Political Contributions
The Act repeals the political contributions tax credit beginning in 1987.

Two-Earner Deduction
The two-earner deduction for working married couples is repealed for tax years after 1986. The adjustments made in the relationship of the standard deduction and rate structure for unmarried individuals and married couples filing joint returns is intended to compensate for the repeal.

Income Averaging
Under the Act, income averaging is repealed for tax years after 1986.

Earned Income Credit
Beginning in calendar year 1988, the Act increases the earned income credit from 11% to 14% of the first $5,714 of earned income. The credit begins to phase out at income levels in excess of $9,000 and is fully phased out for an individual with adjusted gross income or earned income over $17,000.

Unemployment Compensation Benefits
Prior law provided a limited exclusion from income for unemployment compensation benefits paid by a Federal or State program. Under the Act, all unemployment compensation benefits received after December 31, 1986, are taxable.

Provisions Affecting Business and Investments

Reduction in Corporate Tax Rates

The Act lowers the tax rate on a corporation's taxable income from a maximum of 46% to a maximum of 34%. The rate reduction is effective for taxable years beginning on or after July 1, 1987. For taxable years including July 1, 1987, blended rates will apply. The new corporate rate structure for calendar year corporations will be:

Taxable Income	1986	1987	1988
First $25,000	15%	15%	15%
$25,001 - $ 50,000	18%	16½%	15%
$50,001 - $ 75,000	30%	27½%	25%
$75,001 - $100,000	40%	37%	34%
Over $100,000	46%	40%	34%

The Act generally phases out the benefit ($11,250) of the graduated rates on corporations with taxable income over $100,000. The phase out imposes an additional 5% tax on a corporation's taxable income between $100,000 and $335,000 resulting in a marginal income tax rate of 39% in the phaseout range.

Planning Points

Defer income and accelerate deductions to the extent feasible to maximize the benefits of the two-step rate reduction in 1987 and 1988.

Shareholders of closely-held regular corporations (C corporations) should consider electing S corporation status to take advantage of the fact that the individual tax rates are now lower than the corporate tax rates. While S corporations have always presented tax advantages in specific situations, the new rate structure makes S corporations an interesting option for many more closely-held corporations.

Corporate Capital Gain

Under prior law, a corporation's net capital gain was taxed at an alternative rate of 28% if the tax computed using that rate was lower than the corporation's regular tax. Additionally, corporate capital loss was deductible only against corporate capital gain.

Under the Act, the alternative tax rate for the net capital gain of a corporation does not apply to gain included in income in taxable years beginning on or after July 1, 1987. Rather, the capital-gain rate is the same as the highest corporate rate. For gain included in income in earlier taxable years, but after December 31, 1986, the alternative capital gain tax rate is 34%.

Effective Date

Applies to gain properly taken into account under the taxpayer's method of accounting on or after January 1, 1987, without any binding contract exception.

Incentive Stock Options

An employee is not taxed on the grant or exercise of an incentive stock option (ISO) but is generally taxed at capital-gain rates when the stock received on the exercise of the option is sold. Under prior law, to qualify as an ISO, among other requirements, the options must have been exercisable in the order granted and employers could not grant an employee options to acquire stock with a value of more than $100,000 in any one year.

The Act repeals the requirement that the options must be exercised in the order granted. The Act also changes the $100,000 limit on the amount of options that may be granted in any one year to provide that the aggregate fair market value (determined at the time the options are granted) of the stock with respect to which ISOs are exercisable during any taxable year may not exceed $100,000.

Effective Date
Applies to ISOs granted after December 31, 1986.

Tax Straddles
Under the Act, the qualified covered call exception to the loss deferral rule in the straddle provisions is denied to a taxpayer who fails to hold a covered call option for 30 days after the related stock is disposed of at a loss, when gain on the termination or other disposition of the option is included in the subsequent year. The mark-to-market rules of prior law are retained.

The Act amends section 108 of the Tax Reform Act of 1984 to deny taxpayers other than dealers the presumption that they had an economic motivation for entering into straddles prior to the effective date of the straddle provisions of the Economic Recovery Tax Act of 1981.

Effective Date
These provisions apply to positions established after December 31, 1986.

Limitation on Deduction for Meals and Entertainment
Under the Act, the amount of an otherwise allowable deduction for business meals or entertainment must be reduced by 20%. This arbitrary disallowance is intended to approximate the element of personal living expenses that Congress determined is present in all such expenses. The percentage reduction rule applies to all food, beverage and entertainment costs even those incurred in the course of travel away from home; it is applied only after determining the amount otherwise deductible under the various other rules that limit these deductions.

There are seven exceptions to the percentage reduction rule. They are:
1. The full value of the meal or entertainment is included in the recipient's taxable income or is excludable under the fringe benefit rules.
2. If an employee is reimbursed for the cost of a meal or entertainment, the percentage reduction rule applies only to the party making the reimbursement.
3. Traditional employer paid employee recreation expenses, e.g., a company Christmas party.
4. The cost of samples and other promotional activities that are made available to the general public.
5. Expenses for attending a sports event if it qualifies as a charitable fund raising event.
6. The cost of providing meals or entertainment that the taxpayer sells for an adequate and full consideration.

7. During calendar years 1987 and 1988, the cost of a meal that is provided as an integral part of a qualified banquet meeting.

Additional Restrictions on Deductible Meals

Under prior law, if the meal or drinks took place in an atmosphere conducive to a business discussion, expenses for food and beverage were deductible without regard to the *directly-related* or *associated-with* tests that were generally applicable to entertainment expenses. There was no requirement that business actually be discussed either before, during or after the meal.

Under the Act, expenses for meals and drinks will be subject to the same directly-related or associated-with tests that are currently applicable to entertainment expenses. Therefore, for the cost of a meal to be deductible there must be substantial and bona fide business discussions directly preceding, during or directly following the meal. The business discussion requirement cannot be met if the taxpayer or an employee of the taxpayer is not present at the meal. An individual who is away from home on business and who eats alone will not lose the deduction because there is no related business discussion.

Although the Act disallows any deduction for *lavish or extravagant* business meals, it does not define lavish or extravagant.

In addition to these changes, the Conference Committee instructed the Treasury Department to adopt new regulations providing for stricter substantiation requirements for business-meal deductions. The Conference Committee also emphasized that courts may not approximate the amount of a business meal or entertainment expense under the *Cohan* rule.

Need for Substantiation

Under the Act, if business meals or entertainment expenses are claimed on a return and the taxpayer cannot meet the substantiation requirements or fails any of the tests discussed above, negligence or fraud penalties could apply. If the erroneous deduction was caused by a disregard of the law and regulations, the negligence penalty will apply.

Deduction For Tickets

Under the Act, a deduction for the cost of a ticket to any entertainment activity is limited (prior to the application of the 20% reduction rule) to the face value of the ticket. Under this rule, any amount above the face value paid to a scalper or a ticket agent would be completely nondeductible. The only exception to this rule is for tickets to charitable fund raising events, which are exempt from the 20% reduction rule.

Deduction for Educational Travel

Under the Act, no deduction is allowed for travel as a form of education. This rule applies when a travel expense would otherwise be deductible only on the ground that the travel itself serves educational purposes.

Expenses for Nonbusiness Conventions

Under the Act, no deduction is allowed for any expense related to attending an investment seminar, convention or similar meeting. For these expenses to be deductible, they must be ordinary and necessary expenses of carrying on a trade or business.

Skybox Rental

The Act limits the deduction for leasing luxury boxes (skyboxes) at sports arenas for more than one event. The limitation is 80% of the cost of non-luxury box-seat tickets times the number of seats in the skybox. The disallowance is phased in over three years.

Luxury Water Travel

The Act places limitations on the amount that can be deducted for business travel by ocean liner, cruise ship or other form of luxury water transportation. The deduction for each day of sea transportation cannot exceed twice the highest amount of per diem payable to an executive branch federal employee traveling in the continental United States. For example, if the maximum federal per diem rate is $75 per day, the maximum deduction for a six day business trip on an ocean liner would be $900 ($75 x 2 x 6).

The new per diem rule only applies to business travel. Expenses incurred for business conventions, seminars or other meetings held on board a cruise ship are subject to the same rules as under prior law, which either wholly denies the deductions or limits them to no more than $2,000 per the individual attending.

Under the Act, the statutory exceptions to the business-meal percentage reduction rule also apply to the per diem rule for luxury water travel.

Effective Date

All of the provisions dealing with the deductibility of business meals entertainment and travel are effective for taxable years beginning after 1986.

Capital Cost Recovery

Accelerated Cost Recovery System (ACRS)

General

Prior to 1981, property used in a trade or business or held for the production of income was depreciated over its useful life. For property placed in service after 1980, the Tax Reform Act of 1981 introduced the Accelerated Cost Recovery System (ACRS), which generally permitted property to be depreciated at accelerated rates over periods much shorter than its useful life. ACRS also eliminated the concept of nondepreciable salvage value.

The Act modifies ACRS by significantly lengthening the depreciation periods for real property placed in service after 1986. It also lengthens the depreciation period for certain types of long-life equipment. However, for many types of personal property it provides faster depreciation by increasing the depreciation rate from 150% declining balance to 200% declining balance over the same depreciation period. Congress intended the rate increase to partially offset the effect of the repeal of investment tax credit (explained below). Generally, the changes only affect property placed in service after 1986.

One complicating feature of the new ACRS rules is that the ACRS depreciation class of property is generally determined by reference to its Asset Depreciation Range (ADR) guideline class. ADR is an involved system that was in use between 1970 and 1981 primarily by larger corporate taxpayers. As a result, many taxpayers are completely unfamiliar with it.

Under ADR, depreciable assets were grouped in broad classes by type of industry. Depreciation lives (upper limit, midpoint, and lower limit) were prescribed for each class. (See IRS Revenue Procedure 83-35, 1983-1 C.B. 745, for the most current ADR guideline class listing.) To understand the operation of the new ACRS depreciation classes, it will be necessary for taxpayers to become familiar with the ADR class life tables.

The new rules no longer provide a statutory table listing the annual depreciation percentages. Instead, taxpayers must determine the annual percentages themselves based on the applicable property class, depreciation method, and averaging convention.

Classification of Assets, Recovery Methods and Periods

In place of the prior 3-year, 5-year, 10-year and 15-year recovery classes for personal property and the 18-year and 19-year classes for real property, the Act classifies property as follows:

Class	Method	Property Included in Class
3-year	200% declining balance switching to straight line.	Generally, all property with ADR midpoints of four years or less. However, automobiles and light trucks are excluded and horses that were included in the pre-1987 3-year class are included.
5-year	200% declining balance switching to straight line.	Property with ADR midpoints of more than four years and less than 10 years. Automobiles, light trucks, qualified technological equipment, computer-based central office switching equipment, certain renewable energy and biomass property, and R&D property are included.
7-year	200% declining balance switching to straight line.	Property with ADR midpoints of 10 years or more and less than 16 years. Single-purpose agricultural and horticultural structures and property without an ADR midpoint that is not classified elsewhere are included.
10-year	200% declining balance switching to straight line.	Property with ADR midpoints of 16 years or more and less than 20 years.

Class	Method	Property Included in Class
15-year	150% declining balance switching to straight line.	Property with ADR midpoints of 20 years or more and less than 25 years. Sewage and waste-water treatment plants, telephone distribution plants and comparable equipment used for two-way voice and data communications are included.
20-year	150% declining balance switching to straight line.	Property with ADR midpoints of 25 years or more, other than real property with an ADR midpoint 27½ years or more, and including sewer pipes.
27½-yr.	Straight line.	Residential rental property.
31½-yr.	Straight line.	Nonresidential real property.

Taxpayers have the option of electing to use the straight-line depreciation method for 3-year through 20-year property over the ACRS class life.

Planning Point

A taxpayer currently constructing or negotiating the purchase of a building for business or rental use should make every effort to place it in service before the end of 1986. By doing so, the taxpayer will obtain a 19-year depreciation period, rather than a 27 1/2 or 31 1/2-year period. In addition, the new at-risk rules will not apply to real property acquired before 1987.

Averaging Conventions

The Act does not significantly change any of the prior law rules (known as *averaging conventions*) for computing depreciation for the taxable year in which property is placed in service or disposed of.

- Half-Year Convention: Personal property is treated as being placed in service or disposed of at the midpoint of the taxable year. Accordingly, a half-year of depreciation generally is allowed for the taxable year in which property is placed in service or disposed of. This is a change from prior law, under which no depreciation was allowed for personal property in the year of disposition. However, no depreciation is allowed for personal property disposed of in the same taxable year in which it was placed in service.
- Mid-Month Convention: Real property is treated as being placed in service or disposed of in the middle of the month. Accordingly, a half-month of depreciation is allowed for the month disposed of or placed in service.
- Short Taxable Years: For any taxable year of less than 12 months, the ACRS deduction for personal property must be prorated.
- Special Rule for Substantial Property Placed in Service During Last Three Months of Taxable Year: If more than 40% of the aggregate amount of all real and personal property placed in service during the taxable year is

Example (1): Ms. Grey, a self-employed realtor in the highest tax bracket, purchases a $15,000 automobile that will be used 100% for business. Her after-tax cost under the Act would be approximately $10,049, as compared to approximately $6,994 under prior law.

		Prior Law			The Act	
Year	ITC	ACRS	Tax Savings at 50% Tax Rate	ITC	ACRS	Tax Savings at 33% Tax Rate
1	$675*	$ 3,200	$2,275	-0-	$ 2,560	$ 845
2		4,800	2,400		4,100	1,353
3		4,800	2,400		2,450	809
4		1,862	931		1,475	487
5		-0-	-0-		1,475	487
6		-0-	-0-		1,475	487
7		-0-	-0-		1,465	483
Totals		$14,662**	$8,006		$15,000	$4,951

Example (2): Acme Corp., which is taxed at the highest corporate tax rate, purchases a $15,000 automobile that a non-shareholder salesperson will use 100% for business. Its after-tax cost under the Act would be approximately $9,899, as compared to approximately $7,580 under prior law.

		Prior Law			The Act	
Year	ITC	ACRS	Tax Savings at 46% Tax Rate	ITC	ACRS	Tax Savings at 34% Tax Rate
1	$675*	$ 3,200	$2,147	-0-	$ 2,560	$ 870
2		4,800	2,208		4,100	1,394
3		4,800	2,208		2,450	833
4		1,862	857		1,475	502
5		-0-	-0-		1,475	502
6		-0-	-0-		1,475	502
7		-0-	-0-		1,465	498
Totals		$14,662**	$7,420		$15,000	$5,101

* ITC on automobiles is limited to $675
**Depreciable basis reduced by one-half of ITC

Election to Expense Property
Under prior law, a taxpayer could elect to expense, rather than depreciate, up to $5,000 per year of tangible personal property used in a trade or business. The Act makes several changes in the expensing rule for property placed in service after 1986:

- The maximum amount that may be expensed each year is increased to $10,000.
- The $10,000 maximum amount is reduced by the amount of property placed in service during the taxable year that exceeds $200,000.

- The amount that may be expensed is also limited to the amount of taxable income (determined without regard to the deduction for expensed property) derived from any trade or business.
- If property is converted to nonbusiness use *at any time*, the excess of the amount expensed over the ACRS deductions that would have been allowed must be recaptured as ordinary income in the year of conversion.

Comment

As under prior law, on the disposition of personal property, any gain is treated as ordinary income to the extent of previously-allowed depreciation deductions. As a practical matter, because capital gains and ordinary income are taxed at the same rates under the Act, the principal effect of the depreciation recapture rule is to reduce the amount of capital gain against which capital loss may be deducted.

Time for Making Elections

All elections relating to depreciation provisions must be made on the *first* tax return for the taxable year in which the property is placed in service. Once made, an election cannot be revoked without IRS permission.

Effective Date

The ACRS amendments generally apply to property placed in service after 1986. However, a taxpayer may also elect to have the provisions of the Act apply to property placed in service after July 31, 1986.

Transitional rules provide that the pre-1987 ACRS rules will apply to certain property placed in service *after 1986* that was:

- Constructed, reconstructed or acquired pursuant to a written contract that was binding on March 1, 1986, and at all times thereafter. For purposes of the transitional rule, a contract will be treated as binding only if:
    - It is enforceable under state law; and
    - Either does not limit damages for breach of contract, or limits them to an amount equal to at least 5% of the total contract price.
- Constructed or reconstructed by the taxpayer if:
    - The construction or reconstruction began by March 1, 1986; or
    - The lesser of $1 million or 5% of the cost of the property had been incurred or committed by that date.
- An equipped building or plant facility under construction as of March 1, 1986, pursuant to a written specific plan and more than one-half of the cost of the equipped building or facility has been incurred or committed by that date.

The ACRS transitional rules apply only to property with an ADR midpoint class life of at least seven years and to real property. In addition, the property must be placed in service no later than:

Property with ADR Class Life	Date
At least 7 years, but less than 20 years	January 1, 1989
20 years or more and real property	January 1, 1991

Special transitional rules apply to sale-leaseback property, property financed with tax-exempt bonds, qualified solid waste disposal facilities, and a number of specifically-listed projects.

The transitional rules apply even if a taxpayer who entered into a pre-March 1, 1986, binding contract later transfers that contract right to another taxpayer who takes delivery of the property and places it in service. The transferee succeeds to the transitional rule eligibility of the transferor as long as the property was not placed in service by the transferor before the transfer. This rule also applies to the ITC· transitional rule, explained below.

Planning Point

A taxpayer who places property that is *not* grandfathered under the ITC transitional rules in service after July 31, 1986, should consider electing to have the new ACRS rules apply if the property is in the same ACRS class under both the old and new rules. The advantage of an election would be the use of a 200% depreciation rate, rather than a 150% rate.

Finance Leasing Rules

Under prior law, certain leasing transactions that would not otherwise qualify as true leases for tax purposes are treated as leases. The Act repeals the prior law finance leasing rules.

Effective Date

The repeal applies to agreements entered into after 1986. However, property grandfathered under the transitional rules of 1982 and 1984 legislation affecting finance leases would also be grandfathered under the Act.

Repeal of the Regular Investment Tax Credit (ITC)

Under prior law, a taxpayer could claim an investment tax credit (ITC) for any tangible personal property purchased for use in a trade or business or for the production of income. The amount of the ITC was 6% of the basis of property in the 3-year ACRS depreciation class and 10% for all other tangible personal property. A special rule limited the amount of ITC allowable on used property.

The Act generally repeals the *regular* ITC for property placed in service after 1985. However, the ITC for energy property and for qualified rehabilitation expenditures for real property are *not* repealed.

Comment

The Act marks the third time since 1966 that Congress has repealed the ITC. The two previous times, in 1966 and 1969, it was reinstated within two years. If history repeats itself, we can expect to see heavy lobbying to bring back the ITC the next time the economy experiences a downturn.

Effective Date

The ITC repeal applies to property placed in service after December 31, 1985. However, transitional rules allow the ITC for property placed in service after 1985 that was:

- Constructed, reconstructed or acquired pursuant to a written contract that was binding on December 31, 1985, and at all times thereafter.

- Constructed or reconstructed by the taxpayer if:
  - The construction or reconstruction began by December 31, 1985; or
  - The lesser of $1 million or 5% of the cost of the property had been incurred or committed by that date.
- An equipped building or plant facility under construction on December 31, 1985, pursuant to a written specific plan and more than one-half of the costs of the equipped building or facility had been incurred or committed by that date.

The ITC transitional rules only apply to property placed in service no later than:

Property with ADR Midpoint	Date
Less than 5 years	July 1, 1986
At least 5, but less than 7 years	January 1, 1987
At least 7, but less than 20 years	January 1, 1989
20 years or more	January 1, 1991

Special transitional rules apply to sale-leaseback property, qualified solid waste disposal facilities, and a number of individually-listed projects.

Reduction of ITC Carryforwards and ITC Claimed under Transitional Rules

The full amount of the ITC on transitional-rule property may be claimed if the credit can be used in a taxable year that ends before July 1, 1987. However, any ITC for transitional-rule property must be reduced by 35% in any taxable year beginning after June 30, 1987. Similarly, any ITC carryover from a prior taxable year to a taxable year beginning after June 30, 1987, must also be reduced by 35%.

For any taxable year that straddles July 1, 1987, the 35% reduction is prorated in the ratio that the number of months in the taxable year after June 30, 1987, bears to the number of months in the taxable year.

Example: Service Co. has a fiscal year that will end September 30, 1987. Its ITC for transitional-rule property and ITC carryovers in its taxable year ending September 30, 1987, will be:

$$35\% \times 3/12 = 8.75\%$$

For calendar-year taxpayers, the reduction for 1987 is 17.5%.

Modification of ITC for Rehabilitation Expenditures

Prior law provided an investment tax credit for qualified expenditures to rehabilitate older buildings used in a trade or business.

Type of Building	Credit %
Nonresidential buildings at least 30 years old	15%
Nonresidential buildings at least 40 years old	20%
Residential and nonresidential certified historic structures	25%

To qualify under prior law, at least 75% of the existing external walls of the building had to be retained in place as external walls. An alternative test required that at least 75% of the external walls had to be retained in place as *either internal or external* walls, at least 50% of those walls had to be retained as external walls, and at least 75% of the building's *internal* structural framework had to be retained in place.

The Act replaces the prior credit structure with a new credit structure:

Type of Building	*Credit %*
Residential and nonresidential buildings placed in service before 1936, other than certified historic structures	10%
Residential and nonresidential certified historic structures	20%

The Act also requires that the depreciable basis of certified historic structures be reduced by the *full* amount of the credit claimed. Previously, basis had to be reduced for certified historic structures by only one-half of the credit.

In addition, the Act also eliminates the primary test of prior law: That at least 75% of the external walls of the building be retained as external walls. It adopts the prior law alternative test as the sole test for buildings other than certified historic structures. As a result, buildings in which the interior structure is gutted, but the exterior walls are retained, will *not* qualify for the rehabilitation credit. All exterior wall requirements are deleted for certified historic structures because all rehabilitations of certified historic structures are closely regulated by the U.S. Department of the Interior, which negates the need to satisfy the IRS of the project's historical integrity.

Effective Date

The amendments to the rehabilitation credit generally apply to property placed in service after 1986. However, transitional rules provide that the amendments will not apply to property placed in service after 1986 and before 1994 if the rehabilitation was:

- Pursuant to a written contract that was binding on March 1, 1986, or
- In connection with property (including a leasehold interest) acquired before March 2, 1986, or acquired on or after that date pursuant to a written contract that was binding on March 1, 1986, if:
  - The rehabilitation was pursuant to a written contract that was binding on March 1, 1986,
  - A Historic Preservation Certification Application was filed before March 2, 1986, or
  - The lesser of $1,000,000 or 5% of the cost of the rehabilitation was incurred before March 2, 1986, or was required to be incurred pursuant to a written contract that was binding on March 1, 1986.

Most transitional rule property placed in service after 1986 would be subject to a reduction of the credit percentage: 10% rather than 15% and 13% rather than 20%.

For limitations on the use of rehabilitation credits in real estate activities in which the taxpayer is an individual, estate, trust or personal service corporation and is not an active participant in the activity, see page 48.

Tax Credit for Constructing or Rehabilitating Low-Income Housing

Congress concluded that the various tax incentives that existed under prior law were not cost efficient in encouraging investors to build and rehabilitate low-income housing.

The Act provides a new credit for owners of low-income housing projects. The amount of the credit depends upon whether the taxpayer acquires existing housing or whether the housing is newly constructed or rehabilitated. The credit amount is also affected by whether or not the housing project is financed by tax-exempt bonds or other federally-subsidized financing.

Type of Project	*Maximum Credit*
New construction and rehabilitation of existing housing (Unsubsidized)	9% per year for 10 years
New construction and rehabilitation of existing housing (Subsidized)	4% per year for 10 years
Acquisition cost of existing housing	4% per year for 10 years

After 1987, the credit rates will vary slightly, depending on the Applicable Federal Rate. The amount on which the annual credit is computed is the portion of the total depreciable basis of a qualified housing project that reflects the portion of the housing units within the project that are occupied by qualified low-income individuals, as defined by the Act.

Special rules govern qualifications of projects, tenants and expenditures, as well as adjustments to the annual credit rate, compliance provisions and credit recapture.

The low-income housing credit is subject to the limitation on passive-activity losses and credits.

Effective Date

In general, the credit applies to property placed in service after 1986 and before 1990. Under a *sunset provision*, the credit is scheduled to expire for property placed in service after 1989. Special transitional rules apply to the sunset provision.

Corporate Minimum Tax

Under prior law, corporations paid an add-on minimum tax on certain tax preferences. The tax was in addition to the corporation's regular tax. The 15% tax was levied on the excess of the aggregate amount of tax preferences over the regular tax paid or $10,000.

For taxable years beginning in 1987, the Act repeals the corporate add-on minimum tax and creates a new alternative minimum tax that is designed to ensure that a corporation will pay a tax equalling at least 20% of its economic income. The new tax is similar to the individual minimum tax described on page 20. The Act also increases the corporate tax preference cutback from 15% to 20%. Generally, the tax base for the corporate alternative minimum tax is the corporation's regular taxable income increased by its tax preferences for the year and adjusted by recomputing certain deductions to negate the acceleration of the deductions under the regular tax. The resulting amount, called alternative minimum taxable income, is then reduced by an exemption amount and the remainder is subject to a 20% tax. The exemption amount is $40,000, reduced (but not below zero) by 25% of the amount by which alternative minimum taxable income exceeds $150,000. This amount is then offset by the minimum foreign tax credit to arrive at the so-called tentative minimum tax. The amount of minimum tax due is the excess of the tentative minimum tax over the regular tax. However, the regular tax continues to be imposed.

In determining alternative minimum taxable income, a corporation's preferences and adjustments are generally the same as the preferences under prior law together with the following additions:

- Accelerated depreciation is a preference item for all corporations. For *personal* property placed in service after December 31, 1986, the amount of the preference is the excess of regular ACRS depreciation over the depreciation calculated using the 150% declining-balance method and the appropriate ADR period (see p. 33). For *real* property, the excess of regular ACRS depreciation over depreciation calculated using the straight-line method over 40 years is a preference item.

  Regular ACRS depreciation on property placed in service before 1987 continues to be a preference item to the extent that it constituted a preference under prior law.
- For a long-term contract entered into after March 1, 1986, any items related to the contract that were computed under the completed- contract method of accounting for regular tax purposes must be recomputed under the percentage-of-completion method and included in alternative minimum taxable income as recomputed.
- For a disposition of dealer property after March 1, 1986, all gain from the disposition in the year in which the disposition takes place is a preference, even though the dealer used the installment method of accounting for computing gain for regular tax purposes.
- The preference for IDCs applies to all corporations and is the same as under prior law for individuals (see page 20) except that the preference is offset by 65% rather than 100% of net oil and gas income.
- Except for bonds issued on behalf of section 501(c)(3) organizations (charitable organizations), interest on most private purpose tax exempt bonds issued after August 7, 1986 is treated as a preference.
- The untaxed appreciation on charitable contributions of capital gain property is treated as a preference. The preference does not apply to carryovers of the deduction for charitable contributions made before August 16, 1986.

Planning Point
To avoid preference treatment for items such as IDCs, circulation expenditures, and mining exploration and development expenses, taxpayers should consider

electing to spread the deduction over longer periods for regular tax purposes.
- In 1987, 1988, and 1989, one-half of the amount by which the adjusted net book income of the taxpayer exceeds alternative minimum taxable income (determined without regard to this preference and prior to the reduction by NOLs) is a preference. After 1989, adjusted net book income is replaced for this purpose by 75% of the amount of adjusted current earnings that exceeds alternative minimum taxable income.

Example: Invest Corp. has adjusted net book income of $100,000 and alternative minimum taxable income (prior to the inclusion of any amounts as a result of this preference) of $50,000. Adjusted net book income exceeds alternative minimum taxable income by $50,000, one-half of which ($25,000) is added to alternative minimum taxable income to give alternative minimum taxable income for the year of $75,000.

In general, the book income of a corporate taxpayer is the net income or loss set forth on the taxpayer's applicable financial statement. Normally, this amount will be disclosed as part of an income statement. For a corporation that has more than one financial statement, the following order of priority applies to determine the applicable financial statement:
— Financial statements that are required to be filed with the Securities and Exchange Commission (SEC);
— Certified audited income statements used (in the order of priority) for credit purposes, for reporting to shareholders or other owners, or for any other substantial non-tax purpose;
— Financial statements issued to other federal, state or local government agencies; or,
— Lacking any of the above, any financial statement or report that is used (in the order of priority) for credit purposes, for reporting to shareholders, or for any other substantial non-tax purpose.

A corporation that does not file a financial statement with the SEC, a government or governmental agency, or obtain a certified audited income statement may elect to use its earnings and profits for the taxable year as book income. Earnings and profits are determined without reduction for distributions or federal income taxes attributable to the year.

Certain adjustments are then made to book income to arrive at adjusted net book income. They include:
— The book income preference is only determined for companies that are included in a corporation's consolidated income tax return for the year. Thus, for example, the preference does not include foreign companies or section 936 corporations (possessions corporations), that cannot be consolidated for tax purposes. To accomplish the adjustment, the net income and any related consolidated eliminations of companies that are included for financial statement purposes but not for federal income tax purposes will be subtracted and the net income and related eliminations of companies excluded for financial statement purposes but included for Federal income tax purposes will be added.

— A corporation is required to record as an item of book income the amount of any actual or deemed distribution from another corporation if the other corporation is not included in the taxpayer's tax consolidated group.

— Dividends received from a possessions corporation and included in the recipient's book income are to be grossed up, for purposes of measuring book income, by the amount of withholding taxes paid on the dividends. To the extent that the alternative minimum taxable income of the recipient is increased by the inclusion of the dividends (including the gross up) in book income, 50% of the related withholding taxes are treated for AMT purposes as creditable foreign taxes paid by the recipient.

— The financial statement preference is a measurement of the amount by which pre-tax book income exceeds alternative minimum taxable income. Thus, it is necessary to adjust for items of financial statement income and expense that relate to federal or foreign income taxes (that are eligible for the foreign tax credit).

— If different accounting years are used for financial statement and federal income tax purposes, an adjustment to book income is required to ensure conformity.

The Act instructs the IRS to issue regulations requiring the adjustment of net book income to prevent the duplication or omission of any item.

• The foreign tax credit can offset no more than 90% of the AMT liability and disallowed amounts can be carried over. All corporations can use their investment tax credit carryovers to offset up to 25% of their AMT liability.

Net Operating Losses (NOLs)

Net operating losses (NOLs) can be used to offset up to 90% of alternative minimum taxable income. For years beginning after 1986, the amount of the NOL for any taxable year available for AMT purposes is computed by adding back to taxable income the items of tax preference for the year. In computing the amount of deduction for carryover years, the recomputed loss is deducted from alternative minimum taxable income in the carryover year.

Example: In year one, Loss Corp. has $200,000 of income and $350,000 of losses including $100,000 of preference items. The recomputed alternative minimum tax NOL is $50,000. Thus, in year two, the $50,000 recomputed NOL deduction can reduce alternative minimum taxable income.

Subject to the 90% limitation, NOLs arising in pre-1987 years can be carried forward in full to offset alternative minimum taxable income. A corporation's deferred add-on minimum tax liability for pre-1987 years would be forgiven but the corporation's alternative minimum tax NOL carryover would be reduced by the amount of the preferences that gave rise to the add-on minimum tax liability.

Minimum Tax Credit

Generally, any alternative minimum tax paid after 1986 can be credited against the regular tax liability of future years. However, the credit is allowed only for liability arising from deferral preferences, i.e., preferences that do not result in a permanent exclusion of certain income for regular tax purposes. This credit can be carried forward indefinitely. The minimum tax credit cannot be used to reduce minimum tax liability in subsequent years.

Effective Date
Except for the treatment of interest on private activity bonds, these provisions apply to taxable years beginning after December 31, 1986.

Tax Shelters and Real Estate

Under prior law, taxpayers generally were allowed to offset losses from one economic activity against income from another economic activity. For example, a loss from the operation of rental property could be used to offset salary income. The principal exception to the general rule was capital losses, which could only be offset against capital gains (the rule for corporations) or against capital gains plus up to $3,000 of other income (the rule for noncorporate taxpayers).

In the absence of any general restrictions on the use of losses from one activity to offset income from another, many high income individuals and corporations were able to substantially reduce their taxes by investing in tax shelters in which they were merely passive participants. Congress perceived that this extensive use of tax shelters produced several undesirable results:

- It reduced federal revenues.
- It eroded public confidence in the fairness of the tax system. That, in turn, threatened to undermine our tax system, which is based on voluntary compliance.
- It diverted investment from economically productive activities to other activities that merely served tax avoidance goals.

In addition, Congress believed that some of the tax benefits that had been added to the tax code in prior years to encourage certain types of economic activities were primarily benefiting passive investors, such as hobby farmers, rather than taxpayers who were actively engaged in carrying on a trade or business.

To attack the tax shelter problem, Congress adopted a multi-pronged approach. It indirectly reduced the value of tax shelter losses by lowering the tax rates. And, in more direct moves, the Act strengthens the alternative minimum tax on tax-preference income (see page 42), and limits the availability of deductions and credits from activities in which the taxpayer is not an active participant. Further, since tax shelters are typically highly leveraged investments, the Act tightens restrictions on the deductibility of investment interest expense.

Limitation on Losses and Credits from Passive Activities

In General
The Act limits the deduction of passive-activity losses of individuals, estates, trusts and specified personal-service corporations. Following a four-year phase-in period, passive-activity losses generally will only be deductible to the extent of income from passive-activities. Portfolio investment income will not be treated as passive-activity income for purposes of the limitation. Similarly, credits from passive activities generally will be limited to the tax allocable to passive activities. Disallowed losses and credits may be carried forward and used against passive-activity income in subsequent years. Any unused losses may be deducted in the year in which a taxpayer disposes of the entire interest in a passive activity.

Closely-held corporations other than personal service corporations can offset passive-activity losses and credits against active income—but not against portfolio income.

Interest deductions attributable to passive activities are subject to the passive loss rule but not the investment interest limitation.

What Is a Passive Activity?

The Act defines a passive activity as any activity that involves the conduct of any trade or business in which the taxpayer does not materially participate. Rental activities are also specifically defined as passive activities, regardless of the actual participation of the taxpayer. Accordingly, a rental loss will be treated as a passive-activity loss even if the taxpayer materially participates in the operation of the rental property. Operating a hotel or other transient lodging is not treated as a rental activity jf significant services are provided, nor is a short-term equipment rental business, such as an automobile rental agency. However, a long-term lease of equipment or a vehicle generally will be treated as a passive activity.

Under the Act, a limited partnership interest is—by definition—a passive-activity interest. The Act also clarifies that the passive-activity rules apply to R&D activities.

The passive-activity rule does not apply to a working interest in any oil or gas property that a taxpayer owns directly or through an entity that does not limit the taxpayer's liability. This exception applies whether or not the taxpayer materially participates in the oil or gas activity.

What Is Material Participation?

The Act defines the term *material participation* as the taxpayer's involvement in the activity on a regular, continuous and substantial basis. A taxpayer who invests in a business and whose only involvement consists of periodic consultation on general management decisions generally would not satisfy the material participation standard: Direct involvement in the operations of the business is necessary. However, special rules apply to retired farmers.

Factors that the IRS will consider in determining whether a taxpayer materially participated in a business activity include:

- Is the activity the taxpayer's principal business?
- If not, how much time does the taxpayer devote to it?
- How regularly is the taxpayer present at the location where the business activities are conducted?
- What duties are performed?
- Does the taxpayer have knowledge of or experience in the business?

Who is subject to the limitation? The limitation on passive losses and credits applies to individuals, estates, trusts and personal service corporations, i.e., any incorporated service business that is owned 10% or more by shareholder-employees. Although the limitations do not apply directly to partnerships and trusts, they will apply at the partner or beneficiary level if the partner or beneficiary does not materially participate in the business activities of the partnership or trust.

Closely-held corporations other than personal service companies are subject to a modified limitation. They are allowed to deduct passive-activity losses and use passive-activity credits to offset net active business income, but not portfolio income.

How Losses and Credits are Treated

Losses: In general, losses from a passive activity may be deducted only against income from a passive activity. They may not be deducted against other income, including wages, dividends, interest and active business income. A limited exception to this rule applies to a loss from rental real estate and is explained further below.

Example: Mr. White has salary income, income from a limited partnership in which he is a limited partner, and a loss from another partnership in whose business he does not actively participate.

He may offset the partnership loss against the income from the limited partnership, but not against his salary income.

To the extent that there is insufficient passive-activity income to absorb passive-activity losses in any given year, the excess losses may be carried forward indefinitely to future taxable years. However, they may not be carried back to prior taxable years. If there is insufficient passive-activity income in subsequent years to fully absorb the loss carryforwards, the unused losses from a passive-activity may be deducted against the gain (or added to the loss) when the taxpayer finally disposes of his or her entire interest in the activity that gave rise to the unused losses.

Example: Ms. Green has a passive-activity loss in 1987 that exceeds her passive-activity income for the year. She carries the excess 1987 loss forward to 1988 and 1989. She does not have any passive-activity income to offset the loss carryforward in either of those years. Late in 1989, she sells her entire interest in the passive activity that generated the 1987 loss. Ms. Green may reduce her 1989 gain on the sale (or increase her loss on the sale) by the amount of the unused loss carryforward from 1987.

Comment

As the example illustrates, the overall effect of the passive-activity loss limitation rules is not to *disallow* the tax benefits of a loss, but rather to *defer* the timing of those benefits until the taxpayer has completely disposed of the entire interest in the passive-activity in a *fully taxable* transaction. However, the economic present value of the deferred benefit of the losses may be significantly less than the value of current deductions each year.

Credits: Arising from passive activities, credits are generally treated the same as losses. They may not be used to offset tax liability attributable to income other than passive-activity income. The amount of that tax liability is determined by comparing total tax liability (disregarding any credits) with the amount of tax that the taxpayer would pay on taxable income other than net passive income (again, disregarding any credits).

Special rules relating to credits for rehabilitation projects and low-income housing are explained further below.

Passive-activity credits that cannot be used in a given taxable year may be carried forward indefinitely. During the five year phase-in of the limitation on passive activity losses and credits, the *allowable* percentage of an unused passive activity credit may be carried back to the three preceding taxable years under the normal credit carryback rules. However, the percentage of the unused credit that is subject to the limitation may *not* be carried back to prior years. Unlike excess losses, excess credits may *not* be claimed in full in the year in which the taxpayer disposes of the interest in the passive activity. Rather, they would continue to be carried forward until used, if ever.

Example: Mr. Brown is a limited partner in an equipment leasing limited partnership. In 1987, his share of investment tax credit (ITC) from the partnership is $10,000. For other reasons, he has no 1987 tax liability. The 65% of the passive activity ITC that is not subject to the limitation in 1987 under the phase-in rules may be carried back to 1984, 1985 and 1986. However, the 35% of the ITC that is subject to the limitation in 1987 may only be carried forward to subsequent years.

Credits allowable under the passive-activity limitation rules are also subject to the previously existing limitation of the general business credit. They may not exceed the sum of $25,000 plus 75% of the net tax liability in excess of $25,000. In addition, credits allowed under the passive-activity limitation may not be used to reduce the alternative minimum tax.

When an Activity Ceases to Be Passive
If a taxpayer who is a passive participant in an activity later becomes an active participant, losses for any year of active participation are not subject to the limitations. Any losses carried over from passive participation years remain classified as passive-activity losses. However, in addition to being deductible against passive income from other sources, they may also be deducted against any income from the activity after it ceases to be a passive activity.

Example: Mr. Brown, a partner in an art gallery in which he invested before 1987, is not actually involved in carrying on the business during 1987. If the gallery sustains a loss in 1987, the passive-activity loss limitation rules would apply to Mr. Brown. However, if he becomes an active participant in 1988, any loss sustained after he becomes an active participant would be treated as a loss from other than a passive activity. Also, the 1987 loss would be available to offset income, if any, from 1988 and later years.

Treatment of Portfolio Income
Portfolio income, which includes interest, dividends, royalties, and gains from the disposition of investment property (except an interest in a passive activity), is generally thought of as *passive* income. However, for purposes of the passive-activity loss limitation, the Act treats portfolio income as income that is *not* from a passive activity. This is designed to prevent taxpayers from circumventing the limitation by offsetting passive-activity losses against portfolio income either directly or by transferring portfolio securities to a partnership, trust or S corporation.

Example: Ms. Gold has dividend and interest income of $30,000 and a passive-activity loss of $15,000. The passive-activity loss may *not* be offset against the dividend and interest income.

If Ms. Gold transferred her interest in the passive activity to a business partnership in which she is an active partner, the passive-activity losses could not be deducted in determining net income from the business partnership. They would retain their separate character as passive activity losses and would pass through to the partners as a separate item of income or loss.

Special Exception for Losses and Credits from Specified Rental Real Estate Activities

Congress recognized that although rental real estate was frequently used as a tax shelter by high-income individuals, many moderate-income taxpayers also purchased rental real estate to provide supplemental income and retirement security. Additionally, Congress was aware that vacation rental property is extremely important to the local economies of many resort areas of the country.

Because the Act defines any rental activity as a passive activity regardless of the property owner's participation in the operation of the rental property, a special exception was added to the limitation on passive-activity losses to provide a degree of relief to moderate-income taxpayers who own and operate rental real estate. Under this relief provision, an individual may offset up to $25,000 of income that is *not* from passive activities by losses or credits from rental real estate. However, this provision applies *only if* the taxpayer *actively participates* in the rental real estate activity.

The $25,000 amount is phased out for higher-income taxpayers. For purposes of the limitation on *losses*, the $25,000 amount is reduced (but not below zero) by $1 for each $2 of adjusted gross income in excess of $100,000. Thus, it is fully phased out when adjusted gross income exceeds $150,000.

Example (1): Mr. and Mrs. Silver own a rental duplex that they manage. In 1987, they have a $12,000 loss from their rental activity. Their joint adjusted gross income (computed without regard to the rental loss) is $65,000. The Silvers may deduct the full $12,000 rental loss from their $65,000 of adjusted gross income from other sources.

Example (2): Miss Scarlet owns several rental properties that she actively manages. In 1987, she has a rental loss of $30,000 and adjusted gross income from other sources of $110,000. Since her adjusted gross income from other sources exceeds $100,000, Miss Scarlet must reduce her $25,000 maximum rental loss deduction by $5,000, i.e., one-half of other adjusted gross income in excess of $100,000. Accordingly, she may deduct $20,000 of her 1987 rental loss under the $25,000 rental loss exception. Of the remaining $10,000 rental loss, 65% would be deductible in 1987 under the loss limitation phase-in rule and 35% must be carried forward.

However, for purposes of the *credit* limitation, the phase out does not begin until adjusted gross income exceeds $200,000. It is fully phased out when adjusted gross income exceeds $250,000.

For purposes of the $25,000 exception, *active participation* in rental activities is a slightly different concept than *material participation*, as that term is used in the passive-activity test. The active-participation test is intended to be less stringent than the material-participation test. Thus, a taxpayer who owns an interest in rental real estate would be permitted to satisfy the active-participation test by:

- Personally operating the rental property; or
- Hiring a rental agent or real estate management firm to operate the property, so long as the taxpayer participates in making management decisions or arranging for others to provide services, such as repairs. Significant management decisions that would satisfy this test would

include: approving new tenants, deciding on rental terms, approving capital expenditures or repairs, and similar types of decisions.

Planning Point

A taxpayer whose property is managed by a rental agent or real estate management firm should establish procedures with the agent or firm to document the taxpayer's participation in management decisions.

Effective Date

The passive-activity limitations apply to taxable years beginning after 1986. However, for interests in passive activities acquired on or before the date of enactment of the Act, the limitation is phased in over a five-year period. A binding contract to purchase an interest in a passive activity will generally be treated as an acquisition if the activity commenced by the date of enactment or if the contract is as entered into on or before August 16, 1986. For any taxable year beginning in calendar years 1987 through 1990, the portion of the loss or credit that will be disallowed under the phase-in rule is determined in accordance with the following table:

Taxable year beginning in	Percentage Disallowed
1987	35%
1988	60%
1989	80%
1990	90%

For interests in passive activities acquired after the date of enactment of the Act, there is no phase-in period. The limitation on losses from those activities is *fully* effective for taxable years beginning after 1986. The phase-in is also not applicable for purposes of the alternative minimum tax.

Transitional Rule for Low-Income Housing

A special transitional rule temporarily exempts from the passive-activity limitation losses sustained by qualified investors in low-income housing projects. The temporary exemption applies only to investors who are *individuals* and who are required to make payments after December 31, 1986, of 50% or more of their total original obligated investment for their interest in the project. To qualify, the investor must hold, directly or through one or more entities, an interest in a project and satisfy either of the following requirements:

- The project was placed in service *before* August 16, 1986, the investor held an interest (or a binding contract to acquire an interest) in the project on August 16, 1986, and the investor made an initial investment after December 31, 1983; or
- The project was placed in service *after* August 15, 1986, and the investor held an interest (or a binding contract to acquire an interest) in the project on December 31, 1986.

For qualifying investors, the temporary exemption period begins with the taxable year in which the investor made an initial investment in the project and ends with the *earliest* of:

- The sixth taxable year after the taxable year in which the investor made the initial investment;
- The first taxable year after the taxable year in which the investor is obligated to make the last investment; or
- The taxable year preceding the 1st taxable year in which the project ceases to qualify as a low-income housing project.

Planning Points

- Taxpayers should exercise extreme caution in evaluating any new tax shelter investment opportunities. Most tax shelters will not be attractive under the new rules.
- Prospective investments in rental real estate should be evaluated primarily on their potential economic return—especially by taxpayers whose adjusted gross income exceeds $100,000. However, rental property that qualifies for rehabilitation credits or low-income housing credits may still offer some tax benefits to taxpayers with adjusted gross income between $100,000 and $200,000.
- Related-party leases of real estate or equipment, e.g., between a closely-held corporation and its shareholders, should be reexamined in light of the Act to determine what changes, if any, are needed to maintain economic viability as the tax benefits are phased out.
- Participants in tax-shelter limited partnerships should consider investing in income-producing limited partnerships, such as non-leveraged rental real estate, to absorb the passive-activity losses. However, interest on any amount borrowed to finance the investment would be investment interest subject to the limitation on the deduction of investment interest.
- An individual with passive-activity losses and no offsetting passive-activity income may find it advantageous to convert income from an active business into passive- activity income by reducing the level of involvement in the business. Conversely, an individual with passive-activity losses and little or no passive-activity income could attempt, if possible, to convert the passive-activity into an activity in which the individual materially participates. For example, an individual who has invested money in a business, but who is only marginally active in its operation, could increase his or her level of activity—and document that activity. Participation could include working with lenders to obtain financing, regularly meeting with customers and suppliers, participating in business planning, meeting with the business' lawyers and accountants, and becoming involved in marketing activities.
- Interest on debt secured by a taxpayer's principal or second residence is not subject to either the passive-activity limitation or the interest limitation. Accordingly, the portion of mortgage interest on a rental vacation home, i.e. a second residence, that is allocable to rental use would *not* be subject to the passive-activity limitation.
- Buying investment real estate, such as unimproved land, that is neither rented to third parties nor operated as a trade or business would *not* be a

passive-activity. Accordingly, interest on the purchase price would not be subject to the passive-activity loss limitation rules. It would, however, be subject to the investment-interest deduction limitation.

Extension of the At-Risk Limitation to Real Property

The at-risk rules generally limit the loss that an individual or a closely-held corporation may claim from a business or an income-producing activity to the amount that the taxpayer actually has at economic risk in the business or activity. The at-risk amount is the total of the taxpayer's investment plus any debt of the business or activity for which the taxpayer is personally liable or for which the taxpayer's assets are pledged as security.

Similar rules limit that amount of investment tax credit (ITC) that a taxpayer may claim. Generally, a taxpayer must be at risk for property on which ITC is claimed. There is an exception for property financed by certain nonrecourse loans from an unrelated financial institution or commercial lender.

Under prior law, the at-risk limitation on losses did not apply to real estate activities.

The Act extends the at-risk rules to losses arising from real estate activities. However, it also provides—similar to the ITC exception—that a taxpayer will be considered as being at risk for nonrecourse financing that is:

- Secured by property used in the activity;
- Borrowed by the taxpayer in connection with the activity; and
- Loaned or guaranteed by an agency of the federal, state or local government or by an unrelated party that is actively and regularly engaged in the business of lending money or by a related party under terms that are commercially reasonable and on substantially the same terms as loans involving unrelated persons.

Effective Date

This provision applies to losses attributable to property placed in service after December 31, 1986.

Corporate Transactions

Dividend Received Deduction

Under prior law, a corporate shareholder was generally entitled to an 85% deduction for dividends received from another corporation. This deduction resulted in an effective corporate tax rate of 6.9% on the dividends received.

Under the Act, the 85% dividends received deduction is reduced to 80%. The effective corporate tax rate on dividends received is reduced to 6.8% when the corporate tax rate is reduced to 34%. The limitation on the dividends received deduction—85% of taxable income unless there is a current year net operating loss—is reduced to 80% of taxable income.

Effective Date

Applies to dividends received after December 31, 1986.

Stock Basis Reduced for Extraordinary Dividends

Under prior law, a dividend generally had no effect on a shareholder's basis in the stock of the distributing corporation. The 1984 Tax Reform Act required corporations receiving extraordinary dividends to reduce their basis in their stock in the distributing corporation by the nontaxed portion of the dividend unless they held the stock for more than one year. Also, if the stock was held by a corporation for less than 46 days (90 days for certain preferred stock), the 85% dividends received deduction was not available. Days held were not included when the shareholder limited its risk of loss in the stock. These provisions affecting extraordinary dividends have been found to be inadequate deterrents to tax-motivated transactions.

Example: A corporation acquires stock with the intent of receiving an extraordinary dividend that will be subject to tax at an effective 6.9% rate. After payment of the dividend, the price of the acquired stock will generally decline by an amount approximately equal to the dividend. The corporation can then sell the stock at a loss and then offset the loss against capital gain that would otherwise be taxed at a 28% rate.

Under the Act, if stock on which an extraordinary dividend is paid has not been held for at least two years before the date of announcement or agreement about the dividend, a corporate shareholder must reduce its basis in the stock by the nontaxed portion of any extraordinary dividend. The nontaxed portion of an extraordinary dividend includes the amount of the dividends received deduction as well as the amount of the nontaxed appreciation in the property distributed.

An extraordinary dividend generally includes amounts received within an 85-day period that exceed 10% (5% in cases of preferred stock) of the corporation's adjusted basis in a share of stock. When determining if a dividend is extraordinary, a corporation may elect to use the fair market value of the subject stock instead of its adjusted basis. In addition, a redemption of stock that is treated as a dividend for tax purposes will be treated as an extraordinary dividend without regard to the holding period of the stock provided the redemption is pursuant to a partial liquidation or is not pro rata to the shareholders. A special rule provides relief for qualified preferred stock so that, if under the general rule, the dividends may be treated as an extraordinary dividend to the extent that the yield on qualified preferred stock does not exceed 15% of the lower of the stock's adjusted basis or liquidation preference.

Effective Date
Applies generally to dividends announced after July 18, 1986, in tax years ending after that date.

Stock Redemption Payments
Under prior law, some corporations have deducted amounts paid to repurchase their stock to prevent a hostile takeover: so called *green mail payments.* Generally, the court cases have held that *green mail payments* were not deductible.

The Act provides that a corporation may not deduct any amount paid, directly or indirectly, in connection with the repurchase of its own stock except for interest payments. Nondeductible amounts include those paid for legal fees, accounting fees, brokerage fees, and other like expenses, except when paid by open-ended regulated investment companies. This provision also applies to any amount paid to a selling shareholder who agrees not to purchase, finance a purchase, acquire, or in any way be a party or agent to the acquisition of the corporation's stock.

Effective Date
This provision is effective for any amount paid after February 28, 1986.

Net Operating Loss Carryovers
Under prior law, different rules apply to an acquiring corporation's ability to use the net operating losses (NOLs) of an acquired corporation depending on whether the transaction took the form of a taxable purchase or a tax-free reorganization.

When there was a taxable purchase of stock, the NOLs of the acquired corporation were completely eliminated if the corporation did not carry on substantially the same trade or business and the 10 largest shareholders increased their stock ownership by more than 50 percentage points through taxable purchases within a two year period.

A tax-free reorganization would result in the loss of 5% of a NOL carryover for each percentage point that the former shareholders' interest in the continuing corporation as a result of the reorganization was less than 20%. This 20% continuity of loss corporation shareholder interest requirement could be avoided by causing the loss corporation to be acquired by a newly formed subsidiary in exchange for stock of the parent corporation, because the losses would generally be only offset against future income of the acquired corporation.

These NOL carryover rules were perceived as permitting partial recoupment of losses through the tax system. But without a change in ownership, the loss rules only provided an averaging mechanism that worked in conjunction with the annual tax accounting system. In 1976, Congress enacted new rules that became effective on January 1, 1986, and that have now been retroactively repealed. As a result, the pre-1986 rules continue to apply until the effective date of the rules contained in the Act.

Generally, under the Act, if there is more than a 50% change in ownership of a loss corporation over a three-year period, the annual NOL carryover is limited to a prescribed rate times the value of the loss corporation's stock on the date of the ownership change. In addition, the loss corporation's historic business must be continued or a significant portion of its historic business assets must be used in the business for two years after the ownership change.

The annual amount of earnings against which the carryovers may be used cannot exceed the fair market value (FMV) of the loss corporation's stock immediately before the ownership change multiplied by the long-term tax-exempt bond rate. If the full amount of allowable carryovers is not used in a taxable year, the unused amount may be used in succeeding years. The limitation for short taxable years is pro-rated. The FMV of the loss corporation is not increased for contributions to capital that have a tax avoidance purpose or, except as provided by the IRS in regulations, for any capital contribution made within two years of the ownership change.

Example: Losscorp has a NOL carryover of $500,000. Mr. Wealthy purchases in an arm's length transaction all of its stock for $1,000,000 (the purchase establishes Losscorp's FMV). Assuming that the long-term tax-exempt bond rate is 8%, Losscorp may use $80,000 (8% X $1,000,000) of its NOL carryover against each year's taxable income. The same result would apply if Losscorp had merged into unrelated Acquisition Corporation in exchange for 25% of its stock (provided that Acquisition Corporation continues the historic trade or business of Losscorp).

If at least one-third of the FMV of a corporation's assets are nonbusiness assets, the FMV of the corporation is reduced by the excess of the value of its nonbusiness assets over a pro-rata portion of its indebtedness attributable to the nonbusiness assets. Nonbusiness assets are those assets held for investment purposes. Assets held as part of a trade or business, including assets held as reserves for an insurance company or similar assets of a bank, are not non-business assets. If the corporation owns at least 50% of the value and voting power of the stock of a subsidiary, it is deemed to own a ratable share of its subsidiary's assets, i.e., stock or securities in a subsidiary are not treated as nonbusiness assets. Regulated investment companies, real estate investment trusts and real estate mortgage investment conduits are not treated as having substantial nonbusiness assets.

The 50% change in stock ownership test applies to all changes, whether taxable or tax-free. In determining whether there is a change in stock ownership, attribution of ownership rules are applied. Changes in stock ownership include transfers of property in exchange for stock, redemptions of stock, and stock for stock exchanges. Stock that does not participate in the corporation's growth to any significant extent is excluded from being treated as stock. In making the determination as to whether a 50% ownership change has occurred, reference is made to all 5% or greater owners of stock. All less-than-5% owners are grouped together and treated as one shareholder owning more than 5%. However, in a tax-free reorganization (other than a divisive reorganization or a mere reincorpora-tion), the less than 5% shareholders of each corporation are treated as separate shareholders. The IRS is instructed to issue regulations that will treat, in appropriate cases, as separate 5% shareholders those persons receiving stock in a public offering or a recapitalization. Also, in appropriate circumstances, war-rants, the conversion feature of convertible debt and similar interests may be treated as stock.

Example (1): A publicly traded company that is 60% owned by less-than-5% shareholders would not experience an ownership change merely because, within a three-year period, every one of the less-than-5% shareholders sold all of their stock to persons who were not 5% shareholders.

Example (2): Losscorp is acquired by Profitcorp in a tax-free reorganization. In the reorganization, the shareholders of Losscorp receive 30% of Profitcorp's stock. Neither Losscorp nor Profitcorp have any 5% shareholders. Losscorp had an ownership change because the former shareholders of Profitcorp (who are treated as a separate single shareholder) hold 70% of its stock after the reorganization—that is more than 50% of stock of Losscorp than they held before the reorganization (0%). If the shareholders of the Losscorp had received at least 50% of the stock of Profitcorp as a result of the reorganization, there would not have been an ownership change.

These rules do not apply to an ownership change of a corporation that is under the jurisdiction of a bankruptcy court provided the shareholders and creditors own at least 50% of the value and voting power of the stock after the ownership change and the transaction is pursuant to a plan approved by the court. However, the loss carryforward is reduced by one-half of the excess of any indebtedness cancelled over the FMV of the stock received in the exchange. Interest payments on debt that is converted to stock during the three years preceding the ownership change year is not included as part of the loss carryforward. If there is another ownership change during the two succeeding years, no losses may be carried forward to a period after the second ownership change.

Troubled thrift institutions (mutual savings banks, domestic building and loan associations and cooperative banks) that are under the jurisdiction of a federal or state bank board will not be deemed to have an ownership change pursuant to a G reorganization if the shareholders, creditors and depositors retain a 20% interest. Deposits of a troubled thrift that become deposits in the acquiring corporation are treated as stock.

Comment

Corporations with NOLs often undergo shifts in ownership. A corporation may have a nominal FMV aside from the tax value of its NOLs. When there is an ownership change, the new rules could cause the NOLs to be used at a rate sufficiently small to be considered to be of little worth. In addition, the NOLs may be significantly reduced.

If a corporation's net assets have unrecognized appreciation or depreciation by more than 25% of their total value (excluding cash items and marketable securities that have not appreciated or depreciated substantially) as of the date of the 50% change in stock ownership, the corporation will be treated as having a net built-in gain or loss. If there is a net built-in gain and it is recognized during the five years after the ownership change, it increases the amount of income that may be offset by a NOL carryover. If there is a net built-in loss and it is recognized during the five years after the ownership change, it is treated as a loss that existed as of the change of ownership.

Comment

These special rules for built-in gains or losses apply only to the extent of net built-in gains or losses existing at the time of the ownership change.

Planning Points

- If a built-in gain exists, unrecognized losses existing at the time of the ownership change that are recognized during the five-year period may reduce taxable income without regard to any limitation or may reduce the corporation's ability to use its NOL carryover against current year's income.
- If sufficient NOL carryovers exist, it may be wise to recognize built-in gains during the five-year period following the ownership change. This will increase the amount of NOL carryover that may be used during this period.

The limitations on NOL carryovers also apply to unused business credits and research credits, excess foreign tax credits and capital loss carryovers. Additionally, use of the new passive-activity losses and credits and alternative minimum tax credits are limited. Credit carryovers will be limited to offsetting the tax on an amount of taxable income equal to the limitations on NOL carryovers for the taxable year.

Effective Date

This provision is generally effective for stock purchases on or after January 1, 1987, and tax-free transactions pursuant to a plan of reorganization adopted on or after January 1, 1987.

In determining whether an ownership change has occurred, the earliest testing period of stock ownership is May 6, 1986, or, if later, the date of an ownership change during 1986.

Example: 60% of the stock of Losscorp is purchased on June 15, 1986. The remaining 40% of the stock is purchased on January 10, 1987. Since the stock purchase on June 15, 1986, constituted an ownership change, only ownership changes after June 15, 1986, are counted in determining whether an ownership change has occurred after December 31, 1986.

Example: 40% of the stock of Losscorp is purchased on July 1, 1986, and an additional 15% of the stock is purchased on January 15, 1987. An ownership change resulting from the purchase of stock occurs January 15, 1987, and the losses would be limited under the Act.

The provisions applicable to reorganizations of corporations under the jurisdiction of a bankruptcy court do not apply if a petition was filed with the court before August 14, 1986.

Personal Holding Company Income

Personal holding companies (PHCs) are subject to a penalty tax on PHC income that is not distributed to their shareholders. Generally, PHCs are corporations that have more than 50% of their stock owned by five or fewer individuals and at least 60% of whose adjusted ordinary gross income is PHC income.

Courts have held that PHC income includes computer software royalties, regardless of whether the royalties were received in connection with the active conduct of the trade or business of developing the software that generated the royalties. This resulted in closely-held corporations engaged in developing computer software being forced to distribute funds rather than being able to retain funds for future development and expansion.

Under the Act, computer software royalties received by a corporation that is actively engaged in the business of developing computer software will be excluded from PHC income if they exceed 50% of ordinary gross income. To qualify, a company must incur substantial trade or business expenses and must distribute most of its passive income other than computer software royalties.

Effective Date
The provision is effective for royalties received at any time.

Planning Point
Since this provision is retroactive, a corporation that paid PHC tax on its software royalties and meets the new requirements should file a timely claim for refund of the tax paid for any open years.

Liquidating Sales and Distributions

The so-called *General Utilities* rule provides that a corporation does not recognize gain or loss on a sale or distribution of its assets pursuant to a plan of complete liquidation. Over the years this rule was somewhat eroded by various provisions requiring some income recognition in certain circumstances, including the difference between the FIFO and LIFO value of inventory, recapture of certain depreciation deductions, and the excess of liabilities over the adjusted basis of property, if any.

The Act repeals the *General Utilities* rule except to the extent that the liquidation results in distributions to an 80% or greater corporate shareholder. Generally, all sales and distributions of appreciated property will be taxable to the liquidating corporation as if it had sold its property at FMV. The provision will not prevent the tax-free distribution of property to the extent there is no gain or loss to the recipient pursuant to a corporate reorganization.

Liquidating distributions to an 80% or greater corporate shareholder will still not be taxable to the extent property is actually distributed to the controlling corporate shareholder. The property received by the corporate shareholder will have the same basis as the liquidating corporation's basis in the property. Thus, any gain will be recognized by the corporate shareholder if, and when, it disposes of the distributed property.

The exception for liquidating distributions to an 80% or greater corporate shareholder does not apply if the shareholder is a tax-exempt organization and such property is not used by it in an unrelated trade or business immediately after the distribution. If the property ceases to be used in an unrelated trade or business, the tax exempt organization will be taxed at that time.

In addition, the exception for liquidating distributions to an 80% or greater corporate shareholder does not apply if the shareholder is a foreign corporation except to the extent provided in regulations to be issued. It is expected that the regulations may permit nonrecognition if the appreciated property is not being removed from taxation by the United States prior to recognition.

If any property distributed is subject to a liability or the shareholders assume a liability, the FMV of the property will not be treated as less than the liability. Two safeguards have been provided so that taxpayers may not avoid the repeal or otherwise take advantage of this provision, recognize losses in inappropriate situations or inflate the amount of losses actually sustained.

First, no loss will be recognized on distributions to a related person (under the related party rules of section 267) unless the property is distributed to all shareholders on a pro rata basis and the property was not acquired by a capital contribution or from a shareholder in a tax-free exchange for stock within five years preceding the distribution.

Second, if a principal purpose of a contribution to capital or receipt of property from a shareholder in a tax-free exchange in advance of the corporation's liquidation is to recognize a loss at any time upon the sale or distribution of the property then the basis of the property will be reduced, but not below zero, by the excess of the basis of the property over its FMV on such date. It is presumed that transfers within two years of the adoption of a plan of liquidation have such a principal purpose unless regulations are issued to the contrary. Contributions more than two years before the adoption of a plan of liquidation will have such a principal purpose only in the most rare and unusual cases.

The repeal also affects a taxable purchase of at least 80% of a corporation's stock by a corporation that makes a section 338 election. The election will cause the purchased corporation to be treated as though it sold its assets in a taxable transaction. The purchased corporation's assets then have a basis equal to their FMV.

A special provision for a section 338 election permits a corporate purchaser and corporate seller of the stock of an 80% controlled subsidiary to elect to treat the corporate seller as though it sold the assets of the subsidiary, rather than the stock, in a taxable transaction. This special provision is beneficial. Without the special provision, a corporate seller of the stock of an 80% controlled subsidiary would recognize gain or loss on the sale of the stock and the 80% controlled subsidiary would also recognize gain or loss on the deemed taxable sale of its assets.

A corporation that elects S corporation status generally does not pay taxes on its income. Rather, the S corporation's shareholders recognize their pro-rata share of the corporation's income or loss in their individual income tax returns. If a corporation converts to S corporation status after 1986, a corporate level tax will be imposed on any gain that arose before the conversion and is recognized through sale or distribution within 10 years of the conversion. Gains will be presumed to have occurred before the conversion except to the extent the corporation can demonstrate otherwise. The amount of gain is limited to the aggregate net gain existing at the time of conversion. Tax is imposed at the maximum rate applicable to the type of gain recognized. The corporation will be able to offset the gain and the tax by any loss carryovers or credits existing at the time of conversion as if it were still a taxable corporation (C corporation).

Comment
This rule replaces the rules that tax the entire capital gain if a corporation has elected S corporation status within the three preceding tax years. If possible, it may be wise to elect S corporation status for a tax year beginning before 1987 without changing its tax year and avoid this new 10-year rule on gains with respect to appreciation inherent in the assets before conversion.

Effective Date
The provision applies to liquidations completed after December 31, 1986, and section 338 elections for which the qualified stock purchase acquisition date is after December 31, 1986. If a plan of liquidation was adopted or a binding contract entered into for the purchase of stock on or before July 31, 1986, and the liquidation or a purchase of stock for which a section 338 election is made is completed by December 31, 1987, the new provisions will not be applicable.

This provision also does not apply to closely-held companies, i.e., corporations that have a FMV of not more than $5 million and more than 50% of whose stock is owned directly or indirectly by 10 or fewer individuals who have held their stock for at least five years, the liquidation of which is completed by December 31, 1988. A phase-out is provided for companies with a FMV of between $5 and $10 million.

Planning Points
- To avoid the corporate level tax on the appreciation inherent in its assets, a corporation with appreciated assets whose shareholders may have been considering liquidation, sale of the assets or sale of stock should immediately determine whether the company may qualify as a closely-held corporation. This will allow the corporation to side step the requirement of liquidating or selling its stock to a corporate purchaser that does not want to make a section 338 election until December 31, 1988.
- A corporation that does not qualify as a closely-held corporation should consider whether it should liquidate by December 31, 1986, to allow its

shareholders to obtain a basis in its assets equal to their FMV without a corporate level tax on the appreciation. This could be a wise move if the corporation is "for sale."

Caution
Before liquidating, a determination must be made as to the amount of income that will be generated under the exceptions to the *General Utilities* rule, such as depreciation recapture versus the future tax benefits of the higher basis in the assets. Also, the assets distributed to the shareholders must not be transferred to another corporation that may be considered to be continuing the business of the liquidating corporation.

Nonliquidating Distributions of Appreciated Property
Historically, the tax treatment of corporate nonliquidating distributions of property (dividends, redemptions, and partial liquidations) has generally been the same as liquidating distributions. However, in recent years, nonliquidating distributions have been subject to stricter rules, often requiring recognition of gain by the distributing corporation.

The Act generally conforms the treatment of nonliquidating distributions with liquidating distributions. Gain will be recognized by the nonliquidating corporation if appreciated property, other than stock, stock rights or an obligation of the corporation, is distributed with respect to its stock. The only exception to the requirement for recognition of gain is a distribution in redemption of stock by a regulated investment company on the demand of the shareholders.

In addition, a distribution by a U.S. corporation to a foreign person of the stock of a corporation that is engaged in an active trade or business and that would normally qualify as a tax-free spin-off under section 355 will be taxable to the distributing corporation.

Effective Date
Distributions made after December 31, 1986.

Comment
Note that this effective date provision is more restrictive than that for liquidating distributions. For example, closely-held corporations will be taxable beginning in 1987 on nonliquidating distributions, while for liquidating distributions they will not be taxable until 1989.

Liquidations of Subsidiaries
Prior law expanded the definition of eligibility for filing a consolidated income tax return to require that the parent corporation own 80% of the voting power and 80% of the value of the stock. Nonvoting nonparticipating preferred stock which is not convertible was excluded from this test.

The Act conforms the definition of eligibility for the tax-free liquidation of a subsidiary by requiring that 80% of the value as well as 80% of the voting power of the stock of the subsidiary be owned by a corporate shareholder. This provision is generally applicable to distributions pursuant to plans of liquidation adopted after March 28, 1985. Related amendments are also made to the provisions providing for no gain or loss pursuant to a chain of corporations liquidating within one year of the adoption of the plan.

The Act also conforms the definition of a qualified stock purchase for purposes of a section 338 election to require that stock representing at least 80% of the voting power as well as 80% of the value of the stock must be purchased to qualify. A section 338 election treats the assets of the acquired corporation as though they were acquired in a taxable transaction. This provision applies generally to acquisition dates after December 31, 1985.

Technical Corrections

The Act made several technical corrections to corporate provisions enacted in the Tax Reform Act of 1984, including:

- The availability of the dividend received deduction for dividends from portfolio foreign corporation stock to the extent the dividend is effectively connected with a U.S. trade or business (and subject to U.S. tax) is further limited to the extent the foreign corporation's stock is debt-financed.
- The IRS's authority to issue regulations regarding related parties to prevent the avoidance of the provision disallowing the deduction of interest attributable to tax-exempt obligations is only effective for term loans made after July 18,1984 and demand loans outstanding after July 18, 1984 *not* repaid by September 18, 1984.
- The provision that restricts the ability of shareholders of a regulated investment company from effectively converting a short-term capital gain into a long-term capital gain by requiring the holding of the stock for more than six months is extended to apply to tax-exempt interest dividends if the holding period of the stock begins after March 28, 1985. Otherwise, the shareholders would be able to convert a short-term capital gain into a tax-exempt interest dividend.
- In a tax-free reorganization, no gain or loss is recognized by the acquired corporation on a disposition of stock and securities permitted to be received from the acquiring corporation to its shareholders, security holders or creditors pursuant to a plan of reorganization.
- In a tax-free reorganization, gain is recognized by an acquired corporation on the distribution to its shareholders of assets held prior to the reorganization. However, no gain is recognized on the distribution of assets received from the acquiring corporation and distributed to its shareholders or creditors.

Purchase Price Allocations

When the assets of a business are sold for a lump sum, the transaction is viewed as a sale of each individual asset. This has been a source of endless taxpayer controversy with the IRS.

Generally, the seller benefits when a larger portion of the purchase price is allocated to capital assets that will generate capital gain, such as goodwill or land. The buyer benefits from an allocation that results in a higher basis for inventory, which generates ordinary income when sold; for depreciable tangible assets, such as buildings and equipment; and for amortizable intangible assets that have determinable useful lives. In many transactions, a premium in excess of the initial valuation of a business' assets was often paid and reallocated among the assets resulting in a basis in excess of their fair market value.

In early 1986, the IRS issued regulations requiring the use of the so-called residual method of allocation for both buyer and seller when a purchaser of corporate stock elected to treat the transaction as a taxable asset acquisition under section 338. The regulations provide for the allocation, based upon fair market value, of the purchase price to be made to: (1) cash type items; (2) certificates of deposit, readily marketable securities and similar types of items; and (3) all other assets except those in the nature of goodwill and going concern value. The remainder of the purchase price is then allocated to goodwill and going concern value.

Under the Act, the purchase price for an acquisition of the assets of a business must be allocated to the assets by both the buyer and the seller under the same method the IRS required in its section 338 regulations. This provision will apply to the acquisition of assets that as a whole will constitute a trade or business even though they may not constitute all of the business assets of the seller. The IRS is authorized to require detailed information to be reported by the buyer and seller.

Planning Point

This provision will generally reduce controversy with the IRS when a business is purchased. Before finalizing a transaction, the buyer and the seller should agree on the purchase price allocation to avoid controversy when the subsequent tax returns are prepared. This will also allow the proper reporting of the allocation used when the expected information recording mechanism is put in place.

Effective Date

Applies to acquisitions of assets after May 6, 1986, unless the acquisition is pursuant to a binding contract in effect on May 6, 1986.

Accounting Provisions

Limitations on the Use of the Cash Method of Accounting

Under present law, a taxpayer generally can elect on its first income tax return to use any method of accounting for federal income tax purposes that clearly reflects income and that is regularly used in keeping the taxpayer's books and records. Various methods of accounting are allowed, including the cash receipts and disbursements method, the accrual method, certain industry-specific methods, and hybrid methods. Once a taxpayer selects a method of accounting, a change to a different method required the consent of the IRS.

A taxpayer using the cash method of accounting generally recognizes items of income and expense in the taxable year in which funds are received or disbursed. This method could result in the recognition of income and expenses without regard to the taxable year in which the economic events giving rise to the item occurred and, therefore, it is not fully in accord with generally accepted accounting principles.

Under the Act, corporations (other than S corporations) and partnerships where one of the partners is a corporation (other than an S corporation) that previously were permitted to use the cash method of accounting, may not use that method for federal income tax purposes. The new rule also applies to tax-exempt trusts that are subject to the unrelated business income tax and to tax shelters. Additionally, once on the accrual method, a tax shelter generally cannot use the recurring item exception to the economic performance rule.

The following taxpayers can continue to use the cash method of accounting:

- Small businesses: Taxpayers with average annual gross receipts of $5 million or less
- Farming and timber: Businesses other than those that were not allowed to use the cash method of accounting under prior law
- Individuals and certain other entities: Sole proprietorships, S corporations, qualified personal service corporations and qualifying partnerships
  —A qualifying partnership is a partnership that does not have a corporate partner other than an S corporation.
  —A qualified personal service corporation is a corporation in which substantially all the activities consist of the performance of services in the field of health, law, engineering, architecture, accounting, actuarial science, performing arts or consulting, and substantially all (at least 95%) of the value of the stock is owned by specified shareholders including present or retired employees of the corporation or their estates.

Any change from the cash method of accounting required by this provision is treated as a change in the taxpayer's method of accounting initiated by the taxpayer, and does not require IRS consent. Any adjustments to income from this change are to be included in income over a period not to exceed four years. Taxpayers, including tax shelters, can elect to continue to report income from loans, leases, and transactions with related persons entered into before September 29, 1985, on the cash method.

Effective Date
This provision is effective for taxable years beginning after December 31, 1986.

Simplified Dollar Value LIFO Method for Specified Small Businesses
Any taxpayer permitted or required to maintain inventories can elect to value its inventory using the last-in, first-out (LIFO) method. The LIFO method is considered to be the most advantageous method of accounting for inventories in periods of inflation because the costs of the most recent additions to inventory are matched against sales. However, the complexity and greater costs of compliance associated with the LIFO method have discouraged some smaller taxpayers from using the LIFO method.

One method of costing LIFO inventories is the dollar-value method. Under the dollar-value LIFO method, a taxpayer measures changes in its inventories on the basis of total dollars rather than on an item-by-item basis. The dollar value method is centered around the basic concept of pools, which is the grouping together of similar items of physical inventory.

Generally, for wholesalers, retailers, jobbers and distributors. items of inventory are pooled by major lines, types or classes of goods. In the case of manufacturers, all inventory items that represent a natural business unit can be combined into a single pool. Additionally, manufacturers can assign inventory items to one of a number of pools determined by the similarity of items to each other. Under prior law, a taxpayer with average annual gross receipts of no more than $2 million for its three most recent taxable years could elect to use a single pool for all items of inventory.

Under the Act, a new election (made without IRS consent) is provided to allow certain small businesses to use the simplified dollar-value LIFO method. This method permits inventories to be grouped in multiple pools in accordance with the major categories of specified published indices. The change in inventory costs for the taxable year is determined by the change in the published index for the general category to which the pool relates. The computation of the ending LIFO value of the pool is then made using the dollar-value LIFO method. The cumulative index necessary to compute the equivalent dollar values of prior years is developed using the link-chain method.

A taxpayer is eligible to use the simplified dollar-value LIFO method if its average annual gross receipts for its three preceding taxable years (or portion thereof that the taxpayer has been in business) do not exceed $5 million. All members of a controlled group are to be treated as a single taxpayer for the purpose of determining average annual gross receipts. A taxpayer using the simplified dollar-value LIFO method is required to change to a different method in the first year that it fails to meet the $5 million gross receipts test. Any taxpayer that has a valid election in effect under prior law to use the single pool method can revoke that election, or it can continue to use that method provided it continues to meet the requirements for that election.

Effective Date
This provision is effective for taxable years beginning after December 31, 1986.

Installment Sales
Under prior law, gain from most sales of property in which the seller receives deferred payments could be reported on the installment method, unless the seller elected other treatment.

Under the Act, a new proportionate disallowance rule is introduced. This new rule provides that specified installment sellers will have to include in income a portion of a deemed payment amount called *allocable installment indebtedness* (AII). AII is multiplied by the sale's gross profit ratio—computed under the present installment sales rules—to determine the portion of AII that is includible in income as taxable gain.

AII equals: The face amount of applicable installment obligations (AIOs) outstanding at year end divided by the sum of:

1. The face amount of all installment obligations, and

2. The adjusted basis of the taxpayer's other assets.
3. This is multiplied by the taxpayer's average quarterly indebtedness.
4. This is reduced by any AII arising in prior years.

AIOs are those obligations from dealer sales made after February 28, 1986, of all property, and from sales of real property used in a trade or business or held for the production of income, whose sales price is more than $150,000. Installment obligations arising from the sale by an individual of personal use property and property used or produced in a farming business are not AIOs. In later years, gain attributable to AIOs that arose in prior years is not currently recognized to the extent any related payments are less than the obligations' AII. If a year's AII exceeds the year's AIO, additional AII is allocated to prior years' obligations. Excess payments are accounted for under existing installment method rules.

Example: Dealco is a calendar taxable year dealer in real property that commenced operations in 1987. It sells a property at a profit during 1987 for $90,000 taking back the purchaser's note on which full payment is due in 1989. At the end of 1987, the adjusted basis of Dealco's assets other than the installment obligation is $310,000 and its average quarterly indebtedness for the year is $200,000.

    1987: Dealco's AII or deemed payment for 1987 is $45,000 (average quarterly indebtedness of $200,000 times the face amount of AIO of $90,000 divided by the sum of face amount of installment obligations of $90,000 and the adjusted basis of other assets of $310,000).

    1988: Dealco sells another property during 1988 at a profit for $110,000 with the full payment due on the purchaser's note in 1990. At the end of 1988, Dealco's adjusted basis of other assets is $400,000 and average quarterly indebtedness is $300,000. Dealco's AII or deemed payment for 1988 is $55,000 (average quarterly indebtedness of $300,000 times the face amount of AIO of $200,000 divided by the sum of the face amount of installment obligations of $200,000 and the adjusted basis of other assets of $400,000, reduced by the 1987 AII of $45,000).

    1989: Dealco sells another property at a profit for $130,000 in 1989 (payment deferred to a later year), and received the full payment of $90,000 for the 1987 sale. At the end of 1989, Dealco's adjusted basis of other assets is $360,000 and its average quarterly indebtededness is $500,000.

        Before computing the 1989 AII, the prior year's AII must be determined. For the 1987 obligation, the first $45,000 of the $90,000 payment does not lead to the recognition of any additional gain and reduces the AII allocated to that obligation. The remaining $45,000 yields additional gain computed under the current installment method rules. Therefore, the 1989 AII allocable to prior years is $55,000 ($45,000 AII from 1987 plus $55,000 AII from 1988 less the returned 1987 AII of $45,000).

        Dealco's 1989 AII is $145,000 (average quarterly indebtedness of $500,000 times the face amount of AIO of $240,000 divided by the sum of the face amount of installment obligations of $240,000 and basis of other assets of $360,000 reduced by 1988 AII of $55,000.

Because Dealco's 1989 AII of $145,000 exceeds the amount of 1989 AIO, the payments deemed to be received in 1989 are $130,000 allocable to the 1989 installment obligation and $15,000 allocable to the 1988 obligation.

Planning Point

The operation of the proportionate disallowance rule could force dealers and others using the installment method into a tight cash-flow situation similar to what happened to Dealco in 1989. While Dealco received payment of $90,000, it had AII of $145,000 generating additional gain on which tax must be paid without additional cash flowing in. Any business currently using the installment method should review its operations to determine whether it will be able to live comfortably with the new rules. The election must be made on or before the due date (including extensions) of the return.

Dealers can elect out of the proportionate disallowance rule for installment obligations that arise from the sale of timeshares and residential lots. The Act also provides an exception for specified manufacturers of tangible personal property. When a manufacturer or an affiliate sells qualified property to a dealer and the dealer must make payments of principal only when the the property is resold the proportionate disallowance rule does not apply.

The Act prohibits taxpayers from using the installment method for revolving credit plan sales and for sales of certain publicly traded property, e.g., stock or securities traded on an established securities market.

Effective Date

The proportionate disallowance rule is generally effective on or before taxable years ending after December 31, 1986, for sales made on or after March 1, 1986.

For installment obligations arising from dealer sales of real property, gain attributable to AII allocated to installment obligations that arise or are deemed to arise in the first taxable year of the taxpayer ending after December 31, 1986, is taken into account ratably over the three taxable years beginning with the first taxable year. For installment obligations arising from dealer sales of personal property, any increase in tax liability for the first taxable year ending after December 31, 1986, resulting from the application of the proportionate disallowance rule, is treated as being imposed ratably over the three taxable years beginning with the first taxable year.

For AIOs other than installment obligations arising from dealer sales of real or personal property, the proportionate disallowance rule is effective for taxable years ending after December 31, 1986, for sales after August 16, 1986.

The elimination of the installment method for sales on a revolving credit plan is effective for taxable years beginning after December 31, 1986. The provision for sales of publicly traded property is effective for sales after December 31, 1986.

Capitalization Rules for Inventory, Construction and Development Costs

Producers of inventory generally may not currently deduct the production costs incurred in producing the inventory. Instead, the costs must be added to an inventory account and recovered through an offset to the sales price. For inventories of manufacturers, the determination of which costs constituted production costs was made under the full-absorption method. Under this method, substantially all direct production costs were inventoried. However, the treatment of indirect costs varied depending on the type of property produced. Indirect costs were divided into three categories: costs in Category 1 were always included in inventory costs; costs in Category 2 did not have to be included in inventory costs; and costs in Category 3 were included in inventory costs only if they were included in inventory costs for purposes of taxpayer's financial reports.

Under prior law, the direct costs of acquiring, constructing or improving buildings, machinery, equipment or other assets having a useful life beyond the end of a taxable year were not currently deductible. These capital expenditures became part of the basis of the asset and were recovered through depreciation or amortization. However, the proper treatment of many indirect costs incurred in connection with this property was uncertain. Additionally, purchasers of goods for resale were subject to rules that required that only direct acquisition costs be inventoried. Direct acquisition costs included the invoice price of the goods plus transportation costs, less any discounts. Additionally, the proper treatment of many indirect costs incurred in connection with self-constructed property was uncertain.

The Act requires application of a uniform set of capitalization rules to all costs incurred in manufacturing or constructing real or personal property or in purchasing or holding property for resale. Therefore, the new rules apply to inventory, noninventory property produced or held for sale to customers, and to assets or improvements to assets constructed by a taxpayer for its own use in a trade or business or in an activity engaged in for profit.

The uniform capitalization rules are based on the existing rules applicable to extended period long-term contracts. Taxpayers subject to the new rules will be required to capitalize not only direct costs but an allocable portion of most indirect costs that benefit the assets produced or acquired for resale, including general and administrative and overhead costs. Additionally, the uniform capitalization rules apply to all depreciation deductions for federal income tax purposes.

- The change in the rules governing the absorption of costs into inventory is treated as a change in method of accounting. All inventory on hand as of the effective date of this provision must be revalued to reflect the new absorption rules. The revaluation is accomplished by valuing the items included in inventory on the effective date as if the new absorption rules concerning direct and indirect costs had been in effect during prior periods. The difference between the inventory as originally valued and the inventory as revalued is an adjustment to income. If the information to make these determinations is not available, a taxpayer can use estimates based on available data.
- If retailers' and wholesalers' average annual gross receipts for the three preceding years were over $10 million, the uniform capitalization rules apply. The Act requires the IRS to provide a simplified method that taxpayers can elect to use when applying the uniform capitalization rules to property acquired for resale. Under the simplified method, it is

anticipated that taxpayers will initially calculate their inventory balances without regard to the new capitalization rules. Taxpayers will then determine the amounts of additional costs that must be capitalized and add these amounts, along with any other appropriate costs in beginning inventory balances, to the preliminary balances to determine their final balances.

Example: For a taxpayer using the LIFO method, the calculation of a particular year's LIFO index will be made without regard to the new capitalization rules. However, costs capitalized under these rules will be added to the LIFO layers applicable to the various years for which the costs were accumulated.

Storage Costs
Under the simplified method, a taxpayer includes storage costs in inventory based on the ratio of total storage costs for the year to the sum of (1) the beginning inventory balance and (2) gross purchases during the year.

Example: Assume that a FIFO taxpayer incurred $1 million in storage costs during a taxable year, had a beginning inventory balance of $2 million, made gross purchases of $8 million, and had an ending inventory of $3 million. The ratio of storage costs to beginning inventory and purchases is 10% ($1,000,000 divided by $2,000,000 plus $8,000,000). Thus, for each dollar of ending inventory, the taxpayer must capitalize $.10 of storage costs. Ending inventory would be increased by $300,000 and the balance of the storage costs ($700,000) would be included in cost of goods sold.

In the case of a LIFO taxpayer, to the extent ending inventory exceeds beginning inventory, additional capitalized storage costs would be calculated by multiplying the increase in inventory for the year by the applicable ratio. Accordingly, in the above example, if the taxpayer used the LIFO method, an additional $100,000 (10% of $1,000,000) of storage costs would be added to ending inventory. However, for LIFO taxpayers any storage costs that were included in the taxpayer's beginning inventory balance would remain in the taxpayer's ending inventory balance and would not be included in the cost of goods sold for the year.

Purchasing costs
Under the simplified method, these costs are allocated between inventory and cost of goods sold based on the ratio of purchasing costs to gross purchases during the year.

Repackaging and other processing costs
Under the simplified method, these costs are allocated based on the ratio of total repackaging processing, etc. costs to the sum of (1) the beginning inventory balance and (2) gross purchases during the year.

General and administrative expenses allocable in part to the above functions
Under the simplified method, these costs are allocated based on the ratio of direct labor costs incurred in a particular function to gross payroll costs.

Example: The total costs of operating the taxpayer's accounting department for the year was $75,000, direct labor purchasing costs were $500,000 and gross payroll was $1,500,000. The portion of the accounting department cost subject to capitalization in connection with the purchasing function is $25,000, i.e., $500,000 divided by $1,500,000 × $75,000.

Retirement Plan Contributions
Contributions to a pension, profit sharing, or stock bonus plan, unless the contributions relate to past service costs, are considered to be indirect costs that must be capitalized.

Debt Interest
Interest on debt must be capitalized if the debt is incurred or continued to finance the construction or production of (1) real property or (2) other long-lived property under the Act's depreciation system regardless of whether it is constructed for self use or sale. Interest incurred in connection with other property estimated to have a production period of more than two years (one year in case of items costing more than $1 million) is also subject to capitalization. The rules relating to the capitalization of interest do not apply to real or personal property acquired solely for resale.

Items Not Covered
The capitalization rules do not apply to research and experimentation expenditures or to the development and other costs of oil and gas wells or mineral properties. Also, the rules do not apply to property produced under a long-term contract, to specified property produced in a farming business, to the growing of timber, or to taxpayer-produced property for use outside of the taxpayer's trade or business or profit activity.

Effective Dates
For noninventory property that is held primarily for sale to customers, the uniform capitalization rules generally are effective for costs and interest paid or incurred after December 31, 1986, with no restatement of beginning balances or adjustments to income. Self-constructed assets for which substantial construction occurred prior to March 1, 1986, remain subject to the prior law tax accounting rules. The new rules apply to inventory for a taxpayer's first taxable year beginning after December 31, 1986. Any adjustments resulting from the changes in inventory accounting are spread over a period of no more than four years. Net operating losses and tax credit carryovers will offset any positive adjustments.

Long-Term Contracts
A taxpayer with long-term contracts can report income and expenses under the cash or accrual method, or, can elect to have income and expenses attributable to long-term contracts accounted for under the percentage-of-completion method or the completed-contract method. A long-term contract is a building, installation, construction or manufacturing contract that spans two or more taxable years.

Under prior law, the percentage-of-completion method required income to be recognized according to the percentage of the contract completed during the taxable year. All costs attributable to the contract are deducted when incurred. Under the completed-contract method, the entire gross contract price is included in income in the taxable year in which the contract is completed and accepted and all costs properly allocable to the long-term contract are deducted in the year of completion.

The long-term contract rules provide that costs must be allocated between contract and noncontract costs. These rules are similar to those under the full absorption method of accounting. For example, research and development costs that relate to a particular contract need not be capitalized as part of that contract. Additional rules concerning the allocation of costs to long-term contracts apply to extended period long-term contracts (those that are not completed within 24 months). Under the extended period long-term contract rules, specified costs not previously treated as contract costs must be allocated to a contract if they either directly benefit the contract or were incurred because of the contract. Under the extended period long-term contract rules, research and development costs that relate to an extended period long-term contract must be capitalized.

Under the Act, taxpayers may elect to compute income from a long-term contract under one of two methods:

- The percentage-of-completion capitalized-cost method (40% PCM)
- The percentage-of-completion method. Additionally, the Act establishes a new *look-back* method that imposes a deemed interest charge on long term contracts.

Under the revised percentage-of-completion method, revenues from long-term contracts must be included in gross income based on the ratio of contract costs incurred during the year to total projected contract costs. Additionally, *contract costs* incurred during the year are currently deductible. Under the new *look-back* method, interest is payable by or to the taxpayer if the actual profit on a contract allocable to any year varies from the estimated profit used in reporting income.

Under the 40% PCM, a taxpayer must take into account 40% of the items related to the contract under the percentage-of-completion method. The contract costs taken into account in determining the percentage of completion are similar to the costs subject to the uniform capitalization rules including the rules relating to the capitalization of interest (see page 70). Additionally, general and administrative costs attributable to cost-plus contracts and to federal government contracts requiring certification of costs are treated as contract costs.

The remaining 60% of the items under the contract are to be taken into account under the taxpayer's normal method of accounting, capitalizing those costs as required under the uniform capitalization rules. Thus, under the completed-contract method, 60% of the gross contract income will be recognized, and 60% of the contract costs will be deducted at the time the contract is completed. The look-back method is applied to the 40% portion of the contract reported on the percentage-of-completion method.

Independent research and development costs (IR&D) are expressly excepted from the category of capitalizable costs. IR&D costs are costs incurred in the performance of independent research and development other than (1) expenses directly attributable to a long-term contract in existence when the expenses were incurred and (2) any expenses under an agreement to perform research and development.

Small-construction contracts are excepted from the required use of either the percentage-of-completion capitalized-cost method or percentage-of- completion method. Small-construction contracts are contracts for the construction or improvement of real property if the contract is expected to be completed within two years and is performed by a taxpayer whose average annual gross receipts for the three taxable years preceding the taxable year in which the contract is entered into do not exceed $10 million. However, these contracts are still subject to the interest capitalization rules.

Effective date
Applies to contracts entered into after February 28, 1986.

Taxable Years of Partnerships, S Corporations, and Personal Service Corporations

As a general requirement for tax years beginning after 1986, the Act requires that all partnerships, S corporations, and personal service corporations conform their taxable years to the taxable year of their owners.

Partnerships

- A partnership must generally use the taxable year of the partners owning a majority interest (more than 50%) in the partnership profits and capital. If partners owning a majority of the partnership profits and capital do not have the same taxable year, the partnership must adopt the same taxable year as its principal partners. A principal partner is a partner having an interest of 5% or more in the partnership profits or capital. If the principal partners do not have the same taxable year, the partnership must adopt a calendar year.
- There is an exception if a partnership establishes the existence of a business purpose for having a different taxable year to the satisfaction of the IRS. The deferral of income to partners for three months or less is not treated as a business purpose.

Example: Smith Bros., a partnership, has one principal partner, which is a March 31 year-end corporation owning a 10% partnership interest in profits and capital. The remaining partners are calendar-year individuals none of whom could qualify as a principal partner. Under the Act, Smith Bros., would be required to adopt a calendar year, i.e., the taxable year of the majority of its partners.

- A partnership is not required to adopt the taxable year of the majority partners unless partners with the same taxable year have owned a majority interest in the partnership for the three preceding taxable years of the partnership. For this purpose, taxable years of the partnership beginning before the effective date of this provision are taken into account.

S Corporations and Personal Service Corporations

Under the Act, an S corporation must adopt a permitted year, regardless of when the corporation elected to be taxed as an S corporation. A permitted year is generally a calendar year. However, an exception is provided for any other taxable year for which the S corporation establishes a business purpose to the IRS's satisfaction. The deferral of income to shareholders of an S corporation for three months or less is not treated as a business purpose.

A personal service corporation must adopt a calendar year. An exception is also provided for a personal service corporation that establishes a business purpose for having a different taxable year. Personal service corporations cannot deduct payments to employee-owners prior to the taxable year in which the employee-owner would include the payment in gross income regardless of the employee-owner's percentage of stock ownership.

Natural Business Year

Any partnership or S corporation that received permission from the IRS to use a fiscal year (other than a year end that resulted in a three-month or less deferral of income) because the year coincides with its natural business year is allowed to continue the use of that taxable year without further IRS approval. Any partnership, S corporation or personal service corporation can adopt, retain or change to a fiscal year if 25% or more of its gross receipts for the 12-month period in question are recognized in the last two months of its fiscal year and this requirement has been met for three consecutive 12-month periods.

Planning Points
- A partnership, S corporation, or personal service corporation that changes its taxable year because of this provision will be treated as making the change with IRS consent. Each partner in a partnership or shareholder in an S corporation that realizes more than 12 months of income in a single taxable year because of the short taxable year resulting from the change should consider electing to take the excess of income over expenses into account ratably over the first four taxable years beginning after December 31, 1986.
- Because the four-year adjustment period applies only to partners and S corporation shareholders, personal service corporations should consider electing S corporation status, if possible, for a taxable year beginning in 1986 to allow the shareholders to take advantage of the four-year adjustment period.

Effective Date
Applies to taxable years beginning after December 31, 1986.

Reserve for Bad Debts
Taxpayers are allowed a deduction for those debts arising from a trade or business that become wholly or partially worthless during the taxable year. Under prior law, the amount of the deduction was determined using either the specific charge-off method or the reserve method. Additionally, dealers in property were allowed to establish a reserve for losses that resulted from their liability as guarantors, endorsers, or indemnitors on debt that arose as a result of the dealers' sales of property.
- The Act repeals the availability of the reserve method of computing the bad debt deduction for all taxpayers other than commercial banks with assets of $500 million or less and thrift institutions. Therefore, the bad debts of most taxpayers will be deducted when the debt becomes wholly or partially worthless under the specific charge-off method.
- The Act also repeals the reserve method for dealers in real or tangible personal property who guarantee, endorse, or provide indemnity agreements for their customers' debts owed to others.
- A change from the reserve method to the specific charge-off method is treated as a change in method of accounting and the balance in any reserve for bad debts is to be taken into income ratably over four years.

Effecitve Date
Applies to taxable years beginning after December 31, 1986.

Qualified Discount Coupons
For taxable years beginning after December 31, 1986, the Act repeals the election

that allows accrual method taxpayers to deduct the cost of redeeming qualified discount coupons received after the close of the taxable year. As a result, only those redemption costs of discount coupons received during a taxable year will be allowed as a deduction during that taxable year.

Utilities Using Accrual Method of Accounting

The IRS has specifically permitted utilities to use a variation of the accrual method of accounting that recognized income in the taxable year in which a customer's utility meter is read: the cycle meter reading method. For taxable years beginning after December 31, 1986, the Act requires accrual basis utilities to recognize income attributable to the furnishing or services to customers not later than the taxable year in which the services are provided. Concurrently utilities can accrue any deductions for the related cost of furnishing services if economic performance has occurred.

Estimated Tax

Waiver of Penalties

The Act makes several changes that increase tax liabilities retroactively to the beginning of 1986. Consequently, the Act allows corporations until March 15, 1987 (the final filing dates for calendar year returns) to pay their full 1986 income tax liabilities without incurring any additions to tax on account of the underpayments of estimated tax attributable to retroactive changes in the law.

Specified Exempt Organizations

Effective for taxable years beginning after December 31, 1986, private foundations must make quarterly estimated payments of the excise tax on their net investment income. Tax-exempt organizations must do likewise for the tax on unrelated business income. These quarterly payments must be made under the regular rules applying to estimated corporate income taxes.

Research and Experimentation Credit

Under prior law, a research and experimentation (R&D) credit is allowed for 25% of the increase in current year qualified incremental research expenses over the average expenditure for such expenses during the prior three years. The Act extends the available credit until December 31, 1988, restricts the definition of qualified research, reduces the rate to 20% and adds a new university basic-research credit.

Under the Act, only research activities that are intended to produce technologically new or improved business products qualify for the credit. Substantially all of the research activities must relate to the product's functional aspects, such as new or improved functions, performance, reliability or quality. Activities relating to style, taste, cosmetic or seasonal design factors do not qualify. The newly developed or improved business item must be a product, process, computer software, technique, formula or invention offered for sale, lease or license or used by the taxpayer in a trade or business.

The determination of whether new or improved characteristics of a business item are technological in nature depends on whether the process of experimentation fundamentally relies on principles of the physical or biological sciences, engineering or computer science. The term *process of experimentation* means a process involving the evaluation of more than one alternative designed to achieve a result where the means of achieving that result is uncertain at the outset. This may involve developing one or more hypotheses for specific design decisions, testing and analyzing those hypotheses and refining or discarding the hypotheses as part of a sequential design process.

The Act generally repeals the current law provision that treats lease payments for personal property used in qualified research as eligible for the credit; however, payments for the use of computer time remain eligible. It also substantially expands the list of research or research related activities that are excluded from eligibility for the credit.

Under prior law, only 65% of amounts paid to outside persons to perform contract research is includible in qualified research expenses. The Act removes cash payments to universities and tax-exempt scientific research organizations under a written agreement for basic research from the definition of contract research subject to the 65% limit. Instead, the excess of these payments over the sum of the greater of two fixed research expense floors plus any decrease in the inflation-adjusted nonresearch contributions to universities is subject to a new 20% credit: the university basic-research credit. Thus, the Act provides a single R&D credit composed of the 20% incremental-research credit and a new 20% university basic-research credit.

The Act also made several other changes in the treatment of R&D items, the most notable of which are making the R&D credit subject to the general business credit limitation and placing restrictions on the treatment—as qualified research expenses—of expenses incurred to develop computer software for internal use.

Effective Date
The extension of the credit is effective for taxable years ending after December 31, 1985. The other provisions, with the exception of the university basic-research credit, are effective for taxable years beginning after December 31, 1985. The university basic-research credit is effective for taxable years beginning after December 31, 1986.

Charitable Donations of Scientific Equipment
The Act expands the charitable deduction allowed for donations of newly manufactured scientific equipment to include donations to tax-exempt scientific research organizations. The change is effective for taxable years beginning after December 31, 1985.

Agriculture, Energy, and Natural Resources

Agriculture

Soil and Water Conservation Expenditures
The Act limits the deduction of soil and water conservation expenditures incurred after December 31, 1986, to improvements that are consistent with a conservation plan approved by the Soil Conservation Service (SCS) of the Department of Agriculture or, if there is no SCS plan, to amounts that are consistent with a plan of a State conservation agency.

Land Clearing Expenditures
For expenditures incurred after December 31, 1985, the Act repeals the provision
allowing a current deduction for clearing land in preparation for farming. Under
the Act, these expenditures will be added to the basis of the cleared land.

Dispositions of Converted Wetlands
Gain realized on the disposition of wetlands or highly erodible croplands that are
converted after March 1, 1986, to agricultural use (other than livestock grazing)
will be treated as ordinary income. Any loss on the disposition of the land will be
treated as long-term capital loss.

Prepayment of Expenses of Farmers
To the extent the prepaid farming expenses of a farmer using the cash method of
accounting exceed 50% of total nonprepaid farm expenses, amounts paid for
feed, seed, fertilizer, and certain other similar farm items in taxable years after
March 1, 1986, may only be deducted as the items are actually consumed (an
economic performance test).

Preproductive Period Expenses of Farmers
The Act provides, for taxable years starting after December 31, 1986, that the
uniform capitalization rules apply to farmers for their products having a
preproductive period of more than two years. Under a special election, certain
farmers may elect to deduct preproductive period expenses currently.

Discharge of Indebtedness Income for Farmers
Under the Act, income realized after April 9, 1986, from an agreement between a
solvent individual farmer and an unrelated person to discharge a qualified farming
indebtedness is treated as income realized by an insolvent individual, i.e., it will
not be taxable. However, to qualify for this deemed insolvent treatment, a farmer
must reduce any tax attributes (NOLs, basis in property) by the amount of the
income realized.

Energy

The solar energy tax credit is phased out over a three year period at decreasing
rates: 15% for 1986, 12% in 1987, and 10% for 1988. The geothermal energy tax
credit is also phased out over three years at the rates of 15% for 1986, and 10% for
1987 and 1988. The 15% credit for converting ocean thermal energy to useable
energy is extended through 1988. The biomass credit is extended through 1987 at
a 15% rate in 1986, and a 10% rate in 1987, while the wind credit expires on
December 31, 1985.

Oil, Gas and Geothermal Properties, and Hard Minerals

Advance Royalties and Lease Bonuses
Retroactively overruling the holding in a 1984 Supreme Court case, the Act
provides that starting on January 1, 1986, percentage depletion will not be allowed
on payments, such as advance royalties or lease bonuses, without actual
production from the oil, gas or geothermal property.

Comment
An unanswered question remains: Can percentage depletion be taken on the full
advance royalty in the year received regardless of the amount of actual production?

Domestic Intangible Drilling Costs and Mining Exploration Costs

Generally, the prior-law treatment of domestic intangible drilling costs (IDCs) and mining exploration costs is retained except:

- An integrated oil and gas company can elect to expense 70% of its IDCs. The remaining 30% must be amortized over a five-year period.
- A corporate producer of hard minerals will recover 30% of its exploration and development costs using the straight-line method over a five-year period.

Foreign IDCs and Mining Exploration Costs

Under the Act, IDCs and mining exploration and development costs incurred *outside* the United States are to be recovered over 10 years using straight-line amortization, or, at the taxpayer's election, by adding these costs to the cost depletion basis.

Effective Date

These provisions are generally effective for costs paid or incurred after December 31, 1986.

Timber Capital Gain

Because the preferential capital-gain rate is repealed effective for taxable years beginning after December 31, 1986, income from the sale of timber is subject to tax at ordinary income rates. Taxpayers are permitted to revoke existing elections to treat the cutting of timber as a sale or exchange.

Rapid Amortization Provisions

Trademark and Trade Name Expenditures

Under prior law, taxpayers could elect to amortize over a period of at least 60 months expenditures for the acquisition, protection, expansion, registration, or defense of a trademark or trade name. However, no amortization was allowed for an expenditure to purchase an existing trademark or trade name.

The Act repeals the amortization provision. Under the Act, all expenditures for trademarks and trade names must be capitalized. The capitalized costs generally are recoverable only on disposition of the trademark or trade name.

Effective Date

The repeal applies to expenditures paid or incurred after 1986. However, transitional rules allow the amortization of expenditures incurred after 1986 pursuant to a written contract that was binding as of March 1, 1986, or for development, protection, expansion, registration or defense activities commenced as of March 1, 1986, if the lesser of $1 million or 5% of the total cost was incurred or committed by that date, provided the trademark or trade name is placed in service before 1988.

Deduction for Loss in Value of Bus Operating Authorities

For bus line operators affected by the Bus Regulatory Reform Act of 1982, the Act allows the deduction over a 60-month period of the aggregate adjusted basis of all bus operating authorities held by the taxpayer on November 19, 1982, or acquired after that date under a written contract that was binding on that date. A similar deduction will be provided for freight forwarders if their industry is deregulated.

Merchant Marine Capital Construction Fund

The Act coordinates the Internal Revenue Code with the capital construction fund of the Merchant Marine Act of 1936. Changes are made in the tax treatment, for taxable years beginning after 1986, of nonqualified withdrawals from capital construction funds. A 25-year limit is imposed on the amount of time money can remain in a capital construction fund without being withdrawn for a qualified purpose.

Limit On General Business Credit

Under prior law, taxpayers could offset 100% of their tax liability up to $25,000 and up to 85% of their tax liability in excess of $25,000 with the general business credit. The general business credit is the aggregate of the ITC, the targeted jobs credit, the alcohol fuel credit, and the employee stock ownership credit.

The Act reduces the maximum offset from 85% to 75% of tax liability. The lower percentage applies to taxable years beginning after December 31, 1985.

Debt Forgiveness of Solvent Taxpayers

Present law provides that gross income includes income from the discharge of indebtedness. An exception is provided for bankrupts, insolvents, or solvent taxpayers if the discharged indebtedness is qualified business indebtedness. For a solvent taxpayer, the amount of the discharge that would have otherwise been included in gross income had the discharge not been of qualified business indebtedness is applied to reduce the basis of the taxpayer's depreciable property or inventory.

The Act repeals the exclusion from gross income of the forgiveness of qualified business indebtedness for solvent taxpayers.

Effective Date

Applies to discharges of indebtedness after December 31, 1986.

Planning Point

Solvent taxpayers who are in a position to have qualified business indebtedness forgiven should consider having the forgiveness take place in 1986 to avoid the impact of the new Act provision. This should also be considered by insolvent taxpayers who would become solvent as a result of debt forgiveness.

Financial Institutions

Commercial Bank Bad Debt Reserve

The Act continues the prior law bad debt reserve method deduction except that large banks will be required to use the specific charge-off method to compute the deduction for bad debts. A bank is a large bank if, for any taxable year beginning after December 31, 1986, the sum of the average adjusted tax basis of its assets or the sum of the assets of any controlled group in which it is a member exceeds $500 million.

Comment
Once a bank has average adjusted assets in excess of $500 million after 1986, it will continue to be treated as a large bank even though it slips below this threshold in a subsequent taxable year.

Existing bad debt reserves for large banks will be recaptured into operating income over four years beginning in taxable years after December 31, 1986 as follows: 10% in 1987, 20% in 1988, 30% in 1989, and 40% in 1990. If a bank becomes a large bank after 1986, the graduated recapture percentages will apply for the subsequent years.

For the first year a bank is required to recapture its bad debt reserve, it can, if desirous, recapture more than the minimum 10%. The bank could recapture as much as 100% of the reserve. Any remaining reserve is recaptured over the three subsequent taxable years at the approximate rates of 23%, 33% and 44%, respectively.

Comment
If a large bank has expiring net operating losses, an optional acceleration of the bad debt reserve recapture could be beneficial.

Comment
In the taxable year the bank becomes a large bank, it must recapture its prior years' reserve balance into operating income while it can only compute its bad debt deduction on the specific charge-off method. This could cause the bank to experience an unusual shift in its tax liabilities, which will, when the prior reserves are fully recaptured, become more regular.

If a large bank has, for any taxable year, a nonperforming loan percentage exceeding 75%, it is considered a financially-troubled bank and does not have to recapture any of its existing bad debt reserves. The nonperforming loan percentage is the ratio of the sum of the outstanding balances of nonperforming loans as of the close of each quarter of the taxable year to the sum of the amounts of equity as of the close of each quarter.

In addition to the phased-in recapture of prior years' bad debt reserves discussed above, a large bank can elect to use a special cut-off method. This method will not be considered a change of accounting method and may allow the bank to recapture 100% of its reserve in the first year the reserve method is disallowed.

Comment
The Act did not change the repeal of the percentage-of-loans method for computing reserve additions for tax years after 1987.

Thrift Institution Bad Debt Reserves
The reserve method used by thrift institutions was not changed by the Act. Thrifts that use the reserve method to compute their bad debt loss deduction can continue to do so under either the experience method, allowed to small commercial banks, or the percentage of taxable income method. However, beginning in taxable years after December 31, 1986, the maximum percentage of taxable income that a thrift institution can deduct as an addition to reserves for bad debts is reduced from 40% to 8%.

To be eligible for the special treatment of bad debt reserves, at least 60% of the assets of a thrift must be invested in qualifying assets that are the same as the current law definition for domestic building and loan associations, i.e., cash, time deposits, U.S. government obligations, and residential real property loans.

Comments

- A failure of a mutual savings bank, domestic building and loan association or cooperative not-for-profit loan association with at least $500 million in assets to meet the 60% qualifying asset test appears to subject them to the same rules as large banks: the recapture of loan loss reserves, and the denial of the reserve method of computing bad debt deductions.
- By reducing both the bad debt percentage to 8% and the maximum income tax rate to 34%, the Act retains the prior law effective tax rate of 31.28% for thrifts.

Tax-Exempt Obligations

Financial institutions will be denied any interest deduction allocable to carrying tax-exempt obligations acquired after August 7, 1986, for interest incurred for taxable years ending after December 31, 1986. The prior 20% disallowance rule will survive for specified tax-exempt issues by small municipal issuers.

Interest income from certain nongovernmental purpose bonds will be a preference item for the alternative minimum tax. The business untaxed reported profits item included in alternative minimum taxable income will subject some of the previously untaxed municipal interest to the new 20% minimum tax.

Net Operating Losses

Under prior law, there was a special bank carry-back and carry-over provision for net operating losses. For losses incurred in taxable years beginning after December 31, 1986, the Act establishes a three-year carryback and a fifteen-year carryforward. As under prior law, an election can be made to forego the carry-back period.

There is a special rule for net operating losses attributable to deductions for bad debt losses. The Act retains the prior law ten-year carryback and five-year carryforward for this item for taxable years beginning before 1994. The Act also allows thrifts to carry their losses incurred between 1981 and 1986 forward to the succeeding eight, rather than five taxable years.

Cash Method

Financial institutions and finance companies will be subject to the same requirement as other corporations relating to the use of the accrual method of accounting.

Federal Home Loan Bank Dividends

In a transaction in early 1985, the Federal Home Loan Mortgage Corporation (Freddie Mac) distributed a new class of stock to the Federal Home Loan Banks, which in turn distributed the stock to their member institutions. A technical correction to the Tax Reform Act of 1984 provides that the receipt of the Freddie Mac preferred stock distributed in 1985 is taxable income and the distribution is not eligible for a dividends received deduction. Current dividends from post-1984 Freddie Mac earnings are eligible for the dividends received deduction.

Troubled Thrifts

The prior law special provisions facilitating the restructuring and rehabilitating of troubled thrift institutions will expire after 1988. The regular corporate reorganization rules will apply to reorganizations after December 31, 1988.

- A troubled thrift will no longer be able to reorganize tax free without issuing stock. The prior law rule is repealed for mergers and acquisitions after December 31, 1988.
- For reorganizations occurring after December 31, 1988, the rule providing that deposits of an acquired thrift are treated as stock in determining net operating loss carryovers will be repealed.
- Payments by the Federal Savings and Loan Corporation (FSLIC) to troubled domestic building and loan associations after December 31, 1988, will result in a reduction in the basis of assets either acquired with the payment or previously held. In addition, these FSLIC payments will be included in the taxable income of the institution after December 31, 1988. There is an exception to these two rules when the payments are made pursuant to an assistance agreement entered into prior to January 1, 1989. The Act makes clear that there is no disallowance of expenses for any amount paid or incurred by a thrift allocable to tax-exempt FSLIC payments.

Insurance Products and Companies

Insurance Policyholders

Interest on Installment Payments

Under the Act, all amounts paid after the date of enactment by an insurance company to any beneficiary of a life insurance policy at a date later than the death of the insured are included in gross income to the extent that the amount paid exceeds the death benefit. Accordingly, the Act repeals the provision of prior law that excluded the first $1,000 in excess of the death benefit from the gross income of a surviving spouse.

Life Insurance Policy Loans

The Act denies a deduction for interest on policyholder loans from certain life insurance policies owned by a taxpayer that cover the life of an officer or employee. The affected loans are those aggregating more than $50,000 per officer, employee or owner of an interest in any trade or business carried on by the taxpayer. This provision applies to interest on loans under policies purchased after June 20, 1986, in taxable years ending after that date.

Structured Settlements

The Act amends present law to limit *qualified assignments* to those assignments entered into after December 31, 1986, that require the payment of damages on account of a claim for physical injury or physical sickness. Damages on account of a claim for wrongful death are also included.

Life Insurance Companies

Special Life Insurance Company Deduction
Under the Act, the special life insurance company deduction used in computing life insurance company taxable income (LICTI), equal to 20% of the income from insurance businesses, is repealed for taxable years beginning after December 31, 1986.

Insolvent Companies' Losses from Operations
Under the Act, an insolvent life insurance company is permitted to apply its current loss from operations and its unused operating loss carryovers against the increase in its taxable income attributable to amounts deemed distributed from its policyholder surplus account (PSA) in liquidations after November 15, 1985.

Tax-Exempt Organizations Engaged in Insurance Activities
Under the Act, charitable organizations and social welfare organizations are exempt from tax only if an insubstantial part of their activities consist of offering commercial-type insurance. If a substantial part of an affected organization's activities consists of providing commercial-type insurance including annuity contracts, the organization will be treated as engaged in an unrelated trade or business and taxed on the insurance business income under the insurance companies rules.

For taxable years after 1986, Blue Cross and Blue Shield organizations that were tax-exempt under prior law are taxable as if they were taxable insurance companies. However, these companies receive various concessions, such as a fresh start with respect to accounting methods.

Property and Casualty Insurance Companies

Physicians' Mutual Protection Associations
In response to the insurance liability crisis, the Act contains several changes designed to encourage physicians to join malpractice insurance associations that provide coverage at reduced prices. In general, premiums paid to an association are deductible to the extent they do not exceed the cost of commercial insurance and are included in the association's income. A refund of a contribution by an association is deductible to the extent included in the recipient's income. The provision applies to associations in operation before January 1, 1984.

Unearned Premium Reserve
Under the Act, a property and casualty insurance company generally is required to reduce its deduction for unearned premiums by 20%. Additionally, 20% of the unearned premium reserve outstanding at the end of the most recent taxable year beginning before January 1, 1987, is included in income ratably over a six year period commencing with the first taxable year beginning after December 31, 1986.

Treatment of Dividends and Tax-exempt Income
Under the Act, for years beginning after December 31, 1986, the deduction for losses is reduced by 15% of the insurer's tax-exempt interest and the deductible portion of the dividends received. Investments acquired on or before August 8, 1986, are excepted from this provision.

Treatment of Loss Reserves

In general, the Act requires casualty companies to discount their deductions for loss reserves to take into account the time value of money. The deduction for unpaid losses is limited to the amount of *discounted* unpaid losses. The amount of the discounted unpaid losses at the end of any taxable year is determined by using (1) the gross amount to be subjected to discounting, i.e., the undiscounted loss reserve; (2) the pattern of payment of claims, including the duration in years over which the claims will be paid; and (3) the rate of interest to be assumed in calculating the discounted reserve (100% of a five-year rolling average applicable Federal midterm rate).

Effective Date

Applies to taxable years beginning after December 31, 1986.

Protection Against Loss Accounts

For taxable years beginning after December 31, 1986, the deduction for contributions to protection against loss (PAL) accounts for mutual property and casualty companies is repealed. Balances in PAL accounts are included in income as under prior law.

Special Treatment for Small Mutual Companies

Under the Act, property and casualty companies with annual net written premiums or direct written premiums (whichever is greater) that do not exceed $350,000 are exempt from tax. Property and casualty companies with annual net written premiums or direct written premiums (whichever is greater) that exceed $350,000, but do not exceed $1,200,000, may elect to be taxed only on taxable investment income.

Effective Date

This provision is effective for taxable years beginning after December 31, 1986.

Tax-Exempt Bonds

The Act retains the tax exemption for interest on state and local government bonds used to finance traditional governmental operations. Under the Act, however, interest on bonds used to provide conduit financing for activities other than the traditional operations of state and local governmental units (collectively referred to as private activity bonds) is taxable unless the bond falls within one of the following exceptions:

- Qualified section 501(c)(3) bonds, i.e., bonds issued for the benefit of schools, hospitals, and other charitable organizations.
- Bonds used to finance certain exempt facilities, such as airports, docks, wharves, mass commuting facilities, sewage or solid waste disposal facilities, qualified water projects and certain hazardous waste disposal facilities
- Qualified redevelopment bonds, small-issue bonds and student loan bonds
- Qualified mortgage and veterans' mortgage bonds

State Volume Limitations

The Act replaces the separate state volume limitations of prior law for (1) industrial development bonds (IDBs) and student loan bonds and (2) qualified mortgage bonds with a single state volume limitation. In addition, a state's private use portion (in excess of $15 million) of governmental bonds is subject to the new volume limitation. Until December 31, 1987, the limitation per state is the greater of $75 per resident or $250 million per annum after which date the limitation is reduced to $50 per resident or $150 million per annum.

Arbitrage Restrictions

Interest on arbitrage bonds—bonds more than a minor portion of the proceeds of which are invested in materially higher yielding taxable obligations—continues to be taxable. The Act tightens the arbitrage restrictions and extends specified rules to more types of tax-exempt bonds.

Information Reporting

The Act extends to all tax-exempt bonds information reporting requirements similar to the requirements that currently apply to IDBs, student loan bonds, qualified 501(c)(3) bonds, and mortgage revenue bonds.

Effective Date

Applies generally to bonds issued after August 15, 1986. There are, however, provisions affecting tax-exempt bonds with effective dates ranging from September 25, 1985 to September 1, 1986.

Real Estate Investment Trusts (REITs)

The Act amends a number of prior law requirements relating to the rules for qualifying as a real estate investment trust (REIT) and the taxation of REITs.

- An otherwise qualified entity is permitted to elect REIT status even though it has fewer than 100 shareholders or more than 50% of its outstanding stock is owned by five or fewer individuals, provided that the entity was not a REIT in any prior year.
- To elect REIT status, the entity must either have been treated as a REIT for all taxable years beginning after February 28, 1986, or must have no earnings and profits accumulated for any year in which it was in existence and not treated as a REIT.
- An entity electing REIT status is permitted to change its annual accounting period from a fiscal year to a calendar year without IRS permission *if* it has not previously engaged in an active trade or business.
- All the assets, liabilities and items of income, deduction and credit of a qualified subsidiary of a REIT are treated as assets, liabilities and respective items of the REIT.
- Income from qualifying temporary investments will be treated as income that meets the *75% of gross income* test of Code section 856(c)(3) for a one-year period after the receipt of new equity capital.
- Special rules are provided regarding the performance of services relating to rental income, and the classification as rent or interest income of amounts based on the net income of the tenant or debtor.
- The required minimum distribution of a REIT is reduced by a portion of amounts required to be included in income before cash is received.
- A nondeductible 4% excise tax is imposed on underdistributions.

- The rules governing the maximum amount of capital gain dividends that a REIT may pay are revised.
- The penalty tax on deficiency dividends is repealed.

Effective Date

The amendments generally are effective for taxable years beginning after 1986.

Mortgage-Backed Securities—Real Estate Mortgage Investment Conduits (REMICs)

To clarify the federal income tax status of securities representing *packaged mortgages* that are traded on the secondary securities market, the Act creates a new type of entity known as a real estate mortgage investment conduit (REMIC). In general, a REMIC is a fixed pool of mortgages with multiple classes of interests held by investors. Congress intends that REMICs are to be the exclusive means of issuing multiple-class real estate mortgage-backed securities without the imposition of two levels of taxation.

The Act provides rules governing:

- Requirements for qualification to elect to be treated as a REMIC.
- Nonrecognition of gain or loss by the transferor on the transfer to a REMIC of qualified mortgages or other property in exchange for regular or residual interests in the REMIC.
- Nontaxable pass-through entity status of a REMIC.
- Taxation of holders of regular and residual interests in a REMIC.
- Application of the original issue discount rules.
- Liquidation and compliance provisions.

Effective Date

The REMIC provisions generally apply to taxable years beginning after 1986.

Regulated Investment Companies (RICs)

The Act makes several amendments affecting regulated investment companies (RICs), e.g., mutual funds:

- A nondeductible 4% excise tax is imposed on underdistributions.
- Differences in the rate of dividends paid to accounts with initial investments of over $10 million that reflect savings in administrative costs (but not differences in management fees) would not be treated as preferential dividends.
- Qualified business development companies would be allowed to elect RIC status.
- A hedging exception to the *short-short test* is instituted.

Effective Date

In general, the RIC amendments apply to taxable years beginning after 1986. The mandatory calendar taxable year provision applies to a RIC's first taxable year beginning after 1986.

Miscellaneous Provisions

- Membership list income: Income earned by tax-exempt charitable organizations from renting or exchanging lists of members or donors will not be taxed as income from an unrelated trade or business. This provision applies to exchanges and rentals of lists after the date of enactment.

- Cooperative housing corporations: The rules allowing a tenant-shareholder of a cooperative housing corporation to deduct an allocable share of interest and real estate taxes paid by the cooperative are amended and expanded to apply to tenant-shareholders other than individuals. This provision applies to taxable years beginning after 1986.

- Real estate title holding entity: Tax-exempt organizations are permitted to pool their investment funds by investing in real estate through a tax-exempt corporation or trust formed for the purpose of holding title to real estate. This provision applies to taxable years beginning after 1986.

- Removal of barriers to the handicapped: The prior law deduction for up to $35,000 of capital expenditures for the removal of architectural barriers to the handicapped, which expired on December 31, 1985, is reinstated and made permanent. The reinstated deduction applies to expenditures after December 31, 1985.

- Targeted jobs tax credit: The targeted jobs tax credit, which expired on December 31, 1985, is extended for three years until December 31, 1988. However, only the first year's wages are eligible for the credit, and at a reduced rate of 40%. The Act repeals the 25% credit for wages paid to members of targeted groups in the second year of employment. In addition, the Act imposes new restrictions on wages eligible for the credit.

- Orphan drugs: The 50% tax credit for clinical testing of certain drugs for rare diseases (orphan drugs) is extended for three years, through December 31, 1990.

- Trade show income: The exemption for trade show income from the tax on the unrelated trade or business income of certain types of tax-exempt organizations is expanded to apply to a broader range of exempt organizations and more types of trade shows. This provision applies to taxable years beginning after the date of enactment of the Act.

- Reindeer sales: The Reindeer Industry Act of 1937 is retroactively amended to exempt from tax income the sale of reindeer and reindeer products. The Act is inexplicably silent on caribou and musk oxen.

- Distribution of low-cost items by charities: The Act allows tax-exempt organizations that are eligible to receive tax-deductible charitable contributions to make unsolicited distributions of items costing $5 or less in fund-raising activities. Funds raised from the recipients of the items are *not* subject to tax on income from an unrelated trade or business. This provision applies to distributions of items occurring after the date of enactment of the Act.

- Fuel excise taxes: The diesel fuel excise tax may, at the election of a retailer, be imposed on sales from manufacturers and wholesalers to retailers. This provision is effective for sales after the first calendar quarter beginning more than 60 days after the date of enactment (i.e., the first calendar quarter of 1987.)

Effective January 1, 1988, the Act also generally repeals the prior law rules under which collection of the manufacturers excise on gasoline may be deferred to the wholesale level.

Provisions Affecting Foreign Operations

U.S. Based Multinationals

Under the Act, the new U.S. corporate tax rate of 34% will now be significantly lower than the rate imposed by most of our major trading partners: the 35% U.K. corporate rate is an exception. Consequently, corporate management should look for methods of reducing the effective tax rates of its overseas subsidiaries to a tax rate no higher than the U.S. rate. In addition, technical changes to the foreign tax credit will make it more difficult for U.S. multinationals to fully use all the foreign income taxes paid by their foreign subsidiaries as tax credits. Therefore, efficient ways of financing foreign activities will become even more important than they were in the past. An important consideration is the desirability of shifting income producing activities to a low tax jurisdiction, which now includes the United States.

Comment

The senior tax authorities of the major U.S. trading partners are well aware of this reaction to the 1986 Tax Reform Act and have alerted their tax inspectors to look for any shifting methods that do not conform to the local tax laws. The proper coordination of U.S. and foreign tax laws, therefore, becomes even more important.

The Source Rules

The Act makes the following changes in the source rules:

- The current law title passage test will be retained for sourcing sales of inventory property, whether purchased or manufactured in the United States. The source of income of all other sales of personal property will be based on the residence of the vendor. Special rules are provided for sales of depreciable and intangible property, including goodwill and shares in foreign affiliates. Sales by foreign vendors outside of the United States may be taxable as U.S. source income if attributable to a U.S. office or place of business.
- Regulations are to prescribe the source of income from trading in futures contracts, forward contracts, options contracts and other securities.
- The prior law 80/20 rule providing special sourcing rules for dividends and interest paid by a domestic corporation is replaced. Under the Act, to satisfy the 80% test, the foreign source income must be active foreign business income. The active business requirement can be met by attributing a subsidiary's active foreign business to its controlling corporate shareholder. An exception for interest paid to a related party treats a portion of the interest as U.S. source income based on the ratio of U.S. income to worldwide income.
- The exception for bank deposit interest under the source rules is eliminated and replaced with an exemption from withholding for payments made to foreign corporations and individuals.
- The prior allocation rules for transportation within and without the United States is replaced with a new rule that treats up to 50% of all transportation income from U.S.-connected shipping and aircraft operations as U.S.

source income. An employee's personal service income (except on routes
to and from U.S. possessions) continues to be sourced based on the place
where the services are performed. A 4% gross transportation tax is
imposed on U.S. source transportation income derived by a nonresident
alien individual or foreign corporation, subject to a net income election.
The Act contains an exception for income effectively connected with a
U.S. trade or business. A foreign corporation organized in a country that
exempts U.S. citizens and domestic corporations from tax on shipping
income will be exempt from U.S. tax on shipping income if at least 50%
of the value of the foreign corporation is beneficially owned by individuals
that reside in countries that provide reciprocal tax exemptions to the
United States.

- Income from space and oceanic activities is sourced to the country of
residence and a conforming change is made to the definition of Subpart F
shipping income. These amounts do not include income from oil, gas and
extractive activities.
- 50% of the income from the transmission of communications or data into
or out of the United States is treated as U.S. source income and 50% is
foreign source. This rule only applies to U.S. persons, or foreign persons
with a U.S. place of business. However, the IRS is authorized to extend
this rule to controlled foreign corporations.

Effective Date
Applies to taxable years beginning on or after January 1, 1987. A retroactive
exception applies to property sales by foreign taxpayers after March 18, 1986.

Foreign Tax Credit (FTC)

Limitation
The Act retains the overall foreign tax credit (FTC) limitation but adds separate
baskets (see below) for different types of income. New separate limitation income
look-through or tracing rules are established for eligible payments received by
U.S. taxpayers from controlled foreign corporations (CFCs). Eligible payments
include specified interest, passive rents and royalties, dividends (including
Subpart F and deemed dividends on the sale of CFC shares), and investments in
U.S. property. There are exceptions for payments from non-CFCs, related-party
interest and other income derived from an active trade or business.

The separate baskets are:
- Passive income, which includes Subpart F foreign personal holding
company (FPHC) type income and passive foreign investment company
(PFIC) income. Conforming changes for the treatment of passive income
are contained in other foreign provisions. A *high-tax kick-out* rule applies
to exclude income (after allocation of expenses at the U.S. recipient level)
subject to a foreign tax rate in excess of the U.S. tax liability. This income,
except for high withholding tax interest, is included in the overall
limitation basket.
- Shipping income, which includes amounts from foreign leasing and
operating activities of vessels or aircraft. The new sourcing rules (see
above) are applicable when applying the FTC limitation.

- Financial services income, which includes amounts derived from qualified active banking, insurance, financial or similar activities. Financial service income does not include income in the high withholding tax interest, certain passive income and shipping income.
- High withholding tax interest, which applies to all interest derived from related or unrelated persons. If interest is subject to a foreign withholding tax of at least 5%, it is high withholding tax interest. This provision applies to all interest recipients (subject to the export exception) and not just financial institutions.
- Dividends from non-CFCs, or 10% to 50% U.S.-owned foreign corporations. The Act also adds a disallowance for foreign taxes deemed paid by a non-CFC in excess of the 5% limitation on high withholding tax interest.
- The Act adds netting rules that permit interest expense paid or accrued by a CFC to its U.S. shareholder or to a related CFC to offset passive income. The IRS may extend this rule to unrelated persons.
- Interest from financing U.S. exports is treated as overall limitation income rather than as one of the separate baskets.

Effective Date

Applies to taxable years beginning on or after January 1, 1987. Transitional rules include special phase-out exceptions for interest on qualified loans to 33 less-developed countries.

Deemed-Paid Credit

Under prior law, dividends and deemed-paid taxes received from a foreign corporation are based on the payer's accumulated profits, i.e., earnings and profits (E&P) computed on an annual basis. The Act eliminates the E&P layering rules for measuring a foreign corporation's deemed paid taxes and replaces them with a pooling concept. For post-1986 taxable years, the deemed paid foreign taxes are based on a multi-year pool of the payer's post-1986 E&P. Dividends are treated as paid first from post-1986 E&P. Rules for taxes deemed paid by second- and third-tier subsidiaries are similarly determined. The Subpart F deemed-paid credit rules are modified to conform to the new average E&P rules.

Carryovers

Excess foreign taxes for pre-1987 overall limitation income can be carried to post-1986 financial service or shipping income.

The Act modifies the FTC carryback rules so that credits that are excess credits solely because of the rate reductions cannot be carried back to high tax years (40% in 1987, 46% in pre-1987 years). Foreign taxes, except for high withholding taxes, paid in tax years beginning on or after January 1, 1987, are carried back to the overall limitation for pre-1987 tax years of U.S. taxpayers.

Creditable Taxes

Effective for foreign taxes paid or accrued in taxable years beginning on or after January 1, 1986, no FTC is allowed for foreign withholding taxes that are subsidized or abated, directly or indirectly, by operation of foreign law. This provision codifies existing language in the IRS Regulations.

Foreign Losses

For FTC purposes, foreign losses are to be applied against all other foreign baskets before reducing U.S. source income. An excess foreign loss in one basket

proportionately reduces foreign source income in other baskets. Recapture of
excess losses results in a recharacterization of separate basket income. U.S. losses
reduce separate basket income on a pro rata basis.

Allocation and Apportionment of Expenses

Under current IRS regulations, most expenses can be apportioned based on facts
and circumstances on a per-company (rather than a consolidated group) basis.
Under the Act, companies filing a consolidated return apportion expenses on an
affiliated group basis.

An affiliated group must apportion interest expense using the ratio of foreign
assets to total assets of the group; the gross income method will not be available.
An affiliated group includes all domestic subsidiaries (including possession's
corporations). For this purpose, the basis of a 10% owned foreign affiliate is
adjusted for increases or decreases in E&P. Interest expense allocated to foreign
sources also must be allocated to separate FTC baskets.

Expenses not allocable to any class of income are apportioned on the
aggregate, rather than separate or per-company, income of a U.S. affiliated group.
The Act also reinstates and modifies the research and experimentation (R&D)
rules for a one-year period. As modified, 50% of expenses attributable to R&D
performed in the United States is allocable to domestic source income. The
remaining 50% of R&D expenses is apportioned on the basis of sales or gross
income.

Effective Date

Applies to taxable years beginning on or after January 1, 1987. Phase-in
transitional rules apply for interest expenses only. The R&D regulation is
reinstated as modified for one tax year beginning after August 1, 1986, and on or
before August 1, 1987.

Foreign Currency Exchange Gains and Losses

Functional Currency Concept

The Act introduces, for the first time, a comprehensive set of rules governing the
taxation of foreign currency gains and losses. These provisions, which provide
greater certainty for the tax treatment of normal commercial transactions, are
based on the functional currency concept of Financial Accounting Statement No.
52. Under this concept, all determinations have to be made in the taxpayer's
functional currency. The functional currency is automatically the U.S. dollar
except for a qualified business unit (a self-contained foreign operation) in which
case it is the currency:
- Used to keep the books and records
- Of the economic environment in which a significant part of the business
  unit's activities generating revenues and expenses are conducted
- Used to borrow or lend

Presumably, the functional currency of related business units and the degree of
the business unit's integration with those related units is also reviewed.

A business unit that maintains its books and records in a foreign currency can
elect to use the U.S. dollar. To elect, the business unit must either use the
separate-transaction method for all foreign currency transactions or use a

translation method that approximates dollar-based accounting. For hyperinflation-
ary economies, IRS regulations, to be issued, will permit an election to compare
year-end balance sheets using historic exchange rates in foreign currency
transactions for all balance sheet items.

For transactions in other than the functional currency, a disposition of foreign
currency will result in the recognition of gain or loss. The foreign exchange gain
or loss is to be accounted for separately from any gain or loss attributable to the
underlying transaction. This rule continues the dual transaction theory which was
the most acceptable theory under the old law.

Example: When a United States exporter sells its products for a designated
amount of foreign currency units, it determines the selling price at the translation
rate on the date of sale. When it collects its payment, if the foreign currency
exchange rate on the date of payment and the date the account receivable was set
up are different, there is a foreign currency gain or loss.

Gain or loss is generally not recognized until there is a closed and completed
transaction, such as the collection of an account receivable. The foreign currency
gain or loss is generally ordinary income or loss.

Hedging Transactions

Unless the regulations provide otherwise, capital gain or loss treatment will apply
to all futures contracts and options contracts that are capital assets in the hands of
the taxpayer (held for speculation) and are *not* marked-to-market. These assets do
not include hedging transactions or tax straddles. Hedges must be identified as
such before the close of the day on which the transaction is entered into to ensure
ordinary income or loss treatment. Banks consider this to be the date the phone
call was made, even though the substantiating paperwork may take several days to
complete.

Corporate treasurers often borrow foreign currency to take advantage of lower
interest rates. They then hedge their exposure by entering into futures contracts in
the same foreign currency. Economically, any gain or loss on the futures contract
is offset by gain or loss on the repayment of interest and principal. Effectively,
this hedge is an addition or reduction of interest income or expense. The Act
authorizes the IRS to issue regulations providing for integration of all aspects of
hedging transactions into a single transaction. This characterization as interest is
only for foreign exchange purposes. It is not applicable for withholding tax
purposes.

Generally, foreign currency gains or losses will be allocated by reference to the
residence of the taxpayer or qualified business unit on whose books the asset or
liability is reflected. Accordingly, for a U.S. corporation the gain or loss would
be U.S. source. However, the IRS is authorized to issue regulations that treat
hedges differently to avoid possible abuse. A special rule is to be provided for
certain related party loans that have to be marked-to-market annually. On foreign
currency loans that bear interest at a rate at least 10% higher than the applicable
rate for mid-term Federal obligations at the time the loan is made, and that are
made by a U.S. person or a related foreign person to a 10% owned foreign
corporation, any interest income is treated as U.S. source income to the extent of
any loss on the loan caused by the marking-to-market.

Translation of Currencies

If a U.S. taxpayer conducts its activities in a foreign country through a branch, it has to translate its branch results into U.S. dollars. Under prior law, an accounting election could be made to either translate the profit and loss statement or to translate the opening and closing balance sheets and then to compare the two, to determine income earned during the period. Under the Act, the profit and loss method will be mandatory; the net worth or balance sheet method will no longer be acceptable.

To translate the foreign functional currency, it is converted into U.S. dollars using the weighted average exchange rate for the taxable period. Any remittances during the year are ignored. Regulations are to be issued that will limit the deductions for branch losses to the taxpayer's U.S. dollar basis in branch assets. This U.S. dollar basis is deemed to be the original U.S. dollar investment plus subsequent capital contributions and unremitted earnings.

An exchange gain or loss will then be recognized on remittances to the extent the value of the foreign currency differs from its value when earned.

Translation of E&P and Foreign Tax Credits

Under prior law, when a foreign corporation paid a dividend to its U.S. shareholder, the dividend was translated at the rate in effect at the time the dividend was received. The deemed-paid foreign tax credit, which the U.S. corporate shareholders could claim, was determined by translating the foreign tax using the same translation rate. Existing regulations provide rules for determining the accumulated profits of the foreign corporation that were used to determine the deemed-paid foreign tax credit. The accumulated profits of a foreign corporation were computed differently when a dividend was paid, when the subsidiary earned subpart F income, or when the foreign subsidiary was finally sold or liquidated. Because of the differences between subpart F income and ordinary dividends, taxpayers had several planning opportunities.

Under the Act, actual and deemed dividends related to the sale of a foreign subsidiary are translated at the exchange rate on the date the dividend is included in income. Deemed distributions under Subpart F are translated at the weighted average exchange rate for the foreign corporation's taxable year. Deemed-paid foreign taxes are translated into U.S. dollars using the exchange rate on the day the tax is paid. This changes the long standing prior law rule, and provides a greater foreign tax credit when the foreign currency is depreciating vis-a-vis the U.S. dollar, and a smaller foreign tax credit when it is appreciating vis-a-vis the U.S. dollar.

Comment

The great uncertainty in the U.S. tax treatment of foreign currency transactions and translation discouraged many American businesses from engaging in actively managing their foreign exchange risks. Although the Act still contains uncertainties, it provides greater clarity in many areas that were previously uncertain.

Effective Date

Applies to taxable years beginning after December 31, 1986.

Controlled Foreign Corporations (CFCs)

Definition of Tainted Income

Tainted income earned by a controlled foreign corporation (CFC) is subject to current tax in the United States under the Subpart F rules. Under current law, tainted Subpart F income includes passive foreign personal holding company (FPHC) and/or certain base company income. The Act expands the scope of the Subpart F FPHC rules. Note, this expanded category is part of the new FTC separate limitation basket provisions for passive income.

Passive FPHC income includes dividends, rents, royalties and net gains from property that generates passive income or no income at all. In addition, gains from commodity and foreign currency forward and similar transactions and income equivalent to interest are treated as passive income. Exceptions will apply to gains from hedging and gains from trade or business related transactions, including trading by a producer or merchant in commodities.

The Subpart F base company shipping rules contained an exclusion for amounts reinvested in qualified foreign shipping assets. The Act repeals this exclusion, resulting in U.S. shareholders being currently taxed on all tainted Subpart F shipping income earned by a CFC.

Insurance income and amounts equivalent to interest are treated as Subpart F income and are subject to the separate passive income basket. Subpart F insurance income includes amounts derived from insuring or reinsuring property, life or liability risks outside the CFC's country of incorporation.

The Act contains a special rule for Group or industry captive insurance companies that underwrite related party or shareholder risks. Except for publicly traded insurance companies, each U.S. person owning stock in any 25% or more U.S. owned foreign insurance company is taxed on the pro-rata share of the foreign insurance company's income derived from the insuring of the U.S. stockholder's and related parties' risks. An exception applies when the captive is not owned by insured companies. An irrevocable election is available to treat related party insurance income as U.S. effectively-connected taxable income.

Exceptions

Under prior law, the Subpart F rules excepted a CFC from current taxation if one of two tests were met. They were:

1. The CFC was not formed or availed of to reduce U.S. tax. This test had two parts, a subjective facts and circumstances test and an objective *de minimis* test: a CFC is not subject to current tax if it is subject to a foreign tax rate that is at least 90% of the U.S. corporate tax rate.

2. Less than 10% of the CFC's earnings were Subpart F income.

The Act repeals the subjective part of the "not-formed-or-availed" of exception, leaving the 90% *de minimis* test in place. In addition, the Act further restricts the second test by establishing a new standard: a CFC will be excepted if its Subpart F income is less than $1 million or 5% of the CFC's gross income.

Under prior law, an E&P deficit in a member of a chain of corporations could reduce the E&P of the profitable members of the chain. This opportunity is eliminated.

Under prior law, E&P deficits from prior years can be carried forward to offset CFC income in a current period. Under the Act, pre-1987 E&P account deficits cannot be carried forward to offset post-1986 CFC income. Post-1986, or qualified deficits, moreover, can only be carried forward to offset income in the same qualified activity.

Under prior law, a corporation organized in a possession cannot be a CFC. The Act repeals this exception.

Control

Under prior law, the determination of control of a CFC was based solely on the ownership of voting power of a U.S. shareholder in a foreign corporation. The Act redefines control to include ownership of more than 50% in either voting power or value of the total outstanding shares of a foreign corporation.

The control requirements of FPHCs are also extended to apply to ownership by five or fewer individuals of more than 50% of either voting power or the value of the foreign corporation's total outstanding shares.

Passive Foreign Investment Company (PFIC)

The Act adds new rules for taxation of income earned by a U.S. shareholder in a passive foreign investment company (PFIC). These rules apply regardless of the amount of PFIC stock held by a U.S. shareholder. The tax on the sale of PFIC shares is increased by interest on tax-deferred earnings. Investors can elect to treat earnings from qualified electing funds as currently taxable. Exceptions apply for active banking and insurance companies and start-up companies. Income subject to the FPHC and PFIC provisions is treated as a Subpart F inclusion.

Capital Gains Subject to Accumulated Earnings and Personal Holding Company (PHC) Tax

Under prior law, accumulated earnings and personal holding company (PHC) taxable income did not include gain from the sale or exchange of property by a foreign corporation. The Act now provides that net capital gain that is attributable to a U.S. business and is not exempt under a treaty may be included in accumulated earnings or PHC taxable income.

Effective Date

Retroactively applicable to gain or loss realized after February 28, 1986.

Possessions Tax Credit (PTC)

The Act retains the possessions tax credit (PTC) with modifications. In addition, eligibility for the PTC is extended to U.S. Virgin Islands corporations. Under present law, income earned by a possessions corporation is not eligible for the PTC unless the taxpayer elects one of the two optional methods of computing possessions source income: (1) cost sharing or (2) 50/50 profit split. The modifications include:

- The cost sharing amount is the greater of an arms-length royalty or 110% of the cost of the product area research times a fraction, the numerator of which is possession sales and the denominator of which is total sales of the affiliated group (a 10% increase over prior law).
- Under the profit-split method, the amount of product area research expenditures allocated to combined taxable income is increased from 110% to 120% of the expenses.

- The active income test for possessions corporation status is increased from 65% to 75%, and income from loans for assets or projects in Caribbean Basin Initiative countries is qualified possession source income.

Effective Date
Applies to taxable years beginning on or after January 1, 1986.

U.S. Expatriates

For taxable years beginning on or after January 1, 1987, the expatriates' foreign earned income exclusion will be reduced from $80,000 to $70,000 per year. This reduction, in combination with the U.S. tax rate reduction, will increase the cost of expatriate equalization programs. As a result, the employment of third country nationals by U.S. multinationals may increase.

The earned income exclusion and housing allowance is disallowed for amounts attributable to travel in prohibited foreign countries. In addition, travel in prohibited areas does not qualify for either the bona-fide foreign residence or physical presence outside the United States tests used to determine eligibility for the earned income exclusion.

Foreign Taxpayers

Branch Profits Tax

Under current law, the United States uses the so-called *classical tax system*: corporations and their shareholders each pay tax. For foreign shareholders of U.S. corporations, this tax typically takes the form of a withholding tax on dividends paid. Shareholders could avoid this withholding tax by conducting their U.S. activities as a branch of a foreign corporation organized in a country that has a favorable income tax treaty, which eliminates the U.S. tax on dividends paid to non-U.S. shareholders: the so-called *second tier tax*.

The 1986 Tax Reform Act adopts a branch profits tax, similar to one imposed in Canada, that is imposed on remitted profits of the U.S. branch, called the dividend equivalent amount. This tax is imposed at a 30% rate unless reduced by treaty.

In treaty-shopping situations, the treaty is overridden. Treaty-shopping cases are those in which more than 50% in value of the foreign corporation is beneficially owned by nonresidents of the treaty country, or 50% or more of the foreign corporation's income is used to satisfy liabilities to persons who are not either residents of that foreign country or the United States, unless the shares of the corporation are regularly traded on an established securities market in the foreign country or the parent corporation's shares are publicly traded.

The dividend equivalency amount is the current and accumulated *effectively connected* earnings of a U.S. branch that are not reinvested in the United States. This may include income, such as tax-exempt municipal bond interest. It is calculated by comparing the adjusted basis of branch assets (including money) at the end of the year and the beginning of the year taking into consideration all assets and liabilities associated with effectively-connected income. The branch profits tax also applies to the greater of interest paid or deducted by a U.S. branch. Interest is treated as U.S. source income subject to withholding at the 30% or lower treaty rate.

Amounts deducted in excess of the actual branch payments, e.g., allocations of head office interest expenses, are deemed paid to a home country parent and the income tax treaty between the home country and the United States would determine the applicable U.S. withholding tax rate. Foreign corporations that are partners in a U.S. partnership will be subject to this provision, but individual partners will not be.

Foreign corporations that derive more than 25% of their income from a U.S. business would be subject to the second tier tax if a tax treaty prevents the branch tax. For foreign banks doing business in the United States, this percentage was negotiated to prevent subjecting the banks to the second tier withholding tax.

Comment

A treaty nondiscrimination provision based on the U.S. model treaty prevents the United States from imposing the branch profits tax. Many older income tax treaties also contain a nondiscrimination provision that is similar but not identical to the provision in the model income tax treaty.

Although the IRS can distinguish the language to reach different results, the better view is that the intent of the older treaty nondiscrimination provisions is identical to the intent of the provision in the United States model income tax treaty and therefore they should also be interpreted as preventing the branch tax from being imposed.

The following amounts are not subject to the branch tax even though they constitute effectively-connected income:

- Certain earnings derived by a Foreign Sales Corporation (FSC).
- Earnings of foreign transportation carriers that are exempt from U.S. tax pursuant to a treaty or reciprocal exemption.
- Earnings derived from the sale of a U.S. real property holding corporation.
- Earnings of certain corporations organized in a U.S. possession.
- Effectively-connected income of certain captive insurance companies.

Effective Date

Applies to taxable years beginning after December 31, 1986.

Effectively Connected Income

Under prior law, if a cash basis taxpayer received income in a year in which the taxpayer was no longer engaged in the U.S. trade or business that generated the income, it could change its character. This consequence posed both a tax planning opportunity as well as a trap for deferred compensation payments and installment sales transactions. The Act changes this by treating the income as effectively-connected income in the year received if it would have been treated as such had it been taken into account in the year earned.

Effective Date

Applies to taxable years beginning after December 31, 1986.

Tax-Free Exchanges By Expatriates

Under prior law, U.S. citizens who gave up U.S. citizenship for the principal purpose of avoiding U.S. tax could avoid U.S. tax by exchanging property located in the United States for like-kind property located outside the United

States and then selling the foreign property when the expatriate was no longer subject to U.S. tax. This result was reached because the tax only applied to gain realized on the sale of U.S. property. The Act ends the use of tax-free exchanges to avoid tax, by taxing the gain on the sale of property whose basis is determined in whole or in part by reference to the basis of U.S. property.

Effective Date

Applies to the sale or exchange of property received in exchange after September 25, 1985.

Reporting by Foreign-Controlled Corporations

U.S. corporations and foreign corporations with a branch in the United States that are controlled by a foreign person must attach an information report to their return on Form 5472, Information Return of a Foreign-Owned Corporation, reporting all transactions with related corporations. This reporting requirement is extended to transactions with all related persons including foreign partnerships, trusts and individuals.

Effective Date

Applies to taxable years beginning after December 31, 1986.

Foreign Investors in U.S. Partnerships

Partnerships engaged in a U.S. trade or business must withhold on certain distributions to foreign partners. The Act extends the withholding provision to all distributions when 80% or more of the partnership income is U.S. business income to the extent that a foreigner receives a pro-rata portion of the U.S. business income. Fixed and determinable annual and periodic income, such as dividends, interest and similar amounts, would be subject to the 30% or lower treaty rate withholding. Other amounts, such as a distribution of normal business income, as distinguished from investment income, would be subject to a 20% withholding tax.

This withholding tax is not the final tax but merely an estimate of the final tax. The foreign partners will still have to file a tax return on which they will be able to claim the withheld tax as a credit against their ultimate U.S. tax liability.

Effective Date

Applies to taxable years beginning after December 31, 1986.

Foreign Governments

Starting July 1, 1986, the Act codifies the present regulation limiting foreign governments' tax exemptions to investment income. This change does not affect international organizations, such as the United Nations.

Transfer Price for Imports

Although both the IRS and the U.S. Customs Service are part of the U.S. Treasury department, the two were never really effectively coordinated. Under the Act, importers must use a purchase price for tax purposes that is consistent with customs valuation. Appropriate adjustments can still be made when customs pricing rules are different from U.S. tax rules, such as the treatment of freight charges and items of U.S. content returned.

Effective Date
Applies to transactions entered into after March 18, 1986.

Dual Residence Companies
For U.S. tax purposes, a corporation organized in one of the 50 states or the District of Columbia is considered a U.S. corporation. In some other countries, the place of incorporation is ignored. Instead, a resident corporation is one that is managed and controlled within the country. Consequently, it is possible to organize corporations that are considered residents of two countries. These corporations are treated as domestic corporations in both taxing systems.

Under the U.S. consolidated return mechanism, if a dual resident corporation had no income, but only expenses, a deduction that reduces income earned by affiliated companies could be claimed for these expenses. Under the group relief system found in some foreign countries, similar relief could also be claimed in those countries. Under the Act, a loss of a U.S. corporation that is also subject to an income tax of a foreign country cannot be used to reduce the taxable income of any other member of an affiliated group filing a consolidated tax return with the loss company. The plain language of the Act can also cover foreign branches of U.S. corporations. However, the IRS is expected to issue regulations that will not apply this provision if the losses are not actually used to offset the income of a foreign corporation for foreign tax purposes.

Effective Date
Applies to taxable years beginning after December 31, 1986.

Definition of Resident Alien
The 1984 Tax Reform Act significantly changed the definition of a U.S. resident for U.S. income tax purposes by substituting objective day counting rules for the prior subjective rules. These rules caused some professional athletes to cancel scheduled appearances in charitable events because if they appeared, they would have become residents of the United States for income tax purposes. Under the Act, days a professional athlete spends competing in charitable sports events in the United States will not be counted.

Effective Date
Applies to competition days after the date of enactment.

Miscellaneous Provisions

Dividend Received Deduction
U.S. shareholders will benefit from an 80% dividend received deduction for qualified dividends paid by a 10%-owned foreign corporation. Qualified dividends include distributions from earnings of the foreign payer that are subject to U.S. tax or are attributable to dividends received from a U.S. subsidiary of the foreign payer.

Possessions Income
Individual Taxpayers: ● Income earned by U.S. citizens resident in
                                          Panama is not exempt from U.S. tax under the

Panama Canal Treaty or other U.S. legislation.
- Government and certain quasi-government employees in Panama are eligible for allowances and exclusions comparable to those available to other U.S. expatriates.
- The Act establishes guidelines for implementing tax laws in lieu of the mirror tax systems in Guam, American Samoa and the Commonwealth of the Northern Mariana Islands (CNMI). These guidelines preserve the level of income on amounts received from sources within or connected with a possession or derived by a resident of the possession country. Special nondiscrimination and enforcement rules also are adopted.
- The prior law provisions for taxing citizens of possessions are repealed. The Act provides an income exclusion for individuals who are bona-fide possessions residents and derive income from possessions source.
- Alien individuals resident in possession countries, including Puerto Rico, are exempted from U.S. witholding tax on dividends, interest, and other fixed or determinable periodic income.

Corporate Taxpayers:
- If more than 80% of a corporation's income was derived from within a possession and 80% of that income is attributable to trade or business activities, a corporation organized in Guam, American Samoa or the CNMI is not a CFC.
- If a Guam banking corporation elects to be taxed as a U.S. corporation, interest on U.S. obligations it receives will not be subject to U.S. withholding tax.
- If less than 25% of the shares of a corporation organized in Guam, American Samoa, the CNMI or the Virgin Islands are held by a foreign person, and more than 80% of its income is derived from U.S. possession sources and no part of its income is used to satisfy obligations of U.S. or foreign persons, there is no withholding tax imposed on payments from the United States.

U.S. Virgin Islands Income:
- The Act adds a new provision for coordinating the taxation of residents of the United States or the U.S. Virgin Islands. The tax liability of the individual to the United States or the U.S. Virgin Islands will be based on the ratio of U.S.

taxable income to U.S. Virgin Islands taxable income.

- The possessions tax credit rules are amended to permit a Virgin Islands corporation to elect the tax credit mechanism.
- The prior law provisions taxing U.S. Virgin Island source income are repealed. Income earned by a U.S. Virgin Islands corporation from internal sources will be subject to tax only in the U.S. Virgin Islands.
- Taxes collected by the United States will be credited annually to the Treasury of the appropriate possession.

Effective Date
Generally applies to taxable years beginning on or after January 1, 1987. The provisions applying to Guam, American Samoa and the CNMI are effective on the date the new mirror tax law is implemented. The provisions coordinating the tax liability to the United States and the Virgin Islands applies to all other years.

Foreign Sales Corporations (FSCs)

Dividend Received Deduction
The Act extends a dividend received deduction to foreign sales corporation (FSC) earnings from non-effectively connected investment income and carrying charges. As modified, a FSC corporate shareholder is entitled to an 85% dividend received deduction for earnings attributable to FSC qualified interest or carrying charges, which includes interest related to qualified FSC sales, leasing, or service transactions. Presumably, this rate will be reduced to 80% as revised by the Act's amendments to the corporate provisions.

Controlled Group Sales
Under the Act, a FSC's qualified receipts exclude receipts from transactions with another FSC that is a member of the same controlled group. The Act limits this exclusion to transactions in which related FSCs use the 1.83%, or gross receipts safe-haven pricing method. Consequently, related party FSC sales are qualified, if the 23% combined taxable income or an arm's-length pricing method is used for reporting the profit on these transactions.

Related Party Transfer of Intangibles
Under prior law, the IRS has had mixed success on audit in generating additional U.S. source licensing income from transfers of intangibles by U.S. persons to related foreign affiliates. The Act codifies a requirement that the amount of U.S. source income must be commensurate with the income attributable to the intangible.

The Act provides that the IRS can also adjust royalty amounts resulting from a transfer by a foreign related entity to its U.S. subsidiary. Because only the IRS can make these adjustments, foreign based companies can only adjust royalty rates by contract.

The Conference Committee also instructed the IRS to conduct a comprehensive study of the intercompany pricing rules with a view to modifying the existing Regulations. The Conference Committee Report acknowledges the practical aspects of bona-fide cost-sharing arrangements. These provisions are applicable to licenses granted or transfers after November 16, 1985, and are effective for post-1986 tax years.

New Filing Procedures for Potential Immigrants

A U.S. citizen is subject to U.S. tax on worldwide income, regardless of residence. A nonresident alien, who has U.S. source income or income effectively connected with a U.S. trade or business, is liable for U.S. income tax on that income.

The Act adds a new statutory compliance and enforcement procedure for individuals applying for an immigration visa. They must file a statement with the following information: tax identification number, country of residence and whether a U.S. tax return has been filed in the last three years.

Miscellaneous Technical Corrections to 1984 TRA

- The *re-sourcing rules* for FTC purposes are expanded to treat certain domestic corporations as U.S.-owned foreign corporations and are effective March 28, 1985, with a transitional rule.
- An exception is added to the related-party factoring (RPF) rules of Subpart F. Under the 1984 Act, RPF income is treated as interest. As modified, RPF income derived from a trade or service receivable is not interest if the factoring affiliate acquires the receivable from another affiliate organized in the same country and the affiliate's income is attributable to bona-fide business activities outside the United States.
- The FIRPTA rules are retained and extended to distributions by domestic conduit entities to foreign partners or beneficiaries. As modified, a 28% U.S. withholding tax is imposed on distributions of gains attributable to the disposition of U.S. real property interests by a U.S. partnership, estate or trust. The obligation to withhold is effective for dispositions more than 30 days after the enactment date.
- The Act limits the scope of the stapled-stock provisions to U.S. controlled entities. As a result, a stapled entity now can be treated as a foreign corporation if 50% or more of the value and voting power of the foreign corporation's stock is held by non-U.S. persons.

Provisions Affecting Retirement Plans

Individual Retirement Accounts (IRAs)

Under prior law, individuals were allowed to make tax deductible annual contributions of up to $2,000 of earned income to an IRA. If a spouse did not have any earned income, the maximum deduction for the family unit was $2,250.

The Act makes several important changes to the IRA contribution rules.

- Individuals who are not covered by another retirement plan will be able to make a deductible $2,000 contribution annually to an IRA.
- Married taxpayers who are covered by a disqualifying retirement plan will be able to make a deductible annual $2,000 contribution to an IRA provided their adjusted gross income (AGI) is no more than $40,000 ($25,000 for single taxpayers). The IRA deduction will be phased out for married taxpayers with AGI between $40,000 and $50,000 ($25,000 and $35,000 for single taxpayers).
- Provided married taxpayers otherwise qualify for the IRA deduction, a spousal contribution will be able to be made.
- Individuals are covered by a disqualifying retirement plan if:
  —Defined contribution plans (e.g., profit sharing, money purchase pension): They are entitled to an allocation of an employer contribution or forfeiture for their taxable year. The mere allocation of plan earnings does not establish participant status.
  —Defined benefit pension plan: They are eligible to participate under the terms of the plan.
- Individuals who are covered by a disqualifying plan will still be able to contribute, subject to the current limitations, to an IRA, but will not be able to deduct the contribution.

Planning Point

The ability of an otherwise covered individual to make nondeductible contributions to an IRA provides an advantageous tax deferral on the earnings attributable to the IRA contribution.

Effective Date

Applies to taxable years beginning after December 31, 1986.

Cash or Deferred Arrangements (Section 401(k) Plans)

The Act modifies many aspects of the popular cash or deferred arrangements, the commonly called *401(k) plans*. As a result, all plans have to be reviewed to assure that they will be in conformity with the new rules.

Limit on Employee contributions

The Act imposes a new annual limit of $7,000 on an employee's elective contribution to all 401(k) plans in which the employee is a participant. The limit applies to the employee's taxable year, not the plan year. The $7,000 annual limit will be indexed for inflation and move in tandem with the dollar limitation on contributions to defined contribution plans.

Nondiscrimination Test

The Act establishes a new nondiscrimination test for 401(k) plans. Under this test, the average deferral percentage (ADP) for highly-compensated employees may not exceed the greater of:

1. 125% of the ADP for all nonhighly-compensated employees, or
2. The lesser of: (a) 200% of the ADP for the nonhighly-compensated employees, or
   (b) The ADP for the nonhighly-compensated employees plus two percentage points.

A highly-compensated employee is redefined to include individuals with specified ownership interests, employees earning more than $75,000 annually or more than $50,000 annually if they are in the top 20% of employees by compensation, specified officers of the employer, and family members of specified highly-compensated employees.

Comment

When the concentration of employee salaries is less than $50,000, the new definition of a highly-compensated group will make it easier for an employer to meet the nondiscrimination test. In addition, the new annual contribution limitation of $7,000 will effectively decrease the deferral percentage of those in the highly-compensated employee group resulting in a lower average deferral percentage for the group as a whole.

If a plan that does not meet the nondiscrimination test distributes an excess contribution (including related earnings) within 2-1/2 months after the year in which the excess contribution was made, the plan will not lose its tax qualified status. Distributions of excess contributions will not be subject to the additional tax on early withdrawals.

Coverage

Under the Act, a 401(k) plan may no longer require more than one year of service as a condition for an employee's eligibility to participate in the plan.

Tax-Exempt and Government Employers

The Act precludes tax-exempt and government employers from maintaining 401(k) plans. However, those 401(k) plans adopted by tax-exempt employers before July 1, 1986, and by government entities before May 6, 1986, are unaffected by this change. Government employers can continue to maintain and establish salary reduction arrangements—known as eligible state deferred compensation plans—that allow eligible employees to defer the lesser of $7,500 or 33-1/3% of compensation before deferral. This type of plan is extended to tax exempt employers.

Hardship Withdrawals

Under the Act, hardship withdrawals from a 401(k) plan will be limited to an employee's elective contributions, but not with respect to any related earnings. While the definition of a hardship withdrawal remains unchanged, all hardship withdrawals, except those for payment of medical expenses that would otherwise be deductible, will be subject to a 10% excise tax on withdrawals before age 59-1/2.

Effective Date

The rule relating to the annual limit on employee elective contributions is generally effective for taxable years beginning after December 31, 1986. The changes in the nondiscrimination test are effective for plan years beginning after December 31, 1986. The changes in the hardship withdrawal and eligibility rules are generally effective for plan years beginning after December 31, 1988.

Nondiscrimination Test for Employer Matching Contributions and Employee Contributions

The Act imposes the same nondiscrimination test applicable to 401(k) plans to employer matching contributions and employee contributions under both defined contribution plans and defined benefit pension plans. Also, the same definition of a highly-compensated employee that applies to 401(k) plans will now apply to these plans. If the special nondiscrimination test is not satisfied, the plan will not be disqualified if the excess contributions, including attributable income, are distributed by the end of the following plan year. Moreover, the distributed amounts will not be subject to the additional income tax on early withdrawals. A highly- compensated employee will be subject to a 10% excise tax on distributed excess contributions unless the excess amount, including income, is distributed within 2-1/2 months after the close of the plan year to which the excess contributions relate.

Observation

Because of the changes in these rules, a thrift plan could, if the level of participation among the nonhighly compensated employee group is relatively low, find itself with significant excess contributions and the potential for plan disqualification. Furthermore, it appears that as a result of the new nondiscrimination test, the availability of 401(k) plans, and the inclusion of all employee contributions as an annual addition, thrift plans are no longer a viable savings-retirement vehicle.

Effective Date

Applies generally to plan years beginning after December 31, 1988.

Simplified Employee Pensions (SEPs)

Limitations

Under the Act, a simplified employee pension (SEP)—other than a SEP maintained by a tax-exempt entity or a state or local government—can maintain a cash or deferred salary reduction arrangement subject to the same $7,000 annual limit on employee deferral amounts that applies to 401(k) plans. A SEP that maintains a salary reduction arrangement must satisfy the following new requirements:

1. At least 50% of all employees must elect to participate in the plan, and
2. The employer maintaining the SEP cannot have more than 25 employees at any time during the prior plan year.

Special Nondiscrimination Test

A SEP that maintains a salary reduction arrangement is subject to a non-discrimination test limiting the deferral percentage for each highly compensated employee to no more than 125% of the average deferral percentage for all other participants.

Observation

The special non discrimination test for SEP deferrals applies to *each* highly compensated employee, while the test applicable to qualified plan-401(k) arrangements looks to the average deferral percentage for all highly compensated employees as a group.

Contribution Date

Under prior law, to be deductible, a SEP contribution had to be made by the initial due date for filing the employer's tax return. The Act changes this rule so that employer contributions to a SEP will be deductible provided they are made by the due date, *including extensions*, of the employer's tax return.

Integration

The integration rules for nonelective SEP contributors must conform to the general integration rules described at page 106

Effective Date

Applies to plan years beginning after December 31, 1986.

Coverage

The Act modifies the minimum coverage rules for qualified plans by establishing three alternative tests.
1. A plan must cover at least 70% of all nonhighly-compensated employees
2. The percentage of nonhighly-compensated employees covered by the plan must be at least 70% of the percentage of highly compensated employees covered under the plan
3. A plan must satisfy the current law fair cross section test and the average benefit provided for nonhighly compensated employees must be at least 70% of the average benefit provided to highly-compensated employees under all qualified plans maintained by the employer.

Employees who do not satisfy the law's minimum age or service requirements, or are included in a unit of employees covered by a collective bargaining agreement, and certain nonresident aliens need not be taken into account.

The Act also provides for a limited exception from the general rule requiring certain commonly controlled entities to be aggregated for coverage test purposes. An employer that establishes that it operates a separate line of business for bona fide business reasons need not aggregate the employees in that line of business with other employees for coverage purposes.

Effective Date

Applies to plan years beginning after December 31, 1988. A special transitional rule applies in the case of certain dispositions or acquisitions of a business.

Minimum Participation

Under the Act, a plan must benefit no fewer than the lesser of 50 employees or 40% of all employees. An employer may not aggregate its plans, even if comparable, to meet this minimum participation test.

Observation

Because an employer may no longer aggregate two or more plans to satisfy the minimum participation requirements, some employers may find themselves no longer able to establish or continue plans covering only small groups of employees, e.g., separate plans for a law firm's partners, associates and administrative staff.

Vesting

Under the Act, a qualified plan's benefits must vest pursuant to a schedule that is no more restrictive than either of two alternatives. Under the first schedule, a participant's benefits must be fully vested on the completion of five years of service. Under the second schedule, a participant's benefits must be 20% vested after three years of service with the percentage increasing 20% for each year of service thereafter up to 100% after seven years of service. Because class year vesting schedules must meet one of the above schedules, they are effectively precluded under the Act.

Under prior law, a plan participant with a minimum of five years of service had the option of continuing under the plan's prior vesting schedule if the schedule was amended. The Act changes the five years of service requirement to three years of service.

The Act provides that maximum service period for eligibility will be two years, instead of three years as under prior law, if participants are always 100% vested.

Effective Date

The provisions generally are effective for plan years beginning after December 31, 1988.

Social Security Integration

Defined Contribution Plans

The Act modifies the Social Security integration rules for qualified profit sharing, stock bonus and money purchase pension plans by providing that the difference between the contribution rate for compensation in excess of the applicable wage base and the contribution rate for compensation up-to-the-wage-base may not exceed the lesser of: (1) The contribution rate for compensation up to the wage base, or (2) the greater of 5.7% or the employer's old age insurance tax rate.

Example: An integrated profit sharing plan provided for a 3% contribution on compensation up to the wage base and an 8.7% contribution on compensation in excess of the wage base, which complied with prior law. Under the Act, this integration formula would have to be revised so that the contribution rate on excess compensation may not exceed 6%.

Defined Benefit Pension Plans

Excess Plans
The Act modifies the integration rules for defined benefit pension excess plans by providing that the difference between the benefit percentage on compensation *in excess* of the applicable wage base and the benefit percentage on compensation *up to* the wage base may not exceed the lesser of the benefit percentage on compensation *up to* the wage base, or 3/4% multiplied by the number of years of service of the participant taken into account under the plan for benefit purposes, but not more than 35 years. Moreover, any optional form of benefit, preretirement benefit, actuarial factor or other special feature provided for compensation *in excess* of the wage base must also be provided for compensation *up to* the wage base.

Offset Plans
Under new integration rules for a defined benefit pension offset plan, a participant's accrued benefit may not be reduced by more than the lesser of 50% of the benefit without regard to the offset or 3/4% of final overall compensation (disregarding compensation increases of the social security withholding level for each relevant year) multiplied by the years of service of the participant taken into account under the plan for benefit purposes, up to a maximum of 35 years. Special rules require the aggregation of contributions and benefits made on behalf of a highly compensated employee, who participates in two or more plans of the same employer, when applying the new integration rules to each plan.

A special rule allows a defined benefit plan to limit the employer benefit to the excess of the participant's final pay over the Social Security benefit attributable to service with the employer.

Effective Date
Applies to plan years beginning after December 31, 1988.

Benefit Accrual Method for Top-Heavy Plan Determination
The Act imposes a uniform benefit accrual method test for determining top heaviness. This is designed to prevent some employers from avoiding the top-heavy rules by artificially accelerating the accrual of benefits for non-key employees. For the sole purpose of determining whether a defined benefit pension plan is top heavy or super top heavy, benefits will be deemed to accrue no more rapidly for all employees than under the fractional-benefit accrual rule. However, in lieu of using the fractional-benefit accrual rule, benefits may accrue under any accrual method provided that method is used by all plans of the employer.

Effective Date
Applies to plan years beginning after December 31, 1986.

Modification of Benefit Forfeiture Rules
Under prior law, any benefits forfeited under a money-purchase pension plan defined-benefit pension plan had to be used to reduce future employer contributions or to offset plan administration expenses. The Act provides that a money-

purchase pension plan may reallocate forfeitures to the accounts of other plan participants, thereby increasing benefits.

Effective Date

Applies to plan years beginning after December 31, 1985.

Distributions

Minimum Distributions

Under prior law, individuals, other than 5% owners, can defer the distribution of benefits from a qualified retirement plan to the April 1 of the calendar year following the calendar year during which they retire. The Act requires that distributions from all types of qualified plans, tax-sheltered custodial accounts, and tax-sheltered annuities must commence by April 1 of the calendar year following the calendar year in which the individual attains age 70-1/2.

The Act changes the penalty for failing to make a required minimum distribution. A 50% nondeductible excise tax on the difference between the amount that should have been distributed to meet the minimum distribution requirements and the amount actually distributed is imposed on the recipient of the distribution. In limited circumstances, the IRS can waive the excise tax.

Effective Date

Applies generally to plan years beginning on or after January 1, 1989. Those 5% owners protected by a special pre-TEFRA election governing the commencement of distributions will not be subject to the 50% excise tax. In addition, those employees who were not 5% owners in the plan year ending in the calendar year in which they reached age 66-1/2 or in later plan years and who have attained age 70-1/2 by January 1, 1988, may defer the distribution of benefits until actual retirement.

Taxation of Distributions

10-Year Averaging and Capital Gain Treatment

The Act repeals the 10-year averaging tax treatment and phases out, over a six-year period, capital-gain treatment for pre-1974 benefits. It substitutes a five-year averaging tax calculation for a qualifying distribution. However, the five-year averaging will apply to only one distribution that is made after a participant has attained age 59-1/2.

Special Elections

Under the Act, there is a special election for individual distributees who were at least 50 years of age on January 1, 1986. The qualified individuals can use the more beneficial of the new five-year averaging rule together with the new individual income tax rates or the 10-year averaging rules with 1986 tax rates. In addition, an individual who attained age 50 by January 1, 1986, can elect to use capital-gain treatment for pre-1974 benefits subject to a maximum effective income tax rate of 20%, without regard to the six-year phaseout of the capital-gain treatment.

Basis Recovery Rules

Pre-Annuity Starting Date Distribution

Under prior law, distributions of a participant's after-tax contributions made before a participant's annuity starting date were recoverable in full before any taxable earnings were deemed to have been received. The Act modifies this recovery rule to provide that a participant's after-tax contributions will be recovered on a pro-rata basis including the taxable earnings portion attributable to the contributions.

Post-Annuity Starting Date Distribution

Under prior law, if a distribution made after a participant's annuity starting date and made during the first three years equalled or exceeded the amount of a participant's contribution, all distributions were nontaxable until the participant's full contribution was recovered. The Act repeals this special three-year basis recovery rule and replaces it with a new pro-rata recovery rule that provides that each distribution will be treated as part taxable earnings and part nontaxable return of participant contribution.

The Act also limits the amount an annuitant may exclude from the taxable portion of a distribution to the total amount of the participant's contribution. Thus, if benefits continue to be received after an annuitant fully recovered the contribution—possible, for example, under a life annuity—the total amount received will be taxable. If benefits cease before the recipient recovers the full amount of the participant's contribution, the unrecovered amount is deductible on the recipient's final income tax return. Under prior law, a tax deduction for unrecovered contributions was not allowed.

For a distribution from an IRA to which nondeductible contributions were made, the basis recovery rules will follow the pro-rata approach applicable to qualified plans.

Observation

The Act changes the basis recovery rules significantly. For instance, distributees can no longer out-live their life expectancies and continue to treat a portion of the benefits received as a nontaxable recovery of the participants' contributions.

Effective Date

Applies to distributions made after December 31, 1986. The provisions relating to the basis-recovery rules for amounts received before a participant's annuity starting date generally apply to distributions received after July 1, 1986. They do not, however, apply to certain employee contributions made prior to January 1, 1987, under plans that permitted withdrawals on May 5, 1986. The repeal of the special three-year basis recovery rule for post annuity starting date distributions generally applies to individuals whose annuity starting dates are after July 1, 1986.

Early Distributions

Under the Act, an early distribution from any qualified retirement plan (including IRAs, SEPs and 405(b) plans, but not 457 plans) to any participant will be subject to an additional income tax of 10% of the amount of the early distribution. An early distribution is a distribution made prior to the individual's attaining age

59-1/2, death or disability. The 10% penalty tax on pre age 59-1/2 distributions to 5% owners is repealed after 1986.

The Act expressly exempts from the imposition of the additional income tax the following early distributions:

1. Annuity payments over the life or life expectancy of the participant or joint lives of the participant and beneficiary after separation from service.
2. Distributions to an individual who has attained age 55, separated from service and met the plan's requirements for early retirement (not applicable to IRAs or SEPs).
3. Distributions used to pay for deductible medical expenses (not applicable to IRAs or SEPs).

In addition, lump-sum cash outs of less than $3,500 from tax qualified plans are also exempt from the penalty tax.

Effective Date

Applies generally to taxable years beginning after December 31, 1986. However, all participants, who, as of March 15, 1987, received a distribution taxable in 1986 resulting from a separation from service in 1986, can elect to treat the distribution as taxable in 1986, and will not be subject to the additional tax on early distributions. In addition, payments to an alternative payee under a qualified domestic relations order will be exempt from the early distribution tax.

Loans

Under prior law, the amount of a participant's outstanding loan balance from a qualified plan could not, at any given time, exceed $50,000, assuming $50,000 equalled or exceeded one-half of the present value of a participant's vested benefits. The Act modifies the maximum dollar limitation on loans from a qualified plan by reducing the $50,000 limit by the amount of a participant's highest outstanding loan balance during the immediately preceding 12 months.

Observation

This new rule precludes the use of balloon payments or bridge loans to pay off outstanding loan balances in the final year of repayment.

The Act also restricts the use of an extended repayment period, i.e., up to 25 years, to those instances in which the participant uses the proceeds to purchase a principal residence. As a result, loans for home improvements must be repaid over no more than five years.

Interest on plan loans will now be subject to the general rules regarding nondeductibility. Further, interest on loans secured with elective deferrals under 401(k) plans, or on loans to a key employee will be nondeductible regardless of the general rules (see p. 11). Interest payments under a plan loan to a participant will not increase the participant's basis. Therefore, the participant will pay tax on the interest when it is distributed from the plan.

Effective Date

Applies generally to loans entered into after December 31, 1986. Existing loans are subject to the phase-in rules applicable to the general interest deduction rules. The provision regarding the loss of basis applies to interest paid after December 31, 1986, regardless of when the loan was secured.

Limits on Contributions and Benefits

Defined Benefit Plans

Under prior law, the maximum annual benefit under a defined-benefit pension plan commencing no earlier than age 62 was $90,000. The Act modifies this benefit limit by providing that the $90,000 annual benefit begin no earlier than the Social Security retirement age. Benefits that begin before the Social Security retirement age will be subject to an actuarally reduced limit. Thus the $75,000 maximum allowable under prior law at age 55 will probably be significantly reduced. Moreover, the same rule, i.e., actuarial equivalent to $90,000 benefit at Social Security retirement age, would apply to benefits that commence after the Social Security retirement age. The percentage of compensation annual limitation on benefits under á defined-benefit pension plan is unaffected by this modification of the dollar limitation.

Under the Act, an individual must have at least 10 years of plan participation to be entitled to the maximum defined-benefit plan annual dollar limitation. Thus, in contrast with current law, years of service with the employer prior to becoming eligible to participate in the plan will be disregarded, and there will be a 10% reduction in the $90,000 limitation for each year of *participation* less than 10.

Example: An individual with five years of participation will be entitled to a maximum pension benefit of $45,000, i.e., $90,000 x 5/10.

Defined Contribution Plans

The Act maintains the current law limits of the lesser of 25% of compensation or $30,000 on annual additions to a defined contribution plan. However, adjustments to the maximum dollar limitation for cost of living increases will be postponed until the ratio of the defined benefit dollar limit to the defined contribution dollar limit is four to one (the present ratio is three to one—$90,000 to $30,000). When the four to one ratio is reached, increases in the defined contribution dollar limitation will match similar increases in the defined benefit dollar limitation. The Act also revises the definition of the annual addition under a defined contribution plan to include all employee contributions.

Cost-Of-Living Arrangements

The Act places new restrictions on qualified cost-of-living arrangements by limiting the cost-of-living adjustments under these arrangements to changes in indexes prescribed by the IRS, and by generally excluding all key employees except specified officers from participating in a qualified cost-of-living arrangement.

Combined Plan Benefit Limitation-Excess Distributions

While current law limitations on benefits or contributions credited to an employee who participates in both a defined benefit and defined contribution plan continue to apply, the Act imposes an excise tax of 15% on any excess distributions from a qualified retirement plan, e.g., profit sharing, pension, stock bonus; tax-sheltered annuity; IRAs, but not 457 plans. Distributions from these plans or accounts will be taken into account to the extent the recipient includes the amounts distributed in income.

The Act defines an excess distribution as the aggregate amount of distributions made with respect to an individual that exceeds 125% of the defined benefit dollar limitation during any calendar year. An individual who received a lump-sum distribution that will be taxed under the new five-year averaging rule or at capital-gain rates will be subject to a higher ceiling for purposes of computing the amount of any excess distribution. A special rule also applies to a distribution made after a participant's death for determining whether all or part of the amounts distributed constitute an excess distribution.

Includible Compensation
Under the Act, compensation in excess of $200,000 will be disregarded for purposes of benefit or contribution calculations, as well as for employer tax deduction computations. The $200,000 compensation limitation applies to all qualified plans whether or not they are top heavy.

Cost-of-Living Adjustments
Beginning in 1988, the defined benefit plan dollar limitation is scheduled to be adjusted by percentage of the changes in the consumer price index as under prior law. The defined contribution plan limitation will not be adjusted until a four to one ratio is reached between the two dollar limitations, i.e. until the defined benefit limit becomes $120,000.

Effective Date
Applies generally to plan years beginning after December 31, 1986. A special transitional rule applies to those individuals who are participants before January 1, 1987, in a defined benefit pension plan that was in existence on May 6, 1986, under which the participant's accrued benefit cannot be reduced by virtue of the changes in the applicable dollar limitation. In addition, the Act protects specified benefits that accrued before August 1, 1986, from the imposition of the excise tax on excess distributions.

Tax Deduction Limitations

Deduction-Limit Carry Forwards
Under prior law, employers who maintain qualified profit sharing or stock bonus plans could carry forward unused deduction limits from preceding years so as to permit, in some cases, up to a 25% deduction limit. The Act repeals the deduction-limit carry forwards for profit sharing and stock bonus plans. However, deduction-limit carry forwards that were accumulated prior to 1987 can be used to increase the deduction limitations applicable to taxable years beginning after December 31, 1986.

Combined Plan Tax Deduction Limitations
Under prior law, an employer who maintained both a defined benefit pension plan and a profit sharing or a stock bonus plan covering a common participant was permitted to deduct no more than the greater of the amount needed to satisfy minimum funding requirements, or 25% of covered payroll. This combined plan limitation did not apply to the combination of a defined benefit pension plan and

money purchase pension plan. The Act applies the combined plan limitation to any combination of a defined benefit plan and a defined contribution plan covering a common participant.

Effective Date
Applies generally to taxable years beginning after December 31, 1986.

Excise Tax On Reversion

The Act imposes a new 10% nondeductible excise tax on a reversion from any qualified plan. The excise tax does not apply when assets that would otherwise revert to the employer are transferred to an employee stock ownership plan (ESOP) in which at least 50% of the employees who were active participants in the terminated pension plan must be eligible to participate. Amounts transferred to an ESOP must be allocated to the accounts of plan participants immediately or over no more than a seven-year period, or, alternatively, the amounts may be used to repay a securities acquisition loan.

Effective Date
The excise tax applies to reversions received after December 31, 1985, other than those reversions attributable to plan terminations occurring on or before December 31, 1985. The exception to the excise tax for transfers to an ESOP will not apply to reversions received after December 31, 1988.

Miscellaneous Provisions

Profit Sharing Plans
Under prior law, an employer's contributions to a profit sharing plan had to be based on current or accumulated profits. For plan years beginning after December 31, 1985, the Act repeals this requirement. Therefore, an employer can contribute to a profit sharing plan whether or not there are current or accumulated profits.

Cash-Out of Accrued Benefits
The Act provides that for purposes of computing the present value of a participant's accrued benefit, on plan termination, a plan may not use an interest rate greater than the rate employed by the Pension Benefit Guaranty Corporation (PBGC). The plan must apply this rate in computing the first $25,000 of the present value of benefits. In computing the present value of benefits in excess of $25,000, the plan may use an interest rate up to 120% of the rate used by the PBGC in determining the present value of benefits on plan termination.

Effective Date
Applies generally to distributions made after December 31, 1984. However, this provision does not apply to distributions made in plan years beginning after December 31, 1984, and before January 2, 1987, provided the distributions were made in accordance with the Retirement Equity Act of 1984.

Time Required for Plan Amendments
Plans must adopt appropriate plan amendments to conform to the Act by the last day of the first plan year beginning after December 31, 1988. However, a plan must still comply with the Act's provisions as of their effective dates.

Employee Leasing

Current law requires an employer that leases the services of individuals, who are employees of another organization—the leasing organization—to treat the leased employees as their own employees for purposes of satisfying a number of plan qualification requirements. There is an available safe harbor that enables an employer to avoid this treatment of leased employees as the employer's own employees.

The Act modifies this safe harbor provision by:

- Increasing the leasing organization's minimum contribution rate to 10% from 7.5%
- Requiring the leasing organization to cover 100% of its leased employees, i.e., not regular employees, subject to a de minimus compensation requirement
- Providing that the safe harbor may not be availed of if more than 20% of the individuals performing substantial services for the employer are leased employees
- Granting an exemption from the employee leasing record keeping requirments for specified employers

Effective Date

Applies to services rendered after December 31, 1986.

Employee Stock Ownership Plans (ESOPS)

In recent years, Employee stock ownership plans (ESOPs) have emerged as a significant vehicle for financing a wide variety of corporate transactions, e.g., redemption of a retiring shareholder's stock. The Act continues to promote ESOPs as both a tool of corporate finance and a vehicle for employee participation in the ownership of their employers.

Vesting Requirements

Under the Act, ESOPs will be subject to the new alternative minimum vesting schedules.

Limitations on Contributions

Under current law, the applicable dollar limitation for contributions to an ESOP can be increased to $60,000 provided no more than one-third of the contributions are allocated to highly-compensated employees as determined above.

Diversification

The Act requires an ESOP to offer participants who have attained age 55 and completed 10 years of participation the right to shift 25% of their account balance into investment vehicles other than employer securities. The diversification percentage increases to 50% for participants who have reached age 60 and completed 10 years of participation.

To satisfy the diversification requirements, an ESOP must offer eligible participants at least three investment options. Further, an ESOP, in carrying out a diversification request, can:

- Distribute the amount selected for diversification to the participant or

- Substitute an equivalent amount of other assets for the portion of the account balance selected for diversification.

Participants receiving distributions of securities from ESOPs under a diversification election will be permitted to roll over their distributions to an IRA or other qualified plans.

Planning Point

When an ESOP has not invested 100% of its assets in employer securities, a participant's account balance can be diversified by simply reallocating plan assets, other than employer securities, to that account. This enables the ESOP to satisfy its diversification obligation while avoiding the necessity of cashing-out employer securities.

Distribution Restrictions

Timing of Distributions: Unless the employee elects otherwise, the Act requires distributions from an ESOP to begin no later than one year after the end of the plan year during which the participant terminates employment as a result of retirement, death or disability, or that is the fifth plan year following the participant's separation from service, whichever is later. There is an exception to this general rule for distributions of employer securities related to an outstanding ESOP loan. In this situation, distributions from the ESOP may be deferred until the plan year following the plan year during which the loan is repaid in full.

Form of Distribution:

The Act continues the current law's granting to an ESOP participant the right to demand a distribution in employer securities. If the employer securities are not publicly traded, the recipient must be given a right to *put* or sell the securities to the ESOP or the employer.

The Act modifies the period over which the plan can make a distribution. In general, distributions from an ESOP can be made over a period that does not extend beyond five years.

If a participant's account balance exceeds $500,000, there is an exception to the five-year maximum payment period. Under this exception, the payment period is extended one year for each $100,000 (or fraction thereof) by which the participant's account balance exceeds $500,000, up to an additional five years.

A recipient of a lump-sum distribution, who exercises a put option, must be paid equally over a period of no more than five years. An employer must provide adequate security to support the installment payments. A recipient of an installment distribution from an ESOP, who exercises a put on an installment, must be paid within 30 days. However, no security need be provided.

Observation

The requirement that an employer post adequate security to cover deferred ESOP payments could, in fact, create the specifically undesirable effect that deferred payments were supposed to alleviate. The opportunity to pay the put (option) price over time was intended to enable ESOPs and their sponsoring employers to avoid a significant cash flow drain that could result from the exodus of a number of participants desiring to cash-out the employer securities held in their accounts. The security provision could require an employer to encumber assets that may already be subject to a security interest that forbids further collateralization.

Tax-Credit ESOPs

The Act repeals the special tax-credit ESOP for compensation paid or accrued after December 31, 1986. Tax-credit ESOPs that are terminated can distribute employer securities even though the securities were not held in the plan for 84 months before distribution.

Independent Appraiser

Employer securities held by an ESOP must be valued by an independent appraiser whose name must be furnished to IRS.

ESOP Financing

Dividend Payments:

The Act extends an employer's deduction for dividend payments to those amounts used by an ESOP to repay the loan used to acquire employer securities on which the dividends are paid.

Exclusion of Interest:

The Act makes the following modifications to the rules governing the exclusion of interest earned on ESOP loans:

- The interest exclusion is available for loans to an employer if securities equal to the proceeds of a loan are transferred to an ESOP including a nonleveraged ESOP within 30 days of the loan and then allocated to participant accounts within one year of the loan.
- The loan repayment period cannot be more than seven years.
- Interest on a loan *from* a regulated investment company (RIC) to an ESOP will qualify for the exclusion. The excludible portion is 25% of the total interest earned by the RIC.

Effective Date

The provision governing the deductibility of dividends is effective for dividends paid in taxable years beginning after the date of enactment. The provisions relating to the exclusion of interest on ESOP loans are effective for loans used to acquire employer securities after the date of enactment. The distribution, diversification, appraisal, and put option requirements apply to stock acquired by the ESOP after December 31, 1986.

Stock Bonus Plans

The Act makes the put option requirements applicable to all qualified stock bonus plans for stock acquired by the plan after December 31, 1986.

Provisions Making Administrative and Technical Corrections

Information Reporting

Real Estate Transactions

Under prior law, there was no reporting requirement for real estate transactions other than the withholding requirements under the Foreign Investment in Real Property Tax Act (FIRPTA).

The Act requires that real estate transactions be reported in a manner similar to that imposed on brokers for other transactions. As a result, all of the penalties and related provisions that apply to the general broker reporting requirements will also apply to reporting real estate transactions. Real estate transactions will also be subject to backup withholding to the extent provided by regulations.

The person responsible for filing the information return for the transaction (in order of priority) is the:

- Person responsible for closing
- Primary Mortgage Lender
- Seller's Broker
- Buyer's Broker
- Any other person designated by regulation

Comment

This new reporting requirement adds another step to established real estate closing practice. Not only will those responsible have to file a Form 1099 information return, they will also have to obtain the parties' taxpayer identification numbers to avoid the requirement of back-up withholding. This additional paperwork will also have to be explained to the parties to the transaction.

Effective Date

The new reporting requirement is effective for real estate closings on or after January 1, 1987, whether or not implementing regulations have been issued.

Royalties

Under prior law, the payers of royalties were required to file information returns when they made payments of $600 or more to one recipient. The Act requires anyone who pays $10 or more in royalties to a single recipient to file an information return with the IRS and to provide a copy to the recipient. If the recipient of the royalty income fails to provide the payer with a taxpayer identification number (TIN), the royalty payments are subject to backup withholding.

Effective Date

These changes are effective for royalty payments made after December 31, 1986.

Separate Mailing Requirement

Under prior law, the payers of interest, dividends and partronage dividends had to provide copies of information returns to the taxpayers who received the payments.

The taxpayer's copy of the return had to be provided in person or in a separate first-class mailing. Generally, nothing other than the information report was permitted to be enclosed in the envelope.

Under the Act, payers of interest, dividends, patronage dividends and royalty payments can enclose with the copy of the information return the following items: a check, a letter explaining why no check is enclosed, and a statement of the taxpayer's specific account with the payer.

The outside of the envelope containing the copy of the information return and the other allowed enclosures must state: "Important Tax Return Document Enclosed." In addition, each enclosure (other than the copy of the information return) must bear the same imprinted caption. The enclosed information return must be made on an official form. If a mailing contains any other material, such as advertising, promotional material, a quarterly report or an annual report, it is not acceptable.

Effective Date
These changes are effective for information returns that are required to be filed after December 31, 1986.

Federal Contracts
Under the Act, the heads of Federal executive agencies must file an information return indicating the name, address and TIN of each person with which the agency enters into a contract. This new requirement is effective for all contracts signed on or after January 1, 1987, and for all contracts signed prior to that date if they are still in effect on that date.

Tax Exempt Interest
For taxable years beginning after December 31, 1986, taxpayers will have to show the tax-exempt interest received or accrued during the year.

Wage Withholding
Under the Act, an employee must file by October 1, 1987 a Form W-4, Employee's Withholding Allowance Certificate, as revised by the IRS to reflect the Tax Reform Act of 1986 changes. If an employee does not timely file the revised Form W-4, the employer must withhold income taxes as if the employee claimed one allowance if single or two allowances if married.

The Act also repeals the prior law provision that gives the IRS the authority to issue regulations permitting employees to request that the table withholding amount be decreased. This change is effective as of the date of enactment.

Comment
Although there is no immediacy to the necessity of filing new Form W-4s, employers should make sure that when the revised Form W-4 becomes available, they act promptly to have their employees execute the forms.

Tax Shelters

Registration
Under prior law, if the total of the deductions allowed plus 200% of the credits

generated by the shelter exceeded twice the cash actually invested in the shelter, the tax shelter had to register with the IRS .

Under the Act, to conform the tax shelter ratio computation to the new tax rates, the tax credits are to be multiplied by 350%.

Effective Date
Applies to shelters first offered for sale after December 31, 1986.

Reporting and Penalties
The Act makes the following additions and changes to the tax shelter information reporting and penalty provisions:

- The minimum penalty for failing to register a tax shelter is increased from $500 to $10,000 with a maximum of 1% of the amount invested (effective as of the date of enactment).
- The penalty for failing to report a tax shelter TIN on a tax return is increased from $50 to $250 for tax returns filed after the date of enactment.
- The maximum penalty that applies to organizers and sellers of tax shelters for failure to maintain a list of investors is increased from $50,000 to $100,000 effective as of the date of enactment.
- Sham and fraudulent transfers are subject to the special 120% interest charge on underpayments of tax that are attributable to tax-motivated transactions (effective for interest accruing after December 31, 1986).

Penalties

Information Returns
Under prior law, a variety of information returns detailing all wages, most other types of income and some deductions had to be filed with the IRS with a copy given to the taxpayer. Civil penalties were imposed for failing to file an information return with the IRS, for failing to provide a copy to the taxpayer and for failure to furnish the correct taxpayer identification number (TIN). These penalties were generally $50 per return that was not filed and $50 for each copy not given to a taxpayer. The penalty for providing an incorrect TIN was either $5 or $50 (depending on the nature of the failure). Generally higher penalties applied to each failure to file when the failure was due to intentional disregard of the law. The maximum penalty for each category of failure was $50,000. There was no limit on the maximum penalty if the failure to file the information returns was due to intentional disregard of the filing requirements.

Under the Act, the maximum penalty is increased to $100,000 for each failure to file category. Thus, a maximum penalty of $100,000 applies to the failure to file information returns with the IRS, another maximum penalty of $100,000 applies to the failure to supply copies of information returns to taxpayers and another maximum penalty of $100,000 applies to the failure to supply TIN's.

The penalty for intentional failure to report cash transactions that exceed $10,000 is increased to 10% of the amount that should have been reported. Also, the penalty for intentional failure to report exchanges of certain partnership interests or certain dispositions of donated property is changed to 5% of the amount that should have been reported.

The Act adds a new penalty for failing to include correct information or omitting information on an information return filed with the IRS or on the copy given to the taxpayer. The penalty is $5 for each return with missing or incorrect information up to a maximum penalty of $20,000 in any calendar year. The maximum penalty limit does not apply when there is an intentional disregard of the filing requirements. Also, the penalty for failure to include correct information does not apply when the penalty for failure to supply a correct TIN is imposed for that information return. If a taxpayer files information returns that contain so many inaccuracies or omissions that the utility of the document is minimized or eliminated, the IRS may impose the failure to file penalties rather than the missing or incorrect information penalty.

As under prior law, there is an exception from all of these penalties provided the failure is due to reasonable cause and not to willful neglect. The Act retains the standards and special rules of current law that apply to failures related to interest or dividend information returns.

Effective Date
Applicable to information returns due after December 31, 1986.

Failures to Pay Tax
Under prior law, a 1/2% penalty per month was imposed for failure to pay the tax shown as due on a tax return. Under the Act, the failure-to-pay penalty is increased to 1% per month after the IRS notifies the taxpayer that it will levy on the assets of the taxpayer. This increase in the rate of the penalty generally will occur only after the IRS has made repeated efforts to contact the taxpayer by mail. During the period that these initial mailings are made, the penalty for failure to pay will remain at 1/2%.

Effective Date
Applicable to amounts assessed after December 31, 1986, regardless of when the failure to pay began.

Negligence and Fraud
Under prior law, taxpayers were subject to a 5% penalty on the *total* amount of any underpayment of tax if any part of the underpayment was due to negligence or intentional disregard of rules or regulations. A special 50% penalty applied if any part of the underpayment was due to fraud. In both cases, the underpayment was computed at the highest marginal rate applicable to the taxpayer.

Under the Act, the negligence penalty is made applicable to all taxes under the Code. The Act also expands the definition of negligence to include any failure to make a reasonable attempt to comply with the provisions of the Code as well as any careless, reckless or intentional disregard of rules or regulations.

The Act also expands the scope of the special negligence penalty that is currently applicable to failure to include in income interest and dividends shown on an information return to all items subject to information reporting. Thus, if a taxpayer fails to properly include in a return any amount that is reported on an information return, the failure is treated as negligence unless there is clear and convincing contrary evidence. The penalty is imposed on the underpayment attributable to the omitted items.

The Act increases the fraud penalty to 75%, but limits its applicability to the amount of underpayment attributable to fraud. The taxpayer has the burden of proving the part of an underpayment that is not attrributable to fraud.

Effective Date
The changes to the negligence and fraud penalties are applicable to returns whose due dates (without extensions) are after December 31, 1986.

Substantial Understatement of Tax Liability
Under prior law, if taxpayers filed returns that substantially understate the income tax payable for the year, they were subject to a penalty equal to 10% of the underpayment of tax. An understatement was considered substantial if it exceeded the greater of 10% of the tax that should have been shown on the return or $5,000 ($10,000 in the case of most corporations). The penalty did not apply if there was substantial authority for a taxpayer's treatment of the amounts that resulted in the understatement or if the relevant facts with respect to that amount were disclosed on the tax return.

The Act increases the penalty rate from 10% to 20%.

Effective Date
Applicable to returns that are due (without extensions) after December 31, 1986.

Interest Provisions

Differential Interest Rate
Under prior law, the interest paid by the IRS on overpayments of tax and the interest charged to the taxpayer on underpayments was calculated at the same rate. This rate was based on the prime rate and was adjusted every six months.

The Act requires that the IRS pay interest on overpayments at a rate equal to the Federal short-term interest rate plus two percentage points. The IRS must charge interest on underpayments at a rate equal to the Federal short-term interest rate plus three percentage points. The rate must be adjusted quarterly.

Effective Date
The new rates are effective for calculating interest for periods after December 31, 1986.

Interest on Accumulated Earnings Tax
Under prior law, when an IRS audit determined that the accumulated earnings tax was due, interest was charged on the unpaid tax only from the date the IRS demanded payment rather than from the date the return was originally due.

Under the Act, interest will be charged on the underpayment of the accumulated earnings tax from the due date (without regard to extensions) of the income tax return for the year the tax is initially imposed.

Effective Date
The change is effective for returns that are due after December 31, 1985.

Tax Administration

Statute of Limitations

Under the Act, if a dispute between a third party recordkeeper and the IRS concerning access to records under an administrative summons is not settled within six months of the issue of the summons, the statute of limitations is suspended until the issue is resolved. The change is effective on the date of enactment.

Statutory Notice of Deficiency (90-Day Letter)

Under prior law, once the IRS had issued a statutory notice of deficiency (90-day letter), it did not have the authority to withdraw the letter; only a Tax Court decision could alter its effect.

Under the Act, a statutory notice of deficiency may be rescinded on the mutual agreement of the IRS and the taxpayer. A properly rescinded notice is treated as if it never existed. The change is effective for statutory notices of deficiency issued on or after January 1, 1986.

Abatement of Interest Due

Under prior law, the IRS did not have the authority to abate interest charges when all or part of the interest had been caused by IRS errors and delays.

The Act provides that in cases where an IRS official fails to perform a ministerial act in a timely manner or makes an error in performing a ministerial act, the IRS has the authority to abate the interest attributable to the delay. The IRS is required to abate interest on erroneously issued refund checks for less than $50,000 when solely due to an IRS error. The abatement of interest in all other cases is at the discretion of the IRS; it is not intended to be a routine occurrence.

The change is effective for erroneously charged interest on deficiencies or payments for taxable years begining after December 31, 1978.

Compounding Interest

Under prior law, when a waiver of restrictions on assessment of a deficiency was filed, the IRS had 30 days to issue a notice and demand for payment. Failing to do so, interest was not imposed on the deficiency from the 31st day until the notice was issued. However, the compounding of interest previously accrued continued.

Under the Act, both the interest on the deficiency as well as the compounding of interest on the previously accrued interest are suspended starting 30 days after the waiver is filed and continuing until the notice and demand are issued.

The change is effective for interest accruing after December 31, 1982. Taxpayers must file a claim for refund of interest with the IRS to receive repayment of interest.

Service-Connected Disability

The Act prohibits the IRS from levying on any amount payable to an individual as a service-connected disability benefit. The change is effective for payments made after December 31, 1986.

Disclosure of Tax Return Information to Cities

Under the Act, any city with a population in excess of two million that imposes an income or wage tax may receive returns and return information. Any disclosure would be required to be made in the same manner and with the same safeguards as currently apply to disclosures made to a state. The change is effective on the date of enactment.

Tax Litigation

Awards of Attorneys' Fees in Tax Cases

Under prior law, to recover attorneys' fees and court costs, a taxpayer who prevailed in a tax case in any Federal court had to prove that the Government's position was unreasonable. The maximum possible recovery was $25,000.

The Act conforms tax law on recovery of attorneys' fees and court costs more closely to the standards imposed in other Federal cases by the Equal Access to Justice Act. The burden of proof, however, is on the taxpayer.

The Act also removes the limit on the total amount of fees that may be awarded and substitutes a suggested maximum of $75 an hour for attorney's fees; a court—at its discretion—may use a higher rate. For other costs to be recoverable, they must be reasonable. Fees for expert witnessess cannot exceed the rate the Government pays.

Effective Date

The changes are effective for proceedings commencing after December 31, 1985. However, no payments may be made before October 1, 1986.

Exhaustion of Administrative Remedies

Failure of a taxpayer to exhaust available administrative remedies before seeking redress in the Tax Court will be subject to that Court's discretionary penalty for delay; applicable to cases filed after December 31, 1986.

Miscellaneous Technical Corrections

The Act contains a large number of technical corrections to provisions in the Tax Reform Act of 1984 and other prior tax legislation. Some of those technical corrections include:

Tax Benefit Rule

The Act clarifies that if a taxpayer recovers an amount claimed as a deduction in a prior year, the amount is *not* required to be included in income under the tax benefit rule to the extent that the deduction did not reduce the taxpayer's tax liability.

Example: In 1986, Mr. Rose claimed a deduction on his tax return for state income tax withheld from his wages. However, Mr. Rose's 1986 tax liability is determined under the alternative minimum tax rules. In 1987, he receives a refund of a portion of the state income taxes withheld in 1986. The refund is *not* includible in Mr. Rose's 1987 income because he received no tax benefit from the 1986 deduction.

Below-Market Interest Loans

The Act corrects several oversights in the rules that impute a market rate of interest on certain below-market rate loans.

- Loans with indefinite maturities are treated as demand loans rather than term loans.
- Specified term loans on which interest is reduced or forgiven contingent on the borrower's performance of future services are treated as demand loans even if the loan is transferable.
- Semi-annual interest compounding is required for all gift loans and demand loans.
- Low-interest Israeli bonds are exempted from the imputed interest rules.

Deduction For Payments to Related Foreign Party

The Act directs the IRS to issue regulations generally limiting the timing of a deduction for certain payments by a U.S. taxpayer to a related foreign person or entity. Essentially, the regulations would place the U.S. taxpayer on the cash-basis method of accounting for the deduction for the payments.

Vacation Pay Election

Under prior law, an accrual-basis employer with a *non-vested* vacation pay plan could elect to deduct certain advance accruals of vacation pay. Generally, the election had to have been made on the taxpayer's tax return for the first taxable year ending after July 18, 1984. The Act extends the time for making the election to six months after the date of enactment of the Act.

Appendix C— Accounting Methods — Advantages and Disadvantages

Who May Use	When Income Is Taxed	When Expenses Are Deductible	Advantages	Disadvantages
Cash Method				
Any taxpayer — unless inventories necessary to reflect income.	In year cash or property is received. For property, use fair market value.	Year in which payment is made in cash or property. Giving note is not payment; payment can be made with borrowed funds.	You don't pay taxes until you get the income.	You don't always match related income and expenses in one year, thur creating distortions.
Must be used if no records or incomplete ones.	Taxed in year of *constructive receipt*— even if there's no actual receipt (i.e., year income was available to you although you didn't take it).	Certain prepaid expenses must be spread over periods to which they apply even though full amount has been paid; *e.g.*, insurance premiums, rent. But payment for supplies bought in advance is currently deductible.	You can control each year's receipts and payouts and even out income over the years.	You may not have full control over receipts and income may pile up in one year.
Can use in one business although other method is used in other business.			You can keep simple records.	Liquidation or sale of business may create income bunching — all accounts receivable may have to be picked up at one time.
Accrual Method				
Anyone except those with no — or incomplete — books or records.	In year income is earned — i.e., year in which right to income becomes fixed, regardless of year of receipt.	In the year all events have occurred which fix the fact and the amount of your liability, regardless of the year of payment. Effective after 7/18/84, no deduction until "Economic Performance" occurs. See Sec. 461.	It matches income and related expenses and tends to even out your income over the years.	Have less leeway than cash-basis taxpayer to defer or accelerate income or deductions.

Who May Use	When Income Is Taxed	When Expenses Are Deductible	Advantages	Disadvantages
You must use if inventories are necessary to reflect income clearly — unless you can use one of the methods discussed below.	You do not accrue contingent, contested, or uncollectable items. Prepaid amounts are income when received — even if not yet earned. However, some relief is available by a special election to defer the income (see *Rev. Proc. 71-21*).	You do not accrue contingent or contested liabilities. But if you pay a liability and still contest it, you deduct it when you pay it. If you get a recovery later, it's income when recovered.		Can still accelerate deductions, however, by: advancing repairs and advertising expenditures within desired period, purchasing supplies, getting bills for professional services before year-end.

"Hybrid" Method (*see Reg.* §1.446-(c)(1)(iv))

Who May Use	When Income Is Taxed	When Expenses Are Deductible	Advantages	Disadvantages
Any taxpayer if method clearly reflects income and is consistently used.	Accrual method is used in respect of purchases and sales, while cash method is used for all other items of income and expense.		Method is simple: it's not necessary to accrue income items such as interest, dividends. And the bother of accruing small expenses is removed.	Method is not entirely accurate. Since it is a "hybrid" it does not reflect *true* income. However, if consistently used, it gives a fairly good idea of how business is doing.

Who May Use	When Income Is Taxed	When Expenses Are Deductible	Advantages	Disadvantages
Installment Method				
Installment dealers who elect this method. Generally, seller in casual sale of personal property or of real property.	Each year that collections are made, a proportionate amount of each collection (equal to percentage of gross profit on entire sale) is picked up as gross income in the year of collection.	Dealer deducts expenses when paid (cash basis) or incurred (accrual basis). On casual sales, expense of sale reduces sales price, thereby having effect of spreading deduction over period of reporting income.	Income is spread over period of collection—so you do not pay taxes on amounts not yet received. If tax rates decline in future, part of profits will bear a lower tax.	Dealers who switch from accrual to installment basis may have to pay a double tax on some receivables — unless they sell off all receivables before the switch. Tax rates may go up; all depreciation recapture income is taxed in year of sale.
Deferred Payment Sales Method				
Any cash-basis taxpayer on sale of personal property. Any cash or accrual taxpayer on sale of real estate.	At time of sale, seller picks up cash and *fair market value* of buyer's obligations. If total exceeds basis of sold property, difference is taxable. In later years, as obligations are collected, difference between amount received and value at which obligations were picked up originally is taxable at time of collection.	Used generally with casual sales,	Useful in somewhat speculative deals where value of buyer's obligations are contingent on future operations and have little or no ascertainable present value.	You may be in for a long and costly argument with IRS as to value of obligations. Even though original sale gave capital gain, gain on collection of the obligations in future years will be taxable as ordinary income.

Long-Term Contract Methods
Percentage of Completion Method

Who May Use	When Income Is Taxed	When Expenses Are Deductible	Advantages	Disadvantages
Taxpayers who have long-term contracts more than a year to complete — usually construction contracts. There are two long-term contract methods — (1) percentage of completion and (2) completed contract — and IRS permission is needed to switch to or from either.	A portion of the total contract price is taken into account each year according to the percentage of the contract completed that year. Architects' or engineers' certificates are required.	All expenses made during the year allocable to that contract are deducted — with adjustments made for inventories and supplies on hand at the beginning and end of the year.	Income from long-term contract is reflected as earned. Income bunching in one year is avoided.	Accurate estimates of completion are difficult to make in some cases. If expenses are irregular as compared with income, there may be distortion of income in the interim years — although the final total will work out accurately.

Completed Contract Method

Who May Use	When Income Is Taxed	When Expenses Are Deductible	Advantages	Disadvantages
	The entire contract price is picked up as income in the year the contract is completed and accepted.	Expenses allocable to specific contracts (that would exclude general administrative cost) are not deductible until year of completion — when income is picked up.	Income can be reflected more accurately — all the figures are in when the computation is made. Avoids estimates in interim years which may turn out to be wrong.	Bunching of income or losses in one year is possible if a number of profitable or unprofitable contracts are all finished in one year. A steady flow of completed contracts from year to year overcomes this problem. There may be some argument with IRS as to proper year of completion in some cases.

Appendix D

Table of Contents—The Current Text (Accounting and Industry Standards)

Most accounting books and articles, in quoting or referencing the AICPA standards, mention as a source the original number of the APB, ARB, SAS, FASB, etc. Reference to those individual pronouncements often involves the further trace to a prior announcement, which amended a prior one, which amended . . . and so on. Also, every opinion, by itself, is dated and pinpointed in time and cannot in itself indicate *subsequent* changes thereafter. Unless one makes manual changes and references to the opinions as they are amended by later pronouncements, he may be working with a provision which is outdated or voided by a later one.

There is only one adequate timely publication which constantly updates the standards—paragraph by paragraph—as changes occur. This two-volume *Current Text* is published by the Financial Accounting Standards Board. Volumes 3 and 4 *Current Text* replaces the AICPA's four-volume *Professional Standards*.

Material Disclosed in the *Current Text*

The FASB *Current Text* is an integration of currently effective accounting and reporting standards. Material in the *Current Text* is drawn from AICPA Accounting Research Bulletins, APB Opinions, FASB Statements of Financial Accounting Standards, and FASB Interpretations. Those pronouncements are covered by Rule 203 of the Rules of Conduct of the AICPA Code of Professional Ethics, which states:

> *Rule 203—Accounting principles.* A member shall not express an opinion that financial statements are presented in conformity with generally accepted accounting principles if such statements contain any departure from an accounting principle promulgated by the body designated by Council . . . to establish such principles which has a material effect on the statement taken as a whole, unless the member can demonstate that due to unusual circumstances the financial statements would otherwise have been misleading. In such cases, his report must describe the departure, the approximate effects

thereof, if practicable, and the reasons why compliance with the principle would result in a misleading statement.

Interpretation No. 2 of Rule 203 states:

Status of FASB interpretations. Council is authorized under Rule 203 to designate a body to establish accounting principles and has designated the Financial Accounting Standards Board as such body. Council also has resolved that FASB Statements of Financial Accounting Standards, together with those Accounting Research Bulletins and APB Opinions which are not superseded by action of the FASB, constitute accounting principles as contemplated in Rule 203.

In determining the existence of a departure from an accounting principle established by a Statement of Financial Accounting Standards, Accounting Research Bulletin or APB Opinion encompassed by Rule 203, the division of professional ethics will construe such Statement, Bulletin or Opinion in the light of any interpretations thereof issued by the FASB.

The *Current Text* also incorporates the supplemental guidance provided by FASB Technical Bulletins and AICPA Accounting Interpretations.

The *Current Text* does not in any way supersede, change, or otherwise affect the pronouncements from which it is drawn. Although edited by the FASB staff, the abridged text has not been subjected to the FASB's due process procedures used for issuing FASB Statements. The authority of the *Current Text* is derived from the underlying pronouncements, which remain in force.

Material Excluded from the *Current Text*

The *Current Text* does not include FASB Statements of Financial Accounting Concepts, APB Statements, or AICPA Terminology Bulletins. Those documents may be found in *Original Pronouncements through June 1973* and *Original Pronouncements July 1973–June 1st, 1987*, the companion publications to the *Current Text* that contain the complete text of all pronouncements arranged in chronological sequence.

The *Current Text* also does not include AICPA Industry Accounting or Audit Guides or Statements of Position, except as specialized principles in them have been extracted and issued in FASB Statements. Nor are Statements of International Accounting Standards included. All of those documents, however, are available from the American Institute of Certified Public Accountants, 1211 Avenue of the Americas, New York, NY 10036.

The *Current Text* is a condensed version of original pronouncements. Descriptive material, such as information about Exposure Drafts, respondents' comments, background information, and reasons for conclusions and dissents, is generally excluded. However, certain material contained in other than the standards section of an original pronouncement is included to help the reader understand or implement the *Current Text*. Readers wishing to better understand the rationale behind a pronouncement or seeking background information should refer to the original pronouncement from which the related *Current Text* material is drawn. This is easy to do because each paragraph in the *Current Text* contains a source reference to the original pronouncement.

Organization of *Current Text*

The *Current Text* integrates financial accounting and reporting standards according to the major subject areas to which they apply. The subjects are arranged alphabetically in sections that are grouped into two volumes. The first volume (General Standards) contains those standards that are generally applicable to all enterprises; the second volume (Industry Standards) contains specialized standards that are applicable to enterprises operating in specific industries. Each volume presents flowcharts to assist in identifying the disclosure requirements for the sections contained in that volume. A comprehensive Topical Index appears at the end of each volume. The *Current Text* includes disclosure checklists in flowchart form.

Each **section** is identified by an alpha-numeric code. (The numeric part has been arbitrarily selected to allow space for future additions.) The alpha-numeric code in the General Standards volume follows an alpha-numeric-numeric pattern (for example, A99), and the code in the Industry Standards volume follows an alpha-alpha-numeric pattern (for example, Aa9). Each volume has a key cross-reference guide which contains a list of topics arranged alphabetically that might logically be sought under each letter and the section code where each topic can be found.

Paragraphs within each section are numbered consecutively, according to the following numeric format:

Paragraphs .101–.399: Standards
Paragraphs .401–.499: Glossary
Paragraphs .501–.999: Supplemental guidance (not covered by Rule 203)

All **section-paragraph references** are made in the following form: B05.127 or In6.102. For example, B05.127 refers to Section B05, "Balance Sheet Classification: Current Assets and Current Liabilities," paragraph .127, and In6.102 refers to Section In6, "Insurance Industry," paragraph .102.

Terms defined in the **Glossary** for a section are in boldface type the first time they appear in that section.

Source references are provided that indicate the original pronouncements from which material in each paragraph and footnote is derived. They appear in brackets and use the following abbreviations:

FAS   FASB Statement of Financial Accounting Standards
FIN   FASB Interpretation
FTB   FASB Technical Bulletin
CON   FASB Statement of Concepts
APB   AICPA Accounting Principles Board Opinion

ARB   AICPA Accounting Research Bulletin

AIN   AICPA Accounting Interpretation

ch   chapter

fn   footnote

For example, the source reference [FIN21, ¶15, fn3] indicates paragraph 15, footnote 3 of FASB Interpretation No. 21, *Accounting for Leases in a Business Combination*. Similarly, the source reference [AIN-APB11, #8] indicates the eighth AICPA Accounting Interpretation of APB Opinion No. 11, *Accounting for Income Taxes*.

Transitional language and editorial changes that *add* wording to an original pronouncement to maintain a consistent editorial style within the volumes appear in brackets. If an original pronouncement *deletes* wording from a previous pronouncement and it does not provide substitute wording, the amending pronouncement is not included in the source reference described in the preceding paragraph. Only the source reference for the earlier pronouncement is noted. However, Appendix B identifies the sources for all such deletions. Certain editorial deletions have been made to original pronouncements either to maintain a consistent editorial style or for clarity. Those deletions also are not noted. However, in such cases the deletions have not affected the substance of the text. Other changes have been made to conform format (for example, "iii" my have been changed to "c") or terminology, as follows:

Term in *Original Pronouncement*	Term in *Current Text*
should (meaning *must*)	shall
see (in making a reference)	refer to
which (in a restrictive clause)	that
where (not location)	if
when (not specific timing)	if
entity (if used broadly)	enterprise
company	enterprise
corporation	enterprise
earned surplus	retained earnings
capital surplus	additional paid-in capital
additional paid-in surplus	additional paid-in capital

Effective Dates and Transition Provisions of Underlying Pronouncements

The effective dates of FASB Statements of Financial Accounting Standards, FASB Interpretations, APB Opinions, and Accounting Research Bulletins, and the issue dates of AICPA Accounting Interpretations and FASB Technical Bulletins are summarized in Appendix C. That appendix also presents the transition paragraphs of more recent pronouncements whose effective dates and transition provisions are such that they might be initially applied in annual financial statements issued on or after June 1, 1987.

Users can refer to the Table of Contents of the *Current Text* in this Appendix to determine if the requirements of issued pronouncements for accounting and financial reporting standards apply to their particular circumstances. Also, users having a need to reference the standards of prior years can refer to the original pronouncements that were effective for those years.

Changes in original pronouncements as the result of subsequent pronouncements are included in the listing.

Table of Contents—The Current Text*

VOLUME I

Section

An Introduction to the Current Text

GENERAL STANDARDS

Current Text, published by the Financial Accounting Standards Board.

VOLUME II

Section
Disclosure Flowcharts—General Standards

Description and Instructions

Yellow —Disclosure Directory
Green   —General Disclosures
Pink   —Extended Scope Disclosures

INDUSTRY STANDARDS

Key Cross-Reference Guides

Co4 —Contractor Accounting:
  Construction-Type Contracts

Co5 —Contractor Accounting:
  Governmental Contracts

De4 —Development Stage Enterprises

Ed8 —Educational Organizations:
  Colleges and Universities

Em6 —Employee Benefit Funds: Employee
  Health and Welfare Benefit Funds

Fi4 —Finance Companies

Fo6 —Forest Products Industry

Fr3 —Franchising:
  Accounting by Franchisors

He4 —Health Care Industry: Hospitals

In6 —Insurance Industry

In8 —Investment Companies

Mi6 —Mining Industry

Mo4 —Mortgage Banking Activities

Mo6 —Motion Picture Industry

No5 —Nonbusiness Organizations

Oi5 —Oil and Gas Producing Activities

Pe5 —Pension Funds: Accounting and Reporting
  by Defined Benefit Pension Plans

Re1 —Real Estate: Sales

Re2 —Real Estate: Accounting for Costs and Initial Rental Operations of
  Real Estate Projects

Re3 —Real Estate: Other

Re4 —Record and Music Industry

Re6 —Regulated Operations

St4 —Stockbrokerage Industry

Ti7 —Title Plant

Disclosure Flowcharts—Industry Standards

Description and Instructions

Yellow —Disclosure Directory

Blue —Specialized Industry Disclosures

Appendixes

Topical Index

Appendix E

Guide to
Record Retention Requirements

in the Code of
Federal Regulations

Revised as of January 1, 1986

Published by
the Office of the Federal Register
National Archives and
Records Administration

TREASURY DEPARTMENT

Internal Revenue Service

NOTE: The following items refer to requirements issued under the Internal Revenue Code of 1954 which were in effect as of January 1, 1981. All regulations applicable under any provision of law in effect on August 16, 1954, the date of enactment of the 1954 Code, are applicable to the corresponding provisions of the 1954 Code insofar as such regulations are not inconsistent with the 1954 Code, and such regulations remain applicable to the 1954 Code until superseded by regulations under such Code. The Internal Revenue Service points out that the omission from this compilation of any record retention requirement provided for by law or regulation issued thereunder shall not be construed as authority to disregard any such requirement. The Service also points out that persons subject to income tax are bound by the retention requirement given in 26 CFR 1.6001-1 regardless of other requirements which for other purposes allow shorter retention periods.

The record retention requirements of the Internal Revenue Service are divided into the following categories: Income, Estate and Gift, Employment, and Excise Taxes.

Income Tax

26 CFR

The following record requirements have not been assigned a specific record retention period and the general "materiality" rule applies:

1.44c-3(1) Residential energy credit.

To maintain records that clearly identify the energy-conserving components and renewable energy source property with respect to which a residential energy credit is claimed, and substantiate their cost to the taxpayer, any labor costs properly allocable to them paid for by the taxpayer, and the method used for allocating such labor costs.

1.46-1 Component members of a controlled group on December 31 apportionment of $25,000 amount; section 38 property; computation of investment credit and qualified investment.

To keep as a part of its records a copy of the statement containing all the required consents to the apportionment plan.

1.46-3 Persons computing qualified investment in certain section 8 depreciable property.

To maintain sufficient records to determine whether section 47 of the Code, relating to certain dispositions of section 38 property, applies with respect to any asset.

1.47-1 Recomputation of credit allowed by Section 38.

To maintain records which will establish with respect to each item of section 38 property, the following facts: (a) The date the property is disposed of or otherwise ceases to be section 38 property, (b) the estimated useful life which was assigned to the property for computing qualified investment, (c) the month and the taxable year in which property was placed in service, and (d) the basis (or cost), actually or reasonably determined, of the property.

Taxpayers who, for purposes of determining qualified investment, do not use a mortality dispersion table with respect to section 38 assets similar in kind but who consistently assign to such assets separate lives based on the estimated range of years taken into consideration in establishing the average useful life of such assets, must, in addition to the above records, maintain records which will establish to the satisfaction of the district director that such asset has not previously been considered as having been disposed of.

1.47-3 Disposition of cessation of section 38 property by transferee.

Any taxpayer who seeks to establish his interest in a trade or business, shall maintain adequate records to demonstrate his indirect interest after any such transfer or transfers.

1.47-4 Electing small business corporations disposing of section 8 property.

Any taxpayer who seeks to establish his interest in a former electing small business corporation shall maintain adequate records to demonstrate his direct interest after any such transfer or transfers.

1.47–5   Estates and trusts disposing of section 8 property.

Any taxpayer who seeks to establish his interest in an estate or trust, shall maintain adequate records to demonstrate his indirect interest after any such transfer or transfers.

1.47–6   Partnerships section 8 property.

Any taxpayer who seeks to establish his interest in a partnership, shall maintain adequate records to demonstrate his indirect interest after any such transfer or transfers.

1.48–3   Persons selecting used section 38 property, $50,000 cost limitation.

To maintain records which permit specific identification of any item of used section 38 property selected, which was placed in service by the person selecting the property. Each member, other than the filing member, of a controlled group shall retain as part of its records a copy of the apportionment statement which was attached to the filing member's return.

1.48–4   Election of lessor of new section 38 property to treat lessee as purchaser.

The lessor and the lessee shall keep as a part of their records the statements filed with the lessee, signed by the lessor and including the written consent of the lessee.

1.50A–1   Apportionment   of   the   first $25,000 of the work incentive program (WIN) credit among members of a controlled group of corporations.

Each component member of the group shall keep a copy of the statement containing all the required consents.

1.50A–4   Persons claiming that a recomputation of the work incentive program (WIN) credit is not required by the early termination of a participating employee.

To maintain sufficient records to support claim that a termination of

employment falls within the exceptions specified in the section cited.

1.50A–5   Persons   maintaining   that   the transfer of an interest in a former small business corporation for an interest in another entity does not result in a diminution requiring a recapture of the work incentive program (WIN) credit.

To maintain adequate records to demonstrate their indirect interest after any such transfer or transfers.

1.50A–6   Persons   maintaining   that   the transfer of an interest in an estate or trust, for an interest in another entity does not result in a diminution requiring a recapture of the work incentive program (WIN) credit.

To maintain adequate records to demonstrate their indirect interest after any such transfer or transfers.

1.50A–7   Persons   maintaining   that   the transfer of an interest in a partnership for an interest in another entity does not result in a diminution requiring a recapture of the work incentive program (WIN) credit.

To maintain adequate records to demonstrate their indirect interest after any such transfer or transfers.

1.57–5   Persons subject to a minimum tax on items of tax preference.

(a) *General.* To maintain permanent records of all the facts necessary to determine the amounts expended to and adjustments made to property acquired and held for investment, and to maintain permanent records necessary to verify the exercise of a qualified stock option. To maintain records of the amount of debts written off and the amount of the loans outstanding with regard to the reserve for losses on bad debts of financial institutions for the taxable year and the 5 preceding taxable years or such shorter or longer period as appropriate.

(b) *Net operating losses.* To maintain permanent records of all the facts necessary for the first taxable year and each succeeding year in which there is a net operating loss or a net operating loss carryover, including the amount of net operating loss in each such taxable year in which tax preference items exceed the minimum tax exemption, the amount of items for each such taxable year, the amount net operating loss reduces taxable income in any taxable year, and the amount net operating loss is reduced in any taxable year.

1.151-1 Persons not totally blind claiming the additional exemption for blindness.

To retain a copy of the certified opinion of the examining physician skilled in the diseases of the eye that there is no reasonable probability that his visual acuity will ever improve beyond the minimum standards described in section 1.151-1(d)(3) of the regulations.

1.162-17 Persons paying travel or other business expenses incurred by an employee in connection with the performance of his services.

To maintain adequate and detailed records of ordinary and necessary travel, transportation, entertainment, and other similar business expenses, including identification of amount and nature of expenditures, and to keep supporting documents, especially in connection with large or exceptional expenditures.

1.167(a)-7 Persons claiming allowance for depreciation of property used in trade or business or property held for the production of income.

To maintain regular books of accounts or permanent auxiliary records showing for each account the basis of the property, including adjustments necessary to conform to the requirements of section 1016 and other provision of law relating to adjustments to basis, and the depreciation allowances for tax purposes.

1.167(a)-11 Persons claiming allowance for depreciation of property used in trade or business or property held for the production of income.

To maintain records reasonably sufficient to determine facts and circumstances taken into account in estimating salvage value.

1.167(a)-12 Persons claiming allowance for depreciation of property used in trade or business or property held for the production of income.

To maintain books and records for each asset guideline class reasonably sufficient to identify the unadjusted basis, reserve for depreciation and salvage value established for each depreciation account in such asset guidelines class.

1.167(d)-1 Persons claiming allowance for depreciation of property used in trade or business or property held for the production of income.

To retain a sign copy of the agreement as to useful life and rates of depreciation of any property which is subject to the allowance for depreciation.

Retention period: Permanent.

1.167(e)-1 Persons changing method of depreciation of section 1245 or section 1250 property.

To maintain records which permit specific identification of section 1245 or section 1250 property in the account with respect to which the election is made, and any other property in such account. The records shall also show for all the property in the account the date of acquisition, cost or other basis, amounts recovered through depreciation and other allowances, the estimated salvage value, the character of the property, and the remaining useful life of the property.

1.167(j)-3 Persons claiming depreciation with respect to residential rental property.

To maintain a record of the gross rental income derived from a building, and the portion thereof which constitutes gross rental income from dwelling units, in addition to records required under section 1.167(a)-7(c) with respect to property in a depreciation account.

1.167(k)-2 Persons claiming depreciation of expenditures to rehabilitate low-income rental housing.

To maintain detailed records which permit specific identification of the rehabilitation expenditures that are permitted to be allocated to individual dwelling units under the allocation rules and income certifications that must be obtained from tenants who propose to live in rehabilitated dwelling units after the beginning of the certification year.

1.170-2 Persons claiming a deduction for amounts expended in maintaining certain students as a member of household.

To keep adequate records of amounts actually paid in maintaining a student as a member of the household. For certain items, such as food, a record of amounts spent for all members of the household, with an equal portion thereof allocated to each member, will be acceptable.

1.170A-13 Persons claiming deductions for a charitable contribution.

To maintain cancelled checks, receipt, letter, or other communication from the donee charitable organization showing the name of the donee, and the date and amount of the contribution. In the absence of a cancelled check or receipt from the donee charitable organization, other reliable written records showing the name of the donee and the date and amount of the contribution.

1.177-1 Persons electing to treat trademark or trade name expenditures as deferred expenses.

To make an accounting segregation on his books and records of trademark and trade name expenditures, for which the election has been made, sufficient to permit an identification of the character and amount of each expenditure and the amortization period selected for each expenditure.

1.179-4 Persons electing additional first-year depreciation allowance for section 179 property.

To maintain records which permit specific identification of each piece of "section 179 property" and reflect how and from whom such property was acquired.

1.190-3 Election to deduct expenditures for removing architectural and transportation barriers to the handicapped and elderly.

To retain records and documentation, including architectural plans and blueprints, contracts, and building permits, of all facts necessary to determine the amount of any deduction to which the taxpayer is entitled by reason of the election, as well as any adjustment to basis made for expenditures in excess of the amount deductible.

1.263(e)-1 Persons electing to deduct rehabilitation expenditures with respect to certain railroad rolling stock.

To maintain a separate section 263(e) record, as specified in the section cited, for each unit for which rehabilitation expenditures are deducted, and to maintain records for expenditures deducted as incidental repairs and maintenance.

1.265-1 Persons receiving any class of exempt income or holding property or engaging in activities the income from which is exempt.

To keep records of expenses otherwise allowable as deductions which are directly allocable to any class or classes of exempt income and amounts of items or parts of items allocated to each class.

1.274-5 Taxpayer substantiation of expenses for travel, entertainment, and gifts related to active conduct of trade or business.

A taxpayer must substantiate each element of an expenditure by adequate records or sufficient evidence corroborating his own statements. A taxpayer must also be able to substantiate by adequate records or sufficient evidence corroborating his own statements the business use of certain depreciable property used for travel or entertainment or the business use of certain computers for any taxable year during which there may be a recapture of any excess depreciation claimed.

1.302-4 Persons who file a waiver of attribution agreement with respect to a redemption of stock in termination of their interest.

To retain copies of income tax returns and any other records indicating fully the amount of tax which would have been payable had the redemption been treated as a distribution subject to section 301 of the Code.

1.312-15 Corporations using different methods of depreciation for taxable income and earnings and profit.

To maintain records which show the depreciation taken each year and which will allow computation of the adjusted basis of the property in each account using depreciation taken.

1.332-6 Corporations receiving distributions in complete liquidation of subsidiaries.

To keep records showing information with respect to the plan of liquidation and its adoption.

1.333-6 Qualified electing shareholders receiving distributions in complete liquidation of domestic corporations other than collapsible corporations.

To keep records in substantial form showing all facts pertinent to the recognition and treatment of the gain realized upon shares of stock owned at the time of the adoption of the plan of liquidation.

1.341-7 Corporations filing consents under section 341(f)(2) of the Code.

To maintain records adequate to permit identification of their subsection (f) assets.

1.351-3 Persons who participate in a transfer of property to a corporation controlled by the transferor.

To keep records in substantial form showing information to facilitate the determination of gain or loss from a subsequent disposition of stock or securities and other property, if any, received in the exchange.

1.358-5 Exchanges under the final system plan for ConRail.

To maintain records to determine the reallocated basis of each certificate of value or share of stock retained.

1.367(a)-1 Participants in exchange involving a foreign corporation.

To retain a copy of the ruling letter obtained from the Commissioner as authority for treating a foreign corporation as a corporation in determining the extent to which gain on exchange is recognized.

1.368-3 Persons who participate in a tax-free exchange in connection with a corporate reorganization.

To keep records in substantial form showing the cost or other basis of the transferred property and the amount of stock or securities and other property or money received (including any liabilities assumed upon the exchange, or any liabilities to which any of the properties received were subject), in order to facilitate the determination of gain or loss from a subsequent disposition of such stock or securities and other property received from the exchange.

1.371-1 Corporations which are parties to reorganizations in pursuance of court orders in receivership, foreclosure, or similar proceedings, or in proceedings under chapter X of the Bankruptcy Act.

To keep records in substantial form showing the cost or other basis of the transferred property and the amount of stock or securities and other property or money received (including any liabilities assumed upon the exchange), in order to facilitate the determination of gain or loss from a subsequent disposition of such stock or securities and other property received from the exchange.

1.371-2 Persons who exchange stock and securities in corporations in accordance with plans of reorganizations approved by the courts in receivership, foreclosure, or similar proceedings, or in proceedings under chapter X of the Bankruptcy Act.

To keep records in substantial form showing the cost or other basis of the transferred property and the amount of stock or securities and other property money received (including any liabilities assumed upon the exchange), in order to facilitate the determination of gain or loss from a subsequent disposition of such stock or securities and other property received from the exchange.

1.374-3 Railroads participating in a tax-free reorganization.

Records in substantial form must be kept by every railroad corporation which participates in a tax-free exchange in connection with a reorganization under section 374(a) of the Code, showing the cost or other basis of the transferred property and the amount of stock or securities and other property or money received, including any liabilities assumed upon the exchange, in order to facilitate the determination of gain or loss from a subsequent disposition of such stock or securities and other property received from the exchange.

1.381(c)(6)-1 Depreciation allowance carryovers of acquiring corporations in certain corporate acquisitions.

Records shall be maintained in sufficient detail to identify any depreciable property to which section 1.381(c)(6)-1 of the regulations applies and to establish the basis thereof.

1.414(f)-1 Multiemployer plan.

To maintain proof for plan years ending prior to September 3, 1974, that the requirements of section 414(f) of the Code and the regulations are met for each plan year ending prior to that date to the extent necessary to show the applicability of the 75 percent test provided in section 1.414(f)-1(c). For plan years ending after September 2, 1974, to maintain proof that the requirements of section 414(f) of the Code and the regulations are met for 6 immediately preceding plan years.

1.442-1 Persons required to seek the approval of the Commissioner in order to change their annual accounting period.

To keep adequate and accurate records of their taxable income for the short period involved in the change and for the fiscal year proposed.

1.453-1 Persons selling by the installment method.

Installment method. In adopting the installment method of accounting the seller must maintain such records as are necessary to clearly reflect income.

1.453-2 Persons selling personal property by the installment plan.

A dealer who desires to compute income by the installment method shall maintain accounting records in such a manner as to enable an accurate computation to be made by such method. In the case of sales under a revolving credit plan, the dealer must maintain records in sufficient detail to show the method of computing and applying the probability sample.

1.456-7 Prepaid dues income.

A taxpayer who makes an election with respect to prepaid dues income shall maintain books and records in sufficient detail to enable the district director to determine upon audit that additional amounts were included in the taxpayer's gross income for any of the three taxable years preceding the first taxable year to which the election applies.

1.472-2 Persons permitted or required to use the LIFO method of inventory valuation.

To maintain such supplemental and detailed inventory records as will enable the District Director to verify the inventory computations and compliance with section 472 and sections 1.472-1 through 1.472-7.

1.472-8 Persons using dollar-value method of inventory valuation.

To maintain adequate records to support the appropriateness, accuracy, and reliability of the index or link-method.

1.521-1 Farmer's cooperative marketing and purchasing associations.

To keep permanent records of the business done both with members and nonmembers, which show that the association was operating during the taxable year on a cooperative basis in the distribution of patronage dividends to all producers. While under the Code patronage dividends must be paid to all producers on the same basis, this requirement is complied with if an association, instead of paying patronage dividends to non-member producers in cash, keeps permanent records from which the proportionate shares of the patronage dividends due to nonmember producers can be determined, and such shares are made applicable toward the purchase price of a share of stock or of a membership in the association.

1.527-2 Political organizations; segregated funds.

The organization or individual maintaining a segregated fund must keep records that are adequate to verify receipts and disbursements of the fund and identify the exempt function activity for which each expenditure is made.

1.561-2 Corporation claiming deduction for dividends paid.

To keep permanent records necessary (a) to establish that dividends with respect to which the deduction is claimed were actually paid during the taxable year, and (b) to supply the information required to be filed with the income tax return of the corporation. To also keep canceled dividend checks and receipts obtained from shareholders acknowledging payment.

1.585-3 Financial institutions establishing a reserve for losses on loans to banks.

Institutions shall maintain records of the reserve for losses on loans to establish that the Federal income tax returns and amended returns with attached schedules are permanently maintained and that the balance of the reserve can be readily reconciled with the reserves maintained by the financial institution for financial statement purposes, and to establish and maintain a permanent subsidiary ledger reflecting an account for the reserve provided the balance can be readily reconciled with the balance of the reserve for financial statement purposes maintained in any other ledger.

1.593-7 Mutual savings banks, etc., maintaining reserves for bad debts.

To maintain as a permanent part of its regular books of account, an account for: (a) A reserve for losses on nonqualifying loans, (b) a reserve for losses on qualifying real property loans, and (c) if required, a supplemental reserve for losses on loans. A permanent subsidiary ledger containing an account for each of such reserves may be maintained.

1.595-1 Mutual savings banks, etc., making capital improvements on land acquired by foreclosure.

To maintain such records as are necessary to relect clearly, with respect to each particular acquired property, the cost of each capital improvement and whether the taxpayer treated minor capital improvements with respect to such property in the same manner as the acquired property.

1.611-2 Persons claiming allowance for cost depletion of natural gas property without reference to discovery value or percentage depletion.

To keep accurate records of periodical pressure determinations where the annual production is not metered.

1.611-2 Persons claiming an allowance for depletion and depreciation of mineral property, oil and gas wells, and other natural deposits.

To keep a separate account in which shall be accurately recorded the cost or other basis of such property together with subsequent allowable capital additions to each account and all other required adjustments; and, to assemble, segregate, and have readily available at his principal place of business, all the supporting data which is used in compiling certain summary statements required to be attached to returns and such other records as indicated in sections cited.

1.611-3 Persons claiming an allowance for depletion of timber property.

To keep accurate ledger accounts in which shall be recorded the cost or other basis of the property and land together with subsequent allowable capital additions in each account and all other adjustments. In such accounts there shall be set up separately the quantity of timber, the quantity of land, and the quantity of other resources, if any, and a proper part of the total cost or value shall be allocated to each after proper provision for immature timber growth. The timber accounts shall be credited each year with the amount of the charges to the depletion accounts or the amount of the charges to the depletion accounts shall be credited to depletion reserves accounts.

1.613-4 Persons computing gross incomes from mining by use of representative market or field price.

To keep records as to the source of pricing information and relevant supporting data.

1.613-5 Mineral property, taxable income computation, allocation of section 1245 gain.

Taxpayer shall have available permanent records of all the facts necessary to determine with reasonable accuracy the portion of any gain recognized under section 1245(a)(1) of the Code which is properly allocable to the mineral property in respect of which the taxable income is being computed. In the absence of such records, none of the gain recognized under section 1245(a)(1) shall be allocable to such mineral property.

1.613A-6 Transfer of interest in oil or gas property.

To retain records that show the terms of the transfer of an interest in the oil or gas property, any geological and geophysical data in the possession of the transferee or other explanatory data with respect to the property transferred, and any other information that bears upon the question of whether at the time of the transfer the principal value of the property transferred had been demonstrated by prospecting, exploration, and discovery work.

To keep records of the secondary and tertiary processes applied and of the amount of production so resulting.

1.614-3 Persons with separate operating mineral interests in the case of mines.

To maintain adequate records and maps and statements of election as indicated in the section cited.

1.614-6 Persons aggregating operating mineral interests in oil and gas wells in a single tract or parcel of land.

To obtain accurate and reliable information, and keep records with respect thereto, establishing all facts necessary for making the computations prescribed for the fair market value method of determining basis on the aggregation.

1.614-8 Persons electing to treat separate operating mineral interests in oil and gas wells in a single tract or parcel of land as separate properties.

To maintain and have available records and maps sufficient to clearly define the tract or parcel and all of the taxpayer's operating mineral interests therein.

1.642(c)-2 Trustee of trust claiming charitable remainder interest deduction, incompetent grantor.

To retain certificate of incompetency or a copy of the judgment or decree and any modification thereof.

1.642(c)-5 Pooled income fund investing or reinvesting any portion of its properties jointly with other properties.

To maintain records which identify the portion of the total fund which is owned by the pooled income fund and the income earned by, and attributable to, such portion.

1.642(i)-1 Cemetery perpetual care fund trustee; certified statements by cemetery officials.

To retain certified copies of statements by an officer of the cemetery concerning the number of interments sold or the amount of the cemetery's expenditure for care and maintenance.

1.801-8 Life insurance companies issuing contracts with reserves based on segregated asset accounts.

To keep such permanent records and other data relating to such contracts as are necessary to enable the District

Director to determine the correctness of the application of the separate accounting rules and the accuracy of the computations.

1.811–2 Life insurance companies distributing dividends to policyholders.

Every life insurance company claiming a deduction for dividends to policyholders shall keep such permanent records as are necessary to establish the amount of dividends actually paid during the taxable year. Such company shall also keep a copy of the dividend resolution and any necessary supporting data relating to the amounts of dividends declared and to the amounts held or set aside as reserves for dividends to policyholders during the taxable year.

1.820–2 Life insurance companies with respect to the optional treatment of policies reinsured under modified coinsurance contracts.

The reinsured and reinsurer shall maintain as part of their permanent books of account any subsequent amendments to the original modified coinsurance contract between the reinsured and reinsurer.

1.852–4 Regulated investment companies.

To keep a record of the proportion of each capital gain dividend which is gain described in section 1201(d)(1) or (2).

1.852–6 Regulated investment companies.

To maintain permanent records showing the information relative to the actual owners of stock contained in the written statements to be demanded from the shareholders.

1.852–9 Shareholders of regulated investment companies.

To keep copy C of Form 2439 furnished for the regulated investment company's taxable years ending after 1969, and beginning before 1975, to show increases in the shareholder's adjusted basis of shares of such company. In addition, every regulated investment company shall keep a record of the proportion of undistributed capital gains (to which section 1.852–9(a)(1)(iii) applies) which is gain described in section 1201(d)(1) or (2).

1.857–6 Real estate investment trust.

To keep a record of the proportion of each capital dividend which is gain described in section 1201(d)(1) or (2) of the Code for taxable years ending after 1969, and beginning before 1975.

1.857–8 Real estate investment trust.

To keep such records as will disclose the actual ownership of its outstanding stock; to also maintain as part of this trust's records, a list of the persons failing or refusing to comply in whole or in part with the trust demand for written statements.

1.905–2 Persons claiming credit for taxes paid or accrued to foreign countries and possessions of the United States.

To keep readily available for comparison on request the original receipt for each such tax payment, or the original return on which each such accrued tax was based, a duplicate original, or a duly certified or authenticated copy, in case only a sworn copy of a receipt or return is submitted.

1.934–1 Persons or corporations seeking to come within the exception to the limitation on reduction in income tax liability incurred to the Virgin Islands, under section 934 of the Code.

To maintain such records and other documents as are necessary to determine the applicability of the exception.

1.995–5 Domestic international sales corporations (DISC's); foreign investment attributable to producer's loans.

To keep permanent books or records as are sufficient to establish the transactions, amounts, and computations described in the section cited.

1.1012–1 Election to use the average basis method for certain regulated investment company stock.

To maintain records as are necessary to substantiate the average basis (or bases) used on an income tax return in reporting gain or loss from the sale or transfer of shares.

1.1014–4 Executors or other legal representatives of decedents, fiduciaries of trusts under wills, life tenants and other persons to whom a uniform basis with respect to property transmitted at death is applicable.

To make and maintain records showing in detail all deductions, distributions, or other items for which adjustment to basis is required to be made.

1.1015–1 Persons making or receiving gifts of property acquired by gift after December 31, 1920.

To preserve and keep accessible a record of the facts necessary to determine the cost of the property, its fair market value as of the date of the gift, the gift tax attributable to the gift, and, if pertinent, its fair market value as of March 1, 1913, to insure a fair and adequate determination of the proper basis.

1.1081–11 Persons participating in exchanges or distributions made in obedience to orders of the Securities and Exchange Commission.

To keep records in substantial form showing the cost or other basis of the property transferred and the amount of stock or securities and other property (including money) received.

1.1101–4 Stock or security holders records of distribution pursuant to the Bank Holding Company Act of 1956.

Each stock or security holder who receives stock or securities or other property upon a distribution made by a qualified bank holding corporation under section 1101 of the Code shall maintain records of all facts pertinent to the nonrecognition of gain upon such distribution.

1.1232–3 Gain upon sale or exchange of obligations issued at an original issue discount after December 31, 1954.

Taxpayer shall keep a record of the issue price and issue date upon or with each such obligation (if known or reasonably ascertainable by him). If the obligation held is an obligation of the United States received from the United States in an exchange upon which gain or loss is not recognized because of section 1037(a) of the Code

(or so much of section 1031(b) or (c) as relates to section 1037(a)), the taxpayer shall keep sufficient records to determine the issue price of such obligations for purposes of applying section 1.1037–1 of the regulations upon the disposition or redemption of such obligations.

1.1233–1 Persons engaged in arbitrage operations in stock and securities.

To keep records that will clearly show that a transaction has been timely and properly identified as an arbitrage operation. Such identification must ordinarily be entered in the taxpayer's records on the day of the transaction.

1.1234–2 Grantors of straddles.

In the case of a multiple option where the number of options to sell and the number of options to buy are not the same or if the terms of all the options are not identical, the grantor must indicate in his records the individual serial number of, or other characteristic symbol imprinted upon, each of the two individual options which comprise the straddle, or by adopting any other method of identification satisfactory to the Commissioner. Such identification must be made before the expiration of the fifteenth day after the day on which the multiple option is granted and is applicable to multiple options granted after January 24, 1972.

1.1244 Corporations and shareholders with respect to the substantiation of ordinary loss deductions on small business corporation stock.

(a) *Corporations.* The plan to issue stock which qualifies under section 1244 of the Code must appear upon the records of the corporation. In addition, in order to substantiate an ordinary loss deduction claimed by its shareholders, the corporation should maintain records as indicated in section cited.

(b) *Shareholders.* Any person who claims a deduction for an ordinary loss on stock under section 1244 of the Code shall file with the income tax return for the year in which a deduction for the loss is claimed a statement setting forth information indicated in section cited.

In addition, a person who owns "section 1244 stock" in a corporation shall maintain records sufficient to distinguish such stock from any other stock owned in the corporation.

1.1245-2 Recomputed basis of section 1245 property and additional depreciation adjustments to section 1250 property when such property is sold, exchanged, transferred, or involuntarily converted.

To maintain permanent records which include (a) the date and manner in which the property was acquired, (b) the basis on the date the property was acquired and the manner in which the basis was determined, (c) the amount and date of all adjustments to basis, and (d) similar information with respect to other property having an adjusted basis reflecting depreciation or amortization adjustments by the taxpayer, or by another taxpayer on the same or other property.

1.1247-5 Foreign investment companies.

To maintain and preserve such permanent books of account, records, and other documents as are sufficient to establish what its taxable income would be if it were a domestic corporation. Generally, if the books and records are maintained in the manner prescribed by regulations under section 30 of the Investment Company Act of 1940, the requirements shall be considered satisfied.

1.321-1 Persons involved in the liquidation and replacement of LIFO inventories.

To keep detailed records such as will enable the Commissioner, in the examination of the taxpayer's return for the year of replacement, readily to verify the extent of the inventory decrease claimed to be involuntary in character and the facts upon which such claim is based, all subsequent inventory increases and decreases, and all other facts material to the replacement adjustment authorized.

1.1375-4 Records by small business corporations of distributions of previously taxed income and undistributed taxable income.

A small business corporation must keep records of (1) distributions of the net share of the previously taxed income of each shareholder and (2) each person's share of undistributed taxable income. In addition, each shareholder of such corporation shall keep a record of that shareholder's net share of previously taxed income and undistributed taxable income and shall make such record available to the corporation for its information.

1.1441-6 Withholding agents making payment to nonresident aliens, foreign partnerships, or foreign corporations after December 31, 1971, which are subject to a reduced rate or an exemption from tax pursuant to a tax treaty.

To maintain Form 1001, Ownership, Exemption, or Reduced Rate Certificate.

Retention period: *Coupon bond interest:* at least 4 years after the close of the calendar year in which the interest is paid; *Income other than coupon bond interest or dividends:* At least 4 years after the close of the calendar year in which the interest is paid; *Nonresident aliens and foreign corporations:* At leat 4 years after the interest is paid.

1.1461-2 Persons required to withhold tax on nonresident aliens, foreign corporations, and tax-free covenant bonds on payments of income made on and after January 1, 1957.

To keep copies of Forms 1042 and 1042S.

1.1502-3 Affiliated group: Intercompany transactions, accounting for deferred gain or loss.

(1) Maintain permanent records (including work papers) which will properly reflect the amount of deferred gain or loss and enable the group to identify the character and source of the deferred gain or loss to the selling member and apply the applicable restoration rules.

Income Tax

1.6001-1 Persons subject to income tax.

(a) *General.* Except as provided in paragraph (b), any person subject to tax, or any person required to file a return of information with respect to income shall keep such permanent books of account or records, including inventories, as are sufficient to establish the amount of gross income, deductions, credits, or other matters required to be shown by such person in any return of such tax or information.

(b) *Farmers and wage-earners.* Individuals deriving gross income from the business of farming, and individuals whose gross income includes salaries, wages, or similar compensation for personal services rendered, are required to keep such records as will enable the district director to determine the correct amount of income subject to the tax, but it is not necessary that these individuals keep the books of account or records required by paragraph (a).

(c) *Exempt organizations.* In addition to the books and records required by paragraph (a) with respect to the tax imposed on unrelated business income, every organization exempt from tax under section 501(a) of the Code shall keep such permanent books of account or records, including inventories, as are sufficient to show specifically the items of gross income, receipts, and disbursements, and other required information.

(d) *Notice by district director requiring returns, statements, or the keeping of records.* The district director may require any person, by notice served upon them, to make such returns, render such statements, or keep such specific records as will enable the district director to determine whether or not such person is liable for tax under subtitle A of the Code, including qualified State individual income taxes, which are treated pursuant to section 6361(a) of the Code as if they were imposed by chapter 1 of subtitle A.

Retention period: The period that records should be kept varies from a few years to a length of time that may cover more than one taxpayer's lifetime. The general requirement as stated in 26 CFR 1.6001-1 is that records must be kept "so long as the contents thereof may become material in the administration of any internal revenue law." Some books and records of a business may be "material" for tax purposes so long as the business remains in existence, and there may be reasons other than the Federal tax consequences to the individual taxpayer for retaining certain records for an indefinite period. However, the general requirements can be more precisely stated in terms of (1) records of property subject to gain or loss treatment, and (2) records supporting items of income, deductions, and credits.

Records of property for which a basis must be determined to compute gain or loss upon disposition (and depreciation, amortization, or depletion allowed or allowable) must be retained until a taxable disposition is made. Thus, if property is given an exchange basis, i.e. a basis determined by reference to other property held by the person for whom the basis must be determined, all records pertaining to such other property must be retained. After a taxable disposition, the record retention rules explained below will generally apply.

Records of income, deductions, and credits (including gains and losses) appearing on a return should be kept, at a minimum, until the statute of limitations for the return expires. 26 CFR 301.6501(a)-1 provides the general rule that the amount of any tax imposed by the Internal Revenue Code shall be assessed within three years after the return was filed; 26 CFR 301.6511(a)-1 requires that a claim for refund or credit must be filed within three years from the date of filing the return or 2 years after payment, whichever is later. However, there are many exceptions. For example, a 6 year period of limitation applies for assessment if there has been a substantial omission of income and a 7 year period applies for filing a claim for credit or refund relating to bad debts or losses on securities. The period of limitations may be extended by mutual agreement for any length of time, and no statutory period applies if fraud is established or if no return was filed.

Failure to retain records for a sufficient length of time could result, for example, in the assessment of additional tax because of disallowance of deductions or a downward adjustment of basis used in determining gain or loss on the disposition of property.

1.6013-6 Election to treat nonresident alien individual as resident of the United States.

To maintain books, records, and other information reasonably necessary to ascertain the amount of liability for taxes under chapters 1, 5, and 24 of the Code of either spouse for the taxable year. "Adequate records" also includes the granting of access to the books and records.

1.6042-1 Banking institutions, trust companies, or brokerage firms, who elect to file Form 1087, Nominee's Information Return, for each actual owner for whom it acts as nominee.

If the total amount of dividends paid to the actual owner is reported on one Form 1087 (without itemization as to issuing company, class of stock, etc.), the nominee must maintain such records as will permit a prompt substantiation of each payment of dividends made to the actual owner.

A specified record retention period has been established for the following income tax records.

1.414(1)-1 Merger of defined benefit plans.

To maintain sufficient data to create the special schedule of accrued benefits required in the case of certain mergers of defined benefit plans.

Retention period: 5 years after merger, if the plan does not have a spinoff or termination within 5 years.

1.6060-1 Income tax return preparers—employers.

An employer is required to retain a record of the name, taxpayer identification number, and principal place of work during the return period of each income tax return preparer employed (or engaged) at any time during the return period and to make the record available for inspection upon request. The employer may choose any form of documentation to be used as a record of the preparers employed (or engaged) during the return period. Sole proprietors and partnerships are also required to retain a record.

Retention period: 3-year period following the close of the return period to which the record relates.

1.6107-1 Income tax return preparers—returns.

To retain a completed copy of the return or claim for refund, or record, by list, card file, or otherwise, of the name, taxpayer identification number and taxable year of the taxpayer (or nontaxable entity) for whom the refund or claim for refund was prepared and the type of return or claim for refund prepared and the name of the individual preparer required to sign the return or claim for refund.

To retain the copy of a return or claim for refund manually signed by the preparer that is photocopied together with a record of arithmetical errors corrected after signature; the information submitted with respect to a computer-prepared return together with a record of arithmetical and clerical errors corrected; and a manually signed copy of the letter submitted to the Internal Revenue Service with respect to facsimile signatures on a return or claim for a nonresident alien individual together with a record of arithmetical errors corrected after the signature is affixed.

Retention period: 3 years following the close of the return period during which the return or claim for refund was presented for signature to the taxpayer or 3 years following the close of a later return period in which the return became due.

1.6695-1 Income tax return preparers—returns.

See 1.6107-1.

5.852-1 Regulated investment companies and real estate investment trust.

To keep a record of the proportion of each capital gain dividend that is post-October 1978 capital gain and post-1978 capital gain. In addition, every regulated investment company shall keep a record of the proportion of undistributed capital gains (to which this section 5.852-1(c)(2) applies) that is from post-October 1978 capital gain and post-1978 capital gain.

5.857-1 Regulated investment companies and real estate investment trust.

See 5.852-1.

7.367(b)-1 Exchanges involving a foreign corporation that began after December 31, 1977.

A corporation whose earnings and profits are required to be adjusted under sections 7.367(b)-4 through 7.367(b)-12 must keep records adequate to establish the adjustment.

A U.S. person owning a foreign corporation's stock to which an amount is attributed under sections 7.367(b)-4 through 7.367(b)-12 must keep records to establish the amount so attributed.

Estate, Gift, and Generation-Skipping Transfer Taxes

20.6001-1 Executors and donors of estates.

Executors of estates are required to keep records that will enable the district director to determine accurately the amount of the estate tax liability, and they must be available for inspection whenever required. Similarly, the donor of a gift is required to keep records necessary to prepare the gift tax return, and they must be available for inspection whenever required. Thus, an executor must keep detailed records of the affairs of the estate as will enable the district director to determine the amounts of the estate and the generation-skipping transfer tax liabilities, including copies of documents relating to the estate or the transfer, appraisal lists of items included in the gross estate or trust, copies of balance sheets or other financial statements relating to value of stock, and any other information necessary in determining the taxes. Persons making transfers of property by gift must maintain books of account or records necessary to establish the amount of the total gifts and generation-skipping transfers together with the deductions allowable in determining the amounts of the taxable interests and other information required to be shown in the tax returns.

Employment Tax

Retention period: Regulations requiring the retention of employment tax records usually specify the number of years that such records must be retained. For some employment tax records, however, no specific retention period can be established and the "materiality rule" discussed in section 1.600-1 under *Income Tax* must be applied. Under the materiality rule, those records must be retained so long as they may become material in the computation of any tax.

Specific record retention requirements have not been assigned to the following and the materiality rule applies:

31.3121(r)-1 Vow-of-poverty religious orders electing social security coverage for its members.

To maintain records of the details relating to the retirement of each of its members.

A specific record retention period has been established for the following employment tax records:

31.3401(a)-1 Employers required to deduct and withhold income tax on wages which include sick pay.

To keep records with respect to payments (sick pay) made directly to employees under a wage continuation plan, and other information specified in the sections cited.

Retention period: 4 years after the due date of such tax for the return period to which the records relate or the date such tax is paid, whichever is later.

31.6001-1 Employers and employee representatives subject to the Railroad Retirement Tax Act.

To keep records of all remuneration (whether in money or in something which may be used in lieu of money) other than tips, paid to his employees after 1954 for services rendered to him (including "time lost") after 1954 and such other records as specified in section cited.

Retention period: 4 years after the due date of such tax for the return period to which the records relate, or the date such tax is paid, whichever is later.

31.6001-1 Employers and persons who are not employers for purposes of the Federal Unemployment Tax Act.

To maintain records as specified in the section cited to determine the correct liability or nonliability for the tax.

Retention period: 4 years after the due date of such tax for the return period to which the records relate or the date such tax is paid, whichever is later.

31.6001-1 Employers claiming a refund, credit, or abatement of tax under the Federal Insurance Contributions Act or Railroad Retirement Tax Act.

Every employer who has filed a claim for refund, credit, or abatement of employee tax under section 3101 or section 3201 of the Code, or a corresponding provision of prior law, collected from an employee shall retain as part of his records the written receipt of the employee showing the date and amount of the repayment, or the written consent of the employee, whichever is used in support of the claim. Where employee tax was collected under section 3101 of the Code, or a corresponding provision of prior law, from an employee in a calendar year prior to the year in which the credit or refund is claimed, the employer shall also retain as part of his records a written statement from the employee (a) that the employee has not claimed refund or credit of the amount of the overcollection, or if so, such claim has been rejected and (b) that the employee will not claim refund or credit of such amount.

Retention period: 4 years after the date the claim is filed.

31.6001-1 Employers required to deduct and withhold income tax on wages which include sick pay.

See 31.3401(a)-1.

31.6001-1 Employers liable for tax under the Federal Insurance Contributions Act.

To keep records of all remuneration, whether in cash or in a medium other than cash, paid to his employees after 1954 for services (other than agricultural labor which constitutes or is deemed to constitute employment, domestic service in a private home of the employer, or service not in the course of the employer's trade or business) performed for him after 1936; and records of all remuneration in the form of tips received by employees after 1965 and reported to him. Records shall include information specified in section cited.

Retention period: 4 years after the due date of such tax for the return period to which the records relate, or the date such tax is paid, whichever is later.

31.6001-1 Employers required to deduct and withhold income tax on wages paid.

(a) To keep records of all remuneration paid to such employees and tips received by employees and reported to the employer. An employer is required to keep only charge receipts in connection with charged tips (26 U.S.C. 6001 as amended by Pub. L. 95-600). Such records shall show, with respect to such employee, the information specified in the section cited.

(b) To retain the Internal Revenue Service copy and the employee copy of all undeliverable annual withholding statements.

Retention period: 4 years after the due date of such tax for the return period to which the records and statements relate, or the date such tax is paid, whichever is later.

31.6001-1 General record retention requirement for employment taxes.

(a) Persons required by regulations or instructions shall keep copies of any return, schedule, statement, or other document as part of their records.

(b) Any person who claims a refund, credit, or abatement shall keep records as indicated in the section cited.

(c) While not mandatory (except in the case of claims) it is advisable for each employee to keep permanent accurate records as indicated in the section cited.

Retention period: 4 years after the due date of such tax for the return period to which the records relate or the date such tax is paid, whichever is later. In the case of claimants, at least

4 years after the date the claim is filed.

31.6001-1 Repayment by employer of tax erroneously collected from employee under the Federal Insurance Contributions Act or the Railroad Retirement Tax Act and of income tax withheld from wages.

(a) *Before employer files return.* To obtain and keep as part of the records the written receipt of the employee showing the date and amount of the repayment.

(b) *After employer files return.* If the amount of an overcollection is repaid to an employee, the employer shall obtain and keep as part of the records the written receipt of the employee, showing the date and amount of the repayment. If in any calendar year, an employer repays or reimburses an employee in the amount of an overcollection of employee tax under section 3101 of the Code, or a corresponding provision of prior law, which was collected from the employee in a prior calendar year, the employer shall obtain from the employee and keep as part of the records a written statement (a) that the employee has not claimed refund or credit of the amount of the overcollection, or if so, such claim has been rejected, and (b) that the employee will not claim refund or credit of such amount.

Retention period: 4 years after the due date of such tax for the return period to which the records relate, or the date such tax is paid, whichever is the later. The records of claimants shall be maintained for a period of at least 4 years after the date the claim is filed.

31.6001-1 Employers and employee representatives subject to the Railroad Retirement Tax Act.

See 31.6001-3.

31.6001-2 Employers liable for tax under the Federal Insurance Contributions Act.

See 1.6001-1.

31.6001-4 Employers and persons who are not employers for purposes of the Federal Unemployment Tax Act.

See 31.6001-1.

31.6001-5 Employers required to deduct and withhold income tax on wages paid.

See 31.6001-1.

31.6001-5 Employers required to deduct and withhold income tax on wages which include sick pay.

See 31.3401(a)-1.

31.6053-3 Certain large food or beverage establishments reporting tips.

To keep records sufficient to substantiate any information returns, employer statements to employees, applications, or tip allocations made pursuant to section 6053(c).

Retention period: 3 years due date of the return or statement to which they pertain.

31.6053-4T Tipped employees; substantiation requirements.

To maintain sufficient evidence to establish the amount of tip income received during a taxable year. If the employee does not maintain a daily record, other evidence of the amount of tip income received during the year, such as documentary evidence shall constitute sufficient evidence, but only if such other evidence is as credible and as reliable as a daily record.

Retention period: At all time available for inspection by authorized Internal Revenue Officers of employees, and shall be retained so long as the contents thereof may become material in the administration of any Internal Revenue law.

31.6402(a)-2 Employers claiming a refund, credit, or abatement of tax under the Federal Insurance Contributions Act or Railroad Retirement Tax Act.

See 31.6001-1.

31.6413(a)-1 Repayment by employer of tax erroneously collected from employee under the Federal Insurance Contributions Act of the Railroad Retirement Tax Act and of income tax withheld from wages.

See 31.6001-1.

Excise Taxes

Retention period: Regulations requiring retention of excise tax records usually specify the number of years that such records must be retained. For some excise tax records, however, no specific retention period can be established and the "materiality rule" discussed in section 1.6001-1 under *Income Tax* must be applied. Under the materiality rule, these records must be retained so long as they may become material in the computation of any tax.

Specific record retention requirements have not been assigned to the following and the materiality rule applies:

48.4041-7 Allocation of diesel and special fuel from common tank for use in special equipment.

To maintain records that will support the allocation of liquid drawn from the same tank as the one supplying fuel for propulsion of a vehicle, and sold for use or used in a separate motor to operate special equipment.

48.4042-2 Operators of vessels used in commercial waterway transportation.

(a) *General.* To maintain records sufficient to establish the amount of fuel used for taxable purposes including (1) quantity and acquisition date of all liquid fuels acquired for taxable and nontaxable purposes delivered to storage tanks or tanks on vessels, (2) date and quantity of fuel pumped into tanks on each vessel, (3) identification number of name of each vessel using fuel, and (4) departure time and point, route traveled, destination, and arrival time for each vessel.

(b) *Tax exemption.* To maintain records to support any exemption claimed including, where applicable, (1) draft of vessel on each voyage, (2) type of vessel in which fuel consumed and in which cargo transported, and (3) ultimate use of cargo transported.

48.4061(a)-1 Manufacturer selling tax-free vehicles of specified gross vehicle weight.

To maintain a record of the gross vehicle weight rating of each truck, bus, trailer, and semitrailer sold and excluded from tax. A recording of the serial number shall be treated as a record of the article if such rating is indicated by the serial number.

48.4061(a)-5 Manufacturers selling automobile truck bodies and chassis.

To retain records that will substantiate the portion of the total selling price attributable to the body if a completed vehicle with a tax-paid chassis attached to a taxable body.

48.4063-2 Manufacturers or vendors selling light-duty truck parts or accessories tax-free under section 4063(e).

To maintain records on the identity of the purchaser, signed statement of the exempt purpose for purchasing the light-duty truck parts or accessories, and the quantity of light-duty truck parts or accessories sold tax free to each purchaser.

48.4063-2 Persons purchasing light-duty truck parts or accessories tax free under section 4063(e).

To maintain sufficient records to establish that the parts or accessories purchased tax free have actually been resold (or used) on or in connection with the first retail sale of a light-duty truck or have been resold to a second purchaser for such a resale by the second purchaser.

48.4071-2 Manufacturers, producers, or importers selling automobile tires and tread rubber.

To maintain records to establish what portion of the total weight of the finished product represents the tire exclusive of the metal rim or rim base, of exemption certificates, and inventories.

48.4073-3 Manufacturers selling tread rubber tax free under section 4073(c).

To keep exemption certificate and proper records of invoices, orders, etc., relative to tax-free sales.

48.4081-2 Persons selling or purchasing gasoline tax free for the production of gasohol.

(a) *Records of the seller.* To maintain records of the identity of the purchaser, the written statement required to be given to the seller under section 4081(c) of the Code, and the quantity of gasoline sold tax free to each purchaser.

(b) *Records of the purchaser.*

1.To maintain records to establish that the gasoline has actually been used for the production of gasohol.

2.To maintain records to establish that alcohol, of the requisite kind has actually been obtained in quantity sufficient for the production of the full amount of gasohol that could have been produced from the quantity of tax-free gasoline purchased.

48.4093-2 Manufacturers selling and persons purchasing lubricating oil tax free under section 4093(c).

(a) *Manufacturer.* To maintain records on the identity of the purchaser, signed statement of the exempt purpose for purchasing the lubricating oil, and the quantity of lubricating oil sold tax free to each purchaser.

(b) *Purchaser.* To maintain sufficient records to establish that the lubricating oil purchased tax free has actually been mixed with used or waste oil to make rerefined lubricating oil and that the quantity of new lubricating oil used in the mixture meets the requirements cited in the section.

48.4121-1 Producers of coal and lignite.

A producer of both taxable coal and lignite must maintain adequate records to establish the portion of the mineral mined that is exempt from tax.

48.4182-1 Manufacturers, producers, or importers selling pistols, revolvers, other firearms, and shells and cartridges.

To maintain records to substantiate claim for exemption from tax imposed.

48.4221-11 Manufacturers selling or persons buying tires, tubes, or tread rubber tax free to be used on intercity, local, and school buses.

(a) *Manufacturer.* To maintain records on the identity of the purchaser, signed statement of the exempt purpose for purchasing the tires, tubes, or tread rubber, and the quantity of tires, tubes, or tread rubber sold tax free to each purchaser.

(b) *Purchaser.* To maintain sufficient records to establish that the tires, tubes, or tread rubber purchased tax free has actually been used on or in connection with a qualified bus.

48.4221-12 Vendors (including the manufacturers) selling and persons purchasing tax free parts or accessories used on intercity, local, and school buses.

(a) *Vendors (including manufacturers).* To maintain records on the identity of the purchaser, signed statements of the exempt purpose for purchasing the parts or accessories, and the quantity of parts or accessories sold tax free to each purchaser.

(b) *Purchasers.* To establish that the parts or accessories purchased tax free have actually been used on or in connection with an automobile bus or have been resold for such a use.

48.6412-1 Persons filing a claim for floor stocks credit or refund.

To keep dealer's inventory statements; records on articles held by each dealer and any such written consent received from a dealer.

48.6416(b)(2)-4 Persons filing claim for credit or refund of an overpayment in cases of special fuels tax involving exportations, uses, sales, or resales of special fuels.

To maintain supporting evidence.

48.6416(b)(3)-3 Persons filing claim for credit or refund of an overpayment in cases of articles sold tax-paid by manufacturers for further manufacture.

To maintain supporting evidence.

48.6416(b)(4)-1 Persons filing claim for credit or refund of an overpayment in cases of tax-paid tires or inner tubes used for further manufacture.

To maintain supporting evidence.

48.6420-6 Persons filing claim for credit or payment for gasoline used on a farm.

To keep records sufficient to enable the district director to determine whether the person is entitled to credit or payment under section 6420 and if so, the amount of the credit or payment.

Retention period: 3 years.

48.6421(a)-1 Allocation of gasoline for use in special equipment.

To maintain records that will substantiate the allocation of gasoline sold for use or used as a fuel and drawn from the same tank as the one supplying fuel for propulsion of a vehicle and sold for use or used in a separate motor to operate special equipment.

48.6421-7 Persons filing claim for credit or payment for gasoline used for certain nonhighway purposes.

To keep records sufficient to enable the district director to determine whether the person is entitled to credit or payment under section 6421 and if so, the amount of the credit or payment.

Retention period: 3 years.

48.6424-6 Persons filing claim for credit or payment for lubricating oil used in a qualified business used or in a qualified bus.

To keep records sufficient to enable the district director to determine whether the person is entitled to credit or payment under section 6424 and if so, the amount of the credit or payment.

Retention period: 3 years.

48.6427-5 Persons filing claim for credit or payment for diesel or special motor fuels used in intercity, local, or school buses.

To keep records sufficient to enable the district director to determine whether the person is entitled to credit or payment under section 6427 and if so, the amount of the credit or payment.

Retention period: 3 years.

49.4253-11 Persons providing certain communication and transportation services to persons entitled to receive the services exempt from tax.

To maintain exemption certificate and any other documents substantiating the tax exemption for services rendered.

49.4261-6 Carriers furnishing nontaxable transportation services for the United States portion.

To maintain appropriate evidence which will clearly show that the tickets or orders for such transportation were purchased for use in conjunction with connecting transportation from or to a point outside the United States.

51.4995-2 Operators, partnerships, and other disbursers subject to the Crude Oil windfall profit tax provisions.

To maintain a certificate that states the percentage of crude oil that is certified as exempt from tax or subject to a lower rate of tax.

51.4997-1 Persons subject to the crude oil windfall profit tax provisions.

To keep records of all documents, material, and information necessary to the determination of the windfall profit tax including material furnished to other persons, as well as information received from other persons.

55.6001-1 Persons subject to excise tax for certain real estate investment trust taxable income not distributed during the taxable year.

To keep such complete and detailed records as are sufficient to enable the district director to determine accurately the amount of liability under Chapter 44.

145.1-1 Persons filing a claim for credit or refund for floor stocks under the provisions of the Highway Revenue Act of 1982.

To retain the dealer's inventory statements to the extent that the articles (certain trucks, truck trailers, truck parts and accessories and lubricating oil) covered in the inventory statements are covered by the claim. In addition maintain any written consent statements and separate records for all articles held by the dealers.

145.1-2 Manufacturers filing a claim for credit or refund under the provisions of the Highway Revenue Act of 1982.

To maintain supporting evidence.

145.2-6 Persons liable for floor stocks tax on gasoline.

To maintain inventories, copies of returns and other relevant papers and materials, and records of claimants.
Retention period: 3 years.

145.4-6 Persons liable for floor stocks tax on tires.

To keep inventories, copies of returns and other relevant papers and materials and records of claimants.
Retention period: 3 years.

147.2-2 Persons involved in acquisitions of foreign stock or debt obligations; interest equalization tax.

To maintain certificates of American ownership, copies of confirmations of prior American ownership, records of withholding, financial records, and such other documents or records as specified in section cited.

147.4-1 Persons involved in acquisitions of foreign stock or debt obligations; interest equalization tax.

See 147.2-2.

147.5-1 Persons involved in acquisitions of foreign stock or debt obligations; interest equalization tax.

See 147.2-2.

147.5-2 Persons involved in acquisitions of foreign stock or debt obligations; interest equalization tax.

See 147.2-2.

147.7-3 Persons involved in acquisitions of foreign stock or debt obligations; interest equalization tax.

See 147.2-2.

147.7-6 Persons involved in acquisitions of foreign stock or debt obligations; interest equalization tax.

See 147.2-2.

147.7-7 Persons involved in acquisitions of foreign stock or debt obligations; interest equalization tax.

See 147.2-2.

147.7-9 Persons involved in acquisitions of foreign stock or debt obligations; interest equalization tax.

See 147.2-2.

147.8-4 Persons involved in acquisitions of foreign stock or debt obligations; interest equalization tax.

See 147.2-2.

A specific record retention period has been established for the following excise tax records:

41.4481-2 Persons subject to tax on use of certain highway motor vehicles.

To maintain records relating to each vehicle registered, as specified in sections cited; records or documents substantiating any claim for exemption from tax; and records and documents relating to any claim for credit or refund.
Retention period: At least 3 years after date tax becomes due or date tax is paid, whichever is later, or after date claim is filed.

41.6001 Persons subject to tax on use of certain highway motor vehicles.

See 41.4481-2.

44.4403-1 Persons required to pay excise tax on wagering.

To maintain daily records of operations, as required in sections cited, and records of overpayment and of each laid-off wager for which credit or refund is claimed, including copy of required certificate.
Retention period: At least 3 years from date tax becomes due or date wager received or date any credit or refund is claimed.

44.6001-1 Persons required to pay excise tax on wagering.

See 44.4403-1.

46.6001-1 Persons subject to miscellaneous excise taxes payable by return.

To maintain copies of any return, schedule, statement, or other document as part of records, in addition to any record relating to claim of credit or refund.
Retention period: At least 3 years after due date of tax or date tax is paid, whichever is later, or after date claim is filed.

46.6001-4 Persons required to keep records with respect to tax on foreign insurance policies.

To maintain records relating to such policies, including identifying information, gross premium, insurer, and any other records as specified in sections cited.
Retention period: At least 3 years from date any part of tax is due or date tax is paid, whichever is later.

48.4061 Manufacturer or reseller selling taxfree bodies or chassis otherwise taxable.

The manufacturer or reseller must retain the statement and other evidence required from the purchase in a sale of chassis or bodies used as component parts of vehicles not operated as highway vehicles.
Retention period: 3 years from the due date of the tax that would be due if the transaction in question had been a taxable sale.

48.6420(f) Aerial applicators claiming credit or refund of tax on fuels used for farming purposes.

To retain copies of all waivers executed by the owner, tenant, operator of the farm who waives the right to receive a payment.
Retention period: At least 3 years after last date prescribed for filing claim.

154.2-1 Persons transporting property by air.

To maintain exemption certificates, statements, documentary evidence of exportation and any other records as specified in section cited.
Retention period: At least 3 years.

301.6316-6 Persons making payments of estimated tax installments in foreign currency.

Maintain a copy of the statement certified by the foundation, commission, or other person having control of the payments to the taxpayer in nonconvertible foreign currency which are expected to be received during the taxable year for the purpose of exhibiting it to the disbursing officer when making installment deposits of foreign currency.

301.6501(a)-1 Persons subject to income tax.

See 1.6001-1.

301.6501(c)-1 Persons subject to income tax.

See 1.6001-1.

301.6501(e)-1 Persons subject to income tax.

See 1.6001-1.

301.6511(a)-1 Persons subject to income tax.

See 1.6001-1.

301.6511(d)-1 Persons subject to income tax.

See 1.6001-1.

Appendix F
Financial Planning Tables

The following tables, involving the effects of interest factors, are useful in various forms of future business planning.

SIMPLE INTEREST TABLE

SIMPLE INTEREST TABLE

Example of use of this table:
Find amount of $500 in 8 years at 6% simple interest.
From table at 8 yrs. and 6% for $1   1.48
Value in 8 yrs. for $500 (500 x 1.48) $740

Number of Years	3%	4%	5%	6%	7%	8%	9%	10%
					Interest Rate			
1	1.03	1.04	1.05	1.06	1.07	1.08	1.09	1.10
2	1.06	1.08	1.10	1.12	1.14	1.16	1.18	1.20
3	1.09	1.12	1.15	1.18	1.21	1.24	1.27	1.30
4	1.12	1.16	1.20	1.24	1.28	1.32	1.36	1.40
5	1.15	1.20	1.25	1.30	1.35	1.40	1.45	1.50
6	1.18	1.24	1.30	1.36	1.42	1.48	1.54	1.60
7	1.21	1.28	1.35	1.42	1.49	1.56	1.63	1.70
8	1.24	1.32	1.40	1.48	1.56	1.64	1.72	1.80
9	1.27	1.36	1.45	1.54	1.63	1.72	1.81	1.90
10	1.30	1.40	1.50	1.60	1.70	1.80	1.90	2.00
11	1.33	1.44	1.55	1.66	1.77	1.88	1.99	2.10
12	1.36	1.48	1.60	1.72	1.84	1.96	2.08	2.20
13	1.39	1.52	1.65	1.78	1.91	2.04	2.17	2.30
14	1.42	1.56	1.70	1.84	1.98	2.12	2.26	2.40
15	1.45	1.60	1.75	1.90	2.05	2.20	2.35	2.50
16	1.48	1.64	1.80	1.96	2.12	2.28	2.44	2.60
17	1.51	1.68	1.85	2.02	2.19	2.36	2.53	2.70
18	1.54	1.72	1.90	2.08	2.26	2.44	2.62	2.80
19	1.57	1.76	1.95	2.14	2.33	2.52	2.71	2.90
20	1.60	1.80	2.00	2.20	2.40	2.60	2.80	3.00
21	1.63	1.84	2.05	2.26	2.47	2.68	2.89	3.10
22	1.66	1.88	2.10	2.32	2.54	2.76	2.98	3.20
23	1.69	1.92	2.15	2.38	2.61	2.84	3.07	3.30
24	1.72	1.96	2.20	2.44	2.68	2.92	3.16	3.40
25	1.75	2.00	2.25	2.50	2.75	3.00	3.25	3.50
26	1.78	2.04	2.30	2.56	2.82	3.08	3.34	3.60
27	1.81	2.08	2.35	2.62	2.89	3.16	3.43	3.70
28	1.84	2.12	2.40	2.68	2.96	3.24	3.52	3.80
29	1.87	2.16	2.45	2.74	3.03	3.32	3.61	3.90
30	1.90	2.20	2.50	2.80	3.10	3.40	3.70	4.00
31	1.93	2.24	2.55	2.86	3.17	3.48	3.79	4.10
32	1.96	2.28	2.60	2.92	3.24	3.56	3.88	4.20
33	1.99	2.32	2.65	2.98	3.31	3.64	3.97	4.30
34	2.02	2.36	2.70	3.04	3.38	3.72	4.06	4.40
35	2.05	2.40	2.75	3.10	3.45	3.80	4.15	4.50
36	2.08	2.44	2.80	3.16	3.52	3.88	4.24	4.60
37	2.11	2.48	2.85	3.22	3.59	3.96	4.33	4.70
38	2.14	2.52	2.90	3.28	3.66	4.04	4.42	4.80
39	2.17	2.56	2.95	3.34	3.73	4.12	4.51	4.90
40	2.20	2.60	3.00	3.40	3.80	4.20	4.60	5.00

COMPOUND INTEREST TABLE

<u>Example of use of this table:</u>

Find how much $1,000 now in bank will grow to in 14 years at 6% interest.

From table 14 years at 6%	2.2609
Value in 14 years of $1,000	$2,260.9

Interest Rate

Number of Years	6%	6 1/2%	7%	7 1/2%	8%	8 1/2%	9%	9 1/2%
1	1.0600	1.0650	1.0700	1.0750	1.0800	1.0850	1.0900	1.0950
2	1.1236	1.1342	1.1449	1.1556	1.1664	1.1772	1.1881	1.1990
3	1.1910	1.2079	1.2250	1.2422	1.2597	1.2772	1.2950	1.3129
4	1.2624	1.2864	1.3107	1.3354	1.3604	1.3858	1.4115	1.4376
5	1.3332	1.3700	1.4025	1.4356	1.4693	1.5036	1.5386	1.5742
6	1.4135	1.4591	1.5007	1.5433	1.5868	1.6314	1.6771	1.7237
7	1.5030	1.5539	1.6057	1.6590	1.7138	1.7701	1.8230	1.8875
8	1.5938	1.6549	1.7181	1.7834	1.8509	1.9206	1.9925	2.0668
9	1.6894	1.7625	1.8384	1.9172	1.9990	2.0838	2.1718	2.2632
10	1.7908	1.8771	1.9671	2.0610	2.1589	2.2609	2.3673	2.4782
11	1.8982	1.9991	2.1048	2.2156	2.3316	2.4531	2.5804	2.7136
12	2.0121	2.1290	2.2521	2.3817	2.5181	2.6616	2.8126	2.9714
13	2.1329	2.2674	2.4098	2.5604	2.7196	2.8879	3.0658	3.2537
14	2.2609	2.4148	2.5785	2.7524	2.9371	3.1334	3.3417	3.5628
15	2.3965	2.5718	2.7590	2.9588	3.1721	3.3997	3.6424	3.9013
16	2.5403	2.7390	2.9521	3.1807	3.4259	3.6887	3.9703	4.2719
17	2.6927	2.9170	3.1588	3.4193	3.7000	4.0022	4.3276	4.6777
18	2.8543	3.1066	3.3799	3.6758	3.9960	4.3424	4.7171	5.1221
19	3.0255	3.3085	3.6165	3.9514	4.3157	4.7115	5.1416	5.6087
20	3.2075	3.5236	3.8696	4.2478	4.6609	5.1120	5.6044	6.1416
21	3.3995	3.7526	4.1405	4.5664	5.0338	5.5465	6.1088	6.7250
22	3.6035	3.9966	4.4304	4.9089	5.4365	6.0180	6.6586	7.3639
23	3.8197	4.2563	4.7405	5.2770	5.8714	6.5295	7.2578	8.0635
24	4.0489	4.5330	5.0723	5.6728	6.3411	7.0845	7.9110	8.8295
25	4.2918	4.8276	5.4274	6.0983	6.8484	7.6867	8.6230	9.6683
26	4.5493	5.1414	5.8073	6.5557	7.3963	8.3401	9.3991	10.5868
27	4.8223	5.4756	6.2138	7.0473	7.9880	9.0490	10.2450	11.5926
28	5.1116	5.8316	6.6488	7.5759	8.6271	9.8182	11.1671	12.6939
29	5.4183	6.2106	7.1142	8.1441	9.3172	10.6527	12.1721	13.8998
30	5.7434	6.6143	7.6122	8.7549	10.5582	11.5582	13.2676	15.2203
31	6.0881	7.0442	8.1451	9.4115	10.8676	12.5407	14.4617	16.6662
32	6.4533	7.5021	8.7152	10.1174	11.7370	13.6066	15.7633	18.2495
33	6.8408	7.9898	9.3253	10.8762	12.6760	14.7632	17.1820	19.9832
34	7.2510	8.5091	9.9781	11.6919	13.6901	16.0181	18.7284	21.8816
35	7.6860	9.0622	10.6765	12.5688	14.7853	17.3796	20.4139	23.9604
36	8.1479	9.6513	11.4239	13.5115	15.9681	18.8569	22.2512	26.2366
37	8.6360	10.2786	12.2236	14.5249	17.2456	20.4597	24.2538	28.7291
38	9.1542	10.9467	13.0792	15.6142	18.6252	22.1988	26.4366	31.4583
39	9.7035	11.6582	13.9948	16.7853	20.1152	24.0857	28.8159	34.4469
40	10.2857	12.4160	14.9744	18.0442	21.7245	26.1330	31.4094	37.7193

Compound Interest Table (Con't.)

Number of Years	10%	11%	12%	13%	14%	15%	16%	17%
1	1.1000	1.1100	1.1200	1.1300	1.1400	1.1500	1.1600	1.1700
2	1.2100	1.2321	1.2544	1.2769	1.2996	1.3225	1.3456	1.3689
3	1.3310	1.3576	1.4049	1.4428	1.4815	1.5208	1.5608	1.6016
4	1.4647	1.5180	1.5735	1.6304	1.6389	1.7490	1.8106	1.8738
5	1.6105	1.6350	1.7623	1.8424	1.9254	2.0113	2.1003	2.1924
6	1.7715	1.8704	1.9738	2.0819	2.1949	2.3130	2.4363	2.5651
7	1.9487	2.0761	2.2106	2.3526	2.5022	2.6600	2.8262	3.0012
8	2.1435	2.3045	2.4759	2.6584	2.8525	3.0590	3.2784	3.5114
9	2.3579	2.5580	2.7730	3.0040	3.2519	3.5178	3.8029	4.1084
10	2.5937	2.8394	3.1058	3.3945	3.7072	4.0455	4.4114	4.8068
11	2.8531	3.1517	3.4785	3.8358	4.2262	4.6523	5.1172	5.6239
12	3.1384	3.4984	3.8959	4.3345	4.8179	5.3502	5.9360	6.5800
13	3.4522	3.8832	4.3634	4.8980	5.4924	6.1527	6.8857	7.6986
14	3.7974	4.3104	4.8871	5.5347	6.2613	7.0757	7.9875	9.0074
15	4.1772	4.7845	5.4735	6.2542	7.1379	8.1370	9.2655	10.5387
16	4.5949	5.3108	6.1303	7.0673	8.1372	9.3576	10.7480	12.3303
17	5.0544	5.8950	6.8660	7.9860	9.2764	10.7612	12.4676	14.4264
18	5.5599	6.5435	7.6899	9.0242	10.5751	12.3754	14.4625	16.8789
19	6.1159	7.2633	8.6127	10.1974	12.0556	14.2317	16.7765	19.7483
20	6.7274	8.0623	9.6462	11.5230	13.7434	16.3665	19.4607	23.1055
21	7.4002	8.9491	10.8038	13.0210	15.6675	18.8215	22.5744	27.0335
22	8.1402	9.9335	12.1003	14.7138	17.8610	21.6447	26.1863	31.6292
23	8.9543	11.0262	13.5523	16.6266	20.3615	24.8914	30.3762	37.0062
24	9.8497	12.2391	15.1786	18.7880	23.2122	28.6251	35.2364	43.2972
25	10.8347	13.5854	17.0000	21.2305	26.4619	32.9189	40.8742	50.6578
26	11.9181	15.0793	19.0400	23.9905	30.1665	37.8567	47.4141	59.2696
27	13.1099	16.7386	21.3248	27.1092	34.3899	43.5353	55.0003	69.3454
28	14.4209	18.5799	23.8838	30.6334	39.2044	50.0656	63.8004	81.1342
29	15.8630	20.6236	26.7499	34.6158	44.6931	57.5754	74.0085	94.9270
30	17.4494	22.8922	29.9599	39.1158	50.9501	66.2117	85.8498	111.0646
31	19.1943	25.4104	33.5551	44.2009	58.0831	76.1435	99.5858	129.9456
32	21.1137	28.2055	37.5817	49.9470	66.2148	87.5650	115.5195	152.0363
33	23.2251	31.3082	42.0915	56.4402	75.4849	100.6998	134.0027	177.8825
34	25.5476	34.7521	47.1425	63.7774	86.0527	115.8048	155.4431	208.1226
35	28.1024	38.5748	52.7996	72.0685	98.1001	133.1755	180.3140	243.5034
36	30.9128	42.8180	59.1355	81.4374	111.8342	153.1518	209.1643	284.8990
37	34.0039	47.5280	66.2318	92.0242	127.4909	176.1246	242.6306	333.3319
38	37.4048	52.7561	74.1796	103.9874	145.3397	202.5433	281.4515	389.9983
39	41.1447	58.5593	83.0812	117.5057	165.6872	232.9248	326.4837	456.2980
40	45.2592	65.0008	93.0509	132.7815	188.8835	267.8635	378.7211	533.8687

Compound Interest Table (Con't.)

Number of Years	18%	19%	20%	21%	22%	23%	24%	25%
1	1.1800	1.1900	1.2000	1.2100	1.2200	1.2300	1.2400	1.2500
2	1.3924	1.4161	1.4400	1.4641	1.4884	1.5129	1.5376	1.5625
3	1.6430	1.6851	1.7280	1.7715	1.8158	1.8608	1.9066	1.9531
4	1.9387	2.0053	2.0736	2.1435	2.2153	2.2888	2.3642	2.4414
5	2.2877	2.3863	2.4883	2.5937	2.7027	2.8153	2.9316	3.0517
6	2.6995	2.8397	2.9859	3.1384	3.2973	3.4628	3.6352	3.8146
7	3.1854	3.3793	3.5831	3.7974	4.0227	4.2592	4.5076	4.7683
8	3.7588	4.0213	4.2998	4.5949	4.9077	5.2389	5.5895	5.9604
9	4.4354	4.7854	5.1597	5.5599	5.9874	6.4438	6.9309	7.4505
10	5.2338	5.6946	6.1917	6.7274	7.3046	7.9259	8.5944	9.3132
11	6.1759	6.7766	7.4300	8.1402	8.9116	9.7489	10.6570	11.6415
12	7.2875	8.0642	8.9161	9.8497	10.8722	11.9911	13.2147	14.5519
13	8.5993	9.5964	10.6993	11.9181	13.2641	14.7491	16.3863	18.1898
14	10.1472	11.4197	12.8391	14.4209	16.1822	18.1414	20.3190	22.7373
15	11.9737	13.5895	15.4070	17.4494	19.7422	22.3139	25.1956	28.4217
16	14.1290	16.1715	18.4884	21.1137	24.0855	27.4461	31.2425	35.5271
17	16.6722	19.2441	22.1861	25.5476	29.3844	33.7587	38.7408	44.4089
18	19.6732	22.9005	26.6233	30.9126	35.8489	41.5233	48.0385	55.5111
19	23.2144	27.2516	31.9479	37.4043	43.7357	51.0736	59.5678	69.3889
20	27.3930	32.4294	38.3375	45.2592	53.3576	62.8206	73.8641	86.7361
21	32.3237	38.5910	46.0051	54.7636	65.0963	77.2693	91.5915	108.4202
22	38.1420	45.9233	55.2061	66.2640	79.4175	95.0413	113.5735	135.5252
23	45.0076	54.6487	66.2473	80.1795	96.8893	116.9008	140.8311	169.4065
24	53.1090	65.0319	79.4968	97.0172	118.2050	143.7880	174.6306	211.7582
25	62.6686	77.3880	95.3962	117.3908	144.2101	176.8592	216.5419	264.6977
26	73.9488	92.0918	114.4754	142.0429	175.9363	217.5368	268.5120	330.8722
27	87.2597	109.5892	137.3705	171.8719	214.6423	267.5703	332.9549	413.5903
28	102.9665	130.4112	164.8446	207.9650	261.8636	329.1115	412.8641	516.9878
29	121.5005	155.1893	197.8135	251.6377	319.4736	404.8072	511.9515	646.2348
30	143.3708	184.6753	237.3763	304.4816	389.7578	497.9128	634.8199	807.7935
31	169.1773	219.7636	284.8515	368.4227	475.5046	612.4328	787.1767	1009.7419
32	199.6292	261.5187	341.8218	445.7915	580.1156	753.2923	976.0991	1262.1774
33	235.5625	311.2072	410.1862	539.4077	707.7410	926.5496	1210.3629	1577.7218
34	277.9638	370.3366	492.2235	652.6834	863.4441	1139.6560	1500.8500	1972.1522
35	327.9972	440.7006	590.6682	789.7469	1053.4018	1401.7769	1861.0540	2465.1903
36	387.0368	524.4337	708.8018	955.5938	1285.1502	1724.1855	2307.7069	3081.4879
37	456.7034	624.0761	850.5622	1156.2685	1567.8833	2120.7482	2861.5566	3851.8598
38	538.9100	742.6505	1020.6746	1399.0849	1912.8176	2608.5203	3548.3302	4814.8248
39	635.9138	883.7542	1224.8096	1692.8927	2333.6375	3208.4800	4399.9295	6018.5310
40	750.3783	1051.6675	1469.7715	2048.4002	2847.0377	3946.4304	5455.9126	7523.1638

PERIODIC DEPOSIT TABLE

Example of use of this table:
How much is $1,000 a year invested at 6% worth in 20 years?
At 6% for 20 years, the figure is   38.993
For $1,000 a year, the amount is $38,993

Interest Rate

Number of Years	6%	7%	8%	9%	10%	11%	12%	13%
1	1.060	1.070	1.080	1.090	1.100	1.110	1.120	1.130
2	2.183	2.215	2.246	2.278	2.310	2.342	2.374	2.407
3	3.375	3.440	3.506	3.573	3.641	3.710	3.779	3.850
4	4.637	4.751	4.867	4.985	5.105	5.228	5.353	5.480
5	5.975	6.153	6.336	6.523	6.716	6.913	7.115	7.323
6	7.394	7.654	7.923	8.200	8.487	8.783	9.089	9.405
7	8.897	9.260	9.637	10.028	10.436	10.859	11.300	11.757
8	10.491	10.978	11.488	12.021	12.579	13.164	13.776	14.416
9	12.181	12.816	13.487	14.193	14.937	15.722	16.549	17.420
10	13.972	14.784	15.645	16.560	17.531	18.561	19.655	20.814
11	15.870	16.888	17.977	19.141	20.384	21.713	23.133	24.650
12	17.882	19.141	20.495	21.953	23.523	25.212	27.029	28.985
13	20.015	21.550	23.215	25.019	26.975	29.095	31.393	33.883
14	22.276	24.129	26.152	28.361	30.772	33.405	36.280	39.417
15	24.673	26.888	29.324	32.003	34.950	38.190	41.753	45.672
16	27.213	29.840	32.750	35.974	39.545	43.501	47.884	52.739
17	29.906	32.999	36.450	40.301	44.599	49.396	54.750	60.725
18	32.760	36.379	40.446	45.018	50.159	55.939	62.440	69.749
19	35.786	39.995	44.762	50.160	56.275	63.203	71.052	79.947
20	38.993	43.865	49.423	55.765	63.002	71.265	80.699	91.470
21	42.392	48.006	54.457	61.873	70.403	80.214	91.503	104.491
22	45.996	52.436	59.893	68.532	78.543	90.148	103.603	119.205
23	49.816	57.177	65.765	75.790	87.497	101.174	117.155	135.831
24	53.865	62.249	72.106	83.701	97.347	113.413	132.334	154.620
25	58.156	67.676	78.954	92.324	108.182	126.999	149.334	175.850
26	62.706	73.484	86.351	101.723	120.100	142.079	168.374	199.841
27	67.528	79.698	94.339	111.968	133.210	158.817	189.699	226.950
28	72.640	86.347	102.966	123.135	147.631	177.397	213.583	257.583
29	78.058	93.461	112.283	135.308	163.494	198.021	240.333	292.199
30	83.802	101.073	122.346	148.575	180.943	220.913	270.293	331.315
31	89.890	109.218	133.214	163.037	200.138	246.324	303.848	375.516
32	96.343	117.933	144.951	178.800	221.252	274.529	341.429	425.463
33	103.184	127.259	157.627	195.982	244.477	305.837	383.521	481.903
34	110.435	137.237	171.317	214.711	270.024	340.590	430.663	545.681
35	118.121	147.913	186.102	235.125	298.127	379.164	483.463	617.749
36	126.268	159.337	202.070	257.376	329.039	421.982	542.599	699.187
37	134.904	171.561	219.316	281.630	363.043	469.511	608.831	791.211
38	144.058	184.640	237.941	308.066	400.448	522.267	683.010	895.198
39	153.762	198.635	258.057	336.882	441.593	580.826	766.091	1012.704
40	164.048	213.610	279.781	368.292	486.852	645.827	859.142	1145.486

COMPOUND DISCOUNT TABLE

This table shows the present or discounted value of $1 due at a given future time. For example, assume property which will revert to a lessor in 10 years will then be worth $1,000. The present value of this reversion, computed at an assumed rate of 4% on the investment, is found by finding the factor on the 10-year line in the 4% column. The factor .6756 is multiplied by 1000 to obtain the answer of $675.60.

Years	4%	4-1/2%	5%	5-1/2%	6%	6-1/2%	7%	7-1/2%	8%	9%	10%	11%
1	0.9615	0.9569	0.9524	0.9479	0.9434	0.9390	0.9346	0.9302	0.9259	0.9174	0.9091	0.9009
2	.9246	.9157	.9070	.8985	.8900	.8817	.8734	.8653	.8573	.8417	.8264	.8116
3	.8890	.8763	.8638	.8516	.8396	.8278	.8163	.8050	.7938	.7722	.7513	.7312
4	.8548	.8386	.8277	.8072	.7921	.7773	.7629	.7488	.7350	.7084	.6830	.6587
5	.8219	.8025	.7835	.7651	.7473	.7299	.7130	.6966	.6806	.6499	.6209	.5935
6	.7903	.7679	.7462	.7252	.7050	.6853	.6663	.6480	.6302	.5963	.5645	.5346
7	.7599	.7343	.7107	.6874	.6651	.6435	.6227	.6027	.5835	.5470	.5132	.4816
8	.7307	.7032	.6768	.6516	.6274	.6042	.5820	.5607	.5403	.5019	.4665	.4339
9	.7026	.6729	.6446	.6176	.5919	.5673	.5439	.5216	.5002	.4604	.4241	.3909
10	.6756	.6439	.6139	.5854	.5584	.5327	.5083	.4852	.4632	.4224	.3855	.3522
11	.6496	.6162	.5847	.5549	.5268	.5002	.4751	.4514	.4289	.3875	.3505	.3173
12	.6246	.5897	.5568	.5260	.4970	.4697	.4440	.4199	.3971	.3555	.3186	.2858
13	.6006	.5643	.5303	.4986	.4688	.4410	.4150	.3906	.3677	.3262	.2897	.2575
14	.5775	.5400	.5051	.4726	.4423	.4141	.3878	.3633	.3405	.2992	.2633	.2320
15	.5553	.5167	.4810	.4479	.4173	.3888	.3624	.3380	.3152	.2745	.2394	.2090
16	.5339	.4945	.4581	.4246	.3936	.3651	.3387	.3144	.2919	.2519	.2176	.1883
17	.5134	.4732	.4363	.4024	.3714	.3428	.3166	.2924	.2703	.2311	.1978	.1696
18	.4936	.4528	.4155	.3815	.3503	.3219	.2959	.2720	.2502	.2120	.1799	.1528
19	.4746	.4333	.3957	.3616	.3305	.3022	.2765	.2531	.2317	.1945	.1635	.1377
20	.4564	.4146	.3769	.3427	.3118	.2838	.2584	.2354	.2145	.1784	.1486	.1240
21	.4388	.3968	.3589	.3249	.2942	.2665	.2415	.2190	.1987	.1637	.1351	.1117
22	.4220	.3797	.3418	.3079	.2775	.2502	.2257	.2037	.1839	.1502	.1228	.1007
23	.4057	.3633	.3256	.2919	.2618	.2349	.2109	.1895	.1703	.1378	.1117	.0907
24	.3901	.3477	.3101	.2766	.2470	.2206	.1971	.1763	.1577	.1264	.1015	.0817
25	.3751	.3327	.2953	.2622	.2330	.2071	.1842	.1640	.1460	.1160	.0923	.0736
26	.3607	.3184	.2812	.2486	.2198	.1945	.1722	.1525	.1352	.1064	.0829	.0663
27	.3468	.3047	.2678	.2356	.2074	.1826	.1609	.1419	.1252	.0976	.0763	.0597
28	.3335	.2916	.2551	.2233	.1956	.1715	.1504	.1320	.1159	.0895	.0693	.0538

Compound Discount Table (Con't.)

Years	4%	4-1/2%	5%	5-1/2%	6%	6-1/2%	7%	7-1/2%	8%	9%	10%	11%
29	0.3207	0.2790	0.2429	0.2117	0.1846	0.1610	0.1406	0.1228	0.1073	0.0822	0.0630	0.0485
30	.3083	.2670	.2314	.2006	.1741	.1512	.1314	.1142	.0994	.0754	.0573	.0437
31	.2965	.2555	.2204	.1902	.1643	.1420	.1228	.1063	.0920	.0691	.0521	.0394
32	.2851	.2445	.2099	.1803	.1550	.1333	.1147	.0988	.0852	.0634	.0474	.0354
33	.2741	.2340	.1999	.1709	.1462	.1251	.1072	.0919	.0789	.0582	.0431	.0319
34	.2636	.2239	.1904	.1620	.1379	.1175	.1002	.0855	.0730	.0534	.0391	.0288
35	.2534	.2142	.1813	.1535	.1301	.1103	.0937	.0796	.0676	.0490	.0356	.0259
36	.2437	.2050	.1727	.1455	.1227	.1036	.0875	.0740	.0626	.0449	.0323	.0234
37	.2343	.1962	.1644	.1379	.1158	.0973	.0818	.0688	.0580	.0412	.0294	.0210
38	.2253	.1878	.1566	.1307	.1092	.0914	.0765	.0640	.0537	.0378	.0267	.0189
39	.2166	.1797	.1491	.1239	.1031	.0858	.0715	.0596	.0497	.0347	.0243	.0171
40	.2083	.1719	.1420	.1175	.0972	.0805	.0668	.0554	.0460	.0318	.0221	.0154
41	.2003	.1645	.1353	.1113	.0917	.0756	.0624	.0515	.0426	.0292	.0201	.0139
42	.1926	.1574	.1288	.1055	.0865	.0710	.0583	.0480	.0395	.0268	.0183	.0125
43	.1852	.1507	.1227	.1000	.0816	.0667	.0545	.0446	.0365	.0246	.0166	.0112
44	.1780	.1442	.1169	.0948	.0770	.0626	.0509	.0415	.0338	.0225	.0151	.0101
45	.1712	.1380	.1113	.0899	.0726	.0588	.0476	.0386	.0313	.0207	.0137	.0091
46	.1646	.1320	.1060	.0852	.0685	.0552	.0445	.0359	.0290	.0190	.0125	.0082
47	.1583	.1263	.1009	.0807	.0647	.0518	.0416	.0334	.0269	.0174	.0113	.0074
48	.1522	.1209	.0961	.0765	.0610	.0487	.0389	.0311	.0249	.0160	.0103	.0067
49	.1463	.1157	.0916	.0725	.0575	.0457	.0363	.0289	.0230	.0147	.0094	.0060
50	.1407	.1107	.0872	.0688	.0543	.0429	.0339	.0269	.0213	.0134	.0085	.0054
51	.1353	.1059	.0831	.0652	.0512	.0403	.0317	.0250	.0197	.0123	.0077	.00488
52	.1301	.1014	.0791	.0618	.0483	.0378	.0297	.0233	.0183	.0113	.0070	.00440
53	.1251	.0970	.0753	.0586	.0456	.0355	.0277	.0216	.0169	.0104	.0064	.00396
54	.1203	.0928	.0717	.0555	.0430	.0333	.0259	.0201	.0157	.0095	.0058	.00357
55	.1157	.0888	.0683	.0526	.0406	.0313	.0242	.0187	.0145	.0087	.0053	.00322
56	.1112	.0850	.0651	.0499	.0383	.0294	.0226	.0174	.0134	.0080	.0048	.00290
57	.1069	.0814	.0620	.0473	.0361	.0276	.0211	.0162	.0124	.0073	.0044	.00261
58	.1028	.0778	.0590	.0448	.0341	.0259	.0198	.0151	.0115	.0067	.0040	.00235
59	.0989	.0745	.0562	.0425	.0321	.0243	.0185	.0140	.0107	.0062	.0036	.00212
60	.0951	.0713	.0535	.0403	.0303	.0229	.0173	.0130	.0099	.0057	.0033	.00191

PRESENT WORTH TABLE — SINGLE FUTURE PAYMENT

Example of use of this table:
Find how much $10,000 payable in 12 years is worth now at an interest rate of 6%.
From table for 12 years 6%
Present value of $10,000 in 12 years (10,000 × .4970)

.4970
$4.970

Interest Rate

Number of Years	6%	7%	8%	9%	10%	11%	12%	13%
1	0.9434	0.9346	0.9259	0.9174	0.9091	0.9009	0.8929	0.8850
2	0.8900	0.8734	0.8573	0.8417	0.8264	0.8116	0.7972	0.7831
3	0.8396	0.8163	0.7938	0.7722	0.7513	0.7312	0.7118	0.6931
4	0.7921	0.7629	0.7350	0.7084	0.6830	0.6587	0.6355	0.6133
5	0.7473	0.7130	0.6806	0.6499	0.6209	0.5935	0.5674	0.5428
6	0.7050	0.6663	0.6302	0.5963	0.5645	0.5346	0.5066	0.4803
7	0.6651	0.6227	0.5835	0.5470	0.5132	0.4816	0.4523	0.4251
8	0.6274	0.5820	0.5403	0.5019	0.4665	0.4339	0.4039	0.3762
9	0.5919	0.5439	0.5002	0.4604	0.4241	0.3909	0.3606	0.3329
10	0.5584	0.5083	0.4632	0.4224	0.3855	0.3522	0.3220	0.2946
11	0.5268	0.4751	0.4289	0.3875	0.3505	0.3173	0.2875	0.2607
12	0.4970	0.4440	0.3971	0.3555	0.3186	0.2858	0.2567	0.2307
13	0.4688	0.4150	0.3677	0.3262	0.2897	0.2575	0.2292	0.2042
14	0.4423	0.3878	0.3405	0.2992	0.2633	0.2320	0.2046	0.1807
15	0.4173	0.3624	0.3152	0.2745	0.2394	0.2090	0.1827	0.1599
16	0.3936	0.3387	0.2919	0.2519	0.2176	0.1883	0.1631	0.1415
17	0.3714	0.3166	0.2703	0.2311	0.1978	0.1696	0.1456	0.1252
18	0.3503	0.2959	0.2502	0.2120	0.1799	0.1528	0.1300	0.1108
19	0.3305	0.2765	0.2317	0.1945	0.1635	0.1377	0.1161	0.0981
20	0.3118	0.2584	0.2145	0.1784	0.1486	0.1240	0.1037	0.0868
21	0.2942	0.2415	0.1987	0.1637	0.1351	0.1117	0.0926	0.0768
22	0.2775	0.2257	0.1839	0.1502	0.1228	0.1007	0.0826	0.0680
23	0.2618	0.2109	0.1703	0.1378	0.1117	0.0907	0.0738	0.0601
24	0.2470	0.1971	0.1577	0.1264	0.1015	0.0817	0.0660	0.0532
25	0.2330	0.1842	0.1460	0.1160	0.0923	0.0736	0.0588	0.0471
26	0.2198	0.1722	0.1352	0.1064	0.0829	0.0663	0.0525	0.0417
27	0.2074	0.1609	0.1252	0.0976	0.0763	0.0597	0.0470	0.0369
28	0.1956	0.1504	0.1159	0.0895	0.0693	0.0538	0.0420	0.0326
29	0.1846	0.1406	0.1073	0.0822	0.0630	0.0485	0.0374	0.0289
30	0.1741	0.1314	0.0994	0.0754	0.0573	0.0437	0.0334	0.0256
31	0.1643	0.1228	0.0920	0.0691	0.0521	0.0394	0.0298	0.0226
32	0.1550	0.1147	0.0852	0.0634	0.0474	0.0354	0.0266	0.0200
33	0.1462	0.1072	0.0789	0.0582	0.0431	0.0319	0.0238	0.0177
34	0.1379	0.1002	0.0730	0.0534	0.0391	0.0288	0.0212	0.0157
35	0.1301	0.0937	0.0676	0.0490	0.0356	0.0259	0.0189	0.0139
36	0.1227	0.0875	0.0626	0.0449	0.0323	0.0234	0.0169	0.0123
37	0.1158	0.0818	0.0580	0.0412	0.0294	0.0210	0.0151	0.0109
38	0.1092	0.0765	0.0536	0.0378	0.0267	0.0189	0.0135	0.0096
39	0.1031	0.0715	0.0497	0.0347	0.0243	0.0171	0.0120	0.0085
40	0.0972	0.0668	0.0460	0.0318	0.0221	0.0154	0.0107	0.0075

PRESENT WORTH TABLE — PERIODIC FUTURE PAYMENTS

Example of use of this table:

To find the cost now of $1,000 of income per year for 20 years at 7%.

From table for 20 years at 7%   10.5940

Cost of $1,000 per year ($1,000 × 10.5940) $10,594

Interest Rate

Number of Years	6%	7%	8%	9%	10%	11%	12%	13%
1	0.9434	0.9346	0.9259	0.9174	0.9091	0.9009	0.8929	0.8850
2	1.8334	1.8080	1.7833	1.7591	1.7355	1.7125	1.6901	1.6681
3	2.6730	2.6243	2.5771	2.5313	2.4869	2.4437	2.4018	2.3612
4	3.4651	3.3872	3.3121	3.2397	3.1699	3.1024	3.0373	2.9745
5	4.2124	4.1002	3.9927	3.8897	3.7908	3.6959	3.6048	3.5172
6	4.9173	4.7665	4.6229	4.4859	4.3553	4.2305	4.1114	3.9975
7	5.5824	5.3893	5.2064	5.0330	4.8684	4.7122	4.5638	4.4226
8	6.2098	5.9713	5.7466	5.5348	5.3349	5.1461	4.9676	4.7988
9	6.8017	6.5152	6.2469	5.9952	5.7590	5.5370	5.3282	5.1317
10	7.3601	7.0236	6.7101	6.4177	6.1446	5.8892	5.6502	5.4262
11	7.8869	7.4987	7.1390	6.8052	6.4951	6.2065	5.9377	5.6869
12	8.3838	7.9427	7.5361	7.1607	6.8137	6.4924	6.1944	5.9176
13	8.8527	8.3577	7.9038	7.4869	7.1034	6.7499	6.4235	6.1218
14	9.2950	8.7455	8.2442	7.7862	7.3667	6.9819	6.6282	6.3025
15	9.7122	9.1079	8.5595	8.0607	7.6061	7.1909	6.8109	6.4624
16	10.1059	9.4466	8.8514	8.3126	7.8237	7.3792	6.9740	6.6039
17	10.4773	9.7632	9.1216	8.5436	8.0216	7.5488	7.1196	6.7291
18	10.8276	10.0591	9.3719	8.7556	8.2014	7.7016	7.2497	6.8399
19	11.1581	10.3356	9.6036	8.9501	8.3649	7.8393	7.3658	6.9380
20	11.4699	10.5940	9.8181	9.1285	8.5136	7.9633	7.4694	7.0248
21	11.7641	10.8355	10.0168	9.2922	8.6487	8.0751	7.5620	7.1016
22	12.0416	11.0612	10.2007	9.4424	8.7715	8.1757	7.6446	7.1695
23	12.3034	11.2722	10.3711	9.5802	8.8832	8.2664	7.7184	7.2297
24	12.5504	11.4693	10.5288	9.7066	8.9847	8.3481	7.7843	7.2829
25	12.7834	11.6536	10.6748	9.8226	9.0770	8.4217	7.8431	7.3299
26	13.0032	11.8258	10.8100	9.9290	9.1609	8.4881	7.8957	7.3717
27	13.2105	11.9867	10.9352	10.0266	9.2372	8.5478	7.9426	7.4086
28	13.4062	12.1371	11.0511	10.1161	9.3066	8.6016	7.9844	7.4412
29	13.5907	12.2777	11.1584	10.1983	9.3696	8.6501	8.0218	7.4701
30	13.7648	12.4090	11.2578	10.2737	9.4269	8.6938	8.0552	7.4957
31	13.9291	12.5318	11.3498	10.3428	9.4790	8.7331	8.0850	7.5183
32	14.0840	12.6466	11.4350	10.4062	9.5264	8.7686	8.1116	7.5383
33	14.2302	12.7538	11.5139	10.4644	9.5694	8.8005	8.1354	7.5560
34	14.3681	12.8540	11.5869	10.5178	9.6086	8.8293	8.1566	7.5717
35	14.4982	12.9477	11.6546	10.5668	9.6442	8.8552	8.1755	7.5856
36	14.6210	13.0352	11.7172	10.6118	9.6765	8.8786	8.1924	7.5979
37	14.7368	13.1170	11.7752	10.6530	9.7059	8.8996	8.2075	7.6087
38	14.8460	13.1935	11.8289	10.6908	9.7327	8.9186	8.2210	7.6183
39	14.9491	13.2649	11.8786	10.7255	9.7569	8.9357	8.2330	7.6268
40	15.0463	13.3317	11.9246	10.7574	9.7791	8.9511	8.2438	7.6344

SINKING FUND REQUIREMENTS TABLE

Example of use of this table:
   To find the amount of money which must be deposited at the end of each year to grow to $10,000 in 19 years at 8%.
   From table for 19 years at 8%   .02413
   Amount of each deposit ($10,000 × .02413) $241.30

Interest Rate

Number of Years	6%	7%	8%	9%	10%	11%	12%	13%
1	1.00000	1.00000	1.00000	1.00000	1.00000	1.00000	1.00000	1.00000
2	.48544	.48309	.48077	.47847	.47619	.47393	.47169	.46948
3	.31411	.31105	.30803	.30505	.30211	.29921	.29635	.29352
4	.22859	.22523	.22192	.21867	.21547	.21233	.20923	.20619
5	.17740	.17389	.17046	.16709	.16379	.16057	.15741	.15431
6	.14336	.13979	.13632	.13292	.12961	.12638	.12323	.12015
7	.11913	.11555	.11207	.10869	.10541	.10222	.09912	.09611
8	.10104	.09747	.09401	.09067	.08744	.08432	.08130	.07839
9	.08702	.08349	.08008	.07679	.07364	.07060	.06768	.06487
10	.07587	.07238	.06903	.06582	.06275	.05980	.05698	.05429
11	.06679	.06336	.06008	.05695	.05396	.05112	.04846	.04584
12	.05928	.05590	.05269	.04965	.04676	.04403	.04144	.03899
13	.05296	.04965	.04652	.04357	.04078	.03815	.03568	.03335
14	.04758	.04434	.04129	.03843	.03575	.03323	.03087	.02867
15	.04206	.03979	.03683	.03406	.03147	.02907	.02682	.02474
16	.03895	.03586	.03298	.03030	.02782	.02552	.02339	.02143
17	.03544	.03243	.02963	.02705	.02466	.02247	.02046	.01861
18	.03236	.02941	.02670	.02421	.02193	.01984	.01794	.01620
19	.02962	.02675	.02413	.02173	.01955	.01756	.01576	.01413
20	.02718	.02439	.02185	.01955	.01746	.01558	.01388	.01235
21	.02500	.02229	.01983	.01762	.01562	.01384	.01224	.01081
22	.02305	.02041	.01803	.01590	.01401	.01231	.01081	.00948
23	.02128	.01871	.01642	.01438	.01257	.01097	.00956	.00832
24	.01968	.01719	.01498	.01302	.01129	.00979	.00846	.00731
25	.01823	.01581	.01168	.01181	.01017	.00874	.00749	.00643
26	.01690	.01456	.01251	.01072	.00916	.00781	.00665	.00565
27	.01570	.01343	.01145	.00973	.00826	.00699	.00590	.00498
28	.01459	.01239	.01049	.00885	.00745	.00626	.00524	.00439
29	.01358	.01145	.00962	.00806	.00673	.00561	.00466	.00387
30	.01265	.01059	.00883	.00734	.00608	.00502	.00414	.00341
31	.01179	.00979	.00811	.00667	.00549	.00451	.00369	.00301
32	.01100	.00907	.00745	.00609	.00497	.00404	.00328	.00266
33	.01027	.00841	.00685	.00556	.00449	.00363	.00292	.00234
34	.00960	.00779	.00630	.00508	.00407	.00326	.00260	.00207
35	.00897	.00723	.00580	.00464	.00369	.00293	.00232	.00183
36	.00839	.00676	.00534	.00424	.00334	.00263	.00206	.00162
37	.00786	.00624	.00492	.00387	.00303	.00236	.00184	.00143
38	.00736	.00579	.00454	.00354	.00275	.00213	.00164	.00126
39	.00689	.00539	.00419	.00324	.00249	.00191	.00146	.00112
40	.00646	.00501	.00386	.00296	.00226	.00172	.00130	.00099

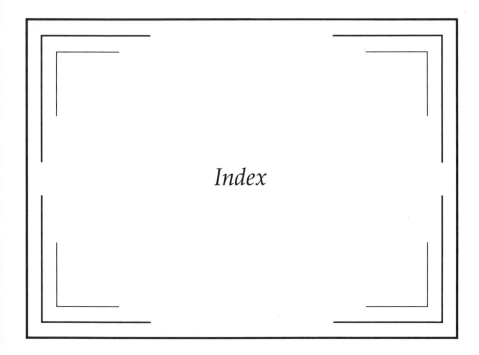

Index

Cost accounting: (*cont.*)
  integration of, 135
  job order systems, 135–36
  model, 130–32
  process cost systems, 135–36
  standard cost systems, 134–35
costs, elements of, 135
cost terminology, 133–34
definition of, 127
direct costing, 140–41
  effect on financial statements, 141
objective of, 127–28
standard costs, 136–40
Cost method, stock acquisitions, 199
Credit risk, 266–67
Cumulative preferred stock, 102
Current assets, 61–75
  assets excluded from, 62–63
  cash, 63–64
  classification of, 61–62
  inventory, 64–73
  marketable securities, 73–75
  See also Non-current assets
Current liabilities, 93–98
  identification of, 93–95
  long-term debt, 95–98
    bond or payment discount, 95
    early extinguishment of debt, 96
    troubled debt restructurings, 96–98

D

Declining-balance method, of depreciation, 80–81, 479
Deferred compensation contracts, 38–39
Deferred compensation plans, 35–37
  compensatory plans, 35–37
  earning per share, 37
  non-compensatory plans, 35
Deferred income, 447
Depletion, 482
Depreciation, 79–82
  basis, 82–83
    allocation of, 83
  methods of, 79–82
    sinking-fund method, 81–82
    straight-line method, 80, 479
    sum-of-years-digits method, 81, 479
    200%-declining-balance method, 80–81, 479
    units-of-production method, 82
Direct costing, 140–41
  effect on financial statements, 141
Direct labor, 135

Direct materials, 135
Discount bonds, 261
Dividends, 474–75
Domestic international sales companies (DISCs), 209

E

Earnings per share, 385–402
  cash receipts and payments
    classification of, 396–98
    computational procedures, 397–98
    direct method of reporting, 398–400
    indirect method of reporting, 400–402
  fact sheet, 386–91
  FASB Statement No. 95, 394–96
    summary, 395–96
    terminology, 394–95
  reporting of, 385–86
  segment reporting, 391–93
    definitions, 392
    segment presentation, 393
Embezzlement, 192–94
Employee benefits, 21–42
  actuarial gains and losses, 37
  companies with more than one plan, 38
  deferred compensation contracts, 38–39
  deferred compensation plans, 35–37
  defined contribution plans, 37–38
  ERISA requirements, 38
  401(k) plans, 40–42
  insured plans, 38
  key-person life insurance, 38
  pension funds, 21–35
  profit-sharing plans, 37
  Social Security benefits and, 38
  See also Expenses
Equipment loans, 244
Equipment obligation bonds, 259
Equity, 99–112, 451–75
  capital, 451
  capitalization
    small business stock, special treatment for, 452–53
    tax benefits of, 451–53
    tax guidelines in, 452
  capital stock, 100–103
    capital stock accounts, 102–3
    common stock, 100–103
    issued for property, 103
    par value, 102–3
    preferred stock, 101–2
    stated capital, 102
  contingency reserves, 105–7